AN EXPOSITION OF THE WHOLE BIBLE

BY G. CAMPBELL MORGAN

STUDIES IN THE PROPHECY OF JEREMIAH
THE WESTMINSTER PULPIT
SEARCHLIGHTS FROM THE WORD
THE SPIRIT OF GOD
NOTES ON THE PSALMS
THE CORINTHIAN LETTERS OF PAUL
THE PARABLES AND METAPHORS OF OUR LORD
THE VOICE OF THE DEVIL
PETER AND THE CHURCH
PREACHING
THE GREAT PHYSICIAN
GREAT CHAPTERS OF THE BIBLE
HOSEA: THE HEART AND HOLINESS OF GOD
THE ANSWERS OF JESUS TO JOB
THE GOSPEL ACCORDING TO MATTHEW
THE GOSPEL ACCORDING TO MARK
THE GOSPEL ACCORDING TO LUKE
THE GOSPEL ACCORDING TO JOHN
THE ACTS OF THE APOSTLES
THE CRISES OF THE CHRIST
THE TEACHING OF CHRIST
LIVING MESSAGES OF THE BOOKS OF THE BIBLE
THE TEN COMMANDMENTS
THE LETTERS OF OUR LORD
THE LIFE OF THE CHRISTIAN

AN EXPOSITION OF THE WHOLE BIBLE

CHAPTER BY CHAPTER IN ONE VOLUME

G. CAMPBELL MORGAN

Fleming H. Revell
A Division of Baker Book House
Grand Rapids, Michigan 49516

The Library of Congress cataloged the original
printing of this title as follows:

Morgan, George Campbell, 1863–1945.
An exposition of the whole Bible, chapter by chapter in one volume. Westwood, N. J. Revell 1959
542 p. 22 cm.

1. Bible—Commentaries. I. Title.
BS491.M62 1959 220.7 59–8719 ‡
Library of Congress

Published by Fleming H. Revell
a division of Baker Book House Company
P.O. Box 6287, Grand Rapids, MI 49516-6287

ISBN: 0-8007-0088-0

Twenty-fifth printing, January 1993

Printed in the United States of America

PREFACE

Why another book of G. Campbell Morgan Biblical exposition? There are two very good reasons for it. One is that *any* exposition from this source has the salty tang of freshness and the ringing tones of eternal truth. The other is that this particular volume reveals so much of the method and purpose of the author as hc approached the Book.

It is "previously unpublished Morgan," in the sense that it has never before appeared in book form. Originally printed in a small British paper—*The Christian*—it was at first entitled "Highways of Biblical Revelation," which gives a clue to its intent. Dr. Morgan was one of those rare Christians who saw the Bible as a whole, and studied it as a whole, and not parts. He had little admiration for those "students" who open the Bible at random, close their eyes and point to a text —and accept the text as God's primary revelation to them. "Some people," he said, "juggle with the Bible. . . . I tried that once, and found my finger pointing to the story of Balaam and his ass. . . . That cured me of juggling the Bible." Nor did he care for the "proof-text" method—that of lifting a fragment out of the context to prove a theological point: "That is *not* Bible study. . . . I can prove anything from the Bible [by] choosing my texts. I can prove that my audience . . . should go out and hang themselves. 'Judas went out and hanged himself.' 'Go, and do thou likewise!' "

He knew the Bible better than most men of his generation, and he saw in its pages something that most of them missed: that in this labyrinthian house of truth one could understand and find his way best by laying hold upon a golden cord that runs from Genesis to Revelation: *the golden cord of revelation and redemption.* Through it all, like Tennyson's "one increasing purpose," ran this emphasis and air.

Unlike the exposition of his *Searchlights of the Word,* in which he cast new light upon various great passages of Scripture, here he binds together *the central thoughts of all the chapters,* as a road-building engineer might bind together main and tributary avenues of travel into a cross-continental highway. Dr. Henry C. Thiessen, in his *Introductory Lectures in Syste-*

matic Theology, puts it thus: "The Bible is to the theologian what nature is to the scientist—a body of unorganized and only partly related facts. God has not seen fit to write the Bible in the form of a Systematic Theology; it remains for us, therefore, to gather together the scattered facts and to build them into a logical system. . . ."

This, Dr. Morgan has done in this volume. It will be, to many, the crowning achievement of his amazing career as princely preacher and inspired teacher of the Word.

THE PUBLISHERS

CONTENTS

PART ONE: OLD TESTAMENT

GENESIS 11
EXODUS 34
LEVITICUS 52
NUMBERS 63
DEUTERONOMY 77
JOSHUA 92
JUDGES 102
RUTH 112
I SAMUEL 115
II SAMUEL 127
I KINGS 137
II KINGS 147
I CHRONICLES 158
II CHRONICLES 170
EZRA 185
NEHEMIAH 191
ESTHER 197
JOB 201
PSALMS 221
PROVERBS 279
ECCLESIASTES 290
THE SONG OF SOLOMON 296
ISAIAH 300
JEREMIAH 321
LAMENTATIONS 341
EZEKIEL 344
DANIEL 366
HOSEA 372
JOEL 378
AMOS 380
OBADIAH 384
JONAH 385
MICAH 387
NAHUM 390
HABAKKUK 392
ZEPHANIAH 394
HAGGAI 396
ZECHARIAH 398
MALACHI 404

PART TWO: NEW TESTAMENT

MATTHEW 409
MARK 424
LUKE 432
JOHN 442
THE ACTS 450
EPISTLE TO THE ROMANS 461
I CORINTHIANS 470
II CORINTHIANS 478
GALATIANS 485
EPHESIANS 489
PHILIPPIANS 493
COLOSSIANS 496
I THESSALONIANS 499
II THESSALONIANS 502
I TIMOTHY 504
II TIMOTHY 507
TITUS 510
PHILEMON 512
TO THE HEBREWS 513
THE EPISTLE OF JAMES 519
I PETER 522
II PETER 525
I JOHN 527
II JOHN 530
III JOHN 531
JUDE 532
REVELATION 533

PART ONE

Old Testament

Genesis

GENESIS 1

The opening sentence of the Book of Genesis is an interpretation of the fact "that what is seen hath not been made out of things which do appear" (Hebrews 11:3), and accounts for the things which are seen. The whole chapter, and, indeed, all subsequent Scripture, must be read in the light of this statement as to origins. This sentence is followed immediately by a declaration, without detail, of a cataclysm which overtook the earth. It then proceeds to show how the God who created, restored the earth to fruitfulness and order. God is here revealed in the threefold fact of His existence. The chaotic earth is seen held in the embrace of the Spirit, who is described as brooding over it. The Word of God is heard expressing the will of God. Thus God is seen speaking the purpose of His mind in word and doing His will through the activity of the Spirit.

The purpose of this restoring process is seen in the creation of an entirely new being, Man. This being is revealed as having direct relationship with God, being made in His image and likeness. Here the deepest truth concerning man's nature, that of its spirituality, is not declared. Consequently there is here no reference to his moral nature, except as both these may be implied in the fact of his being in the image and likeness of God. The chapter reveals a universe rooted in the thought and activity of God, and of man as being His offspring. The acceptation of these declarations gives to the mind a sense of the majesty of all being, thus creating a radiant background against which the darkness of subsequent history will be seen and understood more clearly. Any other view of the universe and man fails to understand the real nature of evil.

GENESIS 2

This chapter gives us a fuller account of man. Three distinct movements are chronicled in the brief but comprehensive account.

First, "Jehovah God formed man of the dust." The Hebrew word "formed" suggests the figure of the potter, molding to shape, material already existing. It is a scientific fact that all the elements in man's physical life are found in the dust of the ground.

Second, "Jehovah God breathed into his nostrils the breath of life." This is the final divine act, mysterious and incomprehensible, indicating the communication to the dust, of the very life of God.

Finally, "man became a living soul." The word *nephesh,* here translated "soul," refers to complete personality.

This being is now placed in an environment which demands his care and cultivation. His relationship as subject to the sovereignty of God is sacramentally symbolized for him in a tree. He can only fulfil the highest function of his being only as he is living and acting within the will of God. By supernatural action, the man is completed in the woman. Here the declaration is most significant. "God created man in His own image, in the image of God created He him; male and female created He them" (1:27). In God are fatherhood and motherhood, parenthood and childhood. This great chapter on human nature ideally reveals it in its relationship with God in being and in purpose. The ultimate meaning of this is not revealed here and will be known only in the ages to come, when, beyond all failure, the divine thought and purpose are fulfilled.

GENESIS 3

Here begins the second section of the Book of Genesis. As the first has answered questions concerning creation, the second replies to questions asked in the presence of sin and suffering and sorrow.

The story of this chapter is simple and yet sublime in its interpretation of human history as we are familiar with it. Man is seen in individual innocence and racial immaturity. To him an evil personality, radiant in appearance, makes an appeal. The appeal, in the last analysis, is a questioning of the goodness and moral integrity of God.

The fall of man consisted in consent to listen to any such appeal and in the consequent failure of faith, which issued in definite breaking of law. At once fear in the human soul is manifested. Faith and fear are mutually exclusive. So long as faith governs, fear is impossible. Man may attempt to hide from God, but he cannot escape Him, in that fact lies man's only hope.

God is revealed wondrously in His dealings with the situation. His first question thrills with pathos, "Where art thou?" In all that followed there is evident the differentiation of the strictest justice. The serpent is cursed. The sentence on the woman is that in the distinctive exercise of her nature, that of motherhood, she shall be wrapped in sorrow. In that connection, however, the first prophetic word of hope was uttered. Of the seed of the woman shall come the Deliverer. The sentence on the man is that, in the highest activity of his life, that of toil, he shall know weariness. Behind all the movements of law there moves the heart of love, and this is finally seen in the exclusion of Adam and Eve from the tree of life in order that they might not perpetuate the conditions into which they had passed as the result of sin.

GENESIS 4

The degeneration of the first man and woman was transmitted, the firstborn being manifestly an inheritor of the fallen nature of his parents. His mother named him Cain, intimating a hope that the seed had come which should bruise the head of the serpent. How little she knew of the nature of her own sin. Thus from the beginning sin manifested a wayward rebelliousness which ever tends to break the heart of fatherhood and motherhood; and experimentally some of the consciousness of the pain of God over their own sin would be revealed to these first parents. Abel means vanity, and suggests the disappointment which had come to Eve.

Sin is seen at once, breaking up the family ideal in the story of Cain and Abel. Death, the penalty of sin, is first executed by the hand of a sinner.

Jehovah intervenes, dealing with Cain in strict justice. His going out from the presence of God was a willful severance of himself from the divine government and from response to its claims.

The chapter records with perfect fidelity the story of human progress, notwithstanding its godlessness. Here begins a history which continues until this hour—marriage, and children, and the building of a city without God. The origin of colonization and commerce is seen in Jabal, who "was the father of such as dwell in tents and have cattle." The initiation of what we may speak of as the fine arts was revealed in Jubal, "the father of all such as handle the harp and pipe." Here, too, we find the beginning of mechanical skill, as Tubal-cain was "the forger of every cutting instrument of brass and iron." In Lamech we have the portrait of a man at the pinnacle of such success. He repeated Cain's sin, but now evidently without any remorse, for in poetic language he is heard defending himself and boasting in his safety.

A third son is born to Adam and Eve, Seth; and the new line commences. Through Abel there is no succession. The posterity of Cain will ultimately be swept away in the Flood. Through Seth the seed of the woman will be preserved toward the ultimate victory.

GENESIS 5

In this chapter we have a condensed account of fifteen centuries in human history. The ruin of the race had come through man's belief in the devil's lie. "Ye shall not surely die." The repetition throughout the chapter of the sentence, "And he died," indicates the vindication of God against the lie of the devil. The chapter with its account of the ages of these men is of value as it reveals how early history was preserved. Adam was yet alive when Methuselah was born, and Methuselah was yet alive when Noah was born. Thus two persons form a link of connection between Adam and Abraham, a span of two thousand years. The story of creation and the fall may have been told by Adam to Methuselah, and by him to Noah. Noah still lived to be contemporary with Terah, the father of Abraham. This, of course, is merely suggestive, but does indicate a possibility.

It will be realized that the supreme glory of this chapter is its brief but wonderful picture of Enoch. One man who though living contemporaneously with Lamech yet lived in conformity with the will of God in life and conduct as it is so remarkably expressed, "Enoch walked with God." As a result of this fellowship in life, he was "translated that he should not see death," God thus indicating, even in the midst of all the darkness, His power to triumph by grace over the consequences of evil when man submits himself to Him on the basis of faith.

GENESIS 6

With the passing of the centuries, the degeneration of the individual and the family became that of society. There had been intermixture between the descendants of Cain and those of Seth, resulting in the Nephilim. These were strong and godless men, ultimately swept away by the Flood.

The description of life is a terrible one. "The wickedness of man was great" that describes the outward condition; "every imagination of the thoughts of his heart was only evil continually" that describes the inward character. The completeness of the depravity is revealed in the use of the words, "every," "only," "continually." God was defied and the flesh with its passions and lusts was regnant.

All this "Jehovah saw." His fiat went

forth that His Spirit should not always strive with man, and the limit of one hundred and twenty years was set.

Amid this degeneration Noah is seen as a man walking with God. With this man God holds communion and brings him into co-operation with Himself for the preservation of a seed and the bearing of testimony.

The closing declaration, "Thus did Noah; according to all that God commanded him, so did he," is a remarkable revelation of his faith.

It was a period of strange experiences. Strong men and godless were living and flourishing in all things mental and material. There is no doubt that for material gain they co-operated with Noah in the building of the Ark, which they must have held in supreme disdain. Nevertheless, in every nail driven and foot of work completed, space was given to them to repent. Noah preached righteousness by the very building of the Ark. Yet it would seem as though none profited, save Noah and his family; and his carpenters were finally destroyed outside the Ark which they had helped to construct.

GENESIS 7

At last the work was completed, and the man who by faith had done that which was evidence of his folly in the eyes of the world entered the Ark, leaving behind him all his possessions.

Then came the swift and final judgment of God against the corrupted race.

The righteousness of this judgment can be challenged only by such as fail to notice carefully the corruption of the race as to its nature and extent. The only way in which it was possible to ensure the eventual purity of the race, and thus realize the divine ideal in its creation was by the destruction of that which was utterly and irrevocably corrupt.

Love, illumined by light, acts not merely in the interests of the present moment, but of all the coming centuries. There is a severity which is of the very essence of tenderness; and the story of the Flood is an instance of the actuality of the love of God.

Questions as to the universality of the Flood are not relevant to the story as it is written in Genesis. All that this story declares is that the destruction was coextensive with the region occupied by man. The Hebrew word used uniformly for "the earth" through this section, *erets,* is used sometimes of the whole earth, sometimes of a part of it, as we may use the word "land." All that this account demands is that we should understand that a corrupt race was swept away and a godly remnant spared.

GENESIS 8

Upborne on the billows of judgment, the Ark rode securely, holding within it the nucleus of a new departure in human history. When the work of judgment was fully accomplished, the waters decreased, and the voice that had commanded Noah to build the Ark and to enter therein called him forth.

What a stupendous moment it was in the history of the race and in the experience of this man when he emerged from what had been practically a prison, and yet the vantage-ground of God for the continuity of His plan and purpose for humanity.

He who by faith had renounced everything in obedience to God, in spite of all appearances, now stepped forth, the sole possessor of the earth. A new day was dawning for humanity, a day of new opportunity in which men would live with history's testimony to the fact of the divine government and judgment, forever speaking to them of the issues of sin and of the impossibility of escape from the government of God.

The first act of Noah as he found

himself delivered from judgment and established in possession was a reaction of response and in itself was most significant. His first look was Godward, and his first act the erection of an altar and the offering of sacrifices.

This attitude and action were answered by a declaration of God which was full of grace. His knowledge of the fact of sin still remaining is declared, but henceforth it was not to be the gauge of His dealing with man. In spite of sin the promise was made that the natural order should continue, seasons come and go, and the day and night should not cease. In other words the declaration was that the earth was not to be involved in the chaos which followed the primal cataclysm (Genesis 1:2), but continue to be the sphere for carrying out His purposes in humanity.

GENESIS 9

The new order in human affairs was initiated by the bestowment of a blessing on Noah and his sons. The first note of change is seen in the word which declared man's relation to the lower orders. In Eden man had governed by love and his own kingliness. With the loss of that kingliness resulting from his disobedience and rebellion, he had lost his true power of dominion, and that must now be exercised by fear and dread directly implanted by God in all the lower orders of life over which man was to rule.

Moreover, an alteration was made in the law of human interrelationship. A sterner rule than family discipline must be set up. Man must now hold the sword of justice, and himself insist on obedience. Another change concerned human sustenance. In addition to the green herb of the past, animal food was permitted under restrictions.

The earth was thus to be repeopled by a race living under new conditions, and at this point a new covenant between God and man came into force. Its terms reminded man that the promises of God are conditional.

A token of the covenant was chosen and established. God appropriated an existing wonder as the sign and seal thereof, the rainbow. The rainbow is born of light falling on raindrops and so is significant of judgment as related to love. Man was to look on this, remembering that God also was looking on it.

The chapter ends with the story of a startlingly sudden plunge into darkness. Noah is seen yielding to fleshly appetite. In the presence of the degradation of their father, the character of the sons was manifest. One, himself degraded, yielded to curiosity. Two, ashamed of the sin of their father, attempted to hide him. The cursing and blessing which fell from the lips of Noah were no capricious passing of sentences. Rather, they formed a clear statement of the tendency of character. The man in the grip of evil moved to slavery, while the man influenced by purity and love proceeded to government and blessing.

GENESIS 10

In this chapter we have a simple and straightforward account of the dispersion of the sons of Noah and their families after the Flood. The descendants of Japheth moved toward the isles or the coastlands. The descendants of Ham moved toward the plains of Shinar and thence on. The descendants of Shem moved toward the hill country of the east.

It is not possible very clearly to define geographically today the districts occupied by various descendants of Noah.

What is clear, however, and to be carefully observed is that their movements were under a direct divine guidance, even though they may not have been conscious of it. Christian ethnologists still claim that all the races of today may be traced back to these revealed origins.

This chapter finds interpretation, in some measure, in the address of Paul on Mars' Hill in which he declared that God "made of one every nation of men to dwell on all the face of the earth, having determined their appointed seasons, and the bounds of their habitation."

GENESIS 11

In this chapter we have the account of a human movement against dispersion. The movement was one of rebellion and was frustrated by divine interposition. The divine intention was the covering of the whole earth. The human action was in opposition to that, as men said, "Lest we be scattered abroad upon the face of the whole earth."

This rebellious purpose was frustrated by the confusion of tongues. Necessarily belief in this story demands belief in the possibility of God's direct intervention in the affairs of men by what we sometimes speak of as supernatural methods. Any argument which is valid against the story of the confusion of tongues at Babel is equally valid against the account of the gift of tongues at Pentecost.

In this chapter we find the history narrowed. The lines of development through Ham and Japheth are omitted and the generations of Shem are given. This marks the selection of that branch of the race from which a man is to be chosen, out of whose loins a new nation is to spring, from which the great Deliverer will come.

In the last section of the chapter we have an account of the movement toward the adoption of a simple faith as the one law of life. Terah moved from Ur of the Chaldees. It is not stated that this was in response to a faith. The fact, however, that it was in the direction of the divine intention would suggest that it was so. Carefully observe these words, however, "And Terah . . . went forth . . . to go into the land of Canaan; and they came unto Haran, and dwelt there." It is the record of a start in a right direction which lacked persistence. Terah paused half way and dwelt at Haran until he died. The true man of faith is seen acting so far under the influence of his father; and bound by the earthly tie he abode with him in Haran.

GENESIS 12

At this point begins the actual historic movement toward the coming of the Redeemer. One man was called to the realization of the true principle of life. The call was personal and purposeful. Abram was commanded to sever the ties of all past associations and to go forth, governed wholly by the will of God. The personal element is clearly marked in the words, "Get thee out . . . I will show thee . . . I will make of thee . . . I will bless thee." It was none the less a purposeful call. The personal going was to result in the creation of a nation through which all the nations of the earth were to be blessed.

Abram's obedience was immediate. Arrived in the land, God appeared to him again and declared that that land was to be given to his seed. All the appearances of the hour were against the possibility of the fulfilment of that promise, for "the Canaanite was then in the land." Faith conquered in spite of appearances as Abram pitched his tent, a sign of possession, and built his altar, a symbol of allegiance.

Once more we confront human failure in Abram's deflection from the life of faith. In the presence of famine he attempted to secure his own safety by going into Egypt. As the result of this we have the startling picture of the chosen mother of the promised Seed in the harem of Pharaoh. God however guards the larger issue of His purpose against the mistakes of the instrument, and by plaguing Pharaoh's house brought about the deliverance of Abram.

It is ever a humbling thing when a man of faith who stands for the principle and purpose of God is rebuked by someone outside the covenant for lack of loyalty to truth. Yet this is exactly what happened in the case of Abram.

GENESIS 13

Thus, delivered by the divine intervention, Abram set his face again toward the line of the divine purpose and returned to Bethel. In this act is seen the victory of faith over failure.

It was at this crisis that the separation came between Abram and Lot. The occasion was strife between herdsmen, but the reason is to be found in the differing principles governing the lives of the two men. Abram was following God. Lot had been following Abram; and while in the deepest desire of his life he was loyal to God, the lack of direct communion seems to have resulted in clouding his vision and lowering his ideals. In the hour of crisis he made his own choice and it was the choice of a man attempting to compromise. The conflict of desire within him is seen in the phrases, "like the garden of Jehovah, like the land of Egypt." If these two things could be made contributory, then success was ensured by all the standards of human measurement.

Abram is seen in direct contrast to Lot in every way. Lot chose for himself. God chose for Abram. Lot chose by sight; "And Lot lifted up his eyes, and beheld." Abram, by faith, chose not to choose; and now Jehovah brought him into the place of sight on the basis of faith: "Lift up now thine eyes." Lot, having chose, obtained, and yet did not possess. Abram, trusting God, received from Him the title deeds to all the land, even including that which Lot had chosen for himself.

Abram immediately moved his tent and built his altar. In this connection the strength of faith is most clearly seen. Dependent on the promise of a seed to be as the dust of the earth, which at this time must have appeared to be contrary to all the probabilities of Nature, he took possession of the land by faith.

GENESIS 14

In this chapter we see Lot and Abram in differing circumstances, resulting in the first case from personal choice, and in the second from the choice of God. Lot was involved in trouble through association. He had chosen his possession, pitched his tent toward Sodom, and finally moved into Sodom. Desiring Sodom's privileges, he had adopted Sodom's policy and had become a sharer in Sodom's peril. Abram, the man for whom God chose, was in the place of separation from peril and was living in quietness and prosperity.

Nevertheless, he went at once to the help of Lot and gained a complete victory over the kings opposing him. Notwithstanding this victory, Lot again moved back into Sodom and took up his abode there.

After the conflict with the kings, the man of faith was refreshed by the appearance of Melchizedek. Very remarkable is this appearance at this time. The only other references to Melchizedek are found in a psalm, and in a New Testament writing where he is named in his priesthood, a type of Christ.

Abram refused the reward which the king of Sodom offered. The blessing of Melchizedek had been all that his heart desired; and in refusing the rewards offered by the king of Sodom, he quoted the very words of Melchizedek, "God Most High, possessor of heaven and earth."

The lessons of this story are obvious.

In the case of Lot it is seen that the voice of God, disobeyed, becomes unheard, and the most startling circumstances fail to arouse the conscience. In the case of Abram it is seen that a right attitude toward God creates a right attitude toward all men. He was eager to help Lot, recognized the superiority of Melchizedek, and was quick to perceive the danger of receiving gifts from the king of Sodom.

GENESIS 15

This is the account of the fourth direct appearance of Jehovah to Abram and evidently it had direct connection with what had immediately preceded. Abram had passed through two conflicts, the first with kings, the second with the suggestion of enrichment from the treasury of Sodom. In both he had been victorous. Now the divine voice declared, first, "I am thy shield," reminding him of how his victory over the kings had been obtained; while the second word, "I am . . . thy exceeding great reward" reminded him that he had lost nothing in refusing the reward offered by the king of Sodom.

In response to this word of God Abram's faith moved to a higher level. He was able to speak to God of the temptation to doubt which was in his heart. He was at once answered with the divine promise of an heir and was commanded to look at the stars to find the measure of the issue, "if thou be able to number them." Abram could not, but God could. So was his seed to be. Looking at the stars, he would know there was order where he could not discover it, number where he could not follow it; purpose where he could not trace it. He believed very literally; he built on God and God counted it to him for righteousness.

Jehovah now repeated the promise that he should inherit the land and in response to Abram's request gave him a sign. It was given in connection with sacrifice. In a horror of great darkness Abram received the revelation of trouble that lay ahead of his people and of an issue out of it. This, by the significant vision of a smoking furnace and a lamp. Abram's request for a sign was the request of faith. Therefore it was granted. When unbelief requests a sign, it is refused.

GENESIS 16

The previous story makes it evident that the principle of faith is the true philosophy of life. It builds on God and is satisfied with Him. It thus becomes the source of all righteousness. Faith, therefore, is the highest activity of reason.

All this stands out in even more startling vividness by contrast in the story contained in this chapter. Here we have the account of the second deflection from faith in the conduct of Abram. It is a sad one and the issue of the failure continued through the following history. The failure of faith consisted in Abram attempting, at the instigation of Sarai, to further the purposes of God by human cleverness and contrivance. The seed was promised and when there appeared no likelihood of the promise being fulfilled on the human level, there was deflection from the divine line for raising seed through Hagar.

The harvest of this folly Abram began to reap almost immediately in the division of his own household and the bitterness that sprang up therein between Sarai and Hagar, and the ultimate flight of Hagar through Sarai's harsh dealing with her. The far-reaching result is found in the story of the posterity of Ishmael as a constant source of trouble to the posterity of Isaac. Where faith fails, evil is wrought, the issues of which are far-reaching.

There is a very beautiful part to this story, however, in the tenderness of God toward Hagar, the wronged one; and in her recognition of Him and consequent naming of the well in the wilderness by which she had in all probability sunk down exhausted. It was called "Beer-lahai-roi," that is, "The Well of the Living One who seeth Me."

GENESIS 17

This chapter gives the account of the fifth appearance of God to Abram in which a divine covenant was made. At this point his name was changed from Abram, which means exalted father, to Abraham, which means, the father of a multitude. The change was significant, as it placed emphasis not upon the importance of the man, but upon the purpose of God through him. Here Jehovah announced Himself as El-Shaddai, the full meaning of which is God all-sufficient.

Abraham yielded himself to the revelation in adoring prostration and thus entered into a yet higher region of fellowship. It was now that the symbol of circumcision was appointed. This was to be an outward and visible sign of an inward and invisible relationship. It is well to remind ourselves that while this rite was indeed the sign of a spiritual relationship, it was by no means capricious and cruel but hygienic and beneficent. Medical science has now set its seal on the value of the rite.

At this point also the name of Sarai was changed to Sarah. The meaning of the old name is uncertain. The meaning of the new is Princess, in that she was to be the mother of nations. Abraham's laughter, unlike Sarah's later, was the laughter of gladness; and if the questions asked seem to suggest doubt, the fact of asking them on his face before God is evidence of the triumph of faith.

It was now that Abraham, in communion, gave expression to something that was evidently pulling at his heart. Ishmael was dear to him. The answer of God was not discipline, but the reaffirmation of a divine purpose. God is ever patient with us when the heart clings in affection to some method which is not His own. However, He never allows the man of faith to have his own way. There is a kindness which would be cruel. There is an apparent cruelty which is of the essence of kindness.

GENESIS 18

This is the account of the sixth appearance of God to Abraham. In it four phases of relationship between God and Abraham are revealed. God visited Abraham and Abraham provided for Him. God bestowed on Abraham and Abraham received from Him. God communicated to Abraham and Abraham answered with the statement of a difficulty. God listened to Abraham and Abraham interceded with Him.

The picture of Abraham providing for the supernatural Visitors is beautiful in its revelation of his love and loyalty; but yet more in its manifestation of the grace of God.

Jehovah now communicated to Abraham His purpose concerning the cities of the Plain and His reasons for making this communication were stated. Abraham was the depository of blessing to the nations. It was fitting that his children should know the meaning of the destruction of Sodom.

Abraham found himself confronted with a difficulty which had to do with the strict justice of God; and his question, "shall not the Judge of all the earth do right?" revealed his anxiety for the vindication of the character of God among the nations. The story of the intercession of Abraham with God on behalf of the cities, in the interest of the righteous, is a wonderful revelation of the patience of

God. He will ever listen to honest intercession, though He knows His ways are infinitely better than the fears that prompt our prayers. The sequel shows that in His action He goes beyond anything we ask. Abraham stopped at ten. Jehovah saved the two or three in whom there was any trace of recognition of Himself.

GENESIS 19

Here the story of the visit of Jehovah and the angels is continued. Here we see the two angels coming to Lot. By this time Lot had attained to a position of eminence in Sodom. The phrase, "sitting in the gate," indicates that. The three Visitors sat and ate with Abraham. The two would hardly enter the dwelling of Lot. Whereas he was anxious to deliver them from the known wickedness of the citizens, it is evident how he had failed in the life of faith. The man who had attempted to compromise with principle is here seen hated of the world, having lost his personal peace, his testimony paralyzed, and utterly unable to influence his city toward righteousness.

The revelation of his failure is most clearly seen in his inability to influence his own family. Moreover, the deterioration of his own character is vividly portrayed. Here, in sight of judgment, he lingered and was saved only as angel hands laid hold on him and practically forced him forth.

The destruction of the cities of the Plain was due to corruption, following godless prosperity. Their cup of iniquity was full. Their unutterable pollution flamed forth in their attitude toward the supernatural Visitors. Over against this terrible failure of Lot, Abraham is seen as the man of faith. He had interceded for Sodom and now stood at the place where he met Jehovah, looking toward the cities of the Plain. Were his prayers unanswered? Nay, verily, for "God remembered Abraham, and sent Lot out of the midst of the overthrow."

GENESIS 20

Once again we have to face Abraham's deflection from faith. We see him journeying south to Gerar. This was the center of a race of men who, having driven out the original possessors of the land, were becoming more and more warlike, and were afterward to be known as the Philistines.

As Abraham approached, an old fear recurred and a former failure was repeated.

These deflections from faith in the life of Abraham did not occur in the great fundamental things, nor in the main essentials of his walk with God; but rather in the application of the principle of faith to the smaller details of life.

As we have said, this was the second time Abraham attempted by his own supposed cleverness to steer clear of a danger he feared; and once again, as in the former case, he ran on the very rocks he dreaded. The result was that the man who stood as a witness for Jehovah was seen by the heathen practicing deceit, and thus suffering the degradation of being censured by Abimelech, the heathen king.

Our deflections from faith occur most often through our failure to allow God to undertake in all the small matters of life. Some trivial business worry, or home difficulty, or personal danger, will drive us to acts that dishonor our Master. The highest activity of faith is that which completely confides in God, not only in crisis, but in the commonplaces of life.

GENESIS 21

At last in God's "set time," and in spite of all natural difficulties, the long-promised son was born. Sarah who at an earlier point had laughed with the laughter of incredulity, now laughed with the laughter of realization.

There is something vivid and startling, even, in the story of Ishmael. It was necessary that, because of an act of unbelief, the son should be cast out in order to carry out the divine purpose. Yet in this act the tenderness of God is revealed in that He "heard the voice of the lad," and sent an angel, promising that he also should become a great nation.

The principal value of the story is that of the part it plays in the history of Abraham. In spite of personal inclination and in simple obedience, he sent forth the child of the bond-woman and leaned back wholly and only on the divine provision for the fulfilment of the promise.

The chapter closes with the account of the covenant made with Abimelech. This covenant was based on Abimelech's clear recognition of the fact that God was with Abraham. Notwithstanding the previous failure of Abraham's faith, which had brought about Abimelech's rebuke, the deeper fact of the existence of his faith had influenced this man and did bring him into covenant relationship with God through Abraham. As the story is written, there seems to be no reason to think that in this covenant made on the basis of the recognition of God there was anything contrary to the purpose of God. I prefer to think of it as revealing the influence that might have been growingly exerted by the people of faith had they been true to God.

GENESIS 22

In this chapter we have the account of the seventh appearing of Jehovah to Abraham and it is that of his supreme testing and consequent bringing into fellowship with God. It must have been in many ways a desolating trial, without apparent reason, coming suddenly and without explanation. Nevertheless, it is the story of the triumph of faith. Abraham passed through the fiercest fire and endured the greatest pressure as his faith was put to the most tremendous strain.

The statement that "God did prove Abraham" is in itself suggestive. He confers honor where He proves. He did not prove Lot. Sodom did that. God proves the man who is proof against Sodom. The outstanding revelation of Abraham is that of one who walking by faith and not by sight rendered active, ready, and quick obedience. The man who really believes in God is always able cheerfully to obey Him, because present sacrifice is set in the light of the necessity for the fulfilment of God's declared purpose. Abraham rested in God rather than in any blessing He bestowed, even though that were Isaac. Faith depending on the divine promises saw beyond the sacrifice and was able to obey.

It may be that the story can never be interpreted in the realm of the natural, and the only thing we can say about it is that through the experience Abraham was brought into fellowship with the God who so loved the world that He gave His only begotten Son.

The testing was followed by the repetition to Abraham of all the great and gracious promises already made to him.

GENESIS 23

We now see Abraham in the midst of personal sorrow, which reveals his character in a remarkable way.

Sarah, who had ever been to him a princess, was now taken from his side, which meant the loss of the strongest human prop to Abraham's faith. It must be remembered that she had been with him along the whole pathway of obedience from Ur of the

Chaldees. She had shared his hours of darkness and his hours of light. Doubtless at times she had been a cause of fear and trembling to him, and his very love for her had brought him to some deflections from faith. But far more often her comradeship had strengthened him.

When she died, Abraham is seen in his action as a man full of the dignity that comes from faith. He was first of all a mourner, shedding the tears which expressed the sorrow and loneliness of his life. Faith never kills affection, and the man was keenly alive to the loss he had sustained.

Yet faith never allows sorrow to overwhelm. He "rose up from before his dead." His next action was definitely one of faith. He did not take Sarah to Ur, but buried her in the land which God had given to him. That faith operated, moreover, in the method he now followed. He was willing to receive the land as a gift from God, but would not receive part of God's gift as a gift from the sons of Heth. Abraham's first actual possession in the land, therefore, was a grave. This in itself is a teaching and a prophecy. God begins where man ends. The sorrows of life reveal a man's true character as perhaps nothing else can. Faith weeps beside the dead and then moves on to fulfilment of duty as it puts a check on sorrow. Faith takes hold of earth's greatest despair, death, and makes it the occasion of a possession which holds within itself all the future.

GENESIS 24

This chapter is complete in itself and is a perfect idyll. Abraham was well stricken in years. Sarah was dead. Isaac, the son of Abraham, was still unmarried. In the interest of the divine program Isaac must not marry a Canaanite nor go back to find a bride among the people who had been left behind. Thus Eliezer was sent to seek a bride among his own kindred. Of course, the story is Eastern, and gives the account of how the quest was undertaken and rewarded.

In this story Laban appears and his masterfulness is manifest in the way he acted as host in the house of his father. Rebekah's consent to go showed her responding to the divine purpose and her willingness to move forward along the divine pathway.

The story of the woman going the long distance toward her new home, and of Isaac, the man of quiet, passive faith, meditating in the field at eventide, is picturesque and full of beauty. Apart from these details of the faraway land, we have here a beautiful picture of an ideal marriage. It is the union of a man and woman on the basis of identity in principle. By faith Isaac waited and by faith Rebekah obeyed. It is, moreover, the union of opposites. In Rebekah faith was adventurous and bold. In Isaac faith was retiring and meek. The two lives were made one on the basis of response to a common principle. Two natures utterly different, yet complementing each other, were united for the fulfilment of a divine purpose. In the story of these two as it proceeds we shall come across failure on both sides, but here the shadows have not gathered, and the faith of Abraham is rewarded in the union of his son, a man of passive faith, with Rebekah, a woman whose faith is adventuresome and bold.

GENESIS 25

The record of the death of Abraham is full of beauty. His life had been spent in the realm of the supernatural, the region of vision, the power of the spiritual. The whole of it is summed up in the words which declared that he died, "an old man, and full." His life was satisfied and rounded out to completion. He had started out to find a land and to found a nation. He died with no possession but a grave, and no sight of his posterity other than his son Isaac and his grandsons Esau and Jacob. Yet he died "full," that is, satisfied.

In this chapter begins the section dealing more especially with the life of Isaac. Two divine appearances are recorded as having been granted to him and in each case they were for ratification. His faith was ever passive rather than active and produced rest rather than initiation.

In the account of the birth of Esau and Jacob the brothers are placed in strong contrast; the first wild and romantic; the second, as the margin reads, "harmless" or "perfect," a dweller in tents. This is an interesting statement at the beginning of a story in which so much will be seen of Jacob that is mean and contemptible. Here, however, is the truth concerning him.

Degeneration in the character of Isaac is evidently marked in the statement that his love for Esau was caused by his eating Esau's venison. Neither Esau nor Jacob is to be admired. The one, profane, allowing the lower side of his nature to master him, sold his birthright to appease physical hunger; the other took advantage of that hunger to obtain the birthright.

GENESIS 26

We have here the account of the first direct divine communication of Jehovah to Isaac. It came in a time of difficulty such as that which had caused his father to go down into Egypt. Warned against repeating that folly, he was thus saved from making his father's mistake. Strangely enough, however, he repeated the folly of his father in Gerar in connection with Abimelech. The story reminds us that there is no richer inheritance into which a man can enter than a godly parentage, but that, after all, every man has to fight his own battles and work out his own salvation.

The quiet patience of Isaac is manifested in the matter of the wells. He first proceeded to dig again the wells of his father Abraham. His servants then dug a new well, for which the Philistine herdsmen contended, and he called it Esek, that is, Contention. Still persevering, they dug another and this was followed by further strife. This well Isaac named Sitnah, which means enmity. Again they dug and no contention followed. All this was the calm persistence of faith.

Returning from Gerar to Beersheba, Jehovah made His second direct communication to Isaac. It would seem as though this communication followed Isaac's return to his own proper place. It was of the nature of the ratification of the covenant, and Isaac at once responded in a way which indicated his fidelity in heart to the principle of faith. He built an altar and pitched a tent. This action was followed by a visit from Abimelech and a covenant between him and Isaac very similar to that made between Abraham and Abimelech.

In the story we see how faith operates in the case of such quieter and less adventurous natures.

GENESIS 27

From this point the history passes to center largely around Jacob. At the beginning, four persons stand out: Isaac, Rebekah, Esau, and Jacob, and not one of them is admirable. Isaac is even more degenerate in his devotion to the physical. Rebekah knows the purpose of God but is not content to wait. Esau is still the same, a man of physical strength, completely centered therein. Jacob is weak as he yields to the suggestion of his mother.

Over the whole is seen the activity of the divine government, overruling deceit and duplicity, so that the purpose of the divine counsel moves forward. Isaac, when the facts are discovered, was seized with a strange trembling, born assuredly of his sense of the overruling majesty of God. The trembling led to the action of faith in which he refused to interfere in the matter of the blessing which he had pronounced unwittingly on Jacob.

Esau's natural reaction was hatred for Jacob, which created anxiety in the mind of Rebekah, and she began to arrange to send Jacob out of the reach of danger.

In all probability Rebekah never saw Jacob again. Her plan was that he should tarry with Laban a few days only, and she distinctly declared her intention to send for him again. But she never did.

GENESIS 28

Here Jacob is seen exiled from his home, flying from Beersheba. In this connection we have the account of the first of the direct divine communications to him. Tired and weary, he reached Luz and during a dream he had a vision which suggested communication between heaven and earth. What impressed Jacob, however, seems not to have been that part of the vision, but the fact that Jehovah was there in that distant place and that He spoke to him. On waking, Jacob declared his new consciousness of the presence of God. It is not to be wondered at that such a revelation filled him with a sense of awe as he cried, "How dreadful is this place."

On the following morning he showed the two sides of his nature. His deep religious conviction and faith were indicated by the erection of a stone and naming the place Beth-el, the House of God. His restless activity was manifested in the bargaining spirit in which he expressed himself. In the vision of the night God had promised to be with him and now he says that if that will be so, he will give a tenth of all he possesses to God. That is faith but on a low level. Nevertheless, there can be no doubt that the memory of the midnight vision remained with him through all the coming days. It is evident that by this appearance he was arrested, and the spirit of his coming to the house of Laban was changed.

GENESIS 29

Pursuing his journey after his experience at Luz, now called Beth-el, Jacob came into "the land of the children of the east." Here the next twenty years of his life were to be spent, during which he amassed his wealth. As presently he himself said, he went out carrying only his staff: "With my staff I passed over this Jordan" (32:10). When he returned, he was wealthy, as his words, again interpreted by the time and place, reveal, ". . . and now I am become two companies."

At this point the story of his dealings with Laban commences. On the human side it is a fascinating account of the conflict of two strong, astute men. There is really little to admire in the methods of either. However, of the two, as we shall see, Laban was the more to be despised. Here, too, we have the beginning of the story of the one great human love in the life of Jacob, the story of his meeting with and eventual winning of Rachel. There is no doubt that it is a pure love story, and all the subsequent history shows how dear to the heart of Jacob was this woman of pastoral life, the shepherdess of her father's sheep.

Laban met Jacob with effusive greetings, and, with the shrewdness that characterized him, there can be no doubt he saw how much he might gain from the services of Jacob. This accounts for the readiness with which he promised him Rachel to wife. The true nature of the man, however, was clearly manifested in the brutal deceit he practiced on Jacob at the end of the seven years. Love, however, is stronger than all opposition and Jacob served Laban another seven years for Rachel. It may be pointed out that he did not wait those seven years, for they were united at once. Nevertheless, he carried out the terms of the bargain.

GENESIS 30

In reading these stories we must never forget that we are looking at things as they were in that far-gone time and must make all necessary allowances for the imperfect light in which these people lived. That, however, does not prevent our seeing how much is chronicled here which contradicts the principle of faith. It is the story of domestic trouble and heart-burning out of which arose actions utterly out of keeping with the life of simple trust. Nevertheless, throughout there is a manifest consciousness of the divine overruling. The interpretation of that government is often at fault, as when Rachel imagined that the son born to Bilhah was in any sense an answer to prayer. That answer came with the birth of Joseph.

At the birth of Joseph, Jacob attempted to break from Laban. Laban, however, realized that Jacob's coming and sojourn with him had brought him great gain; and for pure selfishness he was anxious to retain him. Thus a new compact was entered into between them.

Laban at once attempted to make impossible the enrichment of Jacob by setting three days' journey between the cattle ringstraked, speckled, and spotted, and the rest, giving the former into the hands of his sons, and the latter into the hands of Jacob. It was an attempt to frustrate the possibility of Jacob's gaining anything from the compact. The sequel shows that he had underestimated the shrewdness of his nephew.

Neither side acted admirably; but watching the movement between two schemers, it is impossible to avoid a feeling of satisfaction that Jacob was one too many for Laban. Comparing Jacob with Abraham, however, one sees how much lower was the level of his faith. Abraham had been content to let the scheming Lot choose. Jacob, always believing in God, nevertheless was not able to commit these matters of worldly possession to Him.

GENESIS 31

In the midst of Jacob's success the second divine communication came to him, commanding him to return to the land of his fathers and giving him the promise, "I will be with thee." Thus, after at least twenty years' absence, he set his face again toward home. The same cunning which had been manifested throughout is seen in the stealth with which he broke away from Laban.

Much may happen in twenty years. However, one thing can never happen. The wrongdoing of the past cannot be undone and Jacob started for home with fear, for Esau his brother was yet alive. Nevertheless, the call of God was supreme to him and he went obediently.

Rachel practiced deceit in that she stole the teraphim of her father. This led to one more meeting between Laban and Jacob. After heated controversy, they separated, having erected a stone or a heap and named it Mizpah. It was the symbol of suspicion and called on God to watch between them. It is really a sad spectacle of two men calling on God, not to ratify their comradeship, but to watch over them on behalf of each other in order that neither may wrong the other. The account of the connection between these two men has been full of interest, but its final message is that selfish partnership invariably issues in suspicion and separation.

GENESIS 32

This is unquestionably one of the great chapters of the Bible, and it is significant how constant and powerful is its appeal to all who live on the principle of faith. It gives the account of the third direct communication of God to Jacob.

As he returned to his own land, the same conflicting principles which have been evident throughout are still manifest. His going at all was in direct obedience to the distinct command of God. There was really no other reason to return. He might still have stayed with Laban and outwitted him for his own enrichment. Nevertheless, the manner of his going was characterized by independence and confidence in his own ability. This is seen in the account of the elaborate and carefully calculated preparation he made for meeting Esau. He was ready to placate Esau with presents, and prepared a list of them. However, they were to be used only if Esau was hostile.

This coming back into the land was an event of great importance which Jacob seems to have recognized. When all his own arrangements were made he voluntarily stayed behind and went down to the Jabbok, quite evidently for some dealing with God. Then and there, in the quiet and stillness of the night, God met with him in the form of a man. Wrestling with him, God demonstrated his weakness to Jacob, finally appealing to his spiritual consciousness by crippling him in his body. This is certainly a story of Jacob's victory, but it was a victory won when, conscious of a superior power, he yielded and, with strong crying and tears, out of weakness was made strong. Jacob's limp was a life-long disability, but it was also the patent of his nobility.

GENESIS 33

The morning broke and Jacob—or Israel as he had now become—went forward to meet Esau. How strange a mixture there was in the make-up of this man is once more clearly evident. It is patent that fear of his brother still lurked in his heart and there is a touch of nobleness in his going forward alone to meet him, having set his loved ones behind in two companies. Moreover, his love of Rachel is again manifest as he put her in the second company, so that if Esau met him in anger she, at any rate, might have a better chance to escape.

The chief interest of this story, however, is found in Esau's attitude. In him Jacob met no angry man but a brother. It would appear that Esau had started to meet Jacob with revenge in his heart, as the armed bands suggest. But God has the disposing of all hearts in His own power; and while He had been dealing with Jacob by the brook, probably all unconsciously to Esau, He had been dealing with him too, changing his attitude toward Jacob.

The measure of a man's finding God is ever that of his discovery of a pathway straitened and yet smoothed. Evidently, all Jacob's preparations to appease Esau would have been of no avail, for Esau did not want them. But God had met and dealt with the difficulty for this man who had been brought into submission to Him in the long struggle of the lonely night.

GENESIS 34

When Jacob parted from Esau he should have gone directly to Beth-el. The previous chapter shows that he did not do so but tarried at Shechem. Unquestionably, this was a mistake. There is nothing more perilous than to stay anywhere short of the place to which God is calling, and here we have the account of the sad and tragic reaping from this halt. It gives the story of a defiled daughter and of sons using the instruments of cruelty for vengeance. It is a startling revelation of how the fruits of a man's disobedience may be gathered in the history of his family. How often children have been harmed incalculably, because parents, while believing in God, have tarried at some Shechem of worldly advantage instead of centering life around Beth-el and the altar!

Jacob's complaint to Simeon and Levi was utterly unworthy of a man of faith. It breathed the spirit of selfish fear from first to last. There was no word of jealousy for the honor of God, or of appreciation of the necessity for the purity of the chosen seed. It is wholly indicative of a cowardly fear for himself. Th^ moment faith ceases to be the simple principle of life, selfishness is enthroned; and, instead of the calm courage which is ever the result of obedient faith, there ensues the cowardly fear of personal suffering.

GENESIS 35

God never abandons His children to the forces of evil circumstances resulting from their own folly. The fourth direct communication to Jacob was that which called him back to Beth-el. Again the evidence of his faith in God is found in the fact that his response was immediate. Moreover, its genuineness is evidenced by his destruction of the foreign gods, the quick movement to Beth-el, and the immediate erection there of an altar.

This obedience was followed immediately by the fifth divine communication; only the name Israel was again pronounced. It would seem almost as though Jacob had not entered into the experience of the blessing won by the Jabbok until now. In that night the vision had come to him, and his crippling was evidence of the reality of the divine action. All this, however, had not been translated into victory in the details of his life.

How often this is so. In some great crisis of revelation a larger life is seen, its laws appreciated, and its claims intellectually yielded to. Yet it is not wrought out into the details of life, and so oftentimes its greatest value is gained only through some subsequent experience of failure.

In this fifth of God's direct appearances to Jacob, God not only again declared the new name of the man, but gave him His own name with a new significance. It was the name El-Shaddai, which He had first used to Abraham on the occasion when his name was changed from Abram to Abraham. Its supreme value is its declaration of the all-sufficiency of God.

In this chapter we have also the account of the sorrows following on this experience: the death of Rachel, the sin of Reuben, the death of Isaac. All which things played their part in the final making of the man.

GENESIS 36

This is one of the sections of the biblical literature which all of us are tempted to hurry over, because it appears to be almost exclusively a list of names. We may allow that it appears uninteresting, nevertheless it is of great importance, having a very definite place and value in the highways of history.

The story of the prolific progeny of "that profane person Esau" is at once startling and solemn. The sons of the flesh would seem to have multiplied far faster than the seed of promise. The relationship between these two lines is revealed in a brief and pregnant sentence in the first verse, "Esau . . . is Edom," which is repeated in verse 19, and the fact is emphasized in the closing statement, "This is Esau, the father of the Edomites." These references are evidently intended to draw attention to the origins of the people who through long centuries were antagonistic to Israel.

Though, personally, Jacob escaped

the anger of his brother, the harvests resulting from his deceit were reaped in after years. These harvests of the centuries are full of suggestiveness. They reveal the awful and stupendous greatness of life. The deed of good or evil, of truth or falsehood, done today is not ended, though it is done. There is indeed nothing small.

GENESIS 37

From this point in the sacred narrative, though Jacob appears more than once, for a time the history centers around Joseph, and it is certainly safe to say that in many aspects no more remarkable figure appears on the pages of Old Testament history.

Joseph is seen here, first as the object of his father's love, a love which may surely be accounted for by the fact that he was the first-born of Rachel, and also to the ingenuous simplicity of his disposition and the strong integrity of his character.

If the marginal reading of the Revised Version be correct, and in all probability it is, that his father made him "a long garment with sleeves," this probably suggests his appointment to a position of trust and oversight, for such a garment was the garment of a prince. Naturally imaginative and romantic and given to day dreams, through this avenue God suggested his coming position and power. With simple artlessness he told his dreams to his brethren. The character of the man as subsequently revealed makes it impossible to believe that he had any ulterior motive in this telling of his dreams. The construction his brethren placed on the dreams was undoubtedly the true one; but was most likely arrived at as the result of the position he occupied among them by appointment of his father, and by their interpretation of his feeling by their own jealousies.

The story of his betrayal is at once a revelation of their malice and of the divine determined counsel to move forward to ultimate realization of purpose.

GENESIS 38

The sad and tragic story of Judah's corruption recorded here needs very little comment. It carries its own lessons of the frailty of human nature and of the far-reaching effects of sin.

However, placing it at this point in the history is suggestive and important. Following this revelation, we are observing the first movements of God in the process of regeneration amid the degeneration of the race. So far, we have been occupied almost exclusively with individuals. Gradually the larger outlook on the family and society emerges into view. The conditions which made possible Judah's sin, and the sin in itself, revealed the necessity for another new departure. A marked tendency toward the corruption of the chosen people by unhallowed intercourse with the people of the land was apparent. Had there been no divine over-ruling and had these people been left to themselves, the chosen seed would have inevitably been utterly corrupted and the purposes of God defeated.

While Judah was thus sinning, Joseph was already in Egypt, and so the segregation of the chosen people for a long period was already being prepared by keeping them separate from other people and by the rigid exclusiveness of the Egyptians.

GENESIS 39

Here begins the story of Joseph in Egypt which is so full of interest. Through the malice of his brethren he had been sold into slavery and in such condition we now see him. Here, at the very beginning of the story of his life and work in Egypt, we learn the secret of all his wonderful success, "Jehovah was with him," and also that,

"His master saw that Jehovah was with him."

In those two statements is revealed a man in circumstances which always have been calculated to degrade. He was a slave. Nevertheless, in these very circumstances he so lived as to demonstrate to his master that he was a man having communion with God. Potiphar's conviction resulted in Joseph's promotion.

While it is true that godly men must suffer persecution sooner or later, it is equally true that the life of simple godliness commands the respect and trust even of ungodly men.

Then follows the story of his temptation, a temptation subtle and fierce, presenting itself as it did in the person of one who was supposed to be infinitely Joseph's superior in social position. His quiet and heroic victory bears testimony to the strength of the man who lives with God habitually, even under circumstances of temptation, which are at once subtle and sudden and strong.

Once more his circumstances were changed, and he was a prisoner; and again it is declared, "Jehovah was with him"; and the fact was manifest with practically the same result of promotion to a position of trust. The chapter reveals the fidelity of God to a man who was loyal to Him. Whether in slavery or in prison, in prosperity or adversity, Jehovah was still with Joseph and he was triumphant.

GENESIS 40

The works of God are ever characterized by simplicity. No study is more fascinating in the Divine Oracles or in human experience than the wonderful mosaic of the divine government. If it may be stated reverently, it would seem as though there are no forces or facts on which God does not lay His hand in quiet strength and majesty and make them tributary to the accomplishment of His purpose.

He now worked certainly through the uncertain method of dreams. Prisoners, and Pharaoh, as we shall presently see, were troubled in the night and through such troubling God proceeded in carrying out His designs. When the butler and the baker dreamed and told their dreams to Joseph, he is revealed as a man still dependent on God, declaring that the interpretation of dreams belongs to Him.

There is a human touch in Joseph's request to the butler, "Have me in thy remembrance." He was conscious of the limitation of his life and evidently sighed for liberty as does every healthy man.

There is another human touch, and as natural but sad, in the words, "the . . . butler . . . forgat him." It is good to remember that God did not forget him.

GENESIS 41

Still the divine activity proceeded. Now it was Pharaoh who dreamed, and now the butler remembered. The result was that Joseph was brought before the king, and as he stood in the royal presence he was still the same man, dependent on God and proclaiming his dependence. In answer to the king's declaration that he had heard of his power to interpret dreams, Joseph said, "it is not in me: God will give Pharaoh an answer of peace." He then proceeded to interpret Pharaoh's dreams. The result was that Pharaoh recognized in him "a man in whom the Spirit of God is," and again Joseph was promoted.

It is well to note this repetition. In slavery, in prison, at the court of the king, Jehovah was with His servant. The fact was recognized in turn by Potiphar, the chief keeper, and by Pharaoh. In each case Joseph was placed in power, in the house of his master, in the prison of his confinement, and in the realm of the king.

True godliness will manifest itself and it always commands respect.

Thus the great regenerative movement of God proceeded and things are seen developing toward accomplishment of the divine purpose. One of the chief values of these Old Testament histories is the revelation of these facts. Moreover, this is not merely the story of a condition of affairs that existed long ago. It still exists. In the movements of our age a divine purpose is being wrought out through human history, even though we may not detect it.

GENESIS 42

According to the foretelling of Joseph in interpreting Pharaoh's dreams, the famine came; but through Joseph's executive ability Egypt was provided with corn sufficient not only for its own needs, but equal to the need of other peoples.

At last Joseph's brethren are seen fulfilling his dream of long ago and bowing down in his presence. His conversation with them is revealing. Questioned about themselves, they replied, "We . . . are twelve brethren . . . and one is not." These men were evidently conscious of their guilt. It would seem the memory of the wrong done to their brother long ago had haunted them through the years, recurring with new force in this hour of danger. While their action was utterly evil, yet they referred to their "brother." Though they had no consciousness that the Egyptian governor was their brother, the memory of the sin of long ago sprang up when they found themselves in peril.

When they returned to him without Simeon and communicated the demand of the governor that Benjamin should be brought to him, Jacob's complaint was full of sadness. The old man said, "All these things are against me." It was not the language of faith, and yet surely none of us can criticize him, for the outlook was dark enough. Had he been a man of less subtle faith, perchance he might have been able to say, "All things work together for good."

Though he was not able to say this, the fact remains that the things which seemed to be against him were really working together to give him back his long-lost boy and to carry toward completion those gracious purposes for which he and his father stood. As we study the story we may surely learn the lesson that it is never wise to measure the facts of any hour by the limits of our own vision.

GENESIS 43

All the old characteristics of Jacob are manifest in this account of his proposed method of dealing with the governor of Egypt with whom his sons had had to do. If things were against him, he did not lose confidence in his own ability to manipulate them to his own advantage. He would send a present and so appease the man.

In this action Jacob unconsciously revealed himself. It was his perpetual method of attempting to deal with other men. Always he seems to have thought that the great end of all men was to gain something, and so he imagined that the Egyptian ruler might be bribed into complacency. It is often so that we reveal ourselves in our estimates of others.

The picture of Joseph here is full of beauty. In the sense of worldly power he was now a great man. His position was one of national and even international power and influence. Notwithstanding this, the springs of true life were not dried up. His emotional nature was still quick and active. This is another evidence that he was living in fellowship with God. In some senses the perils of powerful position are subtler and graver than those of slavery and prison. Too often advancement and the ease and luxurious circumstances attendant on it serve to deaden the finer emotions of the soul. Even in such circumstances, however, a man is safe if Jehovah is with him. The rush of emotion which drove Joseph into secrecy for weeping is as sure an evidence of his true greatness as the statesmanlike qualities which had served him in the administration of the affairs of Egypt.

GENESIS 44

Occasionally, criticism of Joseph's action in placing the money and his cup in the sacks of his brethren has been made. To put the matter in the mildest form, surely such criticism reveals a lack of humor. The story is really most natural and beautiful. Such methods are best tested by their ultimate meaning and results. Joseph was preparing for a dramatic ending. One can imagine his quiet enjoyment of the difficulties of his brethren as he played this trick on them. It was a trick which could have been suggested only to a man who still had the heart of a boy. He was arranging for the moment when he would reveal himself and be able to pour out on them all the pent-up love of his heart.

Nobleness and beauty mark Judah's attitude and plea on behalf of his father. Evidently, back of his moving appeal was a keen consciousness of the sin of the past, and, so far as possible, a desire to atone or at least to prevent any further darkening of the last days of the old man. With splendid devotion to this high purpose, Judah asked to be allowed to take the place of Benjamin in the mouth of whose sack the governor's cup had been found.

GENESIS 45

In the account of Joseph's revelation of himself to his brethren, the chief value is in his recognition of the fact that his destiny had been in the hand of God: "It was not you that sent me hither, but God." This capacity for ignoring secondary causes is one of the surest signs of greatness. So it was that Joseph was able to forget and to forgive his brethren for selling him into slavery. It is a consciousness possible only to the life of habitual communion with God.

The important position Joseph occupied in Egypt is clearly seen in Pharaoh's attitude toward Joseph's father and his brothers.

When Jacob heard that his son was alive, his heart was touched to its depth: "It is enough; Joseph my son is yet alive: I will go and see him before I die." Thus he was beginning to find out that under the government of his covenant-keeping God the things he had declared to be against him were really for him. How good it is that when our faith wavers, God does not change His mind or purpose for us. He moves right on in infinite love toward the final good. How much feverish unrest we would be spared if only we would learn from these stories of the past to repose our confidence in God rather than in circumstance and quietly await His time.

GENESIS 46

This chapter should be read in the light of the whole divine movement we are attempting to keep in mind. The migration of Jacob and his sons to Egypt is here distinctly shown to be a part of God's program. At this juncture God appeared and charged him not to be afraid, making him a threefold promise. First, that He would make a great nation of him there, that is, in Egypt. How much lay concealed in that word Jacob perhaps did not understand. In all probability he understood the promise to mean great in numbers. That it had such intention there can be no doubt, but subsequent history shows that it meant far more, for through discipline and suffering the nation was to be made great in other ways than population increase. God reveals to men at any given time only so much as they are able to bear. And yet in case any fear should come to the heart of His servant, He promised him, second, "I will go down with thee"; and, finally, "I will . . . bring thee up." It is interesting to note that God still spoke to him by the old name "Jacob" recognizing that he had not experimentally entered into all that grace had provided for him, and indicating that notwithstanding his failure, God still continued to guide.

Joseph carefully arranged for the segregation of his people which was also undoubtedly part of the divine purpose. He charged them to declare themselves to Pharaoh as shepherds. That ensured the maintenance of the separation of the Egyptians from the Hebrews because "every shepherd is an abomination unto the Egyptians."

GENESIS 47

To watch Jacob is to see a man who alternated between faith and fear. Standing before Pharaoh, his faith in God and his consciousness of his own position in the divine economy were clearly apparent. The less is ever blessed of the greater, and when Jacob gave his blessing to Pharaoh it was undoubtedly with a consciousness of his own relation to a divine program.

Joseph's policy in administering Egyptian affairs must be judged by the times in which he lived. It was a policy which ensured the interests of the king, of the nation, and of the people. It was one of unification and consolidation. So far as Israel was concerned, his action precluded the possibility of their harassment by petty princes. It is equally true that by this very action Joseph made possible what subsequently happened, the enslavement of the whole people by the will of the supreme Pharaoh. Here again the hand of God is seen operating through the Egyptian policy for the immediate safety of His people and then for the discipline and suffering through which they were to pass.

The interchange of names in this story is arresting. Referring to the man, it is said that "Jacob lived in the land of Egypt"; but when referring to his departure, he is called "Israel"; Jacob, in himself; Israel, in the government of God. The writer of the letter to the Hebrews speaks of his faith as manifest only when dying he blessed his sons and worshiped, and even then speaks of him as "Jacob." In the end of this narrative his faith and fear are manifest: his faith, in that he chose to be buried with his fathers; his fear, in that he made Joseph swear so to bury him.

GENESIS 48

The use of the two names is observed once more. Jacob was sick, but, hearing that Joseph was coming to see him, it was Israel that strengthened himself. Once again Jacob was the speaker and in what he said the planning of the schemer was still evident.

Yet how wonderfully the divine overruling is seen, for in Jacob's adoption of Ephraim and Manasseh the redemption of Joseph from Egypt was brought about. Joseph had married an Egyptian woman and occupied a place of peculiar power in Egypt. What more likely than that his sons should be brought up as Egyptians? The action of Jacob in claiming these boys as his retained the succession of Joseph within the border of the people of God.

In the latter part of the story the name is Israel and the whole life of the man was one of faith. Evidently he acted entirely under divine impulse in crossing his hands so that the right lay on Ephraim's head and the left on Manasseh. Thus it is seen that notwithstanding all his faults and failures, this son of Isaac and Abraham was indeed a man of faith and an instrument through whom it was possible for God to carry out His purposes.

GENESIS 49

Before his passing, Jacob, in forecasting the future of his sons, based what he had to say on what he had already seen in them. In some cases the allusions are difficult to follow, and the connection is not easy to see. In others both are unmistakable.

Speaking of Reuben, Jacob declared that pre-eminence of privilege does not necessarily issue in pre-eminence of position. Of Simeon and Levi he declared that cruelty of character ever issues in division and scattering. In Judah he saw the shining of the central hope of himself and Israel. In Zebulun he saw all commercial supremacy and in Issachar the method of the diplomat bending to service in order to secure quietness. Dan, cunning and keen, was to exercise judgeship. Gad, the warlike, Asher, the luxurious, and Naphtali are all referred to.

Most tender and beautiful were Jacob's references to Joseph. He was a fruitful bough, which indicated his realization of possibility. Moreover, his branches were to run over the wall, thus exceeding the bounds of expectation. He was to know persecution but to abide in strength, and the most abundant blessings were pronounced on him. Benjamin was dismissed briefly as characterized by cunning and fierceness.

Then follows the story of Jacob's death, his last charge to his sons being that he should be buried among his own people.

GENESIS 50

Here we have a strange and wonderful sight. Jacob was buried with Egyptian pomp, yet in the land of promise. Thus, at last, after a career checkered from the beginning, Jacob entered into his rest. The study of his life reveals little to his own credit, but much to the strength of the grace of God. Nevertheless the activity of that principle of faith which is ever the basis of divine operation was revealed throughout. Well for us if from the story we learn to avoid his mistakes.

Jacob being dead and buried, Joseph's brethren were afraid. How little they knew their brother's heart. Again, with splendid magnanimity, he triumphed over their fear when he said to them, "Ye meant evil against me; but God meant it for good." It is always the prerogative of one whose life is lived in close relationship with God to be magnanimous toward those who, while attempting to harm him, do, nevertheless, carry out the divine intention of blessing.

At length, Joseph came to his last hour, declaring his confidence that his people would ultimately return to the God-appointed land, and charging them that in the day of their going they should take his bones with them.

Thus ends the Book of Genesis. It is a story of beginnings and not of completions. That which commenced with the majestic phrase, "In the beginning God," ends with the equally suggestive phrase, "a coffin in Egypt." Genesis demands a way out of Egypt for that coffin or else the faith of the man whose bones rest therein was of no effect. The name of the next Book is in itself an answer—Exodus.

Exodus

EXODUS 1

The first word of Exodus, "Now," might with equal accuracy be rendered "And." Either word serves to suggest continuity. The story of Genesis is taken up in Exodus. It begins by recording the prolific and rapid growth of the sons of Jacob in Egypt. They "were fruitful . . . increased abundantly . . . multiplied . . . waxed exceeding mighty . . . the land was filled with them." The progress of God is seen. After the fathers, the children, and the program of God is carried forward. Jacob and his sons lived in their children. Their faults were perpetuated through long generations. It is equally true that the underlying principle of faith continued, and though failure often occurred, seeming to overwhelm faith, the vital principle was never lost.

In the account of the enslavement and oppression of these people, human and divine elements are equally apparent. The policy of the new Pharaoh was politically selfish. He attempted to stay the growth and break the power of the people. How little he understood the infinite Force against which he was setting himself. All the sufferings endured by these people gained for them that strength which even today makes them a people who cannot be destroyed. Luxury ever tends to weakness in national life, while suffering stiffens and strengthens the national character.

EXODUS 2

Here begins the story of Moses. When Pharaoh was beginning to take active steps to oppress the people, God brought to birth the man who was to break Egypt's power. A mother's love is seen scheming for the life of her child. The New Testament tells us that what she did, she did by faith. Was anything more unimportant, judged by all human standards, than the startled cry of a baby? Yet that cry opened the gate of a woman's heart and admitted to the center of Egyptian life the coming deliverer.

Between verses ten and eleven about forty years elapsed. During this period Moses had become learned in all the learning of the Egyptians. At man's estate the forces and fires of his own people flamed in him and the passion to deliver them was born in his heart. This passion was right, but the action was premature. Disappointed, he cut his connection with the court and fled to the wilderness in a mixture of fear and faith. The fear was incidental and transient. The faith was fundamental and abiding.

Again forty years passed. The hour of crisis arrived. The king of Egypt died. In time, despots always do. The children of Israel sighed and cried. Their cry went up into the ears of God. Note the phrases, "And God heard . . . and God remembered . . . and God saw . . . and God took knowledge." These statements do not reveal any awakening or change in the attitude of God. They simply declare what had been perpetually true. Children of faith in every hour of darkness may comfort themselves by knowing that God is not unmindful and that He never forgets His covenant.

EXODUS 3

At last the actual call of God came to Moses. It found him fulfilling a daily duty, keeping the sheep of his father-in-law. There can be no doubt that in the silent solitudes of the wilderness he had meditated on the condition of his people. Forty years, however, changes any man. The fiery impetuosity which characterized him at forty had matured into self-restraint and meekness at eighty.

In the mysterious fire manifestation God said to His servant certain things which lie at the foundation of all that is to follow. "I have seen . . . [I] have heard . . . I know . . . I am come . . . I will send thee." Small wonder that Moses answered, "Who am I?" Does it seem strange that when God had spoken of Himself Moses should be conscious of himself? It is not strange. The light of the divine glory ever reveals man to himself. Hence the cry, "Who am I?" The answer was immediate and full of grace, "Certainly I will be with thee."

The second difficulty immediately presented itself to Moses. He thought of the people to whom he was being sent and inquired, "Whom shall I say has sent me?" In order to act with authority, he was conscious that he himself must know God better. The answer was threefold: first, for himself, "I AM THAT I AM"; second, for Israel, "the God of your fathers"; finally, for Pharaoh, "Jehovah, the God of the Hebrews." To Moses' commission for leadership there was a direct communication of His secret. To the people a Name was given that reminded them of a covenant which could not be broken. Pharaoh could know God only through the chosen people. Thus the difficulties of Moses were recognized but set in the light of a great divine revelation.

EXODUS 4

A further difficulty was now declared. The man who first doubted himself and then doubted because of his ignorance of God now doubted because of the people to whom he was to be sent. God had told him that the people would hearken, but now he questioned this. All fear of man is evidence of feeble faith in God. In the presence of such fear what we need is clearer vision of God. The story shows that God understood and answered the fear of His servant by granting him signs.

Then is revealed the strangest of all the difficulties. Moses returned to the first stated and declared his own weakness and incompetence. At the beginning it was natural, and the answer was one of grace. Now it was unwarranted and God was angry with him. The result was that Aaron was given to him as a mouthpiece. This is a strange and yet recurring experience. Faltering faith is answered by the supply of something that might have been done without, and the result is sorrow.

At last, difficulties having been dealt with, Moses commenced to walk in the path of obedience. Here we have the record of something certainly strange in the way in which it is told. Jehovah meets him on the pathway and seeks to kill him. The explanation is to be found in what follows. There can be no doubt that for some reason unrecorded Moses had failed to carry out the divine instructions concerning circumcision. The lesson is self-evident. No great consecration to service can excuse failure in what may appear to be smaller matters of conduct. Obedience completely established, everything moved forward.

EXODUS 5

Here we have the last picture of the people in bondage. As we follow the history, we shall be particularly interested in noticing the process through which Pharaoh passed. Here Moses and Aaron came to him and uttered the simple requirement of Jehovah in the words, "Let My people go." The answer was immediate, daring, and stubborn. Pharoah declared his ignorance of Jehovah and practically challenged Him as he bluntly said, "I will not let Israel go." His refusal was followed by brutality. He assumed the attitude of insolent ignorance.

As we read the story of the suffering of these people, we cannot wonder at their complaint. Everything surely seemed to be against them and as though the intervention of Moses was turning out for ill rather than good. The whole transaction constituted a trial for Moses in the pathway of faith and obedience. There is a touch of impatience and evidence of wavering faith in what he said in the presence of God. Yet the profounder truth is that there is a remarkable evidence of his faith in his going directly to God with his difficulty. Happy is the man who when he cannot understand the divine movement and, indeed, doubts it has yet faith enough in God Himself to tell Him all his doubt.

EXODUS 6

Here commences the section of Exodus devoted to the subject of national deliverance. Everything began with a solemn charge to Moses. It is first an answer to the complaint which God's servant had uttered in His presence. It was a message of divine self-assertion and, therefore, necessarily a message of grace. Mark the recurrence of the personal pronoun. That is the permanent value of this wonderful passage. The supreme need in every hour of difficulty and depression is a vision of God. To see Him is to see all else in proper proportion and perspective. Moreover, in this passage we have the unfolding of the real value of the name Jehovah.

After this the command to go to Pharaoh was reiterated and a new fear took possession of the heart of Moses which again was expressed in the presence of God. He no longer complained at God's treatment of the people but spoke of his own inability to deliver God's message. That inability was now born of a sense, not as before of his lack of eloquence, but of his uncleanness. He spoke of himself as of uncircumcised lips. As when Isaiah beheld the glory of God he cried, "I am a man of unclean lips"; and as Daniel in the presence of the same glory said, "My comeliness was turned in me into corruption"; and as Job in the presence of the matchless splendor of God said, "Behold, I am of small account"; so Moses became conscious of his own moral imperfection.

EXODUS 7

We have here the record of God's answer to Moses' difficulty. He reaffirmed Himself and charged His servant to speak to Pharaoh the things commanded. Moreover, He foretold the result of the delivery of the message.

Here begins the story of the conflict between Jehovah and Pharaoh. Throughout this entire story two different words are employed, the distinction between which has a vital bearing on the story itself. The first word suggests the idea of giving fixity, or, in the realm of the will, strength. The second indicates willful stubbornness. The condition of Pharaoh on the first visit of Moses and Aaron is described by the first of these words. The Authorized renders it, "He hardened Pharaoh's heart." This should be rendered, He made strong the heart of Pharaoh. Immediately following, Pharaoh's attitude from his own standpoint is revealed. Then the word is "hardened," in the sense of calloused. This distinction must be maintained throughout.

The plagues that fell on Pharaoh came in three sections of three each, followed by a fourth, with only one plague, which was final. The first of the first three is recorded here. Before it fell, Pharaoh was warned in the morning. In this and the two following, terrible discomfort was produced but neither pain nor death.

EXODUS 8

Before the second plague Pharaoh received an opportunity to repent. He was warned of the approach of the plague. The warning had no effect. In the first plague magicians had produced apparently like results and it was so also with this second one. This was their last success. Pharaoh relented and asked for a respite. This was granted and for a reason clearly declared, "That thou mayest know that there is none like unto Jehovah our God." At any sign of turning by Pharaoh the divine mercy turned toward him. Here again Pharaoh hardened, that is, calloused his own heart. Note this was his own act and not God's.

In the coming of the third plague there was a change of method. No warning was given. Pharaoh had broken faith. In the presence of this visitation the magicians confessed their recognition of some power superior to any they knew. Their incompetence and testimony constituted a still further warning to Pharaoh. Nevertheless, again he refused to relent.

Therefore the judgment of God went forward and we have the first of the second cycle of plagues. A new method of impressing the heart of the king was taken by the information that Israel was to be immune. At this point Pharaoh commenced a policy of attempted compromise. He suggested that they should sacrifice in the land. This Moses absolutely refused, declaring it was necessary to separate from Egypt in order to worship. Pharaoh then seemed to give way as he declared his willingness to let them go, but not far. Once again, by his own act, Pharaoh made stubborn his heart and refused to submit.

EXODUS 9

The patient method of God is manifest in that, notwithstanding the fact that Pharaoh had again broken faith, God again warned him. There being no evidence of repentance, the fifth plague fell upon the nation. The fact of the struggle going on in the heart of Pharaoh is seen in that he investigated the condition of Israel and found that they were exempt from the visitation. Nevertheless, he still maintained the attitude of stubborn resistance.

Now the divine method changed. Without warning came the plague of boils, and here it is said that Jehovah hardened the heart of Pharaoh. It is important to notice the word made use of. And "Jehovah made strong the heart of Pharaoh." This is a significant statement, revealing that God strengthened the courage of the man in order that now, when he had stubbornly resisted, he might persist in the conflict to bring the complete victory of Jehovah.

The third cycle of three plagues began with hail. The warning was more explicit than on any previous occasion and an opportunity to escape was given. Some of the Egyptians availed themselves it. Out of the midst of the desolation Pharaoh cried, "I have sinned." The sequence shows that this was not a cry of genuine repentance, but an expression of desire to escape from the plague. The absolute justice and the patience of God are seen in that even though the cry was not a cry of genuine repentance, the plague was withdrawn. When it was withdrawn, we are again told that Pharaoh made heavy his heart, and his heart was made strong. The first word described his own act; the second the act of God, confirming his choice.

EXODUS 10

It would seem at this point that Moses himself was overawed by the fearful process of judgment and so before the next plague God announced to His servant a new reason for the whole movement. It was in order that posterity might have the solemn and awful warnings of the result of persistent rebellion.

Pharaoh was now beyond reason, and God did not reason with him. Pharaoh's servants, apparently more alive than he to his folly, pleaded with him to let the people go. Whereupon he sent for Moses and again attempted a compromise. He suggested that the children be left behind. This being refused, a further plague fell. Still Pharaoh persisted in his rebellion. The final plague of the third cycle fell without warning. In the presence of the appalling darkness, Pharaoh made his fourth and last attempt at compromise by suggesting that their cattle should be left. To this the reply of the servant of God was at once final and conclusive, "There shall not a hoof be left behind." Then Pharaoh's failure aroused his anger. All the evil passion of the man flamed out. He commanded Moses to see his face no more. This is indeed a story of long-continued and determined rebellion against God; first by Pharaoh's own choice, then by that choice ratified by the choice of God as the terrible judgment moved forward.

EXODUS 11

In this brief chapter we have the most solemn account of communion between Jehovah and His servant Moses. Pharaoh had rejected God finally, and God had now finally rejected Pharaoh. Jehovah now announced that He Himself would come with the actual stroke of final punishment. He had sent His messengers, Moses and Aaron, and His ministers, blood, and frogs, and lice; flies, and murrain, and boils; hail, and locusts, and darkness. He had waited patiently for the effect of the plagues, allowing time for Pharaoh to relent and repent, all without producing any effect other than determined and willful and insolent opposition. The time for remedy had passed and now, as an avenging angel, He would Himself pass through the land. In this hour of communion Jehovah's final determination was indicated to Moses, and by him to the Hebrew people, in order to prepare for their departure according to the will and claim of God.

EXODUS 12

While the subjects necessarily intermingle at this point, we turn from the contemplation of the judgments of Jehovah in dealing with Pharaoh to that of deliverance in His dealings with Israel. As these people were now to pass into national constitution, the calendar was altered. A rite was established which was called an ordinance, a feast, a sacrifice. Thus at the very beginning the nation was reminded that it was rooted in the fact of deliverance wrought by God through sacrifice.

The story of the actual exodus is told. It was indeed, as the sacred historian writes, "a night to be much observed." It was a night in which a people passed from slavery to liberty, from under the lash of oppression to the place of power under authority, from degradation to realization of national life. With them passed out a mixed multitude which constituted an element of danger, as tracing their history through subsequent books will show.

That exodus and the Passover feast were prophetic. Long ages were required fully to unfold the meaning, but in fullness of time its symbolism became manifest and Paul was able to write, "Our Passover also hath been sacrificed, even Christ . . . wherefore let us keep the feast."

EXODUS 13

As the Passover feast signified the deliverance from death by obedience, and the sprinkling of blood signified redemption through death, the feast of Unleavened Bread was established in connection with it. This was to be a perpetual memorial of the necessity to abstain from anything and everything which cause disintegration in the national life. The chosen people were to be delivered from slavery into submission to the law of their one and only King.

It is significant that in connection with these feasts we have a distinct statement of the true purpose for establishing them, namely, instruction of the children. This throws light on the true value of symbolism. It is ever intended to arouse interest in the minds of the young in order that, true to their instincts, they may ask for information, which is to be supplied by their elders.

The nation delivered and consecrated is seen at once as under the direct government and guidance of God. "God led them not by the way of the land of the Philistines, although that was near." "But God led the people about." The essential truths revealed here are that He leads and that there is a meaning and purpose in all such guidance. The longer journey was the outcome of His patient desire that they should not be discouraged at the beginning by warfare. It is very arresting that in connection with these movements the story is linked again with that in Genesis. Joseph had died in the faith that such an hour as this would come. He signalized his faith by commandment concerning his bones. The people then moving out from Egypt under divine direction carried those bones with them. As yet they were very far from the possibility of simple faith and needed signs. Hence God gave them the vision of the pillar of cloud by day and the pillar of fire by night.

EXODUS 14

The first movement of the emancipated people was to march into the place of danger. It eventuated in the trial of their faith, as we shall see, but the divine meaning of it was told to Moses and it is full of solemnity. Pharaoh's final judgment must be carried out in such a way as to make its justice evident. The people were brought to a place where it would appear to the proud heart of the obstinate king that he could overcome them in spite of all previous divine intervention. Were ever the madness and blindness of sin persisted in more manifest than in the proud preparation of chariots and armies to overcome and destroy a people for whom God had so wondrously appeared?

The panic of the people is hardly to be wondered at when we think of their circumstances. Moses confronted them with magnificent courage and faith. The story of their deliverance needs no comment. It is full of life and color and dramatic power. The one great truth illustrated is that under divine government there can be no obstacles which cannot be overcome. What solemn awe must have inspired the hearts of the multitudes of Israel as they marched in silent companies along the strange highway, with the cloud of the divine Presence acting as their rear guard and the walls of the sea towering above them on the right hand and on the left. The new nation walked through a threatened death toward a new life in a consciousness of the presence and power of Jehovah from which they could not escape.

EXODUS 15

It was a great and glorious song that rose on the morning air on the far side of the sea. A study of it will reveal it to be a song of the King. It was a high ecstatic moment of national consciousness. In some aspect every movement of it sounds the praise of the King. The reason for the song is God Himself (verses 1, 2). The victory against the proud foe is wholly Jehovah's (verses 3 to 10). The leading of His people is His alone (verses 11-13). The sense of dread that falls on the men of other nations who witnessed the passage is the issue of Jehovah's victory (verses 14-16). Their confidence, now high and hopeful, of finally coming into possession of their inheritance is centered wholly in Him (verses 7, 18).

Now begins the more direct story of Jehovah's guidance of the people. Marah and its bitterness afforded opportunity to discover the resources of Jehovah. Elim was an evidence of His tender care for them.

To those who have eyes to see and hearts to understand, the divine tenderness is manifest along the whole pilgrim pathway.

EXODUS 16

From Elim the people moved into the dreariness of the great wilderness and began to be conscious of the scarcity of some of the things which they had had, even in the midst of Egyptian slavery. There manifested itself a craving for the material which for the moment rendered them unconscious of the value of the spiritual. They plainly declared that bondage with flesh was preferable to liberty with hunger. Very arresting is the attitude and activity of Jehovah toward them. Without rebuke He gave them both bread and flesh.

In the method of the gift of the manna one great lesson is apparent. The people were to understand that their life was to be daily dependence on God. They were to gather each day for five days and on the sixth enough for that day and the Sabbath. Probably there are today some people who may smile at this story of days far distant. The great facts, however, abide to this hour. In the path of obedience every man will find manifestations of the divine Presence and overruling, and that things impossible to him are possible to him with God.

EXODUS 17

Another trial of their faith came to the people in the lack of water. In view of the fact that they had been provided with bread and flesh, it would seem as if they would have learned enough to be able to wait patiently for God. Yet it was not so. It is an arresting and important fact that a present darkness will make men forget the clear light of the past and imminent danger render us unconscious of previous deliverance. Here again the divine patience appears, for Jehovah uttered no word of reproach, but in spite of their impatient unbelief provided water out of the rock for them. Again, in impossible circumstances all things are seen to be possible where God is.

The forward march of the people brought down on them the army of Amalek. To the Israelites this was a new experience. In their first movement God led them in such a way as to avoid the possibility of war (Exodus 13:17). Now they were involved in war. A perfect victory was gained over Amalek and in this first battle the principles of their conflict were revealed. Joshua led men to an actual conflict, while Moses, assisted by Aaron and Hur, prayed. It was a combination of fighting and faith, the manifestation of loyalty to duty combined with dependence on God. Thus came to them a new revelation of God which Moses signified by raising an altar which he named *Jehovah-Nissi* meaning "Jehovah, our Banner."

EXODUS 18

Here we have an interesting interruption of the main narrative. Jethro arrests our attention and compels recognition of certain facts which we are liable to forget, as also were the Israelites of old. This man was evidently of a caliber different from that of the ordinary run of those not included in the divinely created nation. He was at once a prince and a priest. He declared his own faith in Jehovah to be confirmed by the deliverance wrought under the leadership of Moses and he offered sacrifice to Jehovah. Here, as formerly, when Melchizedek met Abraham, we find a recognition of the fact that on the basis of faith and sacrifice it is possible for others than the chosen people to approach God.

The advice Jethro offered Moses was that of a man of excellent common sense. He saw that instead of devoting himself to the more important work of leadership, Moses might also attempt to do work which could well be delegated to others. This is a common mistake. Men called by God to lead are always in danger of attempting to encompass more than they are able. Jethro's advice was reverent in its recognition of the divine authority, "If thou shalt do this thing, and God command thee so." The fact that Moses acted on Jethro's advice is almost certain evidence that he recognized that God was speaking to him through this man. It is well for us to remember that God has different ways of making known His will and the fact that He sometimes comes to us through the advice of others should save us from anything like arrogant self-sufficiency.

EXODUS 19

Here we begin the third great movement in the Book of Exodus. We have seen the people in bondage and have observed them being delivered from that bondage and guided by Jehovah. However, they were still a confused multitude rather than an organized nation. From this point to the end of the Book we have the account of the giving of the constitution and the great work of organization.

The first event was the calling of Moses and the announcement to him of the divine purpose. Jehovah first stated a simple condition to the people, "If ye will obey My voice indeed, and keep My covenant." The promise was most remarkable. The people were to be His "peculiar treasure . . . a kingdom of priests . . . a holy nation." This was a covenant of grace. It declared a great divine intention, but the unpreparedness of the people was shown in their easy declaration that they would keep all the words of Jehovah.

Immediately on this declaration the

tone of Jehovah changed. Moses was sent back to them and the word that followed emphasized the majesty of their King. This they must ever bear in mind and maintain toward Him an attitude of such reverence as must be the outcome of an abiding sense of His power and His purity.

While in our day these ancient methods and manifestations may have ceased, the truths they were intended to indicate abide.

EXODUS 20

Here we have the Ten Words of the moral Law. They are introduced by a proclamation of God concerning Himself: first as to His name, "I am Jehovah"; second, as to His relation to them, "thy God"; and, third, the basis of relationship, His deliverance of them from bondage.

The Ten Words fall into two sections: the first, of four commandments dealing with the relationship between God and man; the second, of six commandments conditioning human interrelationships. The Ten Words constitute a philosophy of life as well as a law. Man's first business is with God. His every other relationship depends on that and, indeed, is created by it.

The effect produced on the people by these words was a sense of fear. They were made conscious of the holiness of God. Because they were sinners, the fear was both natural and necessary. Nevertheless Moses at once on divine authority said to them, "Fear not," which meant that they might "fear" and "sin not." The apparent paradox teaches that when man has the fear of God he need have no other fear.

Finally, the way of God's approach to them was provided. It was the way of the altar and sacrifice. The instructions concerning the altar are revealing. It must be of simple and unmade things, devoid of human workmanship, in which the heart of man might make its boast.

EXODUS 21

At this point we have certain laws which apply the principles of the Decalogue to life. The first movement has to do with the laws of the person. This begins with the relation of slaves to their masters. By these laws slavery was changed into covenant relationship. Henceforward the condition of slaves among the Hebrew people would be in marked distinction to slavery as existing among other peoples. It was the beginning of a great moral movement. The right of a master to service by a definite bond was recognized, but the right of the servant to freedom on fulfilment of the bond was also recognized.

Then followed laws dealing with possible injury of man by man. Life was to be held so sacred that he who took it must forfeit his own. If a killing were premeditated there must be no escape. If the act were unpremeditated, provision was made for a place of refuge. Every detail emphasized the sanctity of human life.

Finally, this sanctity is still in mind in the laws dealing with injury and death wrought by cattle.

It is impossible to read these laws carefully without being impressed with their absolute equity and righteousness and at the same time with their thoroughness. Here, as in other cases, carelessness was never to be an excuse.

EXODUS 22

The laws of property follow. The section really begins with verse 33 of the previous chapter. These laws also began by laying emphasis on the guilt of carelessness. The truth emphasized is that no man must live his life on the basis of selfishness or wholly alone and that wrong inflicted on neighbor by neighbor in the material realm becomes sin against God in the moral realm.

Specific instructions were given on the responsibility of trustees. Within clearly defined limitations, a man is to be held responsible for goods deposited with him.

A group of laws seemingly having no direct sequence or connection follows. Two of them deal with sins of unchastity. Between these occurs a blunt and stern word, "Thou shalt not suffer a sorceress to live." Humanity has ever had a craving after what sometimes is termed the occult. Invariably such traffic is injurious to life.

A law characterized by great tenderness was enunciated for the protection of the stranger, showing that God hears the cry and avenges the sorrows of any oppressed people.

While the rights of property had been carefully safeguarded in previous words, now the inherent rights of life were shown to be superior. Usury was not to be practiced, and necessary things held in pledge must be restored for necessary use.

Closely following on these laws which make serious demands on men, we have words demanding reverence for God expressed in fidelity to Him in the matter of offerings.

EXODUS 23

The enactments now recorded have to do with the administration of justice. A study of them reveals that true justice is always merciful and yet makes sterner demand than any moral code of laws. The divine estimate of justice forbids wresting judgment, accepting bribes, and oppression.

The feasts of the Lord are placed in their relation to the people's social life. The sabbatical year was arranged in the interests of the poor. The rest of the Sabbath is more than selfish, cattle and servants being included in its intention. Community interest underlay the command to observe the three great feasts.

At the close of the section enunciating these laws of application, we have the record of how Jehovah made a gracious promise of that Presence which would lead and guide the people in all the days to come. There can be no question that this Angel Presence was the Angel Jehovah through whom these people received a manifestation of God. The most natural deduction is to identify this mystic Person with Him who eventually became flesh and dwelt among us. This Angel Presence was to ensure blessing to the people and drive out their foes before them.

Concerning the people to be driven out, it is worthy of note that this paragraph shows that "their gods" were their undoing. Everything in the life of a man or a nation depends on the character of its worship. Whatever is worshiped is served. The service ennobles or degrades according to the character of those worshiped.

EXODUS 24

We now come to the story of the preparation for the true order of worship. The elders of Israel were called to approach in company with Moses. So far as it had been received, the law was repeated in their hearing. This was immediately followed by the offering of sacrifice and the shedding of blood. Thus at the very heart of these laws for the conditioning of national life the necessity for sacrifice was solemnly emphasized.

Perhaps there is nothing more august in all the inspired ceremony than the account of the approach of the elders. We are told that "they saw the God of Israel." No description is given of what they saw. It may be that God manifested Himself to these men in the Angel Presence which He had promised. However, in all probability it is better to leave the sublime statement as it stands, remembering that it may be interpreted by the facts which followed. Almost immediately afterward Moses went into yet closer union with God and, as we shall find in a subsequent chapter, notwithstanding that closer union he craved something beyond it. In response, he received the declaration that none could see God and live. Spiritual intelligence will easily understand that there is no contradiction here. These men saw God and yet the infinite and final Essence could not be seen. The vision was characterized for the elders by immunity from judgment, for on them "He laid not His hand," and, moreover, by a sacred act of communion in which they "did eat and drink."

After this, Moses was called to go beyond the elders into the midst of the mount. There we may not follow him. We may see only what the children of Israel saw during those days, an appearance like "a devouring fire." Into that fire Presence Moses passed to receive the law in fuller detail and to see the heavenly things and to learn the pattern of earthly worship.

EXODUS 25

Here we begin consideration of the transactions of the forty days. Moses received instruction concerning a place of worship for the nation. It is important that we attempt to understand what this meant to the people at the time. The great underlying principles are all realized and fulfilled in Christianity.

The instructions began, not with the structure, but with its contents. An Ark was to be prepared and its place was to be at the very center of everything. The Ark with the covering cherubim symbolized that God dwelt among them. The mercy seat above it was a witness to a divine method to God.

The next instructions concerned the table of shewbread. In the East a table was always the symbol of fellowship. Thus the people were reminded of the possibility created of constant communion with God.

Instructions followed concerning the golden candlestick which was a light bearer symbolizing the testimony these people were called on to bear to the outside world. As between themselves and God the propitiatory or mercy seat had made fellowship possible, so between the nation and the world the same provision made testimony a necessity. Light shining in darkness is ever the symbol of holiness and hope. The very form of the candlestick indicated the unity of the people and the diversity of their service and testimony.

These three were the essential pieces of furniture at the center of the national life and religion: first, a meeting place with God on the basis of propitiation, second, a table for fellowship between God and His people, and, finally, a candlestick indicating the office to which they were called.

EXODUS 26

Continuing the outward movement of description from the Ark as center, we have instructions concerning the curtains and coverings which were to constitute the Tabernacle and Tent. There was unquestionably symbolic suggestiveness in everything. Fine twined linen was the symbol of purity, the blue of heavenly glory, the purple of kingly majesty, the scarlet of the richness of created life, while the inwrought cherubim symbolized the highest realization of life.

The boards and bars constituted the solid foundations on which the curtains and the coverings were to rest. These boards were set in sockets of silver made out of the ransom money which the people had brought. Because of its extreme durability, the acacia wood was the symbol of continuity Standing these boards in the sockets of silver symbolized the fact that continuous life is founded in redemption.

In the veil hanging between the Holy Place and the Holy of Holies and in the screen hanging between the court and the Holy Place we have symbols of exclusion. The material and colors of the inner veil spoke of absolute perfection. This veil symbolized that man can draw near to God only by the way of perfection. No man was ever found who could pass that veil in his own right until in fulfilment of the symbolism one Man did go beyond it. When presently the high priest passed behind the veil, he carried with him the blood of propitiation, not merely for the people he represented, but first for himself.

EXODUS 27

Here we have the account of the court surrounding the Tabernacle and the Tent and here again the description begins from the inside. First, the brazen altar is described. It symbolized devotion on the basis of sacrifice. Once more the acacia wood spoke of the necessity for continuous devotion while the brass symbolized the strength of that devotion. As will be seen later on, the sin sacrifice was offered outside the camp. Here its ashes, mingled with offerings, formed the groundwork of acceptance.

The whole court was to be enclosed by curtains of finely twined linen. There was no intermixture of gold or blue, or scarlet, save at the gates of entrance. These exterior curtains were to be upheld by pillars set in sockets of brass and capped by crowns of silver, the whole suggestive of purity based on the strength of government and crowned by the fact of redemption.

The screen to be hung at the entrance was similar to that before the Holy Place. Thus the worshiper, standing outside each entrance, was reminded by the screen of the court, the screen of the Holy Place and the veil of the Most Holy, that there could be no approach to God save on the basis of perfection. No man might pass within the court to reach the altar of devotion save through the symbol of mediation. None might enter the Holy Place for fellowship and testimony but in the same way. None might reach the inner Presence chamber of the manifested Glory except through perfection.

EXODUS 28

The account of the calling and the hallowing of the priests for the exercise of their sacred office is given in detail. The outstanding values are revealed in certain clear statements. That of the purpose of the robing of the priests is stated in the words, ". . . make Aaron's garments to sanctify him, that he may minister unto Me in the priests' office." A careful study of the description of these garments will reveal very much that is important to an understanding of the divine thought concerning priesthood.

Taking them briefly, not in the order here described but in that of the actual robing, we notice first that the undergarments were to be of fine linen, symbolic of the necessity for personal purity. Covering this was the robe of the ephod, all of blue—this in Eastern imagery suggesting the necessity for familiarity with heavenly things. The alternating bell and pomegranate on the skirts of the priest's robe were typical of his obligation to testimony and fruit bearing. Over these was placed the ephod itself, the essential garment of the priestly function, while on the head rested the sacred miter, or priestly crown. Completing the glorious apparel were ornaments of great beauty. Attached to the miter on the head was a plate bearing the inscription, "HOLY TO THE LORD," the significance of which is self-evident. On the shoulders onyx stones engraved with the names of the tribes indicated the office of bearing their burdens. On the heart rested the breastplate, with the names of the tribes inscribed there also on precious stones. In the center of this was the mystic Urim and Thummim. All this was intended to emphasize that the office of the priest was to carry the people on his heart in discovering the divine mind and will concerning them.

EXODUS 29

The hallowing of the priests consisted in a threefold function: ablution, arrayal, and anointing. Approaching with sacrifices and offerings, there was first to be the washing in water and then the arrayal in the holy garments. The ceremony of consecration, with its sacrifices and anointing, emphasized the purity necessary on the part of those exercising the office of the priesthood.

Aaron, cleansed and anointed, proceeded to service, and the ceremonies emphasized that the consecration of the priest must be expressed in actual service. All these rites and ceremonies were to be observed, not by Aaron alone, but also by his sons.

After these instructions concerning the hallowing of the priests, we find instructions concerning the daily offerings. These are dealt with more in detail in the Book of Leviticus. In the provision made for the offering of a lamb morning and evening, together with a meal offering and a drink offering, Jehovah promised that by this means He would meet with them and dwell among them and make them know Him. Thus the truth, at once symbolic and glorious, was to be kept perpetually before the people, that God could meet with them only by way of sacrifice and on condition of their devotion to Himself.

Through all these detailed provisions for the organization of the people it is of the utmost importance that we keep in mind the fuller intention of God that other nations might come to know the blessedness of the people directly governed by Himself.

EXODUS 30

We may come to the description of the altar of incense. It is significant that in the earlier description of the Holy Place, with its furnishing, this altar was not named. It was specifically the altar of priesthood, instructions concerning which were not given until the priest was prepared for service. It completes and crowns the symbolism of the Holy Place. The table of shewbread represented communion with God, the lampstand spoke of testimony to the world, and now the golden altar speaks of the offering of adoration.

Provision was now made for the taking of the sum of the children of Israel and the process was a recognition of redemption. Every one was to provide a half shekel of silver. The rich man's value was expressed by the half shekel, as was also that of the poor man.

Instructions concerning the laver follow. It was to stand at the entrance; in it the priests were to wash before they entered the Holy Place. For continued service in holy things repeated cleansing is necessary. Finally, we have in this chapter instructions concerning the anointing oil and incense. In each case these were compounded of precious things, all of them having significance and suggesting that the best graces of the soul are to merge with the sweetness of the anointing from on high. Very solemn are the injunctions that neither the sacred oil nor the holy incense was to be used in any way for personal gratification.

They are symbols of the soul's relation to God at its highest and must not be degraded.

EXODUS 31

It should be borne in mind that in a certain way, these people were necessarily vulgarized by centuries of slavery and almost certainly devoid of that artistic ability which would enable them to construct the Tabernacle according to pattern. Moreover, they were far removed from the centers of human refinement. They were, however, a people gathered around God, who is ever equal to the task of fitting His people for doing all that His will appoints. Bezalel was filled with the Spirit of God, and the effect of that on him is described. He had "wisdom," that is capacity; "understanding," which indicates progress; and "knowledge," the attainment of skill.

The commandment concerning the Sabbath had already been enunciated in the Law. The insertion of a reference to it at this point is interesting. God had commissioned the people to a work specially sacred. Moreover, He had provided for carrying out the work in the special equipment of certain men. How easy it would have been for them to imagine that in doing this work they might dispense with the Sabbath observance.

This first period of communion between God and Moses ended with giving the two tables of stone written with the finger of God.

EXODUS 32

Immediately following the account of this period of communion between Moses and God we have the record of the sin of the people. When they said, "Up, make us Gods," they were seeking something to represent God rather than seeking a new god. The day after the calf was erected they observed a feast to Jehovah.

In this connection Moses is seen in one of the greatest hours of his life as he stood and pleaded with God. It is to be observed that his plea was not so much on behalf of the people as on behalf of God. He spoke to Him of "Thy people, that Thou hast brought out of the land of Egypt" and then pleaded the covenant made with Abraham, Isaac, and Israel. Undoubtedly Moses was filled with compassion for the people, but his chief concern was for the honor of the name of God. In such a man God found vantage ground for the activity of mercy and the carrying out of purpose.

Another side of Moses' character is revealed in the story of his return to the people. He came in anger, broke the tables of stone, ground the calf to powder, and compelled the people to drink of the water into which it was flung. These actions were far more than a mere outburst of passion. They were followed by inquisition. From this inquisition Moses returned into the presence of God and there confessed the sin of the people, pleading that they might be spared, even though he be blotted out of the Book. God's answer was strict justice and mercy. Moses was commanded to return and lead the people, and it was promised that an angel would lead them.

EXODUS 33

The command to go forward and possess the land was now repeated to the people. It is clear that the people felt that the promise of an angel to be sent before them was the lowering of a privilege. They spoke of it as "evil tidings," and gave expression to their feeling in that they "stripped themselves of their ornaments from mount Horeb onward." It is probable that they never again arrayed themselves with adornments of joy during the wilderness period.

The action of Moses at this point

was full of significance. Whereas the Tabernacle could not yet have been built, there was evidently a temporary tent as the center of worship. This Moses took from the center of the people and pitched it outside the camp, a solemn act symbolizing the removal of the presence of God and the consequent excommunication of the people. At that new center Jehovah spoke unto Moses "face to face, as a man speaketh unto his friend." It was then that Moses asked for some fuller knowledge of God. The gracious promise was given, "My presence shall go with thee, and I will give thee rest." Then the cry of Moses was uttered, "If Thy presence go not with me, carry us not up hence."

That cry was again answered with the promise that God would do as His servant asked. Now, made exceeding bold, Moses asked for a vision of God's glory and in reply was told that God would make all His goodness pass before him. The brightest glory of God is ever seen in the outshining of His grace.

EXODUS 34

Moses was called again into the mount and the promised unveiling was made to him. It consisted of a declaration by God of the truth concerning Himself, first, as to His nature and second, as to His methods with men. In these we have the merging of the two essential truths that God is love and God is light. He is full of compassion and yet absolutely holy, He forgives and yet cannot clear the guilty. It was strange and paradoxical, yet an infinite music, fully interpreted when Moses was superseded finally by the Son of God.

Following these things, the terms of a covenant between the people and God were enunciated. In view of this covenant they were to make no covenant with the people of the land to which they were going. We have no detailed account of the happenings of this second period in the mount, save that the tables of the law were written anew. Probably in holy silence, Moses looked deeply into the nature of God and thereby was further strengthened for the work that lay before him.

He returned to the people, his face radiant with the glory of this solemn period of communion. He was not conscious of the shining of his face until he learned it from the people. After the words of the law had been delivered, he put a veil on his face. It is in the New Testament we learn clearly the purpose of that veiling. "Moses . . . put a veil upon his face, that the children of Israel should not look steadfastly on the end of that which was passing away." Whether Moses understood that the fading of the glory on his face was symbolic of the ultimate passing away of the dispensation of Law it is impossible for us to say. It is equally impossible, however, for us to read this story without rejoicing in the fact that the glory which shines in the faces of those who hold communion with God through Jesus Christ increases ever unto the perfect light.

EXODUS 35

This and the four following chapters contain the account of the actual building of the Tabernacle. At the very commencement the Sabbath obligation was again declared. The people were then called on to bring their offerings, the appeal being made to those who had willing hearts. Giving was to be the outward and sacramental sign of the inward grace of devotion to the will of God. It is noticeable that among the offerings the ornaments of the people were conspicuous. It would seem as though this was the end of the ornaments which they had put off in their contrition. If so it was a double beautiful and sacred ceremony. In the presence of their sin and in deep penitence they had stripped themselves of the signs of a rejoicing people. Henceforward their chief cause of rejoicing would be found in the presence of God among them. This presence was forever symbolized by the Tabernacle of order and beauty. To its construction they brought these symbols of rejoicing.

EXODUS 36

The account of the actual presentation of the offerings to the company of workers inspired of God to use them is full of beauty. All the people offered, but a select number were commissioned for the actual work. These were such as were wise and understanding of heart a fitness which came as a direct gift of God.

The earnestness of the people at this point is made supremely apparent in that they offered more than was needed; indeed, "much more" is the actual word of Scripture.

The work now proceeded, and as in the earlier movements of the Book we have seen something of the symbolism of this center of worship, we now notice only the order in which that work was carried out.

In giving instructions, everything proceeded from the center to the circumference. Here the order is much the same but with slight variations. The place of divine dwelling and revelation was first prepared, and the beginning of this is described. First, the Tabernacle itself; then the Tent which covered it; next the boards and the bars on which the Tabernacle and Tent were raised; and, after that, the veil and the pillars on which it was hung. The supreme thing in the whole structure was this central dwelling place of God and that was made first.

EXODUS 37

In furnishing the Tabernacle and Tent, the work commenced with the furniture of the Holy of Holies. The Ark was first constructed because it was to be the very center, and in itself the foundations of the government of God in righteousness. Then followed the mercy seat, attesting the provision made in the economy of God for approach to Him by sinful man. Long after, a Hebrew singer expressed the significance of this as he sang:

> Surely His salvation is nigh them that fear Him,
> That glory may dwell in our land.
> Mercy and truth are met together;
> Righteousness and peace have kissed each other.
> (Psalm 85:9-10).

After the furniture of the Holy of Holies that of the Holy Place was made. First the table of communion, consequent on the propitiation manifested between the cherubim; then the lampstand, indicating the testimony the communing people were to bear to the outside world. Following this, the altar of incense, at which the people brought into communion and bearing testimony were to offer their sacrifices of praise. Finally, the anointing oil, the perpetual symbol of the truth that fitness for all approach and service comes by the way of divine provision.

EXODUS 38

In the history of construction we now pass to the court itself. Here again the furniture was first prepared. The brazen altar led the way as the symbol of absolute devotion to God. This was followed by the laver, a gracious provision for the constant cleansing of those who were to find their way into the Holy Place for communion and testimony. Then followed the making of the courts, its curtains, its pillars, and its sockets of redemption silver. Finally the screen of embroidered work for the gate was prepared.

The study of this pattern and the work done to carry it out must inevitably lead the thought to the fulfilment of everything symbolized in and through Christ. Whereas there may be fanciful and almost fantastic interpretations, there can be no doubt that everything was intended to teach great lessons and to lead the thought of these people to the spiritual nature of their life under the government of God. If we may use the term with all reverence, lifting it on to the highest level of application, the whole Hebrew economy was that of an elementary education, the employment of the kindergarten method of pictures, leading to underlying and eternal truth.

EXODUS 39

Very full details are given concerning the preparation of the holy garments of the priests, all of which were made strictly according to the pattern.

We then come to the definite statement, "Thus was finished all the work of the tabernacle and the tent of meeting: and the children of Israel did according to all that the Lord commanded Moses; so did they."

The work thus completed was brought by the workmen to Moses for final inspection, and in rapid survey the whole is again mentioned, the story closing with the words, "And Moses saw all the work, and, behold, they had done it; as Jehovah had commanded, even so had they done it: and Moses blessed them."

This almost monotonous repetition of the fact that the work was carried out according to the pattern is full of significance. Everything was intended to teach the people that the one simple basis of relationship between them and God must ever be implicit obedience to the minutest detail of divine instructions. In the economy of God no apparently trivial matter is really trivial or unimportant. Man cannot approach God in any way of his own contriving, and no people have any right to expect God's guidance save as they are devoted to Him and His methods in His worship and His work.

EXODUS 40

In this final movement in the Book of Exodus we find the same constant repetition of the necessity of obeying the divine plan. In the first fifteen verses of the chapter we have an account of the specific command of God concerned with setting up the Tabernacle, anointing it in order, and sanctifying the priests and clothing them in their robes.

In this setting up, everything proceeds from the center outward. First, the Tabernacle was reared, the Ark placed, and the veil hung. Then the table of shewbread was set in its place and the lamps were lighted. That being done, the golden altar was brought in and the door of the Holy Place erected.

In the court the brazen altar was set, then the laver, while around the whole were hung the curtains of the court, and finally the outer gate was erected.

Then all were anointed with the holy oil. The priest was arrayed and anointed and his sons likewise. Everything was ready. Once more it is declared in general terms, "Thus did Moses: according to all that Jehovah commanded him, so did he." That statement is emphasized by the repetition of the words, "as the Lord commanded Moses" no less than seven times.

All being completed, the final declaration fills the soul with awe. The great verity, of which everything was but symbolic, was made real in the consciousness of the people as the glory of the Lord filled the Tabernacle. So great was that glory that Moses was not able to enter the Tent of meeting.

Thus in the march of history the nation is seen organized around the presence and power of Jehovah. The record closes with the simple statement that they went onward with their journeys, guided ever by the presence of God manifested thus at the center of their life and worship.

Leviticus

LEVITICUS 1

The Book of Leviticus is the Book of Laws. It first deals with laws of dedication concerning the offerings, all of which have to do with the divine provision for the people's approach to Jehovah in worship. Five offerings are named. The first, dealt with in this chapter, was the burnt offering, suggesting the need of personal dedication to God. Those who are admitted to the place of worship are such as have utterly failed to render their life to God thus perfectly. Therefore the offering they bring must be slain and burned. In this arrangement was set forth the truth of substitution as being the only way in which a sinning man can draw near to worship. The spiritual sense of the reader will see throughout the whole of these studies how the ideas embodied in the ancient economy found their fulfilment in Christ. It is not the purpose of these notes to dwell on this fact, but rather to attempt to discover the simple significance of the laws to the men to whom they were given, as was the case in our consideration of Exodus.

LEVITICUS 2

In the meal offering was presented another side of the great truth of personal dedication. In itself the offering was of the work of man's hands, the fruits of the ground, the result of civilization, manufacture, and preparation. Through it the people were ever reminded that their approach to God demanded that they offer to Him a perfect service as well as a perfect life. Dedication of life is a condition for service. Service is its true reason and finest expression. A man whose life is imperfect necessarily renders an imperfect service.

If by the burnt offering the truth of substitution for life is taught, in the meal offering the provision of a perfect service in place of an imperfect one is as clearly set forth. In a perfect life there would be no necessity for the sacrificial burnt offering because the life in itself is acceptable to God. That, of course, was the truth about the life of Christ. Moreover, such life has no need of the specific meal offering, for all the service which it renders is perfect. Where life has failed, it can approach only through sacrifice, and where service has failed through the imperfect life, the offering suggesting perfection is necessary.

LEVITICUS 3

In the peace offering new elements are manifest. Here one part was to be burned with fire and thus offered directly to God, while another part was returned from the altar to the worshiper for his own sustenance. In this offering, then, the great fact of acceptance and communion established on the basis of sacrifice and dedication is portrayed. It is indeed the peace offering forevermore speaking of peace established between the worshiper and God.

The basis of this peace is found in the offering through the death of the guiltless for the guilty, and the complete dedication of the worshiper to God. It is therefore the offering suggesting fellowship between God and the worshiper when all the reasons for disagreement have been banished and peace naturally ensues. To the sinner no such place of communion is possible, but in the offerings substitution is revealed as the way of dedication, which, in turn, admits into such communion with God sacrifice characterized by peace.

In these three offerings the sinner has been dealt with as such by nature. In each case the offering has been voluntary. The facts of specific and personal sins have not been dealt with.

LEVITICUS 4

We come now to the consideration of the sin offering. In the light of the divine holiness sin is seen, whether it be willful or not, and provisions must be made for its expiation. In the instructions, arrangements were made for the priest, the congregation as a whole, a ruler, and one of the common people. In each case a bullock was to be taken and a sevenfold ceremony followed. It was surely impossible for any Hebrew to make the offering for sin without being brought into an overwhelming sense of its hatefulness to God, and, moreover, without having suggested to his mind the fact that God does make provision of grace whereby approach is made possible.

An order of responsibility is revealed in that provision is made first for the priest, then for the congregation, then for the ruler, and finally for the individual. While it is recognized that in the priest or the ruler sin is more pernicious on account of the influence each exerts, no man can excuse himself by transferring blame to others. It will be observed that through all these arrangements concerning the sin offering, responsibility is recognized with the knowledge of the sin. It is when a man's sin was made known to him that he was expected to bring his offering. Let it not be thought, however, that sins of which a man is unconscious can be lightly excused. For these, sacrificial provision was also made in the offering on the great Day of Atonement, which will be considered in due course.

LEVITICUS 5

Commentators have not been in agreement in their interpretation of this section, some holding that it deals with the sin offering, some that it is the commencement of the trespass offering. I believe that the section dealing with the trespass offering begins here, notwithstanding that in the course of the passage the word "sin offering" occurs frequently. A careful examination will show that the sin offering merges into the trespass offering in interpretation. Trespass is more than a missing of the mark and refers to positive wrongdoing. In the sins mentioned in this paragraph both kinds are recognized.

In the more positive aspects of the trespass offering, two groups are dealt with: first, trespass against God directly in the matter of the holy things, and, second, trespass against one's neighbor. In the rest of this chapter we have to do with the first of these.

In any sin connected with the holy

things of the Lord ignorance is palpable guilt because the commandments had been given with perfect clearness. In the trespass offering, therefore, it will be observed that there are elements of divine requirement and personal restitution. In cases of willful sin restoration must be made. Thus guilt is canceled through vicarious suffering. In some senses it must also be shared by the loss sustained by the guilty.

LEVITICUS 6

The first movement in this chapter completes the subject of the trespass offering in its application to other men. Carefully observe, however, that such a trespass is also trespass against the Lord: "If any one sin, and commit a trespass against Jehovah, and deal falsely with his neighbor. . . ." Five illustrations are given an examination of which will show that the underlying wrong in each case is violation of truth.

The divine provision for worship having been revealed in the offerings, instructions were now given concerning the method of offering, which will reveal the true attitude of the worshiper. In the burnt offering the priest was charged to observe a threefold carefulness. He must be robed in his garments of pure linen, must employ the ashes which signified expiatory sacrifice, and must guard the holy fire, which is the element by which the offering passes from the giver to God.

In connection with the meal offering there are four points to be noted, an absence of leaven, the agency of fire, the retention of a portion for the priests, and, finally, the perpetuity of the offering. As indicating the complete devotion of the priests the whole of their meal offering was to be consumed, no part being retained for themselves.

The law of the sin offering provided that it should be killed in the place of the burnt offering. In this offering the one supreme care of the worshiper was to be recognition of the fact that it was a most holy thing, no part of which must be defiled. Moreover, the portion of the offering devoted to the purpose of sustenance must be eaten in the Holy Place. Thus the supreme importance of the expiatory method is clearly revealed.

LEVITICUS 7

The law of the trespass offering is practically identical with that of the sin offering. It is impossible to ponder these things without the mind turning to the great and infinite Sacrifice in which all the suggestions of the Mosaic economy were finally fulfilled.

The peace offering was pre-eminently that of communion. In the law of this offering three kinds are recognized: an offering of thanksgiving, an offering in connection with vows, and one which is purely a free-will offering to God. In all these communion is recognized. A stringent requirement in connection with this offering is that no part of them should be allowed to see corruption.

In the final section concerning the laws of dedication, certain principles of observation applicable throughout are repeated and emphasized. First, the fat and the blood were not to be eaten. Further, communion could not be maintained by proxy. Each man for himself must bring in "his own hands" the Lord's portion. While God comes to men directly and individually, He expects to receive from them in like manner. Thus communion is more than general and sentimental. It is personal and immediate.

LEVITICUS 8

At this point the second section of the book commences dealing with the laws of mediation. It opens with a brief historical account of the actual ceremony of the consecration of the priests and Tabernacle and the commencement of worship.

In the sacred rites of consecration it is noticeable that Moses acted. It is an arresting thing to see him thus exercising all the functions of the priestly office, although he was not permanently appointed thereto. The explanation is that he was acting as in the very place of God. God, through His servant, anointed Tabernacle and priests. Thus at the initiation of the order the intermediary between God and the people was a man who, sharing no priestly appointment, was in direct communication with God. The final movements in the sacred rite of the consecration of the priests describes the offering to God, their acceptance through fire, and a fresh anointing of those called to the office of mediation and intercession.

In the fullness of time, the one great Priest did not approach on the basis of sacrifice for Himself, but He did appear as Mediator through sacrifice for the people in the fullness of spiritual power.

LEVITICUS 9

Here we see the priests actually beginning their sacred work. After the gathering of the people, they stood in solemn silence in the presence of Jehovah. Aaron's first act was bringing the sin offering and the burnt offering for himself. He could not be the instrument of mediation between the people and God for worship save as he was brought into right relationship with God.

The first acts of the priests on behalf of the people are now recorded. The offerings brought were presented: first the sin offering, then the burnt offering, then the meal offering, and, finally, the peace offering. The very order of procedure is a revelation of the fundamental principles on the life of worship.

His work completed in the outer court Aaron, accompanied by Moses, passed within the Tent. What took place there is not described. Coming forth again, Moses as representative of God and Aaron as mediating priest, blessed the people and immediately the glory of the Lord was manifested in the sight of the congregation. This was followed by the prostration and worship of the gathered multitude.

Carefully observe this order. Sin put away, life and work devoted, communion made possible; then the priestly blessing, speaking of acceptance, followed by a second blessing, which declared the divine satisfaction as it was accompanied by the manifestation of glory, and so finally the full worship of the people.

LEVITICUS 10

In the record there breaks in a story full of solemn significance. Two sons of Aaron, Nadab, and Abihu were guilty of offering strange fire before the Lord. They were swiftly consumed by fire. The very fire which was the medium of God's acceptance of the offering in worship was the minister of His swift judgment against that which was false. Strangely solemn are the words, "Aaron held his peace." They were his own sons, but his relation to God was superior to his relation to them and his attitude was that of submissive silence.

Closely following these solemn events Moses was charged that Aaron and his sons were to abstain from strong drink. This suggests the possibility that the sin of Nadab and Abihu had been the consequence of their excessive use of wine. Whether this be so or not, the principle is a warning to those devoted to sacred service that they must abstain from any form of false fire.

Moses then repeated instructions already given because of their special value at this juncture. A peril was threatening these men, namely, thinking that in the presence of so severe a judgment they hardly dare partake even of permitted things. The necessity for this is revealed in the fact that Aaron, Ithamar, and Eleazer had not done according to instructions, and Aaron declared he had not dared to do so in view of the things which had befallen him.

LEVITICUS 11

We now reach the section dealing with the laws of separation. The first movement records the laws concerning health. It is impossible to enter here into any detailed dealing with the particular laws concerning sustenance. It may at least be affirmed that these requirements were based on the soundest laws of health. God, who perfectly understands the physical structure of man, knows what is good and what is harmful. There can be very little doubt that a careful examination of these provisions will demonstrate the sanitary wisdom of them all. It is at least remarkable that the general principles revealed in these laws have been accepted by all civilized peoples, although of course in many of their details they are disregarded.

LEVITICUS 12

In this brief section, which deals with the beginning of life, the religious aspect of childbirth is most unquestionably the permanent value. The separation of the woman from the congregation for a period is the suggestion of the recognition of the fact that the race is sinful and of the necessary consequence that every child is born in sin.

The return of the mother to her place in the privileges of worship could be brought about only by the presentation of sin and burnt offerings. While these requirements kept fresh in the mind this sense of sin, the provision of a way of return spoke in the language of hope. If men are born in sin, through expiation and devotion a way is yet made for their restoration to the place of communion with God. Thus at the beginning of every life the appalling need and the gracious provision were brought freshly to mind.

LEVITICUS 13

Here we have a section (chapters 13, 14) wholly devoted to the subject of leprosy. The disease was dealt with as one which is loathsome, whose tendency is to spread, and which is contagious. The whole community must be zealously safeguarded. Therefore, there must be no carelessness in the method of dealing with leprosy.

In the instructions two principles of perpetual importance are manifested. The first is the necessity for guarding the general health of the community and the second is that no injustice be done to the individual in the interests of the community. These two principles are perpetual in their application. The State should ever have the right of inspection and examination. It should, however, use its right with the greatest care that no wrong be done to any individual.

The law provided that there should be most careful distinction made between actual leprosy and that which may appear to be leprosy. When the case was a clearly defined one, the method was drastic in the extreme. The leper was to be separated at once from the whole congregation. Moreover, all garments likely in any way to have become contaminated were to be destroyed by fire.

LEVITICUS 14

The possibility of the restoration of a leper to health was recognized and provision was made accordingly. In the case of the individual, the ceremony was elaborate. The priest must first visit him without the camp. If he found that the man was indeed cured of his leprosy, a religious ceremony initiated the movement of his return to communion. Then ere he was admitted to the camp he must himself be washed and his hair shaved. After seven days of waiting there was to be another guilt offering, the anointing of the man with blood and oil, after which a sin offering, a burnt offering, and a meal offering were to be presented. Then he was restored to worship.

Once more the strictness of the law is revealed in the instructions given as to the cleansing of the house of the leper, which was to be observed in the time ahead when the people would be dwelling in the land.

The reading of this whole section (chapters 13, 14) impresses the mind with the strictness of the law of God concerning such things. It reveals the interest of God in the physical well-being of His people and His unceasing antagonism to everything likely to harm them. In our own day and land the purely Eastern qualities of these laws may seem to have no application, but their permanent values speak with no uncertain sound, teaching us among other things that it is impossible for men to be loyal to God and careless in any measure concerning the laws of sanitation. For example, it is ungodly for a community claiming to be in any sense Christian to tolerate the existence of dwellings which are infected in the slightest degree with what may be harmful to the highest physical condition of the people.

LEVITICUS 15

Chapter fifteen is a strange and solemn one in many ways, dealing as it does with the law of uncleanness as it applies to the question of issues. As in the case of the laws concerning childbirth, here the mind is once more brought face to face with dread and forceful solemnity to the fact of the defilement of the race.

A careful perusal of these requirements reminds us that the procreative faculties are all underneath the curse as the result of race pollution. Whether the exercise of such faculties be natural or unnatural, in the sight of a God of absolute holiness they are tainted with sin. Therefore, for the people of God, most stringent laws were made for cleansing.

This section has a solemn message to all of us concerning the fact of the pollution of our nature at its very fountainhead and the consequently perpetual necessity for cleansing. Such views may not be popular in our own day and generation, but experience perpetually teaches that to forget them or to neglect their solemn warning issues in disastrous results and a paralysis of the possibility of communion with God.

LEVITICUS 16

The great Day of Atonement was perhaps the most important of the whole year in the Hebrew economy. On that day provision was made for dealing with the whole question of sin as known and unknown. When considering the sin and trespass offerings, we saw that in each case, in greater or less degree, the element of accountability was conditioned in knowledge. Sin, however, in the sight of God is still sin, even though committed in ignorance. All such must be dealt with.

Careful instructions were given for the observance of the day. It was the one day in the year on which the high priest entered into the Holy of Holies. Every arrangement was intended to impress the mind with the solemnity of approach to God and to emphasize the fact that man as a sinner has no right of access save as he approaches through sacrifice. It is significant that when the priest entered the Holiest of all he did not wear his gorgeous apparel, but was clothed in a garment of simple and pure white linen. Careful instructions, moreover, were given as to the attitude of the people on that day. They were to rest and afflict their souls, which means that the day must be observed as one of solemn fasting and humiliation in which they would remind themselves of the fact of their sin or the provision made for their cleansing and of the consequent right of approach to God in worship.

LEVITICUS 17

Very definite instructions were given to the priests concerning sacrifices. These provided, first, that all sacrifices must be brought to the door of the Tent of Meeting. This provision at once recognized the unification of the nation around the fact of the divine presence. It reminded the people that worship is possible only along divinely ordained lines and in no isolated independence; and so by making offering of sacrifice there, the possibility of offering worship to strange gods was eliminated.

Then followed the strictest instructions forbidding the eating of blood under any conditions. The reason for this prohibition was carefully given. Blood is the seat of life and God has set it apart, and therefore it is the medium of atonement. The most precious and essential thing in human life was thus sealed to the sacred and holy work of perpetual testimony to the only way in which it is possible for sinning man to be reconciled to God, that is, sacrifice as symbolized in the shedding of blood. In order that this truth might perpetually be present to the mind of the people, the blood of beast and fowl was forevermore to be held sacred and under no circumstances to be eaten.

LEVITICUS 18

At this point in the enunciation of the laws of separation they assume a slightly altered character. So far, the fundamental matters of relationships to God have been the principal note. Now the habits of the life of separation are more particularly dealt with. The enactments here recorded especially recognize the perils which would surround these people on account of the habits and customs of the people by whom they would be surrounded in the land.

In view of these there was first a call to separation in general terms. Jehovah asserted Himself as being their God and distinctly forbade their conforming their actions to the doings either of Egypt or of Canaan, accompanying the commandment with a promise that if they obeyed Him they should live thereby.

Then followed the naming of certain evil practices of the people of these lands, certain abominations which had cursed the whole life of the peoples.

In this connection occurs a most important declaration, explaining the judgment of God upon the people of these lands. It is that the reason for such judgment is to be found in the practice of these abominations with terrible effects produced upon the peoples, so that they were utterly corrupt. All this emphasizes the paramount importance of the insistence on the necessity that the people of God should not be themselves defiled by such practices.

LEVITICUS 19

The more positive habits of separation are insisted on by the repetition of laws already given, with one reiterated emphasis, namely, the fact that the God of this people is Jehovah. There was, first, a general call to holiness based upon the essential reason, "Ye shall be holy; for I Jehovah your God am holy." This is the profoundest reason that can possibly be assigned. The holiness of Jehovah must be exemplified in His people. Every departure from the pathway of holiness is a profaning of the name of God, and in the case of a people thus called to realize and manifest the glory of His Kingship such departure is the most disastrous sin.

It is because of this that we find the almost monotonous repetition throughout this chapter of the solemn declaration, "I am Jehovah." No less than fourteen times does it occur. A people created and governed by God are intended to represent Him and the truth concerning Him to other people. When they fail to do so, His name is blasphemed by that failure. Therefore, in the midst of all the activities of life there must be the perpetual remembrance of whose they are and whom they serve. It will be remembered that in this very connection in his letter to the Romans, when the apostle was dealing with the specific nature of the sin of Israel, he summed everything up by saying, "For the name of God is blasphemed among the Gentiles because of you" (Romans 2:24)

LEVITICUS 20

Once more we have a repetition of laws already enunciated with the same persistent thought of responsibility. In this section we find the death sentence associated with certain forms of disobedience, and thus the fact of responsibility is lifted into a yet more clearly defined importance and lays a new and startling emphasis on the absolute authority of God. All the words which had thus been uttered for conditioning life were definite and positive laws. They were infinitely more than general messages of advice and direction. To disregard them was not merely unwise, it was positively penal and must be visited with actual punishment, and in certain cases with the death penalty.

LEVITICUS 21

The absolute necessity for the strictest separation of the priest from all possibility of defilement is vividly set forth in the laws here enunciated. Standing as he ever did in a place of special nearness to God as the appointed mediator of the people, he must, of all men, manifest in all externals of life and conduct the characteristics of that holiness without which no man can see the Lord. He was strictly forbidden to defile himself by contact with the dead in any form. The only exceptions permitted were in the cases of those who were next of kin to him. In the case of the high priest even such exceptions were not allowed. He must not touch a dead person, even though it be father or mother.

The necessity for rectitude within his family is revealed in the one flaming declaration that if the daughter of a priest defile herself, she profaneth her father and is to be burned with fire.

Moreover, it was provided that no cripple of any sort should exercise the priestly office. Approach to God necessitated perfection in the entire man, and so far as it was possible to reveal this by external symbols, it was done in the case of the priest. A tender recognition of the fact that blame may not attach to the man in the matter of defect is found in the provision that he might eat of the bread of God but must not offer it.

LEVITICUS 22

Instructions already given are now repeated with greater detail and wider application. Not only must the priest himself be free from blemish and defilement, he must see to it that all that which he offered was to be of the same character. Yet again, he was not to exercise hospitality toward those who were unclean or strangers to the covenant of the things which pertained to the House of his God.

These stringent instructions closed with a reaffirmation of the reason, which had been given in other connections, "I am Jehovah . . . I will be hallowed among the children of Israel." Thus these people were never allowed to lose sight of the fact that the deepest purpose of their existence was the manifestation of the truth concerning God. All the degradation existing among the nations was due to the false ideas of God which characterized their life and worship. Jehovah is the God of holiness because He is essentially the God of love. These are the profoundest things that nations can learn. A people created for their manifestation must share in that holiness and in that love. Hence the absolute necessity for entire loyalty in personal life and relative conduct of the men who are to interpret to the surrounding nations the truth concerning God.

LEVITICUS 23

The feasts of Jehovah were national signs and symbols. These were now dealt with. The foremost place was given to the Sabbath. Its constant recurrence, governed not by the natural order, but by the divine enactment, spoke ever of infinite things and eternal values.

The year commenced with the feast of Passover and Unleavened Bread, thus ever reminding the people of the fundamental truths concerning their national existence.

The feast of Firstfruits was to be observed in the land. It marked the fact of possession and was to be characterized by joyfulness.

After a lapse of seven full weeks during which harvest was gathered, the feast of Harvest was observed, this being a recognition that all came from God.

The seventh month was the most sacred month of the year. In it two great ordinances were observed: the Day of Atonement and the feast of Tabernacles, these being preceded by the feast of Trumpets. The Day of Atonement has already been described (chapter 16). Here it is placed among the feasts of Jehovah. All the other feasts were seasons of joy. This was to be a day of affliction. Nevertheless, in the profoundest sense it was a day of feasting and rejoicing. The mourning was the method, but joy was the issue.

The final feast of the year was that of Tabernacles. By dwelling in booths the people were reminded of the pilgrim character of their life under the government of God. It was to be preeminently a feast of joy. Readiness to obey the will of God is the occasion of songs rather than dirges.

LEVITICUS 24

As this chapter is read, it seems at first to be out of place or out of order. Yet undoubtedly it is not so. The fact that we may not be able clearly to see the connection does not warrant its omission or give us any ground for placing it elsewhere.

In it provision was made concerning the oil and the shewbread. It would seem that the ingathering of harvest being complete and the feast thereof arranged for, in the giving of the laws they were thus reminded of the claims of God on their produce, especially in the two matters which indicated their responsibility of light bearing and their privilege of communion.

Here also we have a fragment of

history. It is the story of the blasphemer upon whom punishment fell. It may be that it was inserted here because of its occurrence during the period of the promulgation of the laws. In any case, the point emphasized is that if for any reason a stranger take up his abode within the circle of the divine government, he is amenable to the laws thereof. Among the people under the Kingship of Jehovah taking His name in vain was a most heinous offense, and the man guilty thereof suffered the extreme penalty.

LEVITICUS 25

The last section of the Book of Leviticus is occupied with setting forth laws concerning the outward signs in the land of the proof of possession, together with certain promises and warnings, all ending with instructions concerning making and observing vows.

The signs affecting the land were, first, the Sabbath of the land and, second, redemption in the year of jubilee. These signs served to keep before the people the fact that God is the original Owner and Possessor of the land and that no man can treat it as absolutely his own. In the year of jubilee great human interrelationships were insisted on. The laws of this year of jubilee are carefully set out as they affect the land, dwelling houses, and persons. The only thing to which a man has a right in the land is that which results from his own labor. In the year of jubilee, moreover, the slave was to be liberated, thus reminding men that they could have no absolute and final property in any human being. The law, moreover, emphatically provided that during the period of bondage, the slave was not to be governed with rigor. In these laws the foundations of the social order were firmly laid. The interhuman relationships of both property and possession were conditioned in the fundamental fact of relationship to God.

LEVITICUS 26

In these brief repetitions of laws two gracious promises and solemn warnings were set forth. The laws reiterated were fundamental. There must be no idolatry. There must be perpetual observance of the Sabbath and a constant reverence in the sanctuary. The great promises show how conditions of well-being are ever entirely dependent on obedience to the government of God.

In like manner the warnings show that disobedience will always be followed with calamity.

It is most instructive in the giving of the law, to observe how the declension and wandering of the people was evidently known to the King, and that notwithstanding this fact, these promises of final restoration were made. Thus, while human responsibility is most solemnly enforced, it is done in such a way as to create the conviction that the love of God will prove itself finally victorious over all human failure.

LEVITICUS 27

In this final page of the Book of Leviticus we have something superadded to actual laws and yet of very vital importance. It is concerned with vows. A vow is a promise made to God voluntarily and not in obedience to any divine requirement. That is not to suggest that a vow is wrong. It expresses a devotion of the person or of property to the service of God beyond that which is demanded in the strict economy of relationship. It is not necessary therefore that any such vows should be made, but it is laid down clearly that if they are made, they must be religiously observed.

Vows dealing with the devotion of the person, of beasts, of houses, and of fields are all dealt with, and the great principle is emphasized throughout that though such offerings are voluntary, yet they must be paid to the full. If for any reason whatever one making such a vow desires to be set free from it or to redeem that which he has devoted, he must pay its full value, and something more, according to the appraisements of the priests.

Numbers

NUMBERS 1

The Book of Numbers deals with the wilderness. It is the story of a long discipline resulting from disobedience. History moves forward, for God ever protects His own purposes from the failure of His chosen instruments. The story begins and ends on the margin of the land.

The Book opens with the command of God to number the men of war from twenty years and upwards, and then contains the census of the fighting forces of the nation. The total reached 603,550. The Levites were carefully exempt from this numbering because of their consecration to the sacred service of the Tabernacle, all of which is more particularly dealt with afterwards.

Here, then, we have the first movement in preparation for the coming of the people into the land which God had given to them. As we have constantly seen, the nation had been created to carry out a larger divine purpose. This purpose was, first, necessarily punitive. Corrupt peoples were to be swept out in the interests of purity and the people of God were to be the instrument of the divine visitation. They must be prepared for warfare, which was the reason for taking the census of the men of war.

NUMBERS 2

This host of God was not merely a mob or an aggregation of individuals. It must be a disciplined and ordered company, and here we find the instructions concerning the relative positions to be occupied by the tribes, both in times of encampment and when on the march. It would be an interesting and helpful thing for the reader of this chapter to draw a diagram of the encampment as described.

At the center of everything was the Tabernacle, the very dwelling place of God, as to His manifestation. Around this the Levites were encamped on two sides and at the back. Moses and the priests were to occupy the fourth side close to the courts of worship on the east, confronting the entrance. Outside the enclosure and beyond this encampment of priests and Levites, the tribes of the nation took up their positions. Judah, Issachar, and Zebulun encamped on the east, confronting the entrance to the courts. Ephraim, Manasseh, and Benjamin were on the west; Reuben, Simeon, and Gad on the south; with Dan, Asher, and Naphtali, on the north.

On the march, Judah, Issachar, and Zebulun led. Reuben, Simeon, and Gad followed. Then at the center came the Tabernacle priests and Levites.

These were followed by Ephraim, Manasseh, and Benjamin; Dan, Asher, and Naphtali marching last in order. Whereas this is a technical chapter with a technical note, one great fact stands out, that, whether encamped or on the march, there was a divine order; and that in each case at the center of everything, the Tabernacle took its place.

NUMBERS 3

The account of the arrangements for the service of the Levites is fully and carefully given in this and the following chapter. In the rites are certain matters of principle which are of permanent value. First there is the fact of the separation of this tribe by divine arrangement to the sacred service of the sanctuary. It must ever be borne in mind that the Levites occupied that position in a representative capacity. The original provision was that the first-born in every family should be set apart to the work of priesthood. In all probability for the sake of cohesion and order this tribe was now appointed to represent the first-born. This they did, man for man, their number at this period being twenty-two thousand. When the census of the first-born was taken, it was found that there were 273 more first-born than Levites. These unrepresented first-born were commanded to pay a redemption price devoted to the service of the sanctuary. All these arrangements solemnly emphasized for the people the supreme importance of worship and at the same time revealed to them the orderliness of Jehovah. It is of interest to remember that while Our Lord after the flesh was not of the tribe of Levi, He was the First-born and so, according to the original provision, a Priest.

NUMBERS 4

Continuing the instructions concerning the Levites, we have a minute account of their work in connection with the movement and marching of the people. The family of Kohath were made responsible for carrying the holy furniture. This furniture they were not allowed to see or touch. Aaron and his sons first entered the Holy Place and covered each sacred piece, affixing the staves which were to rest on the shoulders of the Levites. On the march these were in charge of Eleazar, who also carried the anointing oil and the sweet incense.

The duty of carrying the curtains and the tents which constituted the Tabernacle itself devolved on the Gershonites.

The boards and bars and pillars and all other things which formed the foundations on which the sacred hangings rested were committed to the care of the Merarites.

All this is technical, and yet it cannot be studied without realizing how it emphasized the importance of the relation of the people to Jehovah. The sacred symbols of that relationship were to be as carefully guarded on the forward march as when they stood in proper order at the center of the encamped people.

NUMBERS 5

This section is devoted to arrangements emphasizing the necessity for the purity of the camp on the eve of the coming of the people into the land. All that were unclean were put outside the camp. This does not, of course, mean they were left behind to perish, but that they were not allowed to march in their proper place with the tribes of their people. For the time being they were camp followers only, excluded until their purification was ensured according to the provision of the laws already given. Not only must there be ceremonial cleanness but moral rectitude. Under this command, restitution had to be made by all such as had in any way sinned against others.

In this application the possibility of jealousy within the marriage relationship was dealt with. The ordeal of drinking bitter water had no similarity to the ordeals by fire and poison of which we read in the history of the Dark Ages. The drinking of such water was perfectly harmless in itself. It was a challenge to God on the part of the woman to demonstrate her purity as against an unjust charge. There is no doubt that if a woman who had been guilty of infidelity consented to drink this water, evidence of her guilt would have been manifested, not by any action of the water, but by the direct intervention of Jehovah. The great lesson taught here is the necessity for the purity of the people as they were to enter into possession of the land.

NUMBERS 6

Having provided for the purity of the camp by the exclusion of the unclean, special instructions were given concerning cases of personal and voluntary devotion to a life of peculiar separation to God in the instructions concerning the Nazarite. There was absolutely nothing monastic in this order. These men did not separate themselves from the ordinary life of their fellows, yet they did maintain an attitude of special separation, the signs of which were arranged for.

In this connection we have the specific form in which the priestly blessing was to be pronounced on the people. The blessing was to be a threefold utterance of the divine name with a threefold interpretation. The people were to be blessed and kept by Jehovah. Their light was to be the uplifted face of Jehovah and the consequent consciousness of His grace. In the same uplifting of that countenance they were to enter into the experience of peace.

NUMBERS 7

In our division of Numbers into chapters, chapter seven is the longest. It deals with worship and, first of all, with the princes' voluntary offering of their substance to the maintenance of worship. It is to be noticed that this offering was voluntary, not in answer to any compulsion outside even that of divine commandment. Out of their own consciousness of the importance of worship did the princes of the people offer willingly.

It is further to be observed that in each case the giving was equal, thus precluding the possibility of any spirit of rivalry and realizing unity of purpose. Perhaps the matter of simplest and yet greatest interest in this long chapter is the fact that this giving was so carefully chronicled and that in so detailed and elaborate a way. While all the story might have been told in a very few sentences, it is set forth with elaborate attention to detail. Every man is named and every gift is recorded. Thus, while the whole reveals unity of purpose and of equality of giving, in the divine recognition there is a remarkable attention to individual devotion.

NUMBERS 8

Having recorded the acts of the princes in offering their substance, the record proceeded to deal with the setting apart of the Levites as the special order of men whose persons and time were to be given wholly to the service of the sanctuary.

At this point, however, we find introduced a repetition of instructions concerning the lighting of the lamps and a declaration that the instructions were carried out.

In all these final arrangements for purifying worship before the people moved forward to the land, the one symbol which is thus referred to is the symbol of light, which was intended to be a type of the witness bearing of the nation.

Then follow the arrangements for the consecration of the Levites, which were not the same as those for the priests. No anointing oil or blood was used nor was any specific dress provided. The sign of their cleansing was the simple one of water.

Finally, the Levites themselves were offered as wave offerings, passing through the hands of the priests as they entered on their sacred service.

NUMBERS 9

As the time approached for entry to the land, the Passover feast was to be observed. In the arrangements now made, the sweet reasonableness of the government under which the people lived was manifested. Certain men were unable to participate in the feast because of having become defiled and others because of distance from camp. For all such a special provision was made in a second observance of the Passover a month after the regular one.

When everything was ready, the hosts awaited only the divine Will which was to be made known through the cloud. There was to be no movement of the people save in response to the movement of the cloud. It was at once a beneficent and drastic provision. No responsibility rested on the people save that of obedience. They were not called on to consider the time or direction of their march, but it is equally true they were not permitted to object or delay. All of which served to keep the fact of the sovereign authority of Jehovah perpetually before them.

NUMBERS 10

The use of trumpets in the history of the people is full of interest and here we find instructions concerning it. They were intended to call the people to attention, that led to obedience. The blast of the trumpets was ever in the ear of the people authoritative as the voice of God. Each note had suggested its own meaning. Certain calls were to assembly in one place, while others summoned to preparation for the march or for conflict, as the case might be.

As the movement forward commenced, we have the story of how Moses persuaded Hobab and his people to accompany them. He first suggested that it would be advantageous to Hobab, as he said, "Come thou with us, and we will do thee good." This was not successful in winning Hobab. Then Moses said, "Thou shalt be to us instead of eyes," thus appealing to him for his help. This appeal was successful.

The story here closes with the suggestive words which Moses used at the opening and closing of each successive movement of the hosts. They indicated Moses' and the people's profound recognition that everything centered in the presence and government of God, both in regard to the victory of Israel over her enemies and her own eternal safety and well-being.

NUMBERS 11

Here we enter upon the second section in the Book of Numbers, in which is revealed the failure of man. The first evidence was discontent, resulting unquestionably from the hardship of life. This was immediately rebuked by the burning of the fire of the Lord. Moses became an intercessor and the fire abated.

The next incident was more pronounced rebellion. The occasion was the mixed multitude. The explanation of the presence of these people is found in Exodus 12:38. These people hankered after things left behind in Egypt and the people of God were infected by this discontent. Moses, in perplexity, poured out his complaint into the listening ear of Jehovah. The answer of Jehovah to Moses was to appoint elders to assist him in oversight and their equipment by the Spirit. To the people He gave quails. An added comment by a psalmist on this story long after was:

> And He gave them their request,
> But sent leanness into their souls.

Here a principle emerges which is of perpetual application and importance. It is that there are times when God grants an unwarranted request in order that men may learn through experience the folly of their desires.

NUMBERS 12

A third manifestation of discontent and rebellion arose among individuals and leaders. The marriage of Moses to a Cushite woman was the occasion of the revelation of an element of jealousy in the hearts of Miriam and Aaron. They resented the exercise of Moses' authority, evidently desiring to share it with him in greater degree.

Once more the story illustrates a principle. If there be hidden evil, circumstances will sooner or later occur in which it will be outwardly manifest.

The divine method of dealing with this outbreak was stern and majestic. The offenders were summoned to appear before Jehovah and in plainest terms He vindicated His servant. Evidently the chief blame attached to Miriam, Aaron being here, as constantly, weak and easily influenced. The stroke fell upon her. After seven days she was restored. God is ever ready to pardon. Nevertheless, the warning was solemn and severe, showing that rebellion of the leaders of the nation could not be tolerated.

NUMBERS 13

Here we have another story of failure. It is closely associated with the movement of the people toward the promised land. The hour had come in which they should go forward. In this account in Numbers it is stated sending the spies was in obedience to the divine command. However, a comparison of this with the reference to the matter in the first chapter of Deuteronomy will show that the command followed the people's determination to do this very thing. This was in itself an act of suspicion and of practical unbelief. However, as they had decided, so they were commanded to do.

After forty days the men returned. Here perhaps we have the first occasion in history of two reports resulting from one commission, a majority report, and a minority report. Here, as has so often been the case, it was the minority report, rather than the majority report, that was right.

All were agreed on the desirability of the land on which they had looked. The emphasis of the majority, however, is gathered from the word, "Howbeit." They had seen the excellencies of the country, but they had seen the difficulties and beyond these they had seen nothing. The minority had seen, first Jehovah, and then the excellencies, and finally the difficulties. The essential difference is the vision of God. In the one case it was lacking and men were shut out from possession of the desirable by the foes of whom they were afraid. In the other it was present and obstacles were accounted as nothing.

NUMBERS 14

The people were swayed by the opinion of the majority. The call was distinctly heard and the desirability of obedience comprehended. But walled cities appeared impregnable and enemies as giants. The result was that they positively suggested a return to Egypt. The answer of God was the discipline of forty years. In communion with His servant Jehovah asked, "How long will this people despise Me? and how long will they not believe in Me?" In those sentences the real interpretation of disobedience and unbelief lay revealed. In this same communion with Moses, Jehovah suggested that the people should be cast off and a new nation be created of His loyal servant.

This led to a revelation of Moses in his greatness. He besought God to vindicate His power by the exercise of His mercy. The answer was immediate. The people were pardoned but were to be excluded from the land.

The attitude of the people changed as there broke upon them the consciousness of the unutterable folly of their action. Here again, however, their failure was manifest in their decision to go up and possess the land from which God had just excluded them. The result was that they were utterly routed. Israel, guided by God, was an entirely different proposition from Israel attempting to realize the purposes of God without Him. The lessons are obvious and searching.

NUMBERS 15

Once more we have the repetition and enforcement of certain laws already given. Occurring here, this appears somewhat strange. The explanation, I think, is to be found in the opening declaration, "When ye are come into the land." The people were about to turn their faces from the land which they ought at once to have possessed, and in this reiteration of certain provisions for dwelling within it there was at once a prophecy of the ultimate fulfilment of divine intention and a provision for preserving in their minds the principles of the law by which they were to be governed.

What follows illustrates the fact that the people were not perfectly clear whether the laws were to be enforced in the wilderness. One of their number was found gathering sticks on the Sabbath. They did not know what to do with him and put him inward until they found the will of God. They were immediately instructed that the law of the land obtained at once and that a violator of the law was to be visited with the full penalty for his crime.

Immediately following this a provision was made for wearing fringes on the borders of their garments, on which was to be bound a cord of blue. The purpose was distinctly declared. That cord of blue was a symbol of the deepest truth in their national life, that they were under the direct government of heaven. Every time the eye rested on that simple sign the heart was to be reminded of the sublime truth.

NUMBERS 16

Here begins the story of perhaps the strangest and most fully organized opposition that Moses had to encounter. Two elements were at work. The first was ambition and the second was dissatisfaction. The plea of the elders was for equal rights and consequent independence of action. The reply of Moses was a reassertion that his authority was divinely ordained. Sudden and terrible discipline fell upon the people. The whole incident is a warning for all time and for all men against any attempt on the ground of popular right to violate the crown rights of Jehovah.

The last movement in the story is a startling revelation of the blindness of the people and of how far the dissatisfaction had spread. The whole congregation charged that the death of those who had been punished rested on Moses. Again the divine voice threatened the extermination of the people, and immediately a fierce and swift plague afflicted them. Directly it commenced, however, at the instigation of Moses, Aaron, the appointed priest, whose right it was to swing the censer, filled it with fire and sprinkling the incense thereupon passed into the midst of the afflicted people. The mediation prevailed, the plague was stayed, and by that fact and with renewed emphasis, the right of Aaron as priest and the right of Moses as leader were indicated.

NUMBERS 17

That the murmuring of the people against the divine government was an evil thing is emphasized by the fact that a supernatural sign was given in final vindication of Aaron's position. The reason for giving the sign was declared in the words, "I will make to cease from Me the murmurings of the children of Israel, which they murmur against you." The spirit of rebellion manifested itself afterward in different ways and for different reasons, but it seems probable that any complaint against the rights of the God-appointed leadership of Moses and the priesthood of Aaron ceased at this time.

The sign granted was simple, but it was luminously suggestive. Twelve princes representing the twelve tribes were commanded to bring rods having their names inscribed on them and to lay them before the Lord. Aaron's rod budded, blossomed, and bore fruit. These effects were patiently the result of divine action, and thus men were taught that the position of Aaron was not due to anything inherent in him but to the direct appointment and equipment of Jehovah.

NUMBERS 18

Once more we find a repetition of sundry laws which had a direct bearing on the events recorded, and the reason is explicitly stated in the words, "That there be wrath no more upon the children of Israel."

The repeated affirmation of the fact of divine appointment as to the position in service of Aaron and the sons of Levi is an arresting and suggestive matter. Observe such sentences as these: "I give you the priesthood as a service of gift" (verse 7); "I have given them (all the wave-offerings) unto thee, and to thy sons and to thy daughters with thee, as a portion for ever" (verse 11); "I am thy portion and thine inheritance among the children of Israel" (verse 20); "I have given (the tithe) to the Levites" (verse 24).

Thus it was made clear that appointment to the priesthood and possession of its privileges and its peculiar relationship to God, together with provision for the sustenance of all those appointed were by direct divine government and according to divine purpose.

It was finally provided that of the tithe, which was the divinely appointed portion of the Levites, a tithe was to be by them specifically offered to God.

NUMBERS 19

A most interesting arrangement is here described. It was a provision for the sacrifice of a red heifer. Instructions were given for the ceremonial cleansing of the people during the period of their wilderness wanderings. It was at once provision for defilement and a protection for the priesthood.

With solemn ceremony and most minute carefulness, a red heifer was to be sacrificed according to instructions already given in Leviticus concerning other offerings. Then its ashes were to be carefully gathered and kept, in order that they might be mixed in water and used in certain cases of uncleanness.

This provision was followed by instructions on how to deal with those contaminated by contact with, or in the presence of, the dead.

In movements from place to place while the camp was not pitched and the ordinary methods of the ceremonial law could not be observed, cleansing was provided by the use of water in which these ashes were to be intermixed. Thus a gracious provision was made and at the same time the rights and prerogatives of the priesthood were safeguarded. Wherever the people might be, these ashes of the red heifer which had been sacrificed by priestly hands were available for use.

NUMBERS 20

We now reach the record of events at the close of the forty years. The people were again at Kadesh. Here Miriam died and was buried. A study of the district will show that perhaps the severest part of their wandering was reached. They were again without water and murmured against Moses and Aaron. It is remarkable that there was no divine punishment, but God graciously supplied their need. The conspicuous failure at this point was Moses' failure. In the moment of God's gracious action he was ungracious in his attitude toward the people. Because of this breakdown he was eventually excluded from the land.

It was at this point in their history that Aaron died. The account of the transference of his robes of office to his son is that of a solemn and impressive ceremony. The people were reminded that the office of the priesthood was greater than the man. Aaron passed; the priesthood remained. So it continued until at last in the fulness of time there came the Priest who retains the office in the power of an unending life. The death of Aaron was in itself a reminder of the present imperfection of the relationship of the people to God. Nevertheless, the transference of office by divine appointment spoke in no uncertain tones of the abiding tenderness of God and of His provision for the people's access to Him.

NUMBERS 21

The movement forward of the people now brought them into the path of conflict. The way was rough and difficult and the people were discouraged. Again they felt a lusting after Egypt and spoke against God and against Moses. So pronounced was their rebellion that swift judgment fell upon them in the form of the serpents. The provision made in the elevating of the brazen serpent was simple and sublime. That serpent was erected by the command of God. The people were told to look at it. In itself that was an act of obedience and a yielding to the God against whom they had rebelled.

Proceeding on their way they met and overcame Sihon and his Amorite hosts and then gained victory over Og the king of Bashan. At last we find them in the plains of Moab beyond the Jordan at Jericho.

NUMBERS 22

We now come to the story of Balaam. It is evident that he was a remarkable personality. He appears in the story first as a man of integrity, who attempted a literal obedience to the will of God. We are arrested by the fact that he was first forbidden, and afterwards consented, to go in response to the invitation of Balak. The only explanation that is satisfactory is that while desiring to maintain a literal and external obedience, his heart was lusting after the riches promised him by Balak. To this the word of Peter bears witness, "Balaam the son of Beor, who loved the hire of wrong-doing" (II Peter 2:15).

As he went on his journey, a startling and supernatural intervention occurred. Had his heart been set upon doing right for its own sake, he would surely have turned back at that point. His hesitation was revealed in the words, "If it displease Thee, I will get me back again." Therefore permission to proceed was again granted to him, but a limit was set on his speech.

In this story we have again a remarkable illustration of the working of an abiding principle. Man is compelled to work out what is deepest within him, while all the way God works toward changing that internal condition. Circumstances are overruled for the development in outward manifestation of the inward truth. Balaam loved the hire of wrong-doing and so long as that love remained within him, he was driven forward, even though the sin of his action was revealed by the divine interventions.

He returned to Balak and in doing so manifested an external obedience to the will of God in declaring to him that he could speak only the word that God put into his mouth. Underneath there still lurked the love of hire. He attempted to compromise between obedience and this love.

NUMBERS 23

The first of Balaam's prophecies was uttered in the midst of strange surroundings. Sacrifices were offered to heathen gods, while Balaam turned aside to inquire of Jehovah. The result was that we have in his prophesying the first of a series of utterances concerning Israel which are among the most sublime in the whole of Scripture. In this first we have a central declaration,

> Lo, it is a people that dwell alone.

It constitutes a vision of the nation as separated from others because of the divine attitude toward them. The prophecy ended with a sigh which shows how profound was his conviction of the high privilege of the nation.

> . . . Let me die the death of the righteous,
> And let my last end be like his!

Balak now took Balaam to another point of vision. The result was a prophecy which gave yet another view of the people. Of this the central statement is,

> . . . Jehovah his God is with him,
> And the shout of a King is among them.

Thus the people were seen as governed and guided by God and therefore victorious. The burden of this second utterance was the certainty that all the purposes of God must be accomplished when God Himself was King in the midst. The reading of this chapter should conclude at verse twenty-six, as the next section leads to that which follows.

NUMBERS 24

From the closing sentences in chapter twenty-three we learn that Balaam was taken to yet another place of vision, from whence he looked on the desert. The Spirit of God came upon him and again he uttered only the things which God would have him speak. Here the indexing statement is,

> How goodly are thy tents, O Jacob,
> Thy tabernacles, O Israel!

Thus there was given to him the vision of a people victorious and prosperous.

The progressive note of these utterances is self-evident. First, there was revealed a people separated to God, dwelling alone. Second, they were seen as a people governed by God. Finally, they were seen therefore as a people victorious.

All this lead to the fourth and final prophecy of Balaam, the principal note of which is:

> There shall come forth a star out of Jacob.

Thus the far-distant movements of the divine economy were for a moment laid bare to his vision. He beheld a Person shining as a star, swaying a scepter, and conquering as He goes.

The last word having been spoken, Balaam left Balak and went to his place. Having failed to curse the people of God, he set himself to injure them. As John says in his Apocalypse, he "cast a stumbling-block before the children of Israel, to eat things sacrificed to idols, and to commit fornication" (Revelation 2:14). How fearfully he succeeded is shown in the subsequent story.

NUMBERS 25

The influence of Balaam is revealed in what is now recorded. The words of Jesus in His letter to the Church at Pergamum, quoted in our last note, are closely connected with the statement with which this chapter opens. "The people began to play the harlot with the daughters of Moab: for they called the people unto the sacrifices of their gods; and the people did eat, and bowed down to their gods."

This action would appear to have been one of simple neighborliness. Tarrying in the vicinity of the Moabites, they attended their sacrifices and bowed down at their worship. In doing this they were violating the principle of Balaam's first vision of them as a people dwelling alone. It was an act of rebellion against God and so a corruption of the Covenant.

The account of the action of Phinehas the priest is a revelation of how one man in loyalty to God and jealous for His honor may stand against the false attitude of a people. Phinehas dared to refuse to take part in these false conventionalities and visited with immediate and terrible punishment the two notorious wrongdoers. His action stayed the plague and saved the nation.

NUMBERS 26

At this point we begin the third and last movement in the Book of Numbers, that which is devoted to the second numbering of the people and their preparation for taking possession of the land from which they had been excluded for forty years.

We have first the record of historic facts in sequence and all the way an account of how the divine government was insisted upon by the repetition of certain laws with new emphasis and applications. In this particular chapter we have the account of the taking of the census and a record of the families and their numbers.

The record is followed by the account of an instruction given to Moses concerning the division of the land among the tribes, the numbering of the Levites, who possessed no inheritance in the land because they were devoted to the service of God.

An examination of this new census will reveal the omission of many names occurring in the first, while others have taken their place. Thus there is emphasized a marked continuity of purpose, notwithstanding the change of persons.

Two men only of those who long before had come to the same margin of the land were now to pass over into possession. These were Caleb and Joshua, the men who constituted the minority, who saw more than enemies and walled cities because to them the vision of God was unclouded.

NUMBERS 27

An interesting historic incident is here recorded during the wilderness wanderings. One Zelophehad had died, leaving no sons but five daughters. These now petitioned that they might have an inheritance in the land and their petition was granted.

The time for the passing of Moses had now come. In the plan of God it was necessary that the people should pass into the land from which they had been so long excluded. Moses could not enter with them. There is a great tenderness in all God's dealings with him in those closing scenes. The final account of his death is found at the close of Deuteronomy. Here we see him permitted publicly to appoint his successor.

When the call of God came to him to ascend the mountain and view the land and be gathered to his people, the final passion of his heart was that which had so long sustained him in the midst of all the trying circumstance of his work as leader. He thought of the great congregation and of them as the "congregation of Jehovah." He knew, as no other man, their weakness and the necessity for one to succeed him who would lead them according to the will of God. They were indeed but a flock of sheep, and to the mind of Moses, sheep without a shepherd, as they were to the mind of Jesus so long after—men helpless and hopeless. Moses' last prayer, then, was that Jehovah would appoint his successor. The prayer was immediately answered and he had not only the satisfaction already referred to of appointing his successor, but, what was far more important to him, that of knowing that the one so appointed was the man of God's own choice.

NUMBERS 28

This and the next chapter contain a repetition of laws concerning the great religious observances of the nation. This repetition is an orderly statement covering the whole year and, indeed, showing its relationship in every period to spiritual matters. It was thus set forth on the eve of their entering on possession of the land in order that the arrangements for worship might be duly made and properly carried out.

First we have the religious rites appointed for the small time divisions. Daily sacrifices were arranged for (verses 1-8), weekly offerings which were to be made on the Sabbath were named (verses 9, 10), and the monthly offerings appointed (verses 11-15).

A study of these will show how there was an increase in the number of the sacrifices and the importance of the religious rites in each enlarging section of time. Daily, one lamb in the morning and one in the evening; on the Sabbath two he-lambs in addition to the continual burnt offering; in the beginnings of the months two young bullocks, one ram, and seven he-lambs, all in addition to continual burnt offering.

Then follow instructions concerning the observances marking the springtime, the feast of Passover forever reminding them of the divine deliverance by which they had become a nation formed the commencement of the year. Following this, after an interval, came the feast of Pentecost in which the first fruits were offered to God.

NUMBERS 29

Continuing the laws concerning the feasts as they governed the year, the celebrations of the autumn were next dealt with. Three feasts are mentioned —First, the feast of Trumpets (verses 1-6), then the great day of Atonement (verses 7-11), and, finally, more particularly described here than any of the others or than elsewhere, the feast of Tabernacles (verses 12-40).

A study of these arrangements will show again how the increase in sacrifices noticed from the daily offering to the monthly is yet more remarkably manifest in these annual festivals.

Thus the whole year was covered and conditioned by these solemn religious rites and ceremonies. Every day as it broke and passed, every week as it began, every month as it opened, every year both as it commenced and closed was sealed with the sacred matters which ever spoke to the people of the relation they bore to God, as based on sacrifice and expressing itself in service.

NUMBERS 30

In this section the subject of vows was dealt with and principally those of women. A man's vow was declared to be absolutely binding. No provision was made for release. In the case of women this was not so. If a woman dwelling in her father's house took a vow, the father had the power to forbid. If he did not do so, then the vow became binding. In the case of a woman dwelling with her husband, the husband had the like power. Similarly, if he did not exercise it, the vow became binding. In the case of a widow or one divorced, if her vow was made in her widowhood or while she was divorced, it was absolutely binding. If it was made while she dwelt with her husband and he forbad it, she was released. If not, she also was bound by it.

These provisions are most arresting in revealing as they do the divine conception of the importance and necessity for the unity of the household. There must not be two supreme authorities in any family and here as always in the economy of God the responsibility of headship was with the husband and father. It can readily be seen how, were this otherwise, even through religious vows, discord and probable breakup in family life might ensue. Therefore as the nation approached settlement in the land, the integrity of the family was thus carefully safeguarded.

NUMBERS 31

Here we have the story of the end of Balaam. It took place in connection with a war directly resulting from the sin of the people committed through the influence of Balaam. They had corrupted the national life by cohabitation with the women of Midian. This, as specifically stated, resulted from "the counsel of Balaam."

In this war Phinehas led as priest. This is arresting as revealing the peculiar and religious note of the conflict. It was the relationship of the people to God that was imperiled. Phinehas, who on a previous occasion had stayed the plague by his action, now led the twelve thousand chosen men on the mission of judgment. It has been suggested that in all probability some of the actual numbers in this chapter are inaccurate, that in the process of translation and copying, mistakes have been made. That is quite possible. It is, however, a matter of no real moment. The method of this enterprise was most drastic and hard, but, as so constantly in the perusal of the history of those times, it must be interpreted by the age in which it happened. In the fuller light which has come in the process of the ages such methods are unnecessary and therefore are never commanded.

NUMBERS 32

We have here the record of what without doubt was a wrong committed by two and a half tribes, of Moses' failure in judgment, and, consequently, of a grave mistake.

Reuben, Gad, and the half-tribe of Manasseh looked on the lands which recently had been depopulated by the conflict and desired immediate settlement therein. The distinctly avowed purpose of Jehovah for His people was that they should go over Jordan. The request of these two and a half tribes was of the nature of compromise.

There is no account of Moses seeking divine guidance as he had so constantly done. His own first judgment was against granting the request in this matter. He pointed out to the two and a half tribes that in essence it was of the same spirit which their fathers had manifested forty years before and which had resulted in the long and wearying discipline of the wilderness.

They, however, persisted in urging their plea, promising that they would cross the Jordan to help in the conflict there. Moses yielded to them and so permitted their settlement on that side of the river. Subsequent events reveal how wrong the compromise was.

No desire of our own for early and easy realization of peace ought to be allowed to interfere with the declared will of God. No policy of compromise can ever justify a modification of a divine method toward the accomplishment of divine purpose.

NUMBERS 33

An account of the wanderings of the people in the wilderness was written by Moses at the express command of God. It appears as a bare and uninteresting list of names and yet it tells the story of a people guided by God through discipline. In the course of it there are occasional glimpses of light, revelations of varying experiences but of unvarying guidance. Through shadow and through sunshine, through trial and through triumph, by ways that were gracious, they were led with unceasing faithfulness by God.

Thus we are taught that even though He chastise, He continues to conduct and when through our own unbelief we have to pass through the paths of the wilderness He never forsakes us.

This account is followed by a record of the solemn charge to the people in view of their approaching possession of the land. They were to enter by divine appointment and the purpose of which was to be a manifestation of God and of the perfection of His government. Therefore, when they entered the land, every trace of false worship was to be swept away wherever it was found. Moreover, the land was to be divided equitably among them.

The charge was accompanied by warnings uttered in simple terms and yet most solemn and searching. To tolerate and allow to remain what God had ordered to be driven forth would be to retain that which in itself would be a source of continual difficulty and suffering. The most solemn word of all was the last uttered. "And it shall come to pass, that, as I thought to do unto them, so will I do unto you." In these words is revealed an abiding principle, that God's election to blessing is never of persons without reference to conduct, but rather of character which expresses itself in obedience to His will.

NUMBERS 34

One of the terms of the charge already considered, that the people should possess the land and that it should be divided equitably, was now enlarged upon. The division was to be according to divine arrangement and choice. It must be based as to amount on the comparative needs of the tribes. The divisions given were for those who would pass over into the land beyond Jordan according to the divine purpose. Reuben and Gad and the half-tribe of Manasseh were to have no part in that inheritance. Thrice over the words are repeated in reference to them, they "have received." They had made their own choice and it was now ratified. Long after, they were the first to be captured and carried away in the breakup which ensued upon the sin of the whole of the people.

While the arrangements for division were divine, human instruments were appointed to see them carried out. These were the priest Eleazar and the princes of the tribes.

Among these one name arrests our attention. It is Caleb, the man who, with Joshua, forty years earlier had believed in the possibility of doing the will of God in face of difficulties. Now, after the long period of disciplinary experience, he was appointed with Joshua again to take oversight of the partition of the land according to the divine plan.

NUMBERS 35

It will be remembered that the Levites were not permitted to hold any inheritance in the land. Jehovah was the portion of their inheritance. Provision was now made for them. Forty-eight cities scattered throughout the whole land were to be the places of their abode. This scattering of the servants of the Tabernacle through the length and breadth of the land was a beneficent arrangement. Nothing is said of religious service to be rendered by them in their own cities. They were rather to go up in courses to the center of worship. According to the divine purpose, their residence would have an influence for right on the whole life of the nation.

Among these forty-eight cities of the Levites six were to be set apart as cities of refuge. This was a tender and just provision among a people naturally fierce and vindictive. The law of God had made life sacred, and the punishment of taking it had been solemnly declared in the words, "Whoso sheddeth man's blood, by man shall his blood be shed." Nevertheless, there might be extenuating circumstances. For premeditated murder there was to be no final refuge or forgiveness. For killing in haste, that is, unpremeditated killing, provision was made. These cities were not provided that men might evade justice, but rather that justice might be ensured. The fact that a man slayer reached one of these cities did not ensure him against inquiry and investigation. It rather made such inquiry necessary and thus gave him opportunity of explanation and ensured the certainty of just action.

NUMBERS 36

The question of the inheritance of women, which had already occurred through the application of the daughters of Zelophehad, came up once more, raised by the heads of the tribes. It was possible that these women might marry men who were members of other tribes. In such case their inheritance would pass over. It was therefore provided that they must marry only within the border of their own tribe.

Thus closes the Book of Numbers. It is essentially a book of the wilderness. The nation was on the eve of entering the land. The actual history is again taken up in the last chapter of Deuteronomy with the account of the death of Moses.

It is impossible to read this book without being impressed first with the failure of the people. It is a record of long-continued stubbornness and foolishness.

Yet what right have we to think or speak harshly of the people, for the book is also the story of the unwearying patience and perpetual faithfulness of God.

Throughout there is manifest the forward movement of God along the highway of His own purpose. This forward movement is not of man but of Jehovah. The book is a revelation of the sure procedure of God toward the final working out into human history of the regeneration of humanity, the first movements of which were recorded in the close of the Book of Genesis, the central forces of which came in the Incarnation of the Son of God, and the final victories of which are not yet.

Deuteronomy

DEUTERONOMY 1

The Book of Deuteronomy is didactic rather than historic. It consists of a collection of the final utterances of Moses and is a Book of review.

It commences with a discourse in which Moses reviewed the forty years. This occupies chapters 1 to 4, verse 43. The whole journey from Horeb to Kadesh-barnea should have occupied eleven days (verse 2). The distance was not more than 125 miles. Because of unbelief they had spent forty years in the wilderness.

We have in this chapter a review of the first movement from Horeb to Kadesh-barnea. The call which had come to them at Horeb emphasized the fact that they were under the divine government, and indicated the purpose of God that they should go in and possess the land. Looking back, Moses reminded the people of their rebellion in the matter of the spies and of the consequent discipline to which they had been subjected. In doing this he was careful to set all the facts in the light of the government of God. He reminded them that their disturbance at Horeb was due to the direct commandment of God, that even though the way of the wilderness had been a terrible one, they had not been left to grope their way through it alone. God had constantly moved before them, choosing them the place of encampment at every pause, indicating where they should pitch their tents.

It is noticeable that when he now referred to the mission of the spies, he quoted the report of the minority rather than that of the majority.

DEUTERONOMY 2

Continuing his discourse, Moses reviewed the second movement from Kadesh-barnea to Heshbon. The notes which characterized the description of the first period are found also in this review of the second period. All that Moses told them they knew as to the actual facts of the long and tedious road they had traveled in the weary years which were now drawing to a close. The great burden of his message to them was emphasizing the fact of how even amidst such sorrowful and severe discipline they had still been thought of and guided by God. The turning back to the wilderness was under the divine command, and therefore through all the tiresome way God was still with them and they had lacked nothing (verses 3-7).

Now once more at His command

they were approaching the land. With this ending of the discipline God gave them the first manifestation of the power which they had called in question forty years before, in that He placed the fear of them and the dread of them on the peoples of the land.

This great truth that God never forsakes His people, even when they are bearing the chastisements He imposes as the result of their unbelief, is full of comfort for the hearts of His people for all time.

DEUTERONOMY 3

Still continuing his review, Moses dealt with the third movement from Heshbon to Beth-peor. In doing so he continued to emphasize the fact that the power of God had been clearly manifest throughout. He reminded them that they had taken all the cities against which they had been commissioned to go. In doing so and in referring to these cities he used the words which declared that they were "fenced with high walls, gates, and bars."

It is interesting to remember that when the majority report of the spies was given long before, they had declared that the cities were "fenced and very great" (Numbers 13:28). The report, therefore, was so far correct. Moses now showed them how through their first victorious movement against such cities, the mistake of the fear which had characterized them in the past was made manifest.

There is a touch of pathos in the way which Moses referred to his own emotion at this manifestation of power and his desire to go over and possess the land. Whereas this was denied him, the punishment was mingled with a tender mercy in that he was permitted to know that his successor would actually lead the people in. There can be no doubt that the supreme desire of Moses was a desire for the accomplishment of the divine purpose.

DEUTERONOMY 4

On the ground of this survey Moses exhorted the people to be obedient. His appeal was based on the greatness of their God and the perfection of His law. Their whole existence as a nation centered around a spiritual ideal. Therefore, he re-emphasized the importance of their attempting to make no likeness to God.

Looking on into the future, he uttered words which in the light of subsequent history are seen to have been prophetic. He actually foretold the story of the corruption of the people in the land and their ultimate exclusion from it. Nevertheless, he also declared that when they would turn to Him again with a full heart, He would still have mercy on them and restore them.

Finally, he urged them to make comparison of the facts of their national existence with all other history. Their God had spoken to them. Their God had acted for them. Therefore Moses urged them to know that He was God and to keep His commandments.

The end of the chapter briefly records, first, the appointment of three cities of refuge, and then constitutes the beginning of an introduction to the second discourse. This beginning carefully marks the place, time, and subject.

DEUTERONOMY 5

Continuing the introductory part of the great discourse, Moses called on all Israel to attend to "statutes and judgments." In addition to these words, he later employed the word "testimonies." The three words occur together later (6:20). "Testimonies" are the actual words of the law given. "Statutes" are the provisions for worship and the conduct that harmonizes therewith. "Judgments" deal with the arrangements for the administration of justice.

Moses first repeated the ten words of the Decalogue. In doing this it is arresting to observe that concerning the Sabbath the ground of the appeal is no longer God's resting during creation but the people's position as redeemed from Egypt's bondage.

The discourse proceeded in solemn and stately language to recall to the memory of the people the occasion and the method of the giving of the Law. One brief declaration in this connection marked the sufficiency of the Law as given, "He added no more." On the basis of all this he urged them to "observe to do, not turn aside"; but "walk in all the way . . . that it may be well. . . ."

DEUTERONOMY 6

The appeal of Moses was now elaborated in a great statement on the deepest value of the commandment and the corresponding responsibilities of the people. Observe the peculiar form of the opening statement, "Now this is the commandment, the statutes, and the judgments." The very form suggested the unification of plurality and evidently was intended to do so, for it led to the statement, "Jehovah our God is one Jehovah." Here Jehovah was used as name and as title, its supreme value, of course, being that it postulated existence and revealed an attitude of grace.

Immediately following this announcement of the sublime and all-inclusive principle of the unity of Jehovah, Moses dealt with the resulting responsibilities. First, personal love for God and His commandments was insisted upon. Second, the family was in mind, for the children were to be diligently taught these things. Third, these words were to be the subject of conversation in all the activities of life, sitting in the house, walking by the way, lying down, or arising. Moreover, they were to be kept in mind by outward manifestation, bound upon the hand, and between the eyes; written upon the door posts, and upon gates.

The great lawgiver proceeded to make certain applications of these responsibilities of the life they would live when they had come into possession of the land. Three perils would then threaten them. The first would be the peril of prosperity. Moses charged them not to forget their relationship to God. The second would be the peril of adversity. They were not to tempt the Lord as they had at Massah (Exodus 17:1-7). There they had committed the sin of murmuring and strife because of their difficulties. The third peril would be the neglect to keep their relation to God alive in the minds of their children. He charged them, therefore, to take time to teach the children.

DEUTERONOMY 7

Continuing to deal with the responsibilities of the people as they entered the land, Moses insisted upon the absolute necessity for the maintenance of the attitude of separation to God. Stringent instructions were given in this matter. They must not compromise with the people of the land. They must not marry with them because such alliance would result in corruption of the chosen people and their straying after other gods. Moreover, they were to sweep out all the signs of false religion, altars and pillars and Asherim and graven images. Moses reminded them that their God was faithful both in mercy and in discipline, and urged them therefore to be faithful.

Still another peril threatened them. This peril would necessarily grow out of the difficulties of the work that lay before them. It was inevitable that they would become conscious of the number and strength of their foes. If once they permitted their minds to dwell on these things, they would repeat the folly of their fathers, who saw fenced cities and giants rather than God. Moses urged them, therefore, to remember the deliverances already wrought. The central word of this charge is, "for Jehovah thy God is in the midst of thee, a great God and terrible." To be perpetually conscious of this would be to be delivered from the sense of fear in the presence of all opposition.

Moses ended with the solemn warning that in the burning of the images the clothing and drapery also must be destroyed. Everything devoted by God to destruction must be destroyed by the people whom He leads into victory and possession.

DEUTERONOMY 8

Still continuing this discourse, Moses declared that the land when purified of the corrupt people was to be possessed by the people of God as His chosen nation. He showed that the first condition of possession was that they should remember the past with all it had taught them. They must never forget that God had led them and that the way of His leading was purposeful.

All the experiences of the wilderness were in order that they might learn two lessons: first, that they might know their own heart. It is important that we recognize that the meaning of this passage is not that God might know them, but that they might come to know themselves. God knows man perfectly. The important thing is that man should come to know himself.

Out of the humbling that such knowledge must bring to man, a second lesson would be learned, namely, the fact of his need of God and of God's guidance and government.

Therefore, all the chastening and discipline of God resulted from His love. God ever treated man as a man treats his son.

The second principle of possession insisted upon was that the people should live by the Word of God, that is, that they must act on the lessons they had learned and keep the commandments of Him from whom they had received the land as a gift.

Solemnly Moses warned the people against the peril of imagining that their possession of the land was the result of personal effort or thinking that it was by their own strength they had entered therein.

DEUTERONOMY 9

It is interesting to note that as the final announcement of their approaching entrance to the land was made the difficulties which the people had faced at Kadesh-barnea were recognized as still confronting them, and they were shown that these difficulties were not difficulties to God. Moses also insisted that they were not being taken into the land because of their righteousness but as the instruments of God's government of the world.

The truth so declared was further emphasized by a repetition of the sad story of their failure which had manifested itself from the very beginning of their history, their coming out of Egypt. In Horeb they had provoked the Lord to wrath and were saved only by the intervention of Moses. At Taberah the spirit of discontent brought down on them the fire of God. At Massah they had doubted God and provoked Him. At Kibroth-hattaavah they murmured because of their privations. Finally, at Kadesh-barnea they had refused belief in God. All these facts thus massed demonstrated the truth of the affirmation that they were not being brought into the land because they were righteous.

DEUTERONOMY 10

In recounting the story of the writing of the Law the second time, Moses distinctly affirmed that these tables too were written by God Himself. This was the culminating word in all he had said to them concerning their unfaithfulness. Side by side with their failure had been the manifestation of the pity and forbearance of God. They were therefore now being called upon to enter the land in spite of their own unrighteousness because of the compassion of God and His set determination to carry forward His larger purposes through them.

In a passage of great beauty, thrilling with earnestness, Moses made a statement summarizing the truth concerning the requirements of God as His people entered the land. The whole revealed the fact that everything depended on their relationship to Him. They were to fear Him, that is reverence; to walk in His ways, that is obedience; to love Him, that is worship; to serve Him, that is co-operation; to keep His commandments, that is fidelity.

In order to encourage them in such attitudes and activities, he made two great declarations concerning God. The first (verses 14-16) concerned their relationship to Him. He is a great God, possessing all. He is a God of love, having delighted in their fathers and choosing their seed. In consequence of these facts they were called on to maintain the attitude of separation, in the words, "Circumcise . . . the foreskin of your heart."

The second (verses 17-19) declared anew the greatness of God as the Ruler of all things and of His love as it expresses itself in just dealing with the needy and the stranger. These convictions were to create their attitude toward strangers. They were to love them. Finally He made his appeal to them to fear, serve, cleave to, and swear by Jehovah their God.

DEUTERONOMY 11

As Moses concluded his great call to the people to the pathway of obedience, he reminded them what varied experiences they had had from which they knew the nature of the government and power of God.

He wooed them toward obedience by speaking of the excellencies of the land to which they were going and by contrasting it with the land of Egypt from which they had come. Egypt was the place of forced cultivation. The new land was one watered, and loved, and watched by God.

For all material prosperity in this new land they therefore must depend entirely on God, knowing that His answers of blessing would depend in turn on their obedience to His law. He told them that they would move to possession of the land and all its wealth in unhindered power in proportion as they maintained the position of unquestioning obedience.

Very solemnly he called them to remember that he had set clearly before them the way of blessing and the way of cursing, finally ordaining on Mount Gerizim and Mount Ebal, a solemn ceremony of blessing and cursing. Concerning these he gave more detailed instructions at a later period.

DEUTERONOMY 12

Having thus repeated the great words of the Law and called the people to obedience, Moses now proceeded tc deal with the statutes and judgments, and, first, the statutes.

In dealing with these he commenced with the true place of worship. He solemnly charged them what their attitude toward false places of worship must be when they entered the land.

They were to be utterly destroyed without pity and without sparing.

Moses then put into striking contrast their attitude toward the true place of worship, commencing with the words, "Ye shall not do so unto Jehovah your God." To the place of His appointment they were earnestly to seek.

Then he proceeded to emphasize this more particularly. The attendance of the people at the center of worship to be appointed in the land was obligatory. During the wilderness period there had evidently been some laxity in this matter; for he said, "Ye shall not do after all the things which ye do here this day, every man whatsoever is right in his own eyes." This evidently referred to matters of worship and they were thus solemnly charged that in the land there must be regular attendance at the place of the divine appointment. No worship in the home was to be taken as a substitute for public worship. Nevertheless, certain provisions were made for those who might live at a distance.

DEUTERONOMY 13

The discourse commenced in chapter twelve continues with carefully expressed warnings against idolatry, and it is very arresting to note how the ways by which they might be seduced from the pure worship of Jehovah to the false worship of idols were guarded against.

First, there would be the danger of curiosity and therefore they were charged not to inquire after false gods.

Second, there would be a peril of signs and wonders wrought by false prophets. No such sign or wonder must be permitted to withdraw them from the pure worship of Jehovah and, indeed, any such working of signs was pronounced guilty of death.

Third, in all probability there would be the temptation presented by some tie of blood or friendship. These must all be sternly guarded against, and any being seduced in either way were to be slain without pity.

Once more there would be the peril arising from looseness of discipline in these very matters and the people were charged to take active measures against seducers and the seduced. The importance of these severe provisions will be understood as it is remembered that the worship of a people forevermore determines their character and their conduct.

DEUTERONOMY 14

Continuing, Moses proceeded to give the injunctions which revealed his consciousness of this effect of worship on conduct, warning the people against specific evils and urging them anew to observance of matters enjoined by the Law.

In this chapter we find first of all his warning against the seduction of sorrow. The people of the land were accustomed to mutilate themselves in the wildness of their sorrow over the death of friends. All such mutilation was strictly forbidden to the people chosen to be a holy people to the Lord.

Next in order, followed careful instructions on eating, with differentiation between things clean and unclean. Such provisions as these were long looked on as wholly capricious, the result of mere superstitions among the Hebrew people. Today we find men of science coming ever more closely to the teachings of Moses in their views on the subject of human diet. There is no question that every provision was in strict accordance with the laws of health, qualified of course by the climate and conditions existing in that land.

Finally, the chapter contains Moses' instructions on tithing. The people were warned not to neglect it and it was insisted that they must personally present the tithe at the place of the law's appointing. If they lived too far away to carry the produce, they were to turn it into money, which might more easily be carried the long distance.

DEUTERONOMY 15

Here we have provision made for the relief of the poor and the less fortunate at regularly stated intervals. The great ideal is revealed in the words, "There shall be no poor with thee." This, however, was possible only as Moses taught, "If only thou diligently hearken unto the voice of Jehovah thy God. . . ."

In this connection they were charged to make provision for the release of the debtor every seventh year. In all social life will come times of adversity but if this benevolent provision be observed there will never be any absolutely hopeless poverty.

Whereas Moses had said that on the fulfilment of certain conditions there would be no poor, he followed with, "If there be with thee a poor man . . ."; and, later, he affirmed, "The poor shall never cease out of the land."

Therefore, such must be cared for and the fact of this provision of a year of release must not be made an excuse for failing to give immediate help to those who are in need. Solemnly he charged them to obey the command which called for the consecration of the first fruits of herds and flocks to the Lord.

DEUTERONOMY 16

As the section dealing with the statutes commenced with the place of worship, it closed with the restatement of the importance of the great feasts which by their annual recurrence set the whole year in relation to worship.

The year commenced with the Passover. Thus at the beginning the Hebrews were reminded of how their true national existence resulted from their deliverance by God out of Egypt's bondage. The Passover feast must be maintained in the land and observed at the proper center of worship in order that the day of the exodus might be remembered perpetually. Thus their fundamental relationship to God was to be brought to mind at the beginning of every year.

The next event of importance in the consecration of the year was the feast of Pentecost, in which the first fruits of the harvest were to be presented to the Lord, thus reminding them that not only their existence as a nation, but their perpetual sustenance was dependent on the selfsame fact of relationship to Him.

Finally, in this particular application came the feast of Tabernacles. This was to be a time of rejoicing in which master and servant, people and priests, fathers and children, the prosperous and the bereft were all to be included.

On these three occasions all the males were called upon to appear before God and to bring with them gifts. Thus the value and importance of stated and united worship were solemnly enforced on the people as they stood on the threshold of their land.

In this chapter, verse eighteen, we have commenced the section dealing with the subject of judgments. Here Moses commanded the appointment of judges and officers and declared the principles on which they were to act. These were to be those of strict righteousness without any wresting of judgment. There must be no respect of persons and no reception of bribes. There must be no false worship.

DEUTERONOMY 17

Continuing the discourse commenced in the previous chapter, we find insistence on the fact that no false sacrifices must be offered and no false worshipers permitted to approach. For dealing with such, a method was minutely laid down. First there must be careful inquiry and for condemnation there must be three, or at the least two, witnesses. Where cases of peculiar difficulty arose they must be remitted to the priests and to the supreme judge, that is, to the religious and civil court.

Then followed a revelation of the threefold medium through which the government of God must be interpreted—the king, the priest, and the prophet. In dealing with the king the words of Moses were those of prophetic foresight. He saw what would happen in the history of the people after they had come into the land. Therefore the principles of appointment were declared. The king must be chosen of God and be of the people's own nation. He was not to multiply horses, wives, silver, or gold. All these things were characteristic of the kings of the nations round about them, and it was provided that Israel's king must live a simpler life for the fulfilment of a higher ideal. Moreover, he must be a student and doer of the law.

This is a remarkable portrait of God's ideal of kingship. It would be an interesting exercise to measure the kings of men throughout history by this ideal. Such a procedure would inevitably issue in a twofold consciousness. First, we would find that the measure in which the kings of men have conformed to the ideal is the measure in which they have contributed to the strength of national life; and, on the contrary, the measure by which they have violated these principles has been the measure of the disaster resulting from their rule.

DEUTERONOMY 18

In dealing with the priest who was already found among the people by the appointment of God, the fact that he was to have no inheritance in the land was restated. Then a special provision was made for any priest whose heart drove him to some particular service. He also must be cared for by the people.

Finally, turning to the subject of the prophet, Moses enjoined the people to beware of the false and to know the true.

In dealing with the false prophets he described their methods. They would be the practice of secret things, of dealing with the spiritual forces of evil in a professed attempt to discover the will of God.

The true prophet was then promised and described. The description given is brief but graphic. He would be one of themselves, receiving the words of God and uttering them to the people. All the true prophets of God that followed fulfilled this ideal in measure. The proportion in which they spoke to the nation the will of God with authority was the proportion in which they did so.

As we study these words concerning king and priest and prophet, we inevitably realize that the perfect fulfilment in each case came ultimately with the coming of the Son of God. He was at once King of His brethren without inheritance in His own land; Priest, abiding in the service of God and ministered to by the people of God; Prophet of His brethren, speaking the word of God in all fulness and in all purity.

DEUTERONOMY 19

Still with his mind on the fact that the people were coming into the land, Moses made further applications of the laws to the new conditions. His words now had to do with life and land and truth and justice.

Cities of refuge were to be provided in order that in the administration of the law which safeguards human life there should be strict justice. The accidental killing of a man was not to be counted equal to premeditated murder. Deliberate killing was to be followed by the death penalty, the cities of refuge offering no harbor to the guilty.

The words concerning the land were brief but clear. No man was to remove an ancient landmark. The far-reaching importance of this will be understood when it is remembered how absolutely man depends on the land for physical sustenance.

Truth as between man and man in all dealings must be maintained at all costs. Anything in the nature of false witness was to be severely punished.

The final words have in them a note of great severity as they sternly insist on the necessity for the strictest justice in all human interrelationships.

DEUTERONOMY 20

It is necessary to bear in mind that these people were being led into the land not merely to find a possession for themselves as an established nation, but first as the scourge of God against a corrupt and corrupting people. In view of this fact war was inevitable, and therefore particular instructions were now given for the people's guidance in war.

First, they were charged to keep before them the vision of God, which alone would enable them to be free from fear in the presence of the foe. Before they went into battle it was ordained that the priest should authoritatively announce the presence of the authority and power of God.

Then the army itself was to be sifted. Men whose hearts were for the time being set on other things, houses, or vineyards, or wives, were not to go into the fighting line. Moreover, those who failed to see the vision of God and therefore were faint-hearted were to be refused.

Before attacking far-distant cities, an offering of peace was to be made. Where there was submission, a certain measure of leniency was to follow. In the case of the cities which the Lord gave them as an inheritance, the war was to be one of extermination. The reasons for this already have been revealed.

In connection with these commands occurs one of those remarkable evidences of the divine attention to the smallest matters. No trees were to be cut down which were of value to the sustenance of the people.

DEUTERONOMY 21

Sundry laws affecting the life of the people in the land after the conquest were now uttered. The sin of murder was once again dealt with. This time it was the murder of a person which could not be traced to the guilty party. Civic responsibility must be recognized by offering sacrifice.

The question of the marriage of captive women was also dealt with. Should a man set his heart on one of these women, she was to be treated in the most honorable way. The marriage was not to be consummated for a month. If at the close of that time the man were of the same mind, the woman could be married. If not, she was to be allowed to go forth absolutely free.

Then followed laws concerning the inheritance of children. In the existing state of things, it might be that a man would come to hate one of his wives, while he loved another. In such case the children were not to be allowed to suffer. The first-born was to have the rights of the birthright, whether the child of the loved or the hated woman.

While in this way the right of the child was safeguarded, the necessity for parental discipline was enforced, and provision was made that if the child was not amenable to the law of his parents, the city was to act in discipline and in judgment.

Finally, the hatefulness of sin to God was revealed in the injunction that persons hanged on a tree as the result of sin were to be buried immediately.

DEUTERONOMY 22

Here we have the record of the laws conditioning life in love and neighborliness. Every man was enjoined to take care of his brother's lost things if he found them; and he was also to help the hurt animals of his brethren in the hour of their distress.

All unseemliness in dress was forbidden. Men were charged to act in kindness even toward the birds. In building their houses they were to think of others who later might have to use them, and protect them against the possibility of accident by erecting a parapet around the roof.

Three commandments were uttered forbidding admixture. The land must not be sown with two seeds. Plowing must not be done with an ass and ox together. Garments were not to be made of an admixture of wool and linen.

Continuing, the stringency of the Mosaic economy in the matter of chastity is revealed. It may well be carefully studied even today. It may be summarized by declaring that it demands that at all costs the man must be chaste and the woman pure. Moreover, it is made perfectly clear that in the mind of God the sacredness of betrothal is as great as that of the marriage relationship.

DEUTERONOMY 23

Under the Mosaic law certain persons were excluded from worship and others from the camp. Any who in any way violated the requirements of personal perfection in physical matters were not to be allowed to stand among the worshipers. Both the actually maimed and such as were the direct issue of sin were excluded. The Moabite and Ammonite were excluded to the tenth generation because of their refusal to help the people of God in the time of their need and their attempt to harm them in the matter of Balaam. The Edomite and Egyptian were to be excluded to the second generation only. In the case of the first, help had not been rendered in time of need; and in that of the second, Israel must never forget benefits received.

With his eye ever on the future of the people in the land, Moses proceeded to touch upon various subjects to the end of this chapter and through the following two chapters seemingly without any system. Israel was to be a refuge for the oppressed slaves of other people. Usury among brethren was forbidden. Vows, it was plainly declared, must be kept, but it was also made perfectly clear that there was no necessity for making vows. In the case of need a man might eat in his neighbor's vineyards or pluck his standing corn, but no man was allowed to carry away from vineyard or cornfield anything for trade or personal enrichment.

DEUTERONOMY 24

Continuing, we have varied subjects dealt with, revealing the divine thought for the people in many ways. Divorce was recognized and restrained. The sacredness of the marriage relation was recognized by the tender provision that no man must be called on to leave his wife for war or business during the first year. In the matter of creditors and their pledges, nothing must be taken with which a man earned his living. Man-stealing was to be summarily punished with death. A new warning was uttered against leprosy, coupled with the illustration of Miriam, which reminded them that leprosy might be caused any time by disobedience and unholy ambition.

Instructions were given concerning loans and pledges which were full of mercy to the poor, and provided that nothing really necessary for the well-being of anyone should be withheld from him after sundown. Those who were in need were not to be oppressed.

Finally, in all business enterprise the poor were to be had in memory, and reapers and gatherers were to act, not merely for their own profit, but also for the necessities of the poor.

DEUTERONOMY 25

This chapter is a continuation of the two previous ones in giving varied instructions.

Punishments were to be righteously administered and were never to be excessive. It is interesting to notice what excessive punishment is to the mind of God. It is anything which makes our brother appear vile in our sight. Perhaps no word of these varied instructions reveals more clearly than this the divine sense of the rights of personality.

The next word was concerned with the wrong of muzzling the ox that treadeth out the corn. It would seem that whereas undoubtedly this was applicable first to animals, it also had a spiritual significance. At least it was so referred to by Paul (see I Corinthians 9:8-10).

The law of the kinsman redeemer, which provided for the perpetuation of the line of descent in Israel of one dying without issue was enunciated at this time.

Just measures were insisted upon and the people were solemnly warned to maintain their antagonism to Amalek.

Moses' very lack of system or order in setting forth these sundry laws is in itself suggestive. It would seem to say to us that we may approach life in any of its activities or relationships, knowing that God is always interested; and, more, that He has a purpose and a method which it is our business to discover and obey.

DEUTERONOMY 26

Here we have the final movement in the second of these great farewell discourses of Moses. In it the lawgiver lifted his eyes and looked at the land to be possessed, and proceeded to tell the people how they were to worship in the new land.

The first recognition and act of worship necessarily is that of approach to God. Therefore they were instructed to go to the place of worship with the first fruits of the land. Then a formal confession of a threefold nature was to be made; first, the fact of possession was to be stated; second, the helpless origin of the nation was to be remembered: "A Syrian ready to perish was my father"; and, finally, the people's possession of the land was to be acknowledged as the work of Jehovah alone.

With such confession, offerings were to be presented to the Lord and the people to rejoice together.

Then followed a recognition of the other side of worship, which is the true and outward expression of the first. Gifts were to be bestowed on men, the Levites, the strangers, the fatherless, and the widow.

This having been done, prayer again was to be offered to God in which the gifts bestowed on men are spoken of as dedicated to Him.

All this is most suggestive, as it teaches us that our worship can be perfected only in service to our fellow men. The discourse ended with words that reminded the people of their relationship to God. Of the nation it was affirmed, "Thou hast avouched Jehovah this day to be thy God." Of Jehovah it was affirmed, "Jehovah hath avouched thee this day to be a people for His own possession."

DEUTERONOMY 27

We have here the record of something distinctive and arresting. Immediately after the close of the second discourse containing a résumé of laws, Moses and the elders commanded the people that after they entered the land they were to erect on Mount Ebal stones that were to be covered with plaster and have inscribed on them the words of the Law, the reference to the Law there undoubtedly being to the Ten Commandments. Moreover, they were to build an altar on the same mountain.

The action was suggestive. The law insisted on the necessity for obedience, while the altar spoke of the only method of approach to God consequent on disobedience.

Following these instructions, Moses and the Levites charged the people that after they entered on the land there was to be a formal pronouncement of blessing and cursing. The blessings were to be uttered from Mount Gerizim by the children of Leah and Rachael; the cursing from Mount Ebal by the children of the bondwomen. It is noticeable here that the blessings pronounced are not enumerated, but only the curses.

DEUTERONOMY 28

We now come to the commencement of the third discourse of Moses. It was pre-eminently the uttering of solemn warnings in which he laid before the people the results of disobedience and rebellion. He spoke first, however, of the blessings which would follow obedience. They were to have national pre-eminence. Temporal blessings of all kinds would abound. They were to have victory over their enemies in time of war. The purpose of their King, Jehovah, it was plainly declared, was to fill them with joy and make their path prosperous. They could, however, enter into His purpose only by obeying His law.

The effect of disobedience was then described as it would obtain among themselves. Adversity of every kind would overtake them. They would be smitten before their enemies, and persistent disobedience would result in their being driven out of the land into which God had brought them. The description of this expulsion proved eventually to have been a prophecy of what actually happened when they were carried away to Babylon. Continuing to speak prophetically, Moses uttered words which the centuries proved to be a detailed description of the Roman mastery of the land and the ultimate destruction of the city.

In view of so solemn a discourse as this delivered at the close of his period of leadership, it is indeed an appalling thing to think of how these people disobeyed the commandments, rebelled against God, and fulfilled to the letter all Moses had said. There can be but one explanation, and that the one to which the writer of the letter to the Hebrews referred—unbelief. The story is a warning for us, revealing as it does the capacity of man for evil, and how, in spite of the clearest warnings, he is capable of disastrous disobedience. More is needed than the law which indicates the way and more than the prophet who urges obedience.

DEUTERONOMY 29

The fourth discourse of Moses urged the people to be true to the Covenant, the terms of which had been given and are recorded in the previous chapter. It is to be carefully remembered that the first verse of chapter twenty-nine in our arrangement is the last of chapter twenty-eight in the Hebrew Bible. The statement, "These are the words of the covenant," refers to what had already been uttered.

In thus especially appealing to them, Moses first referred to the Lord's deliverances for them, wrought in the past (verses 2-9)—from Egypt, during the wilderness experiences, and in the day of battle on the eve of their coming into possession.

His appeal was to all classes of the community—to the rulers, the people, men, women, children, and also to the servants. There was to be no escape and no excuse.

Then in graphic and burning words he described what must be the result of breaking the Covenant. Recognizing the imperfection of the people and their inability at all times to appreciate the methods of the divine government, he enunciated a principle of far-reaching importance and perpetual application as he declared that the secret or mysterious or hidden things belong to God, while the things revealed were for them and their children.

DEUTERONOMY 30

Continuing his discourse, Moses uttered words thrilling at first with tenderness and urgent appeal.

In the first ten verses of the chapter we have the long look ahead of love. He seems to have seen the people in the conditions which he had predicted must result from disobedience, scattered far off from their own land. He saw them, however, returning in spirit to God as the result of severe discipline. In view of this, he saw how ready God would ever be to receive and pardon them when they thus returned.

It was a great prophetic evangel, the message of which stands true for all time, but the value of which men have even yet hardly appreciated.

Proceeding, Moses reminded the people of the supreme glory of the nation. For them the law of God was not something to be sought out. It was near them, yea, in their hearts.

As the discourse drew to its close, Moses reminded the people of his faithfulness to them in delivering the message of God. His faithfulness he called heaven and earth to witness, and, recognizing that everything depended on their exercise of that power, urged them to choose life.

DEUTERONOMY 31

At the conclusion of his fourth discourse, Moses talked to the people concerning his own departure and encouraged them in view of the fact that they were coming into the land by assuring them of the continued presence and power of God. To Joshua also he spoke words of the same kind.

It is very beautiful to see Moses in his last days on earth attempting in every way in his power to impress on the people the fact that only one thing mattered—that they should remember God and obey Him. Here it is distinctly stated that Moses wrote the words of the Law. This was probably among the last things he did.

In the final movement of this particular chapter we have an account of matters preceding the public uttering of the great song of Moses. First he and Joshua appeared before the Lord in order that Joshua might be officially appointed to succeed Moses as administrator of affairs.

Jehovah then spoke to His servant, telling him that the time had come for him to sleep with his fathers, that the people whom he had led would fulfil his predictions concerning their failure, and that God would visit them with the punishments previously announced.

It was a gloomy outlook for the great leader, but it was the occasion of one of those manifestations of the divine love which are ever full of beauty. He was commanded to write a song, the purpose of which was distinctly stated. The song embodied in the national life would remain, from generation to generation, a haunting memory testifying to truth concerning God. Songs often remain after commandments are forgotten, and it was that this might be so that Moses was instructed to write. The song was written and taught to the people. The Law was written and committed to the priests.

DEUTERONOMY 32

Here we have the song itself. The first part (verses 1-3) consists of a call to attention. Heaven and earth are called to listen while the servant of God proclaims the name of God.

This he does immediately (verses 3, 4), celebrating His greatness, His perfection, His justice, His faithfulness. Briefly he refers to the people (verse 5) and nothing good is said of them.

Proceeding with the song, the tender government of God is illustrated in the figure of the eagle and its method with its young. A consideration of this figure shows that in their methods which may at the moment appear unkind, Love is perpetually working toward the higher development of those on whom it is set.

At this point the song becomes a wail, opening with the startling words, "But Jeshurun waxed fat, and kicked." Prosperity which was wholly due to the goodness of God was made the occasion of rebellion against Him. Consequently the tenderness of love becomes the burning of a fierce anger and benefits are replaced by chastisements. The song ends on the note, "Oh, that they were wise," and shows that if they were, the strength of God would be greater than all the forces of their foes.

The song ended, Moses once more earnestly appealed to the people, declaring that their very life depended on their obedience.

Immediately following, there came to him the final call. It was characterized by both tenderness and severity. The reason for his exclusion from the land was once more declared; and yet he was to die, not amid the mists and mysteries of the valley, but on the mount of vision itself.

DEUTERONOMY 33

Here we have the record of the final words of Moses to the nation. They also take the form of a song. Often he had set before the people cursing and blessing. His last words were of blessing only.

First, in stately and majestic language he affirmed anew the majesty of Jehovah. In the midst of these statements is a word which arrests us: "Yea, He loveth the people." It may be that the Hebrew word there might be rendered "tribes," and that the reference was to Israel. Personally, however, I believe that it was a recognition of the larger purpose of God in dealing with Israel. While it is true that the holy ones are in His hands for safety and at His feet for communion, His purpose is not exhausted in them. "He loveth the people," that is, the nations beyond, and would reach them also in blessing.

The great words of blessing on the tribes follow, Simeon only being omitted. Reuben and Gad are referred to in terms which suggest that they will be saved so as by fire. Levi, having lost all earthly things for the special honor of bearing the Word of God, will receive the reward of such sacrifice. The word concerning Benjamin speaks of the safety of frailty. The choicest things said are those concerning Joseph. His are all "precious things and the good will of Him that dwelt in the bush." His therefore is the portion of government. In Issachar and Zebulun is to be seen triumph over disability. Gad, overcoming at the last, is made a judge. Dan becomes typical of conquest. Naphtali is satisfied. Asher is sustained.

Thus in his final benediction Moses

made the peculiar realization of blessing by the tribes unfold the all-sufficiency of God. The concluding words again affirm the greatness of God manifested in His tenderness and strength toward His people.

DEUTERONOMY 34

Here in all likelihood we have the writing of another hand. The section contains the story of the death of Moses, the equipment of Joshua for his work, with a last tender reference to the great leader and lawgiver.

The passing of Moses was full of beauty. As we have seen, his exclusion from the land towards which his face had so long been set was in fact a punishment. Yet how wonderfully it was tempered with mercy.

His force had not weakened. Everything ended in full strength. He went up to die and Jehovah gave him a vision of the land and buried him in the valley.

The last words are almost of the nature of a wail of sorrow. "And there hath not arisen a prophet . . . like unto Moses."

Notwithstanding this, a promise already had been made by God to Moses and uttered by him in his second discourse, "I will raise thee up a Prophet from among their brethren, like unto thee." Long centuries elapsed and at last that Prophet came, and in His coming was greater than Moses.

Thus ends the last Book of the Pentateuch. The nation created for regeneration among the nations is seen standing on the margin of the possession of their land. The highways of the biblical revelation have led us thus far. The great story will now move on through the history of this people to the coming of the promised One.

Joshua

JOSHUA 1

In the Hebrew division of the Scriptures after the Torah or Law came the Prophets, divided into the Earlier Prophets and the Later Prophets. In this section the first Book is the Book of Joshua. Its content is a continuation of the history of the chosen people. The first division (1-12) tells the story of the conquest of the land.

The link of connection between this Book and the preceding ones is arrestingly shown in the use of the word "therefore," in the charge to Joshua; "Moses My servant is dead; now *therefore* arise." The work of the great leader was completed, but the work of God moves forward. For this Joshua was divinely commissioned. His right of entrance was that God had given the land to His people. His power of entrance was to be that of the divine presence and the consequent inability of any man to stand against him. The conditions of his success were to be that he must be strong and courageous by obedience to the law of God.

Immediately following the account of this commission of Joshua we have his call to the people. It was characterized by urgency and dispatch; "within three days" the hosts were to move forward toward all the conflict and difficulty which had long ago frightened their fathers and turned them back into the wilderness. The call was uttered first to the whole nation and then especially to the Reubenites, the Gadites, and the half-tribe of Manasseh, who had already found their settlement on the wilderness side of the Jordan.

It is interesting to notice here the terms of the response of the people to the call of the new leader. They said "Only Jehovah thy God be with thee, as He was with Moses" (verse 17); "only be strong and of a good courage" (verse 18). The people thus made the same demand on Joshua as Jehovah Himself had already made.

JOSHUA 2

Forty years before this time the spies had been sent out and had brought back to Moses their reports of the land. Of these, Joshua had been one of the two who had brought back a report revealing their recognition of the power of God.

Now Joshua himself once more sent out spies. The whole story, however, reveals the principle of his sending was very different from that underlying the sending of the spies in the time of Moses. As we saw in considering the Book of Numbers, the occasion then was almost certainly one savoring of unbelief. Here it was the action of faith.

Faith, however, is never foolhardiness. It acts with caution. Joshua's vision of God was no dimmer and his courage was evidenced by his attention to all the details of the coming conflict. Whatever the report of the spies might be, he would go forward, but it was important for him as a military leader to know the condition of affairs.

The men thus sent found all they wanted to know from conversation with Rahab. A comparison of what she said to them with the report which they brought to Joshua (verses 9-24) will show that their report was in exact accord with what she told them.

Thus these spies returning to Joshua made it evident that the promise of God that no man should be able to stand before him was being fulfilled; for, according to Rahab, "the fear of you is fallen upon us."

Rahab's action was that of faith (Hebrews 11:31), which was manifested in that she acted on the conviction that had come to her in common with the rest of the people in Jericho concerning this invading army. The men of Jericho shared that conviction but rebelled against it. Rahab recognized the activity of God and yielded to it. That is faith.

JOSHUA 3

The first movement in the actual advance of the people into the land was of such a nature as to impress them with the truth of their positive relation to God. There was nothing in this first advance calculated to give them any cause for personal glorying. They came on to the actual soil of Canaan not by deflecting the course of the intervening river nor by bridging it, but by direct divine intervention. Divine power arrested the rushing river and made a highway for them to the other side.

The method of the divine procedure was intended to magnify Joshua in the sight of Israel by demonstrating to them that God was indeed with him as He had been with Moses.

While the act was wholly God's, it was performed on the fulfilment of certain conditions by the people. Charged so to do by Joshua, they sanctified themselves and thus made possible the action of God. Moreover, they moved in obedience to His command, setting themselves in array, with the priests leading before the parting of the waters.

The crossing of the Jordan was connected with the center of their life, the divine Presence, which was made evident by the pause of the priests and the Ark in the midst of the river bed while the hosts marched past them into possession.

JOSHUA 4

The commands of God required haste in obedience. Haste, however, never means neglect of religious observance. The very fact of their need for the divine guidance made it of supreme importance that the people should take time for worship and the recognition of their relationship with God. Safely over Jordan, with the conflict waiting, the hosts must pause while stones were gathered out of the river bed and erected in a memorial pile on the land to which they now had come.

We shall miss a very great deal of the beauty of this picture if we fail to notice the true reason of this pause and the erection of this pillar. That reason is revealed in verses six and twenty-one. "That this may be a sign among you, that, when your children ask in time to come, . . ." "When your children shall ask their fathers in time to come. . . ." It will be remembered that the same principle held in connection with the establishment of the Passover feast. The ultimate purpose of God lies far out of sight. Ere it is reached, new generations will spring up. Therefore none of the lessons of the present must be lost. They must be perpetuated in memory throughout the coming days. In order that this may be so, Jehovah deliberately arranged for such things as would appeal to the natural curiosity of a child. What more natural than that in days to come children playing or walking near this heap of stones should ask their fathers what it meant. It was for this that the divine arrangement made provision and the people were commanded that when the children asked their questions, they were to be answered. So the story of divine deliverance was retold by fathers to children through all successive generations.

JOSHUA 5

The effect on the people of this crossing of the Jordan is revealed in the words, "Their heart melted, neither was there any spirit in them any more." Therefore time must again be taken for matters distinctly of worship.

During the forty years in the wilderness the rite of circumcision evidently had been neglected. There could be no triumphal progress until this had been corrected. Moreover, the nation, so far as its men were concerned, was now becoming a nation of soldiers who were to conduct a campaign of judgment against the corrupt and depraved people. As there can be no doubt that the rite of circumcision was based on holiness and purity of physical life, we see the importance of its enforcement anew at this juncture.

Following this the great Passover feast was solemnly kept and thus the people were reminded again of the nature of their national existence.

At this time there appeared to Joshua himself the Captain or Prince of the hosts of the Lord, and he was thus made to recognize that his authority and leadership depended on his submission and obedience.

Thus, in different ways before a blow was struck, leader and people were compelled to recognize their dependence on God and the fact that they were but instruments in His hand, moving forward for the accomplishment of His purpose.

JOSHUA 6

All the preparation being completed, the hosts of God moved forward as the scourge of God in judgment on the corrupt peoples of the land.

It is impossible to imagine anything more calculated to impress on these hosts their own absolute weakness than the method of their first victory.

Those marching hosts and those blatant horns were patently utterly inadequate to the work of capturing a city, and by the standards of all ordinary human methods of warfare they were the instruments of foolishness.

Surely the tremendous lesson thus taught at the beginning was that victory must come not by might and not by power.

Yet it is equally true that what happened taught these people their absolute invincibility so long as they were trusting and obedient.

The peril of the lust of plunder was before them and they were solemnly warned against yielding to it.

The days passed as the hosts marched, and at last through the folly of the human method the divine power operated and Jericho was captured.

The salvation of Rahab illustrates for all time the principle upon which men may be saved. It is faith in God, and here as always faith is seen to be conviction yielded to rather than rebelled against.

JOSHUA 7

This chapter opens with a significant and ominous "But." So far we have had the record of remarkable progress —but! We now see the triumphant people defeated and flying and the reason is declared. It was the sin of a man, but it was also the sin of the nation. Israel had now become a nation in very deed, and therefore no one person could act alone. Individualism is a far more tremendous responsibility when it has ceased to be mere individualism. The sin of the one became the sin of the community, and all the hosts of God were defeated and His enterprises checked because one man had disobeyed.

The story of Achan's sin as he told it is full of warning. Mark carefully its progress; "I saw," "I coveted," "I took."

The confession he made was complete, but it was worthless. The reason of its worthlessness lay in the fact that it was never made until there was no escape. Gradually the walls closed around him until not on his own confession, but by the appointed method of divine detection, he was manifested as guilty.

Joshua's cry to God as recorded here was a cry full of agony, and, as in the case of Moses, its deepest note of sorrow was created by his jealousy for the name of God.

Swift and terrible and yet necessary and just was the judgment which fell on the man who had so grievously sinned.

JOSHUA 8

As the result of the severity of the discipline exercised in the case of Achan, the nation returned to obedience, and consequently Jehovah immediately uttered the word of reassurance to Joshua and the campaign moved victoriously forward.

The story of the taking of Ai is one of brilliant military strategy. Thus again the fact was brought into prominence that in prosecuting the work of Jehovah there must ever be a recognition of the value and use of the best in human reason. Strategy without obedience is useless. Obedience includes the use of reason, the employment of common sense, and in a campaign such as that on which Joshua was engaged the employment of strategic methods.

Once more the first victories being won and the gates of entrance to the whole country being secured, Joshua paused to fulfil religious duties.

Among the final instructions given to the people by Moses were those which provided for setting up great stones on which the words of the law were to be written, the erection of an altar on Mount Ebal, the offering of sacrifices, and the uttering of the blessings and curses as appointed. These instructions were now being carried out by Joshua.

JOSHUA 9

The fame and the dread of the people by this time were spreading far and wide. The kings of Canaan, conscious of their danger, formed a league against the oncoming hosts.

However, before they had time to take action, a new peril threatened Israel through the strategy of the Gibeonites. The first mistake made by the princes of Israel in this matter was that they acted alone in receiving the messengers instead of remitting what was a new set of circumstances to God for counsel and guidance.

Moreover, they had been straitly charged to make no covenant with the people of the land. Although it may be urged that they thought in making the covenant with these people they were doing so with those from a great distance, it is yet clear that they approached perilously near direct disobedience.

The deceit being discovered, the action of Joshua was immediate and decisive. He was bound by the letter of his covenant with the Gibeonites, but he condemned them to perpetual servitude, making them hewers of wood and drawers of water. It is interesting to observe that in subsequent history the binding nature of this treaty was recognized and the Gibeonites do not appear anywhere to have made any attempt to corrupt the children of Israel with idolatry.

JOSHUA 10

This action of the Gibeonites in securing their own safety aroused the anger of the confederate kings and they proceeded to act against Gibeon in order to punish it. In their peril the men of Gibeon appealed to Joshua. He instantly responded, for the gathering together of these kings created his opportunity. By forced marches he reached the scene of action. The rout of the kings was complete and was made more terrible by the storm of hail which swept upon them as they fled, killing more than were slain by the Israelitish hosts.

It was in connection with this defeat of the five kings that the day was lengthened for Joshua in answer to his prayer, sun and moon alike standing still at his command. To make this story a merely poetic description of a day not longer but fuller than usual is to declare it untrue, for the method of its telling leaves no doubt that the chronicler intended to record it as supernatural.

This decisive victory broke the ground for fresh triumphs. With the skill of a true general, Joshua followed up his advantage immediately. How long a period is covered by the events recorded, we have no means of knowing. That which is revealed is the determined and victorious movement ever onward until the whole of southern Canaan was in the possession of Israel.

Swiftly and surely the divine judgment was falling on the corrupt peoples, and the possibility of a new era in the history of humanity was being created by the coming of the chosen people into possession of the land.

JOSHUA 11

A new confederacy had now to be faced and fought. Conscious of their peril, the northern kings now joined in an attempt to break the power of those conquering hosts. Turning north, Joshua led an attack upon these kings and utterly routed them. He then turned back to Hazor with like results.

All this did not happen immediately. Indeed, we are told in the text that it had occupied "a long time." In all probability five years had elapsed from the death of Moses to this period.

Thus ended the unity of the action of the hosts of God. "The land had rest from war." Of course, there was still much to be done in the way of conquest, but the power of the enemy was broken and the moment had arrived for the settlement of the land by the tribes of Israel. Afterward there was to be much fighting as occasion demanded, but the great preliminary war of conquest was practically over.

Great capital has often been made of this war of destruction and extermination, but it is manifestly unfair to criticize the action of the Hebrews without remembering what the Scriptures distinctly affirm its reason. Israel was the scourge of God on a corrupt people whose hearts God had hardened, that is, had made strong in order that they might be exterminated (verse 20). The reason and method of this hardening process we saw in the case of Pharaoh in the study of Exodus. The hardening of the heart, as then, resulted from long-continued rebellion and was the natural outcome thereof. Punishment fell only when in the highest interests of posterity the destruction of a people was necessary.

JOSHUA 12

This chapter contains no new matter. It is rather a detailed summary of the extent of the conquest. First the victories under Moses (verses 1-6) and then those under Joshua (verses 7-24). Thus ends the first section of this Book.

The chosen people are now seen in actual possession of the land. The destructive part of the divine work was accomplished. The constructive purposes of God might now go forward.

All grim and soiled and brown with tan,
  I saw a Strong One, in His wrath,
Smiting the godless shrines of man
  Along His path.

I looked; aside the dust-cloud rolled—
  The Waster seemed the Builder too;
Up springing from the ruined Old
  I saw the New.

'Twas but the ruin of the bad—
  The wasting of the wrong and ill;
What e'er of good the old time had
  Was living still.

God works in all things; all obey
  His first propulsion from the night;
Wake thou and watch!—the world is gray
  With morning light!

JOSHUA 13

The second half of the Book of Joshua deals with the settlement of the people in the promised land. Dean Stanley says: "In the Book of Joshua we have what may without offense be termed 'The Domesday Book of the Conquest of Canaan.' Ten chapters of that Book are devoted to a description of the country in which not only are its general features and boundaries laid down, but the names and situations of its towns and villages enumerated with the precision of geographical terms which encourages, and almost compels a minute investigation."

It is not within the purpose of this book to follow such minute investigation, but the student of the Book of Joshua will surely wish to, with the aid of maps. We must, however, observe the relation of all this to the general movement. Now about ninety years old, Joshua was reminded that the conquest was by no means over. There remained much land to be possessed. In order that the chosen people might be able to complete the conquest and perfectly possess the land, it was now to be divided among them, so that the whole area might be covered. In this connection the provision already made for the two and a half tribes east of the Jordan was ratified.

JOSHUA 14

The matter of supreme interest here is, of course, the story of Caleb, who, after forty-five years of waiting, claimed and obtained a definite possession in the land.

His claim was made while there was much still to be done and he urged his unabated vigor as constituting his fitness for the work.

The whole history of Caleb is full of interest and instruction. While perhaps it cannot be positively proven, it is yet most probable that he was a proselyte and a descendant of Esau. His victory at Kadesh-barnea was that of a man who followed the Lord fully. He had seen what all the other spies had seen, but in company with Joshua he had seen more—the fact of the majesty and power of God. He had obtained that victory long ago because he had the courage of his convictions.

The joy of that victory had been his portion for forty-five years of waiting. His ultimate reward had been long postponed but had never been uncertain. Now he came in unabated vigor to its realization. During these long years he would seem to have continued to keep a quiet and retired position, while his friend Joshua had been brought into the place of conspicuous leadership. Joshua's recognition of the claim of his friend and of his right to a choice of possession was quick and generous. He granted him the mountain he asked and blessed him.

JOSHUA 15

In the settlement of the nine and a half tribes, Judah was the first dealt with as being the imperial and kingly tribe. The position allocated to it was the fighting front. It was touched by enemies on three sides; on the east, Moab; on the west, the Philistines; on the south, Edom. Away to the southwest were the Amalekites.

The tribe whose standard was that of the kingly line, and from which that line presently was to spring, was to have its fiber toughened by the sternest discipline—constant watchfulness against the foe and long-continued fighting.

Necessarily, the proximity of these enemies had its peril in another and more insidious source. And, alas, it was in this source that Judah eventually found the elements of her breakup. The fighting line remained loyal longer than the rest, but subsequently even Judah became contaminated with the abominations of the heathen.

God's hosts are never overcome in fair and open fighting with His foes. Friendship with the enemies of God is the enmity against God which brings about corruption and defeat.

Caleb appears once again in this narrative, this time as the man of generosity, readily giving to his daughter at her request the field containing the nether and the upper springs. It is ever remarkable how much that man can give who has found his all in God.

JOSHUA 16

Next in order we have an account of the inheritance of Joseph divided between his sons Ephraim and Manasseh.

The part allotted to Ephraim was a fertile and beautiful district, perhaps in many respects the most desirable in all the country. Nevertheless, it was a place of peculiar difficulty at the time from the fact that it lay still wholly in the power of the Canaanites. The campaigns of Joshua had not perfectly dealt with it and cities possessed by the Canaanites existed.

This, in itself is suggestive so far as Ephraim's responsibility was concerned. The richest tracts of country in the possessions which God intends for His people can be possessed only by victories over the strongest foes. The whole history of Ephraim was a sad one for long centuries and their failure began here and is recorded in the words, "And they drove not out the Canaanites that dwelt in Gezer: but the Canaanites dwell in the midst of Ephraim unto this day, and are become servants to do task-work."

JOSHUA 17

It is interesting to note that in the territory allotted to Manasseh, some of the cities of Ephraim are included; and, moreover, that some of the cities of Manasseh are within the territory of Asher and Issachar. The reason for this may be, in the first case, to mark the unity between Ephraim and Manasseh as the sons of Joseph; and, in the second case, because Asher and Issachar, especially the latter, were not strong enough to subdue the territory committed to them.

Ephraim was discontented with the portion allotted to it and complained to Joshua. The answer he gave was characteristic of him and a revelation of the greatness of his statesmanship. He manifested an understanding of the weakness of these tribes and of the principles on which alone they might become strong. He did not deny their declaration that they were a great people, but with what would seem to have been a touch of irony, he charged them to demonstrate their greatness by taking possession of what they had. He instructed them to go up to the mountains and cut down the trees and drive out their foes. The principle thus revealed is of perpetual application. If the Church of God would possess its possessions it would be far more powerful.

JOSHUA 18

An important event is now recorded. The Tent of Meeting was erected at Shiloh. No reason is given for the choice of Shiloh. It certainly was central to the country and perhaps that is the simplest explanation. That which follows immediately would lead us to believe that after districts had been allotted to Judah, Ephraim, and Manasseh there was some slackness in continuing the work of settlement, for Joshua definitely rebuked the seven tribes for being slow to go up and possess the land. Before doing so, however, this place of worship was erected as the symbol of the deepest truth and principle of their nationality.

In the choice of the seven lots, the first fell to Benjamin. His territory occupied the space between that of Judah and Ephraim. This nearness to Ephraim and Manasseh was according to a natural order, but in process of time Benjamin drew nearer in sympathy to Judah, and at the great division went with Judah altogether.

Benjamin was always looked upon as the least of the tribes of Israel, but it is not to be measured by its size but rather by its caliber. Among its cities it included some that became famous in subsequent history—Jericho, Beth-el, Gibeon, and Mizpeh. Dean Stanley pointed out that even in New Testament times its influence remained, this being revealed partly by the frequency of the name of Saul in Hebrew families. It is interesting that one bearing that name subsequently made his boast in that he was "of the stock of Israel, of the tribe of Benjamin" (Philippians 3:5).

JOSHUA 19

In this chapter we have the account of the distribution of the remainder of the land among the last six tribes—Simeon, Zebulun, Issachar, Asher, Naphtali, and Dan.

Now that all had been provided, Joshua was given a special portion. Moreover, he was given what he asked. The time and the nature of his choice are alike revelations of the character of the man. As to time, he did not ask for a possession until all had been supplied. He was content to wait, taking only when others had received. Then as to the nature of his choice. He asked for Timnath-serah in the hill country of Ephraim. In doing so he chose a city which was hardly a city until it became his. It will be remembered that when Ephraim had complained, Joshua had charged them to go to the mountains and possess their possessions. Now when his opportunity came, he proved that he was prepared to act for himself on the advice he had given. To that very hill country he went, and there is a splended ring of resoluteness in his character in the statement, "He built the city, and dwelt therein."

Thus the conquered country was now divided, and the division was made under the superintendence of Eleazar the priest, Joshua the leader, and the heads of the tribes of the nation. All this, moreover, was done at the door of the Tent of Meeting and in recognition of those great principles of religious life which lay at the heart of the national life.

JOSHUA 20

Having come into possession of the land, the cities of refuge were provided according to arrangements already made. Three were fixed on the west of the Jordan and three on the east. They were so placed as to cover the whole area. Moreover, they were Levitical cities.

Maclear says, "Jewish interpreters tell us how in later times, the roads leading to the cities of refuge were always kept in thorough repair—all obstructions were removed that might stay the flyer's feet or hinder his speed. No hillock was left, no river was allowed over which there was no bridge, and at every turning there were posts erected bearing the word 'Refuge.'"

In this method of dealing with the most heinous of all sins as between man and man, certain interesting principles are manifest. First, God does make a distinction in degrees of guilt. Premeditated murder was to find no sanctuary even in the city of refuge. Second, man must not punish man save after the fullest inquiry. Third, all deliverance was closely connected with the priesthood, which forever stands for sacrificial mediation.

JOSHUA 21

Jacob's prophecy concerning Simeon and Levi:

> I will divide them in Jacob,
> And scatter them in Israel,

was fulfilled in the case of Levi in the distribution of the tribe through all the other tribes. What sounded like a curse thus proved to be a blessing. The presence of the Levites everywhere was intended to serve as a perpetual witness to the relation of the nation to God.

This second division of the Book of Joshua dealing with the settlement of the people ends with a statement that Jehovah gave and they possessed the land. His promises to them had been fulfilled. No man had been able to stand before them. Their enemies had been wholly delivered into their hands. Their responsibilities, however, had not been completely fulfilled. Not yet were all their enemies driven out. Not yet had they fully possessed their possessions. As a matter of fact, they never did completely realize the purpose of God in these matters. The failure, however, was wholly due to their own disobedience, and so the record at this point fittingly closes with the declaration of the fidelity of God. "There failed not aught of any good thing which Jehovah had spoken unto the house of Israel; all came to pass." Failure to possess what God gives is always due to His people and is never the result of His unwillingness or weakness.

JOSHUA 22

We now begin the third and last division of the Book, which tells the story of the final things circling around Joshua's farewell and passing. The first incident recorded is the return of the two and a half tribes to their possessions on the west of the Jordan. As they departed, Joshua addressed them, first commending them for fulfilling the covenant they had made with Moses in helping their brethren. He then charged them concerning the future, that they should be obedient to the commandments of the Law. How they might fulfil this charge he explained in brief and suggestive words, the principal thoughts of which were that they were to love, to walk, to keep, to cleave, to serve.

After their return, they built an altar east of the Jordan. To the erection of this the nine and a half tribes objected, not because they had any fear of their brethren possessing within the actual borders of the land so recently divided, but because the act of erecting an altar seemed to indicate the setting up of a new center of worship. In their protest they invited their brethren to come into the land and possess it if the land allotted to them was unclean and urged them not to commit the sin of departure from God. The reply made was that so far from desiring to set up any new worship, their altar was erected as a sign to their children and to all others that their worship was identical with that of their brethren, who had passed over to the eastern side of the river.

JOSHUA 23

As the time approached for Joshua's passing, he twice gathered the people together and delivered to them his farewell messages.

The first of these is contained in this chapter. Its burden was of the power and faithfulness of God, with the declaration of an earnest desire for the faithfulness of His people to Him.

His references to himself were very brief, the principal ones being, "I am old and well stricken in years," and "I am going the way of all the earth." Only incidentally did he refer to his own work. After having declared that Jehovah had brought them in he said, "Behold, I have allotted unto you these nations"; "I have cut off" your enemies. In contrast to this his references to Jehovah were constant. "Jehovah your God hath done," "Jehovah your God, He will thrust out." Urgently and earnestly he charged, "Therefore, be ye very courgeous to keep and to do all that is written in the book the law of Moses"; "cleave unto Jehovah your God"; closing with the most solemn warnings as to what would happen if they departed from their allegiance.

Perhaps his warnings were more fiery and searching than those of Moses. The address is a wonderful revelation of the strength of the man, and of that strength as consisting in his acute consciousness of the relation of the people to Jehovah and his consequent passion for their loyalty to God's law.

JOSHUA 24

Here we have the record of the final address of Joshua. In it he first concisely and comprehensively traced the Hebrews' history from the call of Abraham and did so in the form of the speech of Jehovah to them. In the brief compass of eleven verses the pronoun "I" as referring to Jehovah occurs no less than seventeen times. The whole movement emphasized the truth that everything of greatness in the history of the people was the result of divine action.

Then he appealed to them with a touch of fine irony. If they would not serve God, he called them to choose whom they would serve, asking them whether they would go back to the gods of their fathers beyond the river or turn to the gods of the Amorites in whose land they were now dwelling. Thus, by presenting the alternatives to loyalty to Jehovah he made patent the foolhardiness of disloyalty. He ended with the declaration of personal decision. "As for me and my house, we will serve Jehovah."

Then we have a dramatic description of what followed. The people declared their choice of God as against any other gods. From an intimate knowledge of them Joshua declared that in spite of their declared choice they were not able to serve God. It was a strange outburst and one wonders whether the tone was of scorn or of intense pity. The subsequent history of the people shows that the words were prophetic. Again the people affirmed their determination to serve the Lord and Joshua called them to put away all strange gods. Everything ended with the making of a covenant and the erection of a memorial.

The Book closes with an account of the death of Joshua and the death of Eleazer. It is significant that in the midst of the darkness of death there was something almost weird and yet full of the suggestion of hope. The bones of Joseph were buried in the land.

Judges

JUDGES 1

The Book of Judges covers historically a period from the death of Joshua to the judgeship of Samuel and the introduction of the monarchy.

It opens with a description of the general condition of affairs at the close of the period of Joshua's leadership. He had led the people into possession of the land but had left them with much to be done ere its final subjugation. Their first act was to seek to know the will of God as to who should commence this final work of conquest. Judah, the kingly tribe, was appointed. Simeon's inheritance lay within the borders of Judah and therefore Simeon acted together with Judah.

The story as here given reveals that whereas the work began in earnest, it gradually weakened. The Lord was with Judah and victories resulted. The Lord was with Joseph and Beth-el was taken. Manasseh and Ephraim and all the rest weakened in the work and Canaanites were left in possession. This false toleration or manifestation of cowardice resulted in their ultimate undoing. The confession of Adoni-bezek (verse 7) is remarkable as revealing the fact that one of their own number was conscious of the corruption which had overtaken the people of the land and of the consequent justice of the divine procedure.

JUDGES 2

The fact of Israel's failure is still further revealed in this chapter. In the first five verses we have the account of the coming of a messenger from Gilgal. This messenger, referred to as "the angel of the Lord," may have been a prophet, for the word rendered "angel" may with equal accuracy be rendered messenger. On the other hand it may have been a special divine and angelic personality.

There was an assembly of the people at Bochim. For what purpose we are not told, but the message brought to them called them back to loyalty to God.

Immediately following this, the historian gives a brief retrospect of the condition of affairs under Joshua, emphasizing that during his life and the life of the elders associated with him the people served the Lord; but that after the passing of these a generation sprang up which did not know the Lord. This of course means not that they were ignorant of the fact of the divine government, but that they were careless about it and disobedient.

This statement is followed by a synopsis of the history which is yet to be set out in greater detail. Here the facts are set forth in the light of the relation the people bore to God. Three movements, the details of which will be found in subsequent sections, are indicated. The first had to do with the sin of the people (verses 11-13), the second with the punishment which followed (verses 14, 15), the third with deliverances (verse 16). Continuing, we find a record of sin repeated (verses 20-23).

This connection of sin, punishment, and deliverance really forms the keynote to the historical movement recorded in the whole of the Book.

JUDGES 3

God left certain nations, a company of stern, implacable enemies, in order to prove Israel. The overruling of God is set forth remarkably in this declaration. The people who had refused to cast out the enemies were now to be taught by long-continued conflict with them the lessons of vital importance to their fulfilment of divine purpose.

In what remains of this chapter, the first two movements of failure, punishment, and deliverance are recorded.

The first of these occupies verses seven to eleven. Their sin is stated definitely as being that they forgot God. The statement suggests a gradual deterioration ending in degeneracy. The punishment for this consisted of eight years of oppression. Under this affliction they cried to God and He heard them, and the first of the judges appeared in the person of Othniel, a relation of Caleb. Of him it is said, "And he judged Israel, and he went out to war." Thus the repentant nation was heard and the divinely appointed deliverer set the nation once again in order. Forty years of rest followed.

Then we have the story of the second declension. At the death of Othniel the people sinned again. This time punishment came through Eglon. An illuminative declaration made here is that Jehovah strengthened Eglon.

The one thing most vividly impressed upon the mind in reading these accounts is the fact of the government of God. After eighteen years they cried to Him again and again He heard. Ehud was the deliverer. Probably Shamgar was associated with him in some way in this work. This deliverance was followed by eighty years of rest.

JUDGES 4

With almost wearisome monotony the story of declension, discipline, and deliverance goes forward. After the eighty years of rest, the children of Israel sinned again, and were delivered into the hands of Jabin. Then followed twenty years of oppression and suffering which became most terrible under Sisera. Once again in penitence the Israelites cried to God and were heard.

The story of deliverance this time is full of romance and poetry because associated with the name of Deborah. One can imagine how this daughter of the people, true child of faith, had suffered under the intolerable consciousness of the degradation of her people. She gained the ear of many in so great a degree that she was appointed to judge the people. In doing this she called Barak to her aid. He, inspired by her teaching, and she, helped by his consecration, went forward and Israel was once more delivered from oppression.

It is interesting at this point to notice the persons who became the agents of the divine deliverance and what is said concerning them. Othniel was clothed with the Spirit of God and driven forth to the work of deliverance. Ehud and Shamgar were illustrations of the individual flaming forth of the spirit of devotion as a result of the bitter consciousness of oppression. The story of Deborah is that of a woman gradually gaining power and inspiring others to action.

JUDGES 5

Here we have preserved for us the great song of Deborah, composed and sung in celebration of the victory. It is full of fire and passion and is a remarkable index to the character of the woman herself. It may be divided into two main parts. First, verses one to eleven is a great chant of confidence, telling the story of the deepest secret of the victories. Everything is attributed to the direct government and activity of God. In it she recognized that the leaders were raised and the people followed as the result of His inspiring. Therefore the song uttered His praise. His doings were celebrated from Seir until the day when Israel lacked warriors. She sang the praise of God because He had governed the governors and the people.

The second part of the song celebrates the victory. In the course of it she poured scorn upon those who failed to respond to the call and to come "to the help of Jehovah against the mighty" and spoke in terms of approval of those who did respond. The song gathers strength as it proceeds and celebrates the victory, and in the midst of the great outburst it curses the neutrals and blesses the woman who struck the blow of death to the tyrant Sisera.

Finally the song rejoiced over the death of the tyrant in language that thrills with Eastern imagery and color. Everything ends with the cry, "So let all Thine enemies perish, O Jehovah"; and the prayer, "But let them that love Him be as the sun when he goeth forth in his might." After this deliverance the land had rest again for forty years.

JUDGES 6

After the passing of these forty years, sin again brought punishment. The people passed under the oppression of Midian. It was oppression of the severest kind and lasted for seven years. A terrible picture is drawn of the people of God hiding in dens and caves and strongholds.

In answer to their cry deliverance began. It came through Gideon. He is revealed as a man continuing his work with the bitterness of the whole situation burning like a fire in his bones. He was conscious of the true relation of the people to Jehovah, but equally conscious of the fact that the conditions obtaining were the result of disobedience to the divine government. The words of the angel to him are very significant, "Go in this thy might." This command can be interpreted only in the light of the words immediately following, "Have not I sent thee?"

Thus the deliverer is seen as a man overwhelmingly conscious of the disastrous condition of affairs and yet as definitely conscious of the divine power. It is ever the man who has a double vision of divine intention and human failure who is the man of might and of valor. Moreover, in the consciousness of his own lowliness and insufficiency we discover another element of the greatness of Gideon. He knew that success did not depend on what he was but on what God was. Therefore, submissively to the divine call he erected his altar and seeing through to the prospect of war he called the altar, "Jehovah is peace." That is the triumph of faith.

His activity resultant on these convictions is recorded. He began at home. The altar of Baal in connection with his father's house was broken down and the worship of God restored. The second movement was to send out the call. It is in connection with this that we have that remarkable statement that "the Spirit of Jehovah came upon Gideon." Having gone so far, it would seem as though for the moment he became overwhelmed with a sense of fear. Such fear, however, never issues in evil when it drives men to God as it drove Gideon. He asked for signs and they were granted to him.

JUDGES 7

This is the story of perhaps one of the most remarkable conflicts in the whole history of the people. As we have seen, it was a time when they had been cruelly oppressed as the result of disobedience. It was of the utmost importance that their deliverance should be evidently by divine action. Nothing would have been more disastrous at that time than for them to have imagined that they were able to extricate themselves from the circumstances in the midst of which they were suffering.

Therefore, by divine direction, the first work Gideon was called on to do was to sift the army. In response to his call to arms, thirty-two thousand had responded. The result shows that they lacked the very attitudes necessary for success in war. The first test imposed was a proclamation that all who were faint-hearted and afraid should return. They were given their opportunity to act voluntarily on this principle. The result was that twenty-two thousand went back.

And still the number was too great because the quality of the men making up the ten thousand lacked something of vital importance. A simple test was imposed which revealed these things. Men who bent down to get a drink of water were not sufficiently alive to the danger. An ambush might surprise them. Men who stooped and caught the water in their hands and lapped it were watchers as well as fighters. In other words, men who took no unnecessary time over necessary things were the men who were needed. This sifting resulted in the return of nine thousand seven hundred. Thus the army of Gideon was reduced to a handful of three hundred.

JUDGES 8

Following the deliverance from the oppression of Midian, Gideon had to deal with internal troubles. The people of Ephraim objected that he had not called them to his help. The men of Succoth and Penuel had refused help in an hour of crisis. Gideon's method with Ephraim was conciliatory and that with the men of Succoth and Penuel was severe.

The last things we read about Gideon are full of interest: one is characterized by great nobility, the other is a revelation of weakness which issued in trouble. When the people virtually desired to make him king, he refused and in his refusal manifested his disinterestedness and his recognition that God was sufficient as King. On the other hand, his making of an ephod suggests that he took to himself some of the functions of the priesthood. While this was probably done out of a sense of the religious failure of the people, the effect produced was evil and resulted in deterioration of the character of Gideon himself.

JUDGES 9

The closing statement of the previous chapter constitutes the introduction to this. The words, "As soon as Gideon was dead" and the declaration that then the people returned to evil courses reveal, first of all, the strength of Gideon and the fact that he had very largely exercised a beneficent influence. They show, also, how practically worthless was the external obedience of the people.

Judgment this time came from within rather than from without. Abimelech, a natural son of Gideon, a man unprincipled and brutal but of great personal force, secured to himself the allegiance of the men of Shechem and practically assumed the position of king. In order to make his position secure he brought about the massacre of all the sons of Gideon, except Jotham, who, escaping, uttered a parabolic prophecy from the height of Mount Gerizim.

This parable was full of a fine scorn for Abimelech, whom Jotham compared to the bramble. In the course of it he indicated the line along which judgment would fall on the sinning people. Abimelech would be the destruction of the men of Shechem and the men of Shechem would be the destruction of Abimelech.

The prophecy of Jotham was not to be immediately fulfilled. The fire smoldered for three years but at last manifested itself. It may well be imagined how such a man's government would be characterized by oppression and tyranny, and the seeds of discontent sown in the hearts of the oppressed people moved towards a harvest of judgment. Gaal, the son of Ebed, took advantage of this discontent to stir up the men of Shechem against Abimelech. Abimelech retaliated with drastic and brutal measures but met his death by the act of a woman who hurled a piece of upper millstone on him. Almost more terrible than the oppression of those from without was this period of judgment by means of internecine strife.

JUDGES 10

Following the death of Abimelech there seems to have been a period of forty years' quietness under the dictatorship of Tola and Jair.

After this there appears to have broken out a period characterized by an almost utter abandonment of the people to idolatry. The list of the forms which this idolatry took is appalling.

Judgment came this time through the Philistines and the men of Ammon and continued for eighteen years.

At last, sore distressed, they cried to God, and for the first time in the history it is recorded that God refused to hear them, reminding them of how repeatedly He had delivered them and they had returned to evil courses.

In the message of His anger, however, there was, as is always the case, clearly evident a purpose of deliverance. He recalled them to a recognition of His power by bidding them seek deliverance from the gods whom they had worshiped. They knew full well the helplessness of these gods in such an hour of distress. The very heart of Jehovah flames out in this connection in a remarkable statement. "His soul was grieved for the misery of Israel."

JUDGES 11

At last deliverance came through Jephthah, whose history is full of interest. He was the son of a harlot and had been thrust out from his inheritance by the legitimate sons of his father. Evidently the iron had entered into his soul and he had gathered to himself a band of men and had become a kind of outlaw freebooter. He was evidently a man of courage and heroic daring, and it is impossible to read the story of the approach of the men of Gilead to him without recognizing that he had certain excellencies of character. He can hardly be measured even by the highest standards of his own time. For some period he had been compelled to live outside the national life. Nevertheless, it is evident that he had his own religious convictions.

Perhaps the chief interest in this story is in the matter of his vow, of which there have been various interpretations. The story seems to leave no room for doubt that he intended to offer a human sacrifice, for when he promised to give what came to the door of his house, the reference can hardly be to an animal. When his daughter appeared, whether he actually slew her or whether, as some commentators believe, he condemned her to perpetual virginity must remain open to question. If indeed he offered her as a sacrifice by death, the question of the morality of his act can be discussed only in the light of his time, and, indeed, in the light of his own personal conviction. Certainly such an act was not justified by the law of Moses. Nevertheless, the impulse was a religious impulse.

JUDGES 12

The men of Ephraim took the same action in the case of Jephthah as they had done in the case of Gideon. After his victory they complained that they had not been called to help. It would seem as though they had become more arrogant as the result of Gideon's conciliatory method with them, for this time they came with the deliberate purpose of war. In Jephthah they found a man of another mold. He did not attempt to conciliate but visited them with the most severe punishment. Two things combined to rouse his anger, first as he reminded them when he and his people had been at strife with the children of Ammon, he had asked the aid of Ephraim and it had been refused. What had offended him and the men of Gilead most deeply, however, was the taunt which Ephraim had used against them, "Ye are fugitives of Ephraim, ye Gileadites, in the midst of Ephraim, and in the midst of Manasseh."

This clearly again reveals the sad disintegration of the nation. The consciousness of the unity of the people seems largely to have been lost. A moment's retrospect here will be of value. After the terrible multiplication of idolatry (chapter 10), God had refused to hear the people and it is questionable whether anything afterward can be spoken of as deliverance. Prior to the raising up of Jephthah, there was a cry to God by the people, but it could hardly be claimed that Jephthah delivered the nation.

JUDGES 13

Once again we read that "Israel again did that which was evil," and once again they were delivered to discipline at the hands of their enemies. In this connection we have one of the strangest stories of the Old Testament, the story of Samson. It is the story of a great opportunity and a disastrous failure in the case of a man who might have wrought a great deliverance but failed.

Everything would seem to have been in his favor. His birth was foretold by an angel visitor. The foretelling led to his special training, for Manoah his father inquired diligently of the angel how he should be trained. These facts make the story of Samson's failure the more terrible. There is an almost weird suggestiveness in the phrase used by the angel concerning him, "He shall begin to save Israel." His ultimate failure was as certainly foreknown as was his opportunity.

Samson seems to stand as a symbol of the nation in his strength and possibility and also in his ruin and comparative failure. This will be seen as we follow the story. In the light of the after years there is a tragic pathos in this account of beginnings. "The Spirit of Jehovah began to move him." Had he but yielded to the impulses of the Spirit, how different a story might have resulted.

JUDGES 14

This is the record of tragic things. The boy Samson had grown to manhood's estate full of strength and passion. Going to Timnah, he saw a woman of the Philistines and desired to take her to wife. His parents attempted to dissuade him, but he allowed himself to be swept by his passion and determined to realize his own desires. All through the transactions connected with this woman, he is seen as a man of animal strength, bold, adventurous, determined, and of sporting propensities. There is nothing to admire in him in all his doings.

Two things, however, in the course of the narrative arrest our attention. First, the statement, "His father and his mother knew not that it was of Jehovah" (verse 4); and, second, the declaration, "The Spirit of Jehovah came mightily upon him" (verse 19). In these statements the fact of the overruling of God is clearly revealed. The phrase, "It was of Jehovah," is used in the sense in which we find it in Joshua 11:20. God makes even the wrath of man praise Him as He compels it to contribute to the accomplishment of His own purpose. This fact, however, in no sense justified the sin of Samson in seeking a wife of the Philistines in violation of the expressed commands of God. The impetuous passion in which he slew thirty men of the Philistines to pay his sporting debt was utterly reprehensible. Yet this also contributed to the purpose of God in the destruction of the Philistines.

JUDGES 15

Here we have the record of further exploits by Samson and once more the circumstances of them were not to his credit.

His revenge on the Philistines in the destruction of their property and their slaughter served in the wider outlook to limit the oppression of the Philistines. The action of the men of Judah in binding him and handing him over to the Philistines was utterly contemptible, and in this connection the great possibility of the man flamed into view. We see him breaking the bonds that bound him and with terrific onslaught, armed only with the jawbone of an ass, slaying a thousand of their number. We are conscious of what he might have done had he been wholly yielded to that "Spirit of Jehovah" who came mightily upon him, instead of being so largely governed by the fires of his own passion.

After this victory there was perhaps a break during which he realized his possibility more perfectly. Miraculously refreshed with water, he revived, and it is said that he judged Israel in the days of the Philistines for twenty years.

JUDGES 16

Here we have the sad and awful account of Samson's relapse and final fall. He went to Gaza. It is easy to imagine how much there must have been in Gaza which should have appealed to one acting for the fulfilment of the divine purpose. There were idolatries and evil things against which he should have flung himself in force. But he did not. He was still swayed by the strength of his animal nature, and the tragic sentence is written, ". . . Samson went to Gaza, and saw there a harlot."

In the midst of his sin, his enemies attempted to imprison him. He broke through by plucking up the gates of the city and carrying them to the top of an adjacent mountain. Even then, however, he did not learn his lesson and we see him in the toils of Delilah. At last she triumphed, and the man who had long since ceased to be in any deep sense a Nazarite was at last shorn of even the outward symbols of his vow.

There is nothing perhaps in the sacred writings at once more pathetically tragic than the vision of Samson with his eyes put out, grinding in the prison house of the Philistines. It is a picture and a parable needing no enforcement of exposition to make it powerful.

At last, out of the depths of his degradation, he cried to God, and in his death struck the heaviest blow at the people from whose oppression he ought to have delivered his people.

At this point ends the history of this Book. It is taken up again in the first Book of Samuel. The remaining chapters of the Book and the Book of Ruth have their chronological place in the period already surveyed.

JUDGES 17

Here begins the final section of the Book of Judges which is of the nature of an appendix. The events here recorded must have taken place closely following the death of Joshua. They give us a picture of the internal condition of the people, and it is probable that they were added with that intention by the historian.

Micah's act was a violation of the second commandment. He made to himself and for his household certain images. In doing so he was not adopting the idolatries of the heathen. His mother's language reveals her recognition of Jehovah as she said, "Blessed be my son of Jehovah." Moreover, Micah's own words, when persuading a Levite to act as his priest, show the same thing, "Now know I that Jehovah will do me good. . . ." The images were intended to aid him in the worship of Jehovah but were distinctly forbidden, as we have said, in the second commandment.

The whole story is a revelation of a degenerate condition. Micah had robbed his mother. On making restitution he accompanied the act, at her instigation, with what she supposed to be a religious movement. The consent of the Levite to become a priest in the house of Micah for the sake of a living is a further revelation of degeneracy. Micah was attempting to maintain his relationship with God by violating the commands of God. The Levite degenerated into an attempt to secure his own material comfort by compromise.

JUDGES 18

The account of the backsliding of individuals is followed by an illustration of its widespread existence among the people. While seeking new territory the Danites found Micah and the condition of things established in his house.

When presently they moved forward to success, they did not hesitate to size Micah's images and capture his priest. The terrible decadence of the religious ideal is startlingly revealed in this whole story.

Deeply embedded in the character of the people was the consciousness of the importance of religion. Micah must worship and the Danites felt the necessity of their enterprise for maintaining some kind of relationship with God. Yet in each case there was the most violent prostitution of religion to purposes of personal prosperity. Micah hoped by the maintenance of some form of worship and the presence of a Levite that Jehovah would be his God, by which he evidently meant that material prosperity would come to him. The Danites, searching for new territory, were anxious to maintain religion.

Wherever religion is acknowledged and adopted merely in order to ensure material prosperity, it suffers degradation. In these stories we have a revelation of the beginnings of those terrible conditions which eventually issued in the ruin of the people.

JUDGES 19

The story of the Levite occupies three chapters and is again a mirror held up to the times, revealing startling moral conditions and showing the conflict of good and evil among them.

In considering the story of this chapter, several things are to be carefully noted. First, we must recognize the imperfection of the times as revealed in the practice of polygamy and concubinage among the chosen people. There is no doubt that their action in these matters was in advance of that of the people of the land. Nevertheless, the fact that a Levite had a concubine in these days was terrible, but we must consider it in the light of the times. When this is done, we notice that the sacredness in which he thought of her relation to him does stand in striking contrast to the loose ideals of the Canaanitish people. Nevertheless, the story does reveal a terrible condition of degeneracy among a section of the chosen people. The action of the men of Gibeah was nothing less than the action of the men of Sodom long before. The drastic and terrible method adopted by the Levite was intended to draw the attention of Israel to the sin of the men and reveals the conscience of the better part of the people concerning purity.

JUDGES 20

The action of the Levite served its purpose. The nation was stirred momentarily to its center. A great moral passion flamed out. Underneath all the degeneracy was a true stratum of religious conviction, which in the presence of the iniquity of the men of Gibeah sprang to life and action.

It is very remarkable how in the case of nations backsliding from religious ideals this is ever true. In the midst of most sordid and debased times, in the presence of some more than usually violent manifestation of evil, the slumbering convictions of the past will flame into new sensitiveness and demand recognition.

In response to the ghastly and bloody appeal of the Levite we see the tribes of Israel gathered together before God seeking to know how to act.

The low level of morality which had manifested itself in so powerful a form could be dealt with by general suffering. The men who were in the wrong were brutally defiant and refused to hand over the sinners. Moreover, they were strong enough at the first to defeat the army of Israel, and once again its hosts are seen in lamentation, waiting before God.

After this, they again went forward, this time to victory and the sore punishment of the sinning people and of those who had condoned their sin.

JUDGES 21

Uninstructed zeal, even in the cause of righteousness, often goes beyond its proper limits. The terrible carnage continued until not above six hundred men of the tribe of Benjamin were left.

Another of those sudden revulsions which characterize the action of inflamed peoples is seen as Israel was suddenly filled with pity for the tribe so nearly exterminated. This pity, then, operated in ways that were wholly unrighteous. Wives were provided for the men of Benjamin by unjustified slaughter at Jabesh-gilead and by the vilest iniquity at Shiloh.

It is impossible to read this appendix to the Book of Judges, and especially the closing part of it, without being impressed with how sad is the condition of any people who act without some definitely fixed principle. Passion moves to purpose only as it is governed by principle. If it lacks that, it will march at one moment in heroic determination to establish high ideals and purity of life, and then almost immediately will burn and express itself in brutality and all manner of evil.

The writer of this Book more than once drew attention to the fact that at that time there was no king in Israel. Undoubtedly he meant by this to trace the lawlessness to the lack of government. The truth was that Israel had lost its immediate relation to its one and only King.

Ruth

RUTH 1

The Book of Ruth stands in striking contrast to the Book of Judges and yet is closely connected with it. In Judges the national outlook has been presented and so dark has it been as to create the impression of universal pollution. The story of Ruth illustrates the truth that God has never left Himself without witness.

During a time of famine, Elimelech, his wife, and two sons went into the country of Moab to find bread and to escape trouble. It is questionable whether their action was justified. Their sons married Moabite women. It is evident, however, that their action was rather blundering than willful rebellion. There they maintained their faith in the one God. When, bereft of her husband and two sons, Naomi turned her face again to her own country, she urged her daughters-in-law to leave her and settle among their own people. This was the occasion of that choice of Ruth which in its devotion and in the manner in which she expressed it has become universally accepted as an illustration of fidelity of love. The story, however, reveals that love for Naomi was not the deepest note in her decision. That was struck when she used the expression, ". . . Thy God [shall be] my God."

The language of Naomi at the home-coming shows that she looked upon the sorrows that had come to her as God's testimony against her and His affliction of her. There was, however, no touch of rebellion in what she said but rather a gracious recognition of chastisement, showing that she had learned the lessons it was intended to teach.

RUTH 2

The women went home to poverty, where the practical problems of life faced them. These were, of course, rendered the more difficult by the fact that Ruth was a Moabitess. Yet she it was who faced the fight and went forth as a gleaner to gather what would suffice for their present sustenance.

The human side of things is beautifully expressed in the words, "Her hap was to light on the portion of the field belonging unto Boaz." All the issues reveal the divine overruling.

In this story of Ruth gleaning the principal interest centers in Boaz. The lines of his picture are few, but they are strong and a man of fine quality is revealed. His greeting to his laborers, "Jehovah be with you," and their ready response, "Jehovah bless thee," reveal the happy relationship between him and those serving him and show him a man of strong and yet natural religious life. His presence in the field, overseeing the affairs of harvest, and his quick recognition of the strange girl gleaning show the man of business capacity. Then all the rest of the story evidences the graciousness of his temper and the greatness of his heart.

In all probability he knew a Moabite woman would not be very cordially welcomed among his people, and therefore he provided for her with assiduous care. His influence is at once seen in the absence of objection among the people and their readiness to cooperate with him.

In short, Boaz stands out as a man of the finest fiber, simple, and strongly living in a degenerate age.

RUTH 3

Necessarily, gleaning as a means of livelihood can last only through harvest time. Consequently, Naomi was anxious about the future, especially Ruth's future.

As the outcome of this anxiety we have the story of her advice to interest Boaz more fully and to bring about a marriage between him and Ruth. Necessarily, the expedient to which she resorted must be judged, as we have so constantly to remember, in the light of her own age. Notwithstanding this, however, it can hardly be characterized as other than doubtful, and on the basis of faith it is difficult to justify it. Yet here again Naomi is seen as acting as the result of an error of judgment rather than in willful disobedience, and the overruling love of God moved on to beneficent issue.

One element, and that perhaps the strongest which this venture reveals, is the confidence which Naomi evidently had in Boaz. In order to provide for the future, her appeal should have been made to one nearer of kin, but the whole attitude of Boaz toward Ruth had inspired such confidence in him that it was through him she hoped for succor. On the whole the story of her venture is rather to the credit of Boaz than to that of Naomi and Ruth.

RUTH 4

The nobility and faithfulness of Boaz are clearly manifested in this story. It is hardly possible to read this Book without being convinced that Boaz had already found himself in love with Ruth, which accounts for the fact that he was ready and willing to take the responsibility of the next of kin. However, there was one who had a prior right and in loyalty to the law of his people Boaz gave him his opportunity.

The picture presented of the gathering of the elders in the gate and the legal statement of the case is interesting. The next of kin had a perfect right to abandon his claim if another were ready to assume it. This he did, and seeing that Boaz was ready to assume responsibility, he was justified in doing so on the ground that he did not desire to run the risk of impoverishing his own family, for it was evident that Boaz was well able to fulfil all the obligations of the case.

The whole story ends with poetic simplicity and beauty. "So Boaz took Ruth, and she became his wife. . . ." Nothing need be added to indicate the joy and reward of two faithful souls. Moreover, Naomi was comforted at last. The women of her own people spoke words of cheer to her, which unquestionably must have been full of comfort as they sang the praise of the one who had chosen to share her affliction and had become the medium of her succor.

There is a stately simplicity in the closing sentences. Of the child born to Ruth and Boaz it is said, "They called his name Obed; he is the father of Jesse, the father of David." In these final words is manifest the divine movement in the history of the chosen people. And yet a larger issue followed as the centuries passed. From this union sprang at last, as to the flesh, Jesus the Messiah.

I Samuel

I SAMUEL 1

The first Book of Samuel covers a period of transition in the history of the nation, dealing with the process from the judges to the kings. The condition of the people under the Judges, as we have seen, was one of degeneracy. It was during this period that they practically rejected God as their one King. The clamor for an earthly king which followed was the natural outcome of this practical rejection. The first movement of the Book deals with the story of Samuel, the last, and in some senses, the best of the judges.

It opens with a simple story, full of ordinary human emotion. Polygamy was still practiced. Elkanah was the husband of two wives, Peninnah, and Hannah. Hannah, persecuted by Peninnah, prayed earnestly that she might no longer be childless, making a vow that if a boy were granted to her he would be consecrated to the Lord. The promised consecration was twofold. It was to be life-long. As a Levite, and the son of a Levite, he would be called on to render a certain period of service, but before his birth his mother dedicated him for life. Her vow, moreover, covered not only the length of this service, but its character, as she promised that he would be a Nazarite. Her prayer was answered, and she fulfilled her vow by presenting the boy to Jehovah.

I SAMUEL 2

We have the record of the song of triumph sung by Hannah, in which she set forth the might and justice of Jehovah. Thus, in the dark and troublous times, Jehovah is seen acting toward deliverance, by answering the prayer of faith as faith operated in the heart of a simple and trusting woman. There is much human passion manifest in her desire, but the fact that she turned to Jehovah is evidence of her trust in Him; and on the basis of that confidence she prepared a way for the future guidance of His people.

The latter part of the chapter gives a vivid picture of two simultaneous movements of degeneration and regeneration in Israel. The condition of the people was waxing worse and worse, but all the while Jehovah is enthroned, and without let or hindrance moving forward in His work of deliverance.

The corruption of the priesthood was appalling. The sons of Eli were securing their own selfish ends in the most terrible fashion. Moreover, they were polluting the very courts of the house of God by the grossest immorality.

Meanwhile, the boy Samuel dwelt in the precincts of the Tabernacle, and in obedience to the instructions of Eli, ministered to the Lord.

It was during this time that a prophetic messenger came to Eli with a word of stern rebuke. While Eli had been loyal to God in his personal life and action, he had not exercised discipline in his own family; and out of a false pity for his sons had tolerated their evil courses. To him, then, were uttered the solemn words, "Them that honour Me I will honour, and they that despise Me shall be lightly esteemed." These words should be pondered in this connection, for they teach us that no human affection must be permitted to intervene between the soul and its absolute loyalty to God.

I SAMUEL 3

At this point in the history came a change, startling, and full of meaning in Samuel's life. In the silence of the night a Voice called him by name. Thrice he answered by going to Eli. At last Eli recognized that the Voice was the Voice of God speaking to the lad, and he told Samuel to answer for himself.

This was the beginning of direct divine communication to him. We have already read that he had ministered before the Lord, and yet that he had not known Him directly until now.

This in itself is a beautiful revelation of the true life of a child. Samuel had obeyed Eli in doing all he commanded him within the Tabernacle courts, and thus had rendered service to the Lord. Now the time had come in which, not through mediation, but directly, he must hear and obey.

The first message entrusted to him was a terrible one for him to deliver, and it is interesting to notice how in his action the two elements of fear and courage were manifested. He was afraid to tell Eli, but when Eli charged him to do so, he told the whole message entrusted to him.

There was a further period of training and growth before Samuel was ready to assume the work of leadership. During that period Jehovah vindicated him by permitting no word he spoke to fall to the ground, that is, to fail of fulfilment. Moreover, he became the instrument through whom God appeared to His people, and through whom the word of Jehovah was delivered to them.

I SAMUEL 4

The crisis of judgment foretold by Samuel to Eli now arrived. It was a Philistine attack on the people, in which large numbers were slain, among them the two sons of Eli. On hearing the news Eli himself died, as did also the wife of one of the sons in giving birth to a boy, whose name in dying she pronounced Ichabod.

It was a terrible and significant name, indicating that the glory of Jehovah had departed.

Perhaps the most significant teaching in this story is derived from a consideration of the action of the men of Israel in the presence of the Philistine attack. Realizing their peril, and hoping in some way to save themselves, they carried the Ark of God into the midst of the fray. It was an entirely superstitious use of the Ark, and was utterly unavailing. The Philistines were afraid, but, strengthening their hearts, went forward, gained a great victory, and captured the Ark itself.

How often men who have neglected God, and the rites and ceremonies of His worship, hope in some crisis to save themselves by superstitious use of some of the holy things of the faith. It is always not only unavailing, but blasphemous. In any hour of peril a genuine return to God is of value; but an attempt to make use of sacred things to procure personal safety is the worst form of blasphemy.

I SAMUEL 5

This is a story of supreme and arresting interest, showing as it does how, when the people of God fail to bear testimony for Him among the nations, He becomes His own witness.

The Ark was not a charm equal to delivering disobedient Israel. It was, however, the center and symbol of their life, and Jehovah would not permit Philistia to trifle with it. If men hold their peace stones will cry out; and if the chosen people are unfaithful to God, then the very Ark, which is the symbol of His presence among them, becomes the instrument, wherever it is brought, of judgment on His enemies.

They first lodged it at Ashdod in the house of the fish-god Dagon, with disastrous results to the idol, which was brought to the ground, and broken. With speed and in fear, the people then carried it to Gath. There judgment fell on the inhabitants which, in all probability, was a plague of mice. While this is not stated in our text, it is found in the Septuagint Version, and the subsequent action of making images of mice makes it probable. In any case, some discomfiture came to the people with the coming of the Ark.

Again they moved it as hastily to Ekron, where painful and troublesome tumors broke out among the people.

Thus, at every move, judgment became more severe, and Philistia found that if she had been able to conquer and break the power of Israel, it was a different matter when she came to deal with Israel's God.

I SAMUEL 6

The authorities in Philistia now called a council, and sought the advice of their diviners. It is intensely interesting to observe how unanimously they recognized the action of Jehovah. Whatever the long years had done for Israel itself, it is perfectly certain that the fear and the dread of Jehovah had been implanted in the hearts of the surrounding peoples.

The counselors advised sending the Ark back, accompanied by offerings intended to indicate their recognition that the plagues of mice and tumors constituted a visitation of God.

The method of sending the Ark back was in the nature of an experiment, and the facts which followed show how conclusively their own test must have proved to them that God had been at work. As the kine drawing the new cart took their way directly to Beth-shemesh, it was clearly evident that God was overruling. That they should go quietly, lowing as they went, was in itself a remarkable fact, for they had not been trained to draw loads. That they should travel away from their calves was even more remarkable, and that they should thus take their way directly to the first city of Israel was conclusive. Joshua of Beth-shemesh received the Ark in a way worthy of an Israelite. He clave the cart for wood, and slew the kine for sacrifice, and worshiped. Moreover, so jealous was he for the honor of the sacred symbol that he smote seventy men who, with curious eyes, had dared to attempt to examine it.

I SAMUEL 7

The Ark found its resting place temporarily at Gibeah, in the house of Abinadab. A dark period of twenty years is passed over without detailed record. It would seem that during all that time Israel was under Philistine rule, without any definite center of worship; for while the Ark was resting in the house of an individual, the Tabernacle was in all probability dismantled.

During this period Samuel was advancing from youth to manhood and approaching the hour of his leadership. This period was ushered in by the people's lamentation after God. Of this Samuel took advantage, calling them to return to Him and put away all strange gods.

They obeyed, and then were summoned to Mizpah. Here, by a direct divine intervention, the power of Philistia was broken, and her cities restored to Israel. Here Samuel erected an altar and called it Ebenezer.

This was a great word uttered in the hearing of the people, "Hitherto hath Jehovah helped us." The "hitherto" included all through which they had passed, not the victories only, but the discipline and the suffering also. This man of clear vision recognized both the fact of the divine government and its beneficent method. Jehovah had helped them through chastisement to sorrow for sin, and through such lamentation to freedom from oppression.

The story of the actual judgeship of Samuel is told in brief words. Ramah was his home, and from thence he journeyed in circuit once a year to Beth-el, Gilgal, and Mizpah, thus maintaining oversight and administering the affairs of the people.

I SAMUEL 8

This first Book of Samuel at this point merges into its second division, which has to do with Saul. First we have the account of the clamor of the people for a king and the divine answer thereto. The occasion for the request on their part was that of the maladministration of the sons of Samuel, and their sinful practices. The real principle underlying their request was their desire to be, as they said, "like all the nations."

This is the revelation of the supreme wrong. They had been chosen to be unlike the nations, a people directly governed by God. In communion, Jehovah made plain to Samuel the real evil in their request when He declared that they had rejected Him from being their King.

I SAMUEL 9

The king is now presented to us, and the story of his selection is told. Saul appears in every way to be a remarkable man. He was of good position, of the tribe of Benjamin; and, moreover, was wealthy. Among all the men of the nation he would appear to have been the finest in physique. He is revealed as a man living strongly, quietly at home, and interested in his father's affairs. Moreover, he was naturally a man of modest disposition, as his account of himself as a member of the least family of the smallest tribe testifies.

In pursuit of his filial duty he was led into contact with Samuel. It was a strange day of communion, that first day of their meeting. Not least among Saul's advantages was his fellowship with the prophet. "So Saul did eat with Samuel that day." The meal itself was suggestive, for Samuel had carefully provided that the shoulder, which is ever symbolic of government, should be placed before Saul. Through this day of first communion Samuel led Saul toward the great announcement which he was about to make to him.

I SAMUEL 10

On the morning of the day following Saul's meeting with and eating with Samuel, Samuel told him of his election by God to be king of the nation. This communication was made when they were quite alone, even the servant in attendance on them having been sent on before. The terms of the appointment were definite and solemn. It is easy to understand how startling a thing it must have been to this man. Three signs ratifying the authority of the appointment were promised, and all were granted. Thus no room was left for doubt in the mind of Saul as to this being the definite call of God.

This took place at Mizpah. How long a time elapsed between this divine appointment and Saul's formal presentation to the people we have no means of knowing. Right here, at the beginning of the story, we have the first manifestation of that weakness of character which eventuated in his ultimate failure. Notwithstanding that he had received so clear a demonstration of the will of God, on the day when he was to be presented to the people he was found hiding away among the baggage. Some have treated this as an evidence of modesty, and as manifesting an excellent trait in his character. It is well that we remember that modesty becomes sin when it prevents any man from stepping at once into a place to which he knows that God is calling him. It is by no means an uncommon failure, and the very fact that modesty is in itself a virtue makes the peril all the more subtle. The standard by which conduct is ever to be measured is the standard of simple loyalty to the will of God. If even a virtue interpose, it thereby becomes a vice.

I SAMUEL 11

It would seem as though Saul, going down as he did to his house in Gibeah, did not take up the active responsibilities of the kingship until the Ammonite invasion occurred. This would seem to have stirred within him, as the Spirit of God came upon him, a sense of responsibility, and he responded thereto. Immediately, in the presence of the danger, and under the divine power of the Spirit, he gathered the people together, and gained a great victory.

The closing sentences of the previous chapter reveal that there were certain men in the kingdom who were rebellious against his appointment. Now, in the day of his victory, the people suggested the punishment of these men. In this connection the possibility of greatness in Saul was manifested, in that he refused to mar the day of God's victory by visiting the traitors with punishment.

At this time Samuel at once took advantage of the accession of Saul to gather the people together at Gilgal, at which gathering he was confirmed in the kingdom.

I SAMUEL 12

At the confirmation of the king appointed by God by the consent of the nation, Samuel delivered what was practically his last address to them.

It was of the nature of a farewell message, in which was there a touch of pathos in his speaking of his past relation with the people.

He first challenged them as to his conduct during the period in which he had walked before them, and then proceeded solemnly to warn them, in view of the new departure in their history now taking place.

In a rapid survey of that history he reminded them of two things; first, the consistent faithfulness of God; and, second, their constant failure. The incident is full of dramatic force as Samuel, in the presence of Saul, charged people with having sinned, in that they had sought a king; and it is the more remarkable because he so spoke to them as to bring home a consciousness of wrong.

However, the thing was done, and he now charged them still to serve and follow Jehovah, and promised tenderly that he would continue to pray for them and instruct them in the right way. His final word was to warn them that if they continued in their waywardness their king would not be able to save them.

It is evident how clear Samuel's vision was of the fundamental truth concerning the people—that they were, and could be, great only as they remained a people governed by God and obedient to Him.

I SAMUEL 13

There is some difficulty concerning the opening sentences of this chapter. Some words seem to be omitted, which make it difficult to place the events recorded in their chronological setting. The Authorized Version reads, "Saul reigned one year, and when he had reigned two years. . . ." The Revised Version reads, "Saul was (thirty) years old when he began to reign, and he reigned two years over Israel." The American Revision reads, "Saul was (forty) years old when he began to reign, and he reigned two years over Israel." Quite evidently at some point in the work of transmission, a word was omitted.

The rest of the chapter, and, indeed, the whole of the following chapter gives us the account of the wars he waged. He first created an army of 3,000 men. The Philistines, who looked on the Hebrews as easy prey, for they were practically without arms, gathered themselves together to attempt to break the power of the chosen people. The enormous strength of the enemy filled the Israelites with fear, and they scattered, hiding themselves in caves and thickets, in rocks, and coverts, and pits.

It was under these circumstances that Saul's self-dependence manifested itself in his offering of sacrifice in the absence, and without the instruction, of Samuel. If such an action does not appear to be very serious, it must be remembered that its peril lay in its manifestation of Saul's insubordination to the will and appointment of God in the smallest matters.

I SAMUEL 14

Here we have a picture of Saul, with a part of the army about him, remaining idle in Gibeah. His son Jonathan moved to action by his sense of the degradation of his people, and his conviction of the strength of Jehovah, made a remarkable attack on the foe, which issued first in the slaughter of twenty men. This sudden onrush on the Philistines in so unexpected a way produced panic throughout all their hosts. As a result of this, Saul and the rest of the people who had been in hiding went forth to the rout of the Philistines.

It was in the midst of all this that again Saul's weakness manifested itself in taking a rash oath that no man should stay to take food. This oath resulted in weakening the people, so that they were unable to accomplish so great a victory as they might have done.

The more terrible effect was that it imperiled the life of Jonathan, and caused the people themselves to sin in their hunger.

Perhaps one of the most interesting facts in connection with this story is the action of the people whereby Jonathan was rescued from the peril that threatened him in consequence of his father's rash oath. It would seem as though, in the general consciousness of the true meaning and value of the vow, they had made considerable advance since the days of Jephthah.

I SAMUEL 15

Saul was commissioned by Jehovah through Samuel to smite Amalek, and it was in connection with this that the sin occurred which filled his cup to the brim and caused him to be rejected.

His campaign was victorious over the whole section of the country, but again he was disobedient, sparing Agag and a part of the spoil.

Samuel's anger at this wrong is a clear revelation of his loyalty to Jehovah. Strong in his consciousness of the supremacy of God over the appointed king, and in his sense of the folly of the king's sin, Samuel went forth to meet the king. When Samuel charged Saul with sin Saul prevaricated, meeting the prophet with what was virtually a lie on his lips, "I have performed the commandment of Jehovah." Then in solemn and sublime words Samuel pronounced him as rejected for the kingship.

There is a striking contrast between Samuel and Saul as they are seen here side by side. Saul, the man of great opportunity, miserably failing and passing through disobedience to ruin. Samuel, rejected long ago of the people, still mighty in his allegiance to God, burning in anger, denouncing in force, and, finally, in a white heat of loyalty, himself hewing Agag to pieces.

This was the last interview between the king and the prophet prior to the latter's death. Very touching is the statement, "Samuel mourned for Saul." Evidently the old man had loved the young man, and had hoped great things from him. When Saul failed, Samuel denounced him without sparing, and then in loneliness mourned over him.

I SAMUEL 16

We now come to the third section of this Book, throughout which David is the principal figure. It would seem that Samuel had given himself over to the sadness occasioned by Saul's failure. Jehovah rebuked him. Perfect conformity to the will of God forbids any kind of prolonged mourning over human failure. If Saul had failed, God had not, and Samuel was now commissioned to arise and anoint His king.

This time the choice was to be made on an entirely new basis. Israel had had a king of physical magnificence, one likely to appeal to their desire for conformity to the ideals of surrounding nations. Jehovah would now appoint a man after His own heart.

The deterioration of Saul became more marked. The chronicler tells us that "an evil spirit from Jehovah troubled him." This is naturally a very arresting and remarkable statement. Its meaning, however, is perfectly clear in its revealing of God's sovereignty of the fact that all the forces of evil, whether they will or no, are still under the government of God.

In preparation for his work as king in the economy of God, David found his way to the court. The occasion of his coming there was the melancholy of the king and his own musical ability. The principal value of this story is its clear revelation of the authority and activity of God in government. Under that government all things are seen moving toward the accomplishment of the divine purpose.

I SAMUEL 17

The story contained in this chapter is one of the most familiar of the Old Testament narratives. It places Saul and David in sharp contrast as each stands out in clear relief.

In the presence of the enemy of his people, notwithstanding his position and his army, Saul is seen to be utterly incompetent. On the other hand, David, without human resources, but conscious of the true greatness of his people, and sure of the strength of his God, went forth to battle with the Philistine champion.

The secret of his strength is revealed in his address to Goliath, "Thou comest to me with a sword, and with a spear, and with a javelin; but I come to thee in the name of Jehovah of hosts, the God of the armies of Israel, which thou hast defied."

Whereas under ordinary circumstances it is the duty of the servants of God to make all preparation possible for action, and to employ every resource available in the prosecution of the divine purpose, a man in an hour of crisis may attempt impossible things and be assured of victory in the name of God.

In the divine economy, Saul was no longer king, and David was. He demonstrated his fitness for the kingly position and power by his victory, which revealed his clear understanding of the true secrets of his people's strength and of the power of God.

I SAMUEL 18

Here, in the account of Jonathan and David, begins one of the most perfect stories of love and friendship in the world. The story is all the more beautiful because of its dark background. Love is in itself essentially beautiful, but its richest colors appear only in shadow and difficulty.

In the account of the beginning of this friendship, it would seem that Jonathan's love for David came first. Indeed, it is questionable whether the story does not redound more to the credit of Jonathan than to David's. Jonathan seems to have been without selfishness. He was the son of Saul, and his friendship for and loyalty to, David, was a sacrifice of his right to the succession.

Coincident with the commencement of this friendship, the hatred of Saul for David seems to have deepened, and become more dangerous to David. He became afraid of David. The reason for this is very revealing: "Jehovah was with David, and was departed from Saul."

There is nothing more common or sadder than the jealousy of the sinful and unsuccessful of those who are blessed and succeed. Saul's hatred manifested itself in wicked schemes to rid himself of his rival.

I SAMUEL 19

Saul's enmity toward David grew, while the friendship between Jonathan and David increased. Saul did all in his power to set both Jonathan and the people against David. He even went so far as to charge them to slay David.

For a while he was persuaded by Jonathan to cease his unholy persecution of David. However, the underlying enmity quickly broke out again, and this time in a direct attempt on David's life.

These were indeed days of bitter testing for the young man anointed to the kingly office, and it was perfectly natural that in the stress and strain of such experiences he should flee to Samuel.

Here he was protected by direct divine intervention of the most remarkable kind. Three companies of Saul's messengers, and at last Saul himself, journeying with the express purpose of capturing David, were taken possession of by the Spirit of God and compelled to prophesy.

I SAMUEL 20

David returned to Jonathan, and there follows an interesting and beautiful account of a time in which these two friends took counsel together about David's peril.

Every incident of the story is full of arresting beauty; Jonathan's deep concern and all he did to help his friend reveal a man of the finest type.

As we have suggested, the whole attitude of Jonathan becomes the more wonderful when we remember that he was the heir apparent to the throne. Moreover, we see not merely his love for David, but his willing co-operation with what he knew to be the will of God. He was aware that God had chosen his friend to be king, and, evidently without any pang of regret, he acquiesced in that divine appointment and remained true to David, loving him more rather than less because he saw in him the anointed of Jehovah.

On account of all this, Saul added

to all his other sins his attempt on the life of his own son. He is revealed as rapidly becoming an irresponsible madman, while David is seen through all the painful discipline as being prepared for the work that lay before him.

I SAMUEL 21

Under such trying stress, the land itself seemed too hot to hold David, and he takes refuge in flight. The story of his period of exile, with its varied experiences, follows. His movements during this time were characterized sometimes by faith and sometimes by fear.

He first found his way to the city of the priests, where Ahimelech fed him with the shewbread, the justification of which, interestingly enough, was declared long after by our Lord Himself in the days of His ministry. David's going to Ahimelech, although an exile, was an action of faith.

We next find him at Gath among the Philistines, with Achish their king. It is impossible to read this without feeling how unworthy a picture he presents. Whereas it is easy to understand his state of mind at the time, it remains true that the picture of God's anointed reduced to the necessity of feigning madness to protect himself is full of sadness. It affords a perpetual warning against the folly of taking refuge from peril among those who are the enemies of God.

I SAMUEL 22

Leaving Gath, David took refuge in the cave of Adullam, where there gathered to him a band of the outcasts of his own people. They are graphically described as those in "distress," in "debt," and "discontented." It is quite possible that the condition of these people was the result of the oppressions they had suffered under Saul. In any case, from the standpoint of Saul's reign, they were considered dangerous people, and were outcast. What happened to them in their contact with David is revealed in the later history, when these men became the mighty men of the new kingdom. So far as David was concerned, this was a far safer position, and a worthier occupation than that to which he had been reduced in the court of Achish.

In the meanwhile Saul filled the cup of his iniquity by ordering the slaughter of the priests because Ahimelech had helped David. One of their number, Abiathar, escaped from the slaughter, and joined David in his hiding place. It is interesting to remember that he remained with David, and was loyal to him throughout his life and reign.

All these experiences of David, both in fear and in faith, experiences as they were of adversity and trial, were undoubtedly preparing him for the responsibilities that were to fall upon him when, in fulfilment of the divine purpose, he became king of the nation.

I SAMUEL 23

The series of happenings recorded in this chapter reveals most vividly the appalling condition of affairs in the kingdom.

Saul, still nominally king, filled with hatred for David, was devoting all his strength to persecuting David; while the affairs of the nation were becoming more and more involved in hopeless confusion.

While David in exile was almost certainly the popular idol of the people, their fickleness was manifested in the mean treachery of both the Keilites and the Ziphites, who were prepared to maintain favor with Saul by delivering up David to him.

David, with the spirit of true patriotism burning in his heart, waged war successfully against the Philistines, the enemies of the nation. It is evident, however, that his exile and persecution were telling on him, and nervous fear was growing in his heart. Nevertheless, his trust in God remained unshaken, and he appealed to God in his hour of trouble.

The most beautiful incident of this period is the meeting of David and Jonathan in the wood. It was their last meeting, and it manifested that Jonathan's love for David was as strong as ever. Jonathan was firmly convinced that David must eventually become king; and, looking forward to when this should be, he attested his willingness to take second place in the kingdom.

I SAMUEL 24

At last Saul was in David's power. It would have been perfectly easy for him to have taken his life. He did not do so, but, withholding his hand, uttered a strong protest against Saul's persecution. There is the passion of the true poet in the wording of the protest, and the changing moods of the human heart are manifest as it proceeds. Beginning with the judicial statement of his innocence of all evil intention, he merged into pleading tones in which memories of old and happier days are evident. These tones, however, almost immediately changed into accents of agony as he declared that Jehovah would avenge him, but that he himself would not lay a hand on Saul. He finally appealed scornfully to the king that he should spend time and strength upon hunting him, one lonely man. The degeneracy of Saul was manifest in the weak and maudlin sentiment with which he addressed David.

I SAMUEL 25

We now have the account of Samuel's death. Notwithstanding all Israel's failure to realize his high ideals, it was impossible that they should not recognize his greatness, and it is easy to believe that their mourning for him was the evidence of genuine sorrow.

The story of Nabal, as here written, is intensely interesting. He was of a type which continues to this time. The whole fact is most forcibly expressed in the word "churlish." David's approach to him was characterized by fine courtesy, which was responded to, not only by refusal to grant the request, but by uncalled-for and unwarranted aspersions.

In the story Abigail stands out as a woman of fine tone and temper, and of keen insight. It is perfectly evident that her principal concern was for David. To save him from a bloody deed was her first intention. In this she was successful, and David recognized the true service she had rendered him.

The chapter ends with the story of his marriage to Abigail, while already he had taken Ahinoam to wife. While it is perfectly true that we have no right to measure David by the standards of our own time, it is equally clear that at this point we have evidence of a weakness which presently was to lead him into the most terrible sin of his life and cause him the greatest difficulty and the acutest suffering.

I SAMUEL 26

Once again we have the account of how David spared the life of Saul. There is no reason at all for the view that this is a repetition of the previous story. A quiet comparison of the two will show many points of difference between them.

After dramatically rebuking Abner for his lack of care of the king, David protested Saul's persecution of himself. Varying interpretations of the meaning of the words of David as recorded in the nineteenth verse have been given. The most natural solution is really the simplest, that in appealing to Saul why he was thus following David, he suggested that if the evil spirit should be a divine visitation Saul should seek to be free from it by making an offering to God.

David's weariness of his exile and persecution inadvertently manifested itself when he declared that if men had stirred up Saul against him they were endeavoring to drive him out from the inheritance of the Lord to serve other gods.

In answer to David's protest, Saul confessed his sin, and, in one sentence, unexpectedly, but nevertheless accurately, declared the whole truth concerning himself when he said, "I have played the fool."

Perhaps this is the briefest and, at the same time, the most accurate autobiography in existence. The statement, possibly quite unintentionally, but nevertheless definitely, had application not merely to his immediate action, but to all his history from the beginning.

I SAMUEL 27

David's sense of his danger increased until he became almost pessimistic, and he said in his heart, "I shall now perish one day by the hand of Saul." And who can wonder at, or blame him? Long and weary indeed had been his period of suffering.

The whole story is parabolic. The anointed king was driven out by the rejected king. All this was repeated long after in the history of the one true King. The difference, however, is marked. No fear ever made the anointed One quail. He also spoke, and often, of the fact that men would kill Him, but always ended with the prophecy of His ultimate resurrection and victory. Moreover, He never crossed over to the Philistines for refuge. This David did, going to live in Gath.

From there he made occasional raids on other ancient enemies of his people, and with success. In order to hide this from those among whom he dwelt he was driven to the expedient of untruth.

When a man is in a false position, no matter how strenuously he may desire to be true to divine purpose, he is inevitably in grave danger of violating some fundamental principle of his loyalty. It is impossible to see David taking refuge in Gath without feeling that he had allowed himself to lose that clear vision of God which had made him invincible against Goliath.

I SAMUEL 28

Perhaps there is no more tragic chapter in the Old Testament history than this. It tells the story of Saul's visit in the day of trouble to a witch of Endor, which was the final act and clearest manifestation of his degradation.

It is strange how this story has been made to serve in defense of things occult, which, as a matter of fact, it condemns. Let it be carefully read, and it becomes perfectly patent that this woman had nothing to do with bringing up Samuel. Still practicing her black art, and that in secret, because of the king's edict against all of her class, she commenced, on the occasion of Saul's visit, to practice the deceptions with which she was familiar. When in response to her incantations, as it seemed, Samuel actually appeared, she was startled beyond measure.

That Samuel actually did appear to Saul there can be no doubt. However, he was sent of God for the express purpose of delivering the terrible message to Saul, to which the king listened in amazement. It was the pronouncement of his doom, and the call from the other side to the spirit of the man who had so utterly and disastrously failed to fulfil his opportunity.

I SAMUEL 29

David's sojourn with Achish resulted in his being compelled to join the Philistine army in its preparations to attack Israel.

It is perfectly natural that the Philistine lords protested against this arrangement. They were familiar with the song which had celebrated David's victories over them, and dared not trust him among them in the day of battle.

Achish seems to have formed high estimate of him, and a strong affection for him, but was compelled to yield to his lords in this matter. Therefore David was dismissed from the Philistine army.

It is perhaps idle to speculate what the result would have been had he remained. In all probability in the crisis he would have turned on those with whom he had fought.

This, however, was not God's purpose, and in the attitude and action of the Philistine lords we have another instance of the overruling of God in the affairs of men. Through it David was delivered from an entanglement into which he had brought himself in his excess of fear.

I SAMUEL 30

Being thus delivered, David returned to Ziklag. In his absence it had been sacked by the Amalekites. Immediately the true spirit of patriotic heroism was stirred within him, and he moved with rapid determination to avenge the wrong.

He was absolutely successful, inflicting punishment on his foes and rescuing from them all who were his own.

It is from this story that the history moves forward into the next Book. Having gathered spoils from his enemies, David sent presents to all the elders of Judah, and by this act undoubtedly prepared the way for establishing himself among them.

We have no warrant for thinking that this was merely an act of policy on David's part to obtain the throne. It would be far nearer the truth to say that recognizing his position as the anointed of God he was burning determination with him to rid his people of their foes, and to enlarge his army by enlisting the sympathy of the leaders of the tribe.

I SAMUEL 31

This closing chapter in the first Book of Samuel is draped in sackcloth and ashes. It gives the account of the end of the career of one of the most disastrous failures on record in Biblical history.

Defeat at the hands of the Philistines drove Saul to tragic desperation. Wounded in the final fight, and fearing that the last blow might come to him by the hand of an enemy, he called upon his armor-bearer to slay him.

When the armor-bearer refused to do so, Saul died by his own hand physically, as he had already slain himself morally by his own sin and folly.

Tragically terrible, and ghastly beyond compare, is the account of the Philistines carrying Saul's head about in token of their triumph and his defeat.

The chief spiritual value of this whole Book consists in the solemn lessons it teaches by the life and failure and death of this man. The story proclaims forevermore that advantages and remarkable opportunities are no guarantees of success unless the heart be firm and steady in allegiance to principle and loyalty to God.

II Samuel

II SAMUEL 1

The second Book of Samuel deals largely with the story of David, and presents the picture of the theocratic monarchy. The first movement records the progress of David to the position which God had appointed for him. While the supreme element manifest throughout this section is that of the divine progress toward accomplishment of the purpose, it is impossible to study it without being impressed with the greatness of David. Neither is it necessary to think of all the actions by which he won the favor of Israel as being dictated merely by policy. Rather they reveal the true character of the man—upright, generous, and of great heart.

At times it would appear as though he acted contrary to his merely political interests, and yet, as events moved on, they prove that there is no policy so powerful as that of integrity and abiding in the will of God.

The story of the death of Saul as told by the Amalekite was evidently a fabrication. There is no doubt he found the dead body of the king and despoiled it in the hope of winning favor with David. For this he paid the severest penalty.

The lamentation of David is full of beauty. Over Saul and Jonathan it is stately and dignified, and merges into extreme tenderness when he sings of his friend Jonathan only.

II SAMUEL 2

The first act of David was to inquire of God what he should do. Without hesitation, his own tribe crowned him king. His attitude toward the men of Jabesh-gilead was in the highest sense politic, and yet was in keeping with his attitude toward the house of Saul. The spirit of Saul, which was antagonistic to David, was perpetuated in Abner, Saul's cousin and captain of the host. He at once set himself to consolidate the house of Israel around the house of Saul. Ish-bosheth was merely a puppet in his hands. While it may be true that Abner did not desire the kingship for himself, it must be remembered that it would have been poor policy on his part to seek for that position. It was easier to gather the people around a son of the dead king.

Thus the kingdom was not actually David's. It had to be gained, and seven years passed before his crowning over the whole nation.

Two remarkable men headed opposing factions in the nation. Joab was a strange and rugged character, at once fierce and faithful. His relation to David forms a strange picture of a troublesome friendship. He was a perpetual source of anxiety, and yet his rugged steadfastness naturally appealed to the king. On the other hand, Abner was strong, resourceful, and courageous. As will be seen later, by his own confession, he had fought through all the years against the knowledge of the purpose of God; and yet in some respects he was more admirable than Joab. Here we have the account of the first battle under these leaders, in which Joab was victorious, but his brother Asahel was slain. Asahel's death entered like iron into the soul of Joab, who never rested until his vengeance was satisfied on Abner.

II SAMUEL 3

The long warfare continued, and the progress of it is declared in the opening verse of this chapter: "And David waxed stronger and stronger, but the house of Saul waxed weaker and weaker."

At last matters in the kingdom of Israel were hastened to a crisis by a quarrel between Abner and Ish-bosheth. The latter seems to have charged the former with a peculiar sin against his rights, a charge without foundation. This would explain Abner's fierce rejoinder. As a result of this he made overtures to David, during which he revealed his knowledge of God's purpose that David should occupy the throne. This is a revelation of the reason of his weakness. No man can hope successfully to bring any purpose to final issue when his own will power is weakened by an inward conviction that he is fighting against God.

Joab took advantage of this opportunity to wreak his vengeance on Abner by slaying him. David was at great pains to disavow all connection with the bloody act. His lamentation was the sincere regret of an upright man that anything should be done to aid an unjust cause.

His action was declared to be pleasing to the people. Thus he was steadily gaining his way into that respect and love which is the greatest element of power for a king.

II SAMUEL 4

Again we have the story of a murder unjustifiable and cruel, prompted solely by the hope of gaining favor with David. Once again the king made it perfectly clear that he had no part in any of these methods of obtaining the kingdom which was his by the gift of God.

His immediate punishment of the men who had murdered his rival proved him to be a man of faith, for faith consistently refuses to make use of subterfuge and injustice to secure the realization of the ends appointed by God.

While all this is true of the attitude of David, it is nevertheless patent that with the death of Abner and Ish-bosheth the very center and strength of the cause of the house of Saul were destroyed.

This leads up to the "Then" with which the next paragraph begins.

II SAMUEL 5

At this point the second section in the first movement of the Book commences. David had won the heart of all Israel by his consistent justice and magnanimity toward those who stood in the way of his coming into full possession of the kingdom. He had mourned for Abner, recognizing his greatness. He had punished the murderers of Ish-bosheth.

It was enough. The people recognized the kingly qualities of the man against whom they had been fighting under the leadership of Abner, and so at last David commenced his reign over the whole nation.

His first victory was the taking of

Jebus. The city was considered impregnable, and in taunt its inhabitants declared it to be defended by the blind and the lame, which, of course, we are not to suppose was actually the case. Against these so-called blind and lame Joab proceeded, and with great gallantry captured the fortress.

It was out of this incident that originated the story attributing to David hatred of the blind and lame. There is no evidence that he had any such hatred, as indeed his action toward Mephibosheth subsequently disproved.

An element of weakness in David manifested itself at this point when, having come into possession of the kingdom, he multiplied his concubines and wives. Of course, here, as always, his action must be measured by his times. This, however, does not prevent a glimpse of that side of his nature which eventually manifested itself in deadly sin.

Two victories were gained over the Philistines, and thus the position of the king was made more secure.

II SAMUEL 6

Victorious in war, David was not unmindful of the central truth of the national life over which he was called to preside. The nation was indeed a theocracy, with the worship of God at its very center.

Believing this, David prepared to bring the Ark into the capital. When he did a startling event occurred.

Contrary to instructions given long before to Moses, the Ark was placed on a new cart. As they started on their way, the oxen drawing the cart stumbled; and one man, daring to stretch forth his hand in an attempt to steady the Ark, was at once smitten with death.

The effect on David of this terrible vindication of the divine majesty was remarkable. He was displeased, and yet afraid. So afraid that for the moment he dared not go forward with his purpose, and, consequently, the Ark rested for three months in the house of Obed-edom.

At last, however, it was taken forward to Jerusalem. The action of David as he danced before it, which called forth the contempt of Michal, was, of course, purely Eastern, and revealed his profound recognition of the true King of his people and his sense of humility before Him.

II SAMUEL 7

The story of David's desire to build the Temple is told here in close connection with that of his bringing the Tabernacle to Jerusalem. It is not necessarily in chronological order, but is fittingly related at this point. David's desire to build the house of God was perfectly natural, and, indeed, proper. So much was this the case that it appealed to Nathan, who advised him to do all that was in his heart.

It was not, however, God's will that he should carry out this work, and the prophet was sent to deliver a message which was neither in agreement with David's desire nor with his own opinion.

Jehovah reminded David of all that He had done for him, and declared His intention of making David's reign permanent. He was not, however, the chosen instrument for building the Temple, which work should be carried out by his son.

The story reveals the triumph of Nathan and David in their ready submission to the declared will of God. The prophet unhesitatingly delivered his message, even though it contradicted his own expressed opinion. David immediately acquiesced in the will of God, and worshiped.

It is of the utmost importance that those called to the service of God in any way should ever test their desires, even the highest and the holiest of them, by His will. Work, apparently excellent in itself, must not be undertaken unless by the expressed direction of God. Time always vindicates the wisdom of the divine procedure.

II SAMUEL 8

Here we have the record of some of the victories of David, again not necessarily in chronological order. There is, however, a very close relation between this account of them and what had preceded.

The story of the king's successes contains more perhaps than is apparent on the surface. By them he strengthened his position and that of his people; but he also gathered treasure. The house of the Lord was still in his mind, and although he knew he would not be permitted to build, he was still gathering in preparation for the work of his son. The chapter ends with the account of the appointment of certain officers of state, by which the internal consolidation of the kingdom was ensured.

The functions of these officers are interesting. One was appointed to lead the army; another to be recorder, or national historian; two were priests, in all probability exercising their functions at two centers; a fifth was scribe or secretary of state; a sixth became the head of David's special bodyguard, which would seem to have been composed of foreigners. Finally, the sons of David were made priests, or as the A.V. has it, "chief rulers," the reference undoubtedly being to positions of civic, rather than religious, authority.

II SAMUEL 9

There is an exquisite tenderness about the story here recorded. David's love for Jonathan was still fresh. One can easily imagine how in the days of his growing prosperity the king would often think of the former strenuous times and of his friend's loyalty to him under circumstances so full of stress and peril.

For David the house of Saul, which had done him so much harm, was redeemed by his love for Jonathan; and he instituted an inquiry whether any were left of this house to whom he might show kindness for the sake of his friend.

The inquiry resulted in the finding of Mephibosheth, whose very lameness was tragic and pathetic, in that it had been caused by the flight of his nurse on the awful day of Jezreel, when his father and grandfather had fallen together.

To him the king restored the lands of Saul, and sat him as an honored guest at his own table. David's own account of his action was that he desired to "show kindness of God unto him." This declaration recalls the words of the covenant made between him and Jonathan long before, in which his friend had charged him to show him "the kindness of the Lord," and also that he should show this same kindness to his house forever.

In all this David appears as a man after God's own heart. The common attitude of human nature would not permit such action. It is ever the kindness of God which heaps favors on representatives of enemies.

II SAMUEL 10

Here we have the record of victories over Ammon and Syria. So far as David is concerned it is interesting in revealing the same spirit of good will in David in his attempt to show kindness to Hanum, and the same elements of strength as a warrior as he led the hosts of Israel against the forces of Syria, and defeated them.

Joab appears once more in all the rugged and terrible strength of his nature. It is interesting to observe that in his arrangements he made no allowance for the possibility of ultimate defeat in his conflict with Ammon. He divided his forces, and did so in order that if the Syrians on the one side should be too strong for him, the army of Abishai, his brother, should help him. Or if, on the other hand, the children of Ammon should be too strong for Abishai, he would help Abishai.

It does not seem to have occurred to him that the combination might have been too much for both of them. In all this the true quality of the soldier is revealed. It recognizes the possibility of defeat at a point, but never that of the poet's final triumph. We are not surprised that Joab was victorious.

This story constitutes the culmination of the account of David's rise to power, and prepares for the terrible story of his fall by showing the general circumstances under which the fall occurred.

II SAMUEL 11

In the whole of the Old Testament literature there is no chapter more tragic or full of solemn and searching warning than this.

Carefully pondering it, we notice the downward steps logically following each other in rapid succession. First, "David tarried at Jerusalem." It was the time of war, and his place was with the army Instead of being there, he had remained behind, in the sphere of temptation. This is not to say that the place of peace is more perilous than that of war, but rather that any place other than that of duty is one of extreme danger.

From this, events moved rapidly but surely onward. In briefest quotation we may indicate the movement: "He saw"; "he sent and inquired"; "he took."

The king had fallen from the high level of purity to sin in yielding to the inner weakness which had already become manifested. One sin led to another, and in all likelihood his sin against Uriah, one of the bravest of his soldiers, was more dastardly than his sin with Bathsheba.

From the merely human standpoint, the unutterable folly of the whole affair is evident as he puts himself in Joab's power by sharing with him the secret of his guilt. Even more fitting than in his own use of them, his words concerning the death of Saul and Jonathan are true, "How are the mighty fallen!"

II SAMUEL 12

A year passed away. The child of Bathsheba was born. We can imagine what that year had been to David. Bathsheba, whom in all probability he truly loved, was with him as his wife; but it is inevitable that he had been haunted by the memory of Uriah and by the fear of Joab.

At last the prophet Nathan came and uttered a parable in which David's sin was portrayed. David uttered his opinion on the side of right. Then, like a flash, the prophet charged David with having committed the sin David had condemned. It was at that moment that the best in David was apparent, as he confessed, "I have sinned." His repentance was genuine and immediate.

That repentance was manifested in his attitude in the presence of the punishment which fell upon him. His child was stricken, and the king mourned, and besought that its life might be spared. This could not be. When the child was dead David worshiped.

Perhaps nothing more perfectly reveals the sincerity of his repentance than this ready acceptance of the stroke by which God refused to answer his prayer.

In the midst of his worship, he said of the child, "I shall go to him, but he shall not return to me." This shows his consciousness of the spiritual world and of the life beyond.

The account of his dealing with the children of Ammon after his victory over them should be read in the light of the margin of the Revised Version, which shows that he placed them in servitude rather than treated them with barbarous cruelty.

II SAMUEL 13

The story of Amnon's sin is of a sin committed by a child of David similar to his own. When the story was told to him, we are told that he was wroth. We are not told that he disciplined Amnon. How could he? He had rendered his arm nerveless by his own sin.

In Amnon we have the picture of one mastered by passion. In pondering the narrative it is said of Jonadab that he was a friend of Amnon. The word "friend" is desecrated by its use in such a connection. Any who out of friendship will aid in the pathway of sin, prove themselves enemies rather than friends. Jonadab might have saved Amnon, even though for the moment he had offended him. The picture of Amnon hating Tamar is common as the story of sin. Passion illegally indulged becomes transmuted into a destructive fire.

The troubles of David continued. Absalom slew Amnon, and then took flight. Absalom probably was moved by mixed motives. He wanted vengeance on the man who had wronged his sister. His subsequent actions, however, show that he saw in Amnon a hindrance to carrying out his own secret ambitions. It is noticeable that Jonadab the "friend," who had aided Amnon, was still on hand, and the same cool, calculating traits were manifest in his character. In all these things David was reaping the result of the sin that had cursed his life, and the full harvest was not yet.

II SAMUEL 14

Opinions widely differ over why Joab set himself to bring Absalom back. The most probable reason is that he "perceived that the king's heart was toward Absalom." There is certainly a strange fascination about this rugged and surly soldier Joab. He never paused at a deed of blood, and yet underneath the rough exterior was a strange tenderness in his regard for David.

David is seen again as desiring to be consistent. In the case of the woman of Tekoa, as in that of Nathan, when he had declared a principle, he stood by it when it was applied to himself. Absalom was brought back, but in the interest of the kingdom his punishment was not wholly removed. He was not allowed to see his father, and did not see him for two years.

We have a remarkable picture of Absalom, evidently a handsome man of physical perfection. He was daring, or we might more aptly describe him as a daredevil. When Joab would not come to him, he set fire to his barley, and so compelled him to come. The result was that he was admitted to the presence of his father, and was embraced by him.

II SAMUEL 15

That Absalom's attitude of obeisance before David was feigned is proved by his conspiracy. That Joab cared nothing personally for Absalom is evident from his refusal to see him any further. Absalom's cunning is manifested in that he waited and plotted four years, ever attempting to turn the heart of the people toward himself. His unscrupulousness, moreover, was shown in that when everything was ripe for action, he proceeded to the overt act of rebellion under cover of religious observance.

Perhaps there is nothing more pathetic in the story of David than his flight from the city. Almost all the essential characteristics of the man were exhibited. Nevertheless, throughout we discover the note of the chastened and humbled spirit, which recognized the righteousness of the suffering following on his sin. His magnanimity was manifested in his suggestion to Itai, the Philistine, that there was no need that he should share the misfortune of his sorrow. Above all, his submission to God was supreme; he said, "If He say thus, I have no delight in thee; behold, here am I, let Him do to me as seemeth good unto Him." He left the city weeping, with covered head and barefoot, these things being the symbols of his penitence. Yet even here he was the astute and far-seeing man, as is evidenced by his leaving behind Abiathar and Zadok, the priests, and Hushai, his friend.

II SAMUEL 16

David's sorrows multiplied. Those recorded here are typical. Ziba, a man who for purely selfish reasons took advantage of temporary trouble to traduce an absent friend, was utterly despicable, and the more so because at the moment the sorrow he brought to the heart of David was his feeling that his kindness toward Mephibosheth was ill requited. Shimei was of a higher type than Ziba, but was mean beyond measure. He struck when his foe was in the dust. David's attitude toward Shimei is remarkable in its revelation of his attitude toward God. He spoke of Shimei as sent to curse him.

As we thus follow David through these days of humiliation and shame, while with him we recognize the perfect justice of all the sufferings that came to him, we nevertheless understand more perfectly that he was indeed a man after God's own heart.

Arriving in Jerusalem, Absalom was surprised to find Hushai, David's friend, still there. He turned from him to Ahithophel for counsel. Ahithophel advised an action which would make the breach between himself and his father permanent, and constituted a supreme claim to the succession. To enter and possess the harem of a king was the right only of his successor.

II SAMUEL 17

Ahithophel counseled immediate warlike activity. As David had not gone far, and could not have gathered round him any large number of men, let a company be sent to capture him, and that immediately. Judging from the human standpoint, had Absalom followed this advice, his rebellion might have been successful. But it is never safe to judge from the human standpoint, or to reckon without God.

Absalom turned to Hushai, who counseled delay and gathering a large army. Hushai's counsel was intended to give David time to gather men around him. The advice ministered to Absalom's vanity. It would be far more spectacular to lead an army in person, and gain a great victory, than to send a small company to capture his father. Absalom's vanity ensured his ruin. How disastrous to his own cause was Absalom's decision is manifest by the action of Ahithophel. He saw the utter folly of what was being done, and, hastening from Jerusalem, came to his own city, set his affairs in order, and ended his life.

II SAMUEL 18

The delay advised by Hushai resulted in multitudes gathering to David, and at last the day of battle between those loyal to him and Absalom's followers arrived. Two men attract our attention, David and Joab. A chastened and almost docile spirit is evident as the king yielded to the constraint of his people, and did not himself lead the hosts. It is conceivable, and, indeed, almost certain, that his love for Absalom caused his action. He earnestly charged those going to battle to deal gently with the young man. It is here that Joab appears in the terrible sternness of his character. He had no pity for Absalom. He knew that Absalom was the center of all the trouble, and directly he learned that Absalom was dead, he sounded a trumpet to stay the battle. He had seen David's action toward his sons characterized by lack of discipline. In the highest interests of the kingdom his hand was raised to slay Absalom.

Everything leads up to, and culminates in, David's wail for Absalom. It was brief, but thrilled with agony. Five times he repeated the two words, "my son." It is as though he had said, He is indeed my son. His weaknesses are my weaknesses, his passions my passions, his sins my sins. The deepest cry escaping from his heart was, "Would God I had died for thee." Here David surely reached the profoundest moment of his suffering. We cannot stand in the presence of that suffering without learning the solemn lessons of parental responsibility it has to teach, not merely in training our children, but in that earlier training of ourselves for their sakes.

II SAMUEL 19

The king's sorrow affected the people. They stole back into Jerusalem silently, instead of with rejoicing, while he was left outside. Once again his words tell of his agony, the deepest note thereof being still revealed in the thrice repeated "my son."

In the midst of his sorrow Joab came to him, again politic, but unsympathetic. There are times when men must rise above the grief of their own repentance and act for the sake of others. This was so now in the case of David, and Joab told him so with almost brutal frankness.

It is arresting to notice that on his return the men who had crossed his path in differing ways during the period of his temporary exile came back to David. Shimei, the man who struck his foe in the dust, came fawning back, and David's magnanimity was shown in sparing his life. Mephibosheth met him with all the signs of mourning for his absence, and David was comforted by his coming. Barzillai, who had helped him, set him back on his way to Jerusalem, and there was a tender parting between them. All this was followed by strife between Judah and Israel over the right of bringing in the king.

II SAMUEL 20

The occasion invariably finds the man for evil as well as for good. Sheba seized the strife between Judah and Israel as an opportunity to attempt to divide the kingdom.

David's hosts went forth against Israel. Once more Joab appears on the scene, and the same relentless ferocity was manifested in his murder of Amasa, coupled with continued loyalty to David, as he proceeded to quell the insurrection.

This was accomplished through the wisdom of a woman by the death of Sheba. Thus David was restored to his true position, and the story ends with the new appointment of officers of state. Joab retained the position of commander-in-chief, having ensured this position by the murder of Amasa. Benaiah was appointed over the bodyguard of the king. Adoram was made the national treasurer. Jehoshaphat became the chronicler, or historian. Sheva was appointed scribe, or secretary of state. Zadok and Abiathar continued in the priesthood, and Ira was made the king's priest, or chief minister.

II SAMUEL 21

As at the close of the Book of Judges, so here, several matters are dealt with not in chronological order, or related, but as illustrating the times which have been under consideration.

In many senses they were the best times in the history of Israel, for during this period the theocratic monarchy was most perfectly realized.

During the reign of Solomon there was more magnificence and material prosperity, but the seeds of dissension sown even under David worked toward the ultimate disruption of the kingdom throughout the whole of that period.

This appendix contains matter which reveals the direct government of God: two utterances of David which reveal his real character; and an account of some of the deeds of the mighty men which shows the heroic spirit of the period.

The account of the famine was written to give a purely national lesson. Saul had broken faith with the Gibeonites, and his guilt action had neither been recognized nor expiated. The sin of the ruling house was the sin of the people, and it was noted by God, and must be accounted for. Hence the famine, which was stayed only when by the sacrifice of the sons of Saul the nation had come to consciousness of its guilt and repented thereof.

II SAMUEL 22

The character of David is revealed in the two psalms recorded here. In the first of these, found in this chapter, we find the deepest things concerning him. It may be well to note its main divisions, with the definite teaching of each.

1. Verses 2-4. Jehovah is declared to be the Source of all strength.
2. Verses 5-16. All deliverances are wrought directly by Jehovah Himself.
3. Verses 17-25. Deliverance is wrought by Jehovah on the condition of righteousness realized in the conduct of His people.
4. Verses 26-28. In these words we have revealed the principles of relationship between God and man. God is to man what man is to God.
5. Verses 29-46. The singer here bears experimental testimony to the truth of the things he has celebrated in song.
6. Verses 47-51. The psalm ends with a fine doxology, setting forth the praise of Jehovah.

Such convictions—of the absolute sovereignty of Jehovah, of His omnipotent power to deliver, of the necessity for obedience to His law, and of assurance that in the case of such obedience He ever acts for His people—constituted the underlying strength of David's character. In all probability this psalm was written before his sin, and if so, it will readily be understood how terrible was his sorrow when he recognized his failure.

II SAMUEL 23

Here we have first, the second psalm, containing David's last recorded words in this connection. They breathe the consciousness of his own failure, and sing of the divine faithfulness. In verses one to four David set forth the true ideal of kingship in most exquisite language. In verse five he recognized that he had not realized the ideal, but declared that nevertheless God had been faithful to His Covenant. In the last movement, verses six and seven, in words that must have been to him full of searching power, he announced what the fate of the wicked inevitably must be.

The reign of David was pre-eminently the heroic age in Israel's history. This is demonstrated in the list of the mighty men and their exploits. It is interesting to remember that these were men who had gathered to him in Adullam, who had been described as men in debt, in danger, and discontented. They were possessed of natural powers, which had been spoiled but now were redeemed and realized.

These were the elements of David's reign. His deepest character, as we have seen, was the result of such convictions as he had given utterance to in the great psalm; and the result of such character on others had been the transformation of strong men who were useless into mighty men who were capable of deeds of heroism. More than all his victories against outside foes, the influence of his life and character on the men nearest to him testify to his essential greatness.

II SAMUEL 24

The Book closes with one other picture, reminding us of the direct government of the people by God in that He visited the king and the nation with punishment for numbering the people.

It has been objected that there was nothing sinful in taking a census, seeing that it had been done before in the history of the people by the direct command of God. But in that very fact lay the contrast between previous numberings and this. *They* were carried out by the command of God. *This* was done from a very different motive. That the act was wrong is evident from David's consciousness that it was so; and in the presence of his confession it is not for us to criticize. Quite evidently the motive explains the sin. While that motive is not explicitly declared, we may certainly gain an understanding of it from the protest of Joab, "Now the Lord thy God add unto the people, how many soever they be, an hundredfold, and may the eyes of my lord the king see it; but why doth my lord the king delight in this thing?" The spirit of vainglory in numbers had taken possession of the people and the king, and there was a tendency to trust in numbers and forget God.

David's choice of his punishment once more revealed his recognition both of the righteousness and tenderness of Jehovah. He willed that the stroke which was to fall, should come directly from the divine hand rather than through any intermediary.

The Book ends with the story of the erection of the altar on the threshing floor of Araunah the Jebusite in which we finally see the man after God's own heart turning the occasion of his sin and its punishment into an occasion of worship.

I Kings

I KINGS 1

The two Books of Kings appear in the Hebrew Bible as one. Together they practically cover the whole period of kingly rule over the ancient people. The first Book deals mainly with events centering around two persons, Solomon and Elijah.

The opening verses of this chapter give the account of the days of David's feebleness. These days created the opportunity for rebellion under Adonijah. A remarkable statement concerning the training of this son of David throws light on his action (verse 6). It may be that the bitterness of his sorrow over Absalom was the cause of his foolish indulgence of Adonijah.

As a result of this rebellion Solomon was crowned before the passing of David. Thus, while the life of David was shadowed to the last, the satisfaction of seeing the divine will carried out in the accession to the throne of Solomon was granted to him.

Solomon's action toward Adonijah was characteristic of the best side of his nature, in which clemency and dignified authority were alike manifest. From the beginning of the story of Solomon it is well to remember he was the child of Bathsheba and David. In some sense, therefore, his inheritance was against him; but it is equally true that he inherited excellences as well as defects. Moreover, what was of greater value was that God was ever on his side when he answered the call of the good within him. Had he completely yielded it he would have found sufficient strength to overcome the evil.

I KINGS 2

In the last charge of David there was first a recognition of the sphere of Solomon's safety. In all probability his personal influence had been great with his son, but now he was going "the way of all the earth." Great responsibilities would devolve upon that son. There was, however, a path of safety. It was absolute loyalty to God. One can imagine how, as David urged this upon his son, his own experience of disobedience would add weight and urgency to all he said.

The remainder of the charge of David, especially concerning Joab and Shimei, has been severely criticized. Much of this criticism would cease if certain simple things were borne in mind. It may be well to state them. First, David knew these men by experience, and appreciated their danger to the state. Second, he had kept his covenant with them, and spared their lives. Third, and this is to be especially noted, he left the matter of how to deal with them in the hands of Solomon. Finally, his words concerning the death of each are in all probability prophetic rather than vindictive.

With Solomon began, in some senses, the most splendid period in Israel's history. The splendor, however, was largely mental and material. The spiritual is noticeably absent. The acts in which he dealt with the leading men in the kingdom in whose hearts were the impulses of treachery were characterized by clemency and yet firmness. Adonijah's request for Abishag must be considered in the light of Eastern custom. Solomon saw in the request a movement toward rebellion, and therefore Adonijah was also slain. Abiathar was deposed from the priesthood. To Shimei an opportunity of life was granted on certain well-defined conditions. He broke his parole, and paid the penalty.

I KINGS 3

The first brief paragraph in this chapter reveals at once Solomon's strength and weakness. He was strong, for he loved the Lord and walked in the statutes of his father David. However, there was the other side of his nature, to which he yielded in undue measure, even at the beginning. His affinity with Pharaoh, and his marriage with his daughter, while politically astute, was a vital mistake from the standpoint of his relationship with God and the divine purposes. It is at once seen how he compromised in that he sacrificed and burned incense in the high places. The perils of mixed motives and a divided heart are terrible indeed.

Early in his reign, Jehovah appeared to him in a dream. With that appearance came Solomon's great opportunity, both to manifest himself, and to obtain the best. His choice was characterized by great wisdom, as it revealed his consciousness of personal incapacity for all the work devolving on him. God's answer to his request was full of gracious and overwhelming kindness. He gave Solomon what he asked, and added the things he might have chosen, yet showed his wisdom in passing by.

Long life, wealth, and victory are all good when they come as bestowment from God. Should a man seek them from selfish motives rather than to fulfil the divine purpose, they would in all probability prove to be curses rather than blessings.

In this chapter Solomon's choice is followed by a beautiful picture in which he is seen exercising the gift for which he had asked and which God had granted to him.

I KINGS 4

Solomon set himself to a careful organization of his kingdom. The system of government as here set forth is characterized by order, and, indeed, is in many ways remarkable. The king was supreme in authority. He gathered around him, however, a company of officers of state, each having his own department, for which he was held responsible.

To express them in the language of today, we might say that they consisted of a high priest, two state secretaries, a national historian, and a commander-in-chief, two other priests, a chief of staff, a personal secretary, who, in this case, was also the king's friend, and a chancellor of the exchequer. Beyond this, were twelve appointed officers, each having his own district, in which he was the representative of the king. The principal duty of each officer was to gather provision for the king's household for one month in the year.

These were the days of the nation's greatest material prosperity. The people lived in merriment, and dwelt safely beneath their own vines and fig trees.

The chapter ends with a declaration of the remarkable learning of Solomon. He was a philosopher, as witness his three thousand proverbs, which are still preserved for us; and a poet of impassioned utterance, as the canticles reveal. Moreover, he was a naturalist, according to this record, being interested in and acquainted with trees, from the cedar to the hyssop, and also with life in all its higher developments.

I KINGS 5

Solomon turned his attention to building the Temple immediately after he had set his kingdom in order. The first movement in this direction was the treaty with Hiram, and sending relays of men to the forests and quarries to prepare the timber and the stones for the structure. This treaty with Hiram was the result of a legacy of friendship which David had bequeathed him.

It is evident that Solomon appreciated the real purpose of his coming to the throne as he declared that he purposed in his heart to build this dwelling place for God in accordance with the divine word spoken to his father. The time was now opportune, for the nation was at peace, Solomon's own description of conditions being very significant, "But now the Lord my God hath given me rest on every side; there is neither adversary, nor evil occurrence."

The greatness of the work thus undertaken is revealed by the final paragraph in the chapter, with its account of the enormous amount of labor employed.

I KINGS 6

This chapter is full of interest, as it gives a somewhat detailed description of the structure of the Temple. In all essentials its actual central building was on the pattern of the Tabernacle. It was, however, twice the size of the Tabernacle, and was built of solid material because it was intended to remain in a permanent position, seeing that the nation was now settled in the land.

Moreover, this settlement was symbolized by the fact that round about the Temple proper many chambers were erected to serve in various ways the interest of the priests and worshipers which had been entirely absent from the Tabernacle.

The time occupied in the construction of the Temple was seven years, during which the actual work of erection in the city went forward in impressive silence.

In this description we have special mention of the oracle, or Holy of Holies; of the golden altar; the doors, and the cherubim. Like the Tabernacle of old, its chief splendor was within, where everything was encased in gold, neither wood nor stone being visible. The magnificence of this small Temple—for small it was by comparison with temples erected in other lands to other gods—may be gathered from the fact that the amount of gold used was six hundred talents.

I KINGS 7

Taking advantage of the treaty with Hiram, Solomon also built a house for himself, the house of the forest of Lebanon, a description of which is given in the commencement of this chapter.

It is surely significant that the chronicler says concerning the Temple, "So he was seven years in building it"; and then, "And Solomon was building his own house thirteen years." Comment is hardly necessary, save, perhaps, to remind ourselves that however strong our zeal may be for the Ark of God, if the time and possessions devoted to our own comfort be greater than those devoted to the service of God, it is sure proof that the master passion is self-centered rather than God-centered.

The remainder of the chapter is occupied with a detailed description of the furniture of the Temple. An examination of this shows that essentially it is the same as the furniture of the Tabernacle, but that it is characterized by greater material magnificence and by durability.

I KINGS 8

The Temple being finished, the great ceremony of dedication commenced. The permanent link between Tabernacle and Temple was the Ark of the Covenant. With great care and impressive ceremony, they had carried the Ark over Jordan into the land. For a long time it had remained at Gilgal, and then was taken to Shiloh. Captured by the Philistines, it had brought discomfiture and defeat. For twenty years it had found a resting place at Kirjathjearim, then for three months in the house of Obed-edom, and at length was brought into the city by David. At last it found its way into a House built by one who desired to be loyal to God, but who nevertheless was in many respects already falling short of the true ideal of submission. That the glory of the Lord filled the House was an evidence of the grace of Jehovah.

When Solomon saw the glory, he uttered a cry of exultation, and then blessed the congregation. Then standing by the altar of burnt-offering, he offered the dedicatory prayer. In its opening he recognized the proved faithfulness of God, and appealed to Him to continue it toward His people. Rising from prayer, the king again pronounced blessing on the people, and expressed an earnest desire for the continued presence of Jehovah. Whereas it is true that the presence of Jehovah was dependent on the obedience of the people, Solomon recognized that it was also true that their obedience was dependent on His presence, as he said, "Let Him not leave us, nor forsake us; that He may incline our hearts unto Him."

Following the blessing came the offerings. At the close of the ceremonies the joyful people returned to their tents. It was the most perfect moment of national realization in the land. The Temple was erected, and the presence of God visibly manifested.

I KINGS 9

Jehovah now appeared to Solomon for the second time, and declared that his prayer was heard and answered, but insisted that there were conditions for the people to fulfil. These conditions were clearly stated, and there were most solemn warnings of what would happen if they were broken.

As we read the story, we know the sad and terrible sequel. Notwithstanding all the divine faithfulness, the conditions were not kept either by king or people, and the penalty was the ultimate destruction of the Temple and the expulsion of the nation from its position and service.

How slow the human heart is to learn this lesson. It would seem to be a perpetual peril in the presence of which men fall, that of recognizing God's faithfulness and rejoicing in it, while yet being unfaithful, so that defeat and disaster are the inevitable issues.

The material magnificence of the kingdom is set forth in the remainder of the chapter. Solomon's present of cities to Hiram, his multiplication of cities throughout his own kingdom, and his creation of a commercial navy, are all chronicled. The elements of failure are to be traced throughout. Hiram was dissatisfied with the cities presented to him. The cities the king built became hotbeds of evil, and the ships introduced to the land things that had evil effect.

I KINGS 10

The Queen of Sheba's visit to Solomon shows how far his fame was spread abroad. Moreover, reports had coupled Solomon's wisdom and greatness with the name of Jehovah. The Queen of Sheba saw what the government of God really meant.

Arriving as she did at the time of the nation's peace and prosperity, she was constrained to speak of Solomon's greatness as exceeding all reports of the prosperity of his kingdom and the happiness of his subjects.

But through all this she clearly saw that everything was due to the overruling of God. This she expressed in words which revealed the clearness with which this truth had been manifest to her. "Blessed be the Lord thy God, which delighted in thee, to set thee on the throne of Israel; because the Lord loved Israel for ever, therefore made He thee king, to do judgment and justice."

Then follows the story of Solomon's wealth, and, considering the times, it is an amazing amount. The story cannot be read, however, without a consciousness that the weaker, if not the baser, side of the king's nature is manifest in the abounding luxury with which he surrounded himself. Display seems to have meant more to him than government. Indeed, one is inclined to feel that as in the case of the de Medici in Florence long after, the subjugation of the people by the throne was maintained by this very lavishness of display. Alas for any people where this is the case.

I KINGS 11

At this point the story of Solomon suddenly changes. The glory passes away, and we observe his rapid degeneracy and doom. The nature of the man had ever a strong animal side. His commercial enterprises led him into contact with surrounding peoples, and he allowed his heart to go after "strange women." The wrong thus begun invaded higher realms. He built temples for these women. There followed the demoralization both of the king and his people, until at last it was written, "The Lord was angry with Solomon." The doom pronounced on him was the inevitable issue of his own folly and sin. The kingdom was to be rent, and pass from him.

The judgment of God begins to operate. "The Lord raised up an adversary unto Solomon, Hadad the Edomite" (verse 14); "God raised up another adversary unto him, Rezon, the son of Eliada" (verse 23); "And Jeroboam . . . he also lifted up his hand against the king" (verse 26).

In all this we have a remarkable illustration of how the judgments of God proceed. Man is never punished for sin but that in the midst of the punishment he may say, "This is the stroke of Jehovah, but it is my own deed and act." The story of the life of Solomon ends with the announcement, "Solomon slept with his fathers, and was buried in the city of David his father." So ends in gloom and failure a life full of promise, and that because the heart of the man turned from its loyalty to God in response to the seductions of his own sinful nature.

I KINGS 12

In this and the four following chapters we have the central section of this Book recording the tragedy of the break-up of the nation and the degradation of the people. It covers a period of about sixty years, from the disruption after the death of Solomon to the corruption of Ahab's reign and the coming of Elijah.

The seed of strife had long been growing, as we have seen. The occasion of the actual division arose on the human side, with Rehoboam's accession and Jeroboam's return to the country. These two men were utterly unworthy, as the folly of the first and the sin of the latter, make manifest. Rehoboam was proud and despotic. His asking for advice was a farce. A man with a prejudice is sure to follow advice which ministers thereto. This despotism led to Jeroboam's protest, and so ultimately to the rending of the kingdom. The sin of Jeroboam which cursed the whole later history of the people was due to his fear and expressed itself in a professed desire to make worship easy for them by establishing a new center.

The matter of chief interest in the story is the vision granted of God sitting high enthroned above human failure, making even the wrath of men to praise Him as He guided the sinning people toward the realization of His own purposes.

I KINGS 13

In this chapter are two lessons of supreme value; first, the patient grace of God, and, second, the solemn responsibility of such as bear His message.

The first of these is brought out in the story of Jeroboam. While he stood at the altar which his sin had erected he was rebuked and smitten. This was really his opportunity for repentance. His heart, however, was set on sin, and therefore he manifested no genuine repentance, but only a selfish desire for healing. Thus the opportunity for repentance became the occasion of the outworking of his own evil determination.

In his dealings with men, God ever leads them to circumstances through which they may either return to Him or by their continuance in sin make more certain their own ultimate doom.

The second lesson is the deception and death of the prophet who had been sent to deliver the Lord's message. While there can be no excuse for the man who lied to him in order to draw him aside, that fact does not for one moment change his responsibility. No direct command of God must be disregarded by His messengers, even if it be true that an angel suggest the change of method. A divine purpose directly communicated must never be set aside by any supposed intermediation of any kind.

I KINGS 14

In the story now recorded God is seen acting in judgment. The sickness of the son of Jeroboam was the first stroke of punishment and in connection therewith the prophet Ahijah uttered the doom of the man who had so grievously sinned.

In the name of God he reminded him through his wife, that his exaltation to power had been by the act of God, and declared that, because of his sin he and all his were to be swept away.

In the meantime, the southern kingdom of Judah was also sinning. Thus so quickly after David the nation was steeped in idolatry, and utterly failed to bear to the surrounding nations testimony to the purity of the divine government, although such testimony constituted the very purpose for which the nation had been created.

To fail to fulfil God's purpose is ever worse than to be merely useless. Peoples unrepentant because of the failure of the chosen become a scourge in the hand of God. This is seen in the invasion and spoliation of Judah by Shishak. The great principle uttered long after by Christ is seen here in its working. Salt which loses its savor is flung out, to be trodden under foot of men, whose corruption it ought to have prevented.

I KINGS 15

In this chapter we have the continuation of a sad story in the kingdoms of Judah and Israel. Under the reign of Abijam the process of deterioration went rapidly forward. He walked in the sins of his father, thus abusing the position he occupied. The corruption was not universal, for God maintained a lamp in the midst of His people, that is to say, there was still a remnant loyal to the divine Covenant which partially checked the development of evil. There was a break in this downward process connected with the accession and long reign of Asa. We are told that his heart was perfect as was that of David, that is to say, that his purpose was good; and, indeed, during his reign certain reforms were carried out. These, however, were by no means complete, for the high places were not removed. Nevertheless, this partial reform under Asa preserved Judah for a time from the spread of the corruption and downfall which occurred in the case of Israel.

Returning to the history of the northern kingdom of Israel, we find a terrible story of corruption, in which the government of God is manifested proceeding in a series of judgments against the continued sin which characterized the reigns of successive kings. Nadab, the son of Jeroboam, reigned for two years, and his influence was wholly evil. He was slain by Baasha, who succeeded him. Baasha carried out the judgment of God on the house of Jeroboam in destroying all his sons, but, nevertheless, himself continued for four and twenty years in the same courses of evil.

I KINGS 16

Here we have the account of how Jehu was called on to exercise judgment against Baasha. This being accomplished, Elah succeeded Baasha on the throne of Israel. He was so corrupt as to be found "drinking himself drunk," and was slain by Zimri, who thus came to the throne. He carried out the judgment of God on the house of Baasha, and after four years of civil war died by his own hand.

All this is indeed appalling. The throne of the chosen people was occupied by men of depraved character who came into power by conspiracy and murder. All the while the wheels of the divine justice ground surely forward, so that murderer was slain by murderer.

After the death of Zimri, there was division in Israel, half the people following Tibni and half gathering to Omri. The victory was with Omri, who for six years continued in courses of evil, and was succeeded by Ahab. The record declares of him, "He was evil above all that were before him." He united Jezebel with himself on the actual throne of power. This alliance was contradictory to the law of God, and she became a veritable scourge to the people. Under their joint reign Israel sank almost to the level of surrounding nations. Its testimony was practically destroyed. There was hardly a ray of light, for although, as subsequent declarations reveal, a remnant still existed loyal to God, its testimony was overwhelmed by abounding wickedness.

I KINGS 17

Here began a new order, the prophetic. Of course there had been prophets before, but with the coming of Elijah the office was elevated to national importance. From this point onwards, in the economy of the divine government, the prophet is superior to the king. Presently we shall find kings whose hearts were set upon reform, but even their work will be due to the inspiration of some prophet of God through whom His will is made known to men.

The sudden appearance of Elijah was startling and dramatic. To this day there are doubts as to his nationality and parentage. In the midst of the prevailing darkness, he flamed like a lightning flash upon history. His first words declared his authority. He affirmed that Jehovah, the God of Israel, lived, and announced that in the message he was about to deliver he was speaking for the enthroned Jehovah. The divine action in sending Elijah, and in the method adopted with regard to him, is very remarkable. All earthly authority and protection were swept aside as being unnecessary. In simplest ways God protected His messenger by the brook and at Zarephath. His first appearance was to pronounce judgment. The nation had become wholly materialized, and the first stroke fell on material things. The heavens were to give no rain. The judgment thus announced fell immediately, while the prophet passed out of sight of court and people to the divine care, which was simple and perfect.

I KINGS 18

In this chapter we have perhaps one of the most familiar stories of the Old Testament. There are, however, certain points of interest especially to be noted. The first is Ahab's connection with Obadiah. As to the loyalty of Obadiah there can be no question, and it is passing strange that this man should be found, chosen, and kept by Ahab at his side. Does it reveal an underlying conviction concerning the true relation of Jehovah to His people? If so, it is all the sadder as showing how a man may be degraded until he uses truth simply to serve his own ends.

The meeting of Ahab and Elijah, and their first words to each other suggest a truth of perpetual value. The troubler of a nation is never one who in loyalty to righteousness proceeds against sin, even though he be an outsider. It is rather he through whose corruption a nation becomes corrupt, who troubles the nation notwithstanding that he is king.

The story of the trial by fire is full of majesty, and needs no comment. Throughout, the lonely figure of Elijah is the center of interest as with calm dignity he stands against the combined evils of corrupt court and priesthood. His vindication by the answering fire of God was complete.

I KINGS 19

The slaughter of the prophets of Baal aroused the ire of Jezebel to such a degree that she sent a direct message full of fury to Elijah. There is no escaping the sadness of his attitude on receiving this threat. The man who had stood erect in the presence of tremendous odds now fled for his life. Full of great beauty is the story of God's method with His overwrought and fearful servant. He first ministered to Elijah's physical need, and then patiently listened to the complaint of his troubled heart, answering that by a revelation of Himself to the prophet. It was a new revelation. Elijah was a man of fire and thunder, and we can quite understand how strange it must have been to him to find that God was in "the sound of gentle stillness."

God ever reveals Himself to men according to their need. To rouse His prophet He is the God of thunder and flame. To comfort his bruised heart He is the God of the still small voice. Nevertheless, Elijah was rebuked for his want of faith, and told that God had reserved seven thousand who had not bowed the knee to Baal. He was then commanded to a strange new work, to anoint Hazael to be king of Syria, Jehu to be king of Israel, and Elisha to succeed himself.

Did he ever fulfil these commissions? We have no record of his having done so. The nearest approach was casting his mantle on Elisha. Perhaps the oft debated question cannot be definitely decided, but it is evident that from this time of faith's failure he was largely set aside. Only once or twice again does he appear.

I KINGS 20

Here begins the actual movement in the downfall of Ahab. Ben-hadad, drunken, profligate, despotic, came in the pride of arms against Samaria. By the voices of prophets Jehovah spoke to Ahab, who, acting under their direction, gained complete victory over his enemies.

Then followed his failure in the very moment of triumph. He made a covenant with the man whom God had devoted to destruction. Pity which produces disobedience to the divine command is sin. In consequence of his disobedience his own doom was uttered, and we are told the king returned heavy and displeased, which we may express as sad and angry. The only way in which any man is able to take advantage of opportunities for repentance offered in the circumstances of his life is by return in heart and soul to loyalty to God. This return Ahab never made.

I KINGS 21

This is a story in the private life of Ahab. Next to his own broad and rich possessions was a vineyard, the inheritance of a man who by comparison with Ahab was poor. Naboth, loyal to the law of God, and standing within his own personal rights, declined to part with his vineyard. Once more we read that the king was sad and angry. But again his heart was not right with God, and consequently he lacked the one sufficient inspiration of rectitude in conduct toward his brother.

His brooding sadness arrested the attention of Jezebel, and he left himself in her hands. The result was the dastardly crime of Naboth's murder.

Then we see Ahab in Naboth's vineyard, apparently in possession. Men, however, do not so easily possess the things they obtain by unrighteous methods. Right there in the coveted garden, with startling abruptness, the rough prophet of Horeb, Elijah, stood before Ahab. One can imagine the mixture of terror and passion in the voice of Ahab as he cried, "Hast thou found me, O mine enemy?" Here again Elijah rose to the dignity of the true prophetic office as in words that must have scorched the inner soul of Ahab he pronounced the doom for his terrible wrongdoing. Filled with fear, Ahab assumed the external attitude of penitence, which in all likelihood was as selfish as was his sin. Yet even this was enough to stay the hand of judgment for the moment. God never smites while the faintest chance remains.

I KINGS 22

The final movement in the downfall of Ahab is here chronicled. Jehoshaphat visited Ahab, who suggested the alliance against the king of Syria. Jehoshaphat suggested an appeal to Jehovah. Ahab produced certain prophets of his own. Jehoshaphat sought a true prophet of the Lord and found Micaiah, who predicted the king's defeat. Evidently in the heart of Ahab there was a suspicion that, much as he hated him, Micaiah was right. By a mean and cowardly act he put Jehoshaphat in the conspicuous place of the battle. An arrow, however, shot at a venture, found its true mark, and Ahab was slain. Thus ended the personal career of the worst man who ever occupied the throne of the chosen people.

The last verses of this book are not in strict chronological order, for the story of Jehoshaphat is resumed in the next book. They serve, however, to give us a general view of Judah and Israel. Jehoshaphat reigned over the former. In all the main set of his government he followed in the footsteps of his father Asa, doing that which was right in the sight of the

Lord. But, like his father, he failed in the completeness of his reform by allowing the high places to remain.

Following Ahab in Israel came Ahaziah, who continued in all the evil ways of his father and mother. He was by no means as strong a man as Ahab, but gave himself wholly to the most abominable idolatry by serving and worshiping Baal.

II Kings

II KINGS 1

The history of the second Book of Kings is a continuation of that contained in the first Book. There everything ended with the dark days immediately following the death of Ahab and the passing into comparative obscurity of Elijah. This book centers first around Elisha.

The condition of things is evident from the opening statement of this chapter. Israel was at war with Moab. Ahaziah, the son of Alah, was on the throne; he was an evil man, and unable to govern because of sickness. He sought counsel from Baal-zebub, the god of Ekron. Elijah, who had been in seclusion, suddenly appeared, protesting against this action of the king. Twice Ahaziah attempted to capture him, and in each case the answer of God on behalf of His servant was a swift judgment of fire. At last Elijah went to the king and pronounced a sentence on him that was immediately carried out.

Thus, while we see the terrible degradation of the nation, we also observe how the testimony of truth was kept alive, and how over the ruin of His people through apostasy God was still governing and moving carrying out His own purpose.

To all such as are in any way called into fellowship with God in service how great a vision this is. There is nothing more calculated to keep the heart firm and steady than this truth perpetually taught through Old Testament history, that God abides, and retains in His own hand the reins of government.

II KINGS 2

There is something pathetic and even weird in these final movement's of Elijah, as we see him accompanied by Elisha, and watched by the prophets. It would seem as though he tried to escape into loneliness for his translation, which he knew was at hand. The man upon whom his mantle had already been cast followed him loyally, determined to stand by him. When presently the chariots and horses of fire conveyed Elijah out of earthly sight the cry of Elisha, "My father, my father, the chariots of Israel and the horsemen thereof!" in all probability borrowed its symbolism from the vision, yet had reference, not to the chariots on which he had looked, but to Elijah. In the vision of Elisha the strength of Israel had lain in the presence of the prophet of God, not in her military equipment, but in the message of truth delivered by the rough yet loyal soul who had now been removed from sight. It was a wail from Elisha's heart, expressing his sense of loss to the nation.

He at once commenced his own ministry, and two incidents are recorded: one beneficent, the healing of the waters; and the other punitive, the destruction of the children. The last is misinterpreted if looked upon as an act of personal vengeance. It was rather an evidence of the sacredness of his office, and of the sin of refusing this method of divine manifestation.

II KINGS 3

At this point the history goes back and describes the beginning of the war with Moab, to which reference was made at the opening of the book. It was a combined movement of Israel and Judah and Edom against Moab.

Elisha's capacity for sternness was manifested in the refusal to deal with the king of Israel. The armies lacked water, and appealed to him. His answer immediately called into prominence the fact of the divine government, that God is still able, in supernatural ways, to make provision for the needs of His people if they will but trust Him. Their faith was called into activity in digging the trenches. The coming of the water was by the act and will of God. Thus the prophet stood for the righteousness of God in his refusal to deal with the king of Israel, and for the beneficent purpose of God in providing water for the armies. He thus stood before them as a veritable prophet, and called them back, if they would but hear it, into true relationship to their one King, Jehovah.

II KINGS 4

The ministry of Elisha stands in many respects in vivid contrast with that of Elijah. There is a gentleness about it which inevitably reminds us of that of the Messiah Himself in His day. Instead of suddenly appearing at critical moments, with thunder and flame, he seems to have moved about among the people, doing good wherever he came. Indeed, the ministries of Elijah and Elisha seem in many ways to suggest the ministries of John the Baptist and Jesus.

In this chapter we have four instances of Elisha's method: his provision for the need of the widow, whose creditors were threatening her; his kindness to the Shunammite woman, who had shown him hospitality; at Gilgal his healing of the pottage; and his feeding of a hundred men with twenty loaves.

During all this time he was at the head of the prophetic schools, and journeying from place to place he became known everywhere as the messenger of God. The simplicity of his life is suggested in the provision which the Shunammite woman, wealthy though she was, made for his evident requirement. His appartment was a little chamber on the wall containing a bed, a table, a stool, and a candlestick. His dignity is manifest in the attitude of the people toward him, especially that of the Shunammite woman, who, in her converse with him, stood in the doorway, recognizing the sacredness of his office.

II KINGS 5

When Elijah had felt that he alone was left loyal to God he had been told of seven thousand who had not bowed the knee to Baal. One of these, or perchance the child of one, stands before us in this narrative in the person of the little maid who, carried captive, yet remembered the prophet of her own land and maintained her confidence in his ability to work wonders. Through her intervention the leper Naaman was sent by the king of Syria to the king of Israel, but the day of the king in Israel as in any sense representing Jehovah had passed away.

Elisha's attitude in this chapter was from beginning to end one of dignified loyalty to God. This is seen first in his message to the king, who was filled with fear at the coming of Naaman. It was manifest, moreover, in his command to the wealthy leper calling for his submission, and was finally evidenced in his absolute refusal to take any personal reward for what had been wrought by God.

To Elisha, Gehazi stands in direct contrast. Governed by selfish desire, he obtained advantage for himself, and then lied to his master. His punishment was swift. He who had sought and obtained the reward which Elisha had declined became himself a leper, white as snow.

II KINGS 6

The incident of the swimming of the iron axe head is interesting, but quite secondary. The chief value of the story lies in its revelation of the influence Elisha was exerting in the nation. The growth of the school of the prophets was most remarkable. It was necessary that they should enlarge their borders, as they had not room to dwell. Their relation to Elisha is clearly manifest.

In an hour of national peril he rose above the gentler works which were chiefly characteristic of his ministry. Revealing the plans of the Syrians, he saved his people from peril. The picture of the prophet shut up within the city in company with his servant is very fine, as it brings to light facts of which Elisha was conscious, but which were not seen ordinarily by men closely associated with him. When his servant cried out in despair at the situation of peril, Elisha prayed that his eyes might be opened; and there appeared to the trembling man that of which the prophet was perpetually conscious, the presence of the flaming hosts of God round about him.

It is in such consciousness as this that a man is strong. If he acts in co-operation with God he knows that

> Hell is nigh, but God is nigher,
> Circling us with hosts of fire.

The siege of Samaria by the Syrians brought about a state of famine which resulted in most fearful conditions. When a woman in her sore distress appealed to the king he became angry with Elisha. In all probability Josephus is right when he suggests that his anger was kindled because Elisha did nothing to relieve the situation.

II KINGS 7

Under these circumstances of famine and the anger of the king the calmness and strength of the prophet were again manifest. It is another revelation of how quiet and strong a man becomes who is in secret fellowship with God. Elisha knew that deliverance was coming, and foretold the end of the siege and the provision of ample food for the needy. All he said was intended to emphasize the importance of faith in God, and in this case we see how in loyalty to this desire he foretold mercy and yet the judgment which was to come on the men who mocked at the possibility of the things he announced.

The incident of the leprous men in this chapter is full of suggestiveness. Their wise decision to take what appeared to be but half a chance of life rather than perish, and their immediate decision to tell the good news and share the benefit which their venture of faith had introduced them to, were wholly excellent.

II KINGS 8

The influence of Elisha is incidentally seen in the converse of the king with Gehazi and the restoration of the lands of the Shunammite woman for the sake of the prophet.

Elisha visited Damascus, where occurred an incident full of remarkable interest. Benhadad had sent Hazael to ask if he would recover from his sickness. Elisha's reply was strange in the extreme. He declared the king would recover, but that he would die; that is to say, he affirmed that his death would not come by his sickness, but that it was imminent in another way. The prophet gazed long and fixedly into the eyes of Hazael. It would seem that he saw far more in the soul of the man than any other had seen, perhaps more than the man himself was conscious of. He gazed until Hazael was ashamed, and then the prophet broke into tears. He was conscious that he stood in the presence of a man who would be the instrument of terrible chastisement to Israel in days to come, and he told him all the story. This insight into a human soul again reminds us of the Messiah who came so long afterward. In all probability Hazael's protest was sincere, yet every word was fulfilled.

In the last part of the chapter we have the story of Judah's corruption. Joram walked in the ways of the house of Ahab, whose daughter Athaliah he married. Ahaziah was the son of the union.

II KINGS 9

The hour had come to carry out the sentence of God on the house of Ahab. The prophet sent one of the sons of the prophets to anoint Jehu. This Jehu, as his history reveals, was a fitting instrument for swift and relentless judgment. He was a furious driver, which was symbolic of his character. He halted at nothing, but swept like a whirlwind from point to point until the things he desired were accomplished. This is startlingly manifest in this chapter.

On the way, having been anointed directly to his work, he slew Joram with his own hands, and, quickly moving back, encompassed the death of Ahaziah, and then proceeded to where Jezebel was still living. Pronouncing upon her the very doom of God, he carried out in detail the sentence pronounced long ago.

It is indeed a terrible chapter in which the truth of the divine government is written no longer in the gentle words of patient mercy, but in flames of fire. At last the day of God's patience had passed, and the devouring sword fell on the chief persons in the household of Ahab, who had done so much to encompass the ruin of His ancient people.

II KINGS 10

Here begins the second section of the Book, that which deals with the rapid and fearful corruption of the whole nation. The story alternates between Israel and Judah, and both sections of the nation sink deeper and ever deeper into sin and decay. Jehu is still to the front as a veritable scourge of God. First he was occupied in the work of sweeping out Ahab's posterity, and it was done with terrific speed. He then turned himself against Baalism, and with a thoroughness that is nothing short of terrible he broke and destroyed it.

Yet the story of Jehu is one of personal failure. When proceeding against Baal worship, his words to Jehonadab, "Come with me, and see my zeal for Jehovah," are in themselves a revelation of a proud spirit. While he was an instrument in the hand of God, nevertheless, strange as it may appear, he was in private life corrupt. "He departed not from the sins of Jeroboam"; he "took no heed to walk in the law of Jehovah." How terrible a warning is the story of this man—that it is possible to be an instrument in the hand of God and yet never be in fellowship with Him.

II KINGS 11

The story now turns to Judah. When Jehu had slain Ahaziah, his mother Athaliah, the sister of Ahab and of his very nature, seized the throne by killing all the seed royal, and for six years swayed the scepter of her terrible power over the kingdom of Judah.

In this wholesale massacre Jehosheba, the daughter of Athaliah, saved Joash. The fact is stated as an incident. How much romance lies behind the six years during which this woman nursed and cared for the young life hidden in the Temple! He must have been but a year old when she fled there with him, for he was but seven when he came to the throne. Jehoiada, the priest, at last took careful measures to ensure the death of Athaliah and the crowning of Joash.

And still the same great truth of the divine overruling flames on the page. Selfish ambition and all evil passions are at work, but over all these God presides and moves still onward toward the consummation.

II KINGS 12

Coming to the throne at seven years of age, Jehoash reigned for forty years. All that was beneficent in his reign would seem to have been directly due to the influence of Jehoiada, the priest, for "he did that which was right in the eyes of the Lord all his days wherein Jehoiada the priest instructed him."

During this period the Temple was rebuilt. In order to do this, there was, first, the correction of official abuses; and then the institution of a voluntary system of giving. Yet the reform was not complete, for the high places were not taken away, and the people were still committing idolatry thereon.

The chapter ends with a threatened invasion by Hazael, and Jehoash, in craven cowardice, bought him off by giving him all the vessels and treasures of the house of God. Such a method of averting attack is always perilous, and transitory in its effect.

II KINGS 13

Under Jehoahaz the story of corruption ran on in Israel. It was the story of continuation of evil as moral, and its consequent continuation as punishment. Readiness of God to forgive is revealed in the parenthesis. A consciousness of the terrible condition of the people seems to have taken possession of the king, and he besought the Lord. In answer to his prayer a saviour was raised up. No particulars are here given. In all probability they are to be found in chapter fourteen.

Jehoahaz was succeeded by Jehoash, the chief event of whose reign was his visit to Elisha. The prophet was now sick and feeble. In the midst of his perplexities, Jehoash went to see him. It is interesting to notice that he addressed him with the selfsame words which Elisha had used of Elijah at the moment of his translation, "My father, my father, the chariots of Israel, and the horsemen thereof!" and here evidently with the same meaning. The king recognized that the true strength of the nation was not its military equipment, but its possession of such as interpreted the will of God. In his intercourse with Elisha the weakness of the king was manifest. While following the prophetic signs, he lacked that passion and consecration which were necessary to the full accomplishment of his purpose. There was no heart in his striking on the ground with the arrows, and the prophet foretold his limitation and ultimate failure.

II KINGS 14

Turning back to Judah, we find Amaziah on the throne. "He did that which was right in the sight of the Lord, yet. . . ." The constantly repeated story of limitation in loyalty is told again. Success attended his arms, but issued in the lifting up of his own heart, and his foolish challenge to Jehoash the king of Israel, whose answer was characterized by contempt for Amaziah and yet evidenced a desire for peace. To this the king of Judah would not yield, with the result that he was defeated, and seems to have been kept a prisoner until the death of Jehoash. He was succeeded by his son Azariah.

In Israel, Jeroboam II occupied the throne. In his life, he also was evil before God. A man of war, he brought about the restoration of some lost territory, restoring the boundary line. This was accomplished under the influence of Jonah, the son of Amittai, who, without doubt, was the one sent to Ninevah. In the Book which bears his name we have only the account of that mission. It is evident, however, that he also exercised a ministry among his own people.

Jeroboam's victories were directly due to God's vision of the affliction of His people. His final doom was not yet pronounced, and in all likelihood Jeroboam was the saviour promised to Jehoahaz, who, for a while, restored a measure of liberty to the nation.

II KINGS 15

The throne of Judah was occupied by Azariah, the Uzziah of Isaiah. In the main, his reign was characterized by obedience to the divine will, yet the people continued in sin, and the king was smitten with leprosy.

Going back to Israel, we find Zechariah succeeded Jeroboam. His life and reign were characterized by sin. Now begins a period the most terrible, in some respects, of all Israel's history. To the throne of Israel man succeeded man by way of murder. Zechariah was slain by Shallum, who thus became king. Shallum, after one month's occupancy of the throne, was slain by Menahem, who, in turn, reigned evilly for ten years.

During this period the Assyrians invaded the land under Pul. Menahem bought them off, and thus became a vassal of Assyria. He was at last succeeded by Pekahiah, his son, who, after reigning for two years in persistent evil, was slain by Pekah. Pekah occupied the throne for twenty years, during which the Assyrians under Tiglathpileser invaded the land, and carried away a section of the people into captivity. At last he was slain by Hoshea.

Can anything be more terrible than this story? What a commentary it is on that first clamor for a king, in which, as Samuel had warned the people, they had rejected God from the place of immediate government. Israel was now practically under a military despotism, downtrodden and oppressed, and yet sinning with high hand against God. The whole situation was terrible in the extreme.

The state of affairs was very little better in Judah than in Israel. Jotham followed Azariah on the throne. Generally, his reign was right, but still evil was permitted in the kingdom. During this time Syria and Israel, under Rezin and Pekah, respectively, made war on Judah. Jotham was followed by Ahaz.

II KINGS 16

Perhaps the sin of Judah had its most awful expression during the reign of Ahaz. The king first sought help from the Assyrians under Tiglathpileser in his time of difficulty, and this was by deliberately placing his neck under the yoke when he said, "I am thy servant and thy son."

This was followed by the awful blasphemy of setting up a heathen altar in the actual courts of the Temple of God. It would seem as though the light of truth were absolutely extinguished. It was not so, however, for it is likely that throughout the whole reigns of Jotham and Ahaz, Isaiah was uttering his message, and that during the reign of Ahaz Micah also was delivering the word of God. So far as the nation or its kings were concerned, the testimony of truth was indeed lost, and the very name of God was being blasphemed among the heathen.

II KINGS 17

While Ahaz occupied the throne of Judah, Hoshea, by the murder of Pekah, succeeded to the throne of Israel. His reign, too, was evil, although he did not descend to the depths of some of those who had preceded him. He was the last of the kings of Israel.

The stroke of the divine judgment, long hanging over the guilty people, fell at last, and Shalmaneser came up against Israel, first making the people tributary, and after three years carrying them away captive.

In this chapter the historian is at great pains to declare why they were thus carried away. The charge is explicitly stated in verses seven to twelve. Disobedience to Jehovah, conformity to the nations from which they had been separated, secret practice of abominations, and eventually public idolatry—these were the sins which finally brought down the stroke of national destruction. These evils they did, moreover, in spite of God's patience and warning. "The Lord testified unto Israel, and unto Judah, by the hand of every prophet, and of every seer." These messages they would not hear. They rejected His statutes, they forsook His commandments, they practiced all the abominations of the heathen. Therefore, "the Lord was very angry," and cast them out. Their sin was first against law, but finally it was against patient love.

In this chapter also we have a remarkable passage having no direct connection with the history which is being traced. It is the story of an attempt made by the king of Assyria to colonize Samaria, from which he had taken captive the children of Israel. It is not easy for any people to take possession of what a divinely appointed nation failed to possess. As the colonists set up their own evil worship, divine judgment fell on them. They endeavored to accommodate their practices to what they conceived to be the manner of the God of the land. It is of these people that the remarkable words were written, "They feared the Lord, and served their own gods." The result necessarily was the degradation of the land and the people.

A most solemn and heart-searching lesson is taught by this paragraph. If God's witnesses fail, the issue is worse than previous conditions. The dreadful mixture of heathen practice and abomination with an attempt to make use of divinely revealed religion produces a corruption more fearful than anything else. Instances of the working of this principle in the history of the Christian Church have not been wanting.

II KINGS 18

We now begin the third section of this Book, which includes the story of the reigns of Hezekiah and Josiah, with a period of reaction and sin between the two. It is remarkable that such a man as Hezekiah could be the son of Ahaz. Yet we must remember that all his life he was under the influence of

Isaiah. Coming to the throne, he personally did right in the sight of the Lord, and immediately instituted reforms more widespread and drastic than had been attempted by any of his predecessors.

One illustration is given of how these reforms operated. So low had the people sunk that the serpent of brass, which Moses had made long before in the wilderness, and which had been carefully preserved, had positively been made an object of worship. Hezekiah called it by its right name, Nehushtan, a piece of brass, and broke it in pieces.

It was in the sixth year of his reign that Israel was carried away into captivity. This in itself, we can readily understand, would have an influence on Judah for a time at least, as there is hardly any doubt that the prophets would carefully point out the real reason of this judgment on the aforesaid tribes.

When Hezekiah had occupied the throne for fourteen years, a most formidable foe appeared in the person of Sennacherib, in the presence of whom Hezekiah manifested a weakness unworthy of him and of the God who had so wonderfully sustained him in his internal reforms. The arrogance of the Assyrian was indeed terrible. By Rab-shakeh he did far more than challenge Hezekiah. He deliberately, and with every evidence of contempt, challenged the God in whom the nation had professed to put its trust. It was impossible that such a challenge should go unanswered. And yet is not Sennacherib the supreme illustration of the fact that the infidelity of the chosen people caused the blasphemy of the heathen? Can we do other than believe that the weakness and failure, to say nothing of the sin of the ancient people, created in the mind of the Assyrians unbelief in the God whom the chosen people professed to believe? Judging the matter wholly by what the chosen people had come to be, one is not surprised at the blasphemy of Sennacherib.

II KINGS 19

In the presence of the undoubted peril, Hezekiah in penitence turned to his old and trusted friend, the prophet Isaiah, and charged him to pray for that remnant of God's people which still remained. He thereupon uttered a prophecy concerning the deliverance which was to come, and thus revealed the fine scorn of a man who lived in communion with God for all such empty boasting as that of Sennacherib. God has need of a very small thing to work His will. Said Isaiah, "He shall hear a rumour." As a matter of fact, this was what actually happened, and because of the rumor Sennacherib withdrew. The very next verse declares it. When Rab-shakeh returned, he found that Sennacherib had heard certain things, which had diverted his attention from Israel to other quarters.

Nevertheless, he returned to the charge, and a letter was sent to Hezekiah. This he spread before the Lord in prayer. Isaiah's answer to Hezekiah, on the warrant of God, was lofty in thought and word. He declared that the chosen people laughed at the challenge of the blasphemer. Moreover, he claimed that the victories of which Sennacherib had boasted were the acts of God against whom he was now setting himself. Said Jehovah, "I know thy sitting down, and thy going out and thy coming in, and thy raging against Me." He declared that judgment was to fall upon the Assyrians, and that God's own people were to be delivered. Following the utterance, the swift judgment of God passed over the army; the great Sennacherib escaped to Nineveh only to be slain in the house of his god.

II KINGS 20

In this chapter we have the account of the last days of Hezekiah. From a severe sickness he was delivered in answer to prayer and by the intervention of the prophet. He again manifested weakness during the Babylonians' visit, by showing them all the treasures of his house. For this he was rebuked by Isaiah, who prophesied that the things they had seen the visitors would ultimately bear away.

At the close of the chapter we have a brief incidental glimpse of the home administration of the king, but we are referred to the Book of Chronicles for particulars. This reign is in very many respects most remarkable, coming as it did in the midst of days so full of darkness, and so terribly characterized by corruption. Everything seemed to be against Hezekiah, and yet perhaps in his loyalty we may see the protesting reaction of the son from a father which does sometimes manifest itself in the life of a man brought under such influence as that of Isaiah. At least, the story reveals how much one man, seriously loyal to truth, may accomplish in the midst of the most adverse and difficult circumstances.

II KINGS 21

Here we have the story of reaction. It manifested itself in two reigns, both utterly evil, Manasseh's, lasting fifty-five years, and Amon's, lasting two years.

The story of Manasseh's sin was not merely of personal wrongdoing, but also of the deliberate undoing of what his father had been at such pains to accomplish. What we have hinted at more than once as issuing from such failure as that of the chosen people is here declared in so many words. Manasseh seduced them to do evil more than did the nations whom the Lord destroyed before the children of Israel. Nothing can be clearer as a warrant for the absolute righteousness of the judgment that fell upon them when they were driven out.

After Manasseh, Amon became king. Some of his servants conspired against him, and slew him. But so utterly depraved had become the people of the land, and so completely were they in sympathy with the evil ways of these evil kings, that they slew the man who had slain Amon.

II KINGS 22

With Josiah's accession came the last attempt at reformation before Judah was finally swept into captivity. Josiah's first act of reformation was to restore the Temple. All that followed grew out of that.

In connection with it came the discovery of the book of the Law. The condition of affairs in Judah may be gathered from this discovery. The nation had become utterly corrupt during the fifty-seven years covering the reigns of Manasseh and Amon. The Temple was neglected and deserted, and it would seem as though neither king nor priest knew of the whereabouts of this book. No doubt they were aware of its existence, but so far had the people grown from recognition of, and response to, the divine government, that the sacred writings had been neglected and the actual Temple copy lost.

The effect of the book on the king revealed his ignorance of its content. Therein he found how far the nation had wandered from the divine ideal, and how terrible were the curses pronounced on them for their wandering. Having a conscience quick and sensitive, he at once realized both the danger threatening them and its cause, and turned for counsel to the prophetess Huldah. Speaking on divine authority, she recognized the sincerity of the king and the corruption of the people; and declared, in effect, that the reformation to follow would be unreal so far as the people were concerned, but that because of Josiah's loyalty to Jehovah he would be gathered in peace to his fathers before the final blow should fall.

II KINGS 23

In this chapter we have a graphic account of the reformation following the discovery of the book of the Law. It was carried out by the splendid enthusiasm and energy of Josiah, and it is interesting to note its process. First came the public reading of the book of the Law. This was followed by a covenant into which all entered to restore the lost order. Immediately succeeding, the work went forward, and a simple reading of the story shows how thoroughly, so far as the king was concerned, the work was done. The Temple was cleansed of all the vessels of false religions, and also of the priests. From one end of the country to the other, the idolatrous idols and altars were swept away.

Following this drastic cleansing of the land, the Passover feast, long neglected, was observed with all its ancient glory. As we have said, as far as Josiah was concerned, this whole procedure was the outcome of sincerity and loyalty. The people, however, were simply following the lead of the king, not under any sense of penitence or return to Jehovah. Therefore God did not turn from His necessary judgment. Josiah had done all he was able to do, and in fulfilment of the prophecy of Huldah was gathered to rest before the final stroke fell. Thus, with fine discrimination God moves forward, delivering the godly from the midst of judgment as it falls upon the godless.

And now, in rapid succession, the judgments fell. Jehoahaz succeeded to the throne, and notwithstanding all that had been done during the reign of Josiah, returned immediately to evil ways in his brief reign of three months. The king of Egypt deposed him, and set Jehoiakim on the throne. However, he reigned only as tributary to Pharaoh. The lesson of righteousness was not learned, and for eleven years this man, no longer king but only the vassal of Egypt, continued his evil way.

II KINGS 24

Jehoiakim became tributary to Babylon under Nebuchadnezzar. The continuity of evil made impossible any respite, and it is solemnly written, "The Lord would not pardon."

In this connection the sins of Jehoiakim are attributed to Manasseh, that is to say that it was during the fifty-five years of Manasseh's reign that the fate of the nation was sealed. His successors continued in his evil way, and that with no trace of repentance or reformation.

Finally, Jehoiachin, who had succeeded to Jehoiakim, was carried away by Nebuchadnezzar, with all the men of war, and rulers who were likely to rebel. In place of Jehoiachin, Nebuchadnezzar made Zedekiah his representative and vassal.

Zedekiah held this position eleven years, during which he continued his evil conduct. In process of time he rebelled against the king of Babylon.

II KINGS 25

The rebellion was easily quelled, and Zedekiah was captured and taken to Babylon. His fate is tragic and awful. With eyes put out, and bound in fetters, he was carried to the court of his conqueror as the type and symbol of the people who had rebelled against God and been broken in pieces. A poor remnant still remained in the land over whom Gedaliah was appointed governor for a brief period. After his murder, the remnant fled to Egypt, and thus the nation called to peculiar position of honor, became a people scattered and peeled, losing all their privileges because of their failure to fulfil responsibility.

On the human side the record ends in tragic and disastrous failure. To those whose eyes are fixed on the eternal Throne it is certain that the divine purpose must be accomplished. Into long years of servitude and suffering these people have passed, still to be watched over by their one and only King, and, according to the covenant of grace, by these very conditions are prepared for co-operation in the ultimate movements of the overruling God.

I Chronicles

I CHRONICLES 1

The two Books of Chronicles cover the period of history already studied in I and II Kings. They record this history, however, from an entirely different standpoint. The outlook is almost exclusively confined to Judah, the chronicler never referring to Israel save in cases of absolute necessity. Moreover, the history of the tribe of Judah is the history of the house of David, all other matters being referred to only as they affect, or are affected by, the Davidic line.

Moreover, the story of these two Books centers around the Temple. The chief matter in David's reign is his interest in preparing for it, while in Solomon's the chief interest is in the building thereof.

The whole period included in these genealogical tables is that from Adam to the restoration under Nehemiah. They are not exhaustive, but serve a clearly defined purpose in that they indicate the divine choice of channels in the accomplishment of the purposes of God. Side issues are traced in certain directions, but only as they touch on the divine progress. This is indicated very clearly in the opening verse. The only son of Adam mentioned is Seth. From him the line is traced through Enoch to Noah. At this point the genealogies of Japheth and Ham are given because of the relation of their descendants to the chosen people of God. The direct line of the divine movement is taken up through Shem, and finds a new departure in Abram. Again there is a digression from Abram in tracing the descent through Ishmael, and of that also through the sons of Keturah. The direct procession continues through Isaac. A third and somewhat elaborate excursion is made for the purpose of tracing the descendants of Esau, who came into such intimate relation to the procedure of God. Israel, however, is the son of Isaac through whom is carried forward the great program. A careful consideration of all this will show that the choice of God was ever based on character.

I CHRONICLES 2

Still the same method is manifest. The twelve sons of Israel are mentioned. All of them are subsequently referred to, with the exception of Dan and Zebulun, of whose descendants this chronicler gives no account. The direct line of interest in tracing the divine method passes through Judah. The process of exclusion still goes forward on the principles of character. Er, the firstborn, is slain because of his evil, and Achar likewise.

Some lines of descent excluded are again traced, and for the same reason as before, that of their relation to the history of the chosen people. From Judah the movement passes through Perez and Hezron to Ram, somewhat indirectly. Then directly through Jesse to David. In the case of Jesse another crisis and a new departure are observed. He had seven sons, but of them the youngest was chosen. David is the one through whom the royal line is to be preserved until it culminates in God's one and only King.

I CHRONICLES 3

The tables now continue to deal with Judah, but have special reference to David. The names of nineteen of his sons are given. Six of them were born in Hebron, and four were the sons of Bathshua. There were nine others. From these nineteen, one, Solomon, is selected; and the descent is traced through him, through the kings of Judah, and right on into the period of captivity.

The peculiar quality of the Book of Chronicles is very evidently marked in this chapter in that in the reference to Solomon and his three brothers no mention whatever is made of the sin of David. They are spoken simply of as the sons of Bathshua, who is, of course, Bathsheba. Indeed, nowhere in the books are any of the sins of David referred to, except the sin of numbering the people. If, as is perhaps likely, these books were written by Ezra, we can perfectly understand these omissions. In the return of the people to their land he was supremely conscious of the government of God and the unbroken continuity of His progress toward the fulfilment of purpose. From this standpoint it was not his business to speak of the sins of the chosen instruments; but, rather, simply to deal with the channels through which the divine procession moved.

I CHRONICLES 4

Here another line from Judah is traced, and must be viewed in the light of the royalty manifest in David. It is the story of the multiplication and settlement of the people who became workers in the great kingdom. Thus we have the descent of such as became workers in fine linen, of the potters, and also of the king's workmen.

Two verses of this section tell the story of one man, and of how he, by prayer and obedience, obtained the favor of God. Incidentally, the story is full of interest. In all likelihood, Jabez was a nephew of Caleb. For some reason his mother had given him this name, which means "bringeth sorrow." Perhaps his knowledge of the meaning of the name had cast a shadow over all his life. Dr. W. E. Barnes says, "The man with the ill-omened name staved off ill-fortune by his prayer." This would seem to be perfectly correct in the light of the fact that in his prayer he asked "that it be not to my sorrow!"

The chief beauty of the story is its revelation of God's interest in individuals. While through these genealogies, and indeed through all the history, we are occupied with those connected with government and the procession of events leading to universal issues, it is refreshing to be halted by the story of one man who took his need directly to God and obtained the answer of God's grace.

I CHRONICLES 5

The words principally attracting attention in this chapter are those connected with the name of Reuben. Here the ultimate light flames on the record:

"the Prince," toward whose advent everything moves, is named.

Yet He does not come through the line of birthright. The birthright was given to Joseph, while the Prince came through Judah. In this connection also the principle of divine selection flames out. The actual firstborn of the sons of Israel was Reuben, but he, through sin, forfeited the birthright, which, as we have seen, passed to Joseph.

In these occasional gleams of light on the progress of events, nothing is clearer than the revelation of the all-seeing God, whose selections are based on His own infinite justice. Such light is at once the occasion of joy and fear in the heart. Confidence is born of the certainty of the divine method. This very assurance must have the effect of solemnizing the heart as it makes clear that no supposed right obtains for one moment in the economy of God if its conditions be violated by the disobedience of men.

I CHRONICLES 6

In this whole chapter, consisting of eighty-one verses, the one subject is the priestly tribe. This in itself reveals the standard from which the history was written. Judah, the kingly tribe, is the only one which has more space devoted to it, occupying, as it does, one hundred and two verses. These, however, center in David.

In the section now under consideration, the sons of Levi, around whom the divisions of the tribe for service were made, are named—Gershon, Kohath, and Merari. Then there follows a list of the priests, which undoubtedly is intended to reveal the ground of Joshua's claim by succession. The list is not complete, for names are omitted here, to be found elsewhere in the Scripture records. The chain, however, is perfectly complete from Aaron to Jehozadak, the father of Jehoshua. After this list has been given, the genealogies return to the three sons of Levi already mentioned, and the subject proceeds in four movements. In the final one the genealogies of each of the sons of Levi culminate in the person of one man, Kohath in Heman, Gershon in Asaph, Merari in Ethan. These were men prominent in the reign of David.

Continuing to deal with the tribe of Levi, the chronicler first described the special work of Aaron and his sons. While the Levites generally had the charge of the whole house of God, the work of the high priests was specifically attendance at the altar of burnt-offering, at the altar of incense in the Holy Place, and in connection with the Day of Atonement. Following this, the chapter is occupied with an account of the arrangements made for the dwelling of the Levites. As we have seen in the consideration of earlier records, this distribution ensured the scattering of the priestly order throughout all the land.

I CHRONICLES 7

In this chapter we have the genealogies of six of the tribes, and again the bias of the chronicler is evident in his treatment. Those tribes more directly associated with Judah have fuller treatment than others. In referring to Issachar, Benjamin, and Asher, both genealogies and the number of fighting men are given. These numbers refer to the time of David, around whose reign all the interest of the Book centers. Of the sons of Issachar it is said that they were mighty men of valor, and among them were the chief men of the nation. Much the same is declared of the sons of Asher, that they were choice and mighty men of valor and chief among the princes. Naphtali is dismissed in a verse. Concerning Manasseh some few names are given and the possessions enumerated. The descendants of the three sons of Benjamin are declared to be mighty men of valor, while Ephraim is distinguished principally by the one name of Joshua, which appears in the course of the record.

I CHRONICLES 8

This whole chapter constitutes a fuller account of the house of Benjamin. It seems to be a collection of names and very little more. Among them, however, after the name of the founder, Benjamin, two stand out conspicuously, Saul and Jonathan. They are almost buried among the rest, and yet most probably constitute the reason of this comparatively large section devoted to the genealogy of the house of Benjamin.

As we have said more than once, the chief interest of the Book centers around David, and everything is made to lead up to him. The friendship of Benjamin for Judah was marked, and here are the two names which touch most intimately the early life of the king. Saul was his implacable foe, Jonathan his choicest friend. The love of the latter very largely compensated for the cruelty of the former.

I CHRONICLES 9

In this chapter the genealogies are completed, that is to say, they here reach the latest point in their history, and refer to the dwellers in Jerusalem after the return from captivity. They are lists of the heads of the families of Judah, Benjamin, the priests, and the Levites.

Immediately following these lists we have an account of the porters and their duties, together with those of the Levites and the priests. In the opening verses of the chapter we are told the reason for Judah being carried away into captivity, and all that follows tells the story of how, under the direction of "very able men for the service of the house of God" (verse 13), an attempt was made to restore the order and worship which had been lost in the captivity.

The chronicler is now about to proceed to the story of the central epoch in this whole history, namely the reign of David. He here repeats with greater detail the important genealogy of Saul as a prelude to the story of his death, which prepares the way for the accession and reign of David.

I CHRONICLES 10

Here in sublime and graphic language is recounted the story of the death of the king chosen by men. It is a terrible picture of a man of magnificent capability going down to utter ruin. Routed by his enemies, he died by his own hand in the midst of the field of defeat.

The reason for such failure is clearly declared. He trespassed against God, and then sought counsel of one who had a familiar spirit. Magnificent indeed was the ruin, but it was ruin. Saul was a man than whom no other had greater opportunities, but his failure was disastrous. Of good standing in the nation, distinctly called and commissioned by God, honored with the friendship of Samuel, surrounded by a band of men whose hearts God had touched, everything was in his favor. From the beginning he failed; step by step he declined in conduct and character, until he went out, dragging his nation into such confusion as threatened its very existence.

I CHRONICLES 11

We now enter on the second section of this Book. In this section there are four movements: the story of David's crowning, the events connected with the Ark of God, the account of David's reign, and, finally, matters concerning the building of the Temple.

The chronicler passes over in silence the story of the seven years in which David reigned over Judah. There may be two reasons for this. First, this is the history of the greatness of David, and begins therefore with his crowning over the whole nation; and, second, it was in connection with that crowning that his activity concerning the Ark and the Temple commenced.

In this chapter the story is first told in simple and yet dignified language of the crowning at Hebron. So far as the people were concerned, this was based on their recognition of the divine appointment. Then comes the account of the taking of Jebus, which became the city of David's heart and the metropolis of the nation.

The chronicle of the mighty men and their deeds is full of color. It is principally interesting in view of what these men were in the days of David's exile. They had gathered to him in the mountain fastnesses, a company of men graphically described as in debt, in danger, and discontented. How wonderfully he had influenced them is seen in their remarkable devotion to him, and still more surprisingly in the heroic character they had developed.

I CHRONICLES 12

Here the story is continued; it thrills with the enthusiasm of the multitudes as they marched under the standard of the new king. Over the list of names flashes light from certain outstanding statements concerning them. In verse two it declares that these men "could use both the right hand and the left." This speaks of the careful training they had received. A little later we have a poetic and remarkable description of the companies gathered around David (verse 8). They were "mighty men of valour . . . trained for war." This suggests disciplined strength. They were men who could use shield and spear, that is, who were able to act on both the defensive and the offensive. Their faces were like lions; they had become a kingly race. They were "as swift as the roes upon the mountains," which describes their perfect fitness. They were, moreover, men of differing capacities, all of which were consecrated to David. Among the sons of Issachar were men who had understanding of the times. Among the sons of Zebulun were men able in the art of war and incapable of treachery.

All these were united by common devotion. Thus the new king entered on his kingdom under the most auspicious circumstances.

I CHRONICLES 13

David's consciousness of the true strength of the kingdom is manifest in his anxiety concerning the Ark of God. This had been at Kirjathjearim, and neglected for long years. He now set himself to bring it into the midst of the people as a recognition of the nation's relationship to Jehovah.

In connection with this action a terrible event taught David a lesson of deep solemnity. If God's order is to be restored, it must be done in His way. The long neglect of the Ark would seem to have rendered these men unfamiliar with all the particular regulations for its removal, which they attempted by a device of their own. The swift death of the man who stretched out a hand to save the Ark was evidence at once of the presence of God among the people, and of the necessity for perfect conformity to His minutest instructions. David was at once angry and afraid. The whole movement was stayed, and the Ark was carried for shelter to the house of Obed-edom.

Most graphically does this story set forth a truth never to be lost sight of by the people of God, that zeal for Him must be according to knowledge. When divine arrangements are made for methods of worship and service, no circumstances must be allowed to be an excuse for a change in such methods.

I CHRONICLES 14

In this chapter a most interesting reference is made to the long commercial friendship with Hiram which commenced with David and was continued into the reign of Solomon. Here again the chronicler is silent concerning the sin of David. It is stated boldly that he took more wives at Jerusalem, and a list of his sons is given. Among these are the sons of Bathsheba. Two victories over the Philistines are described. In each case David took counsel of God whether he should go up to battle against them. In the first case he was told to do so, and victory resulted. It is stated in this connection, which we shall do well to ponder, that the defeated Philistines left their gods behind them. David at once recognized the peril of leaving them among the people, and they were destroyed by fire.

Again, before the second victory David took counsel of God, and was forbidden to go until there should be granted to him the supernatural indication of the sound of marching in the mulberry trees. This would have a twofold effect on the king, first, to keep him conscious of his dependence on God; and, second, to maintain his confidence by the evidence of the presence and activity of God.

I CHRONICLES 15

From this account of bringing the Ark from the house of Obed-edom into the city, it is evident that David had learned the lesson which the death of Uzzah was intended to teach. He declared that the work of carrying the Ark must be the Levites' only. After careful preparation of the Tent for its reception, which would almost certainly be according to the ancient pattern given to Moses, the ceremony of bearing it into its resting place was carried out.

The king's love of music is evident in this story. Companies of instrumentalists and singers were appointed; leaders accompanied the Ark, and with high jubilation it was borne by the priests into the prepared Tent. One shadow fell across the brightness of the day. It was the mockery of Michal, Saul's daughter, for her husband, David. The incident illustrates the perpetual inability of the earthly-minded to appreciate the gladness of the spiritual. The external manifestations of the joy of those who hold communion with God cannot convey to the unenlightened mind the real meaning of that spiritual delight. A meeting for prayer and praise is still held in contempt by those who have no personal knowledge of the peace and joy of the Secret Place of the Most High.

I CHRONICLES 16

The Ark was brought in with great rejoicing, and we have the psalm sung on the occasion. This great psalm of praise sung by the trained musicians is a compilation of parts of three found in the Book of Psalms, and its three movements are distinguished by the three quotations.

The first part consists of the first fifteen verses of Psalm 105. This is a general ascription of praise which merges into a call to remembrance of the works of God, and of His government covenant with the people. A slight change is made. In the psalm from which the quotation is made it is declared that God remembered His Covenant. In the form in which it was sung when the Ark was brought in men are called on to remember that Covenant.

The second movement (verses 23-33) is a quotation from Psalm 96, 1-13. In this the sacrifice of praise moves on to a higher level, and expresses itself in adoration of God for what He is in Himself in majesty.

The third division (verses 34-36) is a quotation of the opening and closing sentences of Psalm 106, verses 1, 47, and 48. Here again praise moves into a yet higher sphere, and consists of an expression of thankfulness to God for what He is in Himself in mercy.

These movements indicate a growth of experience, centering in the presence of the Ark among a people as the symbol of divine interest and nearness. First, it was that around which God led them and made His Covenant with them. Second, it became the assurance of the display of His power and glory under differing circumstances in their history. Finally, its restoration, after a period of neglect, was the sure token of His mercy.

I CHRONICLES 17

The presence of the Ark in the city seems to have created in David the desire to provide for it a permanent and more worthy resting place. He declared his desire to Nathan. The prophet, acting without divine consultation, charged him to go forward. It was a perfectly natural piece of advice, as on the surface the desire of David would necessarily appear to be absolutely commendable.

Both prophet and king, however, had to learn that God's ways are not man's ways. David was brought into the presence of Jehovah, and in the words to which he listened all that God had done for him was made to pass before his mind. The man who desired to build a house for God was reminded that God was building his house for him. The desire to do something for Jehovah was corrected by a vision of what Jehovah had done for him.

The response of David is full of beauty. He at once submitted to the teaching, and took his place as unworthy, and yet as worshiping. He poured out his heart in gratitude to God for all His goodness and His truth, and rested his soul in the promised blessing. It should be noticed at once that while David's desire was not granted, yet when he had thus been brought to the place of a resting worshiper, he was finally permitted to make great preparation for the building of the Temple by his son.

I CHRONICLES 18

With slight variations, this chapter is identical with II Samuel 8. It tells the story of David's victories over surrounding foes by which he made the boundaries of his kingdom secure, and put himself in position to increase his trading facilities. First, he dealt with the Philistines on the southwest, and then turned to the northeast, where he secured a position on the great river. The Edomites were defeated by Joab and Abishai, and so security and opportunity to trade were made certain.

In view of the desire of the king to build the Temple of God, this chapter is of special interest, as it shows how in all these wars David was amassing treasure with that end in view. The Moabites and the Syrians brought presents. Shields of gold and much brass were gathered from the cities and servants of Hadarezer. Vessels of gold and silver and brass were sent by Tou. All these things were dedicated to the Lord.

Thus through all the days of conflict, and notwithstanding the fact that he was not to be personally permitted to build, the desire to accomplish his purpose burned in his heart.

The story suggests to us the possibility of our helping very really the work of God to which, in some respects, we may not be permitted to put our hands. The passion of the heart may have been to go into the foreign field of service, and for some reason the way is blocked, evidently by God. The temptation is to think that therefore we are excluded from that work. Let us rather set ourselves to gather treasure for the work, and so keep the passion burning.

I CHRONICLES 19

David's attempt to deal kindly with the new king of Ammon was misrepresented and resented, and his messengers treated with indignity. The issue was their utter rout under Joab and Abishai, notwithstanding their confederacy with the Syrians.

The chapter ends with the account of the decisive victory of David over Zobah. The conflict would seem to have been thrice renewed. The first campaign resulted in David's capture of a position on the Euphrates (18: 3-8). The second victory was gained over them by Joab when they were the allies of Ammon. They gathered their forces for a final attempt after this defeat, and David overcame them, so that they made peace with him, and became his servants. Thus the consolidation of the kingdom went forward, while all the time the king was gathering treasure for building the Temple.

Victory is in itself a peril to any man. David's victories were the direct result of God's blessing on him. "The Lord gave victory to David whithersoever he went" (18:13). Yet in the midst of them he sinned his greatest sin, and that notwithstanding that in his deepest heart he desired the building of God's house. Constant watchfulness is the only guarantee of safety. Not even true desire and great blessing are sufficient if the heart be not personally watchful.

I CHRONICLES 20

Joab's conquest of the children of Ammon was complete. They were despoiled of their possessions and reduced to servitude. There is practically no doubt that this is the meaning of the story as it is written here. In the Revised Version, verse 3, if the italicized word "them" is omitted, this sense is at once apparent. The people were put to the menial work of cutting with saws, with harrows, and with axes. The last mention of David's wars by the chronicler occupies the latter half of this chapter. It tells of the defeat of the Philistines at Gezer.

There is a statement in the first verse which is full of significance. "But David tarried at Jerusalem." That is the only reference in this Book to the most awful sin and failure of David's career. Its insertion would have no meaning in the purpose of this Book, but we ought not to allow ourselves to forget the warning it affords. Nothing is more subtly dangerous to the man of faith than to remain inactive when the business of God demands that he be out on the field of conflict. How many have found the place of ease to be of deadliest peril when the enterprises of God were calling them to strenuous endeavor. It is a very old adage, and very simple, and we are inclined to smile at it, but it is well to remember, not only in childhood, but to the end of the pathway, that

> Satan finds some mischief still
> For idle hands to do.

If I ought to be at Rabbah with the army, and am not, some Bathsheba waits to work my ruin.

I CHRONICLES 21

The cause of David's action in numbering Israel is distinctly stated to be Satan. Therein lies a revelation of its nature. The one sin of Satan is that of pride and ambition, and this was the sin of David. His victories had resulted in the lifting up of his spirit, and in arrogance he would know the number of the people that he might make his boast therein. In this he persisted, notwithstanding the protest of Joab.

The chief interest of this chapter for us lies in the revelation of the true character of David. His sins were the lapses and accidents of his life.

This is not to condone them. It is, however, to emphasize that the habitual set of his life was far otherwise than these sins suggest, and the deepest truth concerning him is revealed, not by the failures, but by his action afterwards. He confessed his sin frankly; chose to fall into the hands of God rather than any other for punishment; mourned over the death of the people because of his conviction that the sin was his, and refused to offer on the altar anything that had cost him nothing.

These things reveal, in order, his sense of sin and knowledge of himself, his knowledge of God and confidence in God's tender mercies, his love of his people, and his profound sense of what was due to God in worship. He sinned surely, but, after all, he was a man after God's own heart, and this is never more clearly manifest than in these dark days when God dealt with him for his wrongdoing. By comparison with the men of his own time, and the other kings of the nation, he stands pre-eminent in real godliness.

I CHRONICLES 22

In the place where the mercy of God operated in staying the plague resulting from his sin, David chose to build the house of his God. The threshing floor of Ornan the Jebusite was chosen as the site of the Temple. The days were rapidly passing, and the end of David's life was not far off. During these latter days his underlying desire became the supreme matter. In perfect acquiescence with the will of God, he gave up all thought of building, and set himself to preparing everything for another hand to carry out. "So David prepared abundantly before his death." His charge to his son is very beautiful. He frankly told him how God had refused to permit him to build, and named the reason. He was careful to teach Solomon that his appointment to build was of God, and thereby created a solemn sense of responsibility in the matter. Out of personal experience both of failure and of realization, David told his son that the condition of success in the enterprises of God is observance of the statutes and judgments of the Lord. He expressed his conviction, moreover, that the house of God must be "exceeding magnificent, of fame and of glory throughout all countries."

This is a picture of a man who through stress and storm had found his way into the quiet calm assurance of his place in the divine economy. The heats and passions of earlier years were under perfect control, and burned to co-operation with the purpose of God, wholly within the limits of the divine will. It is a condition of peace and power.

I CHRONICLES 23

David's interest in building the Temple and establishing it as the center of worship and of the nation is not only manifest in the material preparation he made in amassing treasure, and carrying out preliminary work in getting the stones ready. He practically abdicated the throne to Solomon, that he might supervise arranging the order of worship. In this chapter the duties of the Levites are set out, and it is declared that this was among David's last acts (verse 27, margin).

The specific work of the Levites is beautifully described by the chronicler in the closing verses of the chapter. They were the servants of the priest and of the house. They were also to stand at morning and evening to praise the Lord. High and holy calling, this. The morning hour of praise expressive of confidence in God and gratitude to Him for all His grace and goodness. Then the busy hours of service, all in the power of that early praise. Finally, the hymn of adoration for the guidance and goodness of the day as the shadows of the evening fell.

It was a high national ideal, and the nation which realizes it will be great indeed. Israel sadly failed later in her history, but the purpose was noble. Never was the true kingliness of David more manifest than when in those last days and acts he sought to make arrangements to consolidate around the Throne of God the kingdom he was so soon to leave.

I CHRONICLES 24

With great care and perfect democracy of choice the courses of the priests were next set in order. There was a tactful mingling in the arrangement of the older and the younger men, so that in this highest and holiest national service the experience of age and the enthusiasm of youth were naturally inspiring.

A description of these men in this chapter is very suggestive. They are called "princes of the sanctuary and princes of God." In neither half of the description is there any thought of their exercising rule. They had no authority over the sanctuary; nor, of necessity, over God. Yet they were princes, and were to exericse authority.

This description indicates the source of their authority rather than its sphere of operation. Their government consisted in their obedience in the sanctuary to the will of God. This is always the only authority of priests. By obedience to all the service of God in the holy places and things, they are to make possible the people's approach to God in order that they (the people) may by direct contact render obedience to His soverign rule.

The true exercises of New Testament priesthood consists in this today. In proportion as we of the kingdom of priests exercise our holy service in perfect submission to the will of God in daily life we exercise the true authority among men of that mediation which attracts them to God, and makes possible their immediate dealing with Him.

I CHRONICLES 25

It is easy to imagine what joy the poet king would take in arranging the song service of the new Temple. Music played a very important part in his career. His musical skill had been his first introduction to Saul, and had put his life in peril in Saul's presence. Then the psalms attributed to him in our collection breathe out the spirit of the varied experiences through which he passed. The days of his simple life as a shepherd, the period of his exile and suffering, the hours of battle and weariness, the triumph of his crowning, the agony of his sin, the joy of pardon, these and many other experiences are reflected in the great collection.

The man of poetic nature would naturally take great delight in making such arrangements for that "magnificent" house of God as would ensure proper and skilful attention in its service of praise. Again, from among the trained the courses were so arranged as to ensure perfect use of all classes, "as well the small as the great, the teacher as the scholar."

This work of praise is thrice described by a somewhat singular, and, in this connection, arresting word, "prophecy." The use of this word here is a revelation of the true value of the service of music in the sanctuary of God. There is no doubt that it is used in its broadest sense of *forthtelling* rather than its more restricted sense of *foretelling*. Therefore, music is at once the medium of expressing praise to God, and telling forth that praise in the hearing of men for their instruction and blessing. This includes the whole sphere, and the two thoughts interact. That is true praise of God which instructs the hearers. That is true musical prophesying which sets forth the praise of God.

I CHRONICLES 26

In no particular did the arrangements of the king fall short. Not only Levites, priests, and singers were arranged for, but porters also, and such as had charge of all the stores set apart for the sacred work. These, moreover, were sons of the first of the nation, as well as of others less known; and the same principle of democratic selection is casting the lots—"as well the small as the great" took part.

It is interesting in this section to note, moreover, how long men had looked forward to building the Temple. In the statement that the dedicated treasure was in the care of Shelomoth, some is specified as set apart by Samuel, some by Saul, some by Abner, and some by Joab. In giving to Solomon the charge to build David had spoken of the treasure he had gathered and said, "Thou mayest add thereto." Now it appears that others before himself also had made contributions to the great whole.

These facts are suggestive and helpful. None of us can ever do a complete thing for God. All His works are too great. Nothing we touch is other than a piece of work begun and dropped ere the weary hands had completed their task. And, in turn, nothing we take up can we complete. But there are always others coming on who will continue the toil, for God's work must be done. Let us count it greatest honor to have touched the work at all, and be content to have put in one day's work thereon between morning and sunset.

I CHRONICLES 27

This chapter gives us an idea of the internal order of the kingdom under the government of David. The courses mentioned in the opening part of the chapter are not mentioned elsewhere in the Old Testament. They may have been the toilers who wrought in some specific work. Perhaps this refers to arrangement made for the labor necessary to build the Temple. Then the rulers of the tribes are named. Following this is a significant statement that in the numbering necessary to organization David was careful not to sin again. He had learned a lesson from experience. Next the rulers of departments are named, and, finally, a list of the chief men in David's household is given.

The chapter is a striking revelation of the fact that David's greatness as a king was not confined to his victories in war. He was no less great in peaceful administration. Tilling the soil, careful cultivation, raising cattle and all that pertained to the internal welfare of his people had his attention, and were arranged for under duly qualified and appointed oversight. There is no room for doubt that under the reign of David the Hebrew people realized their greatest strength, even if they did not reach the height of their magnificence. Truly a wonderful man was David. Fundamentally a man of God, he was also a warrior, a poet, an administrator. With his passing, the day of Hebrew greatness passed its meridian.

I CHRONICLES 28

Here begins the final charge of the greatest of the Hebrew kings to his son Solomon, and to the princes and captains and mighty men of the nation. He first made an impressive declaration of his recognition of the government of God in his own appointment to kingship, and that of his son. This, however, was but the background against which he made the declaration which was nearest his heart concerning the house of God. What evidently gave him unqualified satisfaction was that it was to be built. His rejection as builder and Solomon's appointment, were matters of minor importance.

Therein is seen the deepest stratum in his make-up, that which had compelled even his sins to his ultimate making. Out of this conviction came his charge to his son on the principles which were to govern him in the future. The charge was twofold, "Know God," and "Serve God." This was followed by a promise and a warning equally clear and forceful, "Seek Him, and He will be found of thee." "Forsake Him, He will cast thee off for ever." And again the Temple was uppermost in David's thinking, more important to his heart than the welfare of his son. "Take heed now; for the Lord hath chosen thee to build an house for the sanctuary; be strong and do it."

After the charge David solemnly gave to Solomon the pattern of the house in all its details, ending with the tender assurance that in his obedience Solomon would have the presence of God and the help of willing men. Solomon entered on his reign and work with the highest and best advantages.

I CHRONICLES 29

This is the account of the final stage in the greatest work of David's life, namely, his preparation for building the Temple. The king had a treasure of his own, over and above what he had gathered for the house of God. Because of his affection for the work of God, this treasure also he dedicated thereto. This is illuminative, showing the true method of giving. It is when "my affection" is set on the work of "my God" that "my treasure" is at His disposal. And yet, again, it is when such is the case that any appeal I make to others is likely to be productive of results. Heart-inspired generosity is the most contagious grace. Notice very carefully how this section ends. "Then the people rejoiced, for they had offered willingly, because with a perfect heart they offered willingly to the Lord." To have real delight in the work of God one must give to it. The real pleasure of a great work is consecrated co-operation.

The king now stood amidst his people and exercised a priestly function. He voiced his own and the people's joy in a psalm of great beauty. First, it ascribes all inherent excellencies to Jehovah, and recognizes His throne and Kingdom. Then it recognizes that all the riches and honor which men possess are from Him. Thus it acknowledges the fitness of their giving their best to Him, and at the same time confesses that their very gifts have first been received from Him. This thought is then elaborated in a confession of personal poverty and unworthiness, together with a great outpouring of gladness that of His gifts they had given to Him. The praise merges into a prayer that the state of mind in which they have given may be kept in their remembrance, and for Solomon that he may be kept with perfect heart to accomplish the great work.

In connection with this glad and solemn season of worship and sacrifice Solomon was crowned the second time. Finally, the chronicler declares that David "died in a good old age, full of days, riches, and honour." In very truth it had been a great reign. Through varied experiences the king had come at last to the highest that was in him, and, as Paul declared, "David, after he had in his own generation served the counsel of God, fell on sleep" (Acts 13:36).

II Chronicles

II CHRONICLES 1

After all the careful preparations for building the Temple which we considered in our survey of the previous Book, we now come to the period in which Solomon entered into full possession of his kingdom and took up the great work entrusted to him. He commenced by gathering his people with him at a sacred act of worship. There God met with him in a special vision at night, and tested him by commanding him to ask of Him what he desired. The condition of his heart was clearly manifest in that he sought for the wisdom necessary to accomplish his work in the best possible way. His request showed a sense of responsibility, and also his realization that he could fulfil that responsibility only as he was divinely guided.

God's answer was a beautiful instance of the overflowing love and grace of the divine heart. All the things Solomon set aside for the sake of wisdom also were given him. It is impossible to read this story without the words, "Greater than Solomon," being recalled to the mind, "Seek ye first the kingdom of God and His righteousness, and all these things shall be added unto you." So far as Solomon was concerned, it was a fine beginning.

In the closing verses of the chapter we see on the divine side the fulfilment of the promise of material prosperity. These were the days of Israel's greatest glory in this respect. The language of the chronicler is pictorial and forceful. Gold and silver were as common as stones; and the precious cedar timber was as plenteous as the commoner sycamore. There was nothing wrong in all this, but it created a very subtle peril. Prosperity is always a more insidious danger to men of faith than adversity. It is more than likely that the glamor of such affluence was already working evil in the king's heart, as he multiplied his horses and chariots by traffic with Egypt. Commerce with Egypt is always dangerous to the people of God, and it is a very easy stage from the purchase of horses to the procuring of a wife.

II CHRONICLES 2

The king's devotion to the highest work of his life was, however, unhindered, and the second chapter gives us the story of how he commenced his preparations for doing that work by new commercial treaties with his father's old friend Huram. This was an alliance of a totally different nature. Huram recognized the truth about Israel, that it was a God-governed people, and in responding to Solomon's message plainly declared this to be the case. In Solomon's friendship for his father's friend there was everything that was noble and helpful.

In the record of Solomon's appeal to Huram, king of Tyre, for a skilled worker and for timber, we find his question, "Who is able to build Him a house?" It affords evidence of the greatness and truth of Solomon's conception of God, as the words immediately following show: "seeing heaven and the heaven of heavens cannot contain Him." Yet he was about to build a house for God. He declared its value as he understood it, "only to burn incense before Him." Solomon was under no delusion about God, and therefore made no mistake about the Temple. He never conceived of it as a place to which God would be confined. He did expect, and he received, manifestations of the Presence of God in that house. Its chief value was that it afforded man a place in which he should offer incense, that is, the symbol of adoration, praise, worship, to God.

II CHRONICLES 3

In this and the following chapter we have the account of the building and furnishing of the Temple. In all fundamental essentials it was on the pattern of the Tabernacle which Moses had made. The proportions and relations were identical, but Solomon's Temple was larger. Its symbolism was exactly the same, though its magnificence was far greater. However, ornamentation was admitted which would have interfered with the express command that no likeness of God was to be attempted. It was a dwelling place for the unseen God, and its structure was representative of the way of man's approach to Him rather than revelatory of the nature of Being. That was a mystery beyond the comprehension of the finite mind, and it was a distinguishing element in the Hebrew religion that it made no attempt to explain. Solomon erected this glorious house on the spot chosen by his father. The story is told here in order to give a graphic and comprehensive idea of the splendor of the house itself.

II CHRONICLES 4

The period occupied in building the Temple was seven years (I Kings 6:38). The work being completed with filial and godly care, the king carried into the sacred enclosure all that his father had collected and dedicated to the purpose. Thus nearly half a millennium after the Exodus the chosen people are found in the land, with a king on the throne, and a permanent Temple in the midst of the chief city at the center of the national life. "Permanent," do we say? The only principles of permanence are faithfulness and purity. Already the elements of decay were at work in the heart of the king and among the people.

Nevertheless, the building of the Temple was a link in the chain of events moving surely forward under God to the Advent, "in the fullness of the time" of Him in whom all that the Temple symbolized, and infinitely more, was realized.

II CHRONICLES 5

Construction being completed, the happy and solemn ceremony of dedication by the people and consecration by God followed immediately. With awe-inspiring dignity the Ark of God was carried to its resting place—not a new one, but which for long years had been the very center of the nation's life. Its progress to position was accompanied by vast sacrifices, which spoke eloquently and solemnly of sinful men's only way of approach to God.

Then came a great burst of harmony in which vocal and instrumental music were combined in chanting the song of the goodness and mercy of God.

Thus man's dedication of the house of God was completed, and it was immediately answered by God's consecration. As in the Tabernacle of old, so now in the new Temple, the cloud of glory possessed and filled the sacred place so that the ministrations of the priests had to cease.

There is an order in this which we do well to consider. Work performed according to the divine order, offered in sacrifice and praise, is acceptable to God. Such work He receives by possessing it with His own presence and glory. Such reception ever halts our service, so that, without activity, even of the highest order, we may wonder and worship.

II CHRONICLES 6

In the presence of the manifestation of glory the king pronounced a blessing on the people which merged into, or took the form of, a blessing offered to God, as he recounted the way of the divine guidance, ascribing all the honor to Him alone.

After praise came prayer. This is ever the true order in worship. We too often reverse it, or, even worse, forget praise altogether in our desire to obtain gifts. Prayer preceded by praise is none the less powerful, but more so. In the words of these wonderful petitions Solomon is revealed in the real kingliness of his nature far more than in all the material splendor with which he surrounded himself, and which presently stopped his praise and paralyzed his praying. The true king lived for and in his people, and the breadth of Solomon's thought and desire for those over whom he reigned is graphically set forth. He was conscious of the fundamental necessity for the continued presence and government of God. He thought of his own people in their regular exercises of worship, and in their special seasons of need, through sin, in battle, in drought, in famine. The largeness of the kingly heart included the strangers who would dwell in the territory of the chosen; and, finally, he prayed tenderly for the nation in the days when because of its folly and sin it would be driven away into captivity. The prayer is great in its comprehensiveness and understanding of the heart of God.

II CHRONICLES 7

As the ceremonies had begun with sacrifice and song, so they closed, and it is quite easy to realize how "joyful and glad of heart" the people were as they dispersed. Had only the king and people remained on the high altitude on which they stood that day, their history would have been very different. How deeply we should realize the awful truth, that even in the midst of such high experience the seeds of evil may already be at work in our life.

Solomon's greatest work now being completed, God appeared to him in a second vision, in which He first declared that the work done was accepted, and Solomon's prayer heard and answered. Then with the tenderness and faithfulness of His infinite love He restated for Solomon the conditions of Solomon's safety. Obedience would be rewarded with continuity of blessing. Disobedience, on the other hand, must issue in rejection and disaster.

The words speak to us also. No height attained, no work done, no blessing received, is in itself sufficient to ensure our continuance in favor. Nothing but continued fidelity can do that. The influence of particular and sacred work was over, and therefore new and subtle perils awaited the king. The underlying weaknesses of his nature would now appeal with new force for attention. Either he would hear their appeal, to heed, and yield, and fail; or to refuse, and conquer, and rise. On the eve of the coming struggle God spoke. It was the action of perfect love.

II CHRONICLES 8

Here are recorded some of the doings of the king. He consolidated the internal strength of the nation by building cities. He organized the labor of the conquered peoples in his dominions. He set the Temple worship in order. He enlarged his commercial activities.

It was during this period that he took Pharaoh's daughter to the house he had built for her and gave his reason for doing so. "My wife shall not dwell in the house of David, king of Israel, because the places are holy, whereunto the Ark of Jehovah hath come." These were the words of compromise. Solomon's marriage with the daughter of the king of Egypt was a purely political act, arising out of the affinity he had with her father (I Kings 3:1). There can be no question that this affinity was wrong. God had delivered His people from Egypt, and there was never the slightest need, either military or economic, for it. It was a political seduction which persistently threatened the nation, and which more than once cost them dear. Having made the blunder and become affianced to this woman, Solomon sought to safeguard against the possible religious danger by building her house away from the city of David.

This compromise was a failure, as compromise invariably is. In I Kings 11:1-8 we read that presently Solomon built places of idol worship in Jerusalem for "all his foreign wives." Compromise is pathetic in that it always witnesses a conviction of what is the high and the true, and attempts to ensure its realization while yielding to the low and the false. It is evil, for its invariable issue is that the low and the false ultimately gain the ascendance and the high and the true are abandoned. To build a house for Pharaoh's daughter outside the Holy City is to open its gates sooner or later to Pharaoh's gods.

II CHRONICLES 9

The story of the Queen of Sheba's coming is full of beauty, as it illustrates the true influence of kingship exercised under the government of the eternal King. The fame of Solomon's wisdom attracted her to his court, and she came principally to discuss with him the problems on her mind. "She came to prove Solomon with hard questions." He welcomed her with fine courtesy, and answered her questions to her satisfaction. The matter of principal interest is the effect produced on her by her visit. She wondered at all the magnificence as well as at the king's wisdom; but she saw clearly the reason of it all, and her highest praise was offered to that God through whom Solomon was enthroned, and in whose might and wisdom he was strong and wise.

This is as it should be with all who represent God to men by submission. When our greatness or our wisdom is the final impression we have failed. When our success is so manifested as to reveal the secret of our relationship to God; and, therefore, so as to transfer the praise of men from ourselves to Him, we are fulfilling the true function of life.

The chronicler ends the story of Solomon with an account of the wealth that he gathered, and the magnificence which characterized his reign. The account of the failure and fall is not given. The writer's purpose is served when he has made clear the relationship between loyalty to the Temple of God, with its worship, and success and greatness of king and people. The story immediately following, of disruption and degeneracy, is the result of the failure, and sets forth the same truth from the other side.

II CHRONICLES 10

Despotism is seldom transmissible. That Solomon had been an autocrat and had ruled with a hand of iron under the velvet is evidenced by the words of the men of Israel, "Thy father hath made our yoke grievous." If this is a startling suggestion, history testifies to the likelihood of its correctness. Some of the worst tyrants the world ever had robbed the people of their rights, and kept them passive by the deadly drug of gorgeous displays. So did Lorenzo de Medici in Florence; so did our own Charles I.

With the death of Solomon men breathed anew, and discovered their chains. This was the occasion for a bid for freedom. Jeroboam returned from Egypt to be spokesman of peace. Rehoboam showed his folly in taking the advice of the hot-headed youths of his court. He attempted to continue the despotism of his father, though he lacked his father's refinement and ability to fascinate. The result was immediate. The ten tribes revolted. The nation was riven in twain, and, judging by purely human calculation, Judah was on the verge of a war which would have ended in her defeat.

II CHRONICLES 11

Then God interfered. No human folly has even been permitted to continue long enough to thwart His purpose. Shemaiah, a prophet of God, declared to Rehoboam that the revolt was in the divine plan. Rehoboam immediately obeyed, and the period of the two kingdoms commenced.

This section of the book contains the story of the reign of Rehoboam in Judah. Jeroboam as king of Israel turned the people from Jehovah by his idolatrous practices. The result was that the Levites and those who set their hearts to seek the Lord passed over to Judah, and thus, in the best way, the kingdom was strengthened by the accession of faithful souls. Meanwhile, Rehoboam strengthened his position by building fenced cities throughout his dominions. He was, however, the son of his father; and, even in the years of peace and prosperity, the animal nature came out in the multiplicity of his wives and concubines, until he had practically established, as did his father, a harem on the pattern of the corrupt kings around him.

II CHRONICLES 12

The issue was that Rehoboam "forsook the law of the Lord." The scourge came in the person of Israel's ancient foe, the king of Egypt. The patience of God is ever manifest in His dealing with His people. The repentance of Rehoboam produced, as it always does, a stay of judgment. Yet the kingdom of Judah passed under the yoke of Egypt. Judah was saved, however, from complete destruction, not principally for the sake of the king, nor in answer to his repentance, but because "in Judah there were good things found."

God's judgments are always characterized by fine discrimination. He never destroys the righteous with the wicked. The picture of Rehoboam's substitution of brass for gold is unutterably pathetic. Yet how often do the people of Jehovah masquerade amid imitations because they have lost the things of pure gold through unfaithfulness and sin.

II CHRONICLES 13

In the reign of Abijah there was terrible war between Judah and Israel. The king himself was evil, as the Book of the Kings declares. Here, however, he was speaking and acting for his people. His address, in which he attempted to persuade Israel to submission, is very remarkable. It is a strange mixture of misrepresentation and religion. The misrepresentation is in his statement of the reason for the rebellion of Israel, which culminated in the crowning of Jeroboam. He attributed the rebellion to the influence of evil men whom he described as "sons of Belial."

How often in process of time men misrepresent the reasons from which differences spring. There is no doubt that the contrasts which Abijah drew between the nations were true, and that Judah more nearly represented the true ideal of the nation of God than did Israel. This, however, does not justify his misrepresentation of the real beginning of disaffection in Israel. From the standpoint of righteousness, the condition of Israel was deplorable, and Jeroboam was a veritable incarnation of evil. His method of warfare as here recorded was mean and despicable. To surprise a foe from ambush in the midst of conference is inexpressibly wicked. The God of the nations Himself acts, and the power of Jeroboam was broken utterly by the victory of Judah.

II CHRONICLES 14

In Asa there was a break in the continuity of naughtiness which so singularly characterized the succession of kings. His was a long reign, and though not characterized by the pronounced reforms which obtained under future kings, it did give the nation some glimpses of a better order. He commenced by breaking down false worship so far as he was able, and as a result the land had "quiet before him." He took advantage of the peaceful years to build and wall the cities. In a time of peril resulting from the invasion of the Ethiopians, the king's cry to God was answered by a signal deliverance.

How unfailingly the patience of God is made to appear in these records! The repetition of the fact in notes of exposition becomes almost monotonous. Yet, after all, is it not the monotony of the perfect music of those who with veiled faces chant the story of God's holiness and love? The condition of the chosen people as a whole at this time was terrible. Yet immediately man or nation returned to God with repentance and amendment, He responded with pardon and deliverance. There is a limit to His forbearance; but if this history teaches anything it is that the limit is set where by the act of the sinner, be that sinner man or nation, there is no possibility of return. God never ratifies the hardening of any heart until the hardness is absolute through the action of the sinner.

II CHRONICLES 15

This chapter chronicles with greater detail the occasion and value of the reform wrought in Judah during Asa's reign. Here appears a man mentioned nowhere else. His name was Azariah. Suddenly anointed by the Spirit of God, he appeared to the king, and in a brief prophetic word gave direction to all his life and reign.

If the message was brief, it was yet weighty. As to enunciation of principles, it occupies only half a verse in our Bibles. "The Lord is with you, while ye be with Him; and if ye seek Him, He will be found of you; but if ye forsake Him, He will forsake you." The rest is illustrative application of the principle by reference to then existing conditions, ending with a direct appeal. The principle is of perpetual application. It represents God as unchanging. All apparent changes on His part are really changes in the attitude of men toward Him. Man with God, finds God with him. Man forsaking God, finds that he is forsaken of God.

These are the extremes of the one truth. Between them, not contradicting them, but complementing them, is the declaration that the seeker finds. A recognition of these principles must inspire the heart with courage. It certainly did in Asa's case. Upon the ground of that announcement he purged his country to a large extent, even deposing his mother in his loyalty to the principle.

II CHRONICLES 16

This is a very sad chapter, telling as it does the story of the lapse of a man who, considering the conditions under which he lived, had for six and thirty years been so remarkably true to God. When Baasha, king of Israel, commenced to build Ramah with the express purpose of troubling Judah, Asa, who had so often been led by God, turned to Benhadad for help. It seemed to be a successful policy, for Benhadad spoiled the cities of Israel, and Baasha left his work. Things which appear successful may be in the life of faith most disastrous. As a matter of fact, the Syrians were worse foes of Judah than even Israel; and as Hanani, the seer, told the king, by this act they had escaped out of his hand.

How perpetually men defeat their own ends when either through lack of faith or overconfidence, which are practically the same thing, they attempt to do by policy what God is prepared to do for them in answer to their obedient belief. The story is the sadder in that the king seems to have had no repentance for his wrong. He persecuted the prophet, flinging him into prison. Moreover, in his latter days he became despotic, and even though physical suffering came to him, "he sought not to the Lord," so engrossed was he with the suffering and his attempts to gain relief through the physicians.

II CHRONICLES 17

With the accession of Jehoshaphat a period of definite reformation for Judah commenced. In this chapter we have, first, the account of his own relationship to God, and the resulting blessing that came to him. Then follows an interesting account of what in these latter times would be called special missions, arranged by the king, and conducted through the cities of Judah by representatives of the princes, the Levites, and the priests.

Jehoshaphat put into practice himself, and by these special methods provoked his people to put into practice, the principle which Azariah had declared to his father. Coincident with this activity within, a remarkable fear of the Lord fell on the people without, so that they ceased to make war on Jehoshaphat. Thus God was with the man who was with Him, and the result was opportunity to strengthen the kingdom within by building castles and cities, by commerce, and by carrying out many works.

II CHRONICLES 18

These chapters contain the story of a strange lapse in the history of Jehoshaphat, and also of his repentance and restoration. Ahab was king in Israel, perhaps the most evil that ever sat on the throne. With him Jehoshaphat made affinity. The story of this strange and false union is very interesting. The king of Judah attempted to insist, in the midst of the corruption of the court of Ahab, on the necessity for consulting Jehovah on the proposed campaign to Ramoth-gilead. It was strange company for a man of God to be in, and he barely escaped with his life, and would not have escaped but for the intervention of Jehovah. One nameless man "drew his bow at a venture," as the margin reads, "in his simplicity." It was not even a venture in the sense of an attempt, or a gambling against odds, in the hope of killing the king of Israel. It was done "in his simplicity," that is, artlessly, without any intention other than that of "carrying on" in the ordinary sense of that word. Probably this man already had shot many arrows, and he went on in his simplicity, little knowing that this particular arrow was to be guided through all the confusion straight to its mark by the unerring knowledge and power of God. Yet so it was.

Thus it is seen how the refuge of lies is never hidden from the eyes of God. Men may secrete themselves so that other men may never find them; but when the hour of their judgment has come, God takes hold on some ordinary event and makes it the highway on which He comes to carry out His purpose. "It just happened," says the man of the world. "God did it," says the man of faith.

II CHRONICLES 19

Returning to Jerusalem, Jehoshaphat was rebuked by Jehu, the son of Hanani, in words which it would be well for all of us perpetually to bear in mind: "Shouldest thou help the wicked, and love them that hate the Lord?"

Evidently Jehoshaphat realized his wrong, and showed his repentance in a new mission, to bring his people back to Jehovah and to establish the internal administration of the kingdom in righteousness.

His words addressed to the judges are full of value, and of perpetual application. Those who are called on at any time and in any way to administer justice are acting for God, and not for man. They are not seeking to serve men, but to maintain the strict cause of justice, which is to be measured only by divine standards. With God there is no iniquity, no respect of persons, no taking of bribes. So must it be with those who act as judges. Thus, and thus only, are the true interests of men served. To seek to please men is to be unjust to men. To seek to please God is to be just to men.

II CHRONICLES 20

This chapter gives us the story which perhaps reveals most graphically the simplicity and splendor of the faith of Jehoshaphat. His kingdom was threatened with powerful and terrible invasion. In his extremity he gathered his people about him, and prayed. The prayer is a powerful outpouring of his consciousness of need. He pleaded, as men ever do when in need they come before God, recalled the past evidences of the faithfulness of Jehovah, and confessing his inability to cope with the danger, asked God for His help.

It is a great picture, this king surrounded by the nation, men with their wives and their children. The response was not delayed. The Spirit of God came upon Jahaziel, and the answer was the announcement that all Judah had to do was to stand still and see the salvation of the Lord. Then followed the united worship of the people, and the solemn chanting of praise to God. Discomfiture fell on the foe, without Judah striking a blow. It was a moment bright with light amid the darkness. Once again the arm of the Lord acted for His people as definitely as when in the ancient days it broke the power of Egypt and divided the sea, leading the Hebrews from captivity to freedom.

The closing verses of the chapter contain a brief statement of yet another lapse, in that Jehoshaphat made commercial alliances with Ahaziah, king of Israel. His enterprises were unsuccessful because God broke his ships in pieces.

II CHRONICLES 21

With the passing of Jehoshaphat another period of degeneracy and darkness set in for the kingdom of Judah. He was succeeded by his first-born, Jehoram, who seems to have been a man of utterly evil nature. He attempted to secure the throne by the murder of his brothers. Perhaps the secret of his evil courses lay in the fact that he took to wife the daughter of Ahab. That would seem to be the thought of the chronicler expressed in the words, "He walked in the ways of the kings of Israel, as did the house of Ahab; for he had the daughter of Ahab to wife." Trouble fell on his kingdom in the revolt of Edom and invasion by the Philistines and the Ethiopians.

In the midst of his wickedness a message came to him by writing from Elijah the prophet of fire, who had exercised so powerful an influence against Ahab in the kingdom of Israel. It contained a terrible message of judgment, which was fully carried out after eight years of reign. So evil were his courses that the nation loathed him, and the tragic words were written concerning his death, "he departed without being desired."

II CHRONICLES 22

Jehoram was immediately succeeded by Ahaziah, his youngest son. His reign was brief, lasting only one year, and was influenced for evil by Athaliah, his mother. The story of his death is a solemn warning. It occurred directly through his friendship for the evil house of Ahab. Jehu, acting as the instrument of God's judgment on that house, found princes of Judah, and among them the king, and slew them all.

Then followed dark and terrible days in which the dead king's mother, Athaliah, reigned over the land. Her first act was a revelation of her character. It was the destruction of all the seed royal of the house of Judah. However, no evil anger is sufficient to frustrate divine purpose, and against the wickedness of one woman God set the compassion of another. Jehoshabeath rescued Joash, and for six years with patient persistence nursed him under the shelter of the Temple.

There are hours in human history when it seems as though evil were almost all powerful. It entrenches itself in great strength; it builds up great ramparts; it inaugurates policies of the utmost craft and cleverness. It seems to be able to bind together a kingdom which is invincible. All this is false seeming. There is no finality, no security, in the apparent might of iniquity. Sooner or later, irrevocably, inevitably, the trenches are broken through, the ramparts are flung down, the policies fail, and the kingdom which seemed so secure is dashed to pieces like a potter's vessel by the strength of God, which is ever the strength of righteousness and goodness. Neither powerful autocrat nor mighty confederacy of statesmen can establish a kingdom or an empire by fraud, by violence, by corruption. Other than truth and justice and purity, the things of goodness, which are the things of God, nothing will hold a kingdom or an empire or a commonwealth together in strength.

II CHRONICLES 23

The story of Jehoida is one of devotion and courage. Doubtless he had known of the hiding place of Joash and his nurse. After six years of terrible experience, he took means to bring about the death of Athaliah, and the crowning of the boy, who was the true representative of the house of David.

There is dramatic power in one

statement here concerning Athaliah, "She looked, and behold, the king stood by his pillar at the entrance." The boy king was brought out, anointed, and crowned amid the plaudits of the people. Athaliah, hearing the shoutings, came to the Temple, and "she looked, and, behold, the king stood by his pillar at the entrance." Then she knew the powerlessness of evil. In vain she cried, "Treason! treason!" Her own treason against the true and abiding King of the nation was defeated.

Thus, sooner or later, and in ways equally dramatic, the moment arrives when those who plot and plan against heaven and righteousness find themselves looking at the evidences of the triumph of God and of goodness over all their wickedness.

Jehoiada commenced the reformation which followed during the forty years of the reign of Joash. Thus, in one way or another, God, in unceasing fidelity to His own purposes of love, moved forward toward ultimate realization in spite of the failure of His people.

II CHRONICLES 24

The reform under Joash was really due to the influence of Jehoiada the priest. This is clearly indicated in the statement of the chronicler that "Joash did that which was right in the eyes of the Lord all the days of Jehoiada the priest." During this period the king would seem to have been honestly zealous in endeavoring to re-establish the true worship of God.

The reform center is, as always in this Book, around the Temple. "They set up the House of God in its state, and strengthened it." Worship was maintained while Jehoiada lived. After his death the king passed under the influence of the princes of Judah, and the house of God was forsaken and idolatry again established in the land. The king, who had been zealous in reform, now became determined in his wickedness, refusing to obey the voices of the prophets, and encompassing the death of Zechariah, the son of his old friend, Jehoiada.

The study of the story of Joash offers a striking instance of how a weak man is easily influenced. All such men are illustrations of the absolute importance of strong individual character which can be created only where the soul had direct dealing with God and depends wholly on Him. All merely human influence, whether good or bad, is perilous. If a man has nothing more to lean on than the strength of another good man, and the latter should fail from any cause collapse is almost inevitable. All foundations may fail, save the one. When the will of man is yielded wholly to the will of God, and no other authority is sought or permitted, there is perfect safety. Where this is lacking, every changing tide of circumstances will alter the current of life.

II CHRONICLES 25

The story of the reign of Amaziah opens with a remarkable statement which gives us the key to all that follows. "He did that which was right in the eyes of the Lord, but not with a perfect heart." The general aim of the man was right, but execution was spoiled by imperfection. Nothing is wholly satisfactory to God save the perfect heart, because nothing else can possibly produce the best in man. Amaziah's punishment of his father's murders was tempered with justice. The imperfection of his heart appeared in his alliance with Israel; and then again his right desire in the readiness with which he obeyed the voice of the prophet and broke the alliance even at cost to himself.

Returning from his conquest over the Edomites, he brought back with him the gods of his defeated foes. Again the prophet visited him, and the unutterable folly of such action is declared in the question, "Why hast thou sought after the gods of the people, which have not delivered their own people out of thine hand?" Punishment for this followed in the defeat of Judah by Israel.

The root idea of the Hebrew word translated "perfect" is being whole, complete. Imperfection of heart consists in incomplete surrender. Some chamber of the temple is retained for selfish purposes. What it was in the case of Amaziah we are not told, but the fact remains, that notwithstanding the general direction of his life, either through personal indulgence, or ambition, or carelessness, the whole heart was not set on doing the will of God. One room possessed by the foe inside the fortress is ever the gravest peril. Sooner or later, almost inevitably, the man in that room opens the door for foes without. Thus it was in the case of Amaziah, and thus it is in the case of all who are not wholly devoted.

II CHRONICLES 26

The story of Uzziah's long reign of fifty-two years is most interesting and remarkable. He was a man of strong character, and the early part of his occupancy of the throne was characterized by true prosperity. He was at once victorious in his campaigns against the enemies of the people, and remarkably successful in his internal development of the resources of the nation. A man of war, and a lover of husbandry, he was an ideal ruler. During these early years he went quietly forward in dependence on God.

There came a break, and the story of it is told by the chronicler in the words, "He was marvellously helped till he was strong." How consistently in the pages of history we are taught the perils of prosperity. Man depending upon God is ever independent of all else. In the moment when the heart begins to feel independent of God in its own strength, the strength fails; and unless there be repentance ruin is inevitable. The last years of the reign, so glorious in its beginnings, were years of suffering and sadness. In an evil moment of pride Uzziah entered into the sacred courts, and violated the ordinances of God concerning the offering of sacrifices. He was smitten with leprosy, and lived for the last part of his life a prisoner, isolated from his fellow men.

II CHRONICLES 27

Uzziah was succeeded by Jotham. We have very few details of his reign. In all probability the sixteen years referred to by the chronicler cover a period in which he was exercising authority while his father, Uzziah, was still alive though excluded from the kingly office on account of his leprosy. Jotham continued the work of his father in strengthening the kingdom internally by building, and he was successful in a campaign against the Ammonites.

While there was no definite national reform during his reign, he seems to have gone quietly forward along true lines, and his strength is attributed to the fact that he ordered his ways before Jehovah his God. Perhaps three things helped this man. First, he reigned during the early period in which Isaiah was exercising his prophetic ministry. Second, his mother was almost certainly the daughter of Zadok, the priest. Third, he profited by his father's example—both good and bad, following the good and shunning the evil. All good influences are to be valued, but the ultimate note is always personal. "He ordered his ways." If a man will do this, then he will ever profit by all the influences brought to bear on him, distinguishing between good and evil, and choosing according to the will of God.

II CHRONICLES 28

The whole reign of Ahaz was a period of terrible and rapid degeneracy. With appalling fearlessness the king restored all the evils of idolatry, even including the terrible offering of children to Moloch. In all probability his own son was a victim. As difficulties gathered around, he turned to the king of Assyria for aid, attempting to procure help from him by giving him treasure out of the house of God. The evil of his character is supremely demonstrated in that calamities seemed not to have the effect, as they so often had had among his predecessors, of rousing him to consciousness of his sin. Indeed it is distinctly stated, "In the time of his distress did he trespass yet more against the Lord, this same king Ahaz."

During this period Isaiah was exercising his ministry, and the king was persistently rebellious, absolutely refusing to listen to Isaiah's voice or obey its call. Ahaz was evil by choice, persistent in evil in spite of calamity, blasphemously rebellious notwithstanding the direct warnings of the prophet of God. This attitude of the king made the darkness all the denser.

II CHRONICLES 29

With the accession of Hezekiah a great change came over the life of Judah. Among all the reformers he was perhaps the most remarkable. That this was so in spite of the fact that he was the son of Ahaz is interesting, and leads to inquiry as to the reason. The answer is not far to seek. His mother was Abijah, the daughter of Zechariah, probably the person mentioned by the prophet Isaiah (8:2) as a "faithful witness." This possible friendship of his mother for the prophet, combined with the certainty that up to this time he had been under the influence of Isaiah's ministry, may account for Hezekiah's action on coming to the throne. A man brought up in the atmosphere of the wonderful teaching of Isaiah would naturally inaugurate his reign along lines diametrically opposed to those followed by his father.

The reformation began in Hezekiah's deep consciousness of the wretched condition of the people, and the reason thereof. This is most graphically set forth in his words to the priests and Levites when he called them together. He made no attempt to blame on God the calamities which had overtaken the nation. On the other hand, he traced the story of their sin, and declared that the result was the wrath of God, which had expressed itself in their disasters. He then commenced the work of restoring the order of worship, the first business of which was to cleanse the house. Some idea of the condition of things may be gathered from the fact that the Levites were occupied sixteen whole days in carrying out the accumulated filth from the sacred precincts. This being done, the great ceremony of rededication followed. The consciousness of the true order is manifest in Hezekiah's words, "Now ye have consecrated yourselves . . . bring sacrifices and thank-offerings." The New Testament parallel is found in the words of the apostle to the Corinthians, "First they gave their own selves to the Lord, and to us by the will of God."

II CHRONICLES 30

For a long time the proper feasts of the Lord had not been observed. Hezekiah made arrangements to keep the Passover. It is very beautiful to see how his heart took in the whole nation. In all probability, this Passover was observed before the final passing of the northern kingdom into captivity; and Hezekiah sent messengers throughout Israel as well as Judah, asking them to come up to Jerusalem and take part in the feast. The hopeless corruption of Israel is seen in the statement that "the posts passed from city to city through the country of Ephraim and Manasseh, even unto Zebulun; but they laughed them to scorn, and mocked them."

Nevertheless, a remnant even out of Israel gathered to Judah, and took part in the sacred, solemn observance. It was a motley crowd that gathered, multitudes of the people were utterly ignorant of the divine arrangements for preparation. Again Hezekiah's tenderness was shown in his pity for these people and the prayer he offered. His prayer was answered, and the imperfect method was not punished in the case of those who set their hearts to seek the Lord.

II CHRONICLES 31

The observance of the feast was followed by reorganization of the nation. The remnant gathered from Israel became the pioneers in destroying all that remained of idolatry throughout the cities of Judah, and also in Ephraim and Manasseh. The king set in order the courses of the priests and Levites for the service, and rearranged the offerings according to law. He called for the payment of the tithe, and the response seems to have been widespread and generous.

All this is told in general terms in the chapter. The special value in the work was the thoroughness with which the king carried it out. The closing verse states this, and reveals a truth of constant value. "In every work that he began to do in the service of the house of God, and in the law, and in the commandments, to seek his God, he did it with all his heart, and prospered." In this statement we have a purpose, a method, and a result. His purpose was to seek his God, and this he did in the way of the divine appointment, and with all his heart; and the result was his prosperity.

II CHRONICLES 32

One is almost inevitably halted by the opening statement of the chapter. "After these things, and this faithfulness, Sennacherib, king of Assyria, came." It would seem to be a strange answer of God to the faithfulness of His child, that a strong foe should at this moment invade the kingdom; and yet how often the experience of the people of God is of this nature. Happy was Hezekiah in that in the presence of the peril his heart did not fail. He took immediate action to embarrass the foe by stopping the supply of water, strengthening the fortifications, mobilizing his army, and, finally, by assuring the people, "There is a greater with us than with him."

This attitude of faith was answered by Sennacherib with terrible insults, terrible because they were direct blasphemies against the name of God. At these utterances, more terrible to bear than the fighting without the gates, the king sought refuge in prayer in fellowship with the prophet Isaiah. The answer was quick and final—rout of the enemy and salvation of the people.

The chronicler then briefly relates the story of Hezekiah's illness, and of that failure which characterized his last days. The story is more fully told elsewhere. Notwithstanding the lapses of the latter days, the reign was most remarkable, especially when it is remembered how fearful was the condition into which the nation had come at this time.

II CHRONICLES 33

Manasseh, the son of Hezekiah, seems to have set himself to the most wilful and persistent restoration of every form of abomination. All the things specifically forbidden were set up in the places sacred to the name of Jehovah; and with appalling thoroughness he undid all that his father had done. The strong hand of God was stretched out against him, and with the Assyrian as the scourge the king was carried away in irons, broken and defeated. In his distress the stubborn will seems to have been bent, and he cried to God for help. Manasseh's repentance was evidently the chief subject in the mind of the chronicler, and while his sins are painted faithfully and revealed in all their hideousness, all becomes but background which flings into relief Manasseh's genuine penitence and the ready and gracious response of God.

There is a solemn warning in the history of Amon, who, on coming to the throne, followed the earlier example of his father, and was so utterly corrupt that his own servants conspired against him and slew him. While repentance of personal sin brings ready forgiveness, the influence of the sin is terribly likely to abide.

II CHRONICLES 34

The story of Josiah's reign is full of brightness. The conditions around were very terrible, but in this boy king, especially as he developed to manhood, testimony to the government of God was unmistakable. Ascending to the throne when eight years old, at the age of sixteen he began to seek after God. Four years later he set himself to the actual work of reformation, and there is terrific force in the story of his methods. There was no pity in his heart for the evil things about him, and with the strongest hand, so far as he was able, he swept out the abominations.

At the age of twenty-six he set himself to repair the house of God, during which a remarkable thing happened. While the Temple was being cleansed the book of the Law was discovered. It is impossible to tell whether Hilkiah had known of it, but the story would certainly lead us to suppose that Josiah was quite ignorant of it. When by comparison with its ideals he learned the facts concerning his people, Josiah gathered them together, and publicly made a covenant with God and insisted that the people should abide by it.

II CHRONICLES 35

This chapter gives us the story of the great Passover, in which, following in the steps of Hezekiah, after the cleansing of the land and the restoration of the people Josiah thus restored the great feast of the Exodus.

In the account of the joy following the Passover of Hezekiah, comparison is made with the times of Solomon. Under Josiah this goes further back than Solomon, and declares that none like it was kept by any king.

Following the story of his death we read of the lamentation of the people. Josiah had evidently made himself greatly beloved by them, and the probability is that the reforms he instituted were based on that love rather than on the people's real return to devotion to God. Hence the transitory nature of the reformation, which was so soon followed by the final stages in the corruption even in Judah.

II CHRONICLES 36

This is the record of the final movements in the downward course of Judah. They are graphically given. First Jehoahaz reigned for three months, and was deposed by the king of Egypt. Jehoiakim succeeded by appointment of Pharaoh, and after eleven years of continued evil courses was carried prisoner by Nebuchadnezzar to Babylon.

In turn he was succeeded by Jehoiachin, who persisted in the same evil courses for three months and ten days, and in turn was carried away by Nebuchadnezzar.

Zedekiah, appointed by Nebuchadnezzar to the succession, rebelled against him, and continued the same evil history for eleven years, during which corruption became practically universal, the priests and the people sharing therein. Through all these dark days God still patiently waited, sending His messengers because of His compassion. The men who had rebelled against His government contemned His mercy, until the Chaldeans, a people without compassion, swept down upon them like a terrible scourge, and carried the remnant away captive to Babylon.

The Book closes with a statement of the proclamation of Cyrus, which also opens the Book of Ezra.

Ezra

EZRA 1

The Book of Ezra contains an account of a most important epoch in the history of the people of God. After seventy years of captivity, a return from captivity was made possible by the decree of a Gentile king. This Book gives us the story of that return, and the building of the Temple. It is not consecutive history, for while, with the Book of Nehemiah, it covers a period of about one hundred years, there is a gap of sixty years. There are two main divisions, first, the story of the return under Zerubbabel and the building of the Temple, and then, after sixty years, the story of the coming of Ezra and the work he undertook.

God may seem to tarry in carrying out His purposes. He never abandons them. Indeed, there is a very true sense in which He never tarries even for a moment in carrying them out. The wreck of the chosen nation we have seen in previous books. The people had become scattered and peeled, having lost national position and power, and, to a very large extent, national consciousness. Notwithstanding all this, God still moved on toward His great ultimate purpose of redemption, not merely for these people, but for the world. During the seventy years, through the processes of suffering, He prepared a remnant to return and rebuild and hold the fort until He, the true Seed and Servant, should come.

The history of the return sets forth clearly the truth concerning this overruling of God. He compelled the most unlikely instruments to accomplish His will. Babylon had carried His people into captivity, and so fulfilled His purpose. They had, however, treated the conquered nation with undue severity; and in process of time, in fulfilment of the distinct prophesying of Jeremiah, Cyrus the Persian had broken the power of Babylon. This Cyrus was now chosen and commissioned as the instrument of the chosen people's return. Cyrus's proclamation opened the door. It was the result of divine dealing with him, of which he was conscious. The God who opened the door stirred up men, and made them willing to respond. This is ever so in the divine economy. The opportunity, the willingness to obey and the leaders necessary, all come together under God's direction.

EZRA 2

Chapter two contains the register of those who, taking advantage of Cyrus's decree, turned their faces toward

Jerusalem. The list proceeds in a definite order, from the leaders downward. First, the names of those immediately associated with Zerubbabel (1, 2). Then follow the names of families, with the numbers in each case (3-35); names of the members of the priesthood (36-39); following these the list and numbers of the Levites (40-42); after these the Nethinim (43-54); next the children of Solomon's servants (55-58); beside these, a number who had lost their genealogy (59-63). Verses 64 and 65 give the totals of the people, and then come the lists of the cattle. The whole ends with the statement of the gifts of the people, and the declaration of their settlement in the cities of the land.

An examination of this list is remarkable principally from the small number of Levites who returned. Nearly ten times as many priests as Levites went back to the land. This, of course, was an inversion of the original order. Dr. Ryle says that perhaps this may be explained by the Levites having been especially concerned in the worship at the high places, and the idolatrous forms of worship which the reformation of Josiah had sought to abolish. Another point of interest is the Nethinim. They seem to be prominent in these books of the return, for they are mentioned only once elsewhere. Their origin it is almost impossible to determine. In all probability they were of foreign extraction, but had been admitted to some of the minor forms of service in connection with Levitical work.

EZRA 3

The leaders in this return were evidently conscious of the matters of real importance in the life of the people. Directly they were settled in their cities, the altar of God was established at Jerusalem. The statement, "For fear was upon them because of the people of the countries," has given rise to a great many different interpretations. Perhaps the one that harmonizes best with the whole story is that they were conscious of the fact that in their neglect of the altar of God in the past they had become contaminated by the idolatrous practices of surrounding peoples; and in order to prevent a repetition of such sin they immediately set up the true altar. This is the more likely to be a correct interpretation in view of the fact that whatever failure characterized these people in their history, they never again returned to idolatry.

The first feast they observed, according to the time of year, was the feast of Tabernacles, which was the most joyful of all the feasts of the Lord. They also established all the feasts, and, so far as possible, restored the divinely appointed order of worship. Then immediately they commenced the work of building the Temple. The foundations were laid, and in the second year of the return, with fitting ceremonies of praise, they rejoiced. The mingling of tears and songs is in itself remarkable. Remembering the first house, the old men mourned. This can well be understood when one thinks of the comparative insignificance and poverty of the people as they were gathered back. Yet there was also a great shout of praise, for new hope had taken possession of their hearts.

EZRA 4

In this chapter we have the story of the opposition of the Samaritans, and the consequent cessation of work on the Temple for a time. The historic chronology presents difficulties. The subject is not of vital importance. Perhaps, however, the simplest solution is that in the first five verses we have a general statement of the fact that this opposition continued from the reign of Cyrus to that of Darius; while in verses six to twenty-three there is a more detailed account of the opposition.

The one objection to this solution is that the names of the kings mentioned in verses six to twenty-three are not those given as reigning between Cyrus and Darius, but after Darius. Admitting this difficulty, it seems to me less than that presented by any other attempt to explain this passage, and it is quite unsafe to build any theory definitely on names which may be dynastic rather than personal. However, the principal interest of the chapter for us is the opposition and the forms it took. First was an attempt to induce Zerubbabel and those associated with him to admit into partnership such as were really enemies of the work. This being definitely refused, these enemies set themselves in every way to hinder the work, until at last they were successful in obtaining letters from the reigning monarch interdicting the work. Thus, for a long period the building of the house of God ceased, while building houses for the people went forward unchecked.

EZRA 5

A study of the prophecies of Haggai and Zechariah makes it perfectly evident that the cessation of the work of building was unworthy of the men who had commenced. Judged by all human standards they could fairly urge the difficulties of the situation, and the necessity for obedience to the edict of the reigning king. Judged by the divine standard, as all the burning words of the prophets named make perfectly clear, they had no right to cease.

Under the inspiration of this prophetic message, governor and priest, Zerubbabel and Joshua, commenced the work again. But no sooner did they commence than opposition was raised, and they were challenged. To this challenge, however, they gave no heed, and the reason is graphically stated, "The eye of their God was upon the elders of the Jews." We are not to suppose for a moment that this was something new. That eye had always been upon them, but through the teaching of the prophets, and their rousing call, their consciousness of relationship to God had again been renewed; and they went forward in spite of the challenge of their foes, determined not to cease until the matter had been submitted to Darius, the new king. The copy of the letter sent to him by Tattenai is preserved for us, and is very interesting. It is hardly possible to read it without feeling that there was in the mind of this enemy of the work some suspicion of a friendly feeling existing in the mind of the king toward the Jews. It would seem, however, that he did not believe their story concerning the edict of Cyrus, and appealed to the king that it be sought for, and produced if in existence.

EZRA 6

There can be no doubt that Tattenai felt that finding such a decree was unlikely, if not impossible. That the search must have been thorough is indicated by the place where the roll was found. The searchers naturally commenced in the house of the archives in Babylon, but it was not there. It was found at Achmetha, in the royal palace. It is interesting to think how easily it might not have been found. Naturally, if such a document was not found in the proper libraries, men would abandon their search. However, we cannot read this story without realizing that the eye of the God of Israel was on the elders of the Jews, and that all the peoples were in His hand. The search, therefore, was prosecuted until successful. One can easily imagine with what surprise Tattenai received the answer of Darius, characterized by clearness and determination. The man who would have hindered and stayed the progress of the building was compelled not only not to hinder, but to help with great gifts.

How true it is that when a people obey God they at once ensure His cooperation for the accomplishment of their purposes. At last the Temple was finished and solemnly dedicated to God with sacrificial offerings and songs of thanksgiving. On completion of the Temple the great feast of Passover was observed once more, and followed by that of unleavened bread.

EZRA 7

Here begins the second section of the Book, that which gathers around the doings of Ezra. Between the close of the last chapter and the commencement of this sixty years had passed away. To a very great extent they were uneventful years in the history of the people settled in Jerusalem. That they had largely failed in the realization of the purposes of Zerubbabel is evident from the work done by Ezra, subsequently by Nehemiah. This chapter tells of the coming of Ezra, and there are two verses which very largely explain the movement for us. They are verses ten and twenty-three, in which we discover the individual inspiration of Ezra and Artaxerxes.

While still in Babylon, Ezra was moved to help his people in Jerusalem. In order to do this, he yielded to obedience to the law of God, and so prepared himself for his work of teaching. The verse should not be passed without noticing its suggestiveness for all such as are called, or feel they are called, to teach. The order is, "to seek . . . to do . . . to teach." Verse twenty-three explains the personal reason for the decree and beneficence of Artaxerxes. Why should there be "wrath against the realm of the king and his sons?" It is perfectly evident that he had some very clear consciousness of the power of God. Thus God is seen overruling, and by the creation of different emotions, bringing them into co-operation with each other, and thus with His purpose.

EZRA 8

In this chapter we have, first, a representative list of those who joined Ezra when he went up to Jerusalem. First in order, members of the priestly and royal houses are named (verses 1, 2). Then follows the register and number of the people (verses 3-14). Before the actual march commenced, Ezra gathered together at Ahava those who were to accompany him in order to review them and prepare for the journey. He found that none of the sons of Levi was in the company. Recognizing the necessity for their presence, he paused, and sent to Iddo, who perhaps was in charge of some school of the Levites.

In response to his appeal, certain of their number joined him. The journey before them was full of peril, and the character of Ezra is remarkably revealed in his action at this point. Conscious of the perils, he was yet ashamed to seek help in the way from an earthly king; and therefore proclaimed a fast in which, in humiliation, they waited upon God for His guidance and protection.

In this story there is a fine illustration of the independence and dependence of those who follow the Lord. Of greatest importance to Ezra was the honor of the name of his God. That honor he would not sully by seeking help from an earthly king. The voluntary gifts of the king were welcome, and for this Ezra was thankful. To ask for soldiers would have been tacitly to confess questioning the ability or willingness of God to help. God never fails those who act in full dependence on Him and independently of all others. At last, after a long journey, they arrived in safety at Jerusalem, and made their offerings.

EZRA 9

On Ezra's arrival at Jerusalem complaint was made to him of the failure and sin of the people. What an appalling story it was, that during these sixty years, even though there had been no return to heathen idolatry, God's law against intermingling with the people of the land had been wilfully broken, the chief offenders being the princes and rulers.

The picture of Ezra in the presence of this confession is very fine. It is that of a man so stirred with righteous indignation that he had rent his garments and plucked off his beard. As the storm of his passion subsided he sank in silent astonishment until the evening oblation. Then he fell on his knees before God, and poured out his soul in prayer. It was a wonderful prayer. Beginning with confession of his personal shame, he at once gathered into his outcry the whole of the people, identifying himself with them as he spoke of "our iniquities . . . our guiltiness," and so forth. He went back over all the history in imagination as he knelt before his God, and clearly saw that it had been one long story of failure and of consequent disaster. He then spoke of his consciousness of the grace of God manifest in making possible the return of a remnant of the people through favor of the kings of Persia. Then the surging sorrow of the new failure found expression in free and full confession, until at last, without any petition for deliverance, he cast the people before God with a recognition of His righteousness and of their inability to stand in its presence.

It is a fine revelation of the only attitude in which any man can become a mediator. There is first an overwhelming sense of sin. This is accompanied, and perhaps caused by, that deeper sense of the righteousness and grace of God. It finds expression in agonized and unsparing confession. The passion of the whole movement is evidence of its reality. No man can really know the righteousness of God, and in its light see sin, and remain quiet and calculating and unmoved.

EZRA 10

The sincerity and passion of Ezra's vicarious repentance produced immediate results. The people had gathered about him through the long hours of the day, and it would seem that they became conscious of the enormity of their sin as they saw how this man was so affected by it.

At last, one of their number spoke to him, acknowledging the sin, and suggesting the remedy. Then immediately Ezra became a man of action. He first called the people into sacred covenant, that they would put away the evil thing from among them; and then proceeded to lead them in carrying out their covenant with strict and impartial justice and severity. All the marriages contracted with the women of the land were annulled, and thus by drastic measures the people were brought back to the place of separation. How widespread the evil was is gathered from the list of the names with which the record closes. Priests, Levites, and people had been guilty. None of them was exempt from the reformation, which was carried out with great thoroughness.

The man who sets himself to seek, to do, to teach the law of God invariably brings himself to where sorrow will be his portion and intrepid courage his only strength. If such devotion issue in such experiences, it also is the secret of strength, enabling a man to stand for God, and realize His purpose; and thus, moreover, to be the true friend and deliverer of the people of God.

Nehemiah

NEHEMIAH 1

This is the last Book of Old Testament history. An interval of about twelve years occurred between the reformation under Ezra and the coming of Nehemiah. The story is the continuation of the work commenced by Zerubbabel rebuilding the wall.

With a fine touch of natural and unconscious humility, Nehemiah tells us, in parenthesis only, what his office was at the court of the Gentile king. He was cupbearer. Such a position was one of honor, and admitted the holder not only into the presence of the king, but into relationships of some familiarity. Nehemiah's account of himself in this chapter gives us a splendid illustration of patriotism on the highest level. It is evident, first, that he had no inclination to disown his own people, for he spoke of those who came to the court as "my brethren." In the next place, it is manifest that his consciousness of relationship was a living one, in that he held intercourse with them. Moreover, he was truly interested, and made inquiry concerning Jerusalem.

The news brought to him was full of sadness, and all the man's devotion to his people was manifest in his grief as he heard the sad story. The final proof of true patriotism lay in his recognition of the relationship between his people and God, and in his carrying the burden of God in prayer. The prayer itself was full of beauty, and revealed a correct conception of what prayer under such circumstances ought to be. It opened with confession. Without reserve, he acknowledged the sin of the people, and identified himself with it. He then proceeded to plead the promises of God made to them, and ended with a personal and definite petition that God would give him favor in the eyes of the king.

NEHEMIAH 2

Nehemiah's sadness could not wholly be hidden. He had not been habitually a sad man, as he himself declares; but the sorrow of his nation manifested itself as he stood before the king.

It has been suggested that this was part of his plan. Such an interpretation strains the narrative, for Nehemiah confessed that when the king detected signs of mourning he was filled with fear. Yet through fear a splendid courage manifested itself as he told the king the cause of his grief, and boldly asked to be allowed to go up and help his brethren. The secret of the courage that mastered the fear appears in his statement, "I prayed to the God of heaven, and I said to the king."

His prayer being answered, he took his departure for Jerusalem. His sagacity is displayed through all the subsequent story. It appeared first on his way to Jerusalem. He arrived quietly, and not trusting to the reports which had reached him, he made private investigation. Having ascertained the true state of affairs, he gathered the elders together and called them to arise and build. Opposition was displayed at once by surrounding enemies, and with strong determination Nehemiah made it perfectly clear that no co-operation would be permitted with those who derided the effort. It is impossible to read this story without learning how the work of God should be prosecuted under difficult circumstances.

NEHEMIAH 3

This chapter is supremely interesting in its revelation of method. That it is preserved for us at all shows how system characterized Nehemiah's procedure. The description proceeds round the entire wall of the city. Beginning at the sheep gate near the Temple, through which the sacrifices passed, we pass the fish gate in the merchant quarter, on by the old gate in the ancient part of the city, and come, successively, to the valley gate, the dung gate, the gate of the fountain, the water gate, the horse gate, the east gate, the gate Miphkad, until we arrive again at the sheep gate, where the chapter ends.

It has been said that this is not a complete account. It is far more likely that where difficulties arise in the length of the wall covered by the section, the solution is in the fact that the wall was not everywhere in as bad repair as at some places. The arrangements indicated the necessity for speedy work, and were characterized by a sense of the importance of division of labor, and a fitting apportionment thereof in the matter of persons and neighborhoods.

NEHEMIAH 4

As the work proceeded, the opposition of outsiders turned from derision to anger, but rose no higher at the moment than contempt. However, Nehemiah was conscious of the menace of this attitude, and lifted his heart in prayer to God. An illuminative sentence, "The people had a mind to work," shows how completely Nehemiah had captured and inspired them, and we are therefore not surprised when we read that the wall was half finished.

At this point, however, opposition became very wroth, and organized a conspiracy to hinder the work. Immediately, and with a keen sense of the necessity, Nehemiah says, "We made our prayer, and set a watch." In his method there was neither foolish independence of God nor foolhardy neglect of human responsibility. Everything was done to procure that twofold attitude of simple faith in God and determined dependence on personal endeavor which always makes for victory. How often God's workers fail for lack of one or other of these important elements.

NEHEMIAH 5

A new difficulty now presented itself. This time it arose among the people themselves. The rich among them exacted usury from their poorer brethren to such an extent as to oppress and impoverish them.

Perhaps nowhere in the story does the nobility of Nehemiah's character more clearly manifest itself than here. There is a fine touch in his declaration, "I consulted with myself, and contended with the nobles." His consultation with himself resulted in his determination to set an example of self-denial in that he took no usury, or even the things which were his right as the appointed governor of the people. Such an example produced immediate results in that all the nobles did the same. Thus the people were relieved, and were filled with joy; and consequently went forward with their work with new enthusiasm.

From the position of personal rectitude a man is always strong to deal effectively with wrong in others. Contention with nobles who are violating principles of justice, which is not preceded by consultation with self, is of no avail. When the life is free from all complicity with evil, it is strong to smite it and overcome it in others.

NEHEMIAH 6

In this chapter we have the account of the continuity of opposition to the work of Nehemiah. It moved, however, on to a new plane. Having begun in contempt, and proceeded through conspiracy, it now attempted to accomplish its end by subtlety. Affecting friendship, the enemies of Nehemiah four times proposed conference with him, which he resolutely declined, and pressed forward with his work. This was followed by a slanderous open letter, which he was urged to consider. Again, with singular directness, he denied the slander, and carried on his building.

Finding that he was not to be seduced, they attempted a new method, to fill him with fear, and he was advised to hide. This advice he scorned, and continued to urge the workers. Through the whole period he was harassed by the complicity of certain of the nobles with Tobiah. He was constantly compelled to listen to their stories concerning the excellence of this man.

This whole chapter is a wonderful revelation of the true attitude of the servant of God toward his work. Nothing must be allowed to slacken endeavor or to turn the mind aside from the main purpose. Each of these methods illustrates a peril. Conferences with the enemies of the King about His work are always to be avoided. Slanders concerning the workers and their purpose may be denied, but the work must never cease, even for vindication by argument. With the consciousness of the divine purpose in the heart, no man can secure his own safety by hiding, even in the Temple of God. The perpetual wear of reiterated stories concerning the excellence of those who would hinder the building, must be resisted zealously. In all these things Nehemiah was a conspicuous success.

NEHEMIAH 7

At last the wall was completed by setting up the doors, and placing in order porters, singers, and Levites. In the first few verses of this chapter we have an account of the arrangements for the safety of the city. They are characterized by statesmanlike caution. Through all the country round about there were enemies, and the position of the partially restored city, therefore, was one of perpetual peril. Nehemiah was conscious of this, and made the most careful provision for the hour for opening and closing the city gates, and the arrangement of the watchers.

No greater mistake can ever be made in connection with work for God in difficult places than to lack caution. Carelessness is never a sign of courage. True bravery perpetually prepares for attack. The man who, sword in hand, has built to completion does not imagine that swinging doors indicate that the time for relaxing watchfulness has come.

The rest of the chapter is occupied with a register, which is almost undoubtedly a copy of that in the Book of Ezra. The alterations are few and unimportant, and it is distinctly stated that the register was found.

NEHEMIAH 8

We now come to the second section of the Book, which gives an account of the special reading of the Law, and the reform which followed. Ezra now appears on the scene. There has been some speculation as to why he has not been mentioned before. It may be that he was absent from Jerusalem during the earlier part of the work of Nehemiah, or it may be—which perhaps is more probable—that the work already done was such as he had no direct part in, and that now he appeared in co-operation with Nehemiah in the particular kind of work which was especially his.

In this section we have the account of a most interesting and remarkable religious convention. The first day saw the assembling of the people. The phrase, "gathered as one man," indicates the unity of purpose with which they had come. It was a day given to reading the Law. This was not merely reading aloud passages from the Law, or even the whole book of the Law. It was reading, accompanied by exposition, and the exposition was undertaken by men especially appointed to act with Ezra. It would seem almost as if there were first a public reading, and then a separation of the assembly into groups, while the appointed Levites explained and enforced the terms of the Law. It was a day of conviction, resulting in great sadness among the people as they became conscious of their failure. It was a day of comfort, for Nehemiah and those associated with him, insisted on it. The finding of the Law, and the return of the people to its consideration, were reasons for joy rather than for sadness.

It is almost impossible to read this chapter without being reminded of the words of the Master spoken long afterwards, "Blessed are they that mourn; for they shall be comforted." On the second day there was a smaller gathering of the rulers, who came in order more perfectly to understand the law of God. Here, as always if such gatherings are sincere, an immediate application was made in observing the feast of Tabernacles.

NEHEMIAH 9

After a brief interval, following the feast came the great day of humiliation. The people separated themselves entirely from all who were not actually within the Covenant, and gave themselves to confession and humbling before God. In all this they were led by the Levites, and the chapter is largely filled with the great prayer they offered on this occasion. It may have been especially prepared for them, and used by all of them; or perhaps it is a condensed account of their approach to God on behalf of the humbling of the people.

In the first section (5-15), the prayer was praise, first to God for what He is in Himself in majesty (5, 6), then to Him as the Founder of the nation through the calling of Abraham (7, 8); yet further to Him as the Deliverer from Egypt's bondage (9-11), and, finally, as the One who had guided as well as delivered (12-15).

The second section sets forth His grace in contrast to the repeated failure of the people (16-29). This section is a frank confession of repeated sin, and yet the burden of it is rather His being a God ready to pardon. The last movement in the prayer is definite seeking for His continued goodness and help. It is a fine model of a confessing people's true approach to God. The heart is strengthened in contemplation of His essential glory and constant grace, and out of such consciousness it breathes its cry for help.

NEHEMIAH 10

Following their humiliation, the people entered into a new covenant with God. This covenant was sealed representatively by the priests (3-8), Levites (9-13), rulers (14-27). To its terms all the people agreed (28).

These terms were then set forth in general phrases, and in particular application. Generally the people promised "to walk in God's law . . . to observe and do all the commandments." Particularly the covenant referred to matters in which undoubtedly the people had been in danger of failure, namely, intermarriage with the heathen, neglect of the Sabbath, of Temple maintenance and arrangement, and offering of first fruits and tithes. In the light of the Law, as it was expounded on the day of convocation, and in the power of the approach to God on the day of humiliation, the people entered into covenant on the day of dedication.

NEHEMIAH 11

We now begin the third and final division of the Book, in which is set forth the arrangements made for settlement of the cities. It is the last piece of history which the Old Testament contains. Some revelation of later conditions is obtainable from the study of the prophets, but nothing more is directly written until, after a lapse of four centuries, the history is resumed in the New Testament.

In this chapter begins the account of the settlement of Jerusalem particularly. Perhaps not more than fifty thousand of the people, all told, had returned from captivity. By no means all of these had come to Jerusalem. Many of them were scattered through the surrounding cities. Jerusalem was peculiarly difficult of settlement, in that it was the center of danger and of possible attack. It was therefore arranged that the princes should dwell in the city, and that ten per cent of the people, selected by lot, must take up their abode there. In addition to these, some voluntarily came forward to dwell in the place of danger. These were especially honored by all the people (11:2).

NEHEMIAH 12

Here the story of the settlement of the people in Jerusalem is completed. This is followed by an account of the solemn dedication of the wall. It would seem as though it had been postponed for some considerable time. Differences of opinion exist as to the length of time, some placing the dedication in immediate relation to what succeeds, which undoubtedly happened twelve years after Nehemiah's first coming. Others would place it within a few months of the actual completion of the wall. It is difficult to decide, and the matter is of no moment.

The dedication ceremony proceeded in three stages. First, the two processions of singers who chanted the praises of God; second, the reading of the Law; and, finally, the separation of the mixed multitude from the people of God. Thus the reformers perpetually sought to bring these people back in every way to a recognition of the deepest truth concerning the national life, namely, its relation to God.

NEHEMIAH 13

In this final section we have the account of Nehemiah's last reformation. After building the wall he had evidently gone back to the court of the king. Twelve years later, seeking permission, he returned, and the last deeds recorded were such as reveal the continued strength and loyalty of the man.

Four abuses confronted him. Without the slightest hesitation, or any sign of weakness in his method, he set himself to correct them. Eliashib, the priest, had given place, within the very Temple of God, to the man Tobiah, who had done so much to hinder the work of building the wall. Nehemiah arrived, flung out the occupant and furniture, and restored the chamber to its proper use. He found, in the second place, that the Levites, instead of being able to devote their whole time to the service of the Temple, had to earn their living, because the people had neglected to bring in the tithe. He contended with the nobles, and corrected this abuse. Moreover, he found that the Sabbath of the Lord was violated, and restored the divine order in this matter. Finally, he found that the people had made mixed marriages again, and with characteristic roughness and force he dealt with the matter. No words can better convey the impression than his own: "I contended with them, and cursed them, and smote certain of them, and plucked off their hair, and made them swear by God." One can understand Nehemiah's anger by comparing these abuses, which he had to stop, with the terms of the covenant made by them on the day of dedication (chapter 10).

Esther

ESTHER 1

The events recorded in the Book of Esther occurred between the completion of the Temple and the mission of Ezra (between Ezra 6 and 7). In all likelihood the narrative, as we have it, was taken directly from the Persian records. It is a fragment of secular history taken for sacred purposes. The story reveals the same principle of the overruling of God on behalf of His people which marks all their history.

The first scene is a great feast in the palace of the king. It was characterized by all the gorgeousness peculiar to the East, and resolved itself into drunken revelry. In the midst of this, the king commanded Queen Vashti to appear before him and the assembled nobles. The one redeeming feature in the revelation of conditions at the court of Ahasuerus was Vashti's refusal to obey the king. She paid the price of her loyalty to her womanhood in being deposed. Incidentally, the story reveals the place which woman occupied outside the Covenant of the chosen people. She was at once the plaything and the slave of man.

ESTHER 2

In this chapter we have a revelation of customs obtaining in the household of the king. We can read them with thankfulness that wherever the purifying forces of revealed religion have operated they have forever become impossible.

In the midst of this story Mordecai appears on the scene. Living with him was his cousin, whom he had taken to be his daughter. In carrying out the decree of the king, she was taken to the royal palace in the company of the maidens. Mordecai's action in this matter is open to question. His love for Esther was evident, and the picture of him walking before the court of the women's house indicated his continued interest in her. One can only hope that her presence there was not due to his scheming for place and power. In any case his advice that she should not betray her nationality was questionable, as her position at the court of the king was in grave peril for a daughter of the Covenant. Her beauty captured the king, and she was made queen in place of Vashti. Her presence in the palace was part of that process by which the overruling God preserves His people and frustrates the foe. This overruling is even more remarkable if the action of Mordecai was that of scheming.

ESTHER 3

In this section we have a picture of the procedure of government in the court of the king. Haman was promoted to supreme authority, and the portrait of the man is naturally and vividly presented to us—haughty and imperious, proud and cruel. Mordecai's refusal to bow down to him and do him reverence may in all probability be accounted for by the simple fact that he was a Jew, or perhaps it may be that Mordecai was familiar with facts concerning Haman which made it impossible for him to do him any honor. Be that as it may, the malice of the man was stirred, not merely against Mordecai, but against all his people, and he made use of his influence with the king to obtain authority practically to exterminate them. In the acts of evil men strange and inexplicable factors arise which can be accounted for satisfactorily only by belief in the government of God. The delay of months in carrying out his cruel intention was, in all likelihood, prompted by his desire to make the work of extermination thorough. Yet how wonderfully it gave time for all the events which ended in the deliverance of the people of God.

ESTHER 4

The news of the intended slaughter reached Esther in the royal palace, and she sent to make inquiries. Thus between the extreme need of her people and the king she became a direct link. The custom and law of the court forbade her to approach her lord save at his command. Still, the urgency of the case appealed to her, and with splendid heroism she determined to venture.

Conscious of her need of moral support, she asked that the people might fast with her. There is a note of sacrifice and abandonment in her words, "If I perish, I perish." Her decision was arrived at after strong pressure from Mordecai; and in all probability there is evident in it a desire to save her own life, for he had warned her that she was as greatly in peril as were the rest of her people. Granting all that can be said concerning the motive of her action, the supreme teaching of the story moves on, namely, of the care of God for His people, and of His use of a natural means to deliver them.

ESTHER 5

Here we have the story of Esther's venture and its success. Things might have been very different, but the graciousness of the king, notwithstanding Esther's violation of the law of the palace, was undoubtedly due to the disposition of that God in whose hand are the ways of kings, whether they will or no.

Her request was at first of the simplest. She invited the king and Haman to a banquet. Haman's overweening pride appears in the account which follows. He gathered his friends, and boasted of his riches and advancement; and now of this last favor, that he alone was invited to accompany the king to Esther's banquet. At the back of selfish ambition some cankering pain forever torments. In the case of Haman it was Mordecai's refusal to acknowledge him or do him reverence, and he frankly admitted to his friends that nothing else satisfied him while Mordecai remained in his way. Acting on the advice of wife and friends, he committed the unutterable folly of attempting to make the time of the banquet merry for himself by having first erected a gallows for Mordecai.

ESTHER 6

In the economy of God vast issues follow apparently trivial things. A sleepless night is in itself transient and almost trivial. Yet it has often been a time of revelation and surprise, affecting the after years. In the case of Ahasuerus it was another of the forces by which God moved to preserve His people. To while away its hours, the records were read to the king, and a deed of Mordecai which had passed from his memory led to hasty and strange happenings, which must have filled the heart of Haman with new anger and terror. His enemy was suddenly lifted from obscurity to the most conspicuous position in the kingdom —he had become a man whom the king delighted to honor. In the words of Zeresh, wife of Haman, there was manifest that strange fear of God's ancient people which had wrought so much in their history.

ESTHER 7

Events now moved rapidly forward. By the way of the banquet Haman passed to the gallows. It was a fierce and terrible judgment, and yet characterized by poetic justice. The man who for no reason other than his pride had prepared the gallows for Mordecai found himself suddenly stripped of all authority and ending his career by the very instrument his brutality had prepared for another.

The very core of Haman's hatred for Mordecai was his own self-centered and self-consuming pride and ambition. This was of so masterful a nature that one man's refusal to render homage to him inspired in him such hatred that he was determined to encompass, not the death of that man only, but also of all those who bore blood relation to him. The nets of evil plotting and malicious enterprise swing far out in the tides of human life, but never far enough to enmesh God. He remains beyond them all, and gathering them in the hands of His power He makes them include the men who weave them to destroy others.

ESTHER 8

The deposition and death of Haman issued naturally in the promotion of Mordecai. However, the peril to his people was not yet averted. The royal proclamation had gone forth that on the thirteenth day of the twelfth month the Hebrew people should be exterminated. Under the constitution no royal proclamation could be reversed. Something else must be done to save the people. The king permitted Mordecai to write to his people, allowing them to arm and defend themselves.

It is a wonderful picture of the king's own messengers hurrying through the country with letters, urging the people to be ready against what had been intended to be the fateful day of their slaughter. So strange a happening was it that the Jews were filled with gladness and joy, while a new fear of them fell on the native people, and many of the "people of the land became Jews."

ESTHER 9

In this final section of the Book we have an account, first, of the arrival of the fateful day and all that happened thereon. It was a day when the changed conditions in the case of Haman and Mordecai were revealed throughout the whole of the provinces. Men who had persecuted the Jews and were looking for the opportunity of wreaking their vengeance by royal decree found themselves filling the places which they had intended their foes to occupy.

In memory of the great deliverance the feast of Purim was established. According to Jewish tradition, "all the feasts shall cease in the days of the Messiah, except the feast of Purim." It is a remarkable thing that while there have been breaks in the observance of the other great feasts, and some of them have been practically discontinued, this one has been maintained. It is always a time of rejoicing. The first part of the day is spent in the study of the Book of Esther and its exposition; the second is wholly given over to keeping holiday. Whatever view we may hold of the Book, it is certain that Jewish leaders have treated it as an exposition of the method by which God wrought deliverance for His people even while they were in exile.

ESTHER 10

Here we have the last picture of this man Mordecai. It is a singularly fine one. Whatever may have been questionable in some of the methods he adopted with regard to Esther—and here we are not able to be dogmatic —it is evident that he was of fine character. Probably all the experiences of the goodness of God had brought him to finer life. Evidently he retained the favor of Ahasuerus, for his position was next to the king. This did not alienate him from his own people. He continued to seek their good, and to speak peace to them; and therefore was held in highest honor among them, as well as trusted where he exercised authority.

Perhaps there is no severer test of greatness of soul than advancement in the favor of kings. Too often it has meant the undoing of men who, though poor or in disfavor in high places have remained true. The man who can pass to wealth and position among the great ones of the earth, and still maintain his integrity and his loyalty to his own kith and kin, is ever a great man, and the secrets of such greatness invariably are that the man's roots are in God.

Job

JOB 1

In magnificence of argument and beauty of style this Book is one of the grandest in the divine Library. The story of Job is presented in dramatic form.

It opens with a picture of Job. He is seen in three respects: first, as to character. The opening verses declare him to be "perfect and upright, and one that feared God and eschewed evil." The language is simple, and suggests that high integrity which never fails to command respect. In the second place, he is seen in the midst of his home life, rejoicing in his children, not attempting to stay their festivity, while yet anxious concerning their character. Finally, he is revealed to us as a man of great wealth. The combination is rare and remarkable. The man stands before us, a strong and majestic figure, upright and tender, just and gracious; in the language of the chronicler, the "greatest of all the children of the east."

Then we are confronted with a most startling situation. Heaven is seen in argument with hell about earth. God is heard in defense of a man against Satan. The angel messengers of the Most High are seen gathering to Him in counsel. Among them was one, like them in nature, and yet unlike. He is here named the adversary. His estimate of Job was that his attitude toward God was based on pure selfishness, and that if what Job possessed was taken from him he would cease to be loyal to the throne of God. To the adversary permission was given to deal with the possessions of Job. To this permission bounds were set beyond which he might not go. The person of the patriarch was not to be touched. The storm broke on the head of Job. All the advantage seemed to be with the enemy, for up to a certain point Job was powerless against him. There was, however, an inner citadel which the enemy could not touch. Satan is revealed here in startling light. His malice is seen in the choice of time. He strikes in the midst of festivity. His persistence is manifest in that he proceeds to the uttermost bound of the permission. His limitation is evident in that he cannot transgress that bound.

The answer of Job to the sweeping storm was characterized by heroism and vast breadth of outlook. There was no affectation of stoicism. He was afflicted, and showed it in all the outward signs of mourning. In the midst of these, however, he turned to the highest act of life, and bowed in reverential worship. His words were of the profoundest philosophy. He recognized that man is more than the things he gathers about him. His beginning and his ending are in nakedness. Discerning the hand of the Lord in bane as well as in blessing, he lifted to Him, out of the midst of dire calamity, the sacrifice of praise. Thus the adversary's lie in the council of heaven was disproved.

JOB 2

Again the solemn council met, and again Satan was present. The Most High uttered the same estimate of His servant as before, adding thereto a declaration of Job's victory in the conflict which had taken place. The adversary declared that the limits which God had set had hindered him in the accomplishment of his purpose. Though Job had triumphed over his loss of possession, he was not therefore proven loyal to God. The essential greatness of the man was unimpaired in that his own life had not been touched by weakness. Let him but feel there, and renunciation of God would immediately ensue. It is the devil's perpetual estimate of humanity that flesh is supreme. Once again he was permitted to prove his slander, but again the divine limit was set to the sphere of his operation.

The enemy went forth on his terrible work, and immediately we are presented with the awful picture of the man of God weakened in his personality by the unutterable misery of physical affliction. To this was now added the new and subtle attack of the sympathy of his wife. Her love, utterly misguided it is true, counseled that he die by renouncing God. His answer was characterized by tenderness toward her, and yet by unswerving loyalty to God.

Here the adversary passes out of sight. He has done his dire and dreadful work. His slander is manifestly a lie.

The darkest days of all for Job now began. There is a stimulus in the clash of catastrophe. The very shock and surprise of the strokes create strength in which men triumph. It is in the brooding silence which enwraps the soul afterward that the fiercest fight is waged. To that the patriarch now passed. These verses tell the story of the coming of his friends. There were only three of them, joined presently, perchance, by another, when Elihu came on the scene. While it is true that Job suffered more at the hands of these friends ultimately than by the attacks of the foe, yet some recognition must be made of the goodness of the men. They were admirable, first, because they came at all. Even more were they to be admired because they sat in silence with him for seven days and nights. In overwhelming sorrows, true friendship almost invariably demonstrates itself more perfectly by silence than by speech. And even in spite of the fact that Job's friends caused him sorrow by their words, they are more to be admired because what they thought concerning him they dared to say to him, rather than *about* him to others.

JOB 3

Silent sympathy always creates an opportunity for grief to express itself. Job's outcry was undoubtedly an answer to their sympathy. So far, it was good, and they had helped him. It is always better to tell out the dark questionings of the heart than to brood over them. This lamentation of Job is of the nature of a cry for escape, rather than a description of the oppressing sorrows. In it there are three movements The first consists of a terrible cursing of the day of his birth and the night of his conception (1-10). In it the anguish which hates the very fact of being sobs itself out in agony.

The second consists of lamentation

over his preservation (11-19). In it he contemplated the blessings of death. To him in these hours of living sorrow cessation of being would be, he thought, the greatest blessing, a condition in which men escape the troubles of life.

Finally, existence is lamented in his own particular case, because characterized by such unceasing and irremedial sorrow (20-26). It is a great lamentation, pulsing with pain, expressive of the meanings of the most terrible of all sorrows, the sense of mystery, the inexplicability of it all.

JOB 4

Now begins the great controversy between Job and his friends, which occupies the major portion of the Book. This controversy moves in three cycles. The first, commencing here, runs through chapter fourteen. In it each of the three friends speaks to Job, and is answered by him.

The first speaker, Eliphaz, commenced with a courteous apology for speaking at all, and yet a declaration that he could not withhold himself. After expressing surprise at Job's complaint, and asking if his integrity ought not to be a sufficient guarantee of his safety, he proceeded to a general explanation of the problem of suffering, declaring it to be God's punishment of wickedness, a harvest for which there must have been a previous sowing. He argued the truth of this by insisting on the fact of man's sin in the sight of God. This had been revealed to him in a solitary hour, in the dead of night, by a mystic presence, a form. The inference of this is that Job's suffering was the result of Job's sin.

JOB 5

Proceeding, Eliphaz asked Job to whom he would appeal, to which of the holy ones, that is, as against the truth which he had declared, or in defense of himself. In the light of evident guilt, all vexation and jealousy, such as Job had manifested, constitute such sin as produces final undoing. His attempted explanation of the meaning of suffering he then crystallized into proverbial form:

> Affliction cometh not forth of the dust,
> Neither doth trouble spring out of the ground.

That is to say again that there must have been a sowing for such a harvest.

Eliphaz then proceeded to utter his advice to Job by telling him what *he* would do. *He* "would seek unto God," and to Him commit his cause. This declaration is followed by a passage of great beauty, in which he tells of the faithfulness and might of the Most High. In order to persuade his suffering friend to such action, he described the confidence and ultimate deliverance and restoration which would come to him if his trust was in God. It is all very beautiful, but absolutely short-sighted. Eliphaz had no knowledge of those secret councils in heaven, and was making the mistake of attempting to press all things into the compass of his philosophy.

JOB 6

Job's answer is a magnificent and terrible outcry. First, he speaks of his pain as a protest against the method of Eliphaz. His reply is not to the deduction which Eliphaz' argument suggested, but rather to the charge it made, of unreasonableness and folly manifest in his lamentation. Eliphaz had used terms of strong condemnation. Job declared, in effect, that he did not understand the cry because he did not know the pain. His vexation and calamity should be set over against each other, poised in fair balances. If this were done, the calamity would be found to be so heavy as to excuse even the rashness of speech. The wail is always evidence of a want.

The wild ass does not bray when he has grass, nor the ox low over his fodder. Having declared this, his sorrow seemed to surge on his soul anew, and he cried out for death because his strength was not equal to the strain thus placed upon him. His strength was not "the strength of stones," nor was his "flesh of brass."

Job then turned on his friends with reproaches of fine satire. He had expected kindness, but was disappointed. Here there would seem to be reference not merely to the attitude of Eliphaz, but to that attitude as a culminating cruelty. His eyes were wandering back to olden days, and he spoke of "my brethren," likening them to a brook in the desert to which the traveling caravans turned, only to find them consumed and passed. He declared that his friends were nothing. Reproach merged into a fierce demand that instead of generalization and allusion, there should be definiteness in the charges they made against him. "What," says he, "doth your arguing reprove?" There is a majesty in this impatience with men who philosophize in the presence of agony, and it is impossible to read it without a consciousness of profound sympathy with the suffering man.

JOB 7

Without waiting for their reply, Job broke out into a new lamentation, more bitter than the first, for it came out of a heart whose sorrow was aggravated by the misunderstanding of friends. Indeed, its very strength was a new protest against the only open charge Eliphaz had made, namely, of sin and foolishness in complaining at all.

In this lamentation there are two movements: first, a great complaint concerning the stress and misery of life (1-10), and, second, a complaint directed against God (11-21). The toil of life is strenuous indeed. It is a warfare. Man is a hireling, a servant, whose labor issues in nothing, and whose rest is disturbed with tossing. Nothing is satisfying, for nothing is lasting, and figure is piled on figure to emphasize this: a weaver's shuttle, wind, the look of the eye, the vanishing cloud. There was absolutely no ray of hope in this outlook on life. Because of it Job complained not only of life, but directly against God. It was determined. "I will not refrain . . . I will speak . . . I will complain." How terribly the vision of God was blurred in these days of suffering is illustrated as the man cried out that God would not let him alone, and asked why he must be tried every moment. It is such a cry and complaint that none can understand who has not passed into some sorrow equally severe. In saying this we simply state the fact, and those tempted to criticism of the attitude should remember that God patiently bore and waited, knowing that at the back of the complaint was an unshaken confidence, even though for a moment the surfaces were swept with the hurricanes of doubt blowing up out of the darkness.

JOB 8

In answer to Job, the next of his friends, Bildad, took up the argument. There is greater directness in his speech than in that of Eliphaz. By comparison it lacks in courtesy, but gains in force. He made no reference to Job's attack on his friends, but proceeded to make one statement of the righteousness of God from two standpoints. He first protested against the idea which Job's complaint had seemed to advance, that God's dealings are ever unjust with the righteous (1-7). It would be better for him to recognize that his children had died on account of their sin, and himself turn to God. Next he affirmed that those who forget God can no more flourish than can the rush without mire, or the flag without water. The paths of such as forget God are described with great force (8-19). The two things are then summarized (20):

> God will not cast away a perfect man,
> Neither will He uphold the evildoers.

This is followed by an expression of hope concerning Job. Here again we have the same general thought as appeared in the speech of Eliphaz, namely, that God is righteous, and prospers the just, and punishes evil. No direct charge was made against Job. He was left to make his own deduction and application.

JOB 9

Job now answered Bildad. He first admitted the truth of the general proposition,

> Of a truth I know that it is so;

and then propounded the great question, which he subsequently proceeded to discuss in the light of his own suffering.

> How can a man be just with God?

The question was not the expression of his sense of guilt. The conception which overwhelmed him was that of God, and ere the answer closes it will be seen that in the light of his innocence he could not understand his suffering. His question,

> Who hath hardened himself against Him,
> and prospered?

does not suggest the impotence of rebellion but the folly of contention.

Job then described the power of God. In the bitterness of his soul his consciousness of that power was of a terrific and overwhelming force. This God, moreover, is invisible. His presence is a fact, and yet Job cannot perceive. Finally, He is invincible. Therefore it is useless for a man to attempt to be just with Him.

Still discussing his question, Job spoke of his own condition. It was hopeless. God would not have patience with him, and his very attempt to prove himself innocent would issue in condemnation. Seeing that he seemed to charge this injustice on God, he asked in amazement,

> If it be not He, who then is it?

There was no meeting place between him and God. Full of beauty in the light of the Christian revelation is the cry of this afflicted man in his agony for a daysman who "might lay his hand upon us both."

JOB 10

Notwithstanding all this, Job appealed to God. Turning from his answer to Bildad, he poured out his agony as in the presence of the Most High. It was by no means a hopeful appeal, but it was an appeal. He asked why God can contend with him, and with a terrible and yet sincere daring, born of affliction, he suggested questions: Does God delight in what He is doing? Is God's vision faulty as man's that He cannot see? Are God's days and years brief that He is afraid Job may escape Him?

Following these questions, came his great appeal, which is also in the form of a question. God has made him. Why does He destroy him? This thought he carried out in detail on both sides, describing first his creation, and the graciousness of God's past dealing with him; and then the affliction, and his own inability to plead his cause. Once again he asked why he had been born, and in terrible anguish cried for God to let him alone a little that he might have brief respite ere he passed into death. The deepening of his sorrow is seen in this dark description of death. On a previous occasion it had been a land of rest and cessation, but now it is a place of darkness devoid of order. If we are tempted to criticize, we should ever remember that in the whole Book God lays no charge against His child. Terrible things were these which Job uttered about God, but at least they were honest.

JOB 11

When Job had ceased, Zophar, the last of the three friends, answered him. His method was characterized by even greater plainness than that of Bildad. Indeed, there was a roughness and directness about him absent from his friends' manner. This may either reveal a man of different temperament, or that now, with greater definiteness and daring, Job had denied their philosophy by affirming his innocence.

He first affirmed the necessity for answering, describing Job as "a man full of talk," and declaring that his boastings could not silence his friends. Zophar's complaint against him is expressed in the words:

> Thou sayest, my doctrine is pure,
> And I am clean in thine eyes.

He wished that God would speak. If He would, then Job would know that all his suffering was less than his iniquity. Job had affirmed the wisdom of God, and yet, in the thinking of Zophar, had questioned it. Therefore, in a passage full of beauty, he reaffirmed it, and insisted that this God of wisdom knows men. He intended to declare to Job that even though he might not be conscious of his own sin, yet sin was there, and God saw it.

This is again a restatement of the same philosophy as that of his friends. He was arguing from the suffering of Job to his sin. If Zophar was rough of manner, his desire and hope for Job may be observed, for his description of the prosperity which will come if he but set his heart right is longer and more beautiful than that of either Eliphaz or Bildad.

JOB 12

Job's last reply in this first cycle is to the whole argument, as well as to Zophar's application of it. From beginning to end, it thrills with sarcasm, while it maintains its denial of personal guilt.

In the first movement he treated with contempt his friends' interpretation of God, claiming to know more of Him than they did. In this there are two movements, in the first of which (1-6), he dealt with his friends; in the second (7-25), he turned to the subject of the wisdom and power of God with which they had dealt. His first words reveal his contempt, as in biting sarcasm he says:

> No doubt but ye are the people,
> And wisdom shall die with you.

He then rebuked them, declaring that he was not inferior to them, and yet they had made him a laughingstock. He marked his contempt for them as he affirmed theirs for him.

Turning then to the discussion of the things they had emphasized concerning God, he declared that the knowledge was self-evident. The beast and fowl, the earth and the fishes, are acquainted with these matters. It is knowledge of the simplest that all these things are the works of God and that He sustains them. His wisdom is unquestioned. As to God's power, in a passage full of passion and force, Job described it in nature, and among the great men of the earth, counselors and judges, kings and princes, both speaking and governing, amid the nations themselves, increasing and destroying, uplifting and degrading.

JOB 13

Continuing his answer, Job restated his conviction that his knowledge was not inferior to theirs, and declared that his appeal was to God (1-3). Before making this appeal there is an introductory passage in which he first addressed himself to them in terms of anger (4-12), and then avowed his determination to make his appeal directly to God, and urged two conditions. His contempt for his friends as they are revealed in their attitude toward him knows no bounds. He described them as "forgers of lies," and "physicians of no value"; and proceeded to turn their argument back upon them. They had declared that God is righteous, and visits men according to their deeds. They had been speaking unrighteously for God, and therefore must accept His judgment upon themselves. He finally dismissed all their argument as "proverbs of ashes." Announcing his determination to appeal to God, even though God slay him in this determination, he found some comfort in believing that the godless cannot be heard. He urged two conditions: first, that God withdraw His hand from him; and, second, that He not make him afraid by His terror.

After these preliminary matters, Job's speech becomes a direct appeal to God. He first demanded to know his sins, and why God dealt with him as a leaf, as a moth-eaten garment.

JOB 14

Taking a more general outlook, Job declared that man's life is ever transitory, and full of trouble. This should be a reason why God should pity him, and let him work out the brief period of its duration in quietness (1-6). Naturally, following this, he spoke of what the end of a man's doing is, showing the endlessness thereof. There is hope for a tree that it will bud again, but there is none for a man (7-12). This dark assertion seems to have created in the mind of Job a question of wondering hope,

If a man die, shall he live?

and he declared that if this were so, then he could endure through all the days of warfare (13-15). The whole answer ends in lamentation over his present condition, which is so strangely in contrast to the hope suggested.

Thus ends the first cycle. In it Job's friends had, with differing emphasis, propounded the one general philosophy that God is righteous, and punishes the wicked while He blesses the good. They had left Job to make the personal application. He had denied their philosophy by opposing facts to their arguments. He was not wicked but just, and yet he was afflicted. He could not understand it himself, and while refusing to accept their view, was crying out to God for some explanation.

JOB 15

Here the second cycle of argument begins, and again Eliphaz is the first speaker. It is at once evident that Job's answers had wounded him.

He first criticized Job's manner, charging him with using mere words as arguments. His manner, moreover, had been characterized by unwarranted boldness, and by absence of reverence in the presence of God. In the second place, he criticized Job's claim to wisdom, and, in so doing, he compelled satire to answer satire (*cf.* verse 7 with 12:2). Finally, he formally criticized Job's attitude toward God. How dare he turn his spirit against God, in whose sight the very heavens are unclean?

Turning from his rebuke of Job's attitude, Eliphaz again declared his view of the meaning of his affliction, first arguing the truth of what he said from its antiquity. The whole of what follows may be summarized as a declaration that the wicked suffer. The reason for the suffering is next set forth as rebellion against God (25-28). Apart from the fact that these words did not fit the case of Job, they constitute a magnificent description of the unutterable folly of the man who rebels:

He runneth upon Him with a stiff neck,
Upon the thick bosses of His bucklers.

Finally, Eliphaz declared the punishment of such (29-35). The sharpness of this passage will be detected by noticing how the punishment of the wicked, as Eliphaz described it, was a description of the condition to which Job had come. There is a great change in tone between this address of Eliphaz and the first. There is no tenderness here. The philosophy of life is stated wholly on the negative side, and it was impossible for Job to misunderstand the meaning.

JOB 16

Job immediately answered. His answer dealt less with the argument they suggested than before. While the darkness was still about him, and in some senses the agony of his soul was deepening, yet it is impossible to read the whole of this answer without seeing that through the terrible stress he was at least groping after light, if at the moment we may not say that he saw any gleam of it. He first manifested his impatience with these men. Their philosophy was not new. He had heard many such things. Their comfort was nothing; they were "miserable comforters." Their pertinacity was his chief trouble. The folly of criticizing sorrow from the vantage point of prosperity is declared. Job said that *he* could speak as *they* if they were in his place, but he would not do it. He would attempt to strengthen them.

Following this outburst of scorn, we have a new statement of his grief. It was helped neither by speech nor silence. In describing his suffering he spoke of God's relentless method. In the midst of this he said:

Mine adversary sharpeneth his eyes upon me.

The word is not the same as that translated "Satan," but it indicates an enemy. Whether Job so understood it or not may be very doubtful; but in the light of what we know of the preliminary controversy in heaven it is quite possible to read this section as though he had seen some faint outline of the shadow of the foe.

Immediately following, he said:

God delivereth me to the ungodly.

He was evidently conscious of a definite force against him. Perhaps there was more than he knew in what he said.

Continuing, Job now cried out in his distress, and here again it is most remarkable to see how his faith triumphed over his doubt. He declared that his witness was in heaven. He prayed that God would maintain his right with God.

JOB 17

Job was in the midst of difficulties. About him were mockers, none of whom understood him. He was become "a byword of the people." There was no "wise man." And yet he struggled through the unutterable darkness toward God's vindication. If that is not to come here, then let it come somewhere.

In all the movement of this great answer it would seem as though outlines of the truth were breaking upon Job. He was conscious of the action of God in his sorrows, of an adversary who followed him relentlessly and seemed to tear him pitilessly, even as a wild beast. Somehow, this adversary was connected with the action of God, and yet in the deepest of him Job knew that God was his Witness. His present trouble was that God did not appear for him. He had cried out, but the answer had not come. If he had a hope it was not evident, it could not be seen. He would go down to the dust.

And yet he seems to have got back to his original thought about death. It was rest. There was no clear shining of light, but one can well imagine how in the after-days he would come to recognize that these strivings of the soul and these passionate desires for divine defense were gleams even in the darkness.

JOB 18

Bildad now returned to the charge, and as was the case with Eliphaz it is perfectly evident from his opening rebuke that he was speaking under a sense of annoyance. He was wounded at the wrongs done to himself and his friends in that Job had treated them as "beasts," as "unclean."

He was angry, moreover, because he considered that Job's attitude threatened the moral order with violence, and he reminded Job that stable things could not be changed for his sake.

He then plunged at once into an elaborate declaration that the wicked are punished. This punishment he described in great detail, and with much force. He first declared the preliminary experience of the wicked. His light is "put out." It is a graphic description. His own spirit, "the spark of his fire," does not shine; and the light without is extinguished. Therefore, his steps are straitened, and "his own counsel" destroys him. His pathway without light to death is portrayed. Lacking the light, he falls into all kinds of snares and traps. Following his death he becomes extinct so far as earth is concerned. "His remembrance" perishes. He is "chased out of the world." He leaves behind him no children to enter into his inheritance.

Finally, Bildad declared:

Such are the dwellings of the unrighteous,
And this is the place of him that knoweth
not God.

The application is evident. He had described the circumstances through which Job had been passing as to all outward appearance; and finally said that such circumstances were those of the wicked.

JOB 19

To this terrible accusation Job replied first with a rebuke and a complaint. He demanded how long they would vex him, and declared that if he had erred, his sin was his own. If they would continue, let them know that all his suffering was God's doing.

He then passed into a most terrible description of his condition. He cried for help, but had no answer from on high. As he found no answer in judgment from God, so he received no answer in pity from men.

It is out of the depth of this darkness that another flash of light breaks. Conscious that in his own day he was misjudged and misunderstood, Job expressed a longing that the story could be so written as to make its appeal to the future. In this cry there is evidence of the underlying conviction of the man, that right must ultimately triumph. This deep conviction then expressed itself in words the profoundest value of which in all likelihood Job himself did not at the moment realize. He was certain that his vindicator lived, that somewhere in the future he would come into the midst of earthly surroundings. This led him deeper yet, and he declared his assurance that even though the flesh be destroyed, without it he should see God, and that God would be on his side, for such is the meaning of, "Whom I shall see for myself."

It is impossible for us to read this without seeing how these almost unutterable convictions and strivings were fulfilled. The Vindicator came in the process of time, and His words were written, and human consciousness pronounces for Him today.

JOB 20

With evident haste, Zophar replied. His speech is introduced with an apology for his haste and a confession of his anger. He had heard the reproof, but he was not convinced; and the spirit of his understanding prompted him to reply. His reply is like that of Bildad, but is characterized by even greater force and more terrible description.

He opened with a general declaration on the brevity of wickedness. This he argued by tracing the course of an imaginary person who is godless. In a passage thrilling with passion, he described the instability of evil gains. There is a triumph, but it is short. There is a mounting up, but it is succeeded by swift vanishing. There is a sense of youth, but it becomes dust. There is a sweetness, but it becomes remorse; a swallowing down which ends in vomiting; a getting without rejoicing.

The reason for all this he then declared. The pathway has been one of oppression until the oppressed turned on the oppressor. The final nemesis is fearfully set forth. God turns on him, pursues him with the instruments of judgment. Darkness enwraps him. His sin is set in the light of the heavens, and earth rejects him. The speech ends, as in the case of Bildad, with an application (29). Throughout the description Job had evidently been in mind, and he is left to make the application.

Thus, in the second cycle the proposition made by each man with varying emphasis was that it is the wicked who suffer.

JOB 21

Here, as in the first cycle, Job answered not merely Zophar, but the whole argument. First of all, he set over against their statement and illustrations the fact patent to all that often the wicked are prosperous. This prosperity he described in detail. It is personal, they "live," and "wax mighty." It is continued to their children, who are established. It is manifest in their possessions, "their houses are safe." Their increase is successful. It is seen in their habits, in the dance and the song, and the general circumstances of prosperity. It is evident in their death, for not through long suffering, but in a moment, they go down to Sheol. All this is true in spite of their godlessness. They have exiled God, have not sought His knowledge, have become agnostic, and have denied the benefit of prayer. This prosperity, Job declared, is not due to themselves. His inference is that God had bestowed it, and therefore had not punished the wicked as they have declared He does.

Continuing his answer, Job declared their philosophy to be wholly at fault by asking how often is it true that "the lamp of the wicked is put out." He surmised that they might reply that the judgment falls upon their children, and repudiated such suggestion by declaring that the man who sins is the man who should be punished, and that God has no pleasure in the punishment of posterity. He ended his answer by addressing himself to them more personally. With a touch of satire he suggested that they had learned their philosophy from travelers, and declared their conclusions to be wrong. Therefore their attempted comfort was vain, seeing that their answers contained falsehood. Thus ends the second cycle.

JOB 22

Here begins the third cycle in the controversy, and again Eliphaz is the first speaker. His address consisted of two movements. First, he made a definite charge against Job (1-20); and, second, he made his final appeal to Job (21-30). He approached his charge by practically declaring, in a series of questions, first, that a man's righteousness is no direct gain to God, and consequently that it is inconceivable that God punishes a man for his goodness. He then proceeded to declare the sins which, according to his philosophy, would naturally account for the suffering through which Job had passed. By adroit quotation of some of the things Job had said he attempted to account for the sins Job had committed.

Here Eliphaz made his great mistake. Without proof, save such as he was able to deduce from his own reasoning, he had charged Job with the most terrible crimes. Had his deductions been correct, the advice he now gave would indeed have been the highest and the best. What man needs in order himself to be blessed and to be made a blessing is the knowledge of God. This truth is declared, first, by the statement of human condition, and, consequently, by the declaration of the issues of fulfilment. The whole matter is first stated in the great words:

> Acquaint now thyself with Him, and be at peace;
> Thereby good shall come unto thee.

The method by which the conditions are to be fulfilled is described. The law is to be received. There is to be return by putting away unrighteousness. All human treasure is to be abandoned as worthless. Then the answering God is described. Instead of earthly riches, treasure will be possession of the Almighty. In Him there will be delight, and communion with Him; through Him there will come triumph, and the result will be ability to deliver others.

JOB 23

In answer to Eliphaz, Job took no notice of the terrible charges made against him. That is postponed to a later speech. Rather, he discussed Eliphaz' conception of his view of God as being absent from the affairs of men, and boldly affirmed his own consciousness of the great problem.

As to his own case, he admitted that his complaint was accounted rebellious because his stroke was heavier than his groaning. He sighed after God, and principally for His judgment seat. He would fain stand before Him to plead his cause, but he could not find Him, though he went forward and backward. He was conscious of God's presence, but he could not see Him. Suddenly there flames into the midst of the complaint the most remarkable evidence of the tenacity of his faith. His conclusion concerning God was not as Eliphaz had insinuated. He was aware that God knew the way he was taking. He even affirmed his confidence that he would "come forth," and insisted that he had been loyal to God. Then again faith merged into fearful trembling. Whatever God was doing, he could not persuade Him to desist. He knew God's presence, but it troubled him. He was afraid of Him, because He had not appeared to deliver him.

JOB 24

Passing from the personal aspect of his problem, Job considered it in its wider application. He asked the reason of God's noninterference, and then proceeded to describe the evidences of it. Men still existed whose whole activity was oppression. In other words, Job declared that the things which Eliphaz attributed to him are present in the world, and described them far more graphically than Eliphaz had, ending with the declaration:

Yet God imputeth it not for folly.

Continuing, he declared that the murderer, the adulterer, and the robber, all continued their evil courses with impunity. It was true that they pass and die, and yet, for the time being, they were in security. He ended all by challenging anyone to deny the truth of what he had said. Thus Job admitted, in some sense, the accuracy of Eliphaz' declaration concerning his view of God as absent from the affairs of men, but in his method he treated with silent scorn the imputation cast on him of acting on that view in the way of evil described by his friends. His final challenge was for anyone to prove him wrong in his contention that God does not interfere with the ways of wickedness.

JOB 25

The answer of Bildad is characterized by its brevity, and by the fact that he did not set himself to argue the matter with Job. It is a manifest weakening in the controversy on the side of the friends. Bildad was not prepared to discuss the general truth of what had been said, but he made it perfectly evident that he had no sympathy with the personal application which Job suggested. He contented himself with a general statement, first, of the greatness and government of God; and, second, of the consequent absurdity of man's attempt to defend himself, or claim to be just or clean before God.

As to the first, he briefly affirmed the fact of God's enthronement, and of His administration of all affairs. In the presence of this greatness, before which the moon lacks brightness and the stars are impure, how can man, who is but a worm, be just or clean? The force of the speech is identical with that of Eliphaz. Without argument, Bildad made it perfectly clear that, in his mind, the guilt of Job was established.

JOB 26

We come next to Job's answer. The reply to Bildad occupies but one chapter, which is characterized from beginning to end by scorn for the man who had no more to say. In a series of fierce exclamations Job revealed the impotence of all that his friend had said to help him. Then, to show the poverty of Bildad's argument, he spoke of the greatness of God to prove that he knew it, and even more perfectly than his friends. God's power is exercised in the underworld. The "shades tremble," the grave "is naked," destruction has "no covering." The whole material fabric is upheld simply by His power. The mysteries of controlled waters, and light and darkness are in the sphere of His government. The sweeping storm and its disappearance are alike by His power and spirit. Having thus, in almost overwhelming poetic beauty, suggested his consciousness of the greatness and government of God, Job declared that all these things are but the "outskirts of His ways," that, after all, everything that man is conscious of is but "a whisper" of God. The "thunder of His power" evidently is beyond human comprehension.

JOB 27

There would seem to have been a pause after Job's answer to Bildad. The suggestion is that he waited for Zophar, and seeing that Zophar was silent, he took the initiative, and made general reply.

This reply opens with a protestation of innocence (1-6). This was his direct answer to the charge made by Eliphaz. Its terms are to be carefully noted. He swore by God, while yet repeating his complaint, that God had taken away his right and vexed his soul. He refused to move from the position he had occupied throughout. He would not justify his opponents in the debate. He had been righteous, and he reaffirmed it. From this protestation his answer proceeded in terms of anger. In this imprecation, in which he expressed the desire that his enemy might be as the wicked, the deepest conviction of his soul seems to rise, in spite of himself, and it is in direct contradiction of the complaints he had made of the withdrawal of God from interference in the affairs of men. Summoning all the strength of his faith, he declared that he would teach his opponents "concerning the hand of God," and he now practically took hold of all that they had said about God's visitation on the wicked, and hurled it back on them as an anathema. He splendidly admitted the truth of their philosophy, but denied its application to himself. He thus left the whole problem full of mystery. All the things they had said were true, but they were not true to him. There must be some other way to account for his suffering. These arguments as here stated are not declared, but they are of plain inference from this angry retort on Job's foes.

JOB 28

In a fine passage Job now discussed the question of wisdom. What was supremely lacking in his friends' dealing with him was wisdom to understand. As an introduction to the main statement of his argument, he described man's ability to obtain possession of the precious things of the earth. Silver, gold, and iron are mined, and the description of how man does it is full of beauty. Man opens a shaft. In the midst of his operation he is forgotten by men who pass by. In a path that no bird knows the precious things are found. The beasts are unacquainted with it, but man, overturning the roots of the mountains, cuts out channels, and sees the precious things.

Having thus described man's marvelous ability to do the most difficult things, he then asks:

> But where shall wisdom be found?

The value of wisdom is beyond the power of computation; neither can man discover it. The precious things he can find are of no value in comparison with this precious thing he cannot discover. It must be admitted that wisdom is hid from life and from death. This admission prepares the way for the great declaration, "God understandeth." The evidences of the truth of this are to be found in the observation of the impossible things which God does. He "looketh to the ends of the earth"; He makes "a weight for the wind"; He measures the water; He makes "a decree for the rain."

Finally, Job announced that wisdom in the case of man is "the fear of the Lord" and departure from evil. It is impossible to read this without being conscious that a self-satisfied interpretation of God may be less reverent than an honest expression of inability to explain the mystery of His government.

JOB 29

Job now moved a step forward in his reply. He was still without a solution. That of his friends he utterly repudiated. In order to prepare the way for the utterance of a solemn oath of innocence, he first looked back at old and lost days in order to compare them with his present condition.

In this chapter we have his description of the past. It is introduced with a sigh,

> Oh that I were as in the months of old.

That condition is described first in its relation to God. They were days of fellowship in which Job was conscious of the divine watchfulness and guidance. Then in one sentence which has in it the sob of a great agony, he remembered his children—

My children were about me.

He next referred to the abounding prosperity, and, finally, to the esteem in which he was held by all classes of men, even to the highest. The secret of that esteem is then declared to have been his attitude toward men. He was the friend of all who were in need. Clothed in righteousness, and crowned with justice, he administered the affairs of men so as to punish the oppressor and relieve the oppressed. He then described his consciousness in those days. It was a sense of safety and strength. Finally, he returned to a contemplation of the dignity of his position when men listened to him and waited on him, and he was as a king among them.

JOB 30

Immediately Job passed to the description of his present condition, which is all the more startling as it stands in contrast with what he had said concerning the past. He first described the base who now held him in contempt. In the old days the highest reverenced him. Now the very lowest and basest held him in derision,

Now *I* am become *their* song.
They chase mine honour as the wind.

But yesterday the word of Cæsar might
Have stood against the world; now lies
he there,
And none so poor to do him reverence.

So Shakespeare makes Mark Antony speak over the dead body of Cæsar. In the case of Job the experience was more bitter, for not only did the poor refuse to reverence him, the base despised him, and he had not found refuge in the silence of death.

In the midst of this reviling of the crowd, his actual physical pain is graphically described, and the supreme sorrow of all was that when he cried to God there was no answer, but continuity of affliction. He claimed that his sufferings were justification for his complaint. All this precedes the oath of innocence. Before passing to that, it may be well briefly to review the process of these final addresses. Job first protested his innocence (27: 1-6). Then he poured out his wrath on his enemies (27: 7-23). Following this, he declared man's inability to find wisdom (28). Finally, he contrasted his past (29) with his present (30).

JOB 31

This whole chapter is taken up with Job's solemn oath of innocence. It is his official answer to the line of argument adopted by his three friends. In the process of his declaration he called on God to vindicate him. In the next place he asserted his innocence in his relation to his fellow men. As to his servants, recognizing their equality with him in the sight of God, he had not despised their cause when they had contention with him. Toward the poor he had acted the part not only of justice, but of benevolence. He had not eaten his morsel alone. He was perfectly willing to admit that his uprightness had been born of his fear of God, but it remained a fact.

Finally, he protested his uprightness in his relation with God. There had been no idolatry. His wealth had never been his confidence, neither had he been seduced into the worship of nature, even at its highest—the shining of the sun and the brightness of the moon. Moreover, he had no evil disposition to cause him to rejoice over the sufferings of others, and in this there would seem to be a satirical reference to his friends. Finally, in this connection he denied hypocrisy.

In the midst of this proclamation of

integrity he broke off and finally cried,

> Oh that I had one to hear me!

In parenthesis he declared that he subscribed his signature or mark to his oath, and asked that God should answer him.

The final words, "The words of Job are ended," are generally attributed to the author of the book, or some subsequent editor, or copyist. I cannot see why they do not constitute Job's own last sentence. He had nothing more to say. The mystery was unsolved, and he relapsed into silence, and announced his decision so to do.

JOB 32

The last voice in the earthly controversy is now heard. It is a new voice, and opportunity never comes to Job to answer. Moreover, God in the final movements takes no notice other than that of interruption, and in the epilogue Elihu has no place.

Nevertheless, the long speech of this man is full of interest, and moves as to insight on a higher plane than that of the men who had spoken. In the first five verses Elihu is introduced by the author of the Book. His three friends were silent, because unable to bring conviction of guilt to Job. In the presence of their inability, Elihu, who evidently had heard the whole argument, was moved to anger. This anger was against Job because he had justified himself rather than God. It was against Job's friends because they had been unequal to the task to which they set themselves. In the opening of his speech Elihu made his apology. He had been silent because of his youth. While he had been listening he had come to the conclusion that age is not always wisdom. Addressing himself to the friends, he declared that he had waited, and they had failed, and indicated his intention to adopt a new method. The apology ended with a soliloquy in which he considered the failure of the other men, and spoke of his own consciousness of conviction and readiness to speak.

JOB 33

Elihu began his direct appeal to Job by asking his attention, assuring him of sincerity in motive, and finally declaring that he spoke to him as a comrade, not as a judge, or one who would fill him with terror.

Commencing his argument, he first quoted from what Job had said. In his speeches he had declared that God had afflicted him unjustly, that God was hostile to him and gave no explanation of His method. Proceeding to his answer, Elihu declared that God is greater than man, and therefore that man has no right to ask explanation. This, however, was not all. God does answer. He speaks "once, yea, twice"; and Elihu proceeded to name two ways in which God speaks, first "in a dream," or "vision of the night." Moreover, His purpose in so doing is that He would rescue man rather than destroy him. There is another method. It is suffering. While Job had been complaining that God was not to be found, and had no dealing with him, Elihu suggested that all his affliction was the method of the divine dealing. What he had needed had been an angel or a messenger, an interpreter. If one could be found, then it would be understood that God is gracious, and again man would be restored and would rejoice in his restoration.

It is most likely that Elihu looked upon himself as the necessary interpreter, and here the main contention of his argument took shape. It is that through suffering God is dealing with men to some higher issue. According to this argument, suffering is educational. Elihu ended his first movement by challenging Job to hear him while he spoke, and to answer him if he had anything to say. If he had nothing to say, then he was to be silent while Elihu continued.

JOB 34

Job gave no answer to the challenge, and Elihu proceeded. He first appealed to the wise men, asked that they would listen in order to try his words. He then made two quotations from the things Job had been saying. The first may be summarized as a contention, that he had been afflicted by God notwithstanding his integrity. This quotation is followed by an exclamation in which Elihu declared that in this attitude Job had been in the company of wicked men. The second quotation was one in which Job had suggested that nothing is gained by loyalty to God. Of course, neither of these quotations was direct. They rather summarize the conclusions which Job's arguments seemed to warrant. Elihu immediately set himself to answer both. In this section the first only is dealt with. Elihu affirmed first that God cannot do wickedness. God's authority is beyond all appeal. He cannot be influenced by any low motive. Therefore whatever He does is right.

Elihu proceeded to argue that God's government is based on perfect knowledge. He sees all man's goings. There is no need for Him to institute special trial. His judgments are the outcome of His understanding.

Therefore it is the wisdom of man to submit and learn. This Job had not done, but in what he had said he had at least suggested that God's action had been unjust, and thus rebellion was added to sin.

JOB 35

Turning to the second quotation, Elihu suggested that when Job questioned the advantage of serving God, he set up his righteousness as being "more than God's." He then laid bare the very foundations of the truth concerning the divine sovereignty of God by declaring that there is a sense in which God is unaffected by man. Man's sin does nothing to God, and man's righteousness adds nothing to God.

This view had been advanced before in the controversy. Undoubtedly there is an element of truth in it, and yet the whole revelation of God shows that whereas according to the terms and requirements of Infinite Righteousness God is independent of man, according to the nature of His heart of love, which these men did not perfectly understand, He cannot be independent.

However, proceeding, Elihu declared that the reason why men do not find God is that the motive of their prayer is wrong. It is a cry for help rather than for God Himself. He declared that God will not hear vanity, and charged Job with this wrongness of motive in his search for God.

JOB 36

After answering the arguments of Job, as expressed in the quotations, there would seem to have been a pause. Then Elihu commenced his last address.

He first appealed to Job to hear him, as he was about to speak on God's behalf. He was absolutely sure of his ground, and at once plunged into his theme. This opens and closes with a statement of the greatness of God. The first statement of divine greatness concerns His understanding. This he had already declared, but now he proceeded to apply it. It is not true that God "preserveth . . . the life of the wicked." It is true that "He giveth to the afflicted their right." Such as are right with Him are not immune from suffering. In the midst of such suffering God proposes to teach them their own transgressions, and to instruct them. The issue of suffering is determined by man's response to it. If he listens and abandons iniquity, prosperity is the result. If he hearkens not, he dies and perishes miserably. The whole truth is summarized in the words:

He delivereth the afflicted by his affliction,
And openeth their ear in oppression.

Rising above mere argument, Elihu proceeded to speak again of the greatness of God, first as to manifestation, and then in application to Job. It has been suggested that this last part of Elihu's speech really consists in a word description of what was happening around him at the moment. When presently God speaks, He speaks out of a whirlwind, and the idea is that it was this great storm in its approach and force which Elihu described.

JOB 37

The description of the storm commenced in the previous chapter and is here completed. There is first the drawing up of the water into the clouds, their spreading over the sky, the strange mutterings of the thunder. Then the flash of light, the darkness which follows, again lightning that strikes the mark, and the cattle are seen to be conscious of the storm. Gradually its violence increases, the thunder is louder, and the lightning more vivid. It is a strange mixture in which the south wind and the north are in conflict, and intermixed with rain is ice. The purpose of the storm may be for correction, for the land, or for mercy.

Elihu appealed to Job to hear it, to consider it, to ask himself if he really knew God. Even in the midst of the storm there is a light which men see not, a golden splendor which is the majesty of God.

Elihu was attempting to use the storm to tell Job of his inability to know God, and, therefore, of the folly of his speech against God. It was a great theme, but Elihu was not equal to it, and was interrupted by the voice of the Most High.

JOB 38

Here begins the third movement in the great drama, that which deals with the controversy between Jehovah and Job. Out of the midst of the whirlwind the divine voice speaks. Its first word is a challenge to Elihu. The challenge must be carefully considered. It does not charge Elihu with false interpretation, but with darkening counsel by the use of words which he himself did not perfectly understand. As we have said, his theme is too great for him, and God now deals with it. His method is to unveil His own glory in certain aspects before the understanding of His child. God first speaks of the simplest facts of the material universe, which are sublime beyond the comprehension of man. The first movement has to do with the material universe. Throughout, Jehovah claims that all is of Himself, and that He is interested in all, and suggests Job's ignorance to him. The earth itself is dealt with (4-7), and the sea also (8-11), daybreak in its effect on nature and on man (12-15), the underlying mysteries of the deep (16-18).

Continuing the same line, Jehovah proceeds to speak of the heavens: the first, or atmospheric (19-30); and the second, or stellar (31, 32). In dealing with the first, illustrations of the things which men may observe and cannot explain are suggested: the way of light and darkness, the mysteries of snow and hail, the majesty and sweep of the storm, the origin and method of rain, dew, ice, frost. Similarly, illustrations from the stellar spaces, the chain of the Pleiades, the bands of Orion, the signs of the Zodiac, the going of the Bear. All the while God is suggesting His own knowledge and interest, and the perfect ease of His stupendous activity. The ordinances of the heavens, their influences on earth, the bringing of rains, and the sending forth of lightnings; if man can perchance do any of these things, who then put wisdom in him, or gave him understanding?

Still the unveiling of the divine glory proceeds, but now in its application to the things of life: the feeding of the lioness and the young lions, the fact that the cry of a young raven is prayer in His ears, which He answers with food.

JOB 39

And still the unveiling goes forward: the mystery of the begetting and birth of lower animals, with the sorrows of travail, and the finding of strength; the freedom and wildness and splendid untameableness of the wild ass, the uncontrolled strength of the wild ox; in all these things God reveals Himself as interested, and, moreover, as active. The differing manifestations of foolishness and power and wisdom, as they are evident among birds and beasts, are dealt with. The ostrich rejoicing in the power of her pinions and in her folly abandoning her eggs and her young, is described; and her very foolishness is accounted for by the act of God. He deprived her of wisdom.

There is nothing, then, that happens in these lower realms of life, apart from God's volition. The war horse with his might, but tameable so that he will serve man and come to rejoice amid strange and awful battle scenes and sounds, is yet not of man's creation. All his essential strength is divinely bestowed. The hawk, with wisdom directing it to the south land, and the eagle placing her nest on high, far from the possibility of intrusion, yet in such place of observation as enables her to feed her young, these also are God-guided. Even though in the great dispensation of His government God has committed dominion to man, it is dominion over facts and forces which he has not originated, nor does he sustain.

JOB 40

There is a pause in the unveiling as Jehovah speaks directly to His servant and asks for an answer to the things that He has said. The answer is full of suggestiveness. The man who in mighty speech and strong defiance had been of unbroken spirit in the presence of all the arguments of his friends now cried out,

> Behold, I am of small account.
> What shall I answer Thee?

He has learned the wisdom of, and he listens as Jehovah speaks.

Again Jehovah proceeds, and He charges Job to "gird up" his "loins like a man." In each case there is in this introductory word the suggestion of God's consciousness of man's dignity. The things He has been describing cannot hear or answer this divine wisdom. Job can, and he is called on to exercise these distinctive powers of his humanity. Job had exhibited his folly in that in the midst of all his suffering he had by inference blamed on God's method. This God now challenges, yet not to explain it, but first to suggest to Job that he attempt to occupy God's place in the universe. There is a fine and tender satire in Jehovah's call to Job to assume the reins of government. Let him do this in the moral realm, in which his criticism has been at work. Let him abase and humble the proud and lofty and evil and wicked ones. When Job can do this, then Jehovah will acknowledge that Job's own right hand can save him.

Having challenged Job thus, Jehovah now suggests two experiments. He brings before him two animals, nonmoral, and suggests that Job exercise his authority and power over them. This is much easier than governing men. The material always yields itself to man's government with greater ease than the moral. If this man can be made to feel his absolute weakness in the lower sphere he will naturally deduce therefrom his impotence in the higher things. If he cannot govern these, how can he assume the functions of the One who made them, and perfectly governs them? The description of behemoth leaves very little room for doubt that the animal we know as the hippopotamus is intended.

JOB 41

Leviathan is almost certainly the crocodile, and there is the playfulness of a great tenderness in the suggestions Jehovah makes to Job about these fierce creations. Can Job catch him with a rope or a hook? Will he pray to Job? Will Job make a servant or a plaything of him for himself or his maidens? There is a fine, and yet most tender and humorous, satire in the words of Jehovah!

Lay thine hand upon him;
Remember the battle, and do so no more.

If none dare stir up leviathan, who can stand before God? If Job dare not attempt to catch or subdue or play with this animal, how can he hope to compete with God in governing the universe? Following the question, the description returns to the beast in all the magnificence of his strength, and ends with a picture of men attempting to overcome him with sword, or spear, or dart, or pointed shaft; while all the while, in fierce anger, he holds the citadel of his being, and becomes king over all the sons of pride.

Thus the unveiling of God's own glory ends, not in the higher reaches of the spiritual, but in its exhibition in a beast of the river and the field. It is not the method we would have adopted, but it is the perfect method. For the man who knows God it is necessary only to make his commonest knowledge flame with its true glory for him to learn the sublimest lesson of all.

JOB 42

Job's answer is full of the stateliness of a great submission. As he speaks the words of surrender he appears mightier in his submission than all the things into the presence of which he has been brought. In his confession of the sufficiency of God, of the folly of his own past speech, of his present repentance in the light of God's glory, there is revealed a glory of God not manifest in any other part of the universe described. This surrender is God's victory of vindication. There has been no explanation of pain, but pain is forgotten, and all the circumstances of trial against which the spirit of the man has rebelled are out of sight. He has found himself in relationship to God. What Eliphaz asked him to do, but could not teach him how, he now has done. Acquainted with God, his treasure is laid in the dust, and he has found Jehovah to be his all-sufficient wealth.

The victory being won in the soul of Job, Jehovah deals with his friends. His wrath is kindled against them, and yet it is mingled with mercy. Their intention was right, but their words were wrong. In their attempt to explain God, they had not said of Him "the thing that was right." Notwithstanding all his murmuring, nay, in the very affirmation of his inability to comprehend, Job had spoken profounder truth concerning God than they. God's vindication of him to them is marked by the fact that He speaks of him as "My servant," the same term He used at the beginning. It is also marked in His appointment of His servant as intercessor on their behalf. They had attempted to restore Job to God by philosophy. He is now to be the means of restoring them by prayer. As at the beginning there were things to be said in their favor, so at the close. Their sincerity is shown in the fact that they submit, bring their offerings, and make confession.

Up to this point it would seem as if there had been no change in Job's circumstances. The bands of his captivity were broken in the activity of prayer on behalf of others. All the rest is told in brief sentences. Job had been in the fire, and now he emerged from it, and his latter days on earth were characterized by even greater prosperity than his earlier ones.

In ending our consideration of this great Book, let us not attempt to formulate a philosophy which includes a solution of the problem of pain. This much at least we know, that through it this man gained, and there we leave it.

Psalms

PSALM 1

The master thought of this psalm is the law of Jehovah. The obedient and disobedient are placed in sharp contrast. This contrast is vividly seen by bringing together the first and last words of the psalm—"blessed," "perish." The former word describes the issue of obedience; the latter, the result of disobedience. The conditions of blessedness are stated negatively and positively. Negatively, there must be complete separation from fellowship with those who are disobedient. The graduation in description must not be omitted; "walketh," "standeth," "sitteth"; "counsel," "way," "seat"; "wicked," "sinners," "scornful." The positive condition is twofold delight and meditation in the Law. Moreover, this must be continuous, "day and night."

The experience of the blessed is described under the figure of a tree bearing fruit, with evergreen leaf. Moreover such a man prospers in all he does. Then comes the contrast. Let the statement, "The wicked are not so," be considered in the light of all that has been said, that is, in the former part of the psalm cancel the negations where they stand and insert them where they are not. The condition of the wicked is then summarized and the contrast is perfected. Instead of the tree planted, they are chaff driven away. They will be unable to stand the test of judgment, and therefore are excluded from the assembly of the righteous.

The psalm ends with a summary. "The way of the righteous" is known to Jehovah. "The way of the wicked" perishes, that is, runs out, and is lost in the desert.

PSALM 2

This is the psalm of Jehovah's King. It is impossible to fix the event foı which it was written and to which it first referred. The wider application is perfectly patent. To whatsoever king the words first applied, the singer was looking to the ideal King, and his song has found fulfilment in Christ. It is very interesting to notice how this psalm is interwoven with the thinking of the New Testament. To study it carefully, we must, first of all, discover the speakers in each case.

The psalmist opens with a description of the nations in opposition to Jehovah and His King. This is given in the form of a question why they are in such attitude. He then proceeds to declare the Lord's contempt for them, and in verse 6 Jehovah is the Speaker, announcing that, notwithstanding all their opposition, He has appointed His King. The next section (7-9) gives us the words of the anointed King, who declares the decree of His Kingship. The Son of Jehovah is to receive dominion from His Father and exercise it to subjugate all these opposing forces. The order of procedure is indicated, "inheritance," "possession," "administration." The psalm ends with an appeal to the kings and judges to show their wisdom by submitting themselves to Jehovah's King.

PSALM 3

This is a morning psalm. It is the song of a soul in grave peril as a new day dawns. The consciousness of difficulty is first uttered. Adversaries are increased, and the bitterest part of the pain is that they mock him, declaring,

> There is no help for him in God.

Immediately succeeding, are the words that tell of the sufferer's confidence, and its reason. Jehovah is at once "Shield," and "Glory," and "Lifter up." Between this man and Jehovah communion is established—"I cry," and "He answereth."

Then follows the language of courage. He has "slept" and "awaked," because Jehovah sustained him. In this assurance he will not be afraid of the increased adversaries. Then out of these circumstances of peril and conviction of safety the prayer arises for salvation and is accompanied by the assertion that Jehovah already has heard and answered. A consciousness of the constancy of the divine love has always been the strength of the trusting soul amid circumstances of the greatest peril. If that is lost, all is lost. If that be maintained, no great waters can overwhelm.

PSALM 4

This is a song of the evening. The general circumstances out of which it rises are the same as those of the previous psalm. Now, however, the day into which the singer marched with confidence is over. The evidences of strain are apparent, and yet the dominant thought is of victory won and confidence increased.

The opening words constitute a petition in the midst of which the singer declares that God has delivered him. He appeals to the "sons of men," to those who, according to his morning psalm, declared,

> There is no help for him in God.

He now asks them how long they will turn His glory into dishonor, "love vanity," and "seek after falsehood." The experiences of another day enable him to declare that Jehovah is great. He warns them to "stand in awe," to think of it, and "be still."

The testimony merges into an appeal to those who do not know Jehovah. They are pessimists, dissatisfied in the midst of life, and asking,

> Who will show us any good?

Out of his experience of Jehovah's goodness, he affirms that he has found gladness more than the men who have been in circumstances of material prosperity. The song ends with words that breathe his deep content,

> In peace will I both lay me down and sleep . . . ;

and the reason is that though he is alone, or in solitude, Jehovah makes him dwell safely.

PSALM 5

This is another song of the morning. It opens with language which reveals the reason of the soul's assurance as it faces another day. First are petitions asking the attention of Jehovah. These are followed by words which reveal at once the singer's conception of personal responsibility, and the reason of his confidence in God. As to the former, the day is to be begun in prayer.

O Jehovah, in the morning shalt Thou hear my voice.

It is moreover, to be arranged as in the sight of God,

In the morning will I order my prayer unto Thee, and will keep watch.

The attitude of God toward wickedness and evil men is then declared. This attitude at once makes the singer sure of his safety as against the opposition of evil men, and causes his concern about his own position before God.

Turning his eyes toward the enemies that wait for him, whom he describes, he seeks the divine guidance, desiring most of all to see plainly before his face the way of Jehovah. As he goes forth to meet these enemies, he does so with a prayer that God will defeat their counsels and vindicate those who put their trust in Him. There is no doubt or uncertainty in his heart. The things he asks for he is assured he will receive and with an affirmation of this confidence the song ends.

PSALM 6

This is known as the first of the seven great penitential psalms. It is somewhat weak in its note of true penitence and in this respect is not to be compared with some which follow. It is rather a cry for deliverance from the pain and the sorrow and chastisement than from the sin which causes it.

The first seven verses are full of the misery of the man. He is perfectly conscious of the meaning of his suffering. He knows that it is chastisement, and under the pressure of it he sobs for deliverance. The light breaks on the darkness in his confident consciousness of Jehovah's attention and willingness to help him. If this be considered a psalm of penitence, it is remarkable rather as a revelation of the tender compassion of Jehovah than of the true note of repentance. There is not a single sentence which reveals any profound consciousness of the sinfulness of sin. The saving grace of it, so far as the sinner is concerned, is that it recognizes Jehovah's rebuke and chastening. The supreme desire is to escape from suffering and sorrow. Notwithstanding the shallowness of the sense of sin, the fact of the recognition of the hand of Jehovah seems to be enough, and in answering pity and power the deliverance and the comfort sought are granted.

PSALM 7

This is a song of the singer's confidence and appeal in circumstances of the most trying description. He is persecuted by enemies, some among them being violent and cruel. The basis of their attack would seem to be some charge of wrongdoing they make against him. He vehemently denies the charge and cries to Jehovah for vindication, which he firmly believes the God who tries the hearts of men will surely grant.

In the first part of the psalm the story of personal need is told. The ruthlessness of the foe is the reason for his appeal. The declaration of personal innocence follows. If the charges were true, then would the heaviest judgments be just. They are untrue, as God is witness. Then let Jehovah appear on behalf of the innocent against the guilty.

Then follows the general affirmation of the equity of God on which the singer builds his confidence. God is righteous. The way of wickedness cannot prosper. It creates its own destruction. The pit digged is the grave of the man who digs it. The mischief and violence meditated return as retribution on the evildoer. The psalm is a song of confidence in the reign of God in equity over all men, and the consequent certainly that innocence will be vindicated in this particular case. Thanksgiving is according to Jehovah's righteousness.

PSALM 8

This is a great song of worship. It opens and closes with the same words. These words enclose the psalm, and create its burden. The matters between are proofs of the opening and closing statements. They are two. The manifestation of Jehovah's excellencies in nature and man. These are first briefly stated (1,2), and then more particularly described (3-8). The principal manifestation is in man, which is revealed in both sections. The outlook on nature is toward the encompassing heaven, all the glory of which is expressed in one inclusive thought—Jehovah has set His glory there.

From this the singer turns to little children, in whom he finds a perfection of praise absent from the glorious heaven. It is such as "to still the enemy and the avenger." These two facts are then more particularly considered. The first impression suggests the littleness of man. In the presence of the glorious heaven man seems beneath consideration. Yet it is not so. Man is greater than all. He is but little lower than God. His place is that of dominion. The contemplation of the heaven leads to the consideration of man. This creates in man, first, a wonder at Jehovah's consideration of him. This consideration issues in investigation, and man is found nearer to God than the heavens. The issue is worship. It is the true order of creation. Through man's sin it has been lost. Through Jesus it is being restored.

PSALM 9

The burden of this psalm is thanksgiving for Jehovah's righteous rule by which He has overcome the enemies of the chosen people. It is almost exclusively a song of thanksgiving. There are a few brief petitions, but they are intimately related to the measures of praise. These songs of praise move from the personal to the general. First, deliverances wrought for the singer are celebrated (1-4); then the government of the enthroned Jehovah among the nations, a government based on righteousness, is sung (5-8); and next the tenderness of Jehovah toward the oppressed and His unfailing succor of the needy are declared (9,10). The song of the singer then becomes a cry to others to join in the chorus (11,12). Then follows a cry for mercy which immediately merges into praise, and the thanksgiving moves out in the same order from personal (13,14) to general (15,16). The whole ends with a declaration of the certainty of the divine government and a final prayer for its clear manifestation.

The psalm is a great pattern of praise on a level neglected far too much in our day. We praise God much for His mercy. This is right, but it is a good thing to recognize His righteous rule and to praise Him for that.

PSALM 10

In the Septuagint and other versions, probably the ancient Hebrew, Psalms 9 and 10 appear as one. There is a clear connection between them, but it is that of contrast. In the former the singer has rejoiced in the exercise of Jehovah's rule in the whole earth. In this he mourns what seems to be the abandonment of His own people. There is, first, the protesting cry of the heart against what seems to be divine indifference to the injustice being wrought by the wicked against the poor (1,2). This injustice is then described in detail. It is graphic description of the brutality of earthly rule when it has forgotten God, or says in its ignorance that God has forgotten it.

The picture would fit many times of misrule on the pages of human history.

There is a heart cry to Jehovah, to God to interfere. If the psalm opens in complaint, it closes in confidence. The wicked man is wrong about God. He does see and know. The cry of the oppressed He hears. Deliverance must come, for Jehovah is King. Not once or twice, but often the men of faith have been driven to cry out against the oppression of man by man. Happy is he whose faith causes him to complain directly to Jehovah. The result is ever a renewed consciousness of the certainty of the divine government and the necessary rightness of the ultimate issue.

PSALM 11

This psalm is the answer of faith to the advice of fear. Both are alike conscious of immediate peril. Fear sees only the things that are near. Faith takes in the larger distances. If the things fear sees are indeed all, its advice is excellent. When the things which faith sees are realized, its determination is vindicated. The advice of fear is found in the words beginning, "Flee as a bird," and ending, "What can the righteous do?" The name and thought of God are absent. The peril is seen vividly and accurately. It is wicked in nature; imminent, the wicked bend the bow; subtle, they "shoot in darkness." The very foundations are destroyed. There is nothing now for fear but to flee!

The rest of the psalm is the answer of faith. The first vision of faith is of Jehovah enthroned. That is the supreme foundation. Then He also sees the peril. Do the wicked watch the righteous? Jehovah watches the wicked! Are the righteous tried in the process? Jehovah presides over the trial! Are the wicked going to shoot? So is Jehovah—and rain snares and brimstone! Perhaps among all the psalms none reveals more perfectly the strong hold of faith. It is the man who measures things by the circumstances of the hour who is filled with fear and counsels and practices flight! The man who sees Jehovah enthroned and governing has no panic.

PSALM 12

Out of a consciousness of the terrible evil of his times, the worshiper cries to Jehovah for help. The failure of godly men and faithful souls is always the gravest peril which can threaten a nation or an age. There is no trouble which more heavily afflicts the heart of the trusting. The note here is more characterized by faith than that of Psalm 10. Here is a cry for help but no suggestion that God is indifferent. Indeed, there is an immediate affirmation of confidence in the interest and interference of God. It is very beautiful to notice how, in answer to the cry and the affirmation of confidence, Jehovah speaks so that the singer hears Him and is able to announce Jehovah's response before the song ceases.

This answer of Jehovah is most precious. It promises the preservation of the trusting. The psalmist breaks out in praise of the purity of Jehovah's words and declares that Jehovah will "keep them" and "preserve them." The "them" here refers to the words. There is no promise of widespread revival or renewal. It is the salvation of a remnant and the preservation of His own words which Jehovah promises. Thus the psalm ends with a description of the same condition which it at first describes. It is the cry of a godly soul for help amid prevailing ungodliness and it is answered.

PSALM 13

This little psalm is very full of beauty as it traces the way by which many a tried and tempest-tossed soul has found consolation and strength. First of all, there is the cry almost of despair. Foes are oppressing the men of faith. There seems to be no succor even from Jehovah. Yet carefully note that his faith in Jehovah, who is God, abides. He is able to help. To Him then he cries.

This is a lesson of profound value. If the heart be overburdened and Jehovah seems to hide His face, let the story of woe be told to Him. It is a holy exercise. Men may not understand it. They may even charge us with failing faith; when, as a matter of fact, while all other anchorage crumbles in the storm, faith fastens itself more surely on the Rock. How does the psalm end? With a song of triumph. Yet it is a song of faith, for deliverance is not yet realized. How, then, does the song emerge from the wail? Carefully examine the words:

But I *have* trusted in Thy mercy;
My heart *shall* rejoice in Thy salvation.

That backward look has served to remind the troubled heart of deliverances and a new confidence is born of the memory which utters itself in a song. It is good to "forget the things behind" if memory of them would hinder present consecration. It is also good to remember all the way Jehovah has led us when the day was dark with fear.

PSALM 14

Here the psalmist utters his own consciousness of the meaning of godlessness. In its essence it is folly. The word "fool" here stands for moral perversity rather than intellectual blindness. This is repeated in the declaration, "They are corrupt," and in the statement that their works are abominable. To his own testimony the psalmist adds the statement of the divine outlook on humanity. It is the same. Men do not recognize God and their doings are therefore evil.

The psalmist then looks at certain occasions without naming them. "There" refers to some occasion of God's deliverance of His people. The thought is that when God was recognized by His people their enemies were filled with fear. Then there is a contrasting picture of the oppressed people of God put to shame, "because Jehovah is his refuge"; the thought being that the refuge was neglected and the chosen therefore rejected (see Psalm 53:5). The thought of the whole psalm is of the safety of godliness and the peril of ungodliness. Jehovah cannot be deceived. He knows and this events always prove. The psalm ends with a sigh for the coming of the day of deliverance.

PSALM 15

This psalm declares the terms of friendship between man and Jehovah. The opening questions describe the privileges of friendship. To sojourn does not necessarily mean to stay for a brief time. Length of stay is not suggested by the word, but rather the position of one who receives hospitality, a guest. To dwell is to reside permanently. The picture is of a resident of the City of God, who has free and welcome access to God's presence. To whom are such high privileges granted? The answer is first stated in general terms and then illustrations are given.

In general terms, the friend of God is one whose general deportment is perfect, whose activity is right, whose inner thoughts are pure. The test of all this is in a man's attitude to his fellow man, which is described. The man fulfilling these conditions is never moved from his residence on the holy hill nor excluded from the hospitality of Jehovah's tent. The outcome of true friendship with Jehovah is friendship for man. Therefore the condition for continued friendship with Jehovah is loyal friendship to man.

PSALM 16

This is a song of satisfaction. The singer is not one who is unfamiliar with peril. The opening sentence is a sigh, revealing the consciousness of peril. Toward the close, the shadows of Sheol and the terror of corruption are recognized. Yet these things find a place here only that they may be canceled by the facts which create a sense of triumph over all peril. Jehovah is the one and all-sufficient good and the saints are friends of the singer because they are also friends of Jehovah.

With those who exchange Jehovah for another god the psalmist will have no fellowship. The fact that Jehovah is the supreme good is developed in descriptive measures. He is a present good and the hope of all the future. A present possession, creating pleasant places and perpetual power. As for the future, the last enemies will not overcome. Beyond victory over them is the presence of the King and the place of His right hand with fulness of joy and pleasures forevermore. The hope of this singer found its perfect fulfilment only in the Man of perfect trust, and through Him in all who share His life through the mystery of that death from which He came triumphantly to enter into the eternal joys.

PSALM 17

This psalm is generally conceded to be closely linked with the preceding one. There is an evident similarity of outlook. In each case the singer declares his abstention from complicity with ungodly men. In both psalms God is appealed to, and the final hope of the soul is for fuller communion with Him. Yet, of course, the chief impression of comparison is the contrast. In the former, peril is referred to incidentally. Here, it is described and is the occasion of the outpouring of the soul.

The two exercises of priesthood are exemplified in the psalms. In the first the sacrifices of praise are offered. In this the petitions of need are presented. First, the ground of appeal is the singer's uprightness of heart, and speech, and action. It then moves into another and higher realm, the singer's confidence in God. He is known to be One who saves the trusting. The consciousness of His tenderness appears in the expressions used:

Keep me as the apple of the eye;
Hide me under the shadow of Thy wings.

After a description of the immediate peril the singer again appeals for help, and the song ends with the expression of assured blessing and the declaration of the one and only full satisfaction.

PSALM 18

This is one of the most majestic and beautiful of the worship psalms. It is at once a perfect pattern of praise and therefore a great revelation of the method and might and mercy of God. So clear and simple is it in its movement and language that nothing need be said of it save, perhaps, to suggest an analysis to aid in its study.

Prologue of Praise (1-3). Here the psalmist pours out the gladness and gratitude of his heart which thrills with the highest spirit of adoration.

The Peril and Deliverance (4-19). The terrible nature of the peril is first made clear, and then the story of the might and majesty of Jehovah's process is told and the fact of deliverance declared.

The Principle (20-29). The reason of the divine deliverance is declared and the truth of perpetual importance, that God is to man what man is to God, is affirmed.

The Resultant Confidence (30-45). Again the song breaks forth in almost tumultuous joy. Absolute confidence in God, and assurance of continued triumph are based upon experiences already gained of His goodness.

Epilogue of Praise (46-50). The anthem ends with further sentences which group the benefits conferred on the king by his God and attest his determination to praise God among the nations.

PSALM 19

The burden of this psalm is the twofold revelation of Jehovah. He is revealed in Nature and in law. Yet in Nature Jehovah is revealed as God and not by those especial qualities suggested by the great name Jehovah. Moreover, it is in the law that God is revealed as Jehovah rather than by the facts of His wonder-working power. This differentiation is justified by the names as used. In the first six verses, which deal with the Nature revelation, the name "God" appears once and "Jehovah" not at all. In the last eight verses, which speak of the law revelation, the name "Jehovah" appears seven times and God not at all.

It is one Sovereign Ruler who is revealed and He is referred to by name eight times in all. Nature speaks to Nature. Day has its message to itself and night to itself. Without articulation the message is constantly delivered in the circuit of the sun. To man, higher than all Nature (see Psalm 8), an articulate message is given. A word is spoken. It is the great law of Jehovah, "perfect," "sure," "right," "pure," "clean," "true," "righteous." Mark well the sevenfold description and how perfectly all the needs of man are met. Great and wondrous, God is known in Nature by Nature through the speech of a great silence, and is revealed to man in messages which answer all his questionings and govern all his ways.

PSALM 20

This and the next psalms are certainly closely connected. The first is the prayer of the people on behalf of the king as he goes forth to battle. The first five verses were sung in chorus and express the consciousness of the supreme need in this day of trouble. The foes are gathered, the battle must be fought. Help must come from the sanctuary and strength from Zion. In the name of God the banners must be set up. The next verse is a solo. The voice of the king is heard announcing his confidence in Jehovah. Immediately the chorus takes up the music and contrasts the confidence of the foe in chariots and horses with the confidence of those who follow the king in the name of Jehovah, who is their God.

Following the contrast of confidence is that of issue:

> They are bowed down and fallen;
> But we are risen, and stand upright.

The whole ends with a prayer in such form as recognizes the kingship of Jehovah. Today, the weapons of our warfare are no longer carnal, but we have a conflict to wage and the secrets of strength for us are revealed as clearly here as for those of olden times.

PSALM 21

The battle is over, the victory is won, and the assembled people sing the song of victory. This song, while it celebrates one victory, runs beyond it and praises Jehovah for all He has done for the king. They had prayed, "Grant thee thy heart's desire" (20:4). The prayer is answered and now they sing, "Thou hast given him his heart's desire" (21:2). They had sung of victory because their trust was in the name of Jehovah (20:7,8). Victory has been won and now they celebrate it (21:7-12).

The contrast is very vivid between the king trusting in Jehovah and therefore sustained, supplied, and led in triumph; and the enemies who intended evil against Jehovah and who are swallowed up and destroyed and utterly overcome. From the experience of the king the whole nation learns its lesson. The opening declaration, "The king shall joy in Thy strength," issues in the final prayer, "Be Thou exalted, O Jehovah, in Thy strength: so will we sing and praise Thy power."

Again let us remember our conflict is spiritual and still the ancient hymn is ours, for our King also triumphed through the strength of Jehovah and to our final victories we follow in His train.

PSALM 22

Whatever may have been the local conditions creating this psalm, it has become so perfectly and properly associated with the one Son of God that it is almost impossible to read it in any other way. This and the two following psalms constitute a triptych of tablets on which are written the story of the Christ in His work as Saviour, Shepherd, and Sovereign.

As to this first, seeing that in the supreme mystery of the Passion Jesus quoted the first words, we are justified in reading it in the light of that Cross. It has two great movements. The first admits us, so far as that can be, to the lonely suffering of the One on the altar of sacrifice (verses 1-21). The second brings us into the presence of the joy of the Victor, as through the travail He saw the triumph (verses 22-31). In reverently reading the first, we must understand that all the desolation was the experience of One who had entered into the sinner's place. In rejoicingly reading the second, we must recognize that the height of joy is the ability to proclaim an evangel to those in need. And this is enough to write. For the rest, let the Spirit, who is the one Interpreter of the Christ of God, speak to our hearts and let us in amazement worship and obey.

PSALM 23

In the Messianic application this psalm properly follows that in which the work of the Christ as Saviour is portrayed. It is to those whom He has won through His passion that He becomes known as the Shepherd.

Of course, this psalm, as written, is even more wonderful because of the fact that its author did not live in the light of Jehovah which has come to us through the Incarnation. It shows us how very clearly faith saw through the mists of those preparatory days to some of the most precious things about God. We still read the wonderful words of Jehovah and understand them, but the revelation of Him in Jesus is our interpretation and the psalm becomes richer for that fact. It is an unruffled song of rest. All the circumstances of the pilgrimage, want, weariness, journeyings, wanderings, perplexities, the shadowed mystery of the valleys, the thronging enemies, and the infinite beyond, are present and the singer knows them. They are mentioned however, only to sing of their negation by the graciousness of the Shepherd. Want is canceled. For weariness He has green pastures of rest. On journeys He leads by pleasant ways. From wanderings He restores. Through perplexities He guides and that by right ways. In the valleys of death's shadow His presence cancels fear. In the presence of enemies He makes a feast and is a Host royal in bounty. And finally the path runs on, not into a tangled wilderness but by the King's own palace.

PSALM 24

This is the final psalm of the three, and as in Psalm 22 the words so far exceed the possibility of exhaustion by any circumstances originating them as to create an opinion unanimously in favor of their Messianic application. In this song the Saviour who through suffering triumphed, the Shepherd who through pilgrimage leads His own, is seen ascending to the place of power and authority.

The first movement recognizes the sovereignty of Jehovah over the created world and its inhabitants (verses 1,2). There is, then, a question which recognizes a need. The hill of the Lord which is the place of authority (see Psalm 2:6) is vacant, and it is asked, "Who shall ascend into it?" The answer declares the need for purity of conduct and character. Suddenly the antiphonal chanting of angels breaks forth. Some are accompanying the King as He approaches the place of power. Others wait, guarding the entrance. The first company claims entrance for Him. The second assembly challenges His right. The answer tells of might inherent and of victory in battle, and through the lifted portals we see Him pass and know Him for "Jehovah of hosts." By our calendars, yesterday He passed through Psalm 22. Today He is exercising the office of Psalm 23. Tomorrow, He will exercise finally the authority of Psalm 24.

PSALM 25

The sob of a great sorrow sounds through this psalm. The circumstances of its writings were desolation, affliction, distress, travail, as the latter part especially shows. Yet the main content is full of help to all who are in sorrow. It is far more than a wail saddening all who read it. It is the voice of hope and confidence and tells of succor and of strength.

It has three movements. The first (verses 1-7) and the last (verses 16-22) are prayers uttered out of great need. The central (verses 8-15) is contemplation and declaration of the goodness of God. Thus structurally the psalm is beautiful. Its central glory a revelation of God's goodness and patience (verses 8-10). Then a sob at the heart of everything (verse 11). Immediately an account of the blessedness of the man who trusts. The opening verses contain the prayer of a distressed soul, whose thought of God is revealed in the central portion. The closing verses are the earnest cry of that soul to such a God, and in such confidence the details of the experience of suffering are named.

PSALM 26

The central word of the song may be said to be, "So will I compass Thine altar, O Jehovah" (verse 6)

On either side, conditions of worship are described. First the conditions of personal life necessary to worship (verses 1-16). Afterward the true exercise of worship described (verses 7,8). Then the psalm becomes a prayer for preparation (verses 9-11) and ends with the declaration of assurance (verse 12).

As to conditions of personal life fitting for worship, they may be described as complete separation from evil ways and evil persons. Fellowship with Jehovah is possible only when there is no fellowship with the wicked. Moreover, the Judge must be Jehovah Himself. To Him the singer appeals. In this fact there is great solemnity and great comfort. Jehovah's standards are high, but they are ever far more reasonable than men's.

The exercise of worship at its highest is praise issuing from delight in the dwelling place and glory of God. The prayer for preparation explains the opening words. In its light they are seen to be of the nature of appeal to Jehovah's decision rather than boasting in His presence.

The final prayer for preparation is, "Redeem me, and be merciful unto me." Such a prayer is immediately answered and this the last verse makes plain.

PSALM 27

The real significance of this psalm is the experience of worship. It is somewhat strange that the remarkable contrast between the first (1-6) and second (7-14) parts has given rise to the view that two men have written the psalm, or that if one person is the author he must have written the parts at different times. The psalm reveals the true attitude and exercise of the worshiping soul. Praise and prayer follow each other in their true order: first, the offering of praise due to the consciousness of Jehovah, then pouring out of the heart's need to the One worshiped.

The conception of God revealed in the first half makes possible the abandon of the petitions in the second half. The God who is light, and salvation, and strength, who hides in His pavilion, and lifts the soul onto the rock, is the very One whose face a man forsaken of father and mother, pursued by adversaries, and slandered by enemies, will most easily appeal to. This is the meaning of the injunction of the final verse. When hosannas languish on our tongues it is because we do not begin with Jehovah. To see Him first in the hour of communion and to praise Him is to be able without reserve to pour out all the story of our sorrow in His ear, and to know that when the soul beseeches Him not to cast off it may affirm in confidence,

Jehovah will take me up.

PSALM 28

The affinity between this psalm and the previous one is evident and its placing by the editor here was in all likelihood due to that fact. In Psalm 27, in true order, praise prepares for, and issues in, prayer, the whole ending in an appeal to "wait on Jehovah." The next psalm opens—

Unto Thee, O Jehovah, will I call.

This is not to suggest that the song was written by the same person or immediately. It rather affords an illustration of a song written by one who acted on the principle enjoined. The cry of need is very urgent. The peril is so great that death threatens. Unless Jehovah help there is no help. That the danger arose from enemies is evident from the psalmist's cry to Jehovah for justice.

Suddenly the prayer becomes a song of praise, an act of adoration. The prayer is heard, help is granted, the song begins. That this psalm, with its inverted order of prayer and praise, follows closely that in which the order is praise and prayer is encouraging. The true order is praise and prayer. If the heart is not strong enough for this, let it learn how to praise by speaking first in prayer of its sorrow. The one thing impossible in worship is to compress it within the narrow limits of stated formulas.

PSALM 29

This is a wonderful picture of a storm, viewed from the standpoint of one who is supremely conscious of Jehovah. The great name occurs oftener in this psalm than in any other in this first book, being found no less than eighteen times. Therein is discovered the key to the whole movement. Once the name suggestive of wonder-working might is used—

The God of glory thundereth.

For the rest, this God is seen to be Jehovah of the trusting soul.

From this outlook, all the sublimity and majesty are seen under the control of love, and the singer finds occasion for the highest form of praise in the presence of a storm which otherwise might have filled the heart with terror. The storm is described in the central part of the song (3-9). To the description there is a prelude calling on "the sons of God" to praise (1,2). In the epilogue (10-11), the storm seems to have subsided and the psalmist sings of the one supreme impression produced. Over all the flood Jehovah sat as King. The deductions are simple and yet full of beauty. Jehovah always sits as King. During the storm He will give strength to His people. Following it He will give them peace.

PSALM 30

This is a song of praise for deliverance (1-5) and a meditation on the deliverance and its lessons (6-12), with a final note of praise (12). The phrases descriptive of the trouble are such as to leave little room for doubt that the singer had been sick and nigh unto death—"Thou hast healed me. . . . Thou has brought up my soul from Sheol." Moreover, he believed that the sickness was a divine chastisement and that through it and his deliverance he had found the method of Jehovah—"His anger is but for a moment; . . . weeping may tarry for the night."

The issue of such experience is of the highest, "life," "joy in the morning." The review is full of suggestiveness. Days of prosperity had issued in self-satisfaction. Jehovah had hid His face. That was the moment of His anger and that the night of weeping! There was the return to Jehovah in the cry of anguish. The answer was immediate, mourning became dancing, sackcloth was exchanged for gladness. What was all this for?

"To the end that my glory may sing praise to Thee and not be silent." Self-satisfaction cannot praise Jehovah. Therefore it must be corrected by discipline. The final note of praise shows that through affliction and by deliverance the lesson has been learned.

PSALM 31

In this great song of trust struggling through tears to triumph, we have a fine example of an experience often repeated in the history of the children of faith. There are three divisions. In the first (1-8), the double sense of trust and trial is clearly manifest. In the second (9-18), the trial seems for a time almost to have overcome the trust, so keen is the consciousness thereof. In the last (19-24), trust has completely triumphed and the sense of the singer is the sense of perfect safety in the pavilion of Jehovah.

In the first, the soul of the singer valiantly affirms its confidence and pleads for help. In the second, the affirmation of trust is in a past tense and the present is one of trial and tears. In the last, trust is a condition which needs no formal declaration but sings itself out in victory and gladness. In this song we find the seasons of the soul as we know them all sooner or later. First, autumn with its winds and gathering clouds, yet having sunlight and a golden fruitage even though the breath of death is everywhere (1-8). Then follows winter, chill and lifeless, full of sobs and sighing (9-13). After that the spring with its hope and expectation and its sweeping rains and bursting sun gleams (14-18). At last the glad and golden summer (19-24). We need them all to complete our year!

PSALM 32

This is known as the second of the penitential psalms. It is the song of a man who is rejoicing in the assurance of restoration. Opening with a burst of praise which reveals the experimental knowledge of the happiness of forgiveness (1,2), it proceeds to describe the bitterness of the soul's experience while sin is unconfessed (3,4). Then the way of restoration by confession and the readiness of Jehovah to forgive are declared (5). On the basis of such restoration the soul has access to God and the assurance of His succor in trouble (6,7). Then is sung the message of Jehovah to His child, in which the promise of guidance is made and the condition of submission is stated (8,9).

All ends with an affirmation of the safety of those who trust in Jehovah and a call to men to praise Him.

Among all the psalms there is none which touches deeper things in the life of the soul or more perfectly reveals the method of Jehovah in sin, sorrow, and guidance. He is ready to pardon, able to deliver, and willing to guide.

PSALM 33

This is a triumphant song of praise, opening with a call to vocal and instrumental music. "Rejoice," "praise," "give thanks," "sing praises," "sing," "play"—thus all modes of expression are appealed to.

The praise proceeds and the greatness and goodness of Jehovah are sung in general terms (4-11). The whole of the facts are summarized, His word is right, His work is faithful (4). His character is perfect, combining light—"righteousness and judgment"; and love—"lovingkindness" (5). He is the Creator, full of power so that men should worship (6-9). He is the active King, overruling all the affairs of men (10-11). The song then praises Jehovah as the God of the chosen people (12-19). He chose them and in their interest watches all the sons of men (12-15). His watchfulness of His own is a greater security than armies or horses (16-19). The song ends with an affirmation of trust, an assurance of joy, and a prayer for mercy (20-22). There is a lilt and a lift about this psalm which is of the very essence of gladness.

PSALM 34

In this psalm praise is personal. After the chorus of the last we have a solo full of feeling. It tells of the goodness of Jehovah and that in order that others may know and be helped. The opening declares this. The song is to be perpetual and the meek are to be made glad thereby. Then there is the desire to draw others into the same attitude of praise. It is good to go through simply to find the things Jehovah has done. "He answered me, and delivered me from all my fears." "They looked unto him, and were radiant." "Jehovah heard him and saved him." His eyes "are toward . . . His ears are open." "Jehovah heard, and delivered them." "Jehovah is night." "Jehovah delivereth." "He keepeth." "Jehovah redeemeth."

This is not an exhaustive list, for on the side of human reception many more things are said. It is a song which tells of the nearness, the tender sensitiveness, the ready help, the mighty power of Jehovah on behalf of all who trust Him. It is, moreover, rich in its lack of selfishness. The singer is eager for others to hear, to test, to praise, and he takes time to sing to the children that they also may know the secret of life.

PSALM 35

There is agony in this song. The singer is sore beset with enemies. They are striving with him, fighting against him. They are plotting against him, treacherously spreading a net for his feet. He cries out to Jehovah for help, vowing that he will offer praise for deliverance (verses 1-10). The singer touches deeper depths. The cruelty and oppression are being shown by those whom in the past he has befriended. In their time of trouble he had mourned with them. In the day of his halting they have taken advantage of weakness, still further to wound.

Again he cried to the Lord for rescue and promised to praise Him publicly (verses 11-18). And again the same prayer is offered. The foes are not only cruel and treacherous, they are full of bitterness and taunt and mock the suffering man. In his agony he cried out for help, for the third time promising to praise Him (verses 19-28).

Before we criticize the singer for his attitude toward his foes, let us imagine ourselves in his place. In no sense is the level of spiritual realization in this psalm equal to that in many others. One of the greatest values of the collection is its revelation of how, under all circumstances, the soul may turn to God.

PSALM 36

The antithetical nature of this psalm is self-evident. In the first part (verses 1-4), the reason and expression of the wickedness of the wicked are described. The one and only reason for transgression is that the fear of God is lost. All evil results therefrom.

In contrast to this the advantages of the remembrance of Jehovah are set forth, first, by a description of certain facts concerning Him. One can easily imagine that the psalm was written on some natural height from which the singer looked out on a far-stretching scene in which he saw symbols of truth concerning his God. Note the sweep of vision. The heavens, the skies or clouds, the mountains, the great deep, the river, and, over all, the light.

There is a fine fitness in the interpretation of suggestiveness. The encompassing blue speaks of loving-kindness; the passing clouds in the mystery of their orderliness, of His faithfulness; the mountains suggest His righteousness from which rivers of pleasure flow to mingle in the deep of His judgments. Of all the abundant and varying life He is the Source or Fountain and the sunshine of His face is the light on everything. All ends with a prayer for the continued safety of the divine care and protection.

PSALM 37

This psalm has as its keynote "Fret not." The underlying problem is the prosperity of evil men. It is an astonishment and a perplexity still, troubling many a tried and trusting heart.

The psalmist first declares that all such prosperity is short-lived and then tells the secrets of quietness in spite of the problem. There are first positive injunctions. They may be grouped thus: "Trust in Jehovah," "Delight in Jehovah," "Commit thy way unto Jehovah," "Rest in Jehovah." Then again the fundamental injunction is twice repeated, "Fret not." It is wrong; it is harmful; it is needless. Let the trusting wait. Events will justify the action.

Continuing, the psalmist works out his contrast into greater detail. The prosperity of the wicked has within it the elements of its own destruction and cannot last (verses 12-20). This is all stated by way of contrast. The little of the righteous is better than the abundance of many wicked. This is by no means out of date. It is only to wait long enough and to watch to know that the principle is abiding. Ill-gotten gains and the triumph of wickedness are alike doomed by inherent evil to sure destruction. Then the other side is stated in great fulness (verses 21-31). The way established by Jehovah is sure. There may be failure, but there is restoration. With the more complex civilization in the midst of which we live, perhaps sometimes the righteous have been driven to beg, but even now such cases are surely rare, and after some varied experience I would want to subject him who begs one to somewhat severe cross-examination before accepting his testimony against that of the psalmist. Even if it be granted, the underlying principle remains, that the bread of charity is to be chosen in preference to the wealth of wickedness.

In verses 32-40 we have the final contrast of this psalm. The first statement is of the safety of the righteous against the machinations of the wicked. The way in which this psalm has appealed to men and continues to do so is a proof of how prone the heart is to rebel against the seeming prosperity of the wicked, and also a demonstration of the conviction of men that it is better to trust in Jehovah than to achieve any kind of success by other means. Faith does falter and demand some explanation. It finds all it asks when resolutely it obeys the injunction to trust, delight, commit, rest, wait!

PSALM 38

This is the third of what are known as the penitential psalms. The circumstances of the singer were most distressing. He was suffering from some terrible physical malady, deserted by his friends, and persecuted by his enemies. The deepest bitterness of his soul was caused by his overwhelming sense of his moral pollution. He recognized that all his sufferings were the rebukes and chastisements of Jehovah for his sin. This sense of sin crushed him and in his distress he cried out to Jehovah.

The use of the divine names and titles in this psalm is interesting. The first cry for help is to Jehovah. When he would utter his complaint concerning the desertion of friends and persecution of foes, the singer addresses himself to the Lord as the supreme Being. In his final appeal he both begins and closes with Jehovah, Lord, and God. All the foundations seem to have given way beneath his feet, and with deep contrition and desperate endeavor he strives to take hold of God in all the facts of His being. In this he was right, for so desperate a case demands the help, the government, the might of God. Blessed be His name forever; all are at our disposal.

PSALM 39

Again the circumstances are sorrow and affliction. The attitude of the sufferer is true dignity. If the psalm be taken in connection with the preceding one, it marks an advance, perhaps a gain out of that experience. Then we saw a man crying out for Jehovah and His help. Here is a man still undergoing trial and acutely conscious of it, but he has found the secret place of communion and this conditions his attitudes. Toward his foes he maintains a great silence, the secret of which he presently declares—"I was dumb, I opened not my mouth; because Thou didst it." Yet the things he sees strangely stir him and at last he breaks the silence.

Here again the result of his knowledge of Jehovah is seen in that he speaks to Jehovah and not to his enemies. Thus he sets the strange prosperity of the wicked in relation to God. All the apparent success is seen to be nothing worth and this sorrowful man makes his personal appeal to Jehovah.

PSALM 40

Again we find in this psalm the perfect structure found in Psalm 27. Praise prepares for prayer. The experience has mounted higher than in the preceding song (39). The singer still suffers affliction, but a new consciousness of Jehovah, resulting from having "waited patiently" for Him, inspires a lofty song of praise (verses 1-10). This gives the soul a great freedom to pour out its complaint (verses 11-16), after which an affirmation of faith and a final prayer (verse 17) concludes the psalm.

The patient waiting resulted in the singer's feeling that Jehovah was bending over him and listening to his cry. Then comes a new song which is rightly interpreted at its deepest in the words of the hymn—

> Glory to Thee for all the grace
> I have not tasted yet.

This is expressed in recognition of the

activity of Jehovah God and the certainty that His one purpose for His people is that they should delight in His will and proclaim Him to others.

Then follows the prayer. Sorrow and sin have oppressed the heart beyond the power of its endurance. In distress and yet in confidence, appeal is made to Jehovah. The final word of confidence is very full of beauty—

The Lord thinketh upon me.

PSALM 41

This whole song depends for interpretation on its opening beatitude. The man who is considerate toward the weak, who is compassionate, is blessed. His blessings are then described. Emphasize "him" and "he" and "his" in verses 1 to 3. It will then be seen that all these things come to the man at first described, namely the compassionate man. Then the psalmist confesses his sin. In the light of the beatitude the sin is seen to have been lack of compassion, and this is the secret of the bitter hatred of his enemies, which he proceeds to describe.

Returning to his cry for mercy, his words should be carefully noted (verse 10). What is the meaning of "requite"? Almost all expositors agree it indicates revenge, and then attempt to explain it away. The word may certainly be translated *recompense* and is far oftener used to indicate a kind action than a vindictive one. If that be so here, the consistency of the argument is apparent. The psalmist has failed in compassion, therefore his enemies and even his friends are against him. He asks for Jehovah's mercy, that being raised up he may treat his enemies differently. The Messianic reference is not destroyed. The wrong of those who harmed the Christ is greater because they acted without cause. Even then His prayer, "Father, forgive," harmonizes with this interpretation. His raising up by God was for blessing on men.

PSALM 42

This is the song of an exile and, moreover, of an exile among enemies who have no sympathy with his religious convictions. He cries out after God with all the intensity of one who knows God and cares supremely for the honor of God's name. His greatest grief is their mocking inquiry after his God. By contrast he remembers being in the midst of worshiping multitudes, their leader and companion.

In the midst of his grief he appeals to his own soul in the language of hope and confidence. A great conflict goes on within, for he affirms, "My soul is cast down." Notice carefully the heroism of the man. He makes his trouble and disquietude the occasion of remembering God. Out of the place of exile he turns his thoughts to God. The result is not deadening his sense of sorrow but rather setting it in right relationship to God. Trouble has come in cataracts and waves and billows, but they are all God's own. "Thy cataracts . . . Thy waves . . . Thy billows." When sorrow is set in this relationship, there is a consciousness of love in the daytime; there is in the night a song and a prayer. The trouble is still there, the oppression and reproach of the enemy, but courage and hope and the conviction of coming deliverance continue also. It is a wonderful psalm and has been the song of many an afflicted yet trusting soul.

PSALM 43

This psalm is either a part of the previous one or is closely connected with it. It breathes the same note of confidence, ending with the same words practically as the two parts of the former. It reaches a higher plane in that it refers only to sorrow and mourning in order to protest against them in the light of the certainty of God's deliverance. From prayer for that deliverance, which he has twice in the previous psalm declared to be certain, he passes to affirmation of how, following the leading of God's light and truth, he will go up to worship. Notice the procession to praise as he describes it. To the hill, to the Tabernacles, to the altar, and then the act of praise. Not yet has the answer come. The darkness and the mystery are still about him, but the shining way is seen; and again the soul is forbidden to despair and hope is encouraged in God.

PSALM 44

The final meaning of this psalm is discovered in its last four verses. It is a prayer for deliverance from defeat. Its strength of appeal lies in its recognition of the government of God. He is the Author of good and evil. Of course, evil is used here in the sense of disaster and calamity. The psalmist sings of the God of good first (verses 1-8). There is a double recognition of this. History attests it. The testimony of the fathers affirms it. They had originally come into possession by the act of God (verses 1-3). Then there is personal recognition of it. Trust is to be reposed in nothing save God (verses 4-8). The word "but" indicates a change. The day is one of disaster, and this is recognized as the act of God, "Thou hast cast us off." "Thou makest us to turn back," and so on (verses 9-16). Yet there has been no apostasy. Nay, rather it has been a pathway of suffering for the sake of God and His name (verses 17-22). Light is thrown on this by Paul's use of the words in Romans 8:36.

Then follows the plea for help and deliverance. It is a perfectly honest and reasonable plea, yet the wonderful advance of Christian experience is nowhere more plainly shown than here. The apostle of the new covenant makes no appeal for deliverance, but rather declares that in all these things we are more than conquerors, and affirms that nothing can separate us from the love of God.

PSALM 45

Whether this psalm has, or had, a local application or is wholly idealistic cannot be certainly determined. It matters very little, for it is one of the songs which inevitably is Messianic in its deepest and fullest meaning. After an introduction which speaks of the fulness of his heart, the singer addresses the king, telling of the glory of the king's person, the perfection of his rule, and the beauty of his bride (verses 1-9). He then turns to the bride, and in view of her high calling, counsels her to forget her own people and surrender herself wholly to her husband (verses 10-12). If the king in mind was Solomon and the bride the daughter of Pharaoh, the suggestiveness of the song becomes the more remarkable.

The singer then describes the queen gloriously arrayed for her marriage (verses 13-15) and ends in words of promised blessing to the king. If the inclusive truth of this psalm be larger than we are able to grasp, there is a personal application full of value and full of beauty. It is, as we see, the glory of the Lord that we become ready to renounce all our own people and possessions that we may be wholly to His praise, and so the instruments through whom the royal race is propagated and the glory of the King made known among the generations and the peoples.

PSALM 46

Comment on this great song of confidence seems almost unnecessary so powerfully has it taken hold on the heart of humanity, and so perfectly does it set forth the experience of trusting souls in all ages and in tumultuous times.

The system of the song is worth noting. It is divided into three parts. The first (verses 1-3) is the challenge of confidence. The second (verses 4-7) tells the secret of confidence. The third (verses 8-11) declares the vindication of confidence.

The challenge announces confidence in God as refuge and strength and very present help, and defies fear even in the midst of the wildest upheavals. In days when tempests shake loose all solid things and the restless waters roar and surge till mountains shake, the soul is confident. The secret of the confidence is the consciousness of the nearness of God. He is a river of gladness in the midst of the city. What matters the tumult around? The vindication of confidence is found in observing God's activity in all surrounding things from this place of safety and strength within the city. The twice repeated refrain (verses 7-11) is full of beauty as it reveals the twofold conception of God, which is the deepest note in the music. He is the King of all hosts. He is the God of the individual. Scholars believe, and with every reason, that the refrain should also occur between verses 3 and 4. This certainly perfects the literary form and adds to the beauty of the psalm.

PSALM 47

This is a song of the sovereignty of God. In the Hebrew ceremonial it was pre-eminently the song of the New Year, being repeated seven times ere the sounding of the trumpets which announce the feast.

It opens with an appeal to the peoples to unite in His adoration as the one supreme Ruler. The singer has a true sense of the real mission of the chosen as the appointed rulers of the peoples. Their song is called for, and therefore it is plain that their subjugation is looked on as beneficent to them as well as to Israel. The appeal is renewed to praise the uplifted and enthroned King. A prophetic vision of the ultimate recognition of the Throne of God concludes the psalm.

It has a wide outlook. Not the one nation only, but all the princes are seen submissive to His rule and so become the people of the God of Abraham. This is the true note of rejoicing. Not merely is the safety of the one city the cause of gladness, but the gathering together under the one all-beneficent reign of God of all the peoples. This is rejoicing in hope of the glory of God, far more spacious and perfect than any satisfaction in personal deliverance or safety. If our joy is to be all it ought to be, we must have this largest outlook on the purposes of God.

PSALM 48

In Psalm 46 the dominant note was of confidence, because of the government of God in the midst of His people. This is a song describing the experience resulting from such government. It is the anthem of a city's deliverance from an alliance of hostile kings. The beauty and glory of the city remain, notwithstanding the foes' attack. The intervention of God was of such a nature that the attack failed ere it positively began.

> The kings assembled themselves,
> They passed by together.

They were seized with weakness and fear, and fled. So God had delivered, and the deliverance is a reason for new confidence that the city will be established forever. The singer urges the inhabitants to examine well the city, that the wonder of its preservation may fill the heart with praise, and be the foundation for faith in all the years to come.

We may seem to have lost something in the reading of this psalm, because we cannot place it historically with any certainty. Yet it is so true to a constantly recurring experience of the saints that it is in constant use. Threatening perils massed against us suddenly waver and pass away, smitten by unseen hands, and deliverance comes when we had seen nothing but destruction. Verily great is Jehovah, and greatly to be praised as the God of deliverance.

PSALM 49

This is the song of a principle, and the psalmist commences by calling peoples of all castes and classes to give attention. It denies the power of material wealth, and affirms that of uprightness. There are two things which wealth cannot do. It can neither help a man to escape death, nor can it ensure the life of the one possessing it. The passion of the heart for immortality is manifest in the building of houses and the naming of the land. It is all useless. Man is no more able to secure personal immortality thus than are the beasts which perish. Yet there is a mastery over Sheol and death. It is found in uprightness. The declaration, "The upright shall have dominion over them in the morning," is very difficult to explain if it does not contain the light of hope beyond the grave. The morning is certainly something beyond Sheol and death, and the hope of the upright is in God's deliverance from Sheol. The teaching of the song is simple, and sublime, present, and perpetual.

PSALM 50

The singer addresses himself in the name of God to the whole earth, that it may hear and learn an important lesson. The call is made in the first verse. The final appeal is in verses 22 and 23.

The lesson is that forgetfulness of God issues in gravest peril, while the remembrance which worships ensures the blessing of salvation. Between the call to attention and the final appeal the psalmist sings of the relation between God and His own (verses 2-15), and then of the attitude of God to the wicked. As for the former, they are to be the medium of His praise. God shone forth out of Zion. To do this the saints are to be gathered to Him, that, through them He may be manifested in power and righteousness. Their gathering is not because of any sacrifice they can bring of things already belonging to God, but wholly on the basis of praise and trust. The wicked can have no part in such manifestation of God, and therein lie their chief sin and failure.

This is a thought of most searching power. Our most heinous sin is not the act of wrong done, but the fact that such wrong incapacitates us from fulfilling our highest function of glorifying God, and showing forth His praise.

PSALM 51

This is the first of a number of psalms (eighteen) to which titles are prefaced which connect them with David, eight out of the number having historic references. There is a remarkable fitness in every case between the incident thus indicated and the psalm following; but whether the placing is accurate or not is open to question.

This is indeed one of the great penitential psalms, being the fourth in the seven which are usually so described. It opens with a general cry for pardon that comes out of a deep sense of sin and an equally profound desire for forgiveness. In the first three verses sin is described as "transgression," "iniquity," "sin"; and the mercy sought is to "blot out," "wash," "cleanse." The penitent soul cried for forgiveness on the basis of confession. Suddenly the intensity of conviction deepens as the act of sin is traced back to its reason in the pollution of the nature. This leads to a deeper cry. As the first was for pardon, the second is for purity, for cleansing of heart, and renewal of spirit.

The prayer goes on to seek for the things which follow such cleansing, maintenance of fellowship, and consciousness of joy. Looking on in hope, the song anticipates that service of thanksgiving and praise which will issue from such pardon and purity.

PSALM 52

In this song the attitude of God toward the wicked man who is a tyrant is manifest. The mighty man who boasts himself in mischief is first put in striking contrast to God whose mercy endureth continually. Then follows a description of the mischief in which such a man makes his boast. One is reminded of James' description of the tongue and its fearful power, as the psalmist describes the mischief of evil speech, growing out of an evil nature. The God of mercy destroys the mischiefmaker, and thus demonstrates His mercifulness. God's dealings with such a man will be seen by the righteous, who will understand that the reason for the punishment is that this man was godless.

Suddenly the singer puts himself in contrast with the end of this man because he is in contrast with the attitude of the man. Instead of being rooted up, he is like a tree in the house of God. Instead of trusting in the abundance of riches, he trusts in the mercy of God. The contrast reveals the abiding truth of the unchangeableness of God. All that seems to be different in His dealing with man is due to the difference in man's attitude toward Him.

PSALM 53

This psalm, with slight variations, is found in the first book (Psalm 14). Its introduction a second time necessarily leads us to notice the differences. In all probability the editor incorporated it into this book because of these very changes.

They are, first, the substitution of "God" for "Jehovah" four times. Perhaps the change was made for liturgical use in some special circumstances, in which the desire was to express praise of God as the wonder-working God. All that was true of Jehovah's knowledge of men (see Psalm 14) is true also of God's attitude toward men as the Wonder-worker. He looks on men not only as Helper, but as the supreme One. Not only do the workers of iniquity fail to discover Him as the Helper, they do not call on Him as the mighty One. The other main change is found in verse 5, for the exposition of which see note on Psalm 14.

PSALM 54

The burden of the psalm is expressed in the first two verses. Its reason is described in verse 3, while assurance is the song of what remains.

Taking the second and third sections first, they deal with the sorrow of the soul, and the succor which comes from God. The sorrow is from opposition and persecution by the godless. The description of this is preceded by the prayer which cries for salvation by the name of God, and judgment in His might. No touch of despair is manifest. Over against the strangers risen up against the psalmist, he sets God, who is his Helper. Over against the violent men who seek after his soul he sets the Lord, who upholds the soul. The issue is perfect confidence that God will requite the evil, and destroy the enemy. Already, though perhaps yet in the midst of the peril, he sings the song of deliverance, as though it were already realized. The central sentence of the song is, "God is my Helper." Wherever man is conscious of this fact he is superior to all the opposition of his enemies, and so is able, in the midst of the most difficult circumstances, to sing the song of deliverance.

PSALM 55

This is the outcry of a man of faith in sore peril. The emotional nature is moved to its very center, and tides of deep feeling surge through his soul. He has been cruelly betrayed by his familiar friend, who would seem to have headed a conspiracy against him. It is really a revelation of how fellowship with God leads ultimately to the victory of faith.

Three movements are manifest. The first is fear. Appeal is made to God out of a consciousness of fearfulness, trembling, horror. So terrible is this fear that the man fain would fly away and escape it all (verses 1-8). The troubled heart then breaks forth into fury. So mean is the method of the foe that the anger of the man is aroused, and he cries for vengeance against the oppressor (verses 9-15). He then appeals to God, and at once declares that he is delivered. The wrong of the wicked is no less, but, calmly stated in the light of God, it is a burden to be cast on Him, and the conviction that He will deliver is created. Fear leads only to desire to flee. Fury only emphasizes the consciousness of wrong. Faith alone creates courage.

PSALM 56

The keynote of this psalm is the concluding declaration of the previous one, "I will trust in Thee." Here again are evident the same circumstances of oppression (verses 5-7). The song opens and closes with praise.

The opening (verses 1-4) is a prayer for deliverance which culminates in a note of praise. Notice how it ascends. First, the singer declares that in the hour of fear he will trust. Then he declares he will trust and not be afraid.

The closing movement is wholly of praise. The tenderness of God is exquisitely stated. Wanderings are known to Him, and by Him tears are preserved. Against all adversaries God is for the psalmist. Then again the high note of trust canceling fear is struck, and the psalm ends with a sacrifice of praise.

It is a gracious thing to know God well enough to be able resolutely to trust Him when fear possesses the heart. It is a much finer thing to trust Him so completely as to have no fear. Both ways lead homewards, but the former is low level traveling, while the latter is high level.

PSALM 57

Yet again the theme is the same, but the triumph of trust is even more conspicuous. Compare the opening here with that of the previous song. The cry is the same, but the reason is different. There it was a cry born of the consciousness of the enemy. Here it is born of the vision of God, and of trust in Him. Compare also the wish of Psalm 55:6 with the experience in this case. There the desire was for the inefficient wings of a dove for flight. Here the sense is of the sufficient wings of God for refuge until calamities are past. Now the cry is one of real need, for the opposition is stated in terms as pointed as ever, but all the while it is a song of confidence. In the psalm that speaks of fear and flight the heart is "sore pained." Now in trust it is "fixed," and a rush of praise is the issue.

Faith does not free us from trial, but it does enable us to triumph over it. Moreover, faith lifts us high above the purely personal sense of pain, and creates a passion for the exaltation of God among the nations. The heart at leisure from itself is always the heart fixed in God.

PSALM 58

This is a fine setting forth of the certainty of the judgment of God against wickedness. The psalmist declares its reason (verses 1-5), its process (verses 6-9), and its effect (verses 10, 11).

The whole psalm will be misunderstood save as we carefully note its opening questions. The reason of the judgment is not personal wrong. It is rather the failure of the rulers to administer justice. They are silent when they should speak. Their judgments are not upright. Evil in heart, they lie in word, and poison like serpents, and no charming wins them.

The process of judgment is described in the form of prayer, which shows the sympathy of the singer with the God who is forever against the oppressor. The terms are fierce and terrible, but not more so than are the wrath and stroke of God against such evil men. The effect of the divine judgment is to be the rejoicing of the righteous, the destruction of the wicked, and His vindication among men. It is a sickly sentimentality and a wicked weakness that have more sympathy with the corrupt oppressors than with the anger of God.

PSALM 59

Again we have a song from the midst of peril. The singer is the object of determined, stealthy, and malignant opposition. It is divided into two parts, both ending with the same declaration, "God is my high Tower."

The first (verses 1-9) describes the danger. Without any reason, and with the most relentless determination, the singer's enemies are attempting to encompass his destruction. He announces his determination to wait on his Strength, and declares that God is his high Tower.

The second part is a prayer that God will deal with these foes. Not that they may be slain, but rather that they may be consumed in their own sinning. He then announces his determination to sing praises to his Strength, and the note of the praise is that of the prayer. God is his high Tower!

There is perhaps no more beautiful description of what God is to His tried people. The phrase suggests at once strength and peace. A tower against which all the might of the foe hurls itself in vain. A high tower so that the soul taking refuge in it is lifted far above the turmoil and the strife, and enabled to view from a vantage ground of perfect safety the violence which is futile and the victory of God.

PSALM 60

This is a song out of defeat. It may be divided into three parts. The first is a recognition of the cause of defeat, ending with a prayer (verses 1-5). The second expresses the answer of God in the soul of the singer (verses 6-8). In the third there is a note of helplessness, a cry of need, and a cry of confidence. In the midst of an evidently disastrous defeat, the singer recognizes the government of God. His appeal for help is based on his recognition of the true vocation of the people. They bear a banner for the display of truth. Note the "Selah" at this point, suggesting especial attention to this fact. For the sake of that banner the cry for deliverance is raised.

Then the singer tells of the answer, but the supreme note is "God hath spoken in His holiness."

All the fine imagery which describes triumph follows that declaration. Victory is possible only in holiness. Defeat is ever the issue of sin. All human aid is helpless when God has abandoned the people. The song ends with a cry for help and the declaration of personal assurance.

PSALM 61

In this song there is the same undertone of confidence as in the preceding one. Here, however, it is rather the voice of one man than that of the people. The reference to the king, in verse 6, although in the third person, makes it likely that it was written by David under the stress of trial, most probably at some period of exile from his city.

His longing is for restoration to God rather than to circumstances. All through there seems to breathe a sense of perfect confidence in God, together with a consciousness of present need, and a longing desire for a return to past experience. There is no uncertainty in his mind concerning God's help of him in days that are gone. The very height of the psalm as a prayer is reached when he cries: "O prepare lovingkindness and truth, that they may preserve him." There has been some difficulty as to the word "prepare." Perhaps it ought not to be there. In that case we have an affirmation rather than a petition, which may read: "Lovingkindness and truth shall continually guard him." The one impression from reading the psalm is that of the singer's sense that in the midst of trouble his hope is still in God.

PSALM 62

In this psalm the principle of the last is yet more emphatically expressed. It opens with the declaration:

> My soul waiteth *only* upon God,

and then proceeds in three stanzas to set forth this fact.

The first opens with the words we have already quoted, and is an affirmation of confidence made in the presence of enemies. Indeed, it is addressed to them, declaring the relation of defense which God bears to him, and appealing to them against their malicious onslaught. The sense of his enemies is with him as is evidenced in his words:

> I shall not be greatly moved.

In the second stanza he addresses, first, his own soul, and then appeals to the people, most probably those over whom he rules. To himself he repeats what he has said to his enemies about the relation of God to him; and this time, with his eye fixed on God, he reaches a higher level of confidence, and says:

> I shall not be moved.

Finally, he puts the false helps on which men depend, in contrast with the only Help of man, who is God Himself. The false helps are "men of low degree," "men of high degree," "oppression," "robbery," "riches," and the weakness and uselessness of all are declared.

PSALM 63

Here the conviction which has been the inspiration of the two previous psalms reaches a consummation of expression. The song can hardly be divided, for it runs on in a continuous outpouring of praise. The singer is beset by difficulty and sadness, and yet the statement of this at the beginning and at the close, constitutes a background which throws into clearer relief the sure confidence of the soul in God.

Beginning with the affirmation,

> O God, Thou art my God,

the singer declares his thirst in a dry land for the same visions of God he had seen in the sanctuary in former days. Immediately the song ascends to higher levels. The past is the inspiration of the present. Over all diverse and difficult circumstances it rises in triumph because it knows God. Happy indeed is the soul who is able to make sorrow the occasion of a song, and darkness the opportunity for shining. Two things are necessary for such triumph as this. These are indicated in the opening words of the psalm. First, there must be the consciousness of personal relationship, "O God, Thou art my God"; and, second, there must be earnest seeking after God: "Early will I seek Thee." Relationship must be established. Fellowship must be cultivated.

PSALM 64

This is the cry of distress, and yet not of despair. The singer is beset by wily enemies who plan and plot against him with malicious and persistent determination. In great detail he describes their method. It is secret counsel and studied cruelty. They have one object, to harm the righteous by shooting at him from secret places. They strengthen themselves by declaring that none can see them. This is the singer's distress. The warfare is unequal. His foes are not in the open, but under cover. At verse 7 we have the beginning of his account of the reason why his distress is not despair. Over against his foes' evil determination to shoot at the righteous is the fact that God will shoot at them. That is the security of the trusting soul. In New Testament times the truth is expressed differently, but the principle abides, "If God be for us, who can be against us?" The practical application of this to the righteous is that there is no need for them to attempt to take vengeance on their enemies. Their one care is to trust God. Such trust will issue in gladness, and the inevitable vindication of their faith. In order to do this we ever need to pray as the psalmist does, not so much for deliverance from enemies as for deliverance from fear of them.

PSALM 65

This is a great song of worship. The occasion would seem to be that of a harvest festival. The people are assembled for praise (verses 1-4). God's particular goodness in the harvest is celebrated (verses 5-8). With reference to the assembling of the people the marginal reading is full of beauty:

There shall be silence before Thee and praise.

The same thought is present, though obscure, in the text:

Praise *waiteth* for Thee.

It is the true attitude of worship. Reverent silence preparing for, and issuing in, adoring praise.

There is always a difficulty in the way of worship. "Iniquities prevail." Yet these are not final hindrances, for God purges away transgressions. The way into the silence of praise is described. God chooses, and causes to approach. The man so conducted dwells in the courts of God, and is satisfied with the goodness of His house. That is a fine description of worship in its expression, its method, its experience. The greatness of the power of God is the subject of the worshiper's song, and that power is at the disposal of those who worship. Then, finally, is sung the song of harvest. This is beautiful as a description of God's part therein. Man's toil is not described. It is taken for granted, and is his prayer. God's answer is co-operation by which harvest comes in joy and singing.

PSALM 66

This is one of the most beautiful of the songs of worship. It is divided into two parts by a change from the use of the plural pronoun (verses 1-12) to the use of the singular (verses 13-20).

In the first part all the earth is called on to worship God because of what He has done for His people. This is a recognition of the true function of the people of God, which is to reveal God to the outside nations in such a way as to constrain them to worship. In the second half the worship becomes individual and personal, and yet the same purpose is manifest in the appeal to others to hear. In this case those called on to hear are such as fear God. Thus the testimony of the individual is to strengthen the faith of God's own, in order that they may be more perfectly equipped for their testimony to those without.

In the story of God's dealing with His people there is a recognition of His government through all the differing experiences of their history. By deliverance and by distress, by triumph and trial, He has conducted them to a wealthy place. Very full of comfort is the individual realization, following as it does this larger experience. In the economy of God the lonely man is not lost in the multitude, and the solo of his praise is as precious as is the chorus of the multitude's worship.

PSALM 67

In this psalm there is a fine merging of prayer and praise. Prayer is its dominant note. Moreover, it is prayer on the highest level. It asks for personal blessing, but its deepest passion is that all peoples may be blessed and led to praise. If it was a harvest festival song, as the first part of verse 6 would seem to indicate, then the local occasion is graciously submerged in a far wider outlook. The singer, even more remarkably than in the preceding psalm, recognizes the true function of the Holy Nation.

The word "that," with which verse 2 opens, is of the utmost importance:

That God's way may be known upon
  earth,
His saving health among all nations,

is the ultimate purpose of His heart, and the mission of His people. In order to accomplish this the singer prays for blessing *on* and *through* them—*on* them, "God be merciful unto us, and bless us"; *through* them, "Cause His face to shine with us."

The central desire of the prayer is uttered at its center (verses 3-5); and the method is again indicated at its close (verses 6,7). This is not asking in order to consume gifts on personal lusts. It is rather a passion which is self-emptied, and therefore pure. Such praying hastens the Kingdom.

PSALM 68

This psalm sings the praise of the God of deliverances. It opens with a song of pure praise (verses 1-6). This is then justified by a review of God's past dealings with His people (verses 7-18). Finally, it affirms the present activity of God, and declares confidence in His future succor (verses 19-35).

In the first six verses there is a wonderful description of God in His majesty and meekness, in His might and mercy. The contrasts are remarkable. He scatters His enemies. He is a Father of the fatherless. The wicked perish at His presence. He sets the solitary in families. There is no sense of contradiction. Rather the unity of the apparently dissimilar things is felt at once. His righteousness of the strength of His mercy. His might is the ability of His help. The righteous need have no fear of His strength, but rather rejoice in it, trust in it, and co-operate with it by casting up a highway for Him.

The next section of the psalm (verses 7-18) is a description of God's dealing with His people Israel. The might of His going forth is referred to, and the effect it produced is described. The giving of the constitution and law at Sinai is remembered. Then His preparation of the land for His people and their settlement therein is spoken of, together with the song of the women who thus have found their homes. And still the song moves on to describe how God scattered kings before His people, and moved right onward until in majesty He had entered and possessed the hill of His city, the center of His earthly government. It is a fine setting of history in its relation to the activity of God. It is this view of God enthroned and governing which gives courage to the heart and inspires the songs of victory.

Yet the song does not wholly depend on past history for its strength. The last section (verses 19-35) deals with the present activity of God. He is a present God, and in the days of the singer gives evidence of His power and pity.

Blessed be the Lord who daily beareth *our* burden,
Even the God who is *our* salvation. Selah.
God is unto *us* a God of deliverances.

The appeal of the song to the people of God in all ages in their hours of difficulty is easily understood. It expresses the one and only consciousness which is equal to making a day of darkness and difficulty the occasion of exultation and song.

PSALM 69

Perhaps in no psalm in the whole psalter is the sense of sorrow profounder or more intense than in this. The soul of the singer pours itself out in unrestrained abandonment to the overwhelming and terrible grief which consumes it.

The first half is occupied wholly with a statement of the terrible consciousness. There is first a cry of distress, piercing and passionate (verses 1-6). The circumstances described are of helpless whelming in waters and mire. Yet the chief agony is that God seems to be neglectful of the cry, and a fear fills the heart lest others should be harmed through what they see of the hopelessness and helplessness of his suffering.

In the next movement the singer declares that this suffering has come in the path of loyalty to God (verses 7-12).

Following this declaration, the cry for succor is repeated with new emphasis and passion (verses 13-18). This part of the psalm reveals the condition into which the men of faith sometimes are brought. Yet it contains suggestion of a sorrow profounder than any save One had experienced. Nothing can be conceived more overwhelming than the strange and inexplicable suffering resulting from loyalty to God and zeal for His honor. Undeserved reproach is the most stupendous grief possible to the sensitive soul. Yet even throughout this whole movement, expressive of such intense grief, there is an undertone of confidence in God.

In the presence of that God whose loving-kindness the singer has declared to be good he continues to pour out his complaint. Suddenly the song becomes a passionate cry for vengeance. It is a false view of things which criticises this cry as being unworthy of a man familiar with God. It is really the expression of a righteous desire for judgment against essential wrong. The method which he has described as being used by his adversaries violated the essential and fundamental order of the divine Kingdom. For the sake of that order, and the vindication of God, there must be a place for retribution and vengeance. The passion passes, and a prayer follows which merges into praise, and culminates in a great affirmation of confidence in God.

PSALM 70

This short psalm is a rushing sob of anxious solicitude. There is little restfulness in it. Enemies are engaged in cruel persecution and mockery. It seems as though the singer felt that the strain was becoming too much for him, and in fear lest he should be overcome he cries aloud for God to hasten to his deliverance. The faith of the singer is evident in that he cries to God, and evidently has no room in his heart to question God's ability to keep him. The only question is whether help will arrive in time.

It is not the highest type of faith which is revealed, but we are profoundly thankful to find such a song in this great book of religious poetry. Rightly or wrongly, we often come to just such places of doubt. No doubt exists either of God's ability, or of His interest in and love for us, but is He not trying us beyond the power of our endurance? He is not; but for moments of terrible tension it seems as though He were. Then here is a psalm for such days or hours. Let us take it and use it, knowing that He would far rather have in our song an expression of an honest questioning than any affectation of a confidence not possessed. Moreover, He would rather have from us such a song than silence.

PSALM 71

This is pre-eminently a song of the aged, and, like old age, it is reminiscent. The singer passes from memory to hope, and from experience to praise. No very definite division is possible. Generally speaking, it may be noticed that the first part expresses need, and is principally prayer, while the second half affirms confidence and is principally praise.

The song opens with a prayer for deliverance (verses 1-8). This is not so much a cry out of present distress as a prayer that in the event of trouble the singer may be able to resort to God. The old man is discovered in that the first three verses are almost a direct quotation from a previous psalm (31), perhaps one of his own. His experience of God from birth is his confidence that he will be heard now. This leads the song on in prayer that he may still be helped in age, for he still has adversaries (verses 9-13). Here again are quotations from earlier psalms which the marginal references will aid the reader in discovering.

The singer then rises to higher levels as he tells of his confidence in God, and asks that he may be helped to declare God to the succeeding generation. The psalm is a song of sunset, and it is full of beauty. There are storm clouds in the western sky. Some are spent, and some still threaten; but on all is a light which transfigures them.

PSALM 72

This is a great psalm of the Theocracy. Incidentally the whole perfect order is revealed. God high over all enthroned, and in all actively governing. The king, appointed by God, and gaining his guidance from God, so reigning over his own people as to succor the needy, spoil the oppressor, and secure the prosperity of the righteous; and so reigning that the beneficial influence of the kingship and kingdom are felt over all the earth. Submission to him is followed by deliverance of the poor and helpless, and universal peace and prosperity.

This is the Kingdom for which the world still waits. It is a perfect order which has never yet been established, because the ultimate rule of God has never yet been recognized and obeyed. This was surely all in the view of Jesus when He taught us to pray for the coming of the Kingdom. The One King has come, and men would not have Him to reign. Therefore, notwithstanding all the best and highest efforts of man without Him, the needy are still oppressed, and peace and prosperity are postponed. To us the song of this psalm is a prophecy of hope. We have seen the King, and we know the perfect Kingdom must come, for God cannot be defeated.

PSALM 73

The marginal reading, "Only good is God to Israel," indicates the real value of the song. Israel has no other good, and needs no other. Yet it is not always easy to realize this, and the psalmist tells how he nearly stumbled in view of the prosperity of the wicked, and how he was restored. The first half describes the perplexing vision of the prosperity of the wicked. The whole psalm was written in the light of the conviction expressed in the last half, but it describes first the things which startled and perplexed the soul. The wicked prosper in life, and death itself seems to have no terror for them. They are satisfied, and more than satisfied, and because of these things men deny the knowledge of God, and turn their feet into the way of wickedness, affirming the uselessness of right-doing to procure benefits.

The psalmist now tells the story of how he was delivered. He attempted to unravel the mystery and find out why men succeeded and were satisfied without God. It was too painful, that is, too difficult, for him. He could not solve the riddle. At least he found the true viewpoint. He went into the sanctuary of God. Then everything changed. He ceased to look at the present only. He saw the end of the wicked. A more spacious outlook, taking in the whole issue of things, corrected all the false seeming of the near vision. Yet the sanctuary was also the place where the nearest things were seen most accurately, seen, that is, in relation to the large things. Again he remembered and recognized his own wrong in misjudging God, but was able to affirm God's presence and care; and out of the consciousness the song of praise was born. To see the issue of the near is to understand the real meaning of the near, and this is ever to bring to the heart of the trusting a thanksgiving and a song.

PSALM 74

This is a great complaint, but it is a complaint of faith. Hardly a gleam of light is found throughout. The singer sits in the midst of national desolation and pours out his soul to God in passionate appeal for His help, and protest against His silence and inactivity. This is not the son of an atheist, but the wail of a believer. He has a past experience of God's power and a present conviction thereof. The signs of that power are in day and night, in summer and winter. The one place from which He seems to be absent is the place of His people's distress. The ground of the singer's plea is not the distress of these people finally. It is rather that the enemy reproaches the name of Jehovah and blasphemes it.

In that central complaint the name Jehovah, which is ever suggestive of the essential Helper, emerges, and there only, in the psalm. The master consciousness of the moment is of God the Mighty One, but there is that deeper knowledge of Him as the Helper of the needy. Again, we are thankful that such a psalm has a place here, for it is so true to much human experience. When the heart is hot and restless, and it seems as though God had forsaken His own, he is a wise man who turns to God in song, even though the song be only a complaint.

PSALM 75

If this, and the former psalm, were written by different men and at different periods, then the spiritual sense of the editor is most clearly revealed in their juxtaposition in this book. This is a complete and remarkable answer to that. In form the song is dramatic. It opens with a chorus which is an ascription of praise (verse 1). This is answered directly by God Himself. He declares that in the set time He judges. All the appearances of the hour may be perplexing, but the heart may know that He knows, and awaits only the right moment to act. Chaos may characterize the outlook, but order enwraps it all, for God has set up the pillars (verses 2,3). Then the solo of the confident soul breaks forth, and, addressing the wicked, charges them not to be confident, because God is the judge. In His hand He holds the cup of judgment. Ultimately He abases the wicked, and lifts up the righteous. Therefore the singer's song is ceaseless. In experience such a song as this always succeeds an honest declaration of perplexity made directly to God by a tried, but trusting, soul. The prophecy of Habakkuk is another perfect illustration of the fact.

PSALM 76

The singer celebrates a great victory, recognizing it as the work of God. The song has three movements. In the first, God is seen as the defense of the people (verses 1-3). In the second, His victory over their enemies is declared (verses 4-9). In the third, the truth is summarized, and appeal is made to His people and the surrounding nations to change their attitude toward Him (verses 10-12).

The national life gathers around Him. He is known by the nation; His dwelling place is in their city. The attack made upon them has been broken by the One who dwells in the midst of them. The issue of His judgment is manifest in the blotting out of the enemy. They have ceased to be, having been put to the sleep of death. God's judgements are purposeful, He arose to save the meek, and they are resistless; the enemies are no more. So perfect is His government that by judgment He compels evil to serve His purpose, making the wrath of men to praise Him. To such a God there should be allegiance sworn and rendered by His people, and the surrounding peoples should submit with gifts.

While the weapons of our warfare are spiritual, God is the same in might; and while He is in the midst our defense is sure. No weapon formed against the trusting people can prosper.

PSALM 77

This is a song of the healing of sorrow. It opens with the declaration of determination to cry to God, and then proceeds to explain the reason of this determination. Verse 10 is the pivot on which the whole psalm turns, from a description of an experience of darkness and sorrow to one of gladness and praise. The first part tells of sorrow overwhelming the soul. The second gives a song which is the outcome of a vision that has robbed sorrow of its sting. In the first part, a great infirmity overshadows the sky, and there is no song. In the second, a great song pours itself out, and sorrow is forgotten. The difference is that between a man brooding over trouble and a man seeing high above it the enthroned God. In the first half, self is predominant. In the second, God is seen in His glory. A very simple method with the psalm makes this perfectly clear. In verses 1 to 9 the first personal pronoun occurs twenty-two times, and there are eleven references to God by name, title, and pronoun. In the second, there are only three personal references and twenty-four mentions of God.

The message of the psalm is that to brood on sorrow is to be broken and disheartened, while to see God is to sing on the darkest day. Once we come to know that our years are of His right hand, there is light everywhere, and the song ascends.

PSALM 78

The supreme quantity of this psalm is that throughout all its measures, over against the repeated failure of His people God's persistent patience is set forth in bold relief. The purpose of the psalm, however, is to warn God's people against unfaithfulness by the story of past failure. After announcing his determination the first eight verses declare the purpose of the singer. Things of the past are to be recounted for the sake of the children. Notice very carefully the statement of the latter part of this introduction. It announces the institution in Israel of a method for dealing with the children. The words "testimony" and "law" (verse 5) do not here refer to the Mosaic economy, but to a specific arrangement for transmission of that law. This arrangement was to instruct the children. The value of such instruction was that the new generation would be safeguarded in its hope, its memory, its conduct.

The singer then proceeded with the work of "telling . . . the praises of the Lord." This section recites the disloyalty of the people in spite of the goodness of God, and thus explains the reason of the divine chastisement. The prophetic writings (especially Hosea) show that Ephraim became the leader in the rebellion and disloyalty which cursed the nation, and so, figuratively, and as standing for the rest, Ephraim is here addressed. The description is figurative. The people armed and equipped, were guilty of cowardice. They turned back because they forgot God. Then follows a poetic description of the way in which God delivered them from Egypt and led them in the wilderness. These facts of the guidance of God make their cowardice sinful. This goodness is further traced in His dealing with them step by step.

The fickleness of their obedience is especially set forth. "They believed not . . . He slew them . . . they inquired after Him . . . they lied to Him." Yet God's patience was always manifest. With infinite tenderness He bore with them, and waited for them; forgave them and pitied them. In spite of all, they continued to rebel, and the reason was that they did not remember His hand. The singer then sang anew of the things they had forgotten, of God's signs in Egypt, of His leading them out, and of His bringing them into possession. It would seem almost past belief to us as we read that a people so led could forget. Yet is not this sin of forgetfulness with us perpetually? In some day of danger and perplexity we become so occupied with the immediate peril as utterly to fail to think of past deliverances. Such forgetfulness is of the nature of unbelief in its worst form. It wrongs God, and paralyzes our own prayer.

Even when, in spite of their infidelity, God brought them into possession, they tempted and provoked Him. Then came His seven dealings with them which are described. These dealings are also systematic, and as He refused and chose, it was ever with purposes of blessings in His heart. It is indeed a great song of God's patience, and there is no story more fruitful if men will but learn it. It is questionable whether any of us could escape the charges made here against the people of God; and it is certain that we might all survey our lives, and sing just such a song of God's determined patience and persistence.

PSALM 79

This is a cry of distress. The conditions described are an overwhelming national calamity. The country and the city of God are overrun and spoiled by ruthless enemies. The people have been slain and left without burial. Out of the midst of these circumstances the psalmist prays to God for pardon, help, and deliverance.

There is no present note of praise in the psalm, but there is an undertone of confidence in God. This is the quality of these old songs of the men of faith which makes them living and powerful in an age utterly different from the age in which they were written. A careful perusal of this song will show three things as most evidently forming the deepest conviction of the singer's hope. First there is the sense that all the calamity which has overtaken them is the result of their own sin. Behind this is a great idea of the power and goodness of God. These things need not have been had they been faithful, for God is strong and tender. Again there is the passion for the glory of the divine Name,

Help us, O God of our salvation, for the
glory of Thy name;
And deliver us, and purge away our sins,
for Thy name's sake.
Wherefore should the heathen say, Where
is their God?

Finally, the very fact of the song is a revelation of the underlying confidence in God. In distress the heart seeks its way back to some hiding place, and finds it in the name of God, who, by suffering is dealing with them.

PSALM 80

Again we have a song out of the midst of distress. There is far more light and color about it than in the previous psalm. The circumstances seem not to be any more favorable than those described before. However, there is this difference between the two psalms. The first is occupied mainly with the disastrous condition; this one begins with a prayer which is a recognition of the past relationship of God to His people.

This is, therefore, a great song of God as Shepherd. The aspects of the Shepherd nature dealt with are His guidance and care and protection. The Shepherd of glory, who by the shining of His face reveals the way, and by the stirring up of His might saves from dangers, is appealed to.

Then the figure is changed, and God is the Husbandman. His vine, which He planted and which flourished so perfectly, has become a prey to the ravages of wild beasts and fire. Suddenly the figure ceases, and its meaning is revealed in the words,

Let Thy hand be upon the Man of Thy
right hand,
Upon the Son of man whom Thou madest
strong for Thyself.

The burden of the psalm is expressed in the thrice repeated prayer (verses 3,7,19). The suffering of the people is due to their own sin in turning away from God as Shepherd, Husbandman, and King. Their restoration can come only as He turns them back to Himself. Notice the ascent in these verses in the names which the singer uses for God. "God," "God of hosts," "Jehovah God of hosts."

PSALM 81

This is a psalm for the feast of Trumpets. In the calendar of the Hebrews this feast prepared the way for the Day of Atonement and the feast of Tabernacles. The first day of the seventh month was the feast of Trumpets. The tenth day of the seventh month was Atonement. The fifteenth day of the seventh month was Tabernacles (Leviticus 23).

The psalm opens with a call to the feast of Trumpets, and a declaration of its divine appointment (verses 1-5). Then the singer expresses the attitude of God to His people, and the song proceeds as in the words of Jehovah (verses 6-10). First He tells of His deliverance of them from bondage, and His answer to them at Sinai (verses 6,7). Then He reminds them of the terms of the Covenant with them. He would speak, and they should hearken. They were to have no God but Himself, and He would be to them Jehovah God. They were to open the mouth and He would fill it (verses 8-10). They failed in refusing to hearken and obey, and therefore He abandoned them to their choice (verses 11,12). Finally He expresses His desire that they should return, and declares His ability still to deliver them (verses 13-16).

It is still the same burden of the faithfulness of God, and the unfaithfulness of His people. The people's panic and defeat are always due to their departure from God. The enemies who overcome us are without strength in the conflict against Him. When they overcome us it is because we have departed from Him.

PSALM 82

This psalm is a cry for justice, born of a sense of the maladministration of those in authority. It first announces that God is the supreme Judge. This is a recognition of the perfect equity of the standard of justice. The judges in mind have erred in that they have shown respect for the persons of the wicked, and thus departed from that strict justice which ever characterizes the dealings of the God to whom they are all responsible.

The singer then sets forth the essential functions of the judges. They are especially to care for all those in difficulty and danger. This has not been done, for such people are without knowledge or guidance. The judges have had the name of authority, and its position, but because of their failure they are to be degraded.

The song ends with an appeal to God to arise and judge the earth. This is ever the cry of the man of faith when he stands in the presence of the wrongs and oppressions obtaining among the poor and afflicted. There is nothing the world needs today more than the administration of strict and impartial justice, and there is no greater comfort to the heart than the conviction that the prayer of the psalmist, multiplied ten thousandfold in the passing centuries by all who have been, and still are, conscious of prevailing injustice, will yet be answered. God's day of judgment will be a day of mercy in the largest sense.

PSALM 83

The psalmist has a vision of the confederacy of all the enemies of the people of God. He describes the process, constitution, and purpose of the confederacy. Their enemies have taken counsel together with the avowed purpose to annihilate the very name of Israel. The peoples of the conspiracy are named, and the first part of the psalm ends (verses 1-8).

The song then becomes a definite prayer for the destruction of this confederacy and the confusion of its purpose. Past victories are referred to, and in a strong and overwhelming sense of peril the cry for the divine activity is poured forth. Here again, as constantly, this attitude of the singer must be accounted for according to his own declaration. In describing the confederacy he declares:

> They have consulted together, with one consent,
> Against Thee do they make a covenant.

At the close of the prayer he says:

> That they may know that Thou alone, whose name is JEHOVAH,
> Art the Most High over all the earth.

These singers of the ancient people were all inspired supremely with a passion for the honor of God. With them, as with the prophets, selfish motives were unknown. Selfishness sings no song, and sees no visions. On the other hand, a passion for the glory of God is capable of great sternness as well as of great tenderness.

PSALM 84

This is a pilgrim psalm. It falls into three strophes divided by "Selahs." The first describes the pilgrim's hope (verses 1-4); the second, the pilgrim's experience (verses 5-8); the third, the pilgrim's prayer (verses 9-12).

The hope of the pilgrim is centered in the dwelling place of God. The earthly temple suggests the heavenly home. It is a place of rest and worship. The light of it shines on the pathway, and is the inspiration of the pilgrimage. The experience of the pilgrimage is then described. Faith has an anchorage; it is found in God when the heart is set on the consummation. Faith has an activity; it passes through dry valleys and fills them with springs of refreshment. Faith has an assurance; it goes from strength to strength, confident of finally appearing before God. The pilgrim finally pours out his prayer, and it is full of praise and confidence. Its desire is for a vision of God, which, even though it be the distant view of a doorkeeper, is infinitely to be preferred to all the world has to offer. The lessons of the psalm for all the pilgrims of hope, are, first, that the heart should be set on the upper things; second, that faith may dig wells in the driest places and find the living water; and, finally, that pilgrimage develop strength rather than produce weakness as these conditions are fulfilled.

PSALM 85

This psalm would seem to have been written in a day when some divine deliverance had been wrought for the people of God. Yet the singer is conscious that dispositions not in harmony with the will of God remain in the heart of people; and therefore, they are without joy. And yet, further, he is conscious that God, Jehovah, has purposes of the highest and best for His own, and, moreover, that He will accomplish these purposes.

These three matters are evident in the threefold movement: thanksgiving offered (verses 1-3), petition presented (verses 4-7), and confidence affirmed (verses 8-13). In the thanksgiving the relation between captivity and sin is remembered, and the ending of the first by putting away the second is announced. Yet the imperfection of their loyalty creates the long discipline of sorrow and shame, and the prayer is that God will turn the people to Himself. And this is surely His will, for when the singer pauses to hear what Jehovah will say he hears tender and gracious words telling of salvation, first in the spiritual realm, and then in the material. In this psalm which breathes the spirit of the tender compassion of God the name Jehovah is the predominant note.

PSALM 86

This psalm is peculiar in many ways. Its first peculiarity is that the name of God which dominates is Adonahy, or Lord, which indicates absolute lordship, and by the use of which the singer shows his sense of submission and loyalty. The name Jehovah is used four times, thus revealing the singer's sense of God as Helper; and the name God five times, thus revealing the singer's consciousness of the divine might. The supreme sense, however, is that of divine authority.

The next matter of special note is that while the psalm is a beautiful and consecutive song, it is largely composed of quotations from other psalms, thus revealing the singer's familiarity with them. The references in the Revised Version will enable the reader to trace these quotations.

Finally, the psalm is unique in its method of urging a petition on the ground of some known fact. This is clearly seen if the use of the word "for" is noticed (verses 1-5, 7,10,13). The first four verses indicate the singer's attitude toward God. The last four reveal God's attitude toward him. The revelation for us is the true approach to God in time of need. This must be based on our absolute submission to Him. It must be expressed in harmony with spiritual desires as expressed by the fellowship of the faithful. It must be urged in consecration and courage.

PSALM 87

This is a prophecy. The singer is looking on. The order of the earthly realization of the Kingdom of God is established. First, the city is contemplated at the center of everything, with Jehovah as its God. Then the peoples of the earth are seen in their true relation to that city.

It is a most remarkable utterance. Though brief, it is as comprehensive and full of beauty as any of the inspired predictions. Without specific statement, the sovereignty of God is taken for granted. No argument for this is given. It is a fact beyond dispute, and needs no proof. Thus God has the city of His chosen people as the center and foundation of His administration. His love is set on the city, and her fame is widespread; glorious things are spoken of her. The outcome is seen in the effect on the surrounding peoples. Finally, her ancient enemies are to be born, that is, realize their true life through this governing city of God.

This is the highest function of the chosen people according to the purpose of God. Under His government they are to bring the other nations to Him, so that they also shall find their highest in His Kingdom. This is not a story of Israel conquering by force of arms, but of that higher victory not yet won, when by manifestation and administration of the divine government the peoples will dance and sing in finding their fountains and fulness in God.

PSALM 88

This is a song of sadness from beginning to end. It seems to have no gleam of light or of hope. Commencing with an appeal to Jehovah to hear, it proceeds to describe the terrible sorrows through which the singer is passing. He is whelmed with trouble and nigh unto death. Moreover, he is alone; his acquaintances are put away from him. Death is a terrible outlook, for the singer sees no light in it. Therein God Himself will be unknown, and unable to succor.

Again the song moves in yet profounder notes of sadness, which are like the breaking of great waves over the soul, which seem as though they must silence it utterly. The last declaration is a most terrible one of utter loneliness; "lover and friend" are put away from him, and the final word is "darkness."

This psalm was a foreshadowing of sorrow which, being national, yet reached its fulfilment of realization only in the Messiah. The note of present value, however, is that while, as we said at the beginning, there seems to be no light, there is light everywhere. The singer is in great sorrow, but he comes to Jehovah. He is afraid of going into death, because there Jehovah cannot help him; but he has come there, and therefore still cries out for God. While the sense of God abides, darkness has not triumphed.

PSALM 89

Taken as a whole, this song is one of the finest in the collection as a revelation of how the man of faith is compelled to view calamity. In a poem of great beauty he first sets forth the praises of God (verses 1-37). Then he surveys the present condition of His people, and so creates a contrast (verses 38-52). No present defeat can dim the glory of history as it reveals the facts of the divine majesty. Yet these facts and confidences may be the reason of present inquiry and approach to God.

In the first part, which is a song of praise, the singer tells of the covenant made with David, and then breaks out into adoration. The heavens and the angels witness to God's greatness (verses 5-7). The earth and men also. All nature, the sea and the mountains, the north and the south, are conscious of His power. Under His government the foundations are unshakable, and the method full of tenderness (verses 8-14). It follows naturally that the people who are peculiarly His own are indeed blessed (verses 15-37).

"But," and the word suggests a change, and a great change it is. Instead of the glowing picture of the former verses is a dark one of present experience. The people are scattered, their defenses broken down, their enemies triumphant, and their king is robbed of glory and covered with shame (verses 38-45). Yet all this is spoken of as the work of Jehovah. The key phrase to this portion is, "Thou hast." The mighty One who had found the king and blessed the nation is the One who has broken the nation and cast out the king. On the basis of that conviction the final prayer rises, "How long, Jehovah?" This is the true attitude of the interceding soul in the day of calamity. First, a sense of the greatness and goodness of God. Then the conviction that this same One is visiting the people in discipline. When that is recognized, prayer for deliverance is proper, for it must inevitably be accompanied by a turning back to Jehovah from those things which have been the reason of His punishments.

PSALM 90

The main purpose of this psalm is revealed in the prayer with which it concludes (verses 13-17). This prayer is prefaced by a meditation on the frailty of man (verses 3-12), in the light of the eternity of God (verses 1,2). By this backward method of analysis we gain a conception of the general scheme of the psalm, which now enables us to take the three movements in their orderly sequence.

The eternity of God is described in three stages. First, as measured by the history of His people, He has ever been their dwelling place. Second, as measured by creation, He was before all. Finally, whether the mind travel backward or forward to the vanishing point, He is still God. In this light the frailty of man's being is seen. To God a thousand years are nothing, and in every millennium men appear and pass in a sequence as orderly as that of the grass, and in a life as transitory. This frailty is the more feeble because man is a sinner and therefore out of harmony with God. Yet this very eternity of God is the hope of man in his frailty and sin, and the heart is lifted to Jehovah in prayer that the mornings, the days, the years of brief life may all be set in true relation to Him. Satisfaction, gladness, success in work must all come from man's right relation to the eternal Lord.

PSALM 91

This psalm is one of the greatest possessions of the saints. It is a great song of the safety of those who put their trust in Jehovah, and contains the divine assurance that such faith is fruitful. Very little exposition is necessary. There is a change in the use of pronouns from first to second person twice over, and from third to first at the beginning, and from second to third at the close, which, although it has created some sense of difficulty, is yet a key to analysis of the psalm. Let us set out the scheme of the psalm around these changes, leaving its familiar words to speak for themselves.

v.1. The statement of truth.

v.2. Personal affirmation of realization.

vs.3-8. The address of the singer either to his own soul, or to some other person, or to the nation, in which he affirms the convictions resulting from personal realization of the truth.

v.9a. Repetition of personal realization.

vs.9b-13. Same as verses 3-8.

vs.14,15. Conclusion of psalm, in which the singer with holy boldness expresses, as in the words of Jehovah, the safety of the trusting soul, and thus gives the testimony of God as well as that of man to the truth.

PSALM 92

This is a song of praise. The seemliness of praise is first declared (verses 1-3); and then reasons for it are given (verses 4-15).

Praise is good as the first exercise of the day, and also as the last. *Loving-kindness* in the morning, the sense of all the provision made for us as we face the responsibilities and conflicts of the day. *Faithfulness* at night, the conviction that Jehovah has been true to His Covenant through all the hours of need.

The song proceeds to rejoice, first, in that general and wholly beneficent government of God whereby the wicked are dealt with in judgment. That is a weak and perilous tenderness which permits evil to continue its work of destruction. That is a strong and tender pity which, without relenting, smites evil and destroys it. The song ends with a gracious description of the growth and perennial freshness of the righteous. Planted in the courts of God, they will flourish and grow, and yet know no senility—age with all its wealth of experience and fruitage, but with no failing or weakness.

PSALM 93

There is a great majesty about this song. It celebrates Jehovah's assumption of the throne and government. The form in which the preliminary statements are made conveys the impression, not so much of the eternal sovereignty of the King, as that He has taken up His position and acted on it. The result is that the stability of all things is assured. This assumption of power is but the enforcement of a perpetual fact, for

> Thy throne is established of old;
> Thou art from everlasting.

Moreover, this assumption has not been without opposition, and the figure of the storm-tossed sea is made use of to indicate the strength of this opposition,

> The floods have lifted up against Him.

All this has been of no avail. The King is high above, and therefore, Lord of them.

In all likelihood, this psalm was written after some deliverance by Jehovah of His people; but through the open window the singer, consciously or unconsciously, saw the distant light of another day in which the Kingdom of God will be set up in His might, and the song of an established order shall be the anthem of His praise.

PSALM 94

The position of this song immediately after the song which sets forth the fact of the enthronement of Jehovah is remarkable. It creates a contrast while it suggests a continuity of ideas. The contrast is between the celebration in the previous psalm of the victory of Jehovah over all opposition and the appeal to Him out of circumstances in which His enemies seem to triumph in the second psalm. The continuity of ideas is, however, equally apparent. To whom should His own turn in times of such distress save to the One who sits above the force and fury of the flood?

The psalm has three main movements. First, an appeal to Jehovah the Mighty in the presence of the triumph of the wicked (verses 1-7). This is followed by an address to those who are doubting because of the apparent inactivity of God. They are reminded that God hears, sees, and must act (verses 8-11). Finally, the song again becomes a prayer in which faith makes its great affirmations. The period of waiting is one of blessed chastening. Jehovah cannot ultimately cast off His people. Experience testifies to this. The wrong committed by those apparently victorious enemies makes it impossible to believe that they can have fellowship with God. Therefore, the final words tell of the psalmist's confidence.

PSALM 95

We pause here to note a connection one with another in a group of psalms, *viz.*, 93-100. These eight constitute the songs of the King, arranged in conformity with the needs of the people. The first (93) affirms His enthronement and government. The next (94) expresses the hope of His people even in the midst of trial. Then follow six dealing with the fact of His Kingship in varied ways.

The present one declares His supremacy, and utters a note of warning against what must inevitably hinder His people from realizing the rest of His reign. Calling first for praise to the King, the singer celebrates the King's supremacy. He is above all other authority, and is the God of all nature. He is, moreover, the God of His people, and therefore they should worship in submission and reverence before Him (verses 1-7). Then the warning note follows, reminding them of the sins of their fathers, resulting from failure of faith expressing itself in refusal to bow in submission to God's will. That sin excluded them from rest, and the children are warned to profit by the ancient story. Such a King demands loyalty, and it must express itself in submission to His government.

PSALM 96

There is a beauty about this song which irresistibly appeals to the submissive soul. The previous warning must be heeded in order to sing it. When the personal life is loyal to His throne, the song of God's wide and beneficent dominion thrills with exultation. It moves out in widening circles. The first is that of His own people, and sets forth His supremacy over all the gods of the peoples. They are "things of nought"; He is the Creator, and all things high and beautiful are His (verses 1-6). The second calls upon the nations to recognize His Kingship, and to give Him His due, submitting themselves also in worship and reverence (verses 7-9). The third sweeps the whole earth into its circumference, and rejoices in the equity of His reign.

No study of the devotional literature of these people is possible without an ever recurring consciousness of this far-reaching purpose of God. If the song of the Lord begins in the heart, it always grows into the chorus in which others are included in its music. To know the gracious glory of His reign in personal life is to reveal it to those beyond, and to desire its victories in the utmost reaches.

PSALM 97

The reign of Jehovah, while wholly beneficent in purpose and in ultimate issue, is yet full of terror and of judgment in its process toward the issue. This is also cause for rejoicing. The method of God's judgments is described. They are mysterious—"clouds and darkness are round about Him." They are founded on strictest justice —"Righteousness and judgment are the foundation of His throne." They are forceful—"a fire goeth before Him." The effects of His judgments are declared. His adversaries are destroyed, His glory is revealed, His people are filled with joy. The vision of the certainty, method, and victory of the judgments of the King gives rise to a sense of their underlying reason. He is the Holy One, and all wickedness is hateful to Him, because of the harm it works among His people, for the fierceness of God's holiness is ever His love. Therefore let His saints learn the lesson, and "hate evil." The promise to those who obey is very full of beauty, "light is sown . . . and gladness." It is a figure of the dawn, shedding its light. To walk in light is to be able to discover the true pathway leading toward the desired consummation. To walk in that pathway is to have gladness in the heart indeed.

PSALM 98

Another song of worship on the pattern of Psalm 96, it opens and closes in the same way. A new song and its ultimate reason, the judging of the earth by Jehovah with righteousness and with truth. Here also the circles widen. Beginning with Israel (verses 1-3), the whole earth is included (verses 4-6), and, finally, all nature (verses 7,8).

As the singer rejoices over the salvation of God manifested on behalf of Israel, he emphasizes the fact that it has been wrought by Jehovah alone, "*His* right hand, and *His* holy arm"; these were the only instruments available for, or capable of, working deliverance. In proportion as the vision is filled with the glory of the Lord so the heart is filled with gladness, and the lips with song.

This is as true today as ever. Sometimes it seems as though all singing were out of place, save as faith keeps its eye fixed on the occupied throne of Jehovah. The days are dark and mysterious as ever, and the outlook as full of gloom. Yet "He hath done marvellous things," and "He cometh to judge." This vision of God in the past, and the future creates the song of the present.

PSALM 99

This is a song of the Kingdom of Jehovah as founded on, and administered in, holiness. There are three distinct parts, each ending with practically the same refrain. The first acclaims the King as enthroned (verses 1-3). The second affirms the absolute integrity of His administration (verses 4,5). The third declares the constant and faithful guidance of His own representatives (verses 6-9). Each calls for a response to the affirmation. The enthroned King is to be praised. The governing King is to be exalted and worshiped in submission at His footstool. The guiding King is to be exalted and worshiped in fellowship at His holy hill. Finally, in each case the underlying reason of the King's position and activity, and also therefore of the response, is His holiness. The throne is established in holiness. The guidance is motived in holiness. In the fuller light of the Christian revelation we see the threefold fact in the life of God suggested. The Father enthroned, the Son administering His Kingdom, the Spirit interpreting His will through leaders and circumstances, through pity and through punishment.

PSALM 100

This is the last song of the series, and forms an appropriate conclusion to the movement which commenced in Psalm 93. There the divine assumption of the throne and government was the subject. Here it is the benefits resulting to the whole earth. All lands are called on to sing the song of His reign. The strength of their song is to be their service rendered with gladness. Israel is viewed as the witness to the divine power and goodness. The peoples are supposed to see the position of the chosen people in all its desirability; and they are reminded that their well-being is the result of the government of God.

Then the great invitation is given to the outlying people to enter His gates, to yield to Him, and share in His benefits. This is the true position and witness of God's chosen people, according to His purpose for them, and through them for others. It is a glimpse of a glory not realized by the ancient people. They never learned how to invite the outsider into the place of privilege. Because of their failure to do this, Israel as an earthly people is scattered and peeled. The Church, the spiritual Israel, fulfils, or ought to fulfil, this function.

PSALM 101

A fine sense of the fitness of things is exhibited by the editor of the Psalter in placing this psalm here. Following immediately the songs of the enthroned Jehovah, in which there has been perpetually recurrent the recognition of the holiness of His reign, it describes the true attitude of the earthly ruler who recognizes the sovereignty of God, and how that ought to affect his own life and rule. It is a clear testimony, moreover, to the fact that private life and public life are very closely allied.

It has two movements. The keynote of the first is "within my house" (verse 2), of the second it is "the city of God." Between these there is the closest relation. No man is able to make the city in which he dwells anything like the city of God who does not know how to behave in his own house. This is the true order also. The first thing for every public man to do who would serve his city for God is to order his private life aright before God. The private life which answers the enthroned Jehovah is described first (verses 1-4). It is a life cautious and watchful, refusing to countenance anything contrary to the holiness of Jehovah. The public life is one which respects the same holiness in all matters of administration. Evil workers are to be destroyed, and the counselors of the ruler are to be sought among the faithful of the land.

PSALM 102

This is a song of faith triumphing over affliction. Beginning with a prayer for deliverance, and a statement of the circumstances of suffering in which the singer then was, together with a recognition of those sufferings as the chastisements of Jehovah (verses 1-11), it rises to a great song of hope in the consciousness of the eternity of God and the consequent conviction of the restoration of His own people to favor and blessing (verses 12-22). Finally, it returns to the singer's own suffering, yet recognizes that again as part of the divine process, and gains confidence in setting that also in the light of the eternity of God (verses 23-28).

While there are great beauties in the details of the song, it is this general atmosphere which creates its greatest value for us. Nothing is more calculated to strengthen the heart in suffering, nor inspire the spirit with courage in days of danger and difficulty, than the sense of the eternity of God. In it is found the certainty that the purpose defeated today will yet be completed. In the vision of the eternity of God is revealed the continuity of humanity, and a great sense of the solidarity of the race is created. Let us set our limitations always in the light of Him who is without limitations.

PSALM 103

It seems almost a work of supererogation to write anything about this psalm. It is perhaps the most perfect song of pure praise in the Bible. It has become the common inheritance of all who through suffering and deliverance have learned the goodness of Jehovah. Through centuries it has been sung by glad hearts, and today it is as fresh and full of beauty as ever. It is praise intensive and extensive.

As to its intensity, notice how the entire personality of the singer is recognized. The spirit of the man speaks. He addresses his soul, or mind, and calls it to praise first for spiritual benefits, and then for physical. And again notice how in the sweep of the song things so small as the frame of the physical and its constituent dust are recognized, while yet the immeasurable reaches of East and West are included.

The extensive mercy of Jehovah as evident in the same system is seen in other psalms, but perhaps never so majestically as here. It begins with individual consciousness (verses 1-5), proceeds in recognition of national blessings (verses 6-18), and ends with the inclusion of all the angels, and hosts, and works in the vast dominion of Jehovah. The "my" of personal experience merges into the "our" of social fellowship, and thus culminates in the "all" of universal consciousness. Yet all ends with the personal word, and the perfect music of the psalm is revealed in the fact that it opens and closes on the same note.

PSALM 104

Again we have a great song of praise commencing and closing with the same note of personal praise. While in the former the dominant note is the mercy of Jehovah, here it is His majesty. The former is the song of love to Love. This is the song of loyalty to Royalty.

The psalm opens with a declaration of the essential greatness of God, and then proceeds in poetic language to describe the manifestations of His greatness in creation. All through beneficent purpose is recognized. The springs among the valleys are to quench the thirst of birds and beasts. Grass and herb are for service, and so on throughout.

Then in a burst of praise the singer recognizes the dependence of all on Jehovah. Hiding His face is trouble, and if He withdraw breath death ensues. Finally, the singer cries out for the continuity of the realization of divine purpose everywhere in order that Jehovah may rejoice in His works. To this end he declares he will contribute his personal worship. The conception is full of beauty. The widespread revelation of the power and glory of God makes its appeal to the individual responsibility of the one man.

PSALM 105

This and the following psalm are companion pieces. They reveal the two sides of the relation between God and His people during a long period. This one sings the song of His faithfulness and power; while the next tells the sad story of His people's repeated failure and rebellion.

In singing his praise of God the psalmist opens with an appeal which recognizes the responsibility of those who have received of God's blessing. In order that the doings of God may be proclaimed, he calls on men to "remember," and proceeds to trace the divine hand in their history. First, he goes back to the ancient Covenant and sings of how God cared for them while they were few in the land, rebuking kings for their sake. Then follows a recognition of the government of God as overruling even what appeared so disastrous a matter as the famine. Through that, Joseph received his opportunity, and the people were brought into Egypt, which for the time being was a place of quietness and increase.

The master word in the psalm is the pronoun "He." In constant repetition it shows the one thought uppermost in the mind of the singer. It is the thought of the perpetual activity of God in all those experiences through which His people have passed. It was through the oppression of the Egyptians that Israel passed through a baptism of suffering which toughened the fiber of the national life and prepared them for all that lay ahead.

Finally, the song speaks of their coming into possession of the land. It is a noble song of the might of God and of His fidelity to His people. With unswerving loyalty to His Covenant, in spite of all difficulties, and by means of suffering as well as joy, He moved in their history ever onward. In its function of interpreting history and revealing the orderliness in the economy of God, such a song is prophecy of days and events which seem to be the most calamitous.

PSALM 106

The previous psalm called the people to talk of the "marvellous works" of Jehovah. This one calls to praise, and the reason is that "His mercy endureth for ever." This fact is then illustrated by a declaration of how the people of God have persistently sinned against Him, and how He has patiently borne with them, restoring them constantly to Himself.

The first section (verses 1-31) deals with the history of the people after Egypt, and their sojourn in the wilderness. The description of what happened immediately after the crossing of the Red Sea is graphic:

> Then believed they His words;
> They sang His praise.
> They soon forgot His works;
> They waited not for His counsel.

And so the story runs on through Dathan and Abiram, by way of Horeb, and to Baal Peor. And over against all the unutterable folly of the people are seen the faithfulness and matchless patience of Jehovah.

Continuing the same sad story, the psalmist then turned to the unfaithfulness of the people in the land (verses 32-48). This he begins by referring to Moses' exclusion. This reference seems to be a remarkable recognition of the strength of the man. The fair deduction from the setting of the story seems to be that if he had entered with them some of the things might have been different. The story of their failure in the land is tragic, but the singer evidently recognizes a poetic justice in their calamity. Moses was excluded because of his failure to represent God to His people, but that failure was provoked by their sin; and they, passing into the land without him, were from the beginning in greater or less degree corrupted. Very beautiful is the revelation of God in the statement:

> He made them also to be pitied
> Of all those that carried them captives.

While their persistent and terrible sin made His wrath burn, and His judgment inevitable, yet the love of His heart never ceased toward the people of His choice.

PSALM 107

We now begin the fifth and last book of the Psalter. In this book the music is richest and fullest. It begins in this psalm on the fundamental notes, and, by way of the songs of ascents, rises through major and minor to the final measures of perfect praise contained in the doxology.

The first thirty-two verses contain a wonderful story of redemption, using that word in its sense of deliverance from positions and circumstances of peril. In a prologue the theme of the songs is stated. A people redeemed and gathered by Jehovah is called on to declare the fact. Then followed four strophes in which the redemption is illustrated in four ways. The first illustration is homelessness. The second is bondage. The third is affliction. The last is storm. The homeless Jehovah led to a city of habitation; the enslaved He led into liberty; the afflicted He healed; the storm-tossed He led to calm and a haven.

At verse 33 the psalm changes its tone and becomes meditative. With the facts of divine deliverances still in mind, the underlying principles of divine activity are stated. Things which appear contradictory are evidences of consistency. Jehovah turns fruitful places into a wilderness; He turns the wilderness into a fruitful place. His activities are destructive and constructive. He blesses and multiplies a people. Again they are abased and afflicted. He is the author of good as prosperity, and evil as adversity. He dethrones the high and exalts the lowly. Everything results from the attitude of the men with whom He deals. Upright men are made to rejoice. Men of iniquity are silenced. The concluding words draw attention to the importance of understanding these matters. The wise will give heed to them. The mercies of Jehovah are to be considered. This means much more than they are to be remembered. The Authorized "understand," and the Revised "consider," are both partial interpretations of the Hebrew word. It very literally means to distinguish. That is to say, God's "mercies" or "lovingkindnesses" are to be considered in their method and meaning, that they may be understood and not misinterpreted. They are not capricious, but proceed ever in harmony with fixed principles.

PSALM 108

This psalm is composed of two quotations from former songs. The first part (verses 1-5) is taken from Psalm 62, of which the theme is "God the Refuge in calamity" (verses 7-11). The second part is found in Psalm 60, of which the theme is "God the Hope of His people" (verses 6-12).

This psalm opens with the culmination of the earlier psalm, in which, out of calamity, the singer finds refuge in fixity of heart in God. Here in this book of perfected praise it is the opening declaration in a song of triumph over difficulty and danger. The latter part of this psalm was also the close of Psalm 60, where it was preceded by a detailed description of affliction. The point of interest in this song, then, is the attitude of mind indicated by this selection. The circumstances of the writer would seem to be very similar to those obtaining in the earlier psalms. They are only hinted at in passing. The soul's fixity of heart enables the singer to rejoice from beginning to end. Relation to God affects all the relationships. To be homed in His will and submissive to His throne is to be triumphant under all circumstances. Triumph in the very hour of defeat is the finest, but it is possible only when the heart is fixed in God.

PSALM 109

This is a psalm full of interest. The singer is in a place of terrible suffering because of the implacable hostility of his foes. The passage containing the imprecations (verses 6-19) contains the singer's quotation of what his enemies say about him rather than what he says about them. In a translation published by The Jewish Publication Society of America that fact is clearly shown. They render verses 5 and 20 thus:

They repay me evil for good,
And hatred for my love (saying) . . .
This it is which mine enemies seek to obtain of the Lord,
And those that speak evil against my life.

The opening complaint is:

The mouth of the wicked and the mouth of deceit have they opened against me.

The singer complains:

For my love they are my adversaries

(which the translation already referred to gives as, "In return for my love they persecute me").

Taking this view of the psalm, it is a sob which is also a song. The circumstances are terrible. Perhaps there is nothing harder to bear than false accusations, and these were terrible things that they said and horrible things they desired for the singer. But the heart pours out its complaint to God and ends with a note of praise.

PSALM 110

This psalm is purely Messianic, and was always considered to be so. When Jesus quoted it in His conversation with the rulers it is perfectly evident that they looked on it in that light. It is equally certain that He made use of it in that sense. While we believe the authorship of many of these psalms to be uncertain, we claim that the words of Jesus put the question of authorship in this case beyond dispute.

Then the beauty of the song is seen in all its fulness. David the king sings of Another as Lord and therefore superior to himself. In the first half of the songs (verses 1-4) he sings of the relation of the coming King to Jehovah. The second half (verses 5-7) tells of the might and victory of the appointed King. This division is clearly marked by the names of the psalm. "Jehovah said unto Adonahy," "Jehovah shall send forth," "Jehovah hath sworn, and will not repent," "Adonahy at thy right hand." Both these names or titles are used often of God. Here Jehovah is used of God, and Adonahy of the coming King. This King is appointed by Jehovah. He is strengthened by Jehovah. He is, moreover, a King to whom His people will gather in loyalty and with the perpetual freshness of youth. Moreover, by the will of Jehovah He is to be Priest as well as King. In the might of this divine appointment He is to go forth to conquest. The fulfilment of its every word is realized in Christ.

PSALM 111

This psalm is closely connected with the one which follows it. In this the subject is the greatness and graciousness of Jehovah. In the Hebrew there are ten verses, the first eight having two lines each, and the last two, three lines in each. That makes a total of twenty-two lines. The first letters of these lines constitute the alphabet. Thus it is a song of praise constructed as an alphabetical acrostic.

Another division is the first seven lines which tell of His greatness, the next twelve which proclaim His graciousness, and the last three which declare the wisdom of those who fear Him and act accordingly. This last division prepares the way for the next psalm. The greatness of Jehovah is manifest in His works, the supreme characteristics of which are honor, majesty, and righteousness. The graciousness is evident in all His dealings with His people. These are characterized by compassion and constancy, by uprightness and redemption. In view of such greatness and graciousness, how true it is that to fear Him is wisdom and to do His will evidence of good understanding.

PSALM 112

This song follows immediately upon the last in meaning. While that has set forth the praises of Jehovah as great and gracious, this declares the blessedness of the man who lives in true relation with Jehovah. The connection is clearly seen in the relation of the closing verse of the former, "The fear of Jehovah is the beginning of wisdom," to the opening verse in this "Blessed is the man that feareth Jehovah."

The remarkable thing about this psalm is the way in which in describing the blessed condition of the man who fears Jehovah it uses words which the previous psalm used in describing Jehovah. Of Jehovah the psalmist said:

> His righteousness endureth for ever.

Of the man who fears he says:

> His righteousness endureth for ever.

Jehovah is declared to be "gracious and full of compassion." So also is the upright man. The relation of these psalms sets forth truth which is of perpetual application. A man becomes like his God. When a man's God is blessed, the man also is blessed. To have a great God is to become a great man. True wisdom consists in the maintenance of right relationships with the one God. True happiness consists in becoming like Him who is at once great and gracious.

PSALM 113

This is the first of six psalms which constitute the *Hallel* or Hymn of Praise which the Hebrews sang at Passover, Pentecost, and the Feast of Tabernacles. This group is of special interest to us because it is very probable that these psalms were sung by our Lord and His disciples on that dark night in which He was betrayed. While we shall read them and think of them as the songs of the ancient people, we cannot help thinking of them as uttered by that Voice which was, and is, the perfect music.

This first psalm celebrates the name of Jehovah on two accounts. He is high, yet He is lowly, above the nations and above the heavens, yet humbling Himself to behold the heavens and the earth. This is a startling way of stating the fact. The thing which exalts man, the contemplation and consideration of creation and its glories, humbles God, so far is He above creation in the awful majesty of His essential life. Yet how He humbles Himself! Think of these words passing the lips of Him who "humbled Himself" and became "obedient unto death." Then notice the evidences of God's humility and height. He stoops to lift, for He raiseth the poor, lifteth up the needy, and turns barrenness into the joy of motherhood. Again, think how amid the deepening shadows the Incarnate Word sang with a little band of men of the purpose of His humbling, and try to imagine the joy set before Him, and so approach to an understanding of how He endured.

PSALM 114

This is the second psalm in the *Hallel.* The first set forth the might and mercy of Jehovah. This is pre-eminently a song of His might, and so the name of God is used. If, however, it sings of His might it sings of it as manifested in mercy. It is the song of the Exodus and is full of beauty. The first movement declares that the people passing out of Egypt did so as the result of the presence of God. Among them was His sanctuary, and they were His dominion. Nature recognized His presence, and obeyed His will. The sea fled, Jordan was driven back, mountains and little hills were moved.

The singer asks the reason of this commotion, and without waiting for answer charges the earth to tremble at His presence. Notice that this song includes the whole deliverance, the going out under Moses through the sea and the going in under Joshua through Jordan.

Again, we imagine the great Leader, about to accomplish His exodus, singing these words. Ere long, all nature would be convulsed as He passed out and in, breaking the way through for the oncoming hosts. It is possible in imagination to hear the thrill of triumph as the stately words, so full of spiritual significance, sounded forth in that upper room.

PSALM 115

This third psalm in the *Hallel* is born of passion for the glory of the name of Jehovah. That is its opening note, and all that follows must be explained thereby. The singer's distress is heard in the cry:

> Wherefore should the nations say,
> Where is now their God?

Not first for the welfare of the people does he care, but for the vindication of his God. This is a deep note, and all too rare in our music. We are ever in danger of putting the welfare of man before the glory of God.

The song having uttered its keynote, proceeds in a passage of fine scorn for idols and idol worshipers. These idols have form without power, appearance without life, and the effect of worshiping them is that the worshipers become insensate as they are. Following this, there is a fine appeal to the people of God to trust in Him with confident assurance that He will help. There then pass before the mind of the singer the heavens, God's own habitation; the earth, entrusted to men; and *Sheol,* the place of silence. All ends with a declaration which sounds the note of triumph even over death, for the praise of His people is to continue for evermore.

And again the thought reverts to the upper room, and the Singer whose deepest passion was ever the will of God, and the glory of His name; to the One who was soon going into the silence where no note of praise would be heard; and yet to the One who would turn the silence into song forevermore.

PSALM 116

This is the fourth song of the *Hallel.* In it the note of triumph over death with which the last one closed, is elaborated. Evidently the singer had been in some grave peril in which he had practically despaired of life. From the peril he has been delivered by Jehovah, and now he sings Jehovah's praise.

It has two movements. The first tells of his love, and declares its reason, and its issue (verses 1-9). The second tells of his resulting faith, breaks forth into new exultation, and affirms his determination to praise (verses 10-19). His love is the outcome of Jehovah's love manifested on his behalf, when in the very bonds of death he cried to Him. The issue is that he will walk before Jehovah. His faith thus confirmed, he breaks forth into new song, and dedicates himself afresh to the high service of thanksgiving.

Whatever the local circumstances which give rise to this song, it is evident that all its rich meaning was fulfilled, when in the midst of that little company of perplexed souls the shadows of the One Death already upon Him, Jesus sang this song of prophetic triumph over the sharpness of the hour of passion to which He was passing. He has made it over to all His own as their triumph song over death.

PSALM 117

The fifth song of the *Hallel* is the shortest in the Psalter. In it in a very deep sense is fulfilled the saying so common, that "brevity is the soul of wit." It lives indeed with the wisdom of perfect realization. It is the pure song of the people of Jehovah. It is the song of Israel, the ideal servant of Jehovah. It is addressed to all peoples. They are called on to praise and laud Jehovah because of the greatness of His grace toward His own, and because His truth endureth forever. In the long processes of the centuries Israel never fully realized this ideal.

At last the purpose was consummated in a Person. All the ancient prophecies found in Him their potential fulfilment. In that upper room the song was a solo of actual experience. By the union of grace and truth in and through Jesus the call to praise went out to all nations and peoples. Those who joined Him in the song that night were made able to sing it in following days with meaning and with force, and that is the song with which the Church has gone forth ever since to woo and win the peoples to Jehovah. Ere the work of Jesus be finally completed, the Israel of God will sing that song perfectly, and the nations and peoples will respond.

PSALM 118

This is the sixth and last of the psalms of the *Hallel*. It is the song of perfect victory, undoubtedly arranged to be sung by a triumphal procession as it made its way to the Temple for thanksgiving and worship.

It is almost impossible, however, to trace its divisions in that way. As to its subject matter it may be thus divided:

Introduction. The Call to Praise (verses 1-4).
The threefold Song of Israel, of Aaron, of the People (verses 5-27).
Conclusion (verses 28, 29).

The call is to praise Jehovah specifically for His enduring mercy. It is addressed to Israel as the ideal servant, to the house of Aaron as the priesthood, to all that fear the Lord. To this call Israel personified first replies in a song which sets forth the story of distress and deliverance which had characterized the history of the long years (verses 5-18). Then Aaron as the priest who had the right to enter through all the gates takes up the song, and challenges them to admit him, rejoicing in Jehovah's exaltation of him (verses 19-22). Then the people sing of the marvel of the Lord's doings, and devote themselves to Him (verses 23-27). Finally, the psalmist strikes the note of personal thanksgiving, ending with a call to praise.

This is pre-eminently the triumph song of the Christ, the ideal Servant, the perfect Priest, the Leader of the people. How much all these words meant to Him as He sang them on that night in the upper room!

PSALM 119

Any dealing with this psalm must necessarily be general and not particular. It has been called the psalm of the Law, not inaccurately; but the term, "The Law," should be understood in its widest significance, no fewer than ten Hebrew words being used in referring to the great matter celebrated. These are translated "law," "word," "saying" or "savings," "commandment," "statutes," "ordinances," "precepts," "testimony," "way," "path." A careful consideration of them will reveal one underlying conception. It is the conception of the will of God as that will has been made known to man. Every word reveals some aspect of the will in itself, of the method of its revelation, and its value in human life.

Throughout, moreover, the singer reveals his conception of the value of this great will, both in itself and in its revelation, and utters words showing his determination to be obedient thereto combined with constant prayer to enable him to do so. This attitude is supremely revealed in his declaration:

Oh how love I Thy law!
It is my meditation all the day (verse 97).

His sense of the value of this revealed will of God is perhaps most clearly shown in the words:

Thy word is a lamp unto my feet
And light unto my path (verse 105).

The lamp for the feet is that which illumines the immediate pathway, and the light for the path is that which reveals the general direction.

PSALM 120

The next fifteen psalms appear to have formed a book of themselves bearing the title, "The Songs of Ascents." That collection is incorporated by the editor at this point not without purpose.

The title appearing at the head of each has been variously translated, "A Song of Degrees," "A Song of Ascents," "A Song for the Goings Up." In the Hebrew translation to which we have already referred, it appears as "A song of the ascents," and in the title index in each case the psalm is called "Pilgrim's song."

The meaning of this title has been variously interpreted also. Without referring to the different suggestions made, we shall consider them as songs sung by those pilgrims who went up to Jerusalem to worship. Placing the collection immediately after the great psalm dealing with the perfection of the will of God is significant. Those who know the will of God turn their faces toward the Temple of worship. These songs of desire, and hope, and approach are appropriate for the pilgrims' use as they go up to worship.

The first is wholly the cry of the soul acquainted with the perfection of the will of God. The first declaration is one of experience gained. He looks back, and remembers how he has been heard and answered. His present circumstance is absence from the house of his God. He is dwelling among a people whose motives and activities are contrary to his deepest convictions and desires. Mesech and the tents of Kedar figuratively describe the distance of his abode from the home and center of peace. He is surrounded by lying and deceitful people, such as hate peace and are all for war. His heart turns toward Jehovah and the dwelling of His glory, the holy house of worship. He cries to Jehovah for deliverance, and in the midst of adversity declares his confidence that the judgments of God will operate against the evildoers.

PSALM 121

This song, so full of beauty, marks another stage in the approach of the worshiper in that it sets forth his assurance of the present help of Jehovah. The singer is still far from the appointed place of worship, lifting his eyes toward the distant mountains. He is not far from Jehovah, however. In Jehovah's keeping, even though far from the center of external worship, the pilgrim realizes his safety. He lifts his longing eyes toward the mountains of Zion, where stands the house of his God, and asks:

> From whence shall my help come?

Not from those mountains, precious as they are, but from Jehovah, who is with him even in the valley of distance. He then addresses the singer's heart with words of comfort and assurance. Jehovah keeps His children safe, never slumbering or sleeping in His faithful vigil.

The stately sentences which describe the tender care of Jehovah need no exposition. They are the common language of all who know Jehovah. These two psalms, revealing as they do the consciousness of the difficulty of exile and the heart's confidence in Jehovah prepare for the outburst of the next song for approach to the place of worship as the day dawns.

PSALM 122

This is the song of the pilgrims in anticipation of Jerusalem and the house of worship. It sets forth the glory of the establishment and compacted city where the tribes gather to give thanks to Jehovah. Yet through it all it is evident that the glory of city and Temple consists in the fact that they are the city and house of Jehovah. It is not a song of buildings or of material magnificence. It is rather the song of assembly, of testimony, of judgment, of peace, of prosperity. These all issue from the supreme fact of Jehovah's presence. To Him the tribes are gathered. Their testimony is of His name. The judgment, peace, and prosperity are all the outcome of Jehovah's relation to His people.

The tenses of the song have caused some bewilderment, as they seem to indicate the presence of the worshipers in the city, while yet they suggest the attitude of absence. The affirmation:

Our feet are standing within thy gates,

is confidence of faith. It is the claim of citizenship, even though the citizen has not yet actually reached the city. The call has come to ascend to the house of the Lord, and with songs of praise and prayers for the city the pilgrim prepares to respond, while the hope becomes a present consciousness of the joy of assembly.

PSALM 123

Following the idea of the ascent of the worshiper to the longed-for house of Jehovah we have in this song an expression of the soul's strong confidence in Jehovah. The soul first affirms confidence as an experience, then breathes it as a prayer, and finally tells the circumstances calling forth the cry. Taking the last thing first, we can imagine this pilgrim who has been dwelling in the midst of the ungodly starting toward the place of worship, and by that very fact stirring up anew the scornful contempt of these people. This vexes his soul, but it becomes the occasion of prayer for the mercy of Jehovah.

This prayer, born of such experience, is based on the relation of the pilgrim to Jehovah. To Him, the enthroned One, the eyes are lifted. This is the reaffirmation of the truth sung in the earlier song (Psalm 121). The figures of relationship are full of beauty. The eyes look to Jehovah as to the Master of the household, who commands, and guards, and supplies all the needs of His servants. To set the life toward worship in an ungodly age is ever to be the object of scorn and contempt. What matters it? The eyes of Jehovah's pilgrims are lifted to the throne high set above all the tumult and strife of tongues.

PSALM 124

The journey from the place of exile to the city and Temple of Jehovah has now commenced. The heart of the song is in the words:

Our soul is escaped as a bird out of the
snare of the fowlers.

Escape brings a sense of the dangers left behind, and therefore a keen appreciation of the fact that Jehovah has been acting as Deliverer:

If it had not been the Lord!

What a tone of joy is in that sigh. We often speak of a sigh of relief, and here is one indeed. The thunder of the threatening flood is heard behind. It was a strong tide against which these pilgrims could have had no might. If Jehovah had not helped, how great would have been the calamity! But He has helped, and the sigh which trembles with the consciousness of past peril, merges into the glad song:

Blessed be Jehovah.

This first experience of escape is ever one of great delight. There stretches before the pilgrim a long road yet, and there will be much searching of heart before the final rest is won; but "the snare is broken, and we are escaped" is a song full of rapture, one that prepares the heart for all that waits for it on the way.

PSALM 125

The pilgrims catch the first glimpse of the city toward which their faces are set. The journey is not ended, but from some vantage ground there in the distance is seen the home of the heart. It is founded on rock, and stands out in all the majesty and strength of its assured position. Round about it are the mountains, guarding it against its foes. Over it is the throne of God ensuring a government which gives the righteous their opportunity.

It is an ideal picture, but a true one as to divine intention. Yet it is not of the material fact that the pilgrims sing. All that is but a symbol of the safety and protection and government of the trusting people. Jehovah is their rock foundation, their encompassing protection, their enthroned King. In Him are all their strength and confidence, and on the pathway, with the city seen afar, they sing of Him.

The song merges into a prayer that He will exercise on their behalf all that guidance and deliverance in which they make their boast. As in the previous song they looked back to that from which they had escaped, in this they look forward to that to which they go, and in each case their song is of Jehovah. This is true retrospect and prospect, and both minister to the strength of pilgrimage.

PSALM 126

The general movement of these songs of ascents is preserved in this case by reading the first verse:

> When Jehovah brought back those that returned to Zion.

The pilgrims have looked back, and praised Jehovah for escape. They have looked on, and praised Him for their hope and present sense of security. Now they break forth into an expression of their glad experience. It is all so wonderful, this restoration by Jehovah, that it is hardly believable; it is as though they dreamed. Laughter and singing are the only appropriate expressions of their rejoicing hearts. Even the nations are compelled to recognize the doings of Jehovah on their behalf. Yet in the consciousness of the wonders wrought by Jehovah is created a keen sense of their own imperfection. The deliverance is not yet complete, and the prayer is offered, "Turn again our captivity," or, as Dr. Kirkpatrick translates, "Restore our fortunes." The restoration already in progress is the inspiration of the prayer for its fulfilment.

The song ends with a declaration of confidence that the sorrowful experiences of the past must issue in the realization of all that the pilgrims so earnestly desire.

PSALM 127

The thought of the pilgrim centers on the city toward which his face is turned as the place of home. The strength of the Hebrew people in the past and all that remains of it today largely results from the keen sense of the importance of the home and the family which they ever cherished. The house, the city, labor, all are important to conserving the strength of the family. Toward these the pilgrims look, but as they hope they recognize that, as in the settlement which will make these possible Jehovah is the one Worker, so in these also He is the one and only Strength of His people. He must build the house and guard the city. He must be the Partner in toil, giving to His beloved even when they rest in sleep after toil is over.

That last is a thought full of comfort to the toiler. Jehovah is never weary, and carries on the enterprise while His trusting child gains new strength in sleep. Children, the glory of the home, are His gift, and they become the support and defense of their parents. Thus the pilgrims look forward to the rest which follows exile in the city of God, and recognize that this also, in all its details, will result from His power and working.

PSALM 128

This song naturally follows the one in which Jehovah's relation to the home in building and establishing it is recognized. It is chiefly interesting as it reveals the singer's conception of the relation between the prosperity of the family and that of the city.

As to the home, the condition of its prosperity is declared to be fear of the Lord, walking in His ways.

Then the resulting blessings are promised. This blessedness of home life issues in the good of Jerusalem. The line of development is most important; the God-fearing man, the God-fearing family, the God-fearing city. This song of the worshipers ascending toward the city and Temple is one the application of which is of perpetual importance. The strength of any city lies in its strong family life. The true strength of the family issues from its ordering in the fear of the Lord. It is of real significance that these songs of home and of true civic consciousness are found among those which are sung on the way that leads to worship. It is ever good to carry into the place of our communion with God the interests of home and city. It is only by doing so that we can influence these for their lasting good.

PSALM 129

This song is the song of one who, ascending toward the much desired place of rest and worship, looks back, and sees how in the past Jehovah has delivered from sore perils. The backward look would seem to be inspired by consciousness of present peril, for immediately the song expresses desire for the judgment of Jehovah against those who are described as hating Zion. On the way to the city and Temple those who hate the pilgrims of faith plot and scheme for their overthrow, and it is in the consciousness of this that the song celebrates past deliverances and seeks a continuance of them.

While there is evidently a sense of danger in the mind of the singer, there is an utter absence of despair. It is the true attitude of those who have a rich experience of the faithfulness of God. In times of peril it is good for the pilgrim to strengthen the heart by looking back and remembering past deliverances. Such an experience will inevitably create a present confidence.

His love in time past forbids me to think
He'll leave me at last in trouble to sink;
Each sweet Ebenezer I have in review
Confirms His good pleasure to help me
quite through.

PSALM 130

After the backward look there would fittingly be an inward look as the worshiper approached the place of worship. This is always a disquieting look. There is no confession here of specific sins, but the cry is "out of the depths," and the figure suggests the singer's sense of deep need.

What the cause is may certainly be gathered from the apprehensive sigh:

If Thou, Lord, shouldest mark iniquities,
O Lord, who shall stand?

If the sense is of the nation's distress, it is distinctly conscious of the connection of that distress with sin. All this is background which flings into bright relief the confidence of the soul in Jehovah as a pardoning and redeeming Lord. Some of the most beautiful things in the Psalter, or indeed, in the Bible, are here. It was a Welshman in the midst of the wonderful Revival of 1905 who rendered verse four:

There is forgiveness with Thee—enough to frighten us!

It is not accurate translation, but is fine exposition. The deepest note in all true worship is this sense of "plenteous redemption," and the perfection of Jehovah's love as thus manifested. To mark iniquities would be to fill us with despair. To redeem from all iniquities is to inspire us with hope.

PSALM 131

This is a brief psalm, but it is very full of beauty, as it sets forth the content of a restless soul in the will of God. It follows the last as an advance of experience, and as a sequence. Its peculiar note is not a natural content, but a satisfaction won in spite of all contrary tendencies. The thought of weaning is the dominant one. That for which a child craves, it at last comes to be content without. So the soul of the singer, which once was ambitious and restlessly attempted to walk in ways for which it was not fitted is with God in quietness and content. The secret of victory over feverish ambition is divulged in the psalmist's appeal to Israel to hope in the Lord. That, interpreted in the light of the previous psalm, means that in the gracious sense of His forgiving love, there is the secret of a content which puts an end to all false ambition.

Redemption truly apprehended, is more than forgiveness. It is restoration to the quiet peace of being in harmony with all the forces of the universe, because governed by the will of God.

PSALM 132

The pilgrims stand at the very entrance of the Holy City, and their song is one of strong desire and equally strong confidence. In the first part the desire is expressed (verses 1-10). It is for the fulfilment of David's purpose when, through affliction and at cost, he prepared to build the sanctuary. The idea of the theocracy is in mind as they pray:

Arise, O Lord, into Thy resting place.

Jehovah is to be the Center of gathering, while around Him are priests and saints, and before Him the anointed King. The desire is answered by the assurance of the fidelity of Jehovah to His word (verses 11-18). He has sworn to David, and He will not turn from it. The order is then set forth. The faithful Jehovah, the anointed King, the chosen city, the clothed priests, the rejoicing people, the established kingdom.

Whatever were the circumstances of the writing of this song, its placing here is significant. The worshiping people are to be conscious of the true order of their life, and the true meaning of their approach. A spacious conception of the purpose of God is ever necessary to a true worship. Lacking this, worship may easily degenerate into selfish formalism. Where it is present, every individual is enabled to contribute to the whole, which makes for the complete realization of the ideal.

PSALM 133

At last the pilgrims are in the city. After the long and toilsome march their feet stand in the city of God. The common impulse of all has been the desire to reach the dwelling place of Jehovah, and to worship before His face. This desire has brought them together, and in this nearness of souls gathered by a common purpose there is a new blessing, and of that they sing. In finding Jehovah they have found each other, and as a result of a common loyalty to Him a new social order has been created. Under two figures the singer describes the blessedness of this order. It is like the holy anointing oil. It is like the dew of Hermon. The former suggests joy and richness of experience. The latter describes the freshness and renewal of all life. The source of the new joy is recognized, "Jehovah commanded the blessing."

The first matter of importance in individual life is ever to seek fellowship with God. When this is sought and found, there always follows the realization of the fellowship of the saints. All lack of union among ourselves is due to failure to realize our union with God.

PSALM 134

This is the last of the songs of ascents, and breathes the spirit of rest. As in the previous one, the joy of the fellowship of faithful souls was the burden; here it is the joy of the sense of peace and rest flowing from fellowship with Jehovah. The atmosphere of the song is rest. The sun has sunk in the west. The activity of the day is over. Quietness pervades the city. The pilgrims have found the hour of peace. At the center of the people is the Temple. There priests still keep their vigil.

By night stand in the house of Jehovah.

The last thought of the pilgrim is of the goodness of Jehovah, and the song calls the Temple watchers to bless His name. In the stillness comes back the answer of the priests. It is a blessing on the worshiper. Thus in the silence of night, ere sleep comes, the worshiper blesses Jehovah, and is blessed by Him. It is the fellowship of rest. By faith the pilgrims of today have access to this fellowship every night. There is One Watcher in the Holiest, who never slumbers, and through Him our worship is perpetual. His voice speaks the word of benediction to us in response to our adoration. This is rest indeed.

PSALM 135

After the general movement of this book of the Psalter, which has brought us in thought to the ultimate realization of worship, and before the final psalms of perfected praise, we now have a section (135-144) in which are contained songs of experience, the inspiration of which is in the conceptions of Jehovah, and the way of approach to Him, which the former songs have set forth.

The first of the series is a pure song of praise. It opens with a call to the priests as the representatives of the people to praise (verses 1,2). It proceeds to set forth the reasons for this praise (verses 3-18). The first is what He is in Himself, and the fact that He has chosen His people (verses 3-5). The second is His creative might (verses 6, 7). The third is His deliverance of His people from bondage (verses 8,9). The fourth is His giving them a land (verses 10-12). The fifth is His faithfulness (verse 13). The sixth is His sure judgment and consequent return to His servants (verse 14). The seventh is His superiority as the living One over all the false and dead idols of the nations (verses 15-18). Finally, the song is an appeal to nation, priests, and Levites to unite in His praise.

PSALM 136

This is a song of the age-abiding mercy of Jehovah. It opens and closes with a call to praise, and in its main movements sets forth the reason for such praise. In the opening call the three great names or titles of God are used, namely, Jehovah, Elohim, Adonahy. The first is mentioned in its lonely splendor, as it always is. There is no attempt at qualification or comparison. He is the God of gods. All other mighty beings, false or true, are less than He, and subservient to Him. In the same way He is Lord of lords. The reasons foı praise are found in the manifestations of His power and interest in His people. His power as seen in creation is first sung (verses

1-9). Then His delivering power manifested on behalf of His people (verses 10-15). This naturally merges into the song of His guidance and government of them as He brought them into possession (verses 16-22). And finally His goodness in restoring His people after their decline and wandering (verses 23-25).

The dominant note is mercy as manifest in all the activities of God. To see the love and compassion of God in creation, in deliverance, in government, in restoration, is ever to be constrained to praise.

PSALM 137

This is a song of memory. From the midst of the restoration the singer looks back to days of his people's captivity and sorrow. The picture is graphic. Babylon was far from their own land, and far removed in every way from the city of God and the Temple of Jehovah.

All its material splendor was nothing to the captive souls who were yet faithful to Jehovah. There they sat, with harps hung silently on the willows, and wept. Their taunting captors asked them to sing. Babylon sought to be amused by these people of a strange religion, and the request was in itself an insult to their faith. It was impossible, and they refused to sing the song of Jehovah. To have done so would have been to play traitor to their own lost city and to all that their citizenship stood for. The prayer for vengeance must be interpreted by the first part of the song, with its revelation of the treatment they received. It must, of course, be interpreted by the times in which they lived.

Our times are different. We have more light. And yet it is well to remember that the deepest sense of justice still makes punishment a necessary part of the economy of God. That conception of God which denies the equity of retribution is false.

PSALM 138

The final personal note of this song is reached in the words:

> Jehovah will perfect that which concerneth me.

It opens with consecration to the sacred duty of praise. This consecration has a threefold aspect. It is personal, and thus is expressed in terms of completeness. "With the whole heart" leaves no room for mixed motive or divided devotion. It has in view the surrounding authorities, "before the gods." As a testimony to the supreme God the singer will praise. It is directed "toward the holy Temple," and so is conscious of the true order of worship as ordained. The reason for praise is next declared to be loving-kindness and truth as already proved. The effect of praise is to reveal God to others, who, if they come to know Him, will also praise Him.

The final movement tells of the singer's confidence in the future. This is based on Jehovah's knowledge. He sees the lowly, and the haughty cannot escape Him by distance. Therefore the deliverance of the trusting soul from all coming trouble is assured, and his final perfecting also. The song closes with the affirmation of the enduring mercy of Jehovah, and a petition which reveals the singer's need of the continual help of God.

PSALM 139

The conception of intimate personal relation between God and man is perhaps more remarkably and forcefully dealt with in this song than in any other in the whole collection.

The great facts are first stated. Jehovah's knowledge of personal life is declared. He is familiar with every motion, even to the simplest of downsitting and uprising. He knows thought afar off, that is, in the strange and mystic processes of its making. All ways and words are intimately known to the God who is the nearest environment of human life. And from all this there can be no escape, for the Omniscient is also the Omnipresent. He is in heaven, but Sheol also is full of His presence. Distance is a human term only, and the uttermost parts of the trackless sea are also in the Presence. Darkness is light to Him, and has no hiding place from Him. The deep mysteries of being are not involved to Jehovah, for He presided in wisdom over all the mystic processes of the beginnings of human life. All this does not affright the singer, for he knows the love of Jehovah, and exclaims in glad praise for the preciousness of the unnumbered thoughts of God concerning him.

In view of all this it is hopeless for the wicked to attempt to escape from God, and the singer's desire for separation from all such is the final word of the psalm. The way of separation is a personal choice. He must and will separate himself. Yet he is also dependent on God in this matter, and prays for His examination and leading.

PSALM 140

The previous five psalms have dealt with the absolute sufficiency of Jehovah. In the four which follow a different note is struck. They reveal the need of man and his utter helplessness. Yet they stand over against the former five. The appeal of all of them is made out of dire necessity to absolute Sufficiency. They lead up to another which thrills with thanksgiving as it expresses the consciousness of how perfectly the resources of Jehovah meet the need of man.

The present psalm deals with the subject of foes without. The singer is conscious that he is surrounded by enemies. The song begins on a low level, and rises as it proceeds. The first movement (verses 1-5), describes the malice of the enemies, and ends with prayer for preservation. The second (verses 6-10) commences with earnest prayer, the confidence of which is based on past experiences of deliverance; and it ends with a definite request for the discomfiture of his foes. The final movement (verses 11-13) is an affirmation of faith. The singer is confident that in the government of Jehovah evil men cannot continue. The afflicted will be delivered, and the righteous and upright will be perfectly vindicated.

PSALM 141

In this song the influence of the external troubles on the inner life of the singer is revealed. Throughout it breathes the spirit of fear, lest the soul be seduced from the attitude of whole-hearted loyalty to God. The peril most evidently threatening arises from the enticements of the ungodly, and the psalmist earnestly prays that he may be protected by Jehovah in speech and thought and action.

Without in so many words declaring so, the song clearly reveals that the singer has been sorely tempted to turn aside to ways of ungodly men, to share their hospitality and so escape their hostility. This peril is more subtle than the active opposition of these men, and in this distress he turns to God. This is his safety; that he is able to say:

> Mine eyes are unto Thee, O God the Lord,

is a revelation of the fact that his anchor still holds, not only against the fierce onslaught of enemies, but also against the insidious temptation to turn aside from the path of rectitude in order to escape the vindictive opposition of his enemies. If the former psalm reveals the perils of foes without, this no less clearly deals with the danger of fears within.

PSALM 142

In this psalm human need is yet more vividly set forth. Here is the consciousness resulting from the difficulties described in the previous psalm. Here there is a combination of fighting and fears within and without. The onslaught of the foe and the trembling heart constitute an experience which can be described only as that of a spirit overwhelmed. Two notes run side by side throughout the song. The first is this terrible sense of helplessness and hopelessness so far as man is concerned. The other is the determined application of the helpless soul to Jehovah. There is the utmost urgency in this method. "I cry with my voice . . . I pour out my complaint . . . I show before Him my trouble."

The whole need is gathered up into the tremendous statement:

> Refuge hath failed me; no man careth for my soul.

This is answered by triumphing faith in the words:

> O Jehovah . . . Thou art my refuge.

The song ends with an earnest cry for deliverance, and an affirmation of confidence that the cry will be heard and answered.

PSALM 143

This is the last of the four psalms, and both in respect of the sense of helplessness and of assurance in God it is more vivid and striking than any other of them. So far as human situation is concerned, it is a cry of despair, and a terrible one indeed. Life is smitten, the spirit is overwhelmed, and the whole complaint ends with a statement, "My heart within me is desolate." That final word "desolate" has in it the sob of an unillumined sea.

Yet the psalm opens with an earnest cry to Jehovah, and after the declaration of need is to the end a determined act of faith. In the situation of complete helplessness the soul prepares for its prayer, and the words which indicate the method of preparation are interesting. "I remember . . . I meditate . . . I muse."

The issue of this is immediately declared, "I spread forth my hands unto Thee." The earnestness of the soul is manifest in the urgent petitions which follow. "Make haste, . . . hide not Thy face . . . cause me to hear . . . cause me to know . . . deliver me . . . teach me . . . quicken me." Personal consecration in this endeavor to lay hold on the infinite resource is manifest in the affirmations. "In Thee do I trust . . . I lift up my soul unto Thee . . . I flee unto Thee to hide me," and, finally, "I am Thy servant." Through all the urgency and the earnestness there is also manifest an unshaken confidence. "Thou art my God" is the central word around which all the others center.

PSALM 144

This is a song of triumphant assurance. Its place in the book at this point suggests the invincible experience of trusting souls. In order to appreciate all its value the nine psalms immediately preceding must be borne in mind. Five of them celebrate the sufficiency of God. These are followed by four which declare the utter helplessness of man. The present one immediately follows, and in it the two facts are present; but the divine sufficiency is seen encompassing the human helplessness until it is so lost sight of as hardly to be discoverable.

The opening affirmations thrill with the singer's confidence of ability in the might of Jehovah. There is a conflict, but fear is banished because Jehovah teaches the hands to war and the fingers to fight; and He is all that the soul in conflict needs.

This affirmation is followed by an exclamation of surprise that Jehovah so high should take any account of man, who by comparison is vanity. There is no shadow of doubt in the exclamation, for the song immediately becomes a prayer for the operation of Jehovah's might, for the rescue of the trusting soul.

It then climbs to the higher level of praise in the new song of confidence which ends in a repetition of the prayer for rescue. Finally, the singer describes the peace and prosperity of the people whose God is Jehovah.

PSALM 145

This is a great psalm of praise, standing alone, and serving as an introduction to the last five, which constitute the final anthem of thanksgiving, the expression of perfected praise. It is a solo, but the singer is singing not for himself alone, but for others. The peoples are in mind. It has three movements: an introduction (verses 1-4), a statement of theme (verses 5-9), and the full exercise of thanksgiving (verses 10-21).

The introduction speaks of determination to praise (verse 1), of continuity in praise (verse 2), of reason for praise (verse 3), and of fellowship in praise (verse 4).

The theme is a threefold one: first, the majesty of the divine honor and works (verse 5); second, the might of the acts of God (verses 6,7); third and supremely, the mercy of God (verses 8,9).

Then follows the exercise. First the chorus of the works of Jehovah, and of His saints. This chorus celebrates His glory, His power, His mighty acts, and the majesty of His Kingdom.

The rest of the psalm is a song carrying out the thoughts suggested in the statement of the theme. The majesty of Jehovah is celebrated (verse 13). His might as operating in the uplifting of the fallen is declared (verse 14). Finally, the activity of His mercy is delighted in (verses 15-20). Everything concludes with the reaffirmation of personal determination to praise, and the expression of desire that all flesh should join in the anthem.

PSALM 146

We now come to the final psalms of adoration, each one of which opens and closes with the great call to praise, "Hallelujah, praise the Lord." The theme of this first is the sufficiency of God as the Helper of His people. It opens with the personal note of determination to praise (verses 1,2). As a background, the inability of man to help is declared. He is not to be trusted, for "his breath goeth forth."

In contrast with this helplessness the strength of Jehovah is celebrated as manifested in creation, and the maintenance of order (verse 6) as exercised on behalf of the needy and the oppressed (verses 7-9). Notice the descriptions of the people whom Jehovah helps. "The oppressed . . . the hungry . . . the prisoners . . . the blind . . . they that are bowed down . . . the righteous . . . the strangers . . . the fatherless and widow." Then notice how the divine activity exactly meets the need. "Executeth judgment . . . giveth food . . . looseth . . . openeth the eyes . . . raiseth up . . . loveth . . . preserveth . . . upholdeth." In contrast with the vanishing life of princes and sons of men, Jehovah reigns forever and is the God of Zion to all generations.

PSALM 147

In this psalm, beginning with a call which declares the pleasantness and comeliness of praise (verse 1), the singer first celebrates the divine activity in restoring His people (verses 2-6). He then proceeds to declare how God provides for all human needs (verses 7-11), and finally rejoices in the perfection of His government (verses 12-20).

In the first movement dealing with the restoration of Israel there is a very beautiful suggestion of the interrelation of the pitying power of God. "He healeth the broken-hearted . . . He telleth the number of the stars." In this activity of restoration there is manifest power and wisdom, and strict discrimination in upholding the meek and abasing the wicked. In His providence God provides for all material needs, and yet His purpose in so doing is to create the spiritual attitudes toward Himself in which He supremely delights, His delight being, finally, not in animal strength but in the fear and hope which constitute spiritual strength.

In the last movement there is a fine recognition of His provision of material supply, which is, however, all the way through made parabolic of His sustenance of spiritual strength. Literally, He gives His people "the finest of the wheat," and actually gives snow and hoar frost, and yet all these things are intended to be revelations of the methods by which He sends His commandment and His word, His statutes, and His judgments, for the perfect ordering of life.

PSALM 148

This is the psalm of the whole creation. It has two movements indicated by the words, "from the heavens" (verse 1), and "from the earth" (verse 7).

In the first the scale is a descending one. "In the heights" to "His angels," "sun and moon." Of all of them it is true that He created and established them. In the second the scale is an ascending one, from the deeps and the dragons, through the elements and nature, to the sentient life, and onward through kings and princes and all human beings. From the heights and depths and all that lies between, praise is to be offered to Jehovah, for "His glory is above the earth and heaven."

However, in the mind of the singer this praise is to be perfectly expressed through Israel, a people near unto Him. This is an all-encompassing note of adoration, which one of our more recent singers has perfectly expressed in the lines:—

> The whole creation joins in one
> To bless the sacred Name
> Of Him who sits upon the Throne,
> And to adore the Lamb.

PSALM 149

As the last song ended by the recognition of the place of the saints in expressing the universal praise of Jehovah, this one enlarges the thought by confining itself wholly to the anthem of the saints. "His praise in the assembly of the saints" (verse 1), "Let the saints exult in glory" (verse 5), "This honour have all His saints" (verse 9). The saints are to praise Him as Creator and King. They are to do this with all the abandon of the dance and of music, because Jehovah has taken pleasure in them, and beautified them with salvation. This praise is to be the perpetual attitude of their lives. They are to "exult in glory," and to "sing for joy upon their beds." Their praise is not to be merely chanting words. It is also to be exercise of His will. While the high praises of God are in the mouth of the saints, a two-edged sword is to be in their hand with which to carry out His purposes among the peoples, the kings, and the nobles. The privilege of praise in word and work is an honor especially conferred upon His saints.

PSALM 150

This psalm, which concludes the book and all the Psalter as final doxology, is the most comprehensive and illuminative illustration of perfect praise in the whole Psalter.

The central place of prayer is the sanctuary, that is, the place of divine manifestation, whether the earthly temple or the heavenly matters nothing. The circumference is the firmament of His power, which is the outer confine of human consciousness.

The reason for praise is His mighty acts, whether in creation, redemption, or government. The measure of praise is His excellent greatness, so that it can never end until all the story be exhausted. The method is set forth by a description of the instruments of music constituting a perfect orchestra.

Finally, the one condition of praise is the possession of breath, that is to say, life received from Him must return in praise to Him. The function of life is praise, and the force of praise is life. The note of responsibility and the dignity of choice are alike indicated in the fact that the final psalm is not merely an expression of praise but a call to its exercise. Thus it is seen that the worship which perfectly glorifies God is not mechanical but volitional.

Proverbs

PROVERBS 1

The Book of Proverbs is one of the wisdom books of the Hebrew people. Emotionally and fundamentally, wisdom is the fear of God; intellectually, a knowledge of the manifestations of the divine wisdom; and, volitionally, obedience rendered thereto.

The first verse of this chapter constitutes the title of this Book, and the following six verses contain what we today would speak of as preface. That preface first declares the purpose of the Book in terms so simple as to need no comment (verses 3-5). Then follows a statement of method, which is necessary to a right use of the whole Book (verses 6,7). The beginning of wisdom is the fear of the Lord. The facts of God, and man's relation to Him, must be taken for granted and answered if there is to be any true wisdom. After the preface, the first section of the Book contains general instructions on wisdom which prepare the way for the Proverbs themselves, which come later.

The first instruction is a parental counsel, in which the wisdom of recognizing true friends is set forth in words which urge the habit of loyalty to father and mother; and the folly of forming false friendships is set forth in a series of warnings against them. This wisdom is personified, and her first call is written. It is, first, an appeal to turn from simplicity and scorning and hatred of knowledge, with the promise that she will give knowledge (verses 22,23). This is followed by a warning that wisdom neglected at last refuses to answer (verses 24-32). The call ends with a repeated promise of blessing to those who attend.

PROVERBS 2

From here and through chapter 8 we have a series of parental counsels. These all begin with the address, "My son," and deal with the value of wisdom, and make many practical applications.

The first of these is one of a couplet which deals with wisdom generally, and it has to do with the method of the search for wisdom (verses 1-8), and its value (verses 9-22).

First, as to the method of the search, there must be willingness and desire to know (verses 1,2). To this must be added diligence. The illuminative phrases are "cry," "lift up thy voice," "seek," "search." All indicate desire, expressing itself in devotion. The values are the discerning and discreet heart, which enables a man to understand his pathway, and consequent ability to refuse the friendship of false men and women, who would lead into darkness and death; and the resulting choice of a path of good men, with all the benefits resulting therefrom.

PROVERBS 3

As the former address had to do with the search for wisdom, this, in view of the value of it, is an appeal to cultivate wisdom. The appeal consists of a declaration of its essence (verses 1-10), a description of its excellence (verses 11-20), and a declaration of the safety which it brings (verses 21-35).

The essence of wisdom consists in a determined devotion to the things of wisdom. The inspiration of this is next described as life lived in relation to Jehovah. Perfect trust in Him, perpetual dependence on Him, and worshipful devotion expressed in actual giving, these are of the very essence of wisdom and are to be expressed in the devotion already referred to. No wealth is equal to such wisdom, and the very chastenings of God are precious as they are conducive to gaining it. The excellence of wisdom is proven by the pleasantness and peace it brings to man, and by the fact that Jehovah's works are wrought by it. The safety of the soul who keeps wisdom is seen in absence of stumbling and of fear, in the attitude of beneficence to the needy; in absence of envy of the evil; and in abiding blessedness in the secret, the blessing, the grace, and the glory of Jehovah.

PROVERBS 4

In this chapter there are three addresses. The first is of the nature of personal testimony (verses 1-9). The next two are exhortations to fidelity (verses 10-19 and 20-27). The father urges his own experience. In verses 3-9 he repeats what his father had said to him, and he declares (verses 1,2) that it was good. This personal experience lends urgency to his exhortations to his son. Then, conscious of the temptations which ever beset the path of the young, the father urges the son to be obedient. Temptation must be avoided completely. Finally, the father contrasts the path of the righteous with that of the wicked. The former is like the dawn, which increases in brightness to high noon. The latter is like consistent darkness and constant stumbling.

Again, in a second address, fidelity is urged in terms which indicate the necessity for complete devotion. There must be attention, followed by intention. Wisdom in the heart, persistent looking straight ahead, and untiring caution are necessary to fidelity.

PROVERBS 5

This is a parental exhortation against impurity. It is expressed in words of great delicacy and beauty, but it is none the less urgent and searching. It recognizes one of the most subtle and natural temptations likely to assail the life of the young, and sets it in the light of true wisdom, which begins in the fear of Jehovah and expresses itself in perpetual recognition of Him. The allurement of the strange woman is vividly described, but it is put into immediate contrast with the issue of yielding thereto. It is a change from honey to wormwood, from the smoothness of oil to the sharpness of a sword, from the path of life to the highway of death. The woman's abode is to be shunned, lest the remorse of those who disobey become the portion of the soul. The paralysis caused by impurity is suggested in the advice that the ideal joys of the marriage relation must be hopelessly marred by all sinful indulgence.

Here, as everywhere, wisdom consists in recognizing that human life is ever under the observation, and within the government, of Jehovah. That government insures the taking of the wicked by the cords which they weave out of their own sins. Impurity of conduct may seem to be of silken texture in its enticement. It becomes a hard and unyielding cable when it binds the life in slavery.

PROVERBS 6

The parental exhortations are continued. In this section they are directed against suretyship, indolence, the evil man, and certain specific things which Jehovah hates. The warnings against becoming surety here and elsewhere must be interpreted in the light of the conditions obtaining when they were uttered. The sin of the sluggard is rebuked by the illustration of the ant, who, without the constraint of judge, ruler, or overseer, diligently toils to provide meat for herself.

The description of the worthless person is graphic in the extreme. His methods of communication are not straightforward, but such as suggest deceit and cunning. His influence is that of creating discord.

Then follows a list of things which Jehovah hates. They would seem to give a more detailed description of the "worthless person" already referred to. The "six" and "seven" of the opening statement have their explanation in the description. The six are first stated, and the seventh is that which results, namely, "he that soweth discord among brethren."

This is followed by a parental exhortation. It commences with tender and urgent entreaties to attend to parental counsels, because that counsel is for the good of the son to whom it is addressed. A warning is uttered against the first movement toward sin, desire. "Lust not after her beauty in thy heart." Then the consequences of wrong in social life are set forth. The man who is wronged will take no compensation. His fury will exact the utmost.

PROVERBS 7

This is a second parental exhortation, and consists of a warning against the allurements of the strange woman. A graphic picture of the seduction of a youth void of understanding is given. The woman whom Solomon saw is still in our cities, and, alas, so is the youth void of understanding. The address closes with words of burning which tell the issue. The deceived youth passes to the place of slaughter like an ox, till physical nemesis overtakes him. Like a bird hasting to a snare, without consciousness that it means the ending of life, so goes the simple one to the place of sin. In order that it may not be so, this parental counsel is given. In the hour of sin's glamor it is good for the soul to look through to the end which is in Sheol and the chambers of death. When the voice of the siren is heard, it is good to pause and listen to the moan of the breakers on the shore of darkness and death, for to that shore the way of impurity assuredly leads.

PROVERBS 8

The section containing the instructions of wisdom ends with two discourses, the first of which is the great call of wisdom. This takes up and deals more minutely with the call in the earlier part of the book. It opens with an announcement that wisdom is making its appeal everywhere amid the busy activities of life. Then follows her call.

This is, first, an appeal to men to attend (verses 4-11). This they should do because wisdom speaks excellent things, and speaks in righteousness. Moreover, the words of wisdom are plain and more valuable than all riches.

The foundations of wisdom are next declared (verses 12-14). Essentially, these are prudence, knowledge, discretion. As for man, the foundation of wisdom is the fear of the Lord, which expresses itself in hatred of all He hates. In such wisdom lie the secrets of strength.

Then the values of wisdom are described (verses 15-21). All authority is based on it. It is the lover of such as love it. It yields all highest wealth to such as love it.

Next, wisdom claims age-abiding relation to Deity (verses 22-31). Ere the beginnings of creation, Jehovah possessed wisdom. Through all the processes wisdom wrought with God, and God delighted in wisdom, until man, the crowning glory of all, gave wisdom chief delight. This passage may be set side by side with the prologue to John's Gospel, for fuller understanding.

The call ends with a final appeal (verses 32-38). Those who attend to the call of wisdom are blessed indeed, and those who sin against wisdom wrong their own soul.

PROVERBS 9

The last address is a contrast between wisdom and folly. Each is personified as a woman calling to youth. Wisdom has builded her house, and spread her feast in the high places of the city. She calls to a feast of life. Folly in the garb of the evil woman sits at the door of her house, also in the high places of the city. She also calls to a feast, but it is the feast of death.

Between the two descriptions there is a passage revealing the fact that the effect produced will depend on the attitude of those who hear (verses 7-11). The man who scorns, gets shame, and it is useless to reprove him. What, then, is this first wisdom that expresses itself in willingness to learn, and gains yet greater wisdom? It is the fear of Jehovah and the knowledge of the Holy One. In every city, on every street, by every door of opportunity, these two voices of wisdom and folly are appealing to men. To obey the call of wisdom is to live. To yeld to the clamor of folly is to die. How shall we discern between the voices? By making the fear of Jehovah the central inspiration of life. By yielding the being at its deepest to Him for correction and guidance.

PROVERBS 10

Here begin the proverbs proper. In this collection they are antithetical. They present a sharp contrast between wisdom and folly in the outworking of such in practical life. Seeing that this is indeed a collection of proverbs, there is no direct connection or system save this underlying purpose of contrast. No exposition is possible save to take each proverb and consider it in its separate value. In the majority of instances this is unnecessary, because they are self-evident expositions of one abiding truth.

Through these chapters, therefore, we shall glance only at such as may be somewhat obscure, or such as have a new element of construction or suggestiveness. In this chapter we take four such, *viz.,* 10,15,22,23.

Verse 10. The contrast here is between the method of deceit which causeth sorrow, the winking of the eye, which deceives others; and that of blunt and perhaps unwise speech which, nevertheless, causes only the fall of him who uses it.

Verse 15. This is a plain recognition of the power of wealth, and the paralysis of poverty. It is a wholesome corrective to much nonsense talked today about the blessings of poverty. Wealth may become a curse, but poverty is inherently a destruction.

Verse 22. The antithesis is not so clearly marked here. It is, nevertheless, present to the mind in the contrast between true riches and false.

Verse 23. The text of the Revised Version here surely catches the true contrast. A man of understanding finds sport in wisdom. That is, he gets out of wisdom the same satisfaction that a fool gets out of wickedness.

PROVERBS 11

Verse 7. The antithesis of this proverb is between the condition described and that of one not described, that is to say, the expectation or hope of the wicked lies wholly on this side of the grave, and perishes at death.

Verse 12. The word "despiseth" here must be understood as marking some outward manifestation of contempt. The contrast will then be plain.

Verse 16. The method of this proverb is of comparison rather than of contrast, the idea being that a "gracious woman" will defend honor with the same strength and persistency as "violent men," or "strong men," as the Authorized Version had it, will retain riches. The word "violent" here suggests evil rather than good.

Verse 21. The phrase "hand join in hand" indicates either co-operation in wickedness, or continuity of the same, as from father to son. The latter would seem to be more probable, as affirming the direct contrast to the statement that the "seed of the righteous" shall be delivered.

Verse 22. A ring of gold in a swine's snout is out of place, and a useless waste of precious metal. So also is beauty in a woman who lacks discretion. If the thought of the contrast be carried out a little, it will be recognized that the swine will speedily destroy the luster of the gold, and so a woman lacking discretion will surely destroy her own beauty.

Verse 30. Notice the change from "He that winneth souls is wise" to "He that is wise winneth souls." Essentially the meaning is the same, but this setting makes more graphic the truth that winning souls is not easy. It needs wisdom.

PROVERBS 12

Verse 9. That is to say, it matters little that one is not counted as of any importance by his neighbors if, nevertheless, he is able to keep a servant, that is, to employ someone to minister to his need. That man is in a far worse case who honors himself, that is, keeps up an appearance out of pride, while, nevertheless, he lacks bread.

Verse 12. The contrast here is between the feverish desire for the speculative method of obtaining, symbolized by hunting, with the natural and certain, if slower, process of growing.

Verse 14. This proverb takes for granted that a man's words and works are good, and then teaches that they benefit him as well as those to whom he speaks and for whom he works.

Verse 20. In order to appreciate the antithesis of the proverb it must be recognized that the writer takes it for granted that deceit in the heart is the cause of misery. Men who imagine evil have to practice deceit, which causes unhappiness. Men who counsel peace have joy in the heart.

PROVERBS 13

Verse 2. Compare this with 12:14. As the words of a good man benefit himself as well as others, so the evil deeds of transgressors react upon themselves.

Verse 5. The contrast here between the wicked and the righteous is intense, in that concerning the righteous man the proverb simply states he hateth lying; concerning the wicked it declares that he becomes loathsome. That is to say, a righteous man keeping himself separate from wickedness hates lying. An evil man giving himself over to lying or other forms of sin becomes hated by others.

Verse 8. That is to say that if wealth has its advantages, so also has poverty. The rich man by his wealth may be able to conserve his life, but the poor man escapes the very dangers into which the rich are brought.

Verse 14. In this proverb the words "depart from the snares of death" interpret the action of such as obey the law. Thus by obedience to law a man departs from the snares of death, and so law becomes a fountain of life.

Verse 19. The reason that desire is not accomplished is declared in the second part of this proverb. Men will not pay the price of departing from evil, and so fail of the sweetness of fulfilled desire.

Verse 23. This is the declaration of an abiding truth that there is sustenance in the land, but men are excluded from it by injustice.

PROVERBS 14

Verse 7. The sense of this proverb is entirely altered in the Revision. The Authorized reading would make it mean that if a man is perceived to be devoid of knowledge he should be abandoned. The Revised urges attenton to the foolish man in order that it may be known that he lacks knowledge.

Verse 9. This proverb is decidedly ambiguous. It may mean that foolish men despise guilt in the sense of holding in contempt the guilty, whereas upright men have grace or favor or good will in their heart, that is, even to such as fail. Instead of "sin," the American Standard Revision, renders "trespass offering," and so makes it mean that a religious rite by fools is of no value.

Verse 17. The contrast here is between hastiness of temper and maliciousness. The former leads to acts of folly. The other makes the man guilty of it hated by others.

PROVERBS 15

Verse 11. This is a simple method of drawing attention to God's perfect knowledge of all the deepest and hidden things. If that which is most full of mystery to us is perfectly known to Him, how well He must know our hearts.

Verse 23. This proverb sets forth the satisfaction of being able to say the right thing at the right moment. The explanation of its first part is found in the phrase in the second, "in due season."

Verse 24. A recognition of the two forces of which man is ever conscious—the upward pull and the downward pull with a declaration that wisdom consists in answering the upward.

Verse 27. The "gain" here referred to must mean a bribe. The meaning of the proverb then becomes perfectly plain.

PROVERBS 16

Verse 1. A somewhat obscure proverb which recognizes that man has to exercise his own reason in making his plans, but that he is dependent on the Lord for the answer of the tongue. Dr. Perowne's interpretation is most likely the correct one. He says: "The implied moral of the proverb is, If we cannot do the less without God, do not attempt to do the greater without Him."

Verse 4. This is simply the affirmation of the fact that in the orderliness of the divine economy the harvest must be according to the sowing.

Verse 21. Wisdom is recognized, and where there is ability to impart it, it becomes helpful to others.

Verse 26. That is to say that hunger will make a man work when nothing else will. This is in harmony with the apostolic principle, "If a man will not work, neither let him eat."

Verse 32. This is a proverb that is constantly quoted, and very little believed. If men only recognized that there is more valor and heroism in self-control than in doughty deeds which others acclaim in song and story, how different our world would be.

PROVERBS 17

Verse 3. Two important thoughts are suggested by this proverb. First, that the heart will yield to no force other than that of God. Dross in metal may be discovered and expurged by fire, but evil in the heart can be discovered and dealt with only by God. Second, Jehovah does try the heart.

Verse 5. The first part of this proverb does not teach, as is so often stated, that poverty is from God. Rather, it recognizes the inherent rights of every man in God, notwithstanding his poverty.

Verse 10. The finer the disposition, the less is needed to correct it.

Verse 15. A self-evident statement, and yet one that needs to be made, for in every age there have been those who fall into both forms of wrong.

Verse 24. The contrast here is between "before the face of him" and "the ends of the earth." While it is a sure sign of weakness to see only the things that are near, it is a yet surer sign of folly to be forever looking at far-off things, to the neglect of those close at hand.

PROVERBS 18

Verse 1. The protest of this proverb is against the self-satisfaction which makes a man separate himself from the thoughts and opinions of others. Such a one finally "rages against," or "quarrels with all sound wisdom."

Verse 9. This plainly teaches that there can be no middle course between construction and destruction. Every man is contributing something to the commonwealth, or is a wastrel.

Verses 10 and *11.* Each of these verses taken separately constitutes a perfect proverb; but the force of either is diminished unless we note the antithesis created by considering them together. On the one hand, the true refuge of the soul is declared. On the other, a false refuge is described.

Verse 24. The whole force of this proverb lies in the contrast between the word "friends" and the word "friend." In the first case the word would perhaps be best expressed in modern language by the word "acquaintance." The second word needs to be rendered "lover." The whole teaching of the proverb is that one true friend is a lover, and is worth more than a multitude of acquaintances, who are likely to lead into extravagances and evil courses.

PROVERBS 19

Verse 7. This is the only case in this first collection of proverbs in which we find three clauses. It is certainly most likely that the third clause is incomplete. Something has been lost. If this be not so, then the proverb which sets forth the extremely pitiable condition of the poor ends by declaring that to him the promises of friends are not fulfilled.

Verse 16. Here "he that is careless of his ways" simply means, of course, "he that keepeth not the commandment."

Verse 21. This is a perfectly self-evident assertion, but, as such, important as to warrant a pause in reading it. The one thing in the heart that may be depended upon is the counsel or guidance of Jehovah.

Verse 24. Is it possible to find anywhere a more graphic or sarcastic description of absolute laziness?

Verse 27. The meaning here is that it is better not to learn than to learn to refuse to obey.

PROVERBS 20

Verse 9. This is the eternal challenge which has but one answer. When a man recognizes this he begins to inquire for a Saviour.

Verse 14. "It is bad, it is bad," is the description which the buyer gives of the article of which he wishes to possess himself. The words used today are not identical, but the same buyer is in the markets.

Verse 21. Another of the ancient proverbs to which men need to attend today. It would be well to have this plainly engraved before the eyes of all young men as they enter commercial pursuits.

Verse 25. A sane warning against adding sins to those which are certainly such in the economy of righteousness. There is a widespread tendency today to take vows of abstention, or to make promises without careful inquiry.

PROVERBS 21

Verse 4. The "lamp" of a man's life is his spirit. Where that is exalted and manifests itself in the high look and the proud heart, there is sin. All of which is to say that for a man to follow a self-centered desire without recognition of guidance from God is of the essence of sin.

Verse 18. This proverb could have been written only by a man who had learned the important lesson of taking in broad expanses in his outlook. He declares the supremacy of right in the economy of the world, and that, finally, for the ransom and deliverance of the righteous and upright the wicked and transgressors must be dealt with in judgment.

Verse 27. In this proverb there is a somewhat subtle distinction which is nevertheless one of extreme importance. In any case, the sacrifice of the wicked is an abomination. That is to say, it is abominable for any man who is living wrongly to make an offering to God in the way of worship. That abomination becomes worse when in the offering of the wicked comes from an ulterior motive. For a wicked man to give for his own pleasure is an evil thing; but if he hopes by his gift to win some spiritual favor while he continues in sin, that is a still deeper evil.

PROVERBS 22

Verse 2. The question that naturally arises on reading this is, Where do they meet together? This proverb is often used as having reference to the sanctuary or house of prayer; but a very superficial examination of the actual condition of affairs will show that this use of the proverb is hardly warranted. The answer to the question is that in the sight of God, and in His dealing with them, they meet together. If one is looking for locality, let him look to the day of final judgment.

Verse 6. In this oft-quoted proverb the true sense most certainly is found in the adoption of the marginal readings. It is a declaration of the true philosophy of education. That which is in a child naturally is to be discovered and trained in order that the purpose of its life may be realized.

Verse 11. Again, in this proverb the marginal reading, "that hath grace in his lips," should be adopted. The meaning is that the two qualifications which will ensure the friendship of the king are, first, pureness of heart, and, second, wisdom of expression.

Verse 14. This does not mean that if a man is abhorred of Jehovah he will necessarily fall into this particular pit, but rather that he who does fall therein becomes abhorred of Jehovah. It is a graphic way of setting forth the abomination of unchastity.

PROVERBS 23

At the seventeenth verse of the previous chapter the section of the Book begins in which the method is slightly changed. While the teaching is still proverbial, it takes the form of longer discourses on general themes. The preacher first appeals to his hearer to listen because of the importance of wisdom already set forth. Then follows a discourse on social responsibilities. The behavior of the wise toward different classes is described. The poor are not to be oppressed. Jehovah is their Defender. A man of violent temper is to be let alone lest his way be learned. Suretyship is to be avoided lest it lead to poverty. Established rights in property are to be respected.

Diligence in business admits to positions of influence. When because of his diligence a man is admitted to the company of kings he should practice self-restraint. The possession of wealth is uncertain and is not to be coveted. The hospitality of the evil is not to be accepted. Wisdom is not to be wasted on a fool. The misfortunes of men are not to be used as opportunities to wrong them. Devotion to the acquisition of knowledge is to be maintained. The correction of a child is not to be neglected.

PROVERBS 24

Warnings are uttered against envy, against the formation of evil companionships, against excess in passion, against all false exhilaration; and perperpetual attention to wisdom and earnest endeavor to help those in peril are urged.

The mind of wisdom is then described. It is a mind full of hope, free of enmity, filled with reverent fear. The counsels close with further teaching concerning the social order. Judgment must be just, and wickedness must not be condoned. In proverbial language, the importance of working before rest is indicated. The need for a house and its use must be justified by wisdom before it is built. True neighborliness consists in refusing to consent to wronging a neighbor, and also in being free of a vengeful spirit. A graphic description of the slothful's neglect of his field and vineyard serves as a warning against sloth.

PROVERBS 25

We now come to the second collection of the proverbs of Solomon. These, as the title specifically declares, constitute a posthumous collection gathered in the days of Hezekiah. Speaking generally, the proverbs in this collection are more picturesque than the former. For the most part, *they* are antithetical, and logical. *These* are pictures, and are more perfectly parabolic. In passing over them we shall again note some of the more striking.

Verse 11. The figure is intended to suggest the thought of proper and beautiful setting. Delicate filigree work in silver forms a beautiful setting for apples of gold in that it shows them up in relief, and makes their value patent. So also a word which answers the apple of gold as a supreme value is yet more forceful as it is fitly spoken, that is, artistically.

Verse 20. The proverb indicates the impropriety of making merry in the presence of sorrow. It is wrong in method and serves to increase distress rather than to soothe it.

Verse 27. Much honey produces nausea. So eventually does self-glorification.

PROVERBS 26

Verse 2. Therefore, if the heart knows that a curse is unjust it may rest in the certainty that it cannot harm.

Verses 3-12. In this group of proverbs the fool is the subject. The true method of dealing with him is that of chastisement. Caution is needed in answering him lest his folly be shared; and, on the other hand, lest he be not reproved. The fool is not to be trusted. A parable of a fool is useless. Give a fool honor, and it is to offer it where it is useless. The parable of a fool pierces himself. To hire a fool is to ensure the ruin of work. A fool is pre-eminently a fool because he relishes his folly. The greatest fool is the fool who does not know he is a fool.

Verses 13-16. Four proverbs dealing with the slothful. He is a coward. He is the slave of habit. He is incapable of supporting himself. He is pre-eminently conceited.

Verses 17-23. Here are proverbs describing the evil practices and pernicious effects of the meddlesome man.

Verses 24-28. These proverbs describe the method and punishment of the loveless.

PROVERBS 27

Verse 5. This proverb takes for granted the need for rebuke, and by "love that is hidden" is meant a love which fails to rebuke.

Verse 14. There is nothing more calculated to arouse suspicion than profuse protestations of friendship.

Verses 15, 16. These must be read together. The first part suggests the persistence and wearisomeness of a contentious woman; the second part the inability to hinder her.

Verse 21. There are three interpretations of this proverb. First, that you may know what a man is by the way he bears praise. Second, that you may know what a man is by the things he praises. Third, that a man who treats praise as the fining pot treats silver and gold purges it of unworthy substance.

Verses 23-27. A brief proverbial discourse setting forth the advantages of a simple agricultural life over a life spent in amassing wealth.

PROVERBS 28

Verse 2. "The transgression of a land" must be understood as the opposite of the "state shall be prolonged." Then the proverb means that a multiplicity of princes is an evil, but men of understanding are a benefit.

Verse 13. Like Psalm 32, a remarkable revelation of how far these men saw into the very heart of truth concerning the attitude of God toward the sinner.

Verse 14. The blessedness of caution. The peril of stubbornness.

Verse 20. The man who makes fidelity the master principle will be rewarded. He who makes accumulation of wealth the master passion will be punished.

Verse 27. The latter part of this proverb describes an attitude which is very common, though popularly supposed not to be wrong. To hide the eyes means to refuse to see poverty. It is the sin of those who say they are too sensitive to visit the slums.

PROVERBS 29

Verse 2. The sentiment of this proverb often recurs. On the surface it hardly appears to be true. To observe long issues is to be convinced of the absolute accuracy of the sentiment.

Verse 8. A fine motto for engraving on the walls of the Foreign Office of any nation.

Verse 13. That is to say, all intelligence is a divine gift, whether it be used in righteousness or in wickedness. Sin is always the prostitution of a God-given power to base purposes.

Verse 18. This proverb teaches that the one cohesive principle in national life is the consciousness of God which issues in true social conditions.

Verse 21. This is a simple statement of a fact. Whether it be one of blessing or of evil depends on the Christian's servant. An evil servant treated well assumes the position of a son in arrogance. A good servant treated well assumes the position of a son in devotion.

Verse 24. In this proverb the words, "He heareth the adjuration and uttereth nothing," is a purely technical term of the courts, which means that a man who, while not the actual thief is yet in fellowship with him, will on his oath perjure his soul.

Verse 27. A statement of the necessary and abiding antipathy between righteousness and unrighteousness.

PROVERBS 30

This and the following chapter constitute an appendix to the Book of Proverbs. It is impossible to say who Agur was. In this selection from his writings we have an introduction, in which he affirms the fact of man's little wisdom, and then utters the memorable prayer which reveals his fear of Jehovah and his desire for that balanced life which is one of safety.

From the prayer to the end of the chapter we have his observations on various matters affecting conduct. In this the first section opens with a proverb (verse 10). Then follow descriptions of four evil generations and of "four things" perpetually dissatisfied. The second section opens with a proverb (verse 17), and is followed by four groups of four things. The first four excite wonder, the second four, terror; the third four are little things, but exceeding wise; the final four are stately things. The whole movement ends with a proverb (verses 32,33).

PROVERBS 31

This is the second section of the appendix. There have been many conjectures as to who King Lemuel was, but nothing certainly can be said. It is divided into two parts, the first of which consists of his mother's advice to him. This advice urges him against becoming the slave of passion, warns him that while there may be some excuse for the man who is ready to perish if he take strong drink, it must be utterly avoided by kings and princes. And, finally, she sets before him the first duty of the kingly office, that is, caring for all who are oppressed and needy.

The second half is a beautiful picture of a virtuous woman, and may be supposed to be King Lemuel's picture of his mother. After a fine description of her beauty and her diligence, and the helpful influence she exerted in bringing her husband to places of power, he ends with the declaration:

> Many daughters have done virtuously,
> But thou excellest them all,

and with a blessing on her.

Ecclesiastes

ECCLESIASTES 1

The first verse of this chapter introduces us to the author of the Book. Taken in conjunction with verse 12, it leaves no room for doubt that he is Solomon. In stating his theme he employs phrases which recur through the whole of the Book: "vanity," "what profit?" "under the sun." The statement is a declaration of the emptiness of life when it is wholly conditioned in material things—"under the sun."

In this first section we have a still more particular statement in general terms. The generations come and go while the earth abides. The sun rises and sets. The wind moves in a ceaseless circuit. Rivers run into the sea, only to be returned to the places from which they come. Man comes to the scene with desires which are never satisfied, and passes away into a land of forgetfulness. Some of the declarations are very remarkable for scientific accuracy, even in the light of latter-day discoveries. The circuit of the wind to the south and back again to the north is of but recent discovery. The return of rivers to the mountains by evaporation is also of recent discovery. Yet the intention of this whole passage is to impress on the mind the fact of the constant grind of the mechanism of the universe in the midst of which man lives his brief day and passes out to forget and be forgotten. This is still the view of men of science who lose their vision of the spiritual realities which constitute the upper half of human life.

The discourse proceeded to state the grounds on which such conclusions have been reached. They are twofold. First, the actual experiences of the king; and, second, the widespread observation of other men and of matters in general. Commencing with his own experience, he states first the vanity of knowledge, of mirth, of wealth. As to knowledge, he had applied his heart to seek and search out all the works done under the sun, and had come to the conclusion that they were all vanity, and that knowledge of them was grief. Knowledge unillumined by spiritual consciousness is utterly unsatisfactory.

ECCLESIASTES 2

Turning from the pursuit of knowledge to the pathway of pleasure, the king had given himself up to mirth, seeking the false stimulus of wine. In this also he had been disappointed, finding that mirth was madness, and all pleasure incompetent to satisfy. He next turned to his great possessions, attempting to make such use of them as to bring satisfaction not found elsewhere. He surrounded himself with every kind of luxury, gathered large possessions, gave himself over to music and to women, allowing full reign to all his desires. All this also he had found to be vanity, nothing but a striving after wind, and again he had been driven to the conclusion that there was no profit under the sun.

Once again he tried a new pathway. He turned himself from the things that were almost exclusively physical to those of the mind. These were better, and he found that "wisdom excelleth folly." Yet he also perceived that "one event happeneth to all," both the fool and the wise pass on to death, so that this also ended in disappointment as keen as the others. He then summarized the results of his own experience of life "under the sun" in the terrible words: "I hated life . . . I hated all my labour . . . under the sun." The very exercise of wisdom resulted in gathering results into which the toiler did not enter, but which he left to another. Everything was vanity. The ultimate conclusion of his own experience was that there was nothing better than to eat and drink. The mental attitude to God which is not the result of direct spiritual fellowship is clearly revealed in these conclusions of the preacher. He does not deny God's existence, but recognizes Him as an intelligent Force operating purely for His own pleasure without any reference to the satisfaction of men. Everything is vanity. To live under the sun is to decide at last that the natural thing to do is to take what comes. Materialism necessarily becomes fatalism.

ECCLESIASTES 3

The vanity of life under the sun is evidenced not merely in the experience of the preacher himself, but in the wider outlook which he has been able to take. He now gives us some of the results of that learning in the process of which he had found no personal satisfaction. And first he speaks in greater detail of that mechanism of the universe to which he had referred at the opening of his discourse. There is everywhere a ceaseless routine. Though we have often read some parts of his description as though they were the words of wisdom, there is no doubt that his ceaseless reiteration of the words, "A time . . . a time . . . a time," are intended to indicate his sense of the monotony of things, rather than of their variety. Through all experiences men have to pass because the time comes for them so to do. The doctrine of God deduced from such a conception of the universe is of a Being who is absolutely inexorable, and from whom there can be no escape. He is One who has set eternity in the heart of man, that is, created deep and passionate longings there, and yet has given to man no capacity for finding the thing for which he seeks; and, moreover, there is no escape from this inexorable order. The issue of all this is confusion rather than order. In the place of judgment and of righteousness wickedness exists; and the conclusion is that, after all, man is no better than the beasts.

It must be remembered that all this is absolutely true in the case of men who have no commerce with God through revelation. To discover Him in the universe, and recognize Him is not to be at peace with Him; but to be filled rather with the sense of the vanity of all things, and the impossibility of escape.

ECCLESIASTES 4

From this general survey the preacher returned to examine the condition of the beings whom he had described as being no better than the beasts. He looked out upon them, and saw them in suffering, and concluded that death or nonexistence is preferable to life. He declared, moreover, that toil is nothing worth, as it produces envy and striving. This leads him further to declare the vanity of success under such conditions. The wealthy man stands alone, and in his loneliness is more helpless than are the poor, who yet have comrades. And, finally, this led him to declare the emptiness of kingship. The old king who has become foolish is set aside for the youth who is yet poor and wise. This last reflection is not one of satisfaction, but of cynical despair, for the preacher declares, "This also is vanity, and a striving after wind."

ECCLESIASTES 5

The observation of the religious life brings no truer satisfaction. In this brief passage contempt for religion is not expressed, but there is absolutely no joy or satisfaction manifest. The life is wholly conditioned under the sun. The recognition of God is always irksome. This is based largely on the conception of God which is the inevitable outcome of such life, that conception which we have already seen manifest in the previous words of the king. All the things which he advances here are good so far as they go, but they all need something added to them before they can finally express the qualities of the religious life which give rest to the soul. Nothing is here other than a caution, based on fear. Brief phrases taken from these words will reveal the truth of them. "Keep thy foot when thou goest to the house of God," "Be not rash with thy mouth," "When thou vowest . . . defer not to pay." "Fear God."

Turning again to a general survey of the conditions under which men live, the preacher appealed against surprise at oppression. His reason for the appeal shows how low was his conception of God. He declared that all these things are known to One who is higher than the high, and the deduction he drew is that God does not interfere, that all iniquities are part of the great system. Yet the prosperous are not to be envied, for the man who has possessions does not possess them. Others eat them, and the owner merely beholds them. Indeed, the very care of wealth becomes a reason for restlessness. In view of all these things there is but one attitude, which the preacher advises: Do not hoard anything, but enjoy it. The only answer which God gives a man is the joy he finds in eating and drinking and using for himself the things which he possesses. It is the advice of pure selfishness, but it is always given by those who live wholly "under the sun."

ECCLESIASTES 6

The preacher knows prosperity experimentally far better than poverty. Moreover, by observation he is more familiar with men of wealth than with poor men, and, therefore, he returns to a declaration of the sorrows of the wealthy. A man possessing, cannot possess. Lacking nothing of all he desires, yet he cannot eat thereof. That is to say, he has a craving and desire within him which none of these things can appease. If a man be surrounded by children and yet at last have no burial, it would be better if he had never been born. Though he continue for two millenniums and enjoy no good during their passing, what advantage is there in it, for death is the final goal? In a pregnant phrase he expresses the emptiness of wealth. Wandering desire tells the story of the life of restless attempt to possess the best by the use of material things. After all, man is man, and nothing more, and there is no value in his contending with the Mightier One. If the afterward of life be uncertain, who can tell what is good for its experience? Evidently the thought of the preacher is that the more a man possesses under the sun, the more profoundly conscious does he become of the vanity and vexation of it all.

ECCLESIASTES 7

The preacher now proceeded to the inculcation of indifference toward all the facts of life as the only attitude which is in the least likely to be satisfactory. This he did, first, by a series of maxims. In all of these there is an element of truth, and yet here they express the gravest pessimism, the bitterest disappointment. "A good name is better than precious ointment," and yet "the day of death is better than the day of . . . birth"; and if these two statements are connected, it is easy to see the despair of the preacher, who evidently meant to imply that birth was an opportunity for losing the good name, while death closed such opportunity. He continued by declaring that mourning and sorrow are better than feasting and mirth, because they serve to keep the heart steady or wise, while the latter make it excited and foolish. For the same reason rebuke is better than laughter. The issue of all this is that the patient in spirit is better than the proud in spirit, which, in this connection, simply means that the man who can be stoical and indifferent is better than he who attempts to rise and rule. Therefore the preacher urged suppression of the passion of anger, and that there should be no wasted lament over former days. Wisdom, that is, the power of being indifferent and cautious, is good. He finally calls on men to consider the work of God, who has placed prosperity and adversity side by side with the deliberate intention of hiding from man the issues of his own life. Therefore, take things as they come. In prosperity be joyful, and in adversity be thoughtful.

All this general inculcation of indifference is now emphasized by particular illustration. Righteousness does not always pay. Wickedness sometimes does. Therefore morality is to be a thing of calculation. Men are urged to walk the middle way. "Be not righteous overmuch . . . be not overmuch wicked." Overmuch righteousness may end in destruction. Overmuch wickedness cuts short the days. It is the calm, calculating, self-centered morality of the materialist. Moreover, if men are to find any satisfaction they are to remember that there are no righteous men and to turn a deaf ear to tales. A word of personal testimony urges still further the value of this attitude of indifference. The preacher had tried other ways. He had determined to be wise, but had failed. He had turned to find out by personal experience that wickedness is folly, and in one graphic and startling picture revealing the depths to which he had sunk, he gives the issue. He had found something more bitter than death, the evil woman. After all the excesses of material life, therefore, his final conclusion about humanity is that only one man in a thousand can be found, but that not one woman in a thousand can be found. It is a word full of cynicism, but it is the word of a man who has lived the life which according to his own philosophy is the life of the beast.

ECCLESIASTES 8

In this division, dealing with the evidences of the vanity of life, the preacher sets forth certain deductions. The highest wisdom is submission to things as they are. Who knows anything? he asks. Therefore it is good to recognize the king's authority and yield to it, to recognize the inevitableness of all things and submit to them, to recognize the absolute certainty of death and to abandon one's self to that certainty. Yet in doing all this there will abide in the heart the recognition of abounding injustice. It is manifest in all the ways of men. In a clause which is intended to be a saving one, the preacher declares its existence but absolutely denies its activity. And what is the ultimate issue in all such convictions? "I commended mirth, because a man hath not better thing under the sun, than to eat, and to drink, and to be merry." And this because wisdom is elusive. Man cannot know, therefore he need not try and should abandon himself to the sensual pleasures of the moment. It is all true if a man live "under the sun."

ECCLESIASTES 9

In view of the evidences of the truth of the affirmation, "vanity . . . all is vanity," the preacher now turns to its effect on the mind of the man living "under the sun." He extols this worldly wisdom, which he has already inculcated, and then exemplifies this method. He defends this wisdom and extols it.

First of all, it is to be remembered that all things are in the hand of God. Of course, his doctrine of God is that already dealt with in the earlier part of the discourse. The fact now is that these things being in God's hand, men do not know them, nor can they. The only certain thing is that there is one event to all, righteous and wicked, clean and unclean, the worshiper and the man who fails in worship, the good and the sinner, the swearer and the man who fears an oath. All these are really evil, with madness in their heart in life, and move to death. There is some hope in life, and yet all life at last passes into the utter failure of death. Therefore there is nothing for it other than to enter into the present life, to eat and drink, and to dress, to enter into the experiences of the life of vanity, for there is nothing beyond it. Everything is to be done in the present moment, and for the present moment with might, because there is nothing beyond. Still further, there is very little advantage in the things which men count advantageous. Swiftness, and strength, and wisdom, and skill, of what value are they in view of the fact that as fishes and birds are snared unawares, so at any moment the end of all may come? Wisdom under the sun is granted to be of much relative value, but in the long issues it is of little worth.

ECCLESIASTES 10

How, then, does worldly wisdom work? The preacher shows that its first manifestation is discretion based upon selfishness. This section is a series of brief sayings which are of the nature of proverbs, laying down axioms and enjoining habits. One sinner destroyeth much good. Dead flies spoil the ointment. Do not manifest your folly. Do not fight against the ruler; yield to him. It is admitted that rulers are often foolish. Do not make the weapons of your own destruction. If your weapon is blunt, use strength, but be careful. Do not charm the serpent that has bitten you. Do not talk. Do not do too much. Be temperate. Be diligent. Be accommodating. Be cautious. This is a very condensed analysis of this section. The preacher had no idea of stating things so bluntly as this, but these are the thoughts underlying the more stately language of the discourse. They are plausible indeed, and there is an element of truth and value in them; but, taken as a whole, they are such things as men with no vision of the spiritual will accept. They constitute the essence of worldly wisdom. The inspiration of the whole of them is selfishness. All that is valuable in them might be otherwise inspired, but here they are the outcome of convictions already expressed, that in view of the vanity and emptiness of life man's only wise course is to enter into the present moment in all its fulness and abandon all attempt after deeper satisfaction.

ECCLESIASTES 11

The method of worldly wisdom is not that of discretion only; it is, moreover, that of diligence, and this passage urges such diligence. Again, we have taken more than one text out of this passage to preach the truth of God, and therein we do not necessarily do wrong, for there are high spiritual applications of all these things. However, it must be remembered that here they are related to the outlook which has characterized the whole discourse. We have not yet reached, though we are fast approaching it, the point of correction. The whole of this may be summarized by saying that it teaches the necessity for diligence in the midst of the things of this life, "Cast thy bread upon the waters" is an injunction to the toiler that makes harvest possible. "Give a portion to seven" is advice to use all opportunity speculatively, because one does not know what calamities may be ahead, and because it is well to have provided beforehand for such contingencies. All this is followed by advice not to waste time in attempting to decide improbable things; and, finally the words of verses six and seven may be expressed in latter-day language as, "Get at it"; 'Keep at it"; "Make hay while the sun shines." Almost weirdly this section, setting forth the value and method of worldly wisdom, ends in the same wail of disappointment which has characterized the whole of the discourse. "If a man live many years, let him rejoice in them all; but let him remember the days of darkness, for they shall be many. All that cometh is vanity."

The last division of the Book begins with the ninth verse of this chapter. Its first word, like the first word of the Manifesto of the King in later days, indicates the true thought and desire of God for man: "Rejoice." A statement of life which includes all of truth recognized in the discourse, and yet which far transcends the whole of it, is first made. A man is to enter into life, his own life, and his present life, with avidity; and he is constantly to do so in the sight of God, remembering his relationship to God. Judgment here does not mean punishment but verdict. Everything is to be tested first by the supremacy of God. To attempt to find Him through the medium of our self-pleasing use of life is utterly to fail. To enthrone Him first, and then attempt to find life through Him, is to cancel forever the word "vanity."

ECCLESIASTES 12

The preacher now proceeds in language full of poetic beauty to urge the young to remember their Creator. We then reach the epilogue of the sermon. It first repeats the theme as announced at the beginning, and tells how the preacher, through study and diligence, still attempted to teach the people knowledge; and, finally, in the concluding two verses, a great statement of truth is made, understanding and acting upon which the pessimistic views of life resulting from materialism will never be known. At the center is this statement: "This is the whole of man." The word "duty" has no real place in the sentence. What is the whole of man? "To fear God and keep his commandments." To do this is to find life not merely under the sun, but over it as well, to pass from the imperfect hemisphere into the whole sphere. To do this is to have light on the facts and problems of life which otherwise are dark and dismal.

The Song of Solomon

THE SONG OF SONGS
THE WHOLE BOOK

No Book has been provocative of more controversy than this. The question at issue is as to its place and value in Holy Scripture. While there are different varieties of each, the interpretations may be divided into two main classes, the material and the mystical. Without staying to deal with the many interpretations of either kind, may it not be true that the gravest mistake has been to imagine that either method in itself exhausts the meaning? On the extreme left are those who declare it to be simply a voluptuous Eastern love song. On the extreme right are those who at once say it is a portrayal of the love existing between Christ and His Church.

To take the second view first, whatever the Holy Spirit may have caused this to be written for, as ultimate value it is perfectly certain that Solomon did not see in it all that such interpreters find there. I am not denying that these things are there for us, but merely that Solomon did not write to set forth these things, for the Mystery of the Church was hidden under the whole economy of Hebraism.

On the other hand, if some mystical value is recognized as lying within he purpose of the writer, the songs are at once saved from the possibility of being charged with voluptuousness.

In order to understand the value of the Book it seems to me best to recognize a basis in fact, and an increasing understanding of the deepest values with the process of the centuries.

The basis of fact we shall find by recognizing that these songs are idylls, and that behind them is the actual story of the wooing and winning of a bride. As Dr. Moulton lucidly points out, the idyllic form does not proceed in consecutive order in its description, and it is necessary to construct the story by careful examination of the songs themselves.

They first set forth the love existing between bride and bridegroom.

Now the thought of the relationship of bride and bridegroom as setting forth that existing between Jehovah and Israel is peculiarly Hebrew. In the prophets this is subsequently made clearly manifest. Moreover, Jewish expositors have so interpreted these songs, and it is certainly easily probable that Solomon had some such intention in mind.

In the new dispensation, that of the Church, the same figure is the most glorious in setting forth the nature of the relation existing between Christ and His Church. Some of the most sainted writers of the Christian Church have interpreted these songs in the light of this New Testament truth, such, for instance, as Rutherford and McCheyne. Dr. Adeney, in the *Expositor's Bible,* while arguing against the mystical interpretation, yet says:

> It may be maintained that the experience of Christians has demonstrated the aptness of the expression of the deepest spiritual truths in the imagery of the Song of Solomon.

His later contention that New Testament writers make no use of the poem in this way is of no weight, for we believe in the ever-increasing light on the deepest values of the earlier Scriptures. The fact that Solomon had no intention of setting forth the relation between Christ and His Church is of no moment. If through the songs of human love he did intend to set forth the spiritual idea of the love between Jehovah and His ideal people, the fulfilment of the thought of the songs would come with the working out into history of the realization of that purpose.

The songs should be treated, then, first as simple and yet sublime songs of human affection. When they are thus understood, reverently the thoughts may be lifted into the higher value of setting forth the joys of the communion between the spirit of man and the Spirit of God, and ultimately between the Church and Christ.

OUTLINE NOTES ON

The Song of Solomon

SONG OF SOLOMON 1:1—2:7

In these notes I propose to do nothing more than to indicate the speakers in each case. As songs of human love they need no other exposition. As songs of the spiritual life they are better interpreted experimentally than in any other way. The arrangement, while not strictly that of chapters, does occupy eight days, and thus maintains the one chapter a day.

SONG OF SONGS

A. The Marriage (1:2-7).

I. The Shulamite and the Virgins (1:2-6). Ready for the Wedding.

1. The Bride (1:2-4a). Awaiting the Wedding.
2. The Virgins (1:4b). To the Bride.
3. The Bride (1:4c). In the Bridegroom's House.
4. The Virgins (1:4d). To the Bridegroom.
5. The Bride (1:4e-6).
   a. To the Bridegroom (1:4e).
   b. To the Virgins (1:5,6).

II. The Bride and the Bridegroom (1:7—2:6).

1. The Bride (1:7).
2. The Bridegroom (1:8-10).
3. The Virgins (1:11). To the Bride.
4. The Bride (1:12-14).
5. The Bridegroom (1:15).
6. The Bride (1:16—2:1).
7. The Bridegroom (2:2).
8. The Bride (2:3-6).

III. The Voice of the Singer: Wisdom (2:7).

SONG OF SOLOMON 2:8—3:5

B. The Betrothal (2:8—7:9)

I. Memories of the Wooing (2:8—3:5).

1. The Bride (2:8-14). How the Beloved Came.
2. The Brothers (2:15). Interrupting the Wooing.
3. The Bride (2:16, 17). Answering the Wooer.
4. The Bride (3:1-4). Her Dreams after the Wooing.

II. The Voice of the Singer: Wisdom (3, 5).

SONG OF SOLOMON 3:6—4:15

III. The Actual Betrothal (3:6—4:15).

1. The Singer (3:6-11). The Coming of Solomon.
2. Solomon (4:1-15). The Proposal.

SONG OF SOLOMON 4:16—5:1

3. The Bride (4:16).
   The Acceptance.
4. Solomon (5:1).
   (a) To the Bride (1a).
   (b) To His Retinue (1b).

SONG OF SOLOMON 5:2—6:3

IV. Experiences Following Betrothal (5:2—7:9).
1. The Bride (5:2—6:3).
   The Maiden's Troubled Dream.
   (a) The Coming of the Beloved in the Night (5:2-5).
   (b) The Door Opened, but the Beloved Vanished (5:6a).
   (c) Her Search (5:6b—6:12).
      1. Out in the Streets (6b).
      2. The Ill Treatment of the Watchmen (7).
      3. Appeal to the Women of Jerusalem (8).
      4. Their Answer (9).
      5. Her Description of Her Beloved (10-16).
      6. Inquiry of the Women (6:1).
      7. Her Answer (6:2).
   (d) She Awakes (6:3).

SONG OF SOLOMON 6:4—7:9

2. Solomon (6:4—7:9).
   His Musing.
   (a) Description of the Shulamite (6:4-9a).
   (b) Effect on the Virgins of the Vision of Her (6:9b-13).
   (c) Continued Description (7:1-9).

SONG OF SOLOMON 7:10—8

C. The United Life (7:10—8)

I. The Bride (7:10—8)
   Her Desire to Visit Her Home with Her Bridegroom.
II. The Voice of the Singer: Wisdom (8:4).
III. The Bride and the Bridegroom Together (8:5-14).
   1. The Bridegroom (5).
   2. The Bride (6-12).
      (Quotation from the Brothers, 8:8,9).
      (Answer of the Bride, 8:10-12).
   3. The Bridegroom (13).
   4. The Bride (14).

Isaiah

ISAIAH 1

Isaiah was a prophet to Judah. He exercised his ministry wholly within her borders, and with a view to her correction and comfort. His burdens of the nations were uttered concerning those nations which surrounded Judah, and had harassed her. His outlook was world-wide, and inclusive of the whole purpose of God. Profoundly conscious of the purpose of God that through His people all peoples should be blessed, he saw through all the processes of judgment the ultimate blessing of the whole earth.

The prophecies of judgment fall into three circles: concerning Judah and Jerusalem (1-12), concerning the nations and the world (13-27), concerning the chosen and the world (28-35). This concerning Judah and Jerusalem is separated into two parts by the prophet's vision at the death of Uzziah. In the first five chapters, therefore, we have his messages during the reign of Uzziah.

This first message is of the nature of a great impeachment of the nation, in which the cause of controversy between Jehovah and His people is declared, and the necessity for judgment affirmed. The heavens and earth are summoned to hear the complaint of Jehovah, which is that notwithstanding His love and tenderness His people do not know Him. The prophet appeals to the sinning people, demanding why they will still be stricken. All their suffering is the result of their sin, and yet they rebel more and more. Again voicing the message of Jehovah, he corrects the prevalent and pernicious idea that relation to God is conditioned by external acts of worship. Sacrifices and feasts are nothing worth, and God hates them when unaccompanied by rectitude.

Jehovah now calls His people to reason with Him, and declares that the alternative issue of such reasoning is dependent on their attitude. Because of the fearful corruption of the city judgment is necessary. It will proceed to restoration in the case of those who are obedient; but to reprobation and utter destruction in the case of the transgressors.

ISAIAH 2

Following this broad statement of the case between Jehovah and His people, we have the prophet's great appeal to them. The first part constitutes a vision of the latter days, that condition toward which judgment is to proceed. The Lord's house is established at the center of the national life. His law proceeds from Zion to the peoples of the earth, and the issue is peace.

The prevalent conditions are seen in the light of that latter day, and the prophet appeals to the people to walk in that light. In burning words he describes these evil conditions. The people have become contaminated with the surrounding nations. They are wealthy, and prosperous in all material things. They are steeped in idolatry, and consequently human life, both low and high, is degraded. In order to realize the vision of the latter days, Jehovah will visit His people in judgment. His terror is described in itself and in its operation. As He goes forth in judgment men of all classes are subdued and bend before Him, and the wholesale destruction of idols follows. This description of prevalent corruption and judgment ends with another appeal that it cease.

ISAIAH 3

The prophet now deals with judgment in greater detail, and shows how it will proceed against the rulers and against the women. The judgment in the case of the rulers is to be the destruction of true government and the substitution of incompetent administration, with chaos necessarily resulting. The reason for this, so far as the people are concerned, is the open sin into which they have been led by evil rulers. So far as Jehovah is concerned, He has the cause of the people in His heart, and is against all oppression.

ISAIAH 4

In all human history there has been a close connection between corrupt rulers and frivolous and polluted womanhood. Fierce is the prophet's denunciation of such. Their wantonness and their luxury are to be ended. They are to be visited by physical affliction, and the sweeping out of all the things associated with their corrupt and luxurious life, and by the death of men.

The appeal ends with another description of the days following the judgment. They are to be characterized by material prosperity issuing from moral purity, and by the mighty protection of Jehovah.

ISAIAH 5

With the thought of judgment, and the necessity for it still in mind, the prophet utters his great denunciation. This falls into three parts.

The first is a song of accusation. By the simple and familiar illustration of the rights of the proprietor in his vineyard, the prophet appeals to the listening people. The nature of the parable is such as to compel their assent to the rightness of the judgment indicated. The prophet immediately makes a blunt application of his song as he declares that the "vineyard of the Lord of hosts is the house of Israel, and the men of Judah His pleasant plant."

He then proceeds to utter woes against the prevailing sins of the time. The first is against monopoly, and the consequent oppression of the poor; the second, against the life of dissipation which the rulers were living; the third, against that unbelief which persists in iniquity and scoffs at the idea of divine intervention; the fourth, against that moral confusion which is unable to distinguish between good and evil; the fifth, against the false wisdom which acts without reference to God; the sixth, against the perversion of justice by the judges.

He finally describes the instrument of judgment. The inspiration of judgment is the anger of Jehovah, who calls a people from far. These are then described in their perfect equipment, in their terrible fierceness, and in the overwhelming impetuosity of their onslaught.

ISAIAH 6

We now begin the second part of the first circle of prophecy, which contains the prophecies during the reigns of Jotham and Ahaz. When Uzziah died, Isaiah was called to the exercise of a larger ministry, and was prepared for it by the special vision granted to him.

This vision of the Lord was full of grace and of glory. The majesty of the Most High was manifest in the uplifted and occupied throne, in the solemn chanting of the seraphim, and by the earthquake which made the very foundations of the thresholds tremble. The revelation of grace is as remarkable as that of glory. In answer to the prophet's cry of need, one of the singing seraphim bears to him a live coal from the altar, and his sin is expiated. It is a wonderful unveiling of truth concerning God. The center of all adoring worship, He nevertheless hears the sigh of the sinner in his need, and the song of a seraph's worship ceases in order that the sigh of the sinner may be answered.

Following this vision, the voice of the Lord calls for a messenger, and the prophet, cleansed from his sin, answers. He is then commissioned to the ministry of judgment. In answer to an inquiry on his part, a word is spoken which limits judgment and reveals that the purpose of God in His people is not to be utterly frustrated.

ISAIAH 7

Immediately following this new call of the prophet, we have the account of his encounter with Ahaz. Rezin of Syria and Pekah of Israel had entered into a confederacy against Judah, and a great fear possessed the people. The prophet declares to him that the counsel of these kings shall not prevail if he, that is, Ahaz, will be quiet and trust in God. A sign from Jehovah is offered, but he refuses to ask one. This refusal is an act of unbelief, which the prophet rebukes, and then declares that the sign shall be given, namely, that a child shall be born of a virgin.

This sign had an immediate application, but is the beginning in Isaiah's prophesying of a thought which grows as he proceeds, until it is seen to be Messianic in intention. He ends his message to Ahaz by declaring that judgment will fall on Judah, and proceeds to describe the Assyrian invasion, with its terrible results to the people.

ISAIAH 8

In this section we have the account of how the prophet turns from his more public ministry to devote himself to a small circle of believing souls. This departure was signalized by his writing on a tablet the ominous word, *Maher-shalal-hash-baz,* which means "the spoil speedeth, the prey hasteth."

The prophet then turns to his children, the spiritual children who are faithful witnesses, and his own children. Jehovah declares to him that as the people have refused the gentle method of His persuasion, they are now to be dealt with by the overwhelming method of judgment. In the midst of the uproar Jehovah is to be a sanctuary for those who trust Him, and a rock of offense for the disobedient. The prophet is instructed to bind the testimony and seal the law, and his children are to be for signs and wonders. He then turns to the instruction of this small group of disciples, first describing the false way of seeking familiar spirits and wizards, with disastrous results, and then delivering to them the message of hope.

ISAIAH 9:1—10:4

Here we have the message of hope (verses 1-7) in the glorious picture of the Coming Deliverer, with the equally glorious record of the results of His Coming. It is one of the greatest Messianic passages in the Old Testament.

This is followed immediately by a prophecy of judgment on Israel, which falls into four distinct parts, each ending with the words, "For all this His anger is not turned away, but His hand is stretched out still." For this reason we have included in our reading the first four verses of chapter 10.

In the first he rebukes their pride, and declares that in consequence of it Jehovah will send against them the Syrians and the Philistines. In the second, he announces and denounces their stubbornness of heart, and declares that on account of it Jehovah will destroy their own leaders, and thus visit them with punishment. In the third he describes the prevalence and fierceness of their wickedness, and announces the judgment of civil strife, by which they will consume each other. In the fourth he describes the corruption of the judges and rulers of the people, and declares that they shall be overwhelmed and destroyed by the people.

Through all these measures of judgment the afflicted people manifest stubbornness of heart and persistence in wickedness, so that the anger of Jehovah cannot be turned away, although His afflicting hand continues to be outstretched.

ISAIAH 10:5-34

This is a prophecy of judgment on Assyria, and is full of interest. Assyria is the power which Jehovah is using for the punishment of His people, but because it fails to understand its true relation to God, it, in turn, will be judged.

The prophet first indicates this contrast of intention. Jehovah's intention is that the Assyrian shall be a rod in His hand. The Assyrian intention is to destroy the people of God. He then declares the divine purpose. The Lord will accomplish His work on Jerusalem according to His intention, but then He will punish Assyria. The reason for this is that Assyria acts as though it were strong and independent, forgetting that it is but an instrument in the hand of Jehovah. The punishment is then described.

In view of this judgment the prophet delivers a message to the remnant of Israel. The issue of the Assyrian invasion will be that the remnant will stay on Jehovah. They are therefore not to be afraid, for the scourge will be scourged, and the burden upon the neck of the people of God will depart. This prophecy ends with a graphic description of the Assyrians' approach, and a description of the judgment which will fall on the chosen people by their coming.

ISAIAH 11

In this section the prophet's eyes are lifted toward the light of a far-off day. With judgment imminent, he yet sees the ultimate issue of it all. There is first a description of a Coming One (11). The description of the Coming One is divided into two parts. The first describes Him as the Branch, that is, as David's Son (verses 1-9). His Coming is proclaimed, His anointing by the Spirit of Jehovah is declared, the method of His rule is described, and the glorious results are announced. The prophecy now describes Him as the Root, that is, David's Lord (verses 10-15). Again His Coming is announced, but this time for the uplifting of an ensign that the nations may seek Him. Again His reign is described. The first process is to be the gathering together of the remnant. This is followed by the uplifting of the ensign for the nations. The result will be the restoration of unity between Ephraim and Judah, and their victory over their foes. All this will be accompanied by manifestations of the power of God as their fathers had seen it in connection with the Exodus.

ISAIAH 12

Here we have the songs of the people concerning the deliverances wrought by the victories of Jehovah. The first celebrates the personal blessings of the day described, while the second sets forth the gracious results to the peoples of the world issuing from the restoration of the people of God.

These great and glorious prophecies are not yet fulfilled, but they are as certain of fulfilment as every word of God is sure.

ISAIAH 13:1—14:2

We now commence the second circle of the first division of our book, in which are contained Isaiah's prophecies concerning the nations and the world. The first describes the doom of Babylon. Whereas the word "Babylon" occurs here, there is no doubt Assyria is in view. The prophecy concerning Babylon comes later (21:1-10). This is clearly shown by Dr. Thirtle in his *Old Testament Problems.*

In graphic language the prophet foretells the nearness of judgment. He describes the mustering of the hosts, and then their marching. He next declares the purpose of the judgment. It is to punish evil. Finally he describes the process of judgment. Media is to be against Assyria, and the result will be abiding ruin.

The issue of this judgment is intended to be the restoration of Israel through the compassion of Jehovah. He will yet choose them and set them in their own land. The peoples who have oppressed them will submit themselves to them and serve them, and they will rule over their oppressors.

ISAIAH 14:3-23

Anticipating the great day of restoration, the prophet puts into the mouth of Israel the great parable or song which celebrates the downfall of Assyria. This moves in five distinct strophes. In the first (verses 4-8), the deliverance wrought for the whole earth through the overthrow of Assyria is described. The golden city had been the seat of widespread oppression, and when by the action of Jehovah it is destroyed, the whole earth is at rest. In the second (verses 9-11), the consternation of the underworld at the fall of Assyria is described. All the great dead ones are astonished that at last even Assyria had become weak. In the third, the sin which had culminated in such destruction is revealed (verses 12-15). The sin was that rebellion against God, the ambition which attempted to thwart His purpose and contest with Him the right of empire. The completeness of Assyria's destruction is the subject of the fourth (verses 16-19). While other kings sleep in glory, the king of Assyria is to be flung out unburied as utterly evil. The fifth strophe (verses 20,21) announces the utter extermination of Assyria, even to its name and remnant.

The prophecy concerning Assyria ends with a summary of the sentence which affirms the act of Jehovah and the consequent doom of Assyria. While the first application of this great prophecy was undoubtedly to the actual kingdom of Assyria, it is impossible to study it without seeing how graphically it sets forth the ultimate issue of the principle of rebellion which is based on unbelief.

ISAIAH 14:24—15:9

In this section we have three prophecies: concerning Assyria (14:24-27), concerning Philistia (14:28-32), and the commencement of one concerning

Moab (15). This fragment concerning Assyria consists of the reaffirmation of Jehovah's intention to break its power. The oath of Jehovah is declared, and its irrevocable certainty affirmed.

The fragment concerning Philistia is of the nature of a warning spoken to her. Although she oppresses the people of God, she is herself in peril. She is not to rejoice because the rod that smote her is broken, for there are other forces at the disposal of Jehovah, and they threaten Philistia.

The prophecy concerning Moab commences by describing her desolation. A catastrophe will overtake her in a night, the result of which will be the mourning of her people, and their scattering far and wide. In this chapter, moreover, we have an incidental record of the death of Ahaz.

ISAIAH 16

Continuing the prophecy concerning Moab, the prophet proceeds to describe how in her distress she will appeal to Judah for sanctuary (16: 1-5). This will be refused, and so great will be the distress of Moab that even the prophet breaks out into lamentation at sight of it. He declares that this visitation of Moab is in fulfilment of an ancient prophecy, and at last the time limit is actually set (verses 6-14).

ISAIAH 17

In this section (17-18), we have a prophecy dealing with Damascus and an interlude containing a soliloquy of the prophet. The burden of Damascus (17:1-11) announces its doom. It is evident, however, that the prophet had in mind an alliance which had been entered into between Israel, or Ephraim, and Damascus. The doom of Damascus means the destruction of the fortress of Ephraim.

The prophet then proceeds to describe the judgment of Ephraim, which will issue from the destruction of Damascus; and to declare that the effect will be to compel men to look to Jehovah rather than to idols. The reason for this visitation is that Ephraim had forgotten God.

The soliloquy of the prophet commences here (verses 12-14), and reveals his consciousness of the opposing peoples all about the chosen nation, and of Jehovah as perfect Defense.

ISAIAH 18

This is the second of the prophet's soliloquies, and is of the nature of a proclamation to certain ambassadors who are charged to return to their people and to wait for Jehovah. This charge is delivered because Jehovah has declared that He is waiting, watching, and preparing, that at the right moment He will act in judgment, and the issue will be the subjugation of the opposing peoples.

ISAIAH 19

These two chapters (19,20) contain the burden of Egypt. Its doom is first declared (19:1-15). Jehovah's advent will result in the destruction of idols, in civil war, in failure in counsel, and in the government of the Egyptian people by a cruel lord, a false king. This day of visitation will be one of physical catastrophe. The waters of the Nile will fail, and consequently all industry—fishing, weaving, and building—will be paralyzed. Egypt is to be utterly discomfited by the failure of its rulers, of its people, and of all its enterprises.

ISAIAH 20

Yet the prophet sees hope even for Egypt. He describes the process. The result of the judgment will be fear, and in the case of a part of Egypt at least this will issue in submission to Jehovah. Where this is so, there will be healing, and the prophet finally sees both Egypt and Assyria joined in the worship of Jehovah, and ultimately a triple alliance of Israel, Egypt, and Assyria will be made a blessing in the midst of the earth. From that vision of hope for Egypt he turns to pronouncing against her the doom that is at hand.

ISAIAH 21

In this chapter we have prophecies concerning Babylon, Dumah, and Arabia. With regard to Babylon, the prophet has seen the vision of the whirlwind sweeping against it, and so terrible is it that he is filled with horror. Babylon, all unconscious, is described as given over to carousal. The prophet at the command of Jehovah has been on the watch tower, and has now seen the foe coming against Babylon. He makes this the occasion of warning to his own people.

Very brief but very forceful is the burden of Dumah. The prophet has heard some inquiring voice demanding the hour of the night. In briefest words he answers, declaring that he sees morning and night, and inviting further inquiry.

The burden of Arabia consists of a vision and interpretation. The vision is of a fugitive people. The interpretation is of judgment coming on the children of Kedar within a year.

ISAIAH 22

In the midst of the prophecies concerning the nations occurs one of protest against the indifference of Jerusalem to the prophet's messages. He first describes the joyous people as they stand in contrast to him, with his sorrow and his broken heart. He introduces his description by inquiring what ails them. He then declares it to be a day of discomfiture, and speaks of the gathering armies and of the siege of the city. It was a day in which Jehovah had called to mourning, and they were filled with merriment. This was an unpardonable sin, as it revealed their absolute callousness. Immediately following this protest, the prophet utters his denunciation on Shebna, the ruler, filled with pride, declaring that he would be rejected from his office. His place was to be taken by Eliakim, whose appointment and administration are described. This is another instance in which for us the local application is overshadowed by the Messianic values.

ISAIAH 23

The burden of Tyre opens with a graphic description of her desolation. Her harbors are closed. Her borders are desolate. The sea, which had been her highway, is abandoned, and Egypt, her ally, is affrighted at the report. The desolation is then contemplated, and the inquiry, "Who hath purposed this against Tyre?" is answered. This desolation is the act of Jehovah.

In view of this fact, the utter overthrow is again described. The prophet then declares definitely that for seventy years Tyre is to be forgotten. After seventy years she is to be visited by Jehovah, and restored to a position of affluence. There is no hint of Tyre turning at any time to God. According to this prophecy, when restored she will still play the harlot with the kings of the earth. Her restoration is to be in some way in the economy of God, of service to His own people. Nothing more than this is intended.

ISAIAH 24

In these last chapters of the second circle, the prophet takes a still wider outlook. He sees how all the world is under the government of God. In this chapter the prophet states the fact in general terms, and describes a world-wide desolation determined on by Jehovah. This determination is first declared. Jehovah has spoken the word. After having stated this, the prophet describes the visitation following on this determination. The earth itself is seen to mourn and fade away, devoured by a curse, while all mirth ceases. The city is desolate. As the prophet looks out on this terrible scene, he seems to hear some note of hope. Somewhere the voices of singers are heard. The hope gives way to despair as suddenly as it appears, for there is nothing before the prophet's vision save judgment and desolation. The prophecy of world-wide judgment ends with the declaration that it will be the act of Jehovah, and will issue in His perfect victory.

ISAIAH 25

Immediately following this terrible description is a prophecy which, in the form of praise, declares the activity of Jehovah. The song first offers praise for judgment both in its procedure, as it destroys the false city, and in its results, as by such action God manifests Himself as the Succorer and Helper of the afflicted.

The result of this activity will be spreading the feast in the mountain of the Lord, and His illumination of all the nations, followed by the ending of sorrow and the wiping away of tears.

At last Jehovah's own afflicted people will break forth into a song of praise as they come to know Him; and their enemies, comprehensively spoken of as Moab, will finally be overcome and cast out.

ISAIAH 26

Naturally following this prophecy of praise for the activity of Jehovah is the great song which will be sung in the day of Jehovah's ultimate victory. It is praise for the establishment of the city, and for deliverance. The deep secret of the new condition is the secret of the mind stayed on Jehovah. In Him is the Rock of Ages. He has overcome enemies and established the just.

The song merges into one of praise for this Jehovah. Other lords have had dominion, but it is Jehovah who has increased the nation and enlarged the borders of the land. Again the song becomes one of praise for deliverance. The prophet refers to the pain and travail of the past. The new condition is as resurrection out of such death, and praise is therefore fitting. Remembering that he is still speaking in the midst of judgment, the processes of which must proceed to consummation, the prophet utters a final call to the people of God, urging them to quietness and patience until the indignation be past.

ISAIAH 27

This circle of prophecy ends with a message which describes the process toward ultimate restoration, and announces its certainty. The way to restoration is the way of judgment, and this the prophet first announces in figurative language.

The first issue of judgment will be restoration of God's chosen people, and the prophet refers to this under the figure of the vineyard. This figure stands in striking contrast to that in chapter five. The vineyard of the Lord of hosts is now seen as kept by Him, and watered every moment, and the plant of His choice is seen filling the world with fruit. The process of such restoration is judgment, and the prophet declares this in the next section of the message. A ruined vineyard is always the result of failure, and on such failure the Lord can have no compassion.

The last note is hope. The broken and scattered people are to be brought back at the sound of the trumpet, and are to realize their highest vocation, that is, worshiping Jehovah in their holy mountain at Jerusalem.

ISAIAH 28

Here begins the third and last circle of the first division of the book. It consists of a series of prophecies concerning the chosen people and the world.

In this chapter we have a graphic revelation of the difficulties with which Isaiah had to contend, and of his unswerving loyalty to truth. It falls into four parts. In the first (verses 1-6), the prophet announces the judgment on Ephraim. His glorious beauty is to be consumed before the oncoming scourge. This judgment, however, is to move toward the ultimate victory of Jehovah. The second part (verses 7-13), reveals how the message of the prophet was received. It opens with a vivid picture of an unhallowed carousal, in which priest and prophet alike are overcome by strong drink. Then their taunting of the prophet is recorded, "Whom will he teach knowledge?" To this he answers by declaring that there is another method of speech, and moreover, that there was purpose in the halting method he had adopted. He then warns the scorners of their folly (verses 14-22), describing their false covenant with death, declaring Jehovah's word that it shall be disannuled, and urging them to cease their scorning. Finally (verses 23-29), by a series of remarkable illustrations drawn from agriculture the prophet declares that the judgments of God are methodical and move perpetually to purpose.

ISAIAH 29

This is the first of a series of declamations concerning the chosen people, and sets forth the purpose of Jehovah in judgment. The message opens with a description of the judgment (verses 1-4), and declares how suddenly all the foes of Jerusalem shall be discomfited (verses 5-8). The prophet then breaks out into a mourning description of the condition of the people. They are blind, and unable to understand the messages delivered (verses 9-12). This blindness he declares to be the result of their infidelity to God.

In the remaining part of the prophecy he continues his declaration of the purpose of Jehovah concerning them. After denouncing the conspirators who were attempting to mislead the people, and warning them that they cannot be hidden from Jehovah, he breaks out into a fine description of the coming deliverance. This deliverance is to be characterized by a restoration of sensibility to the people who have been blind and stupid. This is to be followed by a restoration of order in which all the oppressed will obtain the justice which so long has been lacking. And, finally, there will be the restoration of the true order in sanctification of the holy name and establishment of right relationship with Jehovah.

ISAIAH 30

This chapter contains two distinct messages. In the first, the prophet denounces an alliance with Egypt (verses 1-26), and in the second foretells the destruction of Assyria (verses 27-33).

In the matter of the Egyptian alliance the prophet denounces the secret treaty, declares the shame and uselessness of it. He is instructed to write what shall be a testimony against the people. This he does by first describing the rebellious attitude which they have adopted, then by declaring how Jehovah will break in pieces the things in which they trust, and, finally, by indicating what their true attitude should have been, and declaring their refusal to adopt it and their consequent discomfiture. Yet the intention of Jehovah is gracious, and He waits for them until they are restored to the spirit of willingness, and are ready to sweep out idolatry. In answer to this, they are brought back to prosperity, which is described in its relation to the new glory of the land.

The destruction of Assyria is announced by a description of Jehovah coming in judgment. This will be the occasion for His people to sing a song of rejoicing and deliverance, which will result in completely and relentlessly sweeping away the oppressing nation. This prophecy of the destruction of Assyria at this point was intended to show the people of God how unnecessary it was for them to turn to Egypt for help.

ISAIAH 31

The prophet again denounces the alliance with Egypt. He declares that the sin of it is a false trust consequent on the chosen people turning their back on Jehovah. The folly of it is manifest in the fact that all their plotting cannot circumvent Jehovah, who is wise, and will certainly proceed against the workers of iniquity.

He then describes the attitude of Jehovah, first as One in whose power the people are as surely as is the prey in the grasp of the lion, and yet He is determined to protect, to deliver, to preserve Jerusalem. In view of this revelation of the divine attitude the prophet appeals to the people to turn again to Him from whom they had revolted. He anticipates their obedience, and describes how in the day of their return they will cast away their idols. This is their true policy, for when they do this, the Assyrian will fall, not by the sword of man, but by the act of Jehovah.

ISAIAH 32

In this message the prophet describes the reign of the coming King, and then suddenly appeals to the women. He describes the reign of the King as establishment of order and creation of refuge and refreshment for all in distress. The beneficent effects of such a reign are restoration of sensibility and a true sense of values, in which men will know violence and call it by its right name, and recognize true nobility. Evidently conscious of how different were the circumstances in which he was exercising his ministry from those described, he appeals to the women. He calls them to abandon their ease and gird themselves with sackcloth before the devastation of the city. This in order to be restored by the outpouring of the Spirit.

This recognition for the second time of the influence of women in the course of this volume is a revelation of the prophet's keen insight and accurate apprehension of one of the most prolific causes of national disaster. A degraded womanhood always creates a dissipated and enervated manhood.

ISAIAH 33

This chapter celebrates a great victory, and is prophetic of the method of the final triumph. In the first thirteen verses we have the prophet's appeal, in which there are two movements. In the first he describes the foe, lifts his cry to God, and declares his confidence in God. In the second he makes his appeal, describes the need, and announces the divine answer.

Following this is a graphic description of the effect produced by the consciousness of the presence of God as of a fire. The sinners are afraid. The righteous dwell in safety in the midst of its burning. In the rest of the chapter we have in detail the answer of Jehovah to the appeal of His servant. It is the vision of the King and of the land. The coming of the King will mean the safety of such as put their trust in Him. They will muse on the terror, but it will have departed, and the city will be quiet and full of peace.

The prophet then breaks out into an exceedingly beautiful description of the safety of the city, God-delivered and God-governed. Jehovah will be to it a river of defense. In the midst of it He will administer its affairs in justice. With such a God, all the attempts of the enemy to overcome the city are useless. Everywhere there is healing for the people, both physically and spiritually.

ISAIAH 34

This and the following chapter constitute the second part of the final circle of the prophecies of judgment. Terrible indeed is the description of world-wide desolation which this chapter presents. The nations, the people, and the whole earth are summoned to hear. Jehovah declares His indignation, and announces His determination to act in a judgment which will involve the whole earth and the host of heaven.

From this wide outlook, the prophet passes to a description of the judgment of God on Edom, which illustrates the larger truth already declared. In this terrible passage (verses 5-17) the reason of the divine vengeance is revealed in the statement, "For it is the day of the Lord's vengeance, the year of recompense in the controversy of Zion."

ISAIAH 35

The message of this chapter stands in close relation to the message of the preceding one, and yet in almost startling contrast to it. That was a picture of desolation. This is one of restoration. As in the former the whole earth was described as having been brought into confusion and emptiness, this great song opens with a description of the restoration of natural order. In all the beauty and glory of His rule men are to see anew "the glory of Jehovah, the excellency of God." This is to be brought about by the coming of God. It is a message of hope to the weak and the feeble. It is the explanation of the fearful vengeance described in the previous chapter. Through that vengeance God moves to this victory.

The glorious issues of the divine activity are then declared, as they will be realized by His own chosen people. There will be an end of all the spiritual dullness of which the prophet has so consistently reminded them. All material defense will be removed, and a highway will be constructed. Finally the ransomed of the Lord will return, and sorrow and sighing will pass away. According to the whole teaching of the Old Testament concerning the purposes of God, this earthly restoration of His people will issue in world-wide blessing.

ISAIAH 36

This chapter is the first of four which constitute a brief historical interlude. All have to do with Hezekiah and Isaiah. The first two are related to the prophecies of judgment so far as they are of local application. They deal with the invasion under Sennacherib. The last two are related to the prophecies of peace. They deal with Hezekiah's sickness and ultimate folly, and form the historic background to the great utterances which set forth the ultimate purpose of God.

In this first of the four, the story of Sennacherib's invasion and Rabshakeh's mission to the city is chronicled. He first met three representatives of Judah: Eliakim, Shebna, and Joah. He taunted them with their weakness, desiring to bully them into submission by telling them that it was useless for them to trust in Egypt; moreover, that it was useless for them to trust in God, because they were there by His commission, which, of course, was a daring and blasphemous lie. The deputation from Judah attempted to persuade him to speak in Aramaic, as they were afraid that the Jews, hearing such words in their own language, would be filled with panic.

He immediately seized on the suggestion, and spoke to the people assembled on the wall in their own language, warning them against trusting in Hezekiah, promising them plenty in another land, and declaring to them that God was unable to deliver them. The loyalty of the people is manifest in the fact that they remained silent.

ISAIAH 37

Penitently, went Hezekiah immediately into the house of the Lord, while he sent messengers to Isaiah. The prophet sent them back with words of encouragement, declaring that God would deliver them. In the meantime Rabshakeh returned to the king in Assyria, and a letter was dispatched to Hezekiah warning him against being deceived by God. This letter he spread before the Lord, and prayed to Him for deliverance. His prayer was characterized by a great simplicity. It was the simplicity of faith which recognized the throne of God, declared the immediate peril threatening the people, and asked for a deliverance which would vindicate the honor of the name of Jehovah. Isaiah's second and fuller message to Hezekiah's declared that the sin of Sennacherib was blasphemy against the Holy One of Israel, and forgetfulness of the fact that he, too, in all his enterprises was within the sphere of Jehovah's government and power. His judgment was imminent, and his boastings vain.

The chapter ends with an account of the destruction of the Assyrian army by the direct act of God, and the death of Sennacherib at the hands of his sons.

ISAIAH 38

In this chapter we have the story of the sickness of Hezekiah. That sickness would seem to have been intimately connected with the invasion of Sennacherib, for in Isaiah's message to Hezekiah that his prayer was heard it was promised, "I will deliver thee and this city out of the hand of the king of Assyria; and I will defend this city."

The last verse of the chapter tells us that Hezekiah had asked a sign that he should go up to the house of the Lord, this in explanation of the account of the sign of the dial given in verses 7 and 8. The going up to the house referred to is in all probability that described in chapter 37, when he went there penitently in the hour of Rabshakeh's taunting. All this would indicate that his sickness was due to some failure on his part. Turning to the Lord, he sought deliverance, and his life was lengthened by fifteen years. In the middle of the chapter we have the psalm of praise which Hezekiah wrote to celebrate his deliverance. It first describes the days of darkness in which he found himself in the noontide of life, approaching the gates of death. In the second part he breaks out in praise of God for deliverance, and throughout the whole of it there is evident his consciousness that the affliction itself had wrought good in his life. After the deliverance he consecrated himself anew to Jehovah, to His praise, and to His service.

ISAIAH 39

This brief chapter tells the story of Hezekiah's folly. After his recovery an embassy came from Babylon ostensibly to congratulate him. That their real motive was sinister is evident from the attitude of Isaiah when he came to the king and rebuked him. Hezekiah, flattered by their coming, showed them all his treasures, and thus gave away secrets which should have been hidden from their eyes. The prophet rebuked him, and foretold that the very things which he had shown the visitors would one day be carried into Babylon, and that his issue would be eunuchs in the palace of the king of Babylon. All this was literally fulfilled. Hezekiah's answer to the prophet was submission and thankfulness as he recognized that for the remainder of his life at least there would be peace and truth.

ISAIAH 40

We now commence the prophecies of peace, which also fall into three divisions, dealing in turn with the purpose of peace (40-48), the Prince of Peace (49-57), the program of peace (58-66).

The first eleven verses of chapter forty constitute a prologue to the whole Book. This prologue opens with a declaration which indicates the burden of all that is to follow. "Comfort ye, comfort ye My people." It then describes the making of a highway for God along which He will move toward the ultimate accomplishment, and closes with a commission to announce the good tidings to Jerusalem that Jehovah will act as a mighty One, and yet with the tenderness of a Shepherd.

In the remainder of the chapter we have the prophet setting forth the majesty of Jehovah, which forms a fitting introduction to all that follows. This majesty is described essentially in its might, in its wisdom, and in the ease of its government of the nations. It is then described by comparison. The impossibility of making anything that will represent God is declared, and a graphic illustration is given in the case of the graven image or of the idol of wood. It is finally declared to be demonstrated in creation by actual government on earth, and in the heavens, and finally in its method of grace with Israel.

ISAIAH 41

Having thus announced the majesty of Jehovah, the prophet proceeds to utter his general manifesto. This occupies chapters forty-one and forty-two. In chapter forty-one Jehovah challenges the island and the people to come near to judgment, that is, to consider what He has to say. He declares that He, and He alone has raised up the one from the East whose progress is victorious. The confederacy of the people against Cyrus is described, and then the prophet declares Jehovah's purpose of peace for Israel. Israel is the chosen and kept servant of God, upheld against foes, and the prophet predicts the ultimate restoration of the chosen people. Again he challenges the enemies to prove their power by prophetic utterance.

Finally Jehovah declares that it is He who alone can raise up the deliverer, or declare beforehand the fact of His coming. The whole movement of this chapter is a challenge preparatory to the presentation of the Servant of God. It is intended to show that apart from Jehovah the people cannot know the course of events, neither can they produce one strong enough to work deliverance. It opens with the command to keep silence in the presence of God, and closes with a declaration of the weakness and vanity of all that are opposed.

ISAIAH 42

The manifesto now presents the great Servant of Jehovah. His person is first described. His manifestation is announced (verse 1), His mission is declared (verse 1), His method is described (verses 2,3), and His might is affirmed (verse 4).

Then His relation to Jehovah is indicated in the words of Jehovah. He is called, held, kept, and given, and all that for purposes of deliverance. The ultimate purpose is the glory of Jehovah. The prophet immediately breaks forth into a song of confidence, calling on the whole earth to give glory to Jehovah. This is followed by a new declaration of the purpose of Jehovah in His very words. First, His compassion is spoken of. For a long time He had been silent, but now would cry out, and that finally in the interest of peace and his determination to bring deliverance to His people.

The chapter closes with the prophet's appeal to the people in view of the great manifesto. He first describes their failure. Israel is thought of in its purpose in the economy of God, as His servant, but is declared to be blind. To them he appeals to hearken for the time to come, and declares that their suffering has all been the result of their sin.

ISAIAH 43

Following the manifesto, we have in the next three chapters a series of messages of Jehovah. The first declares His perpetual purpose for His people. His constant attitude of love is affirmed in promises which gain their force from the fact that they glance back at past deliverances. Passing through waters, and through rivers, walking through fire, they are to be safe, for they have been safe in such conditions.

Then deliverance is definitely promised, in which the north must give up, and the south must not keep back. The present purpose of God is that the blind people who yet have eyes and the deaf who still have ears should be brought forth. Israel has sadly failed as the servant of God, but her ultimate deliverance and the fulfilment of her vocation as witness are sure because of what God is and of what He is able to do. The declaration ends with the announcement and challenge, "I will work, and who shall reverse it?"

In the second message God's present purpose of deliverance is described in greater detail. For the sake of Israel all her foes are to be destroyed. In the midst of this declaration, and for the encouragement of faith, an appeal is made to past history. "Remember ye not the former things, neither consider the things of old." These things, however, are to be superseded by the new, and the purpose is that the people of Jehovah may set forth His praise. This announcement is followed by an appeal to the people in which their sin is described. God's pardon is promised, and their punishment is again explained.

ISAIAH 44

The beginning of this chapter (verses 1-5) contains the gracious promise of the outpouring of the Spirit of God, and a description of the blessing of refreshment and renewal which will come to Israel, and the consequent influence on other people.

In this message the power of Jehovah is compared with that of idols. Jehovah begins by declaring Himself to be the first and the last, the only God, knowing, and declaring, and appointing. Because these things are so, appeal is made to the people not to fear. Then follows a remarkable passage setting forth the folly of idolatry. Those who make the graven image are vanity, and their work is unprofitable. With fine satire, the whole method is described. Men put their strength into fashioning an idol of metal, and yet become hungry, and there is none to feed them. Others work in wood, making gods out of the residue spared from burning. All are so blind that they do not see the folly of their procedure. Israel is called on to remember and turn to Jehovah, who is the God of redemption as well as the God of creation.

The fourth message (verses 24-28) is a brief one, which yet majestically sets forth the might of Jehovah. He is powerful in the material realm, He governs in the moral, and moves forward toward the restoration of His people, appointing His servant, and declaring His purpose.

ISAIAH 45

The fifth of these messages of Jehovah is a charge to Cyrus. First of all, it utters to him the promises of God which are intended to be his strength in carrying out the divine purpose. These all emphasize the ability and activity of Jehovah. He next declares the purpose for which His servant is called and equipped. It is a twofold purpose. First, for Israel's sake; and, second, in order that the world may know that He alone is God. He then declares His power to be universal, and the charge ends with a protest against objections which may be made to the appointment of Cyrus.

The sixth message is a brief one (verses 14-17), in which Jehovah again declares His purpose for His people. It is that the peoples shall submit themselves, and that Israel shall be saved with an everlasting salvation.

The seventh and final message (verses 18-25) declares His purpose for the ends of the earth. His original purpose was that the world should be inhabited. His purpose for His own people was that they might seek Him, and manifest His righteousness. His purpose for all the peoples is their salvation. Comparing Himself with idols, He declares that in right relation to Him salvation may be found, and in no other way.

ISAIAH 46

This chapter and the next contain the prophecy of the fall of Babylon. This one describes the failure of the gods. It opens with a graphic picture of the idols being hurried away for safety, carried on beasts of burden. In immediate contrast the prophet describes Jehovah as carrying His people, and the contrast is endorsed as He inquires, "To whom will ye liken Me, and make Me equal, and compare Me, that we may be like?" Thus He sets forth the fundamental difference between false gods and the true. They have to be carried. He carries. On the basis of this the prophet appeals to the transgressors to remember it; and to the stout-hearted, that is to the enemies of His people, to hearken, and to understand that He will yet be the Deliverer of His own.

ISAIAH 47

The prophecy is now addressed to Babylon itself, and in language full of force and beauty describes its judgment. The description is fourfold. First, the degradation of the city is foretold. From a proud position it is to descend to grinding and shame.

Moreover, this is to be a position of disgrace. Babylon is to pass into darkness, and no more to be called "The Lady of Kingdoms."

Yet again the judgment is to issue in desolation. The proud city which had made its boast that it could not be moved, and would never know sorrow, is to be made childless and widowed in a day, and this in spite of all sorcery and enchantment.

Finally, the judgment will be the utter destruction of the city. The fire will not be for comfort, but for burning, and all those who had trafficked with the city from her youth will abandon her, there being none to save.

ISAIAH 48

This chapter constitutes the last section of the division dealing with the purpose of peace. It is a great appeal to the people. It first describes Jehovah's methods (verses 1-11). He has had to do with a failing people, a people mentioning His name, but not in truth. His method has been that of prophecy and swift performance on account of their obstinacy, and to prevent them attributing to idols the things wrought by Jehovah. All this He has done for His own name's sake.

This method is illustrated in the calling and coming of the great Servant. The purpose of God is finally set forth. He teaches the people to profit, and the ultimate intention of His teaching is their peace and the abounding of their righteousness. Moreover, notwithstanding their failure, He is the God of redemption, and the prophecy reminds them of how He had led them through deserts, and out of rock had provided waters. The section ends with the declaration: "There is no peace, saith the Lord, unto the wicked." While His purpose is peace, they are thus solemnly warned that it cannot be realized in their experience while they persist in wickedness.

ISAIAH 49

We now commence the section in which the Prince of Peace is most clearly seen. He is revealed first as sustained through suffering (chapters 49-53), and then as singing in triumph (chapters 54-57).

In this section we hear the call of Jehovah to His own Servant, which may be divided into three parts. First, as to His Servant (verses 1-13), the isles and the peoples are commanded to understand that He is called of Jehovah. He is now described as "Israel, in whom I will be glorified," as in contrast to the national Israel, which has so grievously failed. His reply to the call declares how He had labored in vain, and yet His appeal is to Jehovah. This reply is followed by the confirmation of His call in which Jehovah declares that the first purpose of blessing to Jacob was too light a thing for Him, and proceeds to describe the worldwide influence which He will exert.

Then the call is to Zion (verses 14-21). Zion complains that she is forgotten of God, and the reply declares God's unfailing love and certain deliverance. Finally, the call is to Jehovah Himself, who announces His determination of blessing.

ISAIAH 50

Proceeding, Jehovah challenges the people to prove their assertion that they have been forsaken by producing the writing in which God has divorced His people, and declares to them that the reason of their separation was their sin, but that although Jehovah found no man, He Himself is determined on deliverance.

We now come to the answer of the Servant to the call of Jehovah. This is, first of all, a declaration of consecration to the pathway of suffering (verses 4-9). Taught of God, He is prepared to submit Himself to smiting, assured that He will be sustained by Jehovah.

Then commences a description of His ministry of suffering. In this the first thing is the brief word that separates the people. Those who fear the Lord and abide in darkness are bidden to trust. Those that walk in the light of the fire they have kindled are condemned to sorrow.

ISAIAH 51

Three messages to the faithful immediately follow. The first is a call to courage (verses 1-8), in which they are charged to look back to Abraham, to look on to the nearness of God's activity, to look around and be without fear in the presence of opposition.

The next is a cry of courage (verses 9-11), in which they first look up to the arm of the Lord, and then look back and remember how He has delivered, and, finally, look on in the assurance that He will deliver.

The last (verses 12-16) is a great message of comfort. First of all, fear is rebuked as due to forgetfulness of Jehovah, and, finally, Jehovah is pledged by His might to succor and establish His people.

Three messages to the afflicted

people as a whole follow. The first (verses 17-23) calls on Jerusalem to awake, because the end of her suffering is approaching. A graphic picture of that suffering is given in which she has been bereft of her children and overtaken by desolation and destruction. The hour has come in which the cup of staggering and of fury is taken out of her hand and put into the hand of those who afflict her.

ISAIAH 52:1-12

The second message (verses 1-6) calls on Zion to awake and put on her strength and her beautiful garments, because she is to be cleansed of all internal defilement. Though she had been sold into slavery for naught, her redemption is determined on, and she is to know Jehovah as the name of Him who is able to accomplish His purpose.

The third (verses 7-12) describes the return of Jehovah to His people. It is announced by runners and watchmen, and results in an outburst of song. In view of the certainty of this return the prophet calls on the people to cleanse themselves; and finally announces that Jehovah will go before, and the God of Israel will be the rearward.

ISAIAH 52:13—53:12

We begin our reading here because the last three verses of chapter 52 so evidently belong to chapter 53. In this section the prophet describes the completion and issue of the suffering of the Servant of God. He is first seen as exalted and lifted up, and this exaltation is put into contrast with the day of humiliation (52:13-15).

A description of the pathway of suffering (53:1-9) follows. First, the rejected ministry: the Messenger is despised, and His report is not believed. Second, the vicarious suffering, which men looked on as a visitation of God, whereas it was the mystery in which He bore the sins of the people. Finally, the atoning death, in which the Messenger humbled Himself, and was "cut off out of the land of the living," although He was the sinless One who "had done no violence, neither was any deceit in His mouth."

The description ends with another declaration of His ultimate triumph, which clearly reveals the fact that it is based on the suffering which has been described. The Servant of God is seen passing through pain to prosperity, through travail to triumph, through humbling to exaltation. This whole description is absolutely without fulfilment save in the person of the Son of God, for whom the ultimate triumph has not yet been won.

ISAIAH 54

We now come to the section which deals with the triumphant singing resulting from the work of the Servant of God, and this chapter is the song of assurance. It first sets forth the glorious fact of restoration. The people, forsaken on account of their own sin, are to be restored to the sacred relationship to Jehovah, in which He is the husband. The borders are to be enlarged in order that the growth of the people may find room, and all this because the end of forsaking has come. It must not be forgotten that this song of restoration follows immediately the description of the suffering and triumph of the Servant of God.

The second half of the song describes the glory of restoration. The city is to be rebuilt in material magnificence. Its life is to be conditioned in moral rectitude. The children are to be taught of Jehovah. The civic strength is to be righteousness, and all oppression is to be banished.

Finally, the reconstituted people are to be impregnable. No enemy will be able to gain an advantage over them, and no weapon formed against them shall prosper.

ISAIAH 55

Immediately following the song we have the prophet's great appeal. It is made in the consciousness of the victory won by the Servant of the Lord and the consequent possibility of restoration offered to the people. Nevertheless it distinctly sets forth the solemn conditions on which advantage may be taken of the great provision.

It first recognizes the need of the people in the verses which describe their condition as thirsty, as being without money, as spending "money for that which is not bread," and earnestly urges them to turn and listen to Him who has been given as a "Witness to the peoples," as a "Leader and Commander."

In this second part the appeal is made with greater directness, and the terms on which the people may find their way back into relationship with God are distinctly stated.

The whole ends with a description, full of poetry and beauty, of the conditions of fruitfulness and joy and prosperity which must follow return to the Lord and submission to His government.

ISAIAH 56

This division ends with two chapters (56 and 57) which set forth certain aspects of the administration of the Kingdom. The first is intended to comfort those who by recent promises of restoration made to the people of God were likely to be discouraged. Strangers would say, "The Lord will surely separate me from His people," and, in view of the hope of the growth of the nation, the eunuch would declare, "Behold, I am a dry tree." Both these are comforted. To the latter is promised a memorial and a name in the house of God better than that of sons and daughters. The strangers are told that as they join themselves to the Lord, to be His ministers who love His name, they also will be welcomed to His holy mountain. It is a declaration which reveals the prophet's understanding that the coming victory will have a wider application than merely to the chosen people.

While there is welcome for the strangers who submit to the Lord, there is to be the severest judgment of evil, even when it manifests itself among the chosen people. The beasts of the field are summoned to devour the blind watchman and the drunken leaders.

ISAIAH 57

Because of the failure of these blind watchmen and drunken leaders, righteous men perish, while none lay it to heart. Moreover, the people have yielded to the evil influences of such leaders; "sons of the sorceress" are summoned to judgment. Their sin has been exalted and manifest, and their judgment is to be conspicuous and complete.

Yet again the declaration turns to such as are contrite and penitent. Jehovah declares Himself to be the One inhabiting eternity, and yet dwelling with the contrite and humble in spirit. In the case of such His judgment is turned into a ministry of healing. All this again follows, and is dependent on, the suffering Servant as described in the previous section. Again, the division ends with solemn warning against wickedness. Although in the economy of God the Prince is to be sustained and finally victorious, yet there is no peace to the wicked.

ISAIAH 58

We now commence the last division of the book, which deals with the program of peace as it sets forth the conditions, describes the ultimate realization, and insists on a principle of discrimination.

In dealing with conditions the prophet first declares the moral requirements. This message consists of a condemnation of formalism and a description of true religion. Jehovah's charge against the people is that they have observed the external ordinances of religion, and yet have complained that God has not answered them. In reply to this complaint Jehovah charges them with selfishness even in worship, and declares that their prayer is not heard, affirming that He does not accept the prostration of the body which is unaccompanied by affliction of soul.

In a passage full of beauty true religion, with its rewards, is then described. It is expressed in rightness of action, and tenderness, which is rewarded by light, and fellowship, and answered prayer. In these external observances, such as that of the Sabbath, they must be free from all selfishness, and characterized by delight in the Lord. This is followed by true exaltation, and the realization of the promises of Jehovah.

ISAIAH 59

Continuing, the prophet makes confession of moral failure. This he does first by declaring the reason for national suffering. It is not to be found in Jehovah's inability, nor in His unwillingness. The iniquities of the people have separated them and their God.

In a terrible passage, the prophet confesses the appalling corruption, and immediately describes the suffering which followed, the groping in the dark, even though it is noonday; the longing for a salvation which does not come, all of which results from the people's own transgression, as the prophet clearly declares.

Having thus shown that all the suffering of the people resulted from their own sin, and made it evident there must be a return to God if there is to be a return to peace, the prophet now describes how restoration will come. It is to be wholly a victory by Jehovah. It is based on His knowledge of the people's sin, and on the fact that they are unable to provide an intercessor. It is the result of His own action. His arm brings salvation, and necessarily His first work is judgment. Finally, a "Redeemer shall come to Zion," and the results shall be the creation of a new spiritual covenant.

ISAIAH 60

In this and the next two chapters, we have a glorious description of the ultimate realization of the purposes of God. It commences with a declaration of the material prosperity of the people described in the last verses of the previous chapter. The breaking of the new day is first spoken of. The holy nation is a center of light in the midst of surrounding darkness. The glory of Jehovah manifest, nations and kings gather to the new center.

A graphic description of the returning exiles follows. The scattered sons and daughters are seen gathering home, bearing with them the wealth of the nations, and followed by the peoples.

The established city is then seen built by strangers, while surrounding peoples submit themselves, or perish; and Jehovah is known as Saviour, Redeemer, and Mighty One.

The ultimate conditions of the high noon of prosperity are set forth. Material prosperity and moral rectitude are to issue from perfect government. The glory of the people is to be Jehovah Himself, and the issue is perfect gladness. The days of mourning are to be ended, and all weakness change into strength.

ISAIAH 61

Passing from the description of material prosperity, the prophecy describes the inner secret, namely, spiritual realization. This description opens with a new declaration of the Servant of the Lord. The anointed Messenger declares His appointment, and describes His program. All the deliverance described is to be due to the message which He delivers. In the light of the use made of this passage by Christ, it is interesting to consider the program.

"To proclaim the acceptable year of the Lord" is the first item. At that point Jesus ceased His reading in the synagogue. Next will come "the day of vengeance of our God." That will be the period of judgment. Beyond it, "to comfort all that mourn." Therefore the description of the glorious restoration has reference to what still lies in the future. In that future the people of God will be His priests, His ministers. Themselves redeemed from shame and from confusion, they will exert an influence for righteousness among the peoples, who, in their turn, will recognize the truth and submit themselves to it.

ISAIAH 62

Having thus dealt with the material prosperity, and with the spiritual realization, the prophet now describes in greater detail the vocational fulfilment. Speaking as in the midst of circumstances of incompleteness, he declares his desire, and avows his determination neither to hold his peace nor to rest until the people of God fulfil His ideal, so that He is vindicated among the nations. There is no uncertainty in his heart, for he declares his conviction that the people shall yet be called Hephzibah rather than Forsaken, and their land Beulah rather than Desolate.

ISAIAH 63

The last section of Isaiah (63-66) sets forth anew the operation of the principle of discrimination. All the blessing which has been described can result only from holiness, and ere that can be established there must be the period of judgment.

In the first section the prophet describes the Warrior returning from the conflict. While that conflict is described, it is from the standpoint of its completion. One is seen returning with crimson garments, marching in the greatness of His strength. In answer to the prophet's inquiry as to who this is, the Warrior declares, "I that speak in righteousness, mighty to save." This answer reveals the method and the purpose. Again the prophet asks for explanation, and then the conflict is described. It has been one of vengeance, in which all opposing forces have been swept away in order to establish righteousness and bring salvation.

The prophet's sense of the absolute justice of the judgment described is manifest in that he immediately breaks forth into praise of the lovingkindnesses of the Lord. In language full of beauty he describes Jehovah's faithfulness to His people. His description looks back to the days in which, in spite of their rebellion and their grieving of His Holy Spirit, through which He was necessarily made their enemy, He nevertheless carried them, and remembered them, and delivered them.

ISAIAH 64

The praise and confession merge into a prayer in which the sore need of the people is first described, and then a cry full of intense anguish is lifted for the dawning of the day when Jehovah will act in judgment.

Again the prophet strengthens his

own faith as he remembers how God had wrought on behalf of His people in the past. This memory of His faithfulness produces a new sense of their unfaithfulness, and he confesses sin and failure. Out of the midst of desolation and destruction he appeals to Jehovah to act on behalf of His people.

ISAIAH 65

In this chapter we have a graphic description of the working of the principle of discrimination, the sifting of the people by God. There is first a contrast between the false and the true. The rebellious people are described as those who, in spite of all Jehovah's patience, still persist in idolatrous and evil practices. Against these Jehovah is compelled to proceed in strict and severe judgment.

Then follows a description of the remnant, the holy seed, those who are described as the servants of Jehovah. These are not to be destroyed by the wicked, but are to be led out of the places of difficulty into inheritance and prosperity.

The sifting process is next described, and the life of the servants of God and the life of the rebellious are placed in striking contrast: eating as against hunger, drinking as against thirst, rejoicing as against shame, singing as against crying and howling. The result of the sifting of judgment is the establishment of the new order, that establishment of the Kingdom of God which is to be one of joy and justice, of prosperity and peace.

ISAIAH 66

This last chapter is confessedly difficult of interpretation. In it the prophet seems to look beyond all that he has previously described, and to deal with destiny. He first announces anew the fact of the established government of God, and then proceeds to show how that for those who had chosen their own ways He will choose delusions, and that because when He called they did not answer. Those who had trembled at His word He will deliver, in spite of all difficulties.

In the final message the prophet describes the coming of Jehovah with fire, when His chariots will be like the whirlwind. It is a picture of righteous vengeance, proceeding to the establishment of the new heavens and the new earth which are to remain before the Lord.

The last declaration of the great prophecy is one which reminds those who read of the sure and terrible judgment of God on evil, of the one fact which must never be lost sight of, that there can be no peace to the wicked.

Jeremiah

JEREMIAH 1

The first three verses constitute a title page naming the author and giving the dates of the period during which he exercised his ministry. The Book opens with the account of Jeremiah's call, and at once reveals the clearness of that call and his shrinking from the great work. With great patience Jehovah bore with Jeremiah's fear, and encouraged him by words and signs. It is interesting to note how the "I" of Jehovah was set over against the "I" of Jeremiah.

Two signs were granted to him, the first, the almond tree, being life in the midst of death, or spring following winter. In a day when the word of the Lord seemed to be forgotten entirely, Jehovah declared, "I watch over My word to perform it."

The second was a seething cauldron, the sign of coming destruction. After these signs the word of divine command was spoken to Jeremiah, and strength equal to the task awaiting him was promised.

JEREMIAH 2

The first movement in commissioning the called man now commences. He was commanded to utter a great impeachment in the ears of Jerusalem.

This impeachment was threefold. It first declared how Israel had forsaken Jehovah, the fountain of living waters, and hewed out cisterns for themselves. In the second place, Israel was charged with obstinate sinfulness, the meaning of her suffering was declared, the folly of her alliances was pointed out, the guilt of her degeneracy was pronounced, the falseness of her denial of sin was denounced, the helplessness of her gods was declared, and the injustice of her protest was affirmed.

This section moves forward in the form of question and answer. The impeachment ends with a summary, charging Israel with lack of love, obstinate impenitence, and useless alliances.

JEREMIAH 3

Following the impeachment, the prophet appealed to the people to return. This appeal commenced with a declaration that Jehovah's love was greater than man's in that He was willing to receive back the people who had been unfaithful if they would return to Him.

Jeremiah then pointed out the conditions of return, describing the sin of Israel, and of Judah, and appealing to each in turn. Of course, his message was principally to Judah, as he pointed out that because Judah had persisted in her sin, in spite of all she had seen of the evil results in the case of Israel, her attitude was more terrible than that of Israel.

This is followed by the recitation of an ideal confession for the sinning people. Weeping, they make their supplication. Recognizing the vanity of expecting help from any source other than Jehovah, they turn to Him with confession of sin.

JEREMIAH 4

Jehovah immediately promised that if Israel would return, she would be established. Then the prophet declared that judgment was determined on. He appealed to the people to repent, and that not in external manifestation, but actually and in heart. The people are described as panic-stricken because of the imminent peril.

In a parenthesis (verse 10), the prophet's anguish is revealed as he sees the judgment falling. Nevertheless he continued his message, and described the swift attack of the foe, again earnestly appealing to Jerusalem to turn from wickedness.

After this description his anguish again is manifest in a lament (verses 19-26). He was pained at his very heart as he saw the destruction coming, and the more so as he recognized that it was the result of their own sin. The picture which spread itself before his vision was of widespread devastation. Notwithstanding his sorrow, he declared that the judgment was inevitable, because the word of the Lord had been uttered, and warned the people of the anguish which must be their portion in the day of visitation.

JEREMIAH 5

Having thus declared that judgment was determined on, the prophet now carefully declared the reason for it. This was, first, the utter corruption of conduct. Among the people not a man was to be found who was truthful and just. Disappointed in his search, he turned to the great men and the rulers, and they also had "broken the yoke and burst the bands." Therefore judgment was indeed inevitable, and pardon impossible.

The second reason was that they did not believe the message. They had declared that punishment would not fall on them. The declaration of judgment is then repeated, and the terror of it is described. When it falls, if they inquire why Jehovah has thus visited them, the reply would be because they had forsaken Him.

Finally, the reason for final judgment is the revolting and rebellious heart of the people. They were not ignorant, but obstinate. They had eyes, but saw not, and ears, but heard not. They had flung off the fear of God deliberately. Greed had been their curse, and had expressed itself in this persistent rebellion. The whole reason is graphically summarized as "a wonderful and horrible thing." Prophets, priests, and people were united in their sin, and there was no alternative other than that of judgment.

JEREMIAH 6

This judgment the prophet now described. A fierce and relentless foe, acting under the word of Jehovah, is described as coming up against Jerusalem. The prophet declared that the city would be taken, and described the thoroughness of the judgment under the figure of gleaning. All ages would be affected, and the whole land as well as the city be involved.

Again he declared that the reason for this judgment was the complete corruption of the people, their false sense of security, and their utter lack of shame. He appealed to the past to bear witness, but they would not attend. He appealed directly to the present, and they would not hearken. Therefore the sentence was inevitable. Returning to what he had already said, he again announced the coming of the foe from the north and the suffering of the people which would follow.

This message concluded with an account of the word spoken to the prophet by Jehovah in order to strengthen him. His position among the people was like "a tower," or, as the margin has it, "a trier," that is, one who tested them, or "a fortress." His ministry would be fruitless, for the people were grievous revolters, and the ultimate verdict is declared to be that men would call them refuse silver because Jehovah had rejected them.

JEREMIAH 7

With this section the second movement in commissioning the prophet commences. It deals first with the sins of worship. These are first denounced. At the gate of the Temple the prophet rebuked the people for putting their trust in external things, and told them that their true safety lay in amending their ways. He charged them with committing all manner of sin, and yet standing before God in His house, imagining that by this external act they would be delivered and set free to continue in abomination. He bade them take lesson from the history of Shiloh, and from what Jehovah had done with Israel.

So terrible was the condition that the prophet was charged at last not to pray for the people. Their sin was heinous and persistent, therefore all their sacrifices and offerings were refused. For this idolatry of formalism the sentence of judgment was again pronounced. They had defiled the Temple and built Topheth as a place of worship. This Topheth was to become "the valley of Slaughter," and all mirth was to end.

JEREMIAH 8

Utter desolation would overtake them so that death would be chosen rather than life. This sin of idolatry had been aggravated by the people's terrible persistence therein. If men fall it is naturally expected that they will rise, if they wander that they will return. In the case of Jerusalem this had not been so, their backsliding had been perpetual. There was no sign of repentance. The people did not know the ordinance or judgment of the Lord.

Because of this perpetual backsliding the judgment was again pronounced, and with the same care the prophet declared the reason to be their complete corruption, the false healing of their wound by prophet and priest, and their lack of shame. Therefore the judgment was to be complete.

The prophet then voiced the cry of the people in answer to the doom. It was characterized, first, by rebellion against the action of Jehovah, and then by remorse. The message ends with a new declaration of the certainty and imminence of judgment.

The strain of the terrible message on the prophet now became evident as he poured out his soul in lamentation. His perplexity was great, and he was conscious of the offended King, and the unhealing physician, and in his anguish cried out, "Why have they provoked me to anger?"

JEREMIAH 9

In answer to his own question, Jeremiah sighed for some adequate means of expressing the anguish of his heart, and then for escape to some lonely place in the wilderness. All this was in the nature of complaint against God, for he revealed most carefully how conscious he was of the sin of his people, describing it in terrible detail.

To this cry of His servant Jehovah replied in a fivefold declaration. First, that He had no choice but to afflict because of their sin; He next affirmed His own sorrow also, but by a question reminded the prophet that there was a reason for the perishing of the land and the destruction of the city.

In the next place, He plainly stated what the reason was. Their persistent rebellion had made necessary His wrath. He then called the people to lament, but insisted that it should be for right causes. Finally, He proclaimed the true ground of glorifying for man, not in his own wisdom or riches, but in his understanding and knowledge of Jehovah.

JEREMIAH 10

Here begins the third movement in the commissioning of the prophet. In it the sin of idolatry is first dealt with. The prophet revealed the unutterable folly of idolatry in a powerful contrast between idols and Jehovah. He described the vanity of idols. They were the work of the hands of man. They were unable to move, but had to be carried.

In contrast, he declared the majesty of Jehovah. Continuing the contrast, he described the weakness of idols, and the might of the true and living God. The test as between idols and Jehovah he declared to be the test of creation. Gods that had not made the heavens and the earth must perish from the earth and from under the heavens. Jehovah God had made the earth and stretched out the heavens. He, therefore, was the God of power.

Once again, the prophet suggested a contrast, but it is now between the man and idolatry, and the man and Jehovah. The former becomes brutish, while the portion of Jacob is Jehovah Himself. On the sin of idolatry he then pronounced judgment. He next uttered the wail of the people, and ended by a cry of distress to Jehovah in the presence of the destruction of Jacob.

JEREMIAH 11

He then proceeded to deal with the broken Covenant. There came to him from the Lord a special word commissioning him to pronounce a curse on "the man that heareth not the words of this covenant." To this command the prophet answered, "Amen, O Lord."

He was then commanded to proclaim in the cities of Judah and the streets of Jerusalem the failure of the fathers, how God had warned, they had disobeyed, and God therefore had visited them with punishment. This sin of the fathers was being repeated by their sons. They were guilty of a conspiracy in turning back to other gods. Therefore, judgment was determined against them, and they were abandoned of God. The thought of the broken Covenant is carried out in the summary with which the section closes, and under the most tender figure—the marriage relationship. The beloved has no longer place in the house because she has "wrought lewdness." Therefore, Jehovah visits with punishment.

The closing part of this third movement in the process of commissioning Jeremiah is occupied with an account of how Jehovah strengthened him in view of the persecution which was already stirred against him, and of the still severer troubles awaiting him. In the present section we see him in peril among the men of his own city, Anathoth.

JEREMIAH 12

Now we hear the prophet as he appealed to Jehovah to be his Defender, and, finally, we hear the divine determination concerning his evil neighbors.

This peril was revealed to him by Jehovah. It was a plot against his life. He appealed to the Lord, and was told by the declaration of His knowledge of the plot, and of the fact that the severest punishments would be meted out to these men.

The prophet then poured out his soul in questions to God. Why is it, he asked, that the wicked prosper? "How long shall the land mourn?" Jehovah's answer indicated that the things he had seen, and the trials through which he had passed were as nothing to those which awaited him. Those to come were by comparison as horses to footmen, as the swelling of Jordan to a land of peace. Concerning His people Jehovah declared that He had forsaken them. With this statement of the case the prophet agreed. He saw the judgment, and recognized its righteousness. Jehovah then declared that the evil neighbors of the prophet would be plucked up with Judah, but that there would yet be a way of deliverance for them, for He would visit them in compassion.

JEREMIAH 13

The account of this time of communion between Jeremiah and Jehovah ends with the story of how Jehovah gave him two signs, one for himself and one for the people.

That for himself was the sign of the girdle which he was to wear, then to hide by Euphrates, and then to seek in order to see its worthlessness. The significance of the sign was clearly stated to him. The girdle was the emblem of the house of Israel and of the house of Judah.

The second sign was a spoken one in the form of a proverb, "Every bottle shall be filled with wine." This he was to declare in the hearing of the people. Their obvious retort would be, "Do we not know that every bottle shall be filled with wine?" In answer he was commanded to declare that God would fill the rulers with drunkenness, and dash them one against another.

The account closes with the cry of the prophet to the people to hear, the last charge of Jehovah, which is a call to the king and queen mother, Jehoahaz and Hamutal; and an announcement of the coming judgment and its cause, the declaration of the hopelessness of the case, and a final pronouncement of doom.

JEREMIAH 14

We now come to the second division of the Book, that containing the account of the prophet's ministry. This falls into three sections: prophecies before the fall of Jerusalem (14-39), prophecies after the fall of Jerusalem (40-45), and prophecies concerning the nations (46-51).

The first series of messages declares God's determination to punish (14-17). This consists of a parable (14:1-6), an account of a controversy between the prophet and Jehovah (14:7-15), and the new charge delivered to the prophet (16, 17).

The opening parable is a graphic picture of drought. The high and the low alike are affected. The whole ground is barren, and all animal life is suffering.

After the word concerning the drought we have the account of a remarkable controversy between Jeremiah and Jehovah. In language full of stately dignity the prophet appealed to Jehovah not to persecute His people. This appeal was answered by solemn refusal. Because of the persistent wandering of the people the prophet was commanded not to pray for them, Jehovah declaring that

He would not hear them. The prophet then pleaded that the prophets had declared that they should be preserved from evil. To this Jehovah replied that they had lied. Though speaking in His name, they had not been sent by Him, and therefore they would be consumed by sword and famine. Likewise the people to whom they had prophesied must be punished.

Again Jeremiah appealed, inquiring if God had utterly forsaken His people, making confession of sin, and beseeching God's pity on the people for His own name's sake.

JEREMIAH 15

To this great appeal Jehovah again replied by declaring mercy to be impossible, and judgment inevitable, and this on account of the sin of Manasseh which had been persisted in, namely, the rejection of Jehovah by the people. Therefore they had been judged, and judgment must be completed.

On hearing this the prophet cried out in great anguish, and Jehovah promised to strengthen him, while reiterating His determination to punish the people.

Once again the prophet replied, first in resignation, and then in prayer on behalf of himself, which ended with a sigh, indicative of the strain being put on his faith. The controversy ends with Jehovah's promise that if Jeremiah would be true to the word of God, God would be to him a defense and a deliverance.

JEREMIAH 16

The controversy was immediately followed by a new charge to the prophet. Jehovah called him to a life of personal asceticism, commanding that he abstain from both mourning and mirth. That is to say, he was to stand aloof from the people in order to deliver to them the messages of his God. His messages of judgment would provoke inquiry among the people concerning the reason of God's dealings with them. The prophet was charged to make clear to them that these things resulted from their own sin. Yet immediately Jehovah declared to His servant that His purpose in judgment was the ultimate deliverance of the people.

This final word the prophet answered with an affirmation of his confidence in Jehovah, first as to his own personal safety, and then as to the ultimate issue.

JEREMIAH 17

Once again Jehovah declared His determination to deal with the people in judgment, because of the defiant definiteness of their sin. That sin was "written with a pen of iron, and with the point of a diamond." This declaration is followed by a contrast between the man who trusts in man and the "man who trusteth in Jehovah." The first dwells in the midst of desert desolation. The second is rooted by the springs of fruitfulness. This is true notwithstanding contrary appearances. Jehovah is the Searcher of hearts, and ultimately the folly of such as do wickedly must be manifest.

To these words of Jehovah the prophet replied in a great affirmation of faith, and an equally great appeal of need. In grave peril he was conscious of the place of sanctuary, namely, right relationship to the uplifted throne of Jehovah. To forsake Jehovah was to forsake the fountain of living waters. Yet the sense of need was very great, and Jeremiah appealed to Jehovah to give him His word, and to vindicate him in the sight of the people. He was then commissioned to stand in the gate of the people, and offer them the test of the Sabbath, being commanded to warn them of how their fathers failed in this respect, and also to declare to them that if they refused to hearken, the judgment must fall.

JEREMIAH 18

We now come to the second series of messages before the fall of Jerusalem (18-20), which consists of declarations of God's absolute supremacy. In preparation for this, Jeremiah was sent to the house of the potter. There he saw him at work on the wheels. Power was manifest in his manipulation of the clay, and pity in his remaking of the marred vessel.

The explanation was given to him by Jehovah Himself. The house of Israel was as clay in Jehovah's hand. All His will must be accomplished, and the people could not possibly escape His hand. This message Jeremiah was charged to deliver to the men of Judah, but they persisted in evil, and Jehovah declared their sin to be incomparable. The nations might be challenged, but they could produce nothing like it. What, then, remained but that judgment must fall?

The delivery of this message stirred up new opposition to Jeremiah, and a conspiracy was formed against his life. In resentment, he poured out his soul to Jehovah. He had pleaded their cause, and this was the return they made. Therefore it was surely in accord with the necessity of the case that they should be punished, and he appealed to Jehovah to deal with them in the time of His anger.

JEREMIAH 19

Jeremiah was now commissioned to go forth into the valley of the son of Hinnon, taking with him a potter's vessel. His message there was of judgment. Because the people had forsaken Jehovah, and had set up the most fearful abominations, even to the burning of their own sons in the fire, therefore judgment was determined against them.

This declaration of judgment Jeremiah was commanded to emphasize by breaking the vessel in the sight of the people, and declaring that in like manner Jehovah would break the people, and the city. Returning from Topheth, having obeyed this command, he stood in the court of the Lord's house and repeated the declaration of coming judgment.

JEREMIAH 20

The story of the persecution which this action stirred up against him follows. Pashur heard the prophecy, and, smiting the prophet, arrested and imprisoned him. On the following day Jeremiah, being brought out of the stocks, repeated his prophecy of judgment, singling out Pashur for special attention, declaring that on him would fall most severe punishment.

In the midst of this persecution and suffering, the prophet poured out his soul in the presence of Jehovah. Conscious that he had been compelled to declare these things, he complained that he had been the laughingstock of the people, and that the word of Jehovah had made him a reproach. He had declared that he would not mention Jehovah, nor speak any more in His name; but the word had become a burning fire, and he had been compelled to utter it. The tempestuous condition of his mind is seen in that after the complaint there was a sudden outburst of confidence in which he declared that Jehovah was with him, that his enemies should not prevail, and called for a song of praise because of deliverance.

This, however, was immediately followed by an outburst of fear, which stood in strange contrast to his former confidence. He cursed the day of his birth and lamented the continuity of his life. This reveals to us how terrible were the sufferings through which this man passed.

JEREMIAH 21

The final series before the fall of Jerusalem consists of messages delivered to Zedekiah (21-27). The occasion of these was, in the first place, Zedekiah's deputation to the prophet. The scourge which Jeremiah had foretold seemed to be imminent. Nebuchadnezzar, king of Babylon, was approaching. Zedekiah sent to inquire whether he might hope for the interference and deliverance of Jehovah. There was no halting or uncertainty in the answer which the prophet gave to the messengers.

He first foretold the disaster in detail. He then declared that the only alternative offered to them was death or captivity. His final word had to do with the house of the king. He called it to return to rectitude in government. The hopelessness of the situation was evident in the fact that, in spite of this call, the last word of the message pronounced sentence and was the clearest declaration that the doom would be by the will and act of Jehovah.

JEREMIAH 22

The message Jeremiah gave the deputation was not enough. He was commanded to go to the house of the king. This he did, and what he there said occupies the succeeding chapters up to and including chapter twenty-seven.

Arrived at the court, he, first of all, repeated at greater length his call to repentance and warning. The way of repentance is the way of restoration. The way of disobedience is the way of destruction.

He then reviewed in three movements the history of the three predecessors of Zedekiah. First, concerning Jehoahaz, he declared that there was no need to weep for Josiah who had died, but rather for Jehoahaz (that is, Shallum), who had been carried away to die in captivity. Moving on to the reign of Jehoiakim, he described the sin of his unrighteous reign, which was characterized by injustice and oppression. For this sin he had been judged and cast out from Jerusalem. Yet his influence had remained. Finally, the prophet described the doom of Jehoiakim's son Jehoiachin (Coniah), and its reason.

JEREMIAH 23

Having thus passed in review the predecessors of Zedekiah on the throne of Judah, the prophet proceeded to deal with those who had been responsible for the failure of the people, the false kings and prophets. This first section has to do with the kings.

In the divine economy the king has always been a shepherd, but the men who had held the kingly office had destroyed and scattered the sheep. This is the charge of Jehovah against them, and the prophet declared that Jehovah would visit on them the evil of their doings. Moreover, he announced the purpose of God to gather the remnant of His flock and set up over them shepherds who would feed them. In this connection his vision grew clearer, and he announced the coming of One of David's line, who would "reign as King and deal wisely," and through whom the restoration of the ancient people would be accomplished.

He then turned to the prophets. Of these he spoke out of a broken heart as he contemplated the condition of the land. He ascribed this terrible state of things to the profanation of prophet and priest. The judgment of the prophets was consequent on the falseness of the messages they had delivered. In the very presence of judgment they had spoken the lie of peace, declaring to the people that no evil would come upon them. Moreover, they had spoken without divine authority. They had dreamed their own dreams, rather than delivered the messages of Jehovah. Finally, he uttered the tremendous word of the divine judgment, beginning, "I am against the prophets, saith Jehovah." The consequence of false prophesying is unutterable confusion, and ultimately the loss of the word of authority, so that "every man's word shall be his own burden."

This section clearly reveals the prophet's accurate understanding of the process of the nation's corruption. False kings and prophets had led the people into courses of evil resulting from degraded conceptions of God. In their turn the people had willingly followed and listened, refusing the true messages of God, such as had been spoken by Jeremiah and other of the divinely appointed messengers.

JEREMIAH 24

Still speaking to Zedekiah, Jeremiah repeated three prophecies from the past, the first being a vision after Jeconiah's (Jehoiachin's) captivity, the second being a message delivered in the fourth year of Jehoiakim, and the last a yet earlier one, delivered in the beginning of Jehoiakim's reign.

The vision after Jeconiah's captivity was two baskets of figs, the first containing very good, and the second very bad, figs. The basket of good figs symbolized the captives who had been taken to the land of the Chaldeans. From them in the future Jehovah would restore His own. The basket of bad figs represented Zedekiah and those who remained in the land under him. These in the economy of God were devoted to judgment. This reminder of the vision would serve to make plain to Zedekiah the burden which the prophet had to deliver to him.

False prophets were speaking both among the captives and in Jerusalem, and throughout the remainder of Jeremiah's message to Zedekiah, he denied the authority and inspiration of these false teachers, and insisted upon the accuracy of this vision of the baskets of figs.

JEREMIAH 25

Still speaking to Zedekiah, Jeremiah reminded him of the word which came in the fourth year of Jehoiakim. It was a message announcing the judgment of God against Judah, Babylon, the nations, the world.

With regard to Judah, the reason for the judgment was her persistent sin. Notwithstanding that Jehovah had spoken constantly and called them to return to obedience, they had not hearkened. The judgment foretold was the conquest of Judah by Babylon, and her captivity for seventy years.

Moreover, the prophecy foretold the judgment of Babylon after the seventy years by a confederacy of nations and kings. Yet the prophet had seen further afield, and had declared that the judgment of God must ultimately fall on all the nations, and that there could be no escape from it.

Finally, judgment would go forth from nation to nation, until a great tempest would be raised from the uttermost parts of the earth. The severest strokes of this evil would fall on the shepherds, that is, on the kings and rulers. Thus again Zedekiah, reminded of the prophecy delivered in the fourth year of Jehoiakim, would see how inevitable was the doom now threatening himself and Jerusalem.

JEREMIAH 26

Once again Jeremiah repeated a previous message, one delivered yet earlier, "in the beginning of the reign of Jehoiakim." He had then been instructed to stand in the court of the Lord's house, and deliver his message in order to give an opportunity to the people to turn. The message itself warned them against refusing to hearken, and told of their persistent refusal and of the consequent judgment decided against them.

The message excited the hostility of the priests, prophets, and people. Jeremiah then told the story of his trial, saying he had been seized and condemned to die. The princes of Judah however, interfered, and he was placed on trial before them. The priests and the prophets charged him with speaking against the city. He answered that he had but delivered the message of Jehovah. The interference of the princes, and the defense of Jeremiah won the people to his side, and, with the princes, they declared to priests and prophets that he was not worthy of death. Certain of the elders addressed the people, declaring that to slay the prophet of the Lord would be sin, and instanced the cases of Micaiah and Uriah. Jeremiah was preserved by Ahikam.

JEREMIAH 27

Having thus repeated the vision and prophecies of the earlier times, Jeremiah again addressed himself directly to Zedekiah. There can be no doubt that the marginal reading of 27:1 must be adopted, and the word "Zedekiah" substituted for "Jehoiakim." Having shown by his vision of the baskets of figs what was determined against Judah in the way of punishment, through Babylon, the prophet now announced Jehovah's attitude in this matter. He was charged to make bands and bars. Evidently one of these the prophet wore himself, while the rest were sent to the messengers.

These messengers represented a confederacy of kings formed to resist Nebuchadnezzar. The prophet declared that all such attempts would be useless. Jehovah was absolutely supreme in governing the world, and had given the lands into the hands of Nebuchadnezzar. Those who refused to submit to him would be punished in other ways, but still by the direct act of Jehovah. Jeremiah warned these messengers therefore to pay no attention to their prophets, nor any who told them that they should not serve the king of Babylon. The divine fiat had gone forth, and the only way of escape from suffering was to bend the neck to the yoke of the king of Babylon. Those who would do so would be allowed to remain in their own land.

After this address to the messengers of all the kings, the prophet directed his attention especially to Zedekiah, urging him to submit to the king of Babylon. Again he earnestly warned Zedekiah against listening to the false prophets who were declaring that the threatened invasion and victory of Nebuchadnezzar would never occur. He suggested this test to the prophets, that they make intercession to the Lord of hosts that the vessels of Jehovah should not go to Babylon. It was an ironical suggestion, as is evidenced by the fact that he immediately declared that the word of Jehovah had irrevocably gone forth that these things should be carried into Babylon and remain there until Jehovah visited them and restored them to their own place.

JEREMIAH 28

This and the following chapter have to do with the direct relations between Jeremiah and the false prophets against whom Jeremiah so solemnly warned Zedekiah.

In this chapter we have the account of the incident between Hananiah and Jeremiah. In the house of Jehovah Hananiah told Jeremiah that Jehovah had declared that within two full years He would restore the vessels and the people, breaking the yoke of the king of Babylon. Evidently deceived, Jeremiah assented, and yet it is evident that he was not assured, for he declared to Hananiah that the only proof of divine authority was the fulfilment of prediction. He was, however, so far persuaded as to allow Hananiah to take the bar from off his neck and break it. This was done publicly, and Hananiah declared to the people that Jehovah would break the yoke of Nebuchadnezzar within two years.

Immediately the word of the Lord came to Jeremiah, contradicting all that Hananiah had declared. It is evident from the story that Jeremiah's failure was a mistake of judgment rather than any deviation from loyalty to duty. Punishment fell not on him but on Hananiah, because he had made the people to trust in a lie.

JEREMIAH 29

As a result of this false prophesying, Jeremiah sent a letter to the exiles. It is evident that they also were disturbed. The letter instructed them, first, concerning their present position, advising them to settle in Babylon and beware of false prophets. It then proceeded to declare what the future would be. Deliverance was in the purpose of God for them, but it would not be accomplished until after seventy years. The promise of deliverance then is full of tenderness and of beauty. It ended by a detailed repetition of the sentence of Jehovah against the people, and a stern denunciation of the prophets, accompanied by a prophecy of their doom.

One of the prophets among the exiles, Shemaiah, wrote to Zephaniah the priest, protesting against his inactivity and declaring that his duty was to put Jeremiah in the stocks and shackles. This letter Zephaniah showed to Jeremiah, who, acting under the direction of Jehovah, sent to all those in captivity, denouncing Shemaiah and foretelling his doom.

JEREMIAH 30

Following this action of the prophet a word of Jehovah came to him which he was especially commanded to write in a book. In a remarkable way it first set forth two things side by side. The first and fundamental was the ultimate determination of God to accomplish His purpose, and restore His people. The second was the appalling condition of the people, so that there was no hope for them except this determination of God.

In setting forth the love that will not let His people go, in spite of all their waywardness and folly, this first movement stands without a rival in all the words of the prophets.

JEREMIAH 31

Continuing, the prophet dealt with the issues of restoration. He first described the restoration of the city. After affirming the ancient love of Jehovah for His people, he foretold the building of the city, and the planting of "vineyards upon the mountains of Samaria," proceeding to describe the return to the city and the country of the penitent people. He then turned to the surrounding nations, and declared to them the fact that Jehovah had ransomed and redeemed Jacob, foretold their prosperity and rejoicing, and the absolute satisfaction with which He would fill them.

The next movement tells of the passing of sorrow. The prophet first described that sorrow, and then uttered the promise of Jehovah which was intended to assuage the grief and stay the tears. He put into the mouth of Ephraim the language which indicated his sense of the meaning of his chastisement, and declared his repentance, and again affirmed God's memory on him and determination to have mercy on him. He then broke in on the poem with an urgent appeal to the people to turn from backsliding into the way of God's restoration.

Taking up the song again, he celebrated the new contentment which would take possession of the people in the day of return. It would be contentment with the divine government and administration. All the proverbs which seemed to reflect upon Jehovah would be abandoned. He then described the new covenant out of which the new contentment would grow. It would no longer be like the external one made with the fathers, but spiritual and internal, and based on an intimate knowledge of Jehovah.

The last movement of the song consists of the prophet's statement of the oath of restoration in which Jehovah appealed to the signs in the heavens, and repeated His promise of deliverance.

JEREMIAH 32

The next of the prophecies of hope consists of the account of Jeremiah's purchase of a field in Anathoth, with the interpretation of the suggestiveness of the action. While he was still in prison through the opposition of Zedekiah, the word of the Lord came to him, informing him of the coming of Hanamel his cousin, requesting him to buy a field in Anathoth. Knowing that this was the will of God, he purchased the field, and declared in the presence of witnesses that his purchase was a sign that houses and fields and vineyards would yet be bought in the land.

Notwithstanding this, the outlook seemed so contrary to any such expectation that Jeremiah inquired of the Lord how the prophecy he had uttered could be fulfilled. This inquiry was introduced by an ascription of praise to God, and a description of the wonder of His dealing with His people.

Jehovah's answer to his inquiry consisted, first, of an all-inclusive general affirmation of His Being and power, coupled with an inquiry whether anything was too hard for Him. The word of the Lord then proceeded to declare to Jeremiah the certainty of the judgment which he had already foretold, and the reasons for it.

Finally, that word of the Lord announced the divine determination to gather His people together from all the countries, and declared the resulting restoration of prosperity, so that what Jeremiah had declared to his cousin and the witnesses would become true.

JEREMIAH 33

Following the story of the purchase of the field in Anathoth, with its signification, is a song of the ultimate restoration therein foretold.

The song first celebrates the restoration of the people and the cities. This is described in its moral and material aspects, and in that order. The people are to be cleansed from their iniquity, and the city is to become "a name of joy" to Jehovah in the consciousness of all the peoples of the earth. The moral restoration will be manifested in a material one. The place, waste and desolate and without inhabitant, will again become the center of family life, and of joy and of prosperity. The establishment of the restored order is to be associated with the coming of One who is described as the "Branch of righteousness." In His Person the two offices of King and Priest are to be united, and the result of His administration will be that Judah shall be saved and Jerusalem dwell safely.

Again the promise is confirmed by the solemn affirmation of Jehovah that if men can break His Covenant of day and night, then also may His covenant with David and with the priests be broken. The promise is not only sure but gracious, and as the host of heaven cannot be numbered so will the seed of His servant be multiplied. Jehovah declares Himself to be conscious of the murmuring and unbelief of the people which finds expression in their declaration that Jehovah has cast off the kingly and priestly families. He declares again that in spite of such unbelief, His Covenant with His ancient servants is as sure as day and night.

JEREMIAH 34

Chapters thirty-four and thirty-five contain prophecies of the siege. The armies of Nebuchadnezzar were round about Jerusalem, and Jehovah declared to Zedekiah that the king of Babylon would be successful, that the city would be taken and burned with fire, and that he himself would be carried captive to Babylon. Nevertheless, the word of Jehovah concerning Zedekiah was that he should not die by the sword, but in peace.

The next prophecy is a denunciation of the king for the false covenant he had made with the man servants and maid servants. Freedom had been promised to them, but they had been compelled to return to subjection and to slavery. This was a sin against the express Covenant God had made with His people, that the slaves should be set free every seventh year.

Because of this breaking of the Covenant and oppression of the people, Jehovah would fling them out, as the prophet satirically declared, to the liberty of the sword, pestilence, and famine. In this prophecy one of the sins which characterized the times is clearly manifest—oppression of the poor and helpless, against which the indignation of Jehovah is graphically set forth.

JEREMIAH 35

The last of these prophecies of the siege consists of telling the story of the Rechabites and applying it to the existing conditions. Jeremiah told how in the days of Jehoiakim he had been charged to bring the Rechabites into the house of Jehovah and test them in the matter of drinking wine. This he had done, but they, in loyalty to the command of their father, refused. They declared that they had been true to the instructions of Jonadab, the son of Rechab, taking no wine, sowing no seed, and dwelling in tents until the armies of Nebuchadnezzar had come into the land. On account of their presence, they had come into Jerusalem, but still refused to drink wine.

Jeremiah then placed the loyalty of these men to the commands of Jonadab in contrast with the disloyalty of his people to Jehovah. He had spoken the word of Jehovah to them with perpetual earnestness, but they had refused to listen or obey. Therefore Jehovah had determined judgment against them for their disobedience and persistent rebellion.

The prophecy ends with a promise made by Jeremiah to the Rechabites on behalf of Jehovah that because they had been true to the commandment of Jonadab they would have continued representation before Jehovah.

JEREMIAH 36

This chapter constitutes an interpolation in the chronological order of Jeremiah's prophesying. In detail it tells the story of the writing of the words of Jeremiah in a book to which he had incidentally made reference in his introduction to the prophecies of hope. The command had come to him in the fourth year of the reign of Jehoiakim. He had called Baruch, to whom he had committed the deed of the purchase of the field in Anathoth, and had dictated to him all the words committed to him by Jehovah, commanding him when he had written them to go into the house of Jehovah on the fast day and read them in the hearing of the people. He was to do this because Jeremiah was unable to go.

In the fifth year of Jehoiakim's reign these words were read by Baruch at a fast proclaimed by the people. Micaiah, who heard the reading, found his way into the assembly of the princes and rehearsed to them what he had heard. They sent Jehudi to bring Baruch to them. He came and read to them the same words. Sending Baruch away, charging him to hide with Jeremiah, they retained the roll and told the king of its contents. At last Jehudi read it to the king, who angrily mutilated it and burned it in the brazier. It is possible to mutilate and even destroy a sacred writing, but it is not possible to make of none effect any word of Jehovah. Again Jeremiah dictated the messages to Baruch, adding many words to them, so that the writing was perpetuated, but Jehoiakim was doomed.

JEREMIAH 37

This and the two following chapters contain the history of the siege up to the fall of the city. In the first part of this chapter Jeremiah was free. Zedekiah occupied the throne, but was disobedient to the messages of Jehovah. Pharaoh's army had come out of Egypt, and, believing that the movement of Pharaoh was directed against themselves, the Chaldeans who were besieging the city departed for a season.

Then Jeremiah delivered a message to Zedekiah, charging him not to be deceived by the appearance of the moment, declaring the ultimate victory of the Chaldeans over Jerusalem. In the interval of the absence of the Chaldean army, Jeremiah left Jerusalem and went to Bethlehem on family business. There he was arrested on the charge of falling away to the Chaldeans, his constant prophecy of their victory evidently being interpreted as proof of his sympathy with them. From the prison Zedekiah brought him to inquire if he had anything to say. He immediately answered by declaring against the certainty of the victory over the king of Babylon. At the same time he protested against the treatment which he had received, and asked that he might not be sent back to the dungeon from which he had been brought. This request was granted by Zedekiah, but Jeremiah was kept a prisoner in the court of the guard.

JEREMIAH 38

Under these circumstances he continued to foretell the victory of the Chaldeans, with the result that the anger of the princes was stirred up against him, and he was cast into a most loathsome dungeon. From that dungeon he was released through the intercession of Ebed-melech, an Ethiopian eunuch, who evidently was in favor with Zedekiah. Again the king sought an interview with him, charging him to hide nothing from him as to the future. Jeremiah advised him earnestly to submit to Babylon, warning him that if he did not do so the women of his household would eventually heap reproaches upon him because of the visitation which would overtake the city and the people.

Nothing is more marked throughout all this story than the absolute and unswerving loyalty of Jeremiah to the message of judgment which he was called on to deliver. In the hour when it seemed as though it could not be fulfilled because the Chaldean army had temporarily left the neighborhood, in spite of the angry opposition of the princes and his suffering, and notwithstanding all the temptations created by his access to the king, he never swerved. However clear at times was his vision of an ultimate restoration of the people by Jehovah, he knew that at the moment punishment was in the purpose of God from which there could be no escape; yet not for one moment did he attempt to hide the fact.

JEREMIAH 39

This chapter records the fall of Jerusalem. After a long siege lasting from the tenth month of the ninth year of Zedekiah's reign until the fourth month of the eleventh year, at last "a breach was made in the city," and the princes of Babylon entered. Zedekiah, with the men of war surrounding him, immediately fled, but he was arrested and brought before Nebuchadnezzar. His sons were slain before his eyes, and then his eyes were put out. This was followed by the sack of the city. The king of Babylon charged his captain of the guard, Nebuzaradan, to afford protection to Jeremiah. This was done by committing him to the care of Gedaliah, who was appointed to be governor of the subjected and broken people.

Very interesting is the last paragraph of the chapter which tells of how, before the fall of the city, Jeremiah was charged by Jehovah to visit Ebed-melech, through whose instrumentality he had been delivered from the dungeon, and promise him protection in the day of calamity. It is a revelation of the fact that when the judgment of God is abroad as vengeance it never proceeds without discrimination, and that those who put their trust in Him are thought upon graciously and delivered.

JEREMIAH 40

Chapters forty and forty-one, which contain the prophecies of Jeremiah after the fall of Jerusalem, constitute his last messages to the chosen people. These fall into two parts—first, prophecies against going into Egypt, and, second, prophecies in Egypt.

Jeremiah was evidently taken with the captives, but was released, and Nebuzaradan offered him his choice between going into Babylon and settling anywhere in the land he chose. Jeremiah chose to go to Gedaliah, the governor appointed by the king of Babylon over the cities of Judah. To him certain of the people submitted, and he sought to restore order. There gathered back many of the Jews who were scattered in the surrounding countries. It was reported to the governor by Johanan that Ishmael was there as the emissary of the king of the children of Ammon, and that with intent to take his life. Gedaliah refused to believe the story, and declined to allow Johanan to take the life of Ishmael as he desired to do. This chapter gives us some idea of the appalling condition of affairs. All the rulers and leading men had been carried captive to Babylon. Only the poorest were left, and among them was a spirit of disaffection threatening to manifest itself in many ways.

JEREMIAH 41

Johanan's story proved to be true, and by the basest treachery Ishmael, with a handful of men, murdered Gedaliah and a number of others, and carried away the rest captive, intending to take them to the king of the children of Ammon. However, Johanan, who evidently had been watching and waiting, gathered a band of men and went after Ishmael. Ishmael escaped, but Johanan delivered the people from the threat. Afraid of the Chaldeans, they dwelt near Bethlehem, and purposed going into Egypt.

Again we are impressed with the terrible plight of the people. Although the purpose of Ishmael to carry them away to the children of Ammon had been frustrated, yet the man who had been the instrument of the deliverance, Johanan, was now proposing, in contravention of the divine purpose and arrangement, to take them into Egypt. Those in authority, or who were assuming authority, were violating the fundamental principle of faith, and acting merely according to what seemed to be the wisest policy. It is a terrible revelation of the degradation of the chosen people.

JEREMIAH 42

Before going forward, Johanan and those associated with him, gathered to Jeremiah, and asked that he pray for them and seek divine guidance. He consented at once to their request, and they promised obedience to whatever command was laid upon them. Ten days elapsed, and then Jeremiah delivered the message of the Lord in answer to Johanan.

It was a distinct command to remain in the land, and not to go into Egypt. Divine protection was promised them if they were obedient, but they were warned solemnly that if they went to Egypt in the hope of escaping from war and hunger, they would find there both the sword and famine.

The end of Jeremiah's message shows that he knew, in all probability by divine revelation, that the prayer they had asked him to offer for them had not been honest. He seems to have known that, in spite of his message, they would go down into Egypt, and he told them so; and finally declared to them that they would die in Egypt by the sword, famine, and pestilence.

JEREMIAH 43

The accuracy of Jeremiah's judgment of the people was immediately manifest. Their leaders charged him with having spoken falsely under the inspiration of Baruch, and immediately all of them passed over into Egypt, taking with them both Jeremiah and Baruch. Again the intrepid courage of the man is manifest, for while he, with perhaps Baruch, to all appearances stood alone, he immediately continued his ministry of denunciation and warning.

At Tahpanhes he announced the coming of Nebuchadnezzar, the king of Babylon, against Egypt, and foretold Nebuchadnezzar's complete victory over all that power in which these men had chosen to put their trust. They had fled to Egypt to escape from Babylon. Babylon was to become victorious over Egypt. Thus Jeremiah declared to them, in effect, the utter folly of any attempt to escape finally from the government of God. Willingly abiding therein, they would have been safe in the land, even under the dominion of Babylon. Departing therefrom, in fear of Babylon, they found themselves in the very place where Babylon was again to set up its authority by the victory of war.

JEREMIAH 44

The next prophecy in Egypt was of a fiery protest against the persistent rebellion of the people of God. The prophet reminded them of the patience of God, and of how His anger had already been poured out on Jerusalem, and declared that the rebellious remnant which had found its way into Egypt would be wholly cut off.

This message was answered by a defiant and persistent declaration of rebellion, in which they misinterpreted their own history by declaring that all the evils that had befallen them resulted from attacks on idolatry, and deliberately declared their intention to continue their idolatrous practices.

This drew from Jeremiah his final prophecy, in which he answered their argument by declaring that their sorrows were the result of their idolatry rather than, as they affirmed, the result of turning from idols. He foretold the determined judgment of God, saying that they would be consumed, only a small remnant escaping from Egypt; and ended by announcing that the sign of Jehovah to them would be the defeat of Pharaoh-Hophra, and his being handed over to those who sought his life.

JEREMIAH 45

The messages of Jeremiah to the chosen people practically ended with the last chapter. Before coming to his messages concerning the surrounding nations we have the brief story told in this chapter of the special word which he was charged to speak to Baruch when he wrote his words in a book in the fourth year of Jehoiakim.

A perusal of this message makes it evident that this faithful ally of the prophet had become depressed. If this message was delivered to him in the fourth year of Jehoiakim, it was evidently before the book was actually written and the words read. His lamentation suggests that he was depressed over the circumstances in which he lived, and the word which Jeremiah was commissioned to speak to him, charging him not to seek great things for himself, would lead us to suppose that the emphasis in his lamentation is to be placed on the word "me"—"Woe is *me* now." Evidently he had been overwhelmed with the sorrows of his people, and had hoped to do something to deliver them. In his aspiration there had been something of self-seeking. Yet he had been sincere, and therefore a word of rebuke and comfort was spoken to him. He was reminded of Jehovah's right to deal as He thought best with the people; but he was also promised protection in the difficult circumstances. Such a word as this would prepare him for writing the words of Jeremiah, and the reading of them which fell to his lot.

JEREMIAH 46

The third and last section of the division containing the account of the prophet's ministry is occupied with his messages concerning the nations.

The first of these has to do with Egypt, and consists of two prophecies. The earlier one described the army of Egypt in its preparation and advance, and declared that this proud preparation of Egypt for battle was but the coming of the day of Jehovah's vengeance against Egypt. In general terms he predicted her doom, declaring that there would be no healing for her, and that the nations would hear of her shame.

The second distinctly predicted the defeat of Egypt by Nebuchadnezzar, and yet affirmed that the king of Babylon would be but the instrument in the hand of Jehovah. In graphic and lofty language he described the coming of the foe and the discomfiture of Egypt, and carefully ascribed everything to the determinate counsel and activity of Jehovah. This prophecy ends with a message of comfort to Jacob, who, while afflicted, is yet not to be utterly destroyed, but to be corrected by judgment.

JEREMIAH 47

In this brief chapter we find the word concerning the Philistines. It consists of foretelling a scourge coming against them from the north which would utterly break their power. In figurative language, the prophet described the sorrow which would overtake the proud yet broken people.

JEREMIAH 48

The word of the Lord concerning Moab is a judgment, which nevertheless closes with a gleam of hope. The judgment is described, first, from the standpoint of the scourge. The widespread extent of it is foretold, and the affliction and helplessness are graphically set forth.

The judgment is then spoken of from the standpoint of Moab, that is to say, the long security of Moab and his freedom from affliction are recognized, as is also his self-confidence. In contrast with this, the judgment is announced. All his past security is to end and his strength is to vanish. Finally, in a long passage full of tremendous power, the judgment of Moab from the standpoint of the onlooker is described. Surrounding nations are called on to observe and to lament, while yet they recognize the justice of the judgment, as it is a punishment for Moab for the sin of magnifying himself against the Lord.

The prophet himself, observing the judgment, broke out into mourning and lamentation, with sobs describing the desolation, until at last, in one brief sentence, he announced the promise of Jehovah that finally He would restore the captivity of Moab, and indicated that until that time of the divine intervention the judgment of Moab must continue.

JEREMIAH 49

Against the children of Ammon Jeremiah raised a protest because their king was in possession of Gad. He declared that by the fierce judgment of war, they were to be dispossessed and driven forth. The message ends with a gleam of hope, in which the prophet foretold that again the children of Ammon would be made captive.

Concerning Edom, destruction is foretold, in spite of her wisdom. The reference to wisdom in Teman may be a satirical literary allusion to the fact that it was the birthplace of Eliphaz, the counselor of Job. The destruction is described in figurative language, and the prophet declared that notwithstanding the arrogancy and security of the people, Jehovah would bring them down into the dust. The destruction of Edom is intended to be a warning to the whole earth.

Damascus is described in her decay, and in the destruction determined against her by the Lord of hosts. This reference to Damascus is brief, for it does not seem that in Jeremiah's time there was anything like intimate relationship of any sort between her and the chosen people. It is evident, however, that as his vision swept the horizon, Jeremiah saw that she also was within the circle of the divine government, and that judgment was determined against her.

Kedar and Hazor represent the Arab peoples, the former such as were nomadic, the latter those who dwelt in settled centers, and yet not in walled cities. Against both of these Nebuchadnezzar, the king of Babylon, was to be the instrument of judgment.

The prophecy against Elam is of a judgment, ending once more with a gleam of hope. Of Elam nothing can be said with any certainty. Again, it is evident in the far-reaching vision of Jeremiah she was seen as under divine displeasure, and consequently to be visited by divine judgment.

JEREMIAH 50

The last of the prophecies concerning the nations has to do with Babylon. Throughout the whole of Jeremiah's prophetic utterances, she has been seen as the instrument of God's judgment. Finally, on account of her own sin and corruption, that judgment must inevitably fall upon her. That is the great burden of the message. It is perfectly evident throughout that the prophet had in mind the nations of Judah and Israel, and what he said concerning Babylon had its direct bearing on these as the people of God.

The prophecy falls into two parts, the first contained in chapter fifty foretelling Babylon's doom and Israel's deliverance; the second, in chapter fifty-one, indicating Israel's responsibility in view of this doom determined on Babylon. The paragraph (verses 1-20) contains the first movement of the first prophecy, in which, in general terms, the prophet announced the coming overthrow of Babylon, and foretold the repentant return of the children of Israel and Judah. He then more definitely described the destruction of the city of Babylon itself. A confederacy of nations would come against her and destroy her, and that because she had rejoiced and been wanton in her dealing with the people of God. That people, though scattered and driven away, would be gathered and restored, while the iniquity of Israel and the sins of Judah would be pardoned.

The prophecy increases in power as it proceeds, as Jeremiah foretold the completeness of the overthrow determined against Babylon. The completeness he described as consisting in the utter humbling of her pride, and the absolute destruction of her power. He recognized that Babylon had been the instrument in the hand of Jehovah as he referred to her as "the hammer of the whole earth." But the hammer is broken, and Babylon become a desolation. He described the destruction of her strong men as bullocks going to the slaughter. Escaping captives announce in Zion the vengeance of Jehovah. Her overthrow is to be according to all that she herself had done, and the prophet reveals the reason for the divine vengeance. "She hath been proud against Jehovah" The hammer had practically turned in rebellion against the hand that held it. There fore the pride of Babylon was to be humbled. All the things in which Babylon had put her trust, her multitudes, her princes, her wise men, her mighty men, her horses, her chariots, "the mingled people that are in the midst of her," her treasures, her waters, are seen as under the destroying sword of Jehovah, doomed to destruction as complete as that of Sodom and Gomorrah. The instrument in the hand of Jehovah is described as people from the north, but the prophet emphatically and with great clearness declared that the judgment is to be accomplished by the invincible Jehovah.

JEREMIAH 51

In the second movement of the prophecy which deals with Babylon's doom and Israel's responsibility, Jeremiah first repeated his declarations concerning the determination of Jehovah to bring about the complete overthrow of Babylon, and thus to ensure the deliverance of His people.

Then, in a passage full of force and beauty, Jeremiah described the invincibility of Jehovah. He is the Creator, the very sounding of whose voice creates tumult in the heavens, and all the forces of nature are under His control. By comparison with Him man is brutish, and the gods which he makes are vanity and delusion. In this connection the description of the greatness of Jehovah by contrast with the false gods is intended to indicate the certainty of the ultimate victory of His people over the people who trust in idols. Proceeding to describe the judgment, he again, and at greater length, recognized that Babylon was an instrument in the hand of Jehovah which He had used for judgment. Jeremiah was viewing Babylon as she then was, at the height of her power. Yet against her Jehovah declared Himself, and so complete will be her destruction that she is to become a desolation without inhabitant.

Continuing, the prophet at length declared that the purpose of the divine judgment of Babylon was the ultimate deliverance of His people. Zion is personified as uttering her complaint against Babylon, describing the cruelty practiced against her. This complaint is answered by the declaration of Jehovah that He will plead the cause of His people, making her desolation a desert, and delivering from her captivity a people whom she had oppressed.

Jeremiah then addressed himself in the name of Jehovah to the people of God, calling on them to go out of the midst of Babylon, and to turn their faces again to Jerusalem. He ended his prophecy concerning Babylon with a reaffirmation of the absolute certainty of her ultimate doom. This prophecy closes with an account of the charge which Jeremiah gave to Seraiah, to write these words and read them in Babylon. This happened in the fourth year of the reign of Zedekiah, when Seraiah, who was the brother of Baruch (32:12), accompanied the king on a visit to Babylon. Thus if, as is probable, Zedekiah was acquainted with this prophecy concerning Babylon, one can understand his repeated questioning of Jeremiah in the latter days of the siege concerning the ultimate issue of Babylon's attack on the city.

JEREMIAH 52

The last chapter of the Book of Jeremiah consists of a historical appendix written, as the final words of the previous chapter show, by another hand. It first gives a brief account of the capture of the city, tracing the main events which led up thereto in the reign of Zedekiah, and giving the account of how he was arrested, compelled to look on the execution of his sons, had his own eyes put out, and was carried in fetters to Babylon, where he abode in prison until his death.

It then describes with some detail the sack of the city and the oppression of the people, detailing how the materials and vessels of the house of the Lord were carried away by the victorious army, and the priests and the leaders of the people slain at Riblah.

The forlorn condition of the people may be gathered from the list which this appendix gives of Nebuchadnezzar's captives. All told, they numbered 4,600. The last item of the history tells how Jehoiachin, who had already been in captivity eleven years when the city fell, was taken out of prison twenty-six years later by Evilmerodach, and given a large measure of privilege and liberty in the city of Babylon until his death.

Lamentations

LAMENTATIONS 1

In the Septuagint, the Lamentations are prefixed with the words, "And it came to pass that after Israel had been carried away captive, and Jerusalem made desolate, Jeremiah sat weeping, and lamented this lament over Jerusalem and said. . . ."

In this brief Book of Lamentation the spirit of the man is strikingly revealed. There is no exultation over the fulfilment of his predictions, and there is a twofold loyalty manifest throughout, first to God in the confession of sin, and then to his people in the expression of their sorrow.

In this first poem there are two clearly defined movements. The first (verses 1-11) describes the desolation of the city, as to her relationships with other nations, and as to her internal condition, declaring the cause to be that "she hath grievously sinned." Under the figure of a widow sitting solitary, the prophet describes the city. "She that was great" has "become tributary," and is loverless and comfortless. Within, her desolation is overwhelming. The Temple is deserted, and her beauty has departed. With great care the prophet sets forth the cause of her affliction. She had "grievously sinned," and has forgotten her latter end; and the prophet ends this description of the desolation by identifying himself with the sorrow and the sin in the words, "See, O Lord, and behold; for I am become vile."

In the second movement (verses 12-22) the city, personified, bewails her affliction, appealing to the passer-by, and describing her sorrow; then confesses the justice of the desolation which has overtaken her, crying to Jehovah for sympathy and deliverance.

LAMENTATIONS 2

In the second poem, the prophet dealt with the sources of the sorrow he had described. Again affirming that it was the result of the direct action of Jehovah, he proceeded to describe it in its material and spiritual aspects. Habitations of Jacob are destroyed, princes are profaned, the people are slain. Such are the material judgments. The place of worship is destroyed, the solemn assemblies are forgotten, the sanctuary is abhorred, king, princes, prophets, and people are degraded.

After this recognition of the act of Jehovah in judgment the prophet broke out into a description of the affliction in iniquity as to the actual suffering endured, and the even more painful contempt of the nations. He identified himself with the people in all their sufferings, and recognized the contempt of the nations as fulfilling the word which Jehovah had spoken. Finally, he uttered an appeal of penitence in which there are two movements. The first is his appeal to the people, in which he urged them to repentance, and the turning of the life to God. The second is the appeal of the people to Jehovah, in which again the story of affliction is told.

LAMENTATIONS 3

In this central and longest poem, Jeremiah identified himself completely with the experiences of his people. In the first movement, in language which throbs with pain, he described his own sorrows, recognizing through all the action of Jehovah, as the almost monotonous repetition of the pronoun "He" reveals. Here he most evidently recognized the relation of sorrow to sin. All the intermediate instruments of punishment are out of sight. Every stroke falls from the hand of God, as the opening declaration suggests, "I am the man that hath seen affliction by the rod of His wrath." This is indeed the recognition of the method of Jehovah in judgment. Such recognition compelled the ending of the dirge by an affirmation of hope. The remembered afflictions of God create assurance of deliverance.

The next movement is one wholly of assurance, in which the prophet, having in the previous section recognized Jehovah's activity in judgment, now recognized His activity in mercy. The passage is full of beauty, as it deals with that tender compassion of God which had never been absent even in the work of punishment. This recognition of mercy ends with an expression of submission to judgment, and a consequent song of hope strong in its confidence.

The third movement of identification is one of appeal. Again the prophet first recognized the justice of the divine visitation, and then earnestly appealed to the people to turn to God in true penitence, ending with a declaration of his sense of the national sorrow and of his personal and immediate share in it.

The last movement of the song is again one wholly of assurance. The prophet celebrated the deliverances already wrought for him by Jehovah. From the lowest dungeons he had lifted his cry, and had been heard. Against all the devices of his enemies Jehovah had pleaded his cause. The reproaches that they had heaped on him Jehovah had heard. These past deliverances created his assurance that Jehovah would yet act on behalf of His people and destroy their enemies from under the heavens.

LAMENTATIONS 4

The fourth poem is for the most part a dirge of desolation, which nevertheless ends in a song of hope. Jeremiah first described the disaster in Zion, declaring that it all arose as the result of the sin of the people, which was greater than that of Sodom. He then described the degradation of the people. From the perfection of health her nobles have degenerated into men on whom the stamp of an unutterable disease is clearly set.

All this has resulted from the sins of the prophets and the iniquities of the priests. Those who have guided men in the purity of their lives were blind and polluted to such an extent that the people held them in contempt, cried after them, "Unclean," and besought them to depart.

The prophet then proceeded to deal with the folly of the men who had sought help from the nations, describing the useless looking of the eyes for help, and then the remorselessness of the enemies who hunted and pursued them to death. He ended with a satirical address to Edom, calling upon her to rejoice, but declaring that the cup should pass to her also, and a final word of hope for Zion in that the punishment of her iniquity was accomplished.

LAMENTATIONS 5

The final poem is an appeal out of sorrow to Jehovah. Speaking on behalf of the whole nation, the prophet called on Jehovah to remember. He described the actual desolation, telling of the affliction of all classes of the people—the women, the maidens, the princes, the elders, the young men, the children, and of the consequently prevalent sorrow, recognizing that all this was the result of sin.

Then, in a last brief and yet forceful word, he prayed Jehovah to turn the people unto Himself. This he introduced by a declaration of his confidence in the perpetual enthronement of Jehovah. It was a cry which recognized the last helplessness of man, namely, his inability even to repent. "Turn Thou us unto Thee, O Lord, and we shall be turned."

The final word of the Lamentations was a wail out of the then existing distress. "But Thou hast utterly rejected us; Thou art very wroth against us."

Ezekiel

EZEKIEL 1

The Book opens with the account of the prophet's preparation, and falls into two sections, the first describing the visions he saw, and the second the voice he heard.

Verses 2 and 3 in this chapter, which are really parenthetical, may be treated as a title page. This gives the date, states that the word came expressly to him, and indicates the place in which he saw the visions and heard the voice.

The visions were inclusively visions of God. They proceeded in four manifestations. The first was of a cloud swept into sight by a stormy wind, surrounded by brightness, and continually flashing forth in glory. The second was of four living ones out of the midst of this fire, who moved in rhythmic unity. The third was of wheels rotating in harmony with each other, and in co-operation with the movements of the living ones. The fourth was, first, of a firmament, overarching the ceaseless activity of the living ones. Above the firmament a voice was heard, and then the likeness of a throne was seen, and, finally, a Person was manifested of the nature of fire, surrounded by a glory like that of the rainbow.

In the presence of the manifested glory Ezekiel fell on his face. The very mystery of the visions spoke of the awfulness of the God with whom he had to deal, and their forms suggested majesty, order, activity, and personality.

EZEKIEL 2

As the prophet lay prostrate, he heard a voice commanding him to stand on his feet, and he was immediately empowered to do so by the entrance of the Spirit. He was then commissioned to deliver the message of God to the children of Israel, who were described as having transgressed against Jehovah, and as being "impudent and stiff-hearted." He was charged to deliver the message of God whether they would hear, or whether they would forbear. The difficulty of his work was recognized, and the prophet was warned not to be rebellious as they had been. The commission was ratified by the symbolism of a roll handed to Ezekiel.

EZEKIEL 3

This roll he was commanded to eat. The writing on the roll was a roll of lamentations and mourning and woe. The prophet declared that having eaten the roll, he found it in his mouth "as honey for sweetness," and by this declaration reveals that whereas the ministry he was about to exercise would be difficult, yet he himself was in perfect accord with the purpose of God and found delight in His will. It may be also that he already recognized that beyond the reprobation with which he would have to deal, restoration was in the purpose of God.

After eating the roll the prophet still heard the voice speaking to him, announcing what his equipment for the fulfilment of his mission would be, warning him of the difficulties awaiting him, in that the house of Israel would not hearken, having become hard of forehead, and stiff of heart, promising him that he would be strengthened for his work by similar hardness of face and of forehead, and charging him to be loyal to the word of the Lord. Then in an interval he was lifted up by the Spirit, and heard a great ascription of praise to the glory of Jehovah, and again was made conscious of the activity of Deity by the symbolism of the wings of the living creatures and the noise of the wheels. In bitterness and heat of spirit he came to the midst of the captives, where he sat "astonished" for seven days.

The word of Jehovah then came to him again, laying on him his responsibilities anew. He was reminded of the source of the message, and told that his first responsibility was hearing, and his second, speech; and, moreover, that if he failed the blood of the unwarned would be required at his hands. Once again he was called into the plain, where he saw the glory of Jehovah, as he had seen it by the river. The Spirit strengthening him, a double charge was laid on him, the first of which was silence, and the second, speech.

EZEKIEL 4

The second division of the Book contains the messages of the prophet concerning the reprobation of the chosen nation. These fall into three parts. In the first, by symbolism and speech he described the results of reprobation. In the second he declared its reason. In the last he proclaimed its righteousness. The results of reprobation were first symbolically set forth in four signs. These were immediately followed by general denunciations. Finally, the cause of the coming judgment and its process were dealt with at length.

In the present chapter three of the signs are described. The first was a tile on which the prophet was charged to portray a city. Around this he was to depict the process of siege. Having done this, he was to place between himself and the model a flat piece of iron. This sign was intended to foretell the taking of Jerusalem by an army, by the will, and under the direction, of Jehovah, whose representative in the sign Ezekiel was.

The second sign consisted of a posture. For 390 days he was charged to lie on his left side, and for forty days on his right, prophesying against Jerusalem during the whole period. It was a long and tedious process of bearing the iniquity of the house of Israel in the sense of confessing it, and so revealing the reason for the siege and the judgment.

The third sign was the food which he should eat during the period. It was to be of the simplest and scantiest, and cooked in such a way as to indicate uncleanness. The sign was intended to predict the famine and desolation which would accompany the judgment against Jerusalem.

EZEKIEL 5

In this chapter we have the description of the last of the four signs. The prophet was commanded to take a sword, sharpened as a barber's razor, and therewith to cut off his hair and his beard. The hair thus taken was to be weighed, and divided into three parts. The first was to be burned in the midst of the city at the expiration of the siege; the second was to be smitten with the sword round about the city; and the third to be scattered to the wind. Finally, a few hairs were to be gathered and bound in his skirt, and of them some were to be cast into the fire.

The explanation of the sign was then given at length to Ezekiel. Jerusalem, set in the midst of the nations, had rebelled against Jehovah, and for this He was against her. A third part of the people was to die by pestilence in the midst of the city, another third would die in battle round about her; the remaining third would be scattered to the winds.

EZEKIEL 6

These signs were followed by denunciations growing naturally out of what they had taught. In general terms, the prophet first foretold the coming judgment of the sword against the whole land, and the consequent scattering of the people. It was distinctly declared that in this process of judgment Jehovah would preserve a remnant of those who would escape from the destruction of Jerusalem, and in whose mind the judgment would remain, producing repentance, and the conviction that the word of God was not in vain.

The prophet was then charged to deliver this message of the sword with all the outward signs of vehemence and passion, and to make perfectly clear that vengeance moved toward the purpose of restoring a knowledge of Jehovah to those who had forgotten Him. The reference to the remnant in the course of this first denunciation explains the final action in the fourth sign, that is, the gathering of a few scattered hairs and binding them in the skirts of the prophet's garment.

Ezekiel's consciousness of the underlying cause of the reprobation of the chosen people is evident through all this section, in which he describes its results. Israel had fallen out of fellowship with God, and had ceased to know Him. Presently this is dealt with in greater detail, but it is interesting to notice the prophet's recognition of it throughout the whole of these messages.

EZEKIEL 7

The second denunciation dealt with the completeness of judgment. Its keynote was expressed in the words, "an end." The prophet declared that an end on the land and the people had been determined on, emphasizing that this final judgment would be accomplished by the act of God in order that they might know Him.

The prophet then proceeded to describe that end. Its first manifestation would be the paralysis of the people, so that when the trumpet was blown for the battle, and all was ready, none would move forward, being overcome by terror and grief. Such a method of judgment would be a clear demonstration of the activity of Jehovah. For a people armed and ready for battle to be suddenly smitten with a nameless terror and an overwhelming consciousness of weakness would be, to use the terms of our own day, phenomenal and supernatural. This paralysis of courage would issue in an overwhelming sense of poverty, not in the absolute lack of silver and gold, but in a wild casting away of silver in the streets and a sense of the uncleanness of gold, because these material riches would be useless as means of deliverance from Jehovah's wrath. All this would finally produce the confession of overwhelming perplexity, and no interpreter would be found. This second denunciation ended as did the first, by indicating the purpose of the vengeance. "They shall know that I am the Lord."

EZEKIEL 8

We now come to the last prophecy dealing with the results of reprobation. It consists of a long and detailed description of the cause and process of judgment. Its first movement came to the prophet as he sat in his own house in the presence of the elders of Judah. He felt the pressure of the divine hand on him, and saw an appearance as of fire.

He was then lifted between earth and heaven, and there was revealed to him the awful idolatries practiced in Jerusalem. He saw at the entrance of the inner court of the house of God "the image of jealousy," which means that there was set up an image which provoked Jehovah to jealousy. His special attention was called to this as revealing the reason why Jehovah departed from His sanctuary.

He was then bidden to dig a hole in the wall, and through a door which he discovered there he saw the elders of Israel burning incense before creeping things, abominable beasts and idols, so far had they passed from conscious fellowship with God as to imagine that He had forsaken the earth and they were not seen.

Yet again the prophet saw the depravity of the women of Israel who were weeping for Tammuz, the significance of which weeping is suggested in Milton's lines:

The love-tale
Infected Zion's daughters with like heat;
Whose wanton passions in the sacred
 porch
Ezekiel saw.

Finally, in the inner court the prophet saw men with their backs turned toward the Temple, worshiping the sun. Because of this utter corruption of the people, Jehovah would proceed in judgment, in spite of all the loud crying of the people.

EZEKIEL 9

The next section of the message most remarkably reveals the fact of the divine discrimination in judgment. The prophet was charged in the vision to cause those who had charge over the city to draw near, armed with weapons of destruction. In response, six men came from the way of the upper gate, and a seventh, clothed in linen, with a writer's inkhorn by his side. The glory of the God of Israel had departed from the center of the Temple to the threshold of the house.

These men were now charged to pass through the midst of the city, and slay the inhabitants. The man with the inkhorn, however, went through the midst of the city first, setting a mark on the foreheads of such as mourned the abominations which had been described. The six men followed him, slaying utterly, beginning at the house, and moving through the city. In this terrible process of judgment all those on whom the mark was found—those who in their hearts mourned the evil existing in the city—were spared.

The vision of judgment appalled the prophet, so that falling on his face, he cried out in intercession. He was answered by the declaration that the sin of Israel and Judah was great, and that therefore the judgment was irrevocable.

EZEKIEL 10

The prophet next described the process of judgment. First, a preliminary vision was granted to him. The man with the inkhorn who had passed through the midst of the city, setting his mark on the sighing and crying men, was commanded to pass in between the whirling wheels and gather coals of fire in his hand and scatter them over the city.

Then appeared the glory of Jehovah over the threshold of the house, and the sound of the wings of the cherubim was heard. Visions of the glory of God, similar to those which the prophet had seen by the Chebar, now were granted to him, but they were viewed as having close association with the process of judgment, which he was about to describe. The man who gathered his fire to scatter on Jerusalem went into the midst of these wheels, and the visible glory of Jehovah as it departed from the threshold was closely associated with the wheels and the cherubim. The whole of the vision of the glory of God moved from the inner court of the Temple beyond the eastern gate of its outer court.

EZEKIEL 11

The prophet was now lifted by the Spirit, and brought to the east gate, that is, to the place whither the glory of God had departed. There he saw a conclave of five and twenty men presided over by princes of the people, who were devising iniquity, that is, plotting against the king of Babylon. They declared that they were safe in their city.

Instructed of the Spirit, Ezekiel uttered a denunciation of them, and declared God's vengeance against them. Taking up their figure of the cauldron and the flesh, he declared that they should be brought forth from the midst thereof, and that on account of their sin.

As he prophesied, one of the princes died, and Ezekiel, filled with amazement, fell on his face before Jehovah, and appealed to Him for intercession. This appeal was answered by the declaration that Jehovah would protect those scattered among the nations, Himself being to them a sanctuary in the countries where they had come. He promised, moreover, that eventually He would restore them to the land of Israel, and that in their coming they would be morally and spiritually cleansed and restored, but that vengeance would inevitably fall on such as were persistent in their sin. Again, a vision of the glory of God departing from the city was granted to him. Returning from these visions, he uttered in the hearing of the captives all the things that the Lord had showed him.

EZEKIEL 12

The prophet was next commanded to act in the sight of the people as an exile going forth from his country, preparing "stuff for removing," and carrying it forth from place to place. He obeyed the command, and its intention was fulfilled when the people inquired what he meant.

In response, he foretold the capture of the people and the princes in Jerusalem, and their being taken to Babylon, declaring that the prince (Zedekiah) would be taken captive to Babylon, but that he would not see it. This, of course, was fulfilled when Zedekiah's eyes were put out when he was taken.

Moreover, the prophet was charged to adopt another sign, that is, eating and drinking his bread and water with fear and with carefulness, and by that sign to foretell the desolations which would fall on the inhabitants of Jerusalem. The unbelief of the people had manifested itself in proverbs, one of which declared the failure of prophecy, and another, the postponement of its fulfilment to far distant times. In answer to this Ezekiel was charged to announce the imminence of the divine visitation and the fulfilment of every word that had been spoken.

EZEKIEL 13

The next movement in the prophesying was a denunciation of false prophets and prophetesses. The prophets were not inspired by the Spirit of God, but followed their own spirit. In so doing they had, like foxes, destroyed the very fences of the vineyard of God instead of restoring and strengthening them. They had spoken in the name of the Lord without His authority. In the place of divine inspiration had been the divination of wickedness. Because of this, Jehovah was against them, and they would be cut off from the council of His people and from the land of Israel. Their immediate sin had been promising peace when judgment was determined. By their messages they had given a false sense of security, which Ezekiel likened to a wall built with untempered mortar. Against this Jehovah would proceed as a stormy wind, in fury sweeping it down with those who built it.

The prophetesses had been guilty of the same evil prophesying "out of their own heart" the things which pleased the people, and that for their own enrichment. Against them also Jehovah would proceed, delivering the people out of their hand.

This burden against the false prophets and prophetesses ended once more with the declaration of purpose, "Ye shall know that I am the Lord." It is a graphic setting forth of the awful peril of misrepresenting Jehovah. There is no deadlier sin than to profess to speak His messages, and at the same time be motivated by anything other than the glory of His name.

EZEKIEL 14

Certain of the elders of Israel now came to Ezekiel, evidently to hear what message he had to deliver to them. The word of the Lord revealed to him that whatever their outward attitude might be, they were at heart idolaters, and he was charged to declare to them that while idolatry remained in their heart they were necessarily estranged from Jehovah. He was to appeal to them to return to Jehovah, and to make perfectly clear that so long as they retained idolatry in their heart the only answer of Jehovah to them must be punishment, warning them that if they listened to the messages of false prophets, they and the prophets would be destroyed together.

This determined attitude of judgment was then explained to Ezekiel, first by a statement of principle. That statement was that in days of wilful and persistent corruption men as righteous as Noah, Daniel, and Job could not prevent the operation of vengeance, but only save their own souls by their righteousness. This statement of principle, while insisting on the inevitableness of judgment, did, nevertheless, also clearly reveal the justice and discrimination of the divine method. If Noah, Daniel, and Job were unable to prevent the judgment, they themselves would be saved by their righteousness. The twofold truth was then even more clearly brought forth in the direct application of the principle to Jerusalem. Four sore judgments were determined against the city, but a remnant would be delivered, and escaping to Ezekiel would comfort him, as they proved that all that the Lord had done had been not without cause.

EZEKIEL 15

This final word on the results of reprobation leads naturally to the part of the prophecy dealing with the reason thereof. This reason is first set forth under two general figures; second, in the form of a riddle; third, as an answer to a false excuse; and, finally, in a great lament.

The figures were familiar because they had been used by former prophets. The first figure was of the vine. Its uselessness as a tree was declared. It provided no wood which men could work, not even a pin on which a vessel might be hung, the meaning of this most evidently being that the one and only value of a vine is its fruit. How worse than useless then is it when burned.

The application of the figure was made immediately to the inhabitants of Jerusalem, who were to be given to the fire because of their trespass. The connection of this prophecy with the song of Isaiah is evident. According to that song the judgment against the men of Judah was due to the fact that when Jehovah looked for grapes they brought forth wild grapes.

EZEKIEL 16

The second figure was that of the adulteress, and this the prophet wrought out at great length. Jerusalem was arraigned on account of her abominations, which were described under the figure of that spiritual adultery and harlotry which Hosea had so graphically and powerfully set forth.

Ezekiel traced the whole history of the city. Her origin was of the land of the Canaanite, an Amorite her father, and a Hittite her mother. She was an abandoned child, born and forsaken. In this condition of helplessness she was found and nurtured by Jehovah. The prophet's description of the tender care of Jehovah is full of beauty. At maturity the child was taken in marriage, and loaded with benefits. The renown of the glory of her state and apparel "went forth among the nations." Then came the downfall, and in words of living fire the prophet dealt with the awful unfaithfulness of the wife as she trusted in her beauty and turned to harlotry, in which she prostituted her husband's wealth. All the gifts which had been lavished on her in love she turned into the means of prosecuting her evil courses. The harlotry of Jerusalem had been worse than the common in which the harlot receives gifts, in that she had bestowed gifts to seduce others. Even the daughters of Philistia were ashamed of her lewdness.

Because of the hatefulness of the sin, the punishment of Jerusalem would be terrible. The method would be to turn her lovers against her, that is, those whom she had seduced. With terrible vengeance they would come on her and strip her of all her orments and her clothing, exposing her to shame. In proverbs of contempt she would be spoken of as the daughter of her mother the Hittite, as a sister of Samaria and Sodom. Yet the prophet declared that Jerusalem had been more corrupt than either of these. Jerusalem's sin had been the more heinous in that she had professed to set the standard for her sisters, whereas she had been more abominable than they. Yet all this shame to be brought on the guilty city was in order that she might repent and turn to God, and so return to her former state. In this again Hosea's thought of the restoration of the sinning wife is evident. The last movement in this terrible story is that in which the prophet foretold the restoration of the wife by Jehovah's remembrance of the Covenant and re-establishment of it.

EZEKIEL 17

Commanded by Jehovah, the prophet then put forth a riddle. A great eagle came on Lebanon, and took off the top of the cedar, planting the young twigs in a land of traffic, a city of merchants. Moreover, he carried away the seed of the land, and planted it in a fruitful soil, where it became a spreading vine. There was also another great eagle toward which the vine bent its roots, that he might water it. For this act of treachery the vine was denounced by command of Jehovah. Its judgment was that it should be plucked up by the roots. and be withered by the east wind.

The riddle was then explained. The first eagle was the king of Babylon, who carried away the king of Jerusalem, and planted the seed royal in Babylon. The second eagle was the king of Egypt, whose help Zedekiah sought, who, in consequence, was punished by Jehovah. The riddle ended with the promise of Jehovah that ultimately He would plant again a cedar in the mountain height of Israel, as a result of which there would be universal recognition of the activity of Jehovah. The paragraph very remarkably sets forth that the government of God is established over all the nations and operates through all their operations.

EZEKIEL 18

The next prophecy was directed against the false attitude of mind obtaining among the exiled people, which had expressed itself in a proverb, "The fathers have eaten sour grapes, and the children's teeth are set on edge." By the use of this proverb they intended to lay the blame of their present suffering on their fathers. While recognizing all the evil which had befallen them as the result of sin, they maintained the attitude of injured innocence, declaring, in effect, that they were bearing the punishment of sins which they had not committed. This the prophet denied, first by setting forth illustrative principles which may thus be summarized. All souls have direct dealings with God, seeing that they are His. The righteous man lives. The wicked son of a righteous man dies. The righteous son of a wicked man lives. In unequivocal terms the prophet then deliberately declared that the son does not bear the iniquity of the father, nor the father that of the son. In this first line of argument in rebutting the false proverb, the prophet laid all his emphasis on personal responsibility. The argument is at once a revelation of the strict justice of God in dealing with men, and of man's opportunity and obligation of immediate dealing with God.

The prophet then proceeded to show how gracious this opportunity is. If the wicked man turns from wickedness to righteousness, his sins are to be forgiven and he is to live, because Jehovah has no pleasure in the death of the wicked. On the other hand, if the righteous man turn from his righteousness to sin, his past righteousness is of no avail and he is to die. Israel declared that the way of Jehovah was not equal. To this Ezekiel replied that the ways of Israel were unequal, and that what appeared to be unequal in the judgment of God was the result of the inequality of their attitude toward Him.

The prophet then appealed to the house of Israel to turn from transgression, and declared again that Jehovah had "no pleasure in the death of him that dieth." The responsibility and opportunity of a sinning people is set forth in the appeal to make for themselves a new heart and a new spirit, and in the declaration that by turning they would live.

EZEKIEL 19

The last section in the prophet's revelation of the righteousness of reprobation consists of his lament over the fallen princes of Judah. He first referred to Jehoahaz, the son and successor of Josiah, who was carried captive to Egypt. His mother, Judah, the prophet described as a lioness couched among lions, and nourishing her whelps. One of them was ensnared, and brought to Egypt. The mother disappointed, took another of her whelps. The reference here is undoubtedly to Jehoiachin, who, after a brief reign in which he won certain victories, was carried away captive to Babylon.

The last movement in the lament

has to do with the failure of Zedekiah and the ruin wrought by him. The mother is now likened to a vine which once was fruitful, and out of which grew strong rods as rulers. Her present condition is then described in contrast. Plucked up in fury, her strong rulers ceased, and out of her rods went forth a fire that destroyed. That is to say, Judah's final destruction had come through those having rule over her, and the reference undoubtedly was to Zedekiah.

EZEKIEL 20

In this final section of the prophecies dealing with reprobation, the prophet in a series of messages set forth the righteousness thereof. In the seventh year of the reign of Jehoiachin, that is four years before the fall of Jerusalem, certain elders of Israel went down to Ezekiel to inquire of the Lord.

The prophet was commissioned to declare to them that God would not be inquired of by them, and at the same time he was charged to make known to them the righteousness of the judgment falling on them. This he did, first by reviewing the past history of Israel. Israel had been delivered from Egypt and charged to put away all its abominations. They had rebelled, and had been punished. All this God had wrought for His name's sake, and in the interests of the nations. In the wilderness He gave them His statutes and showed them His judgments. There again they rebelled against Him, and He visited them with punishment. This also He wrought for His name's sake and in the interest of the nations. Their children He spared in the wilderness, and charged them to take warning by the failure of their fathers, urging them to walk in His statutes. Again the children rebelled against Him, and He punished them. and all this He wrought for His name's sake, and in the interests of the nations.

The prophet then passed to an examination of the more recent history. He first described how their fathers, having been brought into the land, had sinned in turning to its idolatries. This sin of the fathers had been repeated by the sons. Therefore the Lord would not be inquired of them. Having thus made clear to the elders that God would not be inquired of, he proceeded to announce the program of Jehovah concerning them. He would establish the fact of His Kingship over them by gathering them to the wilderness. What was meant by the wilderness the prophet then explained as he described their passing under the rod, and the process of purging them of those in their midst who were in rebellion against Him. The result of this wilderness process would be ultimately the restoration of Israel, and the sanctification of Jehovah in them in the sight of all the nations. Israel would have new understanding of Jehovah, and come to know that the perpetual reason for His operation was the glory of His name, and not merely punishing them for their evil ways, that is to say, the punishment of Jehovah was never merely vindictive, but always a process moving toward the realization of His original intention of good to the nations of the earth.

After the delivery of this message to the elders of Israel the prophet was commissioned to set his face toward the south and prophesy against its forest. The burden of the message was announcing that an unquenchable fire, kindled by Jehovah, would utterly destroy it. The parabolic nature of this charge perplexed the prophet, and he complained to Jehovah that the people said of him that he was a speaker of parables.

EZEKIEL 21

The commission was then repeated in terms of explanation. Ezekiel was to set his face against Jerusalem, and prophesy against the land of Israel, declaring that Jehovah would draw His sword out of its sheath in order to proceed in ultimate judgment against the sinning people.

Moreover, Ezekiel was charged that his message was to be delivered with all the tokens of overwhelming anguish, which tokens should in themselves constitute a sign which he was to interpret to the people as the anguish which must inevitably overtake them in the day of calamity.

All this had prepared the way for the song of the sword. First, in graphic language the prophet described the sword itself, sharpened and furbished, and ready to the hand of the slayer. This song was immediately followed by an interpretation. The king of Babylon was seen approaching. He came to a place where the ways parted, one leading to Rabbah of the children of Ammon, the other to Jerusalem. There he used divination with arrows, and consulted the teraphim. The lot fell on Jerusalem, and toward that he proceeded with all the instruments of siege.

Then the prince of Israel was addressed. Charged with sin, his judgment was announced, and the fact that Jehovah would continue to overturn until the coming of the rightful King. When at the parting of the ways the king of Babylon turned toward Jerusalem it would seem as though Ammon had drawn a sword, in all likelihood with the intention of taking part in the vengeance about to fall on Jerusalem. The prophet uttered the word which commanded Ammon to sheathe that sword, and declared that the judgment of Jehovah was against it.

EZEKIEL 22

The next movement described the utter evil of the city. Its fundamental sins of bloodshed and idolatry were named and denounced, and the resultant evils were described. These consisted of the oppression of the people by the princes, of despising holy things and of profanation of the Sabbath, of terrible and widespread impurity, and of active and iniquitous greed. On account of these things the judgment of Jehovah would be terrible, and the people were challenged whether they could endure Jehovah's dealing with them. Again the truth was emphasized that the method of judgment was characterized by a procedure toward the fulfilment of purpose, by the figure of the refining of metals in the furnace of fire.

Again the prophet described the corruption of the inhabitants, first in a general statement under the figure of an unwatered land, that is, having no teaching, and the figure of the polluted springs, that is, having no prophets. He then proceeded to make particular charges against priests, princes, prophets, and people. The priests had failed to discriminate between things unclean and clean. The princes had cruelly oppressed for selfish ends. The prophets had uttered false words of hope. The people had been guilty of oppressing the poor, and needy, and the stranger. He then concluded by describing the utter hopelessness of the case. There was no man to stand in the gap, therefore the fire of wrath must proceed on its way.

EZEKIEL 23

The next prophecy dealt with the sins of Samaria and Jerusalem under the figures of two women, Oholah and Oholibah. The prophet first described their sins. Samaria was charged with unfaithfulness in her confederacy with the Assyrians in that she allowed herself to be seduced by their wealth and their strength, from her loyalty to Jehovah. He also reminded her of her former confederacy with Judah. In consequence of this double sin she was handed over to the Assyrians who overcame and oppressed her.

The sin of Jerusalem was even more heinous than that of Samaria, and that notwithstanding the judgment she had seen falling on Samaria. She also made confederacy with Assyria, and subsequently more directly with Egypt, wherein she violated her Covenant with Jehovah. Against her also therefore Jehovah raised up those with whom she had been in unholy alliance, bringing them against her in full force, and allowing them to despoil and strip her.

Proceeding at the command of Jehovah, the prophet pronounced judgment on Oholah and Oholibah. In terrible language he again described the wickedness of the alliances formed between these two cities and the surrounding nations. Righteous men would judge them with the judgment of adulteresses. Under the figure of the Hebrew method of dealing with the sin of adultery, namely, stoning, the prophet described an assembly against these cities, carrying out this judgment, and destroying the people utterly. Again the purpose was declared to be to make lewdness cease out of the land in the interests of other cities here referred to under the figure of women, all this still in order to vindicate the honor of Jehovah.

EZEKIEL 24

The final prophecy in this division described the coming destruction of the city. This was first done under the parable of a cauldron set on a fire, filled with water, and made to boil. The prophet applied his figure directly, declaring that Jerusalem was indeed a cauldron. It will be remembered that the conspirators seen by the prophet on an earlier occasion had declared that Jerusalem was a cauldron, and they the flesh, and by that had intended to indicate their safety. Ezekiel would seem now to turn to their own figure and use it against them, making it indicate, not safety but judgment, as he foretold the certainty of the coming destruction of Jerusalem and its people.

At this time the prophet was bereft of his wife, and commanded to give no external manifestation of grief. He obeyed the command and so unusual was his attitude in the presence of grief that the people inquired what he meant. He answered that Jehovah was about to visit them with calamity so dire that they would not be able to find relief in mourning or weeping.

The prophet was then told that the news of the fall of the city would be conveyed to him, and that in that day his mouth would be opened, and he would be able to speak with assurance the messages of Jehovah.

EZEKIEL 25

The last division of the prophecy deals with the subject of the ultimate restoration of the chosen nation. It falls into three sections. The first has to do with the nations, the second with the nation, and the last describes the restored order.

The prophecies concerning the nations fall into three groups. The first pronounced the doom of four, the second the doom of two, and the third the doom of one.

The doom of four dealt with Ammon, Moab, Edom, and Philistia. The children of Ammon had exulted over the destruction of the sanctuary and mocked Israel in the days of her desolation, and Judah when she went into captivity. Therefore Ammon was to be overcome by the children of the East. Moab and Seir had witnessed the degradation of Judah, and rejoiced therein, and judgment was determined against them. Edom had been brutal in her treatment of Judah, taking vengeance on her. Therefore the land of Edom was to be made desolate and her people cut off. Philistia had taken vengeance with perpetual enmity, and therefore vengeance was determined against her.

It is to be especially and particularly noticed that each of these dooms ends with the same thought. By judgment on the people who have failed to recognize Jehovah through the government of His own people, He will make them know that He is Jehovah.

EZEKIEL 26

The doom of the two dealt with Tyre and Sidon, but principally with Tyre. Concerning her, the prophet first made a general statement describing her sin, and the judgment determined against her, declaring that the purpose was that she also would know Jehovah. The sin of Tyre had finally expressed itself in her rejoicing over the downfall of Jerusalem, and her expectation of enrichment therefrom. On account of this the prophet declared that Jehovah was against Tyre, and that He would so utterly destroy her that she would be but a bare rock on which fishermen would spread their nets.

He then proceeded to describe in detail the process of judgment. Nebuchadrezzar would come with his armies and his engines of war and completely overthrow the city, making spoil of her riches and laying all her glory in the dust. So terrible would be her downfall that all the princes of the sea would be filled with fear and astonishment, and lament over her.

This prophecy was fulfilled with absolute accuracy of detail. The historic account of the downfall of Tyre is remarkable reading in the light of Ezekiel's foretelling.

EZEKIEL 27

At the command of Jehovah, Ezekiel then took up a lamentation for Tyre. This took the form of a pictorial representation of her as a gallant ship trafficking among the nations and ultimately wrecked, to the consternation of all that beheld. The subjects set forth under the figure are her commercial supremacy, enterprises, and ruin. Her supremacy was ensured by the fact that she sat at the entrances of the sea, and the wealth of the nations round about had contributed to that result, until Tyre sat in pride, declaring, "I am perfect in beauty." Her commercial enterprises were far-reaching. Her own wise men acted as pilots, that is, directed these enterprises. Men from other nations served her both commercially and in her army. She dealt in raw material, in manufactured articles, and in things of beauty. Judah and Israel had been among those who had traded with her. It is a remarkable description of vast enterprises successfully carried on, until Tyre became very glorious in the heart of the seas.

In a passage full of picturesque beauty, the prophet described the whelming of Tyre in the great waters, and her breaking by the east wind, in a fall in which all those associated with her were involved. So terrible was the fall that the men of the surrounding nations gathered, and gazed in consternation, while they lamented and were afraid in the presence of the overthrow.

EZEKIEL 28

The prophecy concerning Tyre ended with a message to its prince and a lamentation for its king. A distinction must be drawn between these two. Most evidently the prince was the then reigning king, Ithobal. Great difficulty has been felt with regard to the remarkable description of the king which follows. It is most likely that from his height of inspired vision the prophet saw behind the actually reigning prince the awful personality of Satan, whose instrument Ithobal was. All the language used in reference to the king perfectly falls in with this interpretation of the prophet's meaning. Ezekiel declared that the sin of the prince was pride of heart, expressing itself finally in that he thought of himself as a god, and boasted accordingly. That he was a remarkable person is revealed by Ezekiel's declaration that he was wiser than Daniel. By this wisdom he had achieved the successes already described, and on account of it his heart had become lifted up. His judgment was to be that by humiliation and destruction, even to the pit, he would learn that he was a "man, and not God."

The prophet then took up his lamentation over the king of Tyre, of whom he declared that he sealed up the sum, being full of wisdom and perfect in beauty. He described his original appointment by God in poetic language full of suggestiveness. He then declared that his sin began in the day when unrighteousness was found in him, and violence became his method. On account of this unrighteousness he was cast out of the mountain of God. Because of his pride he was cast down in the presence of kings. For the multitude of his iniquities a fire devoured him, and he was burnt to ashes.

In this passage we have the prophet's message to Satan, and a brief parenthesis in which he declared the ultimate restoration of Israel. Satan would be involved in the overthrow of Tyre, and in the midst of her Jehovah would be glorified. All this was in order that there should be no more "a pricking brier" to the house of Israel.

This final declaration led the prophet to utter the brief word concerning the ultimate restoration of Israel. He declared in the name of Jehovah that the scattered ones would be gathered and set apart in the midst of the nations, dwelling securely there, and that in order that the people should know that Jehovah was their God.

EZEKIEL 29

Ezekiel then uttered the doom of one. Egypt had been the principal foe of the people of God, and against her were uttered seven prophecies, which are placed here in an order of purpose rather than in the order of delivery. Again the prophet constantly insisted that the purpose of judgment was to make Jehovah known.

The first prophecy was against Pharaoh and all Egypt. The sin of Pharaoh was inclusively and poetically described pride, which claimed the river as his own creation. This description included the thought of Pharaoh as a great fish living in the river, and at once the folly of his claim is manifest. Ezekiel then foretold Pharaoh's doom. This monster would be taken from his river, and cast on the land, where his flesh would become meat for the beasts of the earth and the fowls of the heaven. In this day of humiliation Egypt would know the folly of Israel when leaning on her for strength. Ezekiel then proceeded to describe the judgment as the coming of a sword on the land of Egypt, and the scattering of its people among the nations. After forty days he declared that Jehovah would gather them again, and in their own land make them a degraded people, no more to rule over the nations.

The second prophecy was brief, foretelling that the instrument of judgment would be Nebuchadrezzar, and that the capture of Egypt would be his wage for the defeat of Tyre.

EZEKIEL 30

The third prophecy described the process by which Nebuchadrezzar would accomplish the purpose of Jehovah. It opens with an introductory word announcing the nearness of the day of the Lord, and foretelling the anguish which would fall on all the peoples in the hour of Egypt's overthrow. This anguish would be caused by the fact that all who had helped her would be made desolate, thus sharing in her judgment. As for Egypt itself, the stroke of Jehovah would fall on the land, whose rivers would be dried as it passed under the domination of evil men. The stroke would also fall on the idols, and finally on all the great cities of the land.

The fourth prophecy was directed against the power of Pharaoh. Judgment against him was described as the breaking of his arm, for which breaking there would be no healing, and therefore he would have no power to hold the sword. This would be accomplished by the king of Babylon, and Ezekiel contrasted his power with the weakness of Pharaoh by declaring that Jehovah would strengthen his arms, so that he might hold the sword and execute His judgment on the land of Egypt. Thus the Egyptians would be scattered among the nations, and dispersed through the countries. Again, each of these prophecies concludes with the clear declaration of purpose, "They shall know that I am Jehovah."

EZEKIEL 31

The fifth prophecy was directed against the greatness of Pharaoh. Ezekiel was commanded to address himself to Pharaoh and his multitudes. This he did, first by describing his greatness. He first asked, "Whom art thou like in thy greatness?" To this inquiry he replied by describing the greatness of the Assyrian, the intention evidently being that Pharaoh should apply that description to himself. The greatness of Assyria was set forth under the figure of a stately tree in Lebanon, overtopping all the rest, nourished by the waters that ran about its roots, so great that all the fowls took refuge in its branches and the beasts of the earth beneath its shadow, so fair that all the trees of Eden envied him.

The prophet then foretold the destruction of this greatness, first by the same figure, and then by a graphic and awful picture of the descent of Pharaoh into Sheol. The fallen tree, with its broken branches lying by all the water courses, so that the fowls of the heaven dwelt in the ruin and the beasts lay down on the branches, set forth the earthly side of the destruction of Egypt. So great had the power of Egypt been that when Pharaoh and his hosts descended to the underworld all nature was moved. The waters were stayed, and Lebanon mourned, while yet the trees of Eden were comforted. The direct application of these figures to Pharaoh closed the fifth prophecy.

EZEKIEL 32

The sixth prophecy followed the fifth after an interval of nearly two years, but was closely associated with it, in that it consisted of a lamentation for Pharaoh whose doom was first described as the taking of a dragon in the seas and casting him forth on the land. The effect of this downfall would be widespread, bringing desolation to his own land, supplying booty to other lands, and making men everywhere tremble in the presence of the judgment of Jehovah.

This prophecy was uttered almost immediately after the fall of Jerusalem, just when certain of the people of God were turning their faces toward Egypt in the hope of help. It is quite evident that the intention of the prophet was not merely to foretell the doom of Egypt, but preeminently to warn those people of God who in the day of His judgment of them were hoping for succor and relief from Egypt.

The seventh and final prophecy against Egypt was uttered about two weeks after the sixth, and consisted of a wail for the multitudes of Egypt, in which the descent to death was portrayed, and all the companies of the dead from among the nations were represented as companions of Pharaoh and his hosts in the underworld. This was a terrible and awe-inspiring message, being, in effect, a funeral song in which the prophet in imagination watched the descent of Pharaoh and his hosts to the underworld. The proud head of the ancient enemy of the people of God is described as going out through death into corruption. As he passes into the dark and awful underworld he finds himself in the company of the slain multitudes of Asshur, and Elam, of Meshech and Tubal, of Edom and Sidon.

The prophet's declaration that "Pharaoh shall see them, and shall be comforted," is appalling, as it reveals that the only comfort that can come to him is the profound sense of the operation of infinite justice in the punishment of all, himself included, who have been guilty of the abominations which have issued in the judgment of Jehovah.

EZEKIEL 33

Ezekiel next delivered a series of messages concerning the chosen nation. The first message described the function and responsibilities of the prophet under the figure of a watchman. In the day of danger a watchman was appointed to give notice of the approach of an enemy. If he did his duty and his warning was not heeded, the blood of the slain would be on their own heads. If he failed to give warning and people were slain their blood would be on his head. That was the position occupied by Ezekiel. Set by Jehovah as a watchman for Israel, his duty was to hear the word from the mouth of the Lord and deliver it to the people. If he did so, and the wicked persisted in wickedness, the soul of the prophet would be delivered.

He was then to declare to the people who were lamenting the judgment of their sins that Jehovah had no pleasure in the death of the wicked, but rather that the wicked should turn from his ways and live. Past acts of righteousness would not atone for present transgression. Past sin would be pardoned if the sinner turned to Jehovah. On the basis of this announcement the prophet defended Jehovah against the people who charged Him with being unequal in His ways.

Immediately after the delivery of this message, fugitives from the sack of Jerusalem came to the prophet. This had been foretold (24:25-27), and the prophet had been instructed that when they came his mouth would be opened and he would be no more dumb. This prophecy he now declared was fulfilled, and he opened his mouth and foretold that desolation of the land was still determined, and that even those left in the waste places would be destroyed.

This message closed with a rebuke of the people, who, aroused and even interested by the messages of the prophet, had gathered together to hear them, being interested in them as those would be who listened to a lovely song and a pleasant voice and capable playing on an instrument. Their interest was sensual rather than spiritual. The difference between the two may always be detected by the consequent attitude of those who hear. Sensuality hears and does nothing. Spirituality hears and obeys.

EZEKIEL 34

The next prophecy dealt ultimately with the one Shepherd. It opened with an indictment of the false shepherds through whom all these evil things had happened to the people. Their sin had been that they had ministered to themselves. Feeding themselves and clothing themselves, they had not fed the sheep, neither had they ministered to the diseased and the sick and the broken and the needy. The result of the failure of the shepherds was that the people were scattered, and had become a prey of the beasts of the field. Because of all this, Jehovah was against the shepherds, and would deliver the sheep.

That deliverance the prophet then described in language full of beauty. Jehovah said, "I Myself, even I, will search . . . and seek . . . and deliver . . . and bring them out . . . and gather them . . . bring them in . . . and feed them . . . and cause them to lie down . . . and bind up . . . and strengthen."

Continuing the same message, the prophet proceeded to declare that the action of Jehovah would be not merely delivering, but also governing. In the gracious words declaring His shepherd care, the last statement was, "I will feed them in judgment." That is explained in the following paragraph, in which the discrimination and administration of Jehovah are manifest, in that He judges between cattle and cattle, and prevents the strong from treading down the pasture to the injury of the weak.

Finally, there was the gracious and glorious promise of the one Shepherd, for the description of whom the prophet borrowed the name of the king who had most perfectly realized in the history of the people the purpose of God. In the fulness of time the one Shepherd appeared, and in a mystery of iniquity the sheep whom He would have gathered flung Him out to the beasts. The men of Israel, "by the hands of lawless men did crucify and slay," and they have been scattered more widely and terribly than ever.

EZEKIEL 35

The prophet next described the new order by contrasting Mount Seir with the mountains of Israel. Jehovah announced Himself as against Mount Seir, and as stretching out His hand in order to make it a desolation and an astonishment. The sin of Mount Seir had been perpetual and persistent enmity to the children of Israel, and that even in the time of their calamity. Therefore its judgment would be perpetual desolation. Mount Seir had lusted to possess the lands of Israel and Judah. And because of their envy judgment would fall on them and they would be dispossessed of their own lands, and be made desolate.

EZEKIEL 36

In contrast with Mount Seir the prophet placed the mountains of Israel, as he delivered the word of the Lord to them. They had been the scorn of their enemies, who had made them desolate and swallowed them up. Therefore Jehovah would proceed against these enemies, and deliver Israel from their oppression. As a result of such deliverance, the whole land, its mountains and its hills, its water courses and its valleys would be made abundantly fruitful. Men would be multiplied, the cities inhabited, and the waste places built.

In the midst of this promise of deliverance comes a great revelation of the secret of all: "Behold, I am for you." The prophet was then charged to explain this prediction of ultimate restoration by first affirming that their own sin caused their suffering.

Then anew and with greater clearness, he declared the reason for their restoration. Jehovah had pity for His holy name, and both by reprobation and restoration moved toward the sanctification of His name among the nations.

The prophet then declared the method of their restoration. Gathered by God out of all countries, the people would be cleansed inwardly and spiritually, and be enabled to do right by being brought into a new fellowship with the Spirit of God.

The results of the restoration would be their repentance and the return of all that prosperity which through sin they had forfeited, and, consequently, a renewal of their witness to the nations round about of truth concerning Jehovah.

EZEKIEL 37

The wonderful vision of the valley filled with bones was now granted to the prophet. As he gazed on them, he was asked, "Son of man, can these bones live?" His utter abandonment to God, even in the matter of his conception, was evident in his reply, "O Lord God, Thou knowest." Over these bones he was then told to prophesy, commanding the people to hear the word of the Lord, proclaiming to them the promise that breath should enter into them and flesh be restored to them. He obeyed, and beheld the bones coming together, and being clothed with sinews and with flesh. As yet the wonder had proceeded only so far as the restoration of dry and scattered bones to corpses.

Again he was commanded to prophesy to the wind, calling it to come and breathe on the slain so that they might live. He obeyed, and beheld the corpses standing on their feet, a living army. This vision was the outcome of a proverb current among the people, "Our bones are dried up and our hope is lost, we are clean cut off." The application of the vision was made in the declaration that God would bring His people from their graves, and make them live.

Having thus foretold the renewal of the people, the prophet was instructed to take two sticks and inscribe on them for Judah and for Joseph, and all the house of Israel. These he was to join together, so that they should be one stick in his hand. When the people inquired what he meant by this, he was to tell them that the purpose of God was not only renewal, but also reunion.

The prophet then repeated the promise of the coming of the one Shepherd, under whose rule Jehovah's original intention for His people would be fulfilled. With them He would make a covenant of peace, and, as symbolized in the ancient economy, would dwell in the midst of them forevermore.

Again the underlying purpose of the whole history of Israel is revealed in the final promise, "The nations shall know that I am Jehovah."

EZEKIEL 38

The final message concerning the nation dealt with matters far removed from the times of the prophet. In the dim distance he saw Gog of the land of Magog, prince of Rosh, Meshech, and Tubal, gathering against Israel. He saw them, however, gathering under divine compulsion to this very manifestation of antagonism, the message of Jehovah plainly declaring, "I will turn thee about and put hooks into thy jaws, and bring thee forth." This last antagonism would consist of a confederacy of Magog and other nations from the uttermost part of the earth. Their coming would be terrible, like a storm.

As the prophet looked into the future he saw the prophecy of Zechariah fulfilled in the case of Jerusalem, for she dwelt securely without walls, and was a city of villages. Against this safely-dwelling people a vast confederacy would move in malice. The prophet then showed that their coming ostensibly against Israel would really be a definite and positive act of rebellion against Jehovah. Therefore His wrath would proceed against them with the result so constantly referred to, that Jehovah would magnify Himself and sanctify Himself, and make Himself known in the eyes of many nations.

EZEKIEL 39

Having thus described the order of events in the far distant future, the prophet proceeded to utter in greater detail his prophecy of the antagonism of God to those who thus would gather themselves against His anointed people. He first made it perfectly clear that the destruction of Gog would be by the direct act of Jehovah, and that in order that His holy name should be profaned no more the nations would know that He was the Holy One in Israel. This destruction, moreover, would be complete. The burial place of the last confederacy against Jehovah and Israel would be Israel itself. The judgment would be characterized by fearfulness and terror, as God would establish His rule, and set His glory forth by His last method of judgment, among the peoples who had not been persuaded in any other way.

The last word in the messages dealing with the one nation is a repetition of the promise that Jehovah would bring again the captivity of Jacob, and have mercy on the whole house of Israel, and be jealous for His holy name. In that day of restoration, dwelling securely in their land, they would still bear their shame, that is to say, repentance for past failure would be profound, even in the day of restoration. By that attitude of mind Jehovah would be sanctified among them in the sight of the nations, but they would have the infinite healing of His unveiled face, and the abiding energy of His outpoured Spirit.

EZEKIEL 40

This final section must be studied in relation to all that has immediately preceded it, wherein the spiritual restoration and cleansing of the people had been foretold. The picture of the restored order of worship results therefrom. It is a little difficult to distinguish between the material and the spiritual in Ezekiel's description in this last part. It is clear that the new condition will be characterized by such fellowship with the eternal and spiritual orders as to be completely under their dominion.

The prophet's description of the new Temple commenced with the courts. In the first paragraph is a general description of the outer courts. It deals, first, with the wall which surrounded the whole Temple buildings, with the gate on the east, through which Jehovah would enter as He returned to the Temple; with the lodges, and then with the outer court and the buildings connected with it.

Still dealing with the Temple courts, the prophet now described the inner. The gates of these corresponded with those of the outer court, and are described, with the lodges and the arches. Within this inner court were the arrangements for the sacrificial ceremonies, the tables and books. Therein also were the chambers for the singers and the priests. The measurement of the court was given, and the fact that the altar stood therein. Finally, the prophet described the porch of the house itself, giving its dimensions, and referring to the two pillars, which undoubtedly responded to the two named Jachin and Boaz in the temple of Solomon.

EZEKIEL 41

Passing to the Temple proper, the prophet portrayed it first from the outside, describing the actual Temple, with its Holy Place, and Holy of Holies, then the side chambers; and, finally, another separate building, ending with the general dimensions of the inner court, the house buildings, and the separate building.

This was followed by a description of the woodwork within, and its ornamentation. The technicalities are difficult to follow, but it is clear that the general effect of the beautiful work was of cherubim and palm trees, which symbolized the perfection of spiritual appreciation and material well-being.

It is interesting to notice the two types of life represented by the two faces of the cherubim, one being a man and the other a young lion. Interpreted by the earlier symbolism of the prophecy, this suggested perfect realization of created life, and its perfect exercise in kingly dominion.

Both the Holy Place and the Holiest of all were entered by two-leaved doors, each of the leaves being again divided, making them what we would call folding doors. These too were adorned with cherubim and palm trees.

EZEKIEL 42

The next section of description deals with the general scheme of buildings surrounding the Temple proper. On the north and south sides were chambers, which are described. These were the holy chambers for the use of the priests, in which they ate the holy things, kept all the materials for the offerings, and changed their garments for the work of their sacred office.

Finally, the outside measurements of the whole Temple buildings were given. Passing through the east gate, the angel accompanying Ezekiel measured the east side, the north side, the south side, and the west side, each of which was 500 reeds. In all probability, in harmony with other measurements given, the word "cubits" should be substituted for "reeds."

EZEKIEL 43

The prophet's next vision was of Jehovah's return to the Temple. Again he beheld a vision and heard a voice. The visions which he had seen by the river Chebar appeared again. The same glory on which he had gazed when he came to destroy the city, that is, to utter his predictions concerning its destruction, appeared in this great hour of restoration, when Jehovah, so long exiled from His Temple, returned to it. The voice of Jehovah was as the sound of many waters, but in speaking to Ezekiel it became the voice of a man, and declared that Jehovah had taken up His abode in the house, that He would dwell in the midst of Israel forever, and that she should no more defile His holy name.

In the sequence of the prophecy a parenthesis occurs in which Ezekiel was charged to show the house of Israel this future glory, in order that they might be ashamed of their iniquities. To those who were ashamed, he was, moreover, charged to make known in detail the form and fashion of the house, and to declare its law.

Returning to the sequence of the message concerning the return of Jehovah, the prophet described the altar of burnt-offering, giving its measurements and a description of the ceremonies of its consecration and of its use.

EZEKIEL 44

The next section described the service of the new Temple. It commenced with the command that the eastern gate, through which Jehovah entered, must be kept closed, and that no man should be allowed to pass through it. The only exception to this rule was that the prince should eat his bread in the gate of Jehovah's entrance.

Again the prophet beheld the glory of the Lord, and was solemnly charged to pay special attention to the ordinances of the house of the Lord and the laws thereof, which were about to be given to him. These ordinances provided, first, that under no circumstances should aliens or the uncircumcised in the heart or flesh serve in the sanctuary of Jehovah. This had been the sin of the past, and must not be repeated.

The Levites who had gone astray in the olden days, and who had been punished on account of their iniquity, while being excluded from the office of the priest, were, nevertheless, to be restored to the charge of the house and all its service. The sons of Zadok who had remained faithful to the charge of the sanctuary in the days of Israel's unfaithfulness and apostasy were appointed to stand as priests before Jehovah in the new Temple. They were instructed about the garments they were to wear in the exercise of their office, their duties of teaching the people to distinguish between holy and common, their purification after necessary defilement by contact with the dead, and, finally, that they were to have no inheritance among the people, finding all they needed in Jehovah and His service.

EZEKIEL 45:1-17

Seeing that the priests were to have no inheritance, the next section of the prophecy dealt fittingly with the method of their support. After the distribution of the land, a description of which followed later, a lot was to be set apart at its very center as an oblation to the Lord, and was to be looked on as holy land. Of this one part was to be for the maintenance of the priests and another for the Levites. On each side of this holy square of territory, land was to be set apart for the prince, and the princes of Jehovah were to oppress the people no more.

The prophet immediately followed with Jehovah's charge to the princes. Their duty was to cease violence and taking spoil, and executing judgment and justice. The standards of weight and measurement were then given, and the provision for the offerings of the prince was described. These offerings were provided by the people for the burnt-offerings and the meal-offerings and the drink-offerings, and it was the prince's duty to provide these things for the priests out of this resource.

EZEKIEL 45:18—46

This passage constitutes one paragraph dealing with the arrangements for the feasts, and appointed times and seasons. Twice a year the sacred ceremony of cleansing the sanctuary was to be performed, on the first day of the first month, and on the first day of the seventh month. In this provision the holiness of God is insisted upon, in that it is an atonement for the house on the behalf, not of any individuals, or of specific sins, but "for everyone that erreth, and for him that is simple."

The Passover feast was still to be observed, and also the feast of Tabernacles. In addition to these great festivals, arrangements were made for the ceremonial observance of sabbaths, and of months, and also for the daily offerings.

In this connection instructions followed which made it impossible for the prince at any time to alienate ultimately his inheritance in the land. What he gave to his sons must be of his own inheritance, in order that the people be not disinherited. Ezekiel was conducted by the angel through the boiling houses in which the servants of the sanctuary were to prepare that portion of the offerings of which the people were to partake.

EZEKIEL 47

Again Ezekiel was taken to the door of the house, and there beheld the wonderful symbolic river. Its source was the sanctuary. It proceeded under the threshold, and past the altar, and outward in an eastward course, a steadily growing stream. A thousand cubits beyond the place of its emergence it was ankle deep, a thousand farther it reached the knees, a thousand farther the loins were covered, and a thousand farther it became, in the stately language of the prophet, "a river that I could not pass through; for the waters were risen, waters to swim in, a river that could not be passed through."

Having observed this growth, the prophet was taken back to the brink of the river, and then in language full of poetic beauty he described its effect. Trees were seen growing on either bank. The angel told him that the waters went down into the Arabah, and ultimately into the sea, and that its waters would be healed by the inflow of the river of life. The inclusive statement of the effect is stated in the words, "Everything shall live whithersoever the river goeth."

Following the vision of the river, the prophet received instructions concerning the new division of the land, the possessions of the tribes running from east to west. The country thus divided would belong to the tribes of Israel, and any stranger dwelling therein was to have an inheritance in the land in common with the children of Israel.

EZEKIEL 48

The disposition of the tribes in relation to the sanctuary was then given. On the north of the sacred land Dan, Asher, Naphtali, Manasseh, Ephraim, Reuben, and Judah were to find their possessions, and in that order from north to south. In the sacred land itself, at the very center, stood the sanctuary, and the priests' possession was immediately round about it. On the north of the land of the sanctuary and the priests, was the possession of the Levites, while on its south were the city and its adjacent lands. On the east and the west of all these was the princes' portion. Then to the south of the sacred land lay the portions of Benjamin, Simeon, Issachar, Zebulun, Gad, and in that order from north to south.

The last vision granted to Ezekiel was of the city at the south of the sacred land, having three gates toward each of the points of the compass, on which were inscribed the names of the tribes of Israel.

The final words of this prophet of hope announced the name of the city, "Jehovah-Shammah," signifying, "The Lord is there." Thus the lonely witness to the glory of God, in exile in Babylon, rejoiced "in hope of the glory of God."

It is a fit and exquisite termination to this most wonderful book. Ezekiel had been arrested and inspired by visions of the essential glory of God, which he was able to describe only in terms full of majestic suggestiveness, which even to this day we read with great reverence and wonder. He had observed the reprobation of his people, and had seen that at its deepest it consisted in the fact that Jehovah had withdrawn Himself from them. Through all the clouds and darkness in the midst of which he lived, he had looked on to the people's restoration, and had seen that it consisted in the return of Jehovah to their midst, and all the burden of his message ended with the simple and sublime word, "Jehovah is there."

Daniel

DANIEL 1

During the reign of Nebuchadnezzar Daniel came into favor and power. The king seems to have been impressed by the people he had conquered. He desired that some of the choicest of their young men be included among his own confidential servants.

Among those selected were four especially named, among whom was Daniel. They were set apart for training and preparation for their official duties. This training lasted three years. They had special physical attention, and their food and drink were supplied from the king's table.

Daniel at once manifested his strength of character in purposing to abstain from the king's meat and wine. He was courteous, but he asked for a ten days' test. The test vindicated his purpose, and he and his friends were allowed to proceed with their training. At the end of that training they were presented to Nebuchadnezzar, were approved by him, and appointed to positions in the kingdom.

DANIEL 2

In the second year of his reign Nebuchadnezzar, troubled by dreams and unable to sleep, called together his enchanters and sorcerers to explain his dreams one of which troubled him especially. Their difficulty was that the king could not recall the dream. It had left an impression on his mind, but none of the details remained in his memory. Of course, his demand was the unreasonable one of a despot, and yet the claims these men made, if true, ought to have enabled them to discover the dream as well as to interpret it. Such was the king's opinion, and he made it a test case, declaring that if they were unable to do what he asked, he would know that they were lying and corrupt. They failed, Nebuchadnezzar was furious, and commanded the destruction of them all. In this decree the Hebrew youths were involved.

Daniel, through the king's captain, sought and obtained an interview with the king, asking for time, and promising to interpret the dream. The request being granted, he at once gathered his friends together, and they betook themselves to prayer. In answer the secret was revealed to Daniel in a vision at night, and in his gratitude he praised the name of Jehovah in what was practically a psalm full of beauty. He then charged the king's captain, Arioch, not to destroy the wise men, as he was able to interpret the king's dream.

Daniel was immediately brought into the king's presence, and first, in language full of confidence and dignity, ascribed to God the glory of the interpretion he was about to give. He exonerated the wise men from any blame for their inability to interpret the dream, and declared the truth concerning the God of heaven, who was able to reveal secrets, and who by this dream intended to make known to the king the course of events in the history of his people. He then vividly described the image of the king's dream, and proceeded to interpret its meaning. Tracing the progress of events through the successive kingdoms of Babylon, Media, and Persia, Greece, Rome, the ten kingdoms, and the final setting up of the Kingdom of Heaven, he showed how there would be a process of deterioration, which would merge into the establishment of the new order. This interpretation convinced Nebuchadnezzar, who at once recognized the supremacy of God, and rewarded Daniel by setting him over the province and the wise men.

DANIEL 3

The next story is of the pride of Nebuchadnezzar in setting up in the plain of Dura a great golden image. This may have been connected with the interpretation of the dream Daniel had given. The head of gold in the image of Nebuchadnezzar's dream symbolized Babylon. Nebuchadnezzar's image was all of gold, and perhaps revealed his conception of the power of Babylon, and therefore was of the nature either of unbelief in the accuracy of the prediction or of rebellion against it. To this image he commanded all peoples to bow down in worship. This would also explain the attitude of the dauntless three who declined to bend their knee to the image. In the first place, it was an act of idolatry, and, moreover, such obeisance on their part might have been construed into a recognition of the continuity of the power of Babylon, of which the divine revelation to Daniel had predicted the downfall.

With splendid heroism they cast themselves on God, and were supernaturally delivered from the fierce fire of the furnace, the king seeing One so glorious in mien with them in the fire, that even he described Him as being "like a son of the gods." This deliverance more deeply impressed Nebuchadnezzar, and he decreed that no word should be spoken against the God of Shadrach, Meshach, and Abednego, and promoted them in the province of Babylon.

DANIEL 4

The last story connected with the reign of Nebuchadnezzar consisted of the king's own manifesto, setting forth the dealings of the Most High God with him.

The opening ascription of praise is most remarkable when it is remembered that it expressed the conviction of so mighty a monarch as Nebuchadnezzar. The story of the dream which troubled him follows. It came to him in the midst of prosperity and ease in his palace. His magicians were unable to give him an interpretation, and Daniel was brought before him. To him he minutely described his vision.

The fact that the king recalled that his dream was symbolic is evidenced by the change to the use of the masculine pronoun, and the declaration that his heart was to be changed from man's and become like a beast's.

Daniel was "astonished," evidently because he immediately saw the application of the dream to the king, and commenced his interpretation with the courteous address, expressive of his sense of the calamity about to fall on the king. Nevertheless, in loyalty to truth he interpreted its meaning to the king.

He then appealed to Nebuchadnezzar to turn from sin and show mercy to the poor in order that his tranquility might be lengthened.

A year later the dream was fulfilled. Nebuchadnezzar did not obey the appeal of Daniel, and while he was boasting that he had built the great city, Babylon, by his own power and for his own glory a voice came from heaven to tell him that the kingdom was departed from him, and that all that Daniel had foretold would be fulfilled. He was immediately stricken with madness and driven out from among men to dwell and eat with the beasts of the field.

Finally, his reason returning, Nebuchadnezzar recognized the God of heaven and was restored to his kingdom, praising the King of Heaven whose works are true and whose ways are judgment.

DANIEL 5

The next scene is cast in the reign of Belshazzar. He had succeeded to the throne of his father, and was a man of profligate habits. No details are given of his reign, but a graphic picture is set before us of the carousal which revealed the man, and was the occasion of the final manifestation of his sin, and of the consequent judgment of God.

Having gathered together a thousand of his lords, his wives, and his concubines, he was guilty of the unutterable folly of using in drunken revelry the sacred vessels from the Temple of God. Thereupon appeared a mystic hand, writing on the wall the doom of himself and his kingdom.

As in the reign of his father, the wise men were unable to interpret the meaning of the writing; and Daniel, evidently not now near to the king, who seemed not to know him, was sent for.

Daniel was full of dignity and heroic loyalty to God. With clear, incisive words, he first declined all the king's gifts, and then charged him with his guilt. Continuing, he proclaimed God as seated high over the thrones of earth, and interpreted the writing as indicating God's knowledge of the kingdom, and His determination to end it and divide it among the Medes and Persians.

DANIEL 6

The last section in the historic portion of the Book is in the reign of Darius. He reorganized the government and distributed the administration among twenty satraps, who, in turn, were responsible to three presidents. Of these Daniel was one, and he was so distinguished by an excellent spirit that Darius proposed to set him over the whole realm. This naturally stirred up jealousy among the other presidents and satraps, who cunningly planned Daniel's downfall.

Knowing that they would be unable to find anything against him save his relationship to his God, they induced the king to sign a decree that for a period of thirty days no one should ask a petition of God or man, save of the king. This was intended to flatter the king, and to bring Daniel into discredit with him, for his habit of prayer was evidently well known. Daniel's loyalty never swerved. He continued to observe the seasons and acts of worship as had been his custom.

Unable to escape from his own decree, the king was reluctantly compelled to commit Daniel to the den of lions. How high his esteem for Daniel was is evidenced by his spending a night of mourning and fasting.

The supremacy of God over all the kings and councils of earth was manifest in the supernatural deliverance of His servant, which issued in a proclamation by Darius.

DANIEL 7

We come now to the second half of the Book, which consists of visions, with their interpretations, granted to Daniel through three reigns. During the reign of Belshazzar two visions were granted to him, which constitute the prophetic light of that particular period.

The first of these was of four beasts rising from the sea, the last of which had ten horns. In their midst arose another, which destroyed them. The vision then became a vision of the setting of thrones, and the appearing of the glory of One who overcame the beasts and received dominion and glory, and a Kingdom.

These visions troubled Daniel, but an interpretation was given to him, first in general terms. The beasts symbolized four kings, and the final vision indicated that the saints of the Most High would yet receive and possess the Kingdom for ever and for ever. A particular interpretation of the meaning of the fourth beast and the horns, was vouchsafed to him, and the ultimate value was again declared to be the setting forth of the truth of the government of Jehovah, and the ultimate establishment of His Kingdom over all others. The whole matter troubled the prophet, but he kept it in his heart.

DANIEL 8

Two years later, in the third year of king Belshazzar's reign, another vision came to Daniel. It was of a ram with two horns pushing westward, northward, and southward. As Daniel watched, a he goat attacked the ram, and overcame him, and magnified himself. Four horns appeared, out of one of which came another, which grew until it had broken down the sanctuary. A voice of a holy one inquired how long this would continue, and the answer was given to Daniel.

Again he pondered the vision, and sought to understand it, and an interpretation was given to him. The two-horned ram represented the united power of Media and Persia, the rough he goat was the king of Greece. Against him a fierce one would arise, succeeding through policy, but ultimately being broken without hand.

DANIEL 9

In the first year of the reign of Darius, Daniel, who was evidently not only a man of prayer, but a diligent student of the prophetic writings, became conscious that the seventy years of judgment on Jerusalem foretold by Jeremiah were drawing to a close. He therefore set himself to seek the Lord by personal prayer and penitence on behalf of his people, making confession of their sin, and pleading their cause. He besought the Lord that the reproaches which had fallen on Jerusalem be put away, and, as men of vision had so often done, he based his plea on the honor of the Lord.

The language of this intercessory prayer reveals a man familiar with God in all the highest meaning of that word, and therefore keenly conscious of the sinfulness of the rebellion and failure of his own people.

During this intercession Gabriel came to him, declaring to him, first of all, that he was "greatly beloved," urging him to consider the matter, and understand the vision. He then made a revelation to him concerning the divine program. Seventy weeks were decreed on the people and the city. These were divided into three periods, the first of seven weeks, the second of sixty-two weeks, and the third of one week.

DANIEL 10

The last things were revealed to Daniel in the reign of Cyrus. For three whole weeks he mourned and fasted as the result of a revelation to him of a great warfare. At the close of that period there appeared to him, by the side of the great river Hiddekel, a glorious Person. The description, when compared with that of John in Patmos, leaves no doubt that in this chapter we have the account of one of the Christophanies of the Old Testament. So radiant was the revelation that Daniel was reduced to weakness in the presence of it and filled with an overwhelming sense of awe.

While prostrate in the dust, he felt the touch of a hand and was lifted into the position of obeisance and adoration. He who had thus appeared to him and touched him then addressed him in words full of tenderness, bidding him not to fear, declaring that his loyalty to God was known and valued.

The glorious One then proceeded to foretell the history of Daniel's people in the latter days. There is a touch of mystic wonder about this story as this glorious One speaks of having been with the kings of Persia, of being in conflict with principalities, having dominion over earthly kingdoms, and being helped by a prince Michael, evidently of spiritual nature rather than a material manifestation.

DANIEL 11

The foretelling of the glorious One is contained in this chapter. It covered a period to the time of Antiochus Epiphanes, and finally referred to the Messianic kingdom.

There would be yet three kings in Persia, and also a fourth, "richer than they all." The fourth would "stir up all against the realm of Greece." This undoubtedly would refer to Xerxes.

Following the fourth there would be another, whose kingdom would be broken and scattered. Here the reference was to Alexander. Beyond that, there would be long conflict between the kings of the North and those of the South, until the coming of One who would cause an exactor to pass through the glory of the Kingdom, whose regime would be brief, and would end neither in anger nor in battle.

The reign of one contemptible in person, but gaining the kingdom by flatteries, is described at greatest length. There can be no doubt that the one referred to was Antiochus Epiphanes. His character and his methods were described. He would be unscrupulous, deceitful, and cruel, but the phrase, "even for a time," indicated that this man also would be within the government of God, and unable to proceed beyond the limit marked for him.

His campaigns against Egypt were foretold, together with his ultimate withdrawal, and his methods of deceit and corruption against the people of God. During the period of his oppression there would be a period of "a little help," the reference being to the rising under the Maccabees. Ultimately the king of the South would contend with him, but would be overwhelmed by him. As a result, Antiochus Epiphanes would set forth on a new campaign of conquest, and finally perish on his way to Jerusalem.

DANIEL 12

The last things are then foretold. Michael, the great prince, would stand up for the children of God's people, and there would ensue a time of trouble such as never had been. Beyond that there would be a resurrection, and the dawning of a new age. This prophecy was literally fulfilled under the Roman power. ?

Daniel was charged to shut the book and seal it to the time of the end. He heard the man clothed in linen swear in mystic language by Him that liveth that these things would be for "a time, times, and a half," that the things finally foretold would be fulfilled only when the end of the breaking of the power of the holy people had come.

Filled with a sense of the mystery of the things he had seen and heard, the prophet inquired, "O, my lord, what shall be the issue of these things?" The answer was that the words were shut up and sealed to the time of the end, and he was urged to go his way, that is, to attend to his own duty, and fulfil his own responsibility. Moreover, he was assured that blessing would be granted to those who waited, that he himself would rest, and yet stand in his lot at the end of the days.

Hosea

HOSEA 1–2:1

The statement with which this prophecy opens, "When the Lord spake at the first," is a declaration by Hosea long after the events. Looking back, he understood that the impulse which resulted in the heart agony was also part of the divine method of teaching him. There is no reason to believe that Gomer was outwardly impure in the days when Hosea married her. If impurity were in her heart, Hosea did not know it, and it was not apparent during the early days of their married life.

In the picture of their domestic life the important matter is its revelation of Hosea's national consciousness. Three children were born to him, and there is still no reason to believe that during this period Gomer was unfaithful. In naming the children he revealed his conviction concerning the condition of his nation. Living in close fellowship with God, he saw his people in the light of the divine purpose, and as the children were born, named them in such a way as to indicate his profound convictions. Jezreel means the threatened judgment; Lo-ruhamah means mercy not obtained; Lo-ammi means cast out, not my people. While the outlook was dark, the section ends with words which show that, in spite of all contradictory appearances, the prophet's faith in the final fulfilment of the first divine purposes was unshaken.

HOSEA 2:2-23

No details of the unfaithfulness of Gomer are given, but in the second movement the prophet is seen nursing his own agony, and by that process learning the true nature of the sin of his people as God knew and felt it. All that Hosea said concerning Gomer was also the language of Jehovah concerning Israel. As she had violated her covenant with him, so had Israel with Jehovah. He charged her with the worst form of infidelity, harlotry, which is sinning for a price; and apparent in the charge is the mingling of the awful anger of wounded love, with a suggestion of pity and mercy.

In the latter part of this section the prophet speaks for Jehovah only, the tragedy in his own life being the background of illustration. The divine attitude was severe and tender. Jehovah would hedge up the way of His people, and their vain search after the fruits of harlotry is graphically described. In tenderness He would lead them to the wilderness, speaking to their heart, and in the valley of Achor open before them a door of hope. The prophet's confidence in this method is manifested in his prediction that Israel would yet answer, as in the days of her youth, that her betrothal to Jehovah would be forever, and that she would be described as Ruhamah instead of Loruhamah, as Ammi instead of Loammi.

HOSEA 3

Finally, the prophet was commanded to love and find and restore his sinning and wandering bride. Through his obedience he entered into fellowship with the amazing tenderness of God, and was thereby prepared to deliver the messages which followed. It must have been a startling command, "Go ye, love a woman . . . an adulteress," but its explanation was found in the words, "even as the Lord loveth the children of Israel." Hosea was commanded to exercise love in spite of his wife's sin, in order that he might learn God's attitude toward Israel. He obeyed, and the price he paid for her was the price of a slave, which in all probability she had become by this time.

The covenant he made with her was that she should enter on a period of seclusion, in which she would be neither harlot nor wife, and that he would be so toward her. The national interpretation of this covenant was that during Israel's time of penitence she would be deprived of both the true and the false, the king or prince, sacrifice or pillar, ephod or teraphim. The ultimate issue would be Israel's return to all the honors and blessings of union with God.

Thus equipped, the prophet was prepared to deliver his messages, all of which sounded the notes of sin, of love, and of judgment.

HOSEA 4

In any attempt to analyze and tabulate the teaching in this second division of the Book it must be remembered that the prophetic utterances cannot be treated as verbatim reports. As they here appear, they are rather the gathering up of the notes or leading ideas of a long period of preaching. These notes fall into three distinct cycles, pollution and its cause, pollution and its punishment, and the love of Jehovah.

In dealing with pollution and its cause the prophet first preferred a general charge against the nation. Israel was summoned to attend and hear the word of the Lord, because He had a controversy with the people. They were charged with being without truth and mercy and knowledge of God, which resulted in the spread of all kinds of evil. The result was to be seen in the mourning land, the languishing people, and man's loss of dominion over nature. The prophet next declared the cause of the sin, and more carefully described the results. The cause was the pollution of the priests. Priest and prophet stumbled, and the people were destroyed for lack of knowledge. As the priests multiplied they sinned, and their glory was turned to shame. The result was the pollution of the people. The example of the priests issued in lack of understanding. The prophet declared that God would not punish for the smaller offense of physical harlotry, but for the more terrible outrage of spiritual adultery which lay behind it. In this connection he counseled Judah to take warning from the terrible example of Israel.

HOSEA 5

Having thus declared the cause of pollution, the prophet's next message was especially addressed to priest, people, and king. First to the priests and the king as elders, and consequently responsible, but to the people also as having been guilty of following the false lead. The message affirmed the divine knowledge of the condition of affairs. Ephraim had committed whoredom; Israel was defiled. Thus the outward doings and the inward condition were recognized. The inevitable judgment was announced.

Ephraim and Israel would stumble, Judah also. There would be a fruitless search after God when it was too late.

The prophet then dealt more particularly with the judgment, and indicated a threefold method. The first would be by the moth and rottenness. These were already at work. They were the emblems of slow destruction. Ephraim, conscious of their presence, had turned to Assyria for help. The second would be by the young lion, suggestive of the new character of strong, devouring judgment determined against the sinning people. The final method of judgment would be the most terrible of all—the withdrawal of God from His people, out of which affliction the prophet declared they would seek His face.

HOSEA 6

Here we have the prophet's appeal in consequence of the judgment threatened. It was first a message calling the people to return to Jehovah. It was based on the certainty of divine pity; and a promise of certain prosperity if the people did return to Him.

However, it is impossible to read this message without discovering its Messianic values, for all that the prophet declared finds its fulfilment in the Christ by way of His First and Second Advents. There are two appeals: the first, "Come, and let us return"; the second, "Let us know, let us follow on to know." The argument for the first is the suffering of Another. "He hath torn, and He will heal us; He hath smitten, and He will bind us up." Resurrection, "After two days will He revive us; on the third day He will raise us up, and we shall live before Him." The argument for the second suggests the things that follow suffering and resurrection, which may be stated thus: Ascension, "His going forth is sure as the morning"; Pentecost, "He shall come unto us as the rain"; the Second Advent, "As the latter rain that watereth the earth."

The second cycle of the prophecy deals with pollution and its punishment. The prophet first stated the case as between Jehovah and His people. The divine attitude was declared to be perplexity. In the presence of the shallowness of their goodness, which was like the morning cloud, or early dew, Jehovah exclaimed, "What shall I do?" He had adopted different methods for their welfare, hewing them by the prophets, slaying them by words, proceeding against them in judgment. What He desired to produce in them as the character of mercy was knowledge of Himself rather than their burnt offerings.

The response to this attitude had been persistent transgression and treachery, and the proofs were to be found in Gilead and Shechem, both of which cities were, in all probability, cities of refuge. The former had been polluted, and the latter filled with lewdness, and even the priests were guilty of murder. Israel had committed the horrible sin of whoredom with Egypt. From Judah also would come a harvest in the day of restoration.

HOSEA 7

The prophet then declared more particularly the true state of affairs. The divine desire to heal was frustrated by the pollution and the people's persistent ignoring of God. Hosea graphically described the widespread pollution. The king, the princess, and the judges were corrupt. All were affected as by the heat of wine and the leaven of evil.

With reference to the widespread influence of Ephraim, the prophet described the tribe as mixing among the people. This ancient tribe was like a cake not turned, a symbol of utter failure, undeveloped on one side, and burned on the other. Moreover, it was, like a silly dove in its manifestation of fear and cowardice. The statement of the case was concluded by a declaration of the utter folly of the people. God was scourging them toward redemption, and in the process they were howling, assembling, and yet continuing in rebellion.

HOSEA 8

From this statement of the case the prophet turned to the pronouncement of judgment. This he did by adopting the figure of the trumpet lifted to the mouth, on which five blasts were sounded, in each of which some aspect of the sin of the people was set forth as revealing the reason for judgment.

The first blast declared the coming judgment under the figure of an eagle, the reason being the transgressions and trespass of the people.

The second blast emphasized Israel's sin of rebellion in that they had set up kings and princes without the authority of Jehovah, and had made idols.

The third blast dealt with Israel's idolatry. She had set up the calf of Samaria, which Jehovah had cast off and broken in pieces. She had been guilty of sowing the wind, that is, emptiness; and therefore she must reap the whirlwind, that is, the force of emptiness.

The fourth blast anounced Israel's alliances. She had gone to Assyria like a wild ass, alone, and her judgment was that her hire among the nations had resulted in diminishing her.

The fifth blast drew attention to the altars of sin which had been raised contrary to light, and by which sacrifice had been violated, and therefore judgment was announced.

HOSEA 9

The judgment was then described in detail. Its first note was of the death of joy. Israel could not find her joy like other peoples. She had gone whoring from God, loving hire on every threshing floor. Having known Jehovah, nothing to which she turned in turning from Him satisfied.

The second note was the actual exile, to which she must pass, back to the slavery of Egypt and Assyria, away from the offerings and feasts of the Lord.

The third was the cessation of prophecy. In the estimation of the debased people the prophet would be a fool, and the spiritual man, mad. Thus the means of testing themselves would be corrupted.

The fourth declared the nemesis of fornication. The prophet traced the growth of this pollution from its beginnings at Baal Peor, and clearly set forth the inevitable deterioration in numbers and strength of a people abandoned to impurity.

The fifth and last would be the final casting out of the people of God because they had failed to listen to His appeals, and as a result they would become wanderers among the nations.

HOSEA 10

The section dealing with pollution and its punishment closes with the prophet's recapitulation and appeal.

The whole case is first stated under the figure of the vine. Israel was a luxuriant vine, and of God's planting, which had turned its fruitfulness to evil account, and it was therefore doomed to His judgment. The result of this judgment would be the lament of the people that they had no king able to save them. The prophet declared that the reason for this was that they had used vain words in swearing falsely, and therefore that judgment would produce terror and mourning, shame and destruction, so that they would cry to the mountains and rocks to cover them and to fall on them. The sin of Israel had been from the days of Gibeah, and therefore Jehovah would chastise them, setting a rider upon Ephraim which would compel the people to the tasks of slavery. The last word here was of earnest and passionate appeal to return to loyalty.

HOSEA 11:1-11

The third cycle of the prophecy sets forth the love which Jehovah had for His people, notwithstanding their sin. This section sets forth Jehovah's love toward His sinning people, and, for the most part, is the speech of Jehovah Himself. Thrice in the course of Jehovah's message to the people, the prophet interpolates words of his own. In studying the section it is necessary to take the words of Jehovah in sequence, and then the interpolations of the prophet in sequence also.

The message of Jehovah falls into three clearly marked movements, which deal, respectively, with the present in the light of past love, the present in the light of present love, the present in the light of future love.

In the first, Jehovah reminded the people of all His past love for them in words full of tenderness, setting their present condition in its light, and crying, "How shall I give thee up?" His own inquiry was answered by the determined declaration of the ultimate triumph of love and the restoration of the people.

HOSEA 11:12; 12:1,7-11; 13:2-14

In the second movement Jehovah set the present sin in the light of His present love. The sin of Ephraim and the sin of Judah, if the marginal reading be adopted, are both declared. The sin of Ephraim is then more distinctly stated, and its pride and impertinence declared. Yet love would triumph over all. Jehovah declared Himself to be the God who had delivered Israel from Egypt, and who would yet again deliver, being true to the messages of the prophets, to the visions of seers, to the similitudes of the ministry of the prophets.

Finally, the present condition of Israel is set in the light of the future love of Jehovah. Opening with the question, "Is Gilead iniquity?" He immediately answered by declaring, "They are altogether vanity," "they sin more and more," charging them with determined persistence in idolatry. Because of abounding sin, judgment was absolutely unavoidable. Yet love would triumph by the way of the wilderness. They had sinned against love in the strength of love's gifts. Jehovah would therefore come against them in terrible judgment, and that because Israel was against God. The sin of Ephraim would create His sorrow. Nevertheless, at last the almighty strength of love would overcome even death and the grave.

HOSEA 12:2-6,12—13:1,15,16

Turning from this main line of the divine message, we now examine the prophet's interpolations. These set forth the history of Israel indicating their relation to Jehovah, and pronounce judgment. They form a remarkable obligato accompaniment in a minor key to the majestic love song of Jehovah, and constitute a contrasting introduction to the final message of the prophet.

The first of them reveals the prophet's sense of Jehovah's controversy with Judah, and his just dealings with Jacob.

The second was reminiscent of Jacob's history, and made a deduction and an appeal.

The third traced the progress of Israel to death, beginning with the flight to the field of Aram, through the exodus from Egypt and preservation to the present, in which Ephraim was exalted in Israel, offended in Baal, and died.

The last declared the doom. It was indeed the last word of man, the pronouncement of awful judgment, and constituted the plea of "guilty," to which the answer of Jehovah as revealed in His message was of the victory of love.

HOSEA 14

The cycle closes with the final call of the prophet, and the promise of Jehovah. The call was to the people to return, because by iniquity they had fallen. The method suggested was to bring the words of penitence, forsaking all false gods, in confidence that mercy would be found in Jehovah. To this Jehovah answered in a message full of hope, declaring, first, that He would restore, because His anger was turned away.

Then in a passage full of exquisite beauty He announced His determination to renew His people and the surrounding nations. He would be as the dew to Israel, which thus would be made fruitful again, and they that dwelt under His shadow would enter into the blessedness. In response to this Ephraim is represented as breaking out into speech which is the language of full and perfect reinstatement.

The prophet closes with a brief word which constitutes an application of the teaching of his message for all time, affirming the ways of Jehovah to be right, and the destiny of man to be determined by his relation thereto.

Joel

JOEL 1

Joel was especially a prophet to Judah. The burden of his message was the Day of the Lord. It seems to be one remarkable utterance rather than notes of a ministry covering a long period. A terrible locust plague which had devastated the entire country was the occasion of its deliverance. Joel spoke of things which were evident to those whom he addressed, then predicted an immediate judgment, and finally looked far on to the ultimate Day of the Lord.

In the first division are two sections. The prophet interpreted the meaning of the actual locust plague, and said it was the sign of yet severer judgment that was imminent. In dealing with the actual plague he uttered a call to contemplation, and to humiliation.

The call to contemplation was addressed, in the first place, to the old men, and then to all the inhabitants. In his description of the desolation the names, "palmer-worm," "locust," "canker-worm," "caterpillar," all refer to locusts. The reference may be to different stages in the development of the locust, or to different varieties of the same family. The thought in the prophet's mind was of the complete destruction by the pest. Singling out the drunkards, the worshipers, the husbandmen, and the vinedressers, he reminded them of the completeness of the devastation, showing how it had affected all classes.

In the call to humiliation he began with the priests, calling them to penitence in the presence of the depletion of the house of God. Then addressing the people, he summoned them to sanctify a fast, and charged them to cry to Jehovah, declaring as his reason the truth which had been the burden of his message, "The day of the Lord is at hand." Finally, he voiced the cry of the people in penitence, "Oh Lord, to Thee do I cry."

JOEL 2:1-27

Having thus dealt with the actual visitation and its terrible devastation, and having called the people into the place of humiliation, the prophet rose to a higher level, and interpreted the visitation as indicating a deeper and more terrible judgment threatening them. In doing this, he made use of the figure of the blowing of a trumpet.

The first blast sounded a note of alarm as it announced the approach of the Day of Jehovah. With the figure of the locusts still in mind, the prophet described the swift, irresistible, and all-consuming character of the armies which were about to come as the scourge of God, being careful to declare that this whole movement would be under the command of Jehovah. However, the prophet declared that God still waited in patience and mercy. If the people would return to Him, He would spare them.

The second blast of the trumpet called the people to assemble in repentance. The character of the assembly was to be that of a fast, and its constitution the actual gathering together of all the people, from the youngest to the oldest. Being assembled, they were to cry for mercy, the ultimate reason being that the nations should not say, "Where is their God?" To such an act Jehovah would respond in grace.

JOEL 2:28—3

Finally the prophet moved on to a yet higher level, and dealt wholly with things to come. The great word introducing the section is "afterward." Some of the things foretold have now been fulfilled, some are still in the future.

In looking toward the distant Day of Jehovah, Joel saw an intervening period of an entirely different character. This he described, ending his message with a declaration concerning the Day of the Lord, which was the real burden on his spirit. Of the intervening period he declared that its initiation would result from the outpouring of the Spirit upon all flesh. It would be characterized by prophecy, dreams, and visions. The signs of the end of this period and the approach of the Day of the Lord would be "wonders in the heavens and in the earth." From the terrors of the Day, those who called on the name of the Lord were to be delivered.

This is a perfect description of the Pentecostal age in which we now live, with a statement of the signs which will precede its end and a declaration of the way of deliverance from the terrors immediately to follow.

Finally the prophet saw in the far distance the ultimate Day of Jehovah. The last vision of the prophet is the complete fulfilment of the divine purpose in and through God's people, in which Jehovah will dwell in Zion—a city holy and full of prosperity.

Amos

AMOS 1—2:3

The second verse of this first chapter gives the key to the book. Jehovah declared Himself in judgment.

Beginning at the point farthest from Israel, the prophet delivered his messages to the nations as such. Each in turn passes before Jehovah, and receives sentence.

The sin of Syria was cruelty. At last, sentence was uttered; the flame would devour, all defense would be useless, and the people would be driven into captivity.

The sin of Philistia had been the slave trade. Here, as before, and as in each subsequent case, the form of the declaration reveals the exhausted patience of God. Philistia would be visited with the devouring flame, her inhabitants be cut off, and even the remnant would perish. Phœnicia's special guilt had been that in spite of the covenant made, she had acted as a slave agent. Edom was doomed for determined and revengeful unforgiveness. The children of Ammon were specially denounced for cruelty based upon cupidity.

Moab's chief wickedness had been her shocking and vindictive hatred.

AMOS 2:4-16

Having thus uttered the word of God concerning the surrounding nations, thereby revealing the fact of His government over all, the prophet turned to Judah, and declared that she also was to share the doom of the other nations, because she had despised the law of Jehovah and had not kept His statutes.

Finally, he spoke to Israel. All the foregoing had been in preparation for this. He described the sins of Israel in detail and with almost startling directness. He charged the people with injustice, avarice, oppression, immorality, profanity, blasphemy, and sacrilege. Moreover, he said that their sin had been very greatly aggravated by the privileges which they had enjoyed. They had seen the Amorites destroyed before them for the very sins which they themselves had subsequently committed. They had been brought up out of Egypt and so knew the power of Jehovah. They had raised up their sons for false prophets and young men for Nazarites, and had silenced the true prophets. The sentence against them was that of oppression and judgment, from which there would be no possibility of escape.

AMOS 3

Having thus uttered the declamations of Jehovah's judgment on all the nations, the prophet delivered his special message to Israel in a series of three discourses. In each the introductory word is, "Hear this word."

The first discourse consists of a statement of Jehovah's verdict and sentence. It opens with a simple announcement that the privileged people were to be punished; their privileges were named, and their punishment described.

In view of the probability that the people would object to his message, the prophet, in an interpolation, defended himself. By a series of seven questions he illustrated a principle which may thus be stated—an effect proves a cause. The illustrations may be summarized thus: communion proves agreement; the lion roaring proves the prey; the cry of the young lion proves the prey possessed; the fall of a bird proves the bait; the springing of the snare proves the bird to be taken; the trumpet proves alarm; calamity in the city proves Jehovah. From this principle the prophet deduced an application: Jehovah hath roared, therefore fear; Jehovah hath spoken, therefore prophesy.

Turning back to the main argument, Amos proclaimed the punishment of the privileged and declared its reason. The reason was stated to the heathen, who were invited to witness the justice of the doom.

AMOS 4

The second discourse consists of Jehovah's summons to the people.

It commences with a severe and terrible indictment of the women. He addressed them as "Ye kine of Bashan," which reveals the degradation of womanhood to mere animalism. The prophet described their doings, declaring that they oppressed the poor and crushed the needy, and said unto their lords, "Bring and let us drink." Their doom would be that they would be taken away with hooks, that is, in shame and helplessness, and in the presence of judgment would take refuge in wild flight.

He then uttered the final summons to the people. In this call there was a piece of stinging satire. They were to come to Bethel to transgress, to Gilgal to multiply transgression. Their sacrifices they were to offer every morning instead of once a year, their tithe every third day instead of every third year, their sacrifice was to be leavened; they were to make free-will offerings and publish them.

Jehovah then described His patience and their perversity. He had spoken to them by famine, by drought, by blasting and mildew, by pestilence and sword, by earthquake. After each description, Jehovah declared, "Yet have ye not returned to Me." All this culminated in a great call, "Prepare to meet thy God."

AMOS 5

The third discourse was a description of Jehovah's judgment. This opened with a lamentation for the virgin of Israel, "The virgin of Israel is fallen, she shall no more rise, she is cast down upon her land, there is none to raise her up." This lamentation the prophet followed with a sequence of explanations, each introduced by the formula, "Thus saith the Lord."

The first declared the coming decrease in population. Only a tithe of them would be spared.

The second recounted the history of God's past calls to the people. He had appealed to them to seek Him, and live. They had refused, hating the reprover in the gate, and abhorring him that spoke uprightly. The results had been that they oppressed the poor, and judgment was determined against them in consequence. Yet another call came to them to hate the evil and love the good. The last announced the doom the people would suffer if they refused to answer the calls of God's patience, the whole procedure of judgment being graphically summarized in the declaration, "I will pass through the midst of them."

Finally, he pronounced the double woe. Two classes of the sinning people were addressed. First, those who desired "the day of the Lord," most evidently the hypocrites, according to the description. They were religionists who kept feasts, observed solemn assemblies, brought burnt meal, and peace offerings, sang songs and made melody with viols; but who, nevertheless, were living a life of sin. With tremendous force the prophet described God's attitude toward such, "I hate, I despise . . . I will take no delight . . . I will not accept . . . neither will I regard . . . I will not hear." Jehovah's call was for righteousness and judgment. "The day of the Lord" for the hypocrites would be a day of darkness and destruction.

AMOS 6

From the formalists the prophet turned toward those who had lost all sense of the spiritual and the moral, and were indifferent, those were "at ease in Zion," and "secure upon the mountains of Samaria." He had in mind the national leaders, "the notable men of the chief of the nation." Zion and Samaria were the headquarters of the kingdoms of Israel and Judah. Here the rulers were living in luxury, and abandoned to animalism, having lost all consciousness of their relationship to Jehovah, with its consequent demands on life and conduct. It would seem that they had given up all reference to "the Day of the Lord," being careless concerning it, and probably disbelieving in it.

On such, the prophet declared the coming of the swift and terrible judgments of Jehovah.

AMOS 7

In this division the prophet gave a fivefold vision of judgment, introduced in the first four cases by the words, "The Lord God showed me." The last vision was of Jehovah Himself.

The vision of the locusts declared judgment to be threatened, and restrained in answer to intercession.

The vision of the fire had the same significance. The prophet saw the devouring fire and interceded. His intercession was answered by Jehovah's repentance, and the judgment was restrained.

The vision of the plumbline is different. Jehovah was seen standing by a wall, testing it with a plumbline. Having done so, He appealed to the prophet. No charge was made, but it is evident that as Amos beheld, he realized all the irregularities the plumbline revealed. There was no intercession. Doom was determined. So long as prophecy was mingled with messages of mercy, it was tolerated by the people. Directly that element was missing, hostility broke forth. Amaziah was an impostor, and yet held the position of priest of Bethel. He reported to Jeroboam what Amos was saying, advising his exile. Moreover, he attempted to appeal to the fear of Amos, and advised him to flee to Judah. The answer of Amos was full of dignity, born of the consciousness of the divine authority of his commission. He declared that he was no prophet, but that Jehovah had taken him and spoken to him, thus he had become a prophet in very deed. Then, answering Amaziah, he declared that God's judgment would overtake Amaziah.

AMOS 8

The next vision, that of the basket of summer fruit, indicated the imminence of the judgment. Jehovah declared that the end was come, that He would not pass by them any more.

This announcement was followed by the prophet's impassioned address to the moneymakers, in which he first declared the effect of their lust for gain. They swallowed the needy, and caused the poor to fail. He described the intensity of that lust; the new moon and sabbath were irksome.

Then followed a figurative description of judgment which declared Jehovah's perpetual consciousness of these things, and His consequent retribution. The final judgment would be a famine of hearing the words of the Lord, as a result of which there would be eager and fruitless search for substitutes, followed by the fainting of the youth for lack.

AMOS 9

The final vision was of judgment executed. In this there was no symbol, no sign. We hear the manifesto of Jehovah Himself. It is one of the most awe-inspiring visions of the whole Bible.

The message proceeded in two phases. First, announcement of judgment, irrevocable and irresistible; second, announcement of the procedure as reasonable and discriminative. Jehovah is seen standing by the altar, declaring the stroke of destruction to be inevitable, and all attempts at escape futile, because He has proceeded to act. While the judgment is to be reasonable and discriminative, the claims in which Israel had trusted were nothing. They became as children of Ethiopians. Philistines and Syrians had also been led by God. The eyes of Jehovah were on the sinful kingdom. The sifting process must go forward, but no grain of wheat should perish. The phrase "in that day" indicates the closing message of restoration, and all that is to precede it.

It is now declared that the reason of the divine judgment is not revenge, but the only way in which it is possible to usher in the restored order on which the heart of God is set. The process of restoration is described as threefold. First, preliminary: "I will raise up . . . that they may possess"; second: progressive, "I will bring again the captivity . . . they shall build the waste cities . . . plant vineyards . . . make gardens"; finally, permanent: "I will plant them . . . they shall no more be plucked up."

Obadiah

OBADIAH

There is no personal history of Obadiah, and it is impossible to fix accurately the date of his prophecy. The only ground on which it may be fixed is the capture of Jerusalem, to which reference is so clearly made. Certain passages in Jeremiah, apparently quoted from this book, make it probable that the capture referred to is that by Nebuchadnezzar. The corrected tense in verses 12-24 in the Revised Version, "Look not," instead of, "Thou shouldest not have looked," would seem to indicate that the prophecy was uttered before the fall of Jerusalem, and not after it.

At that time the nation was a hive of political disturbance. The people were divided into factions. Fierce passions characterized them, and evil counsels prevailed. The whole nation was rushing headlong toward a great catastrophe. Obadiah had a vision of the attitude of Edom toward the chosen people in their calamity, and his message concerned them. It was not spoken to Edom, but to Israel, and was intended as a word of comfort for those who, loyal to Jehovah, were yet suffering with the whole nation. Its message falls into two parts: verses 2-16, the judgment of Edom; verses 17-21, the restoration of Israel.

Jonah

JONAH 1

In narrating his own experience on his mission to Nineveh, Jonah intended to teach his people the lesson of the inclusiveness of the divine government, and thus to rebuke their exclusive attitude toward surrounding peoples. The Book naturally falls into two parts. In this first division we have the prophet's account of Jehovah's command, his disobedience, and the divine interposition. Evidently he had no doubt that the command was from Jehovah. The charge to deliver a message to a city outside the covenant, and one, moreover, which was the center of a power which had been oppressive and cruel, must have been startling to Jonah. His attempt to escape was an act of wilful disobedience. Outside the path of duty he recognized that he was chargeable to himself, and with a touch of fine, if mistaken, independence, he paid his fare to Tarshish.

His going out from the presence of the Lord did not, however, ensure his escape from the Lord's control. Jehovah sent out a wind which endangered the ship in which Jonah was a passenger. The incidents of the storm are full of interest. Terrified by the storm, and at their wits' end, the crew made every effort to save Jonah's life. However, God, who had sent out the wind, presided over the casting of the lots, and at last Jonah was cast into the deep. There he was received by the fish, *prepared.*

JONAH 2

In the midst of the strange and awful circumstances in which he found himself, Jonah poured out his soul in anguish to Jehovah. The prayer as chronicled for us consists of quotations from the Book of Psalms. It is exactly the kind of cry which a man familiar with the sacred penitential writings of his people would utter in such circumstances.

Perhaps the most remarkable note about the prayer is its note of triumph. While it is distinctly asserted that he prayed out of the fish's belly, and while all his quotations indicate the darkness and horror into which he had come, taken as a whole it is an expression of absolute confidence in God and in His deliverance.

The probability is that the prayer as recorded expressed the final stage of Jonah's spiritual experience in the realm of darkness. "When my soul fainted within me I remembered the Lord, and my prayer came in unto Thee, into Thine holy temple," is a quotation aptly indicating the period at which it was uttered. In view of the use made by Christ of this experience of Jonah, the prayer becomes all the more interesting, especially in its allusions to what were undoubtedly Messianic psalms.

JONAH 3

Immediately Jonah was again charged to go to Nineveh. There is a fine revelation of the patient grace of God toward His servant in the statement, "The word of the Lord came unto Jonah the second time." With a new sense of the authority of Jehovah, Jonah arose and obeyed.

It was a strange and startling thing for Nineveh, this arrival of a man who had been cast into the deep; and it is easy to understand how the monotony of his declaration, that within forty days Nineveh would be destroyed, would fill the hearts of the people with terror. They heard; they believed; they were filled with fear, and repented, from the greatest to the least. Their repentance was answered by the repentance of God, so that the doom was averted and the city spared.

JONAH 4

The final picture of the controversy between Jonah and Jehovah reveals most vividly, through Jonah, the attitude of the ancient people which his story was intended to correct, and Jehovah's care for, and patience with, all sinning peoples, which they so little understood. The prophet went out of the city, and in distress and resentment sat in a booth of his own making to watch the course of events.

Again the overruling of Jehovah was manifest in the *prepared* gourd, the *prepared* worm, and the *prepared* sultry east wind. So great were the anger and anguish of the prophet that he fainted, and asked again that he might die. Jehovah repeated His question, but with a new application, "Doest thou well to be angry for the gourd?" He who had been angry that the city was not destroyed, was angry that the gourd was destroyed; and he answered the inquiry by affirming, "I do well to be angry, even unto death."

Thus the last picture we have of Jonah is of a man still out of harmony with the tender mercy of God, and the last vision of Jehovah is of a God full of pity and compassion even for a city such as Nineveh, and willing to spare it if it returned to Him in penitence.

Micah

MICAH 1

The first message of Micah consists of a summons, a proclamation of Jehovah, and a prophetic message based on the proclamation. This division ends with an account of the interruption of the false prophets, and finally the promise of ultimate deliverance.

In the summons the prophet had clearly in mind the attitude of Jehovah toward the whole earth. All peoples are called upon to attend. Israel was Jehovah's medium of teaching, if not in blessing, then in judgment. He witnesses among the nations by His dealings with Israel. The description of His coming forth from His place is full of poetic beauty. Under the figure of a great upheaval of nature the prophet described the advent of God.

The proclamation of Jehovah first declares the cause of judgment. It is "for the transgression of Jacob . . . for the sins of the house of Israel." The reason for judgment is the apostasy of the nation as evidenced in the cities. Jehovah next describes the course of judgment, commencing with the destruction of false religion. The city wherein was gathered the wealth and wherein authority was exercised was to be demolished, and the religion of apostasy swept away.

On the basis of this proclamation the prophet delivers his message. It opens with a personal lamentation expressive of his own grief concerning the incurable wounds of the people.

This is followed by a wailing description of the judgment. The passage is a strange mixture of grief and satire. At the calamity the prophet was grieved. Because of the sin he was angry. This merging of agony and anger flashes in satire. The connection of contrast is not easy to discover. A translation of the proper names appearing in this section may enable the reader to discover the remarkable play on words which runs through it.

MICAH 2

Following this the prophet states the cause of the imminent judgment. The sin consists in devising evil at night and practicing it in the morning, and the abuse of authority. Covetousness, expressing itself in oppression, was the peculiar sin of the rulers. Against this Jehovah proceeds in just retribution, "I devise an evil."

The prophet then describes the mockery of observers who would imitate their sorrow, and finally declares that they will be utterly dispossessed.

In the midst of his prophesying Micah was interrupted by false prophets, who charged him not to prophesy, protesting against his message, basing their objection to his announcement of judgment on the fact of God's goodness. To this objection Micah, in the name of Jehovah, answers that the changed attitude of His people toward Him accounts for Jehovah's change toward them. His people had risen up as an enemy.

He then charged the people to depart, declaring that such teaching could not give them rest, and then breaking out in indignant satire against the people who allowed themselves to be misled by false prophets.

This first message uttered in the hearing of the nations concerning the chosen people, closes with words spoken directly to Jacob. Its burden is evidently forthcoming deliverances, but as to detail it is undefined.

MICAH 3

Addressing himself directly to the rulers of the people, in this second message the prophet describes their peculiar sin, and announces the coming judgment. He then foretells the coming of the one true Ruler, and the consequent deliverance.

In dealing with the sins of the rulers, he first addresses the heads or princes, charging them with being corrupt. As to character, they hate the good, and as to conduct they spoil the people.

Turning to the prophets, he declares that their sin is that they make the people to err, exercising their sacred office for their own welfare. If they were fed, they were prepared to cry peace; if they were not fed, they made war. Judgment must overtake them in kind. Micah defends his own ministry by contrasting it with others.

He finally deals with all the ruling classes, and his summary of their sin is forceful. The heads judge for reward; the priests teach for hire; the prophets divine for money. As a result of their sin, judgment must fall on Zion and Jerusalem.

MICAH 4—5:1

From this scene of a corrupt people governed by corrupt rulers, the prophet lifts his eyes, and looking into the future sees the day when under true government deliverance will be wrought and the divine order be established. In this look ahead he saw the mountain of Jehovah's house established and the peoples flowing into it. Out of Zion the Lord would come forth, and the word of the Lord from Jerusalem. The result of this establishment of divine authority would be cessation of war, and peaceful possession of the land, with all its benefits.

In the light of this future deliverance the prophet addresses himself to the present. In the midst of affliction there was assurance. Even while the cry of pain and travail was heard, there was hope. He declares that there was to be yet further pain and suffering, but that the day of deliverance is certain.

MICAH 5:2-15

Having thus described the coming deliverance, Micah utters the wonderful prophecy concerning the Deliverer and the deliverance under His administration.

The Person of the Deliverer is first described. He is One whose goings forth are from of old, and when He comes it will be to Bethlehem-Ephrathah.

Next, His program is described. Its first movement will be abandoning the people, and the second gathering and feeding them.

The central declaration of the whole prophecy is found in this connection, "This Man shall be peace."

The local application of the foretelling is seen in the fact that Micah described the victory as one over Assyria. Its far-reaching value has become perfectly evident by the literal and local fulfilment. Concerning this coming deliverance the prophet then utters the word of Jehovah which declares that in that day all the false confidence which had ruined the people through the period of their sin and unbelief will be destroyed.

MICAH 6

This closing section is dramatic and magnificent. The prophet summoned Israel and the mountains to hear the controversy of Jehovah with His people. The key-word is "Jehovah . . . will plead."

From that point the address falls into dramatic form. It sets forth the controversy in which Jehovah, the prophet, and the people take part. Jehovah utters a plaintive appeal in which He asks His people what He has done to weary them. In answer, the people inquire how they may appear before Him, in view of the complaint made against them in His appeal. The prophet answers the inquiry, telling them what Jehovah required of them. Immediately the voice of Jehovah is heard crying to the city, and describing its aims, declaring them to be the reason of His visitation. This constitutes a terrible charge against them. The sins of the city's wickedness are in the city, in its treasures of wickedness, and in its false weights and measures. The rich men are rich through oppression, and all the sore and grievous judgments of God are the result of this wickedness.

MICAH 7

Following the charge, the people break into a lamentation which is of the nature of a confession, submission to judgment and hope. The prophet answers the cry with a message of hope, which, however, ends with the consciousness of the necessity for judgment.

Following this, the people pray for the guidance of Jehovah, and Jehovah answers with a promise that He will guide them as of old. Then the prophet in faith repeats Jehovah's promise.

The last movement is a great final doxology, uttered by all the people, which celebrates the patience of God and His certain restoration of His people. The prophet's message of hope is an exclamatory description of a new day, when the walls will be built, and the boundaries will be set far beyond the existing limitations, a day in which the people will gather from other countries and cities.

Thus the message of Micah centered on the subject of authority. The prophet arraigns and condemns the authority of those who had departed from the true standards of government, whether the princes, prophets, or priests; and foretold the coming of the true Ruler, under whom all false confidences would be destroyed and the true order restored.

Nahum

NAHUM 1

The prophet preceded the announcement of a verdict of vengeance by a section dealing wholly with Jehovah Himself. As to His character, He is a God of vengeance, and yet the central fact of His nature is that He is slow to anger.

Under the figure of a storm the prophet set forth the overwhelming majesty of Jehovah. The description of the storm moves in two sections: a hurricane on the sea, a simoon over the land.

He finally described the method of God: toward His friends He is "good, a stronghold"; for His foes, "He will make a full end."

Addressing himself to Nineveh, the prophet inquired, "What do ye imagine against the Lord?" This hints at the deepest sin of Nineveh, namely, that she had set herself up wilfully against the power of God. In answer to his own question, Nahum affirmed the irresistible nature of the judgment which must fall on the city, and finally made his central charge against her, "There is one gone forth out of thee, that imagineth evil against the Lord, that counselleth wickedness." This charge, in all probability, referred to the blasphemous boasts of Sennacherib, chronicled in Isaiah 36: 18-20, and 37: 10-13. As other prophets had summoned the nations to attend to God's controversy with Israel, Nahum addressed himself to the chosen people, declaring that the yoke of Assyria would be broken.

The last word in this first section was addressed to Judah. The verdict of vengeance on Nineveh was an evangel to Judah.

NAHUM 2

Having thus announced the verdict, the prophet described the process of vengeance. He declared that the "hammer" had come up aginst Nineveh, and ironically advised her to prepare. He then detailed the process of Nineveh's destruction.

The interpretations of this description greatly differ. I suggest that it falls into three clearly defined parts. First, the conflict (verses 3-5); second, the conquest (verses 6-9); finally, the consummation (verse 10).

The picture of the conflict is graphic. We first see the attacking army outside the walls, then the defending host inside the city.

Next, the battle itself is described. The conquest of the city is secured by the act of God, "The gates of the rivers are opened." Continuing, Nahum described the city under the figure of a woman and her attendants. They flee, and the enemy captures the spoil.

Finally, the consummation of judgment is announced. Nineveh "is empty, and void, and waste." The utter collapse of the people was set forth in figurative language. The prophet then immediately broke forth into exultation. The den of the lions was gone, all the cruelty of Nineveh was at an end. Moreover, the prophet recognized this as the righteous act of God. It was His act of vengeance. He was against Nineveh, therefore the overthrow was complete.

NAHUM 3

The last part of the prophecy is devoted wholly to the vindication of Jehovah's action against Nineveh, and is a fitting defense of the introductory declarations concerning His character.

In the first movement the prophet describes Nineveh as a "bloody city," evil and cruel. A graphic description of vengeance, consisting of seven illustrations, follows.

In the second movement he more particularly describes both the vice and the vengeance. The national method was whoredom, that is, idolatrous practices; and witchcraft, that is, deceptive methods. The national influence had been in selling nations and families. Jehovah's vengeance was then described, and also its unquestioned righteousness in the inquiry, "Who will bemoan her? Whence shall I seek comforters for thee?"

In the third movement vice and vengeance are dealt with in yet greater detail. Addressing himself to Nineveh, Nahum inquired, "Art thou better than No-amon?" The argument was that No-amon, or Thebes, which was not so corrupt as Nineveh, had been destroyed, notwithstanding her strength. How much more certain then, in view of her greater corruption, was the destruction of Nineveh! In the case of Thebes strength had been of no avail. In the case of Nineveh her corruption had canceled her strength. The vengeance of Jehovah was then set forth.

The last section is a weird description of the destruction of Assyria. The shepherds, the nobles, and the people are dealt with in judgment. The universal verdict agrees as to the righteousness of the judgment. There is to be no healing, and because of the universal oppression exercised by Assyria there will be great rejoicing over her downfall.

Habakkuk

HABAKKUK 1—2:4

In this first division of the Book we have the prophet's statement of the problems which vexed his soul. The first was the apparent indifference of Jehovah both to his prayer and to the condition of prevailing evil. To this Jehovah replied that He was at work, but that the prophet would not believe if he were told. He then proceeded to declare explicitly that His method was that of raising the Chaldeans as a scourge against His people.

This answer of Jehovah, while strengthening the faith of the prophet, immediately created a new problem—that Jehovah should use such an instrument, for, notwithstanding all Israel's sin, she was more righteous than the Chaldeans.

The answer came immediately. The prophet was first commanded to write, and to make his writing plain for easy reading. The vision granted to him was stated in the words, "Behold, his soul is puffed up, it is not upright in him; but the just shall live by his faith." That is the central revelation of the prophecy. It is a contrast between the "puffed up" and the "just." The former is not upright, and therefore is condemned; the latter acts on faith, and therefore lives. The first is self-centered, and therefore doomed; the second is God-centered, and therefore permanent. This was the declaration of a great principle, which the prophet was left to work out in application to all the problems by which he was surrounded.

From this point the prophecy becomes a proclamation of the contrast, and therefore an affirmation of faith in spite of appearances.

HABAKKUK 2:5-20

The proclamations fall into two parts. The first is concerned with the "puffed up," the second concerns the righteous.

The "puffed up" are described as haughty, ambitious, conquering, against whom the prophet pronounces certain woes.

In considering these the progress is to be carefully noted. The first was against ambition, which was described. The judgment pronounced against it was a revolt of the oppressed, and retribution in kind. The second was against covetousness, that lust for possession at the expense of others. Judgment was to be the subjugated people rising against the oppressor, the stones and beams of the house testifying. The third was against violence, the infliction of cruel sufferings on the subjugated. Judgment was that the very cities so built should be destroyed. The fourth was against insolence, the brutal act of making a man drunk, and then making sport of him. Its judgment was to be retribution in kind. The fifth was against idolatry, the description of which was wholly satirical. Its judgment was declared to be unanswering gods.

The final statement of the prophet in this connection declared that he had found the solution, "The Lord is in His holy temple." The apparent strength of wickedness is false. Jehovah reigns.

HABAKKUK 3

In the proclamation concerning the righteous, the majesty of Jehovah and the consequent triumph of His people are set forth. It consists of a psalm which is a prayer.

In the first movement the prophet declared his recognition of the divine interference, and his consequent fear. He then proceeded to celebrate the greatness of Jehovah as manifest in His dealings with His ancient people.

The last section of the psalm expressed the fear and the faith of the just. The contemplation of the judgment of the "puffed up" had filled the prophet with fear, yet he triumphed in God. Describing the circumstances of utter desolation, he declared his determination to rejoice, and announced his reason for this determination.

Zephaniah

ZEPHANIAH 1

The first movement of the prophecy is the prophet's declaration of the coming judgment of Jehovah. This he announced in general terms, then described more particularly its procedure and character.

This description opened with a comprehensive announcement, "I will utterly consume all things from off the face of the ground, saith Jehovah." Zephaniah then showed that to be a description of the creation in so far as it had become evil: man and the sphere of his dominion, the stumbling-blocks, with the wicked and the race, were to be consumed. The local application was that judgment would descend on Judah and Jerusalem, falling on those who had practiced idolatry, those who had indulged in mixed worship, those who had backslidden from following the Lord, and those who had never sought or inquired after Him.

Proceeding to describe more particularly the judgment, the prophet announced the presence of Jehovah for the purpose of judgment. The stroke of that judgment would fall first on the princes, then on the extortioners, also on the merchantmen, and, finally, on those who were living on their wealth in idleness and indifference.

The prophet finally gave a graphic description of the day in which men would walk as blind, none being able to deliver them because Jehovah would make "an end . . . a terrible end, of all them that dwell in the land."

ZEPHANIAH 2

After this declaration, the prophet uttered his great appeal, first to the nation as a whole, calling on it to pull itself together before the opportunity for repentance should pass, before the hour of judgment should arrive.

As though conscious that that larger appeal would be unavailing, he turned to the remnant, to such as were the "meek of the earth," and urged them to renewed devotion. This appeal he enforced by argument, in which he again set forth the fact of the coming judgment on the nations, interspersing his declaration with words of hope concerning the remnant.

He first addressed the nations on the West, proclaiming that they would be utterly destroyed, and that in their place the remnant of the house of Judah would feed their flocks.

He next turned to the nations on

the East, declaring that they would become a perpetual desolation, and that the remnant would inhabit their lands.

He then turned to those on the South, announcing that they would be slain by the sword.

Finally, he declared that those on the North would be destroyed and their cities made a desolation.

ZEPHANIAH 3

In this chapter the prophet yet more clearly set forth the sin of the people, and spoke of the hopelessness of the case from the human standpoint. This gave him his opportunity to announce the victory of God, who, notwithstanding the utter failure of His people, would ultimately accomplish the purpose of His love for them.

The address opened with a declaration of woe against Jerusalem, which the prophet described as rebellious, polluted, and oppressing. In the presence of this utter hopelessness the prophet cried, "Therefore wait for Me, saith Jehovah." This was the first gleam of hope. The very hopelessness and sin of the people made divine action necessary, and the action would be judgment. The judgment, however, would be but the prelude, for no sooner had the prophet declared it to be inevitable than he proceeded to describe the ultimate restoration.

From this point the prophecy is clearly Messianic. Zephaniah gave no picture of the suffering Servant, nor any hint of His method. He dealt only with the ultimate result.

He then addressed himself to the remnant, charging them to sing and rejoice because their enemy would be cast out, and their true King Jehovah be established in the midst of them. He next called them to true courage and to service.

The prophecy reaches its highest level as Zephaniah describes the attitude of God in poetic language under the figure of motherhood. Jehovah in the midst of His people will rejoice, and from the silence of love will proceed to the song of His own satisfaction.

Haggai

HAGGAI 1

The prophet Haggai delivered his first message on the first day of the sixth month in the second year of the reign of Darius. It was addressed especially to those in authority. The people were excusing themselves from building by saying that the time had not come. The prophet replied by reminding them that they were dwelling in their own ceiled houses, while the house of God was lying waste. He called them to consider their ways, reminding them of the long-continued material failure in which they had lived.

He then urged them to build the house of God, declaring that all the failure to which he had already referred was of the nature of divine punishment for their neglect of His house.

There was an immediate response to Haggai's appeal, first by the governor and priest, and then by the people. This response was followed, first, by a word of encouragement, in which the prophet declared that Jehovah was with them, and, second, by new enthusiasm among the people.

HAGGAI 2

About seven weeks later Haggai delivered his second message. This was addressed to Zerubbabel the governor, Joshua the priest, and all the people. A comparison of Ezra 3:13 with this message will show how certain of the old men who remembered the former house lamented the comparative inferiority of this. This memory tended to dishearten the people, and the prophet appealed to them to be strong and to work, promising in His name Jehovah's immediate presence and help.

On the basis of this promise Haggai then rose to the height of a more gracious one. The central phrase of this larger promise is difficult of interpretation, "The desire [singular] . . . shall come [plural]." Perhaps the simplest explanation is in the use made of the connected words in the letter to the Hebrews (12:25-29). It is evident that in this promise there is a revelation of an order of divine procedure which is manifested in the method of both the First and Second Advents of the Messiah. That order may thus be briefly summarized, "I will shake," "the desire shall come," "peace."

About two months later Haggai delivered his third message. In this the people are addressed through a colloquy with the priests. The content of this prophecy shows that after three months of hard building there were still no signs of material rewards, and the people were again disheartened in consequence thereof. As a result of his questioning of the priests and their answers, Haggai taught the people that because of their past sin their present obedience could not immediately result in material prosperity. Yet the final word of this third message is a promise of blessing, "From this day will I bless you."

The last message of Haggai was delivered on the same day as the third, and was an enforcement and explanation of the final promise, "I will bless you." It consists, first, of a repetition of the declaration of Jehovah's determination to shake, carried out in greater detail, in order to reveal that He would destroy all false authority and power; and, finally, of the promise of the establishment of true authority.

Zechariah

ZECHARIAH 1

About a month after Haggai's second message, in which he had encouraged the people who were in danger of being disheartened by the memory of the past, Zechariah uttered his first prophetic word. He gave them another view of the past, intended to warn them. He reminded them that Jehovah was sore displeased with their fathers, and warned them not to walk in the same sins. Thus Haggai encouraged them by looking on to the new spiritual glory, while Zechariah exhorted them by looking back to the past of disobedience.

Two months after Haggai had delivered his last message, Zechariah delivered his great message consisting of eight symbolic visions.

Under the figure of the myrtle trees Israel is described as "in the bottom," or, far better, as the margin reads, "in the shady place." It is the day of her overshadowing, but she is still watched. The whole earth is sitting still and at rest. The angel watcher appeals to Jehovah on behalf of Jerusalem and the cities of Judah, and is answered with "comfortable words." These words declare Jehovah's determination to deliver and re-establish His people. This vision, therefore, is a picture of Israel as she long has been, and still is, outcast from privilege and position, yet never forgotten by Jehovah, who declares His determination ultimately to return to her with mercies, and to restore her to favor.

The second vision of horns and smiths, while indefinite as to detail, yet carries its own explanation. The horn is a symbol of power, and the four stand for the powers which have scattered the chosen people. The smiths are the symbol of that which destroys power, and stand for those who are to break the power of the horns.

The vision thus foretells the ultimate overthrow of the enemies of the purpose of God, and therefore stands in immediate and striking contrast to the one preceding it. As we have seen, there the chosen people are in the shady place, cast out, without influence or power among the nations. The second, while not entering into any detailed account of the instrument to be used, does, nevertheless, symbolize that ultimately those who have oppressed the people of God will be broken in power, and thus the oppressed people be delivered.

ZECHARIAH 2

The vision of the measuring line reveals the condition of Jerusalem which will result from the overthrow of her enemies. The young man with a measuring line goes forth to measure the restored city, and is prevented from doing so by an angel messenger, who, in figurative language, tells him that Jerusalem will be such that it will be impossible to measure.

The nature of that prosperity is indicated in the statement that Jehovah's presence will make walls unnecessary, and its extent be so vast as to make walls impossible. In view of this remarkable vision of ultimate prosperity, the prophet calls the scattered people to return, and tells them to rejoice that Jehovah will dwell in their midst.

ZECHARIAH 3

As the first three visions dealt principally with the material side of Israel's tribulation and restoration, the remaining five dealt pre-eminently with her moral and spiritual influence.

In vision the prophet saw Joshua, who was then the actual high priest, standing before the angel of the Lord, but clothed in filthy garments, while at his right hand Satan stood at his adversary, that is, as one pleading against the cause which Joshua represented. The filthy garments were removed, and in their place a fair miter was set on his head, and he was clothed with rich apparel.

While this vision applied to one who in priestly function would wear the garments of the nation's pollution, and change them for the miter and the garments of access, it pre-eminently set forth that the nation which had failed through sin would be restored by moral cleansing to the priestly position and function of access to God and mediation. The accomplishment of this glorious restoration is associated with the bringing forth of the Branch, and the removal of iniquity.

ZECHARIAH 4

The vision of the candlestick immediately following sets forth Israel as fulfilling the divine intention. In the divinely appointed ritual of Israel's worship the candlestick stood in the holy place, creating the only symbol of Israel's true position as light-bearer amid the darkness.

The two olive trees, as Zechariah described them, referred immediately and locally to Zerubbabel and Joshua, the governor and the priest under whom the Temple had been rebuilt and its worship restored, but ultimately to the offices of king and priest as they would be realized and fulfilled in the person of the Messiah. Here, as always in Scripture, the golden oil symbolized the Spirit of God by whom anointing is possessed for co-operation with God in service, the teaching being that the Spirit would be communicated to Israel through the King and Priest, and thus her light would shine in the darkness.

ZECHARIAH 5

The vision of the flying roll represents the principle of law as it will be administered by Israel when she fulfils the true ideal. It must be considered as a sequence following the realization of those preceding. Israel, cleansed and anointed by the Spirit, becomes again a moral standard and influence among the peoples. The law is a curse on evil in action and in speech, not merely pronounced, but active. Thus while Israel in realization is to stand as priest, mediating, and as light-bearer, illuminating, she is also to affirm and apply the principle of law in the world.

The vision of the application of law

is immediately followed by one showing the result. The ephah is the symbol of commerce, and, according to the distinct prophecy, the woman sitting in the midst of the ephah is the personification of wickedness. Thus the principle of wickedness is to find its last vantage ground in commerce. This ephah dominated by wickedness is borne into the land of Shinar, where the tower of Babel was erected and the city of Babylon was built.

The teaching of the vision, therefore, is that even in the administration of the ultimate, the spirit of lawlessness will exist, finding its vantage ground, as we have seen, in commerce, but that it will be restricted in its operations, being compelled to occupy its own house in its own land on its own basis.

ZECHARIAH 6

In the last vision the prophet observed four chariots, coming out from between two mountains of brass, one drawn by red horses, one by black horses, one by white horses, and one by grizzled horses.

Inquiring of the angel the meaning of the vision, the prophet was instructed that the chariots symbolized the four spirits of heaven going forth from the presence of the Lord to walk to and fro in the earth. It is the final revelation of the method of the restored order. In the day of restoration the administrative forces of righteousness will be spiritual.

After the delivery of this second message of visions the prophet was distinctly charged to observe a great symbolic ceremony. Skilled workmen prepared crowns of silver and of gold. These were set on the head of Joshua, the son of Jehozadak, the high priest. To him thus crowned the prophet repeated his prediction of the coming Man whose name is the Branch, through whom the predictions made in the message of the visions would be fulfilled. Ultimately He would build the Temple of the Lord. His office would be dual: He would be both Priest and King; and it was promised that the "counsel of peace shall be between them both," that is to say, the resulting peace would accrue from the union of the kingly and priestly functions in the one Person.

This ceremony was intended to inspire the men of Joshua's own age with hope and confidence in the ultimate victory of Jehovah. Therefore the crowns which Joshua wore during the ceremony were retained for a memorial in the Temple of the Lord.

The final words of Zechariah in this connection reveal the purpose in all that he had said. It was that the work of Temple building should be continued.

ZECHARIAH 7

The third message of Zechariah was uttered nearly two years later. It was a fourfold answer to an inquiry made by the people concerning the necessity for observing certain fasts.

The history of these fasts is contained in II Kings 25. One was established in the tenth month, in connection with the siege of the city. The next, which occurred in the fourth month, commemorated the taking of the city. The third, held in the fifth month, was in memory of the burning of the city, and the last was in the seventh month, the month in which Gedaliah was murdered.

The inquiry was confined to the fast of the fifth month, whether it was necessary to continue its observance. The answer of the prophet was delivered in four statements of what Jehovah had said to him. The first of these answers declared that the fasts had been instituted, not by divine command, but entirely on the initiative of the people themselves. It declared also that they should consider the messages which had been delivered to them before the occasion which gave rise to the fasts of which they now complained.

The second answer reminded them that God sought justice and mercy rather than the observance of self-appointed fasts. It also reminded them that they had refused to hear the call of justice, and therefore all the evil things which had befallen the city had resulted. The inference was that had they been obedient, the occasions for these fasts would never have arisen.

ZECHARIAH 8

The third answer was full of grace. It declared that God was jealous for Zion, that He had returned to it, and that therefore its prosperity was assured, notwithstanding that these people saw only the devastation which caused their lamentation. Because of the certainty of this restoration, the prophet appealed to the remnant to be strong and build, promising them in the name of Jehovah that instead of being a curse they would become a blessing. Reaffirming this divine intention to restore, the prophet called the people back to what the second answer had declared God sought, namely, the execution of justice and the manifestation of mercy.

The final answer to the questions suggested by the deputation consisted, first, of the declaration that Jehovah would turn all their self-appointed fasts into feasts. These fasts were named. Historically the institution of the fasts had commenced in the tenth month of a certain year, and ended in the seventh month of the next year. In this declaration the prophet deals with them as they occur in the months of one year, beginning with the fast of the fourth month, which celebrated the taking of the city; the fast of the fifth, which commemorated the burning of the city; the fast of the seventh, which had to do with the murder of Gedaliah; and, finally, the fast of the tenth, which commemorated the siege of the city, and historically was the first of the four. This arrangement opened the way for the prophet's further declaration, that when God turned the fasts into feasts He would do it by becoming to the house of Judah joy and gladness and cheerful feasts, with the result that the city of Jerusalem would become the center to which many peoples and the inhabitants of many cities would go to seek Jehovah. It was a gracious and glorious setting forth of the realization of their true ideal by the people of God whereby men of other nations and other peoples would cast in their lot with them because of their consciousness that God was with them.

ZECHARIAH 9

Here begins the second division of the prophecy in which there are two messages. The first the prophet described as "the burden of the word of the Lord upon the land of Hadrach"; it deals with the rejection of the anointed King. In the first movement the prophet announced the coming of the King. He foretold the preservation of the city of Jerusalem in the days when Syria, Phœnicia, and Philistia would be overcome by the enemy, who, acting under Jehovah, would thus execute His judgments on them.

This prophecy was in large measure fulfilled by the coming of Alexander the Great. He captured Damascus and Sidon, and, after a siege of seven months, Tyre itself. He then marched against Gaza and razed it to the ground. In the course of this campaign he passed Jerusalem more than once, but never attacked it. Thus, according to the prophecy of Zechariah, the city was preserved for the coming of the true King. That coming he then foretold, calling on

Zion and Jerusalem to rejoice, declaring the character of the King, and announcing His complete victory.

The prophet proceeded to describe the King's program. He foretold Zion's coming triumph against Greece under the direct guidance and by the might of Jehovah. This prophecy was fulfilled in the victory of Judas Maccabaeus over Antiochus Epiphanes.

ZECHARIAH 10

This victory led him to describe the yet greater and final victory of the people of God. He introduced this description by appealing to Zion to ask help of Jehovah, and immediately declaring Jehovah's intention to accomplish their deliverance. As a result, the people would be strengthened.

Finally, speaking in the name of Jehovah, the prophet described Jehovah's regathering of the people. "I will hiss for them . . . I will sow them . . . I will bring them out . . . I will bring them into . . . I will strengthen them."

ZECHARIAH 11

The last movement of the message described the rejection of the King.

The prophet first foretold the coming of judgment under the figure of the Roman fire devouring the people and spoiling the glory of the false shepherds.

The reason for this judgment was the rejection of the anointed King. This King is portrayed as having two staves, one called Beauty, which signified grace, and the other, Bands, which signified union. This true Shepherd rejected the false, and then was Himself rejected of the people. It is noticeable that the prophet spoke of that rejection from the standpoint of divine interference. Beauty was cut asunder, the price being thirty pieces of silver, and the result was the breaking asunder of Bands. The result of this rejection of the true Shepherd would be the restoration of the false, and the consequent affliction of the people.

The last note of this message pronounced woe on the worthless shepherds. Thus the prophet foresaw the Roman victory over the chosen people following their abandonment of their true King.

ZECHARIAH 12

The second message has to do with things wholly future. The King spoke of in the previous message, whose rejection was there foretold, is now seen coming into His kingdom. This the prophet described in two movements, which are complementary.

In the first he looked at the opposing nations as they will be dealt with in judgment, and at the Israel of God, as she will be restored through the acknowledgment of her true, though rejected, King, and by her own spiritual cleansing.

In the second movement he viewed the same events from the standpoint of the King, beginning with His rejection, and then describing His Coming, day, process, and administration.

The final victories of the King over the nations and the saving of the people of God are described. By the strength of Jehovah operating through His people the strength of the nations is discomfited, and perfect victory is assured. This victory over the nations will issue in the restoration of the spiritual Israel to supremacy under the government of One whom they had pierced.

ZECHARIAH 13

This, however, will be brought about when, recognizing their sin, the chosen people repent with mourning. In that day, by way of a fountain opened to them, they will be cleansed from all the things which have defiled and degraded them.

ZECHARIAH 14

The prophet finally described the ultimate victories of the King, commencing with a description of the smiting of the Shepherd and the scattering of the sheep. Of this scattering a remnant would be loyal, and they would become the people of Jehovah.

The prophet then described the ultimate day of the Lord, which would be ushered in by Jehovah coming to the Mount of Olives in the Person of His King. This advent would initiate the new processes of the settlement of the land, and the cleansing of Jerusalem by judgment, to be followed by the establishment of the Kingdom, in which all nations would gather to Jerusalem as a center of worship, those refusing being punished, while all life would be consecrated.

Malachi

MALACHI 1

After the introductory word, which really constitutes the title page of the prophecy, the message begins almost abruptly with the tender and sensitive word of Jehovah to His people, "I have loved you." This is the real burden of the prophecy; everything is to be viewed in the light thereof.

Then the prophet, in an equally brief sentence, indicated the attitude of the people toward Jehovah. "Wherein hast Thou loved us?" The only possible explanation of such a question is that the people, conscious of the difference between their national position and their past greatness, and of the apparent failure of fulfilment of the prophetic promises, questioned the love of Jehovah. This skeptical question the prophet answered by reminding them of Jehovah's love for Jacob and His hatred of Esau; of His destruction of Edom, and His deliverance of Israel.

Having thus made his fundamental statement, the prophet proceeded to utter his formal accusations. These fall into three groups, those against the priests, those against the people, and those against the nation in general.

MALACHI 2

In dealing with the priests, he declared their corruption, and indicated the line of their punishment. He charged them with profanity, in that they had despised the name of Jehovah; with sacrilege, in that they had offered polluted bread on His altar; with greed, in that none of them was found willing to open the doors of His house for nought; and with weariness, in that they had "snuffed at" the whole system of worship as "a weariness."

In a study of these accusations against the priests it is most evident that they resented the charges against them, as the recurrence of the question, "Wherein?" shows. This makes it evident that the prophet was protesting against a formalism which was devoid of reality. He therefore uttered Jehovah's threatenings against the priests. Their blessings were to be cursed, and the punishment for their corruption would be the contempt of the people.

In this declaration occurs a passage full of beauty, describing the true ideal of the priesthood.

The prophet specifically charged the people with two sins, and in each case pronounced judgment on them. He introduced this charge by enunciating the principle of the common relationship of all to God as Father, and announcing the consequent sin of dealing treacherously with each other.

The first specific sin was the mixed marriages of the people. The second was the prevalence of divorce. Finally, the whole nation was charged with accommodating doctrine to the deterioration of conduct. While failing ethically, the people were saying that notwithstanding their evil doing, Jehovah delighted in the people, and they were inquiring skeptically, "Where is the God of judgment?"

MALACHI 3

The last division of the Book contains the prophet's announcement of the coming of Messiah. It falls into three sections, one dealing with the coming One, one dealing with the Coming Day, and one uttering the closing words.

The prophet announced the advent of Jehovah's Messenger, describing His Person and the process of His administration, and finally declaring the principle of the unchangeableness of Jehovah.

He next appealed to the nation generally, calling the people, to return, and then making a twofold charge against them of robbery and of blasphemy. To each of these they responded with the same inquiry, "Wherein?" and thus showed that like the priests, they were observing formalities of religion while being deficient in true spiritual life.

In all this widespread apostasy a remnant still remained loyal to Jehovah, whom the prophet described, and then addressed, declaring to them Jehovah's knowledge of them and determination concerning them.

MALACHI 4

All this leads to his great declaration concerning the coming day. This day he described in its twofold effect. Toward the wicked it would be a day of burning and of destruction. Toward the righteous it would be a day of healing and of salvation.

The closing words of the prophet called on the people to remember the law of Moses, promised that a herald would come before the day of the Lord, and ended with a solemn suggestion of judgment.

So the word ends. Malachi's voice ceases. He had described the people's condition and told them of God's infinite love; and he makes this final announcement, that God is not abandoning them nor the world, that the day is coming when the Sun will rise. He declares to them the different results produced on two conditions of life, and then with pathos in every tone of his voice he utters the divine words, "I will send you Elijah before that day, to turn your heart to the fathers, and the heart of the fathers to the children, lest God smite the earth with a curse."

PART TWO

New Testament

Matthew

MATTHEW 1

The Gospel of Matthew portrays Jesus as King. It reveals Him as realizing in His Person, and enunciating in His teaching the great principles which had been the peculiar deposit and glory of the ancient people. They were created a nation for the revelation of the beauty and beneficence of the Kingdom of Heaven established on earth, and in this Gospel the King is seen and heard, enunciating its laws, distributing its benefits, and laying its foundations in His life and death.

The first verse gives the title of the genealogy of Jesus rather than of the Gospel of Matthew. This genealogy is remarkable. It is Jewish in its outlook, tracing to Abraham, and is Jesus' legal genealogy resulting from His adoption by Joseph. It overleaps the Jewish boundary in Rahab, and Jewish prejudice in the introduction of women. By this genealogy the coming of Jesus is connected with the history of the ancient people, and yet it is shown to be distinct from it, for He came miraculously. The system could not produce Him. He came to crown the system and transform it. So came the KING, but His name was called JESUS, for the Kingdom had disintegrated and been devastated by sin, and He must begin by saving His people from their sins.

MATTHEW 2

The Kingdom was not ready for the King, so a reception for Him was not arranged and organized by those who should have been waiting for Him. They were in rebellion. The King's advent was heralded by a star, and a few subject souls of a nation other than the chosen were guided by it to the King, and, notwithstanding the poverty of His earthly surroundings, they poured out their gifts—gold, frankincense, and myrrh. The underworld of evil was moved to its center, and found vent through the false king, Herod, in his slaughter of the innocents. Heaven and hell were thus moved at Jesus' coming, and those on earth nearest to each in some way recognized the fact. The great crown remained in ignorance.

MATTHEW 3

Here ends the old prophetic line, John being the last of the Hebrew prophets. It found a fitting end in the stern ascetic who roused the nation and with vehement passion denounced their rebellion, and announced the King in the words, "Repent ye, for the Kingdom of Heaven is at hand." The herald graphically proclaimed the nature of the King's work. Scattering and destructive, witness the fan and the fire. Purifying and constructive, witness the cleansing and the gathering. What a thrill must have passed through the Baptist as he laid his hands on Jesus for that baptism which numbered Him with transgressors and indicated His choice of that identification, with the death it involved. Surely John's consciousness of sin gave rise to the protest, "I have need to be baptized of Thee, and comest Thou to me?"

The King now comes forth from the seclusion of the life at Nazareth, where He had lived wholly within the will of God. His first public act was obedience to the voice of God as it speaks to His nation, and He is baptized "to fulfil all righteousness." Thus He recognized social responsibility, and graciously identified Himself with the needs of His people. The opening heavens and the divine voice immediately followed. In Psalm 2:7-11 is written the great prophecy. By the divine proclamation at the baptism God announced the presence of the King, and set the seal of His approval on the years already lived. The kingly character creates the kingly capacity.

MATTHEW 4

"Then." After the heavens opened, hell is opened. The King must not only be in perfect harmony with the order and beauty of the heavens, He must face all the disorder and ugliness of the abyss. Goodness at its highest He knows, and is; evil at its lowest He must face, and overcome. And so in the wilderness He stands as humanity's representative between the two, responding to the one and refusing the other. How gloriously He won the battle and bruised the head of the serpent. Every vulnerable point was attacked: hunger, trust, and responsibility. When these are held, no other avenue through which the foe can assault the citadel of the human will remains. The need of material sustenance, the spirit's confidence in God, and the carrying out of a divine commission in a divine way—every gate our Captain held, and the foe, defeated, left Him.

The King now commenced His preaching, and in the same words as the Baptist had used, "Repent ye, for the Kingdom of Heaven is at hand." He, however, went further than John, who could only announce and point to another. Jesus immediately followed the announcement with the word spoken to individuals, "Follow Me," thus claiming the position of King. That kingly word includes repentance and the Kingdom.

The narrative shows how, in the early stages of His work, men were attracted by the material benefits of His kingly rule rather than by the spiritual principles He revealed. How blind men are! Had they sought only the spiritual, He would have ensured them the material. Grasping only for the lower, they lost both.

MATTHEW 5

In the three chapters beginning here we have the *Magna Charta* of the Kingdom. This chapter opens with a great revelation of its supreme condition. Character is everything. The first word is suggestive, "Happy." That marks the divine will for man. It also announces that human happiness is conditioned in character. A sevenfold happiness is named. Such character is contradictory to the spirit of every age apart from the Kingship of God, and will result in "persecution." So the King adds an eighth beatitude, and that a double one, for those who because of their loyalty endure suffering.

Such character will result in influence, and that is the divine intention.

This is marked by three figures. Salt—that is the opposite to corruption, that which prevents the progress of corruption. Light—that is the gift of guidance, so that those who have lost their way may find the path home. A city—that is the realization of social order and good government. The people who live in the beatitudes will realize this threefold law of influence.

The moral code followed. It first recognized the divinity of the Mosaic economy. The Revised Version has an important alteration. Instead of, "Ye have heard that it was said *by* them," it reads, "*to* them," thus more clearly marking this recognition. Moses was the mouthpiece, not the author of the words of law which he uttered. The righteousness which the King comes to make possible does not destroy the old, it fulfils; that is, fills to the full. Neither will the requirements of the new law be less exacting than the regulations of the Pharisee, they will go far beyond—exceed them, touching not only the details of externalities, but the fiber and temper of hidden life.

The first requirement deals with murder. The old said, "Thou shalt not kill." The new declares anger deserves judgment; that is, in the Revised Version the words, "without a cause" are relegated to the margin. "Raca," a term of contempt, deserves the discipline of the highest court. "Fool," a term of insult, deserves Gehenna. Thus no room is left for murder. The supervision of the Kingdom does not begin by arresting a criminal with blood-red hands; it arrests the man in whom the murder spirit is just born.

Of adultery, the old said, "Thou shalt not commit." The new declares, Thou hast sinned in that thou hast looked with desire. These are the most searching words concerning impurity that ever were uttered.

The old safeguarded oaths. The new forbids. The same danger is recognized, taking the name of God to a falsehood, and perjury in any form. In the new Kingdom, character will make the oath unnecessary, and therefore simple affirmation or negation will be sufficient.

Of revenge, the old said, Insist on your own right, and loving your neighbor, hate your enemy, and so secure your safety. The new says, Suffer wrong, and lavish your love on all.

Of temper, the new temper is the outcome of the new relationship to God, and is of love. The love, moreover, is not that kind which "alters when it alteration finds." Its strength is to be in itself, not in the object.

MATTHEW 6

In the first verse the Revised Version has substituted the word "righteousness" for "alms," "a reading approved of, almost unanimously, by the great editors and critics" (Morrison). This is a statement of a new motive for conduct. The application of the principle laid down in verse 1 to the subject of alms follows. The secret alms is known to God, who sees in secret. A subject of the King no longer desirous of the applause of his fellow men quietly and secretly helps the needy, and the deed is recognized by God, and is recompensed by Him.

Here the same principle is applied to prayer. Prayer is the soul dealing with God, and when one prays in order to attract the attention of men it is blasphemy. The prayer given as an example is perfect. The first three petitions move wholly in the realm of the divine purpose. Man must seek first the Kingdom of God. The second three voice man's probationary needs. The whole prayer is social. The singular pronoun is absent. Man enters the presence of the Father, and then prays as one of the great family.

The true reason for fasting is in

the opportunity it affords for a clearer vision of God, which should ever manifest itself in new gladness of face.

The King warns His people against laying up for themselves earthly treasures. The Master does not say it is wrong to possess earthly treasure. He does say it is wrong to lay it up for self. We are to hold it as stewards.

The next saying gives a great principle of life. The emphasis in verse 24 should be on the word "serve." That word marks the true relationship existing between Mammon and the man who is given over to it. The man imagines he is compelling Mammon to serve him. As a matter of fact, he is serving Mammon, and the service precludes the possibility of his serving God. "Therefore," that is to say, all that follows is based on the principles of the foregoing statement. Anxiety concerning the things of life is slavery to those things, and it is wrong and futile. There is a subject for anxiety, and that is declared in the words, "seek the Kingdom," "serve God." The warning is against worry, not work.

MATTHEW 7

After thus enunciating the laws of the Kingdom, and bringing men into the realm of direct dealing with God, the King authoritatively set up the standard of judgment. No man is to be his brother's judge. He cannot, first because he can never know all the facts of the case, and, further, because his own need is so great that any time occupied in censorious criticism is so much taken from the all-important work of attending to his own "beam." And yet there is to be discrimination in dealing with holy things, for "dogs" and "swine" have no understanding of their value.

Just as the bewildered soul is on the verge of crying out, "Who is sufficient for these things?" there comes a glorious announcement of an open treasure house. The things enjoined are, indeed, too hard for us in our own strength. Then "ask, seek, knock," and in every case the promise is simple and sublime, "It shall be given," "Ye shall find," "It shall be opened."

Then our Lord gave His invitation to His Kingdom. The entrance is through a strait gate. Character and conduct are supreme. The proof of loyalty is always in the fruit borne, never in the profession made, or the works done. A profession that is not sincere is profanation; and service rendered that has not a pure motive is sacrilege. What of those who enter that strait gate, and, hearing the words of the King—do them? To them is ensured a permanence of character no storms or waves can wreck. What of those who, hearing the words, disregard them? To them all building is folly, for the sandy foundations of wrong motives will cause irremedial ruin in the day of testing. What wonder that the crowds were astonished at such teaching!

Here ends the Manifesto of the King, the Great Charter of humanity. When presently man shall rest in perfect peace and joy, it will be within the sacred circle of this unfolding of law.

MATTHEW 8

The King passed down from the mountain and from teaching in order that He might bring the Kingdom nearer to His people, and give them examples of its benefits. What a wondrous application of His power—leprosy, palsy, fever, all fly before Him, and mark the cosmopolitanism of His giving—a leper, a Roman, a woman, all the despised in the Jewish mind. In that wonderful evening, when the crowds gathered, and the King took their infirmities and bore their diseases, what a radiant revelation He gave them of the power and love of His heart, and therefore of the privilege of entering His Kingdom.

A time of sifting and testing followed. Men who would follow Him, but— They have had their successors all down the years, as also have the Gadarenes, who, when He interfered with their illicit trading, formally requested Him to depart, notwithstanding that He had left on their shores a man whom by His coming He had transformed from the curse of the countryside into a law-abiding citizen. Even the disciples most closely associated with Him had so little confidence they did not believe in His power unless they saw Him at work. They must wake Him to still the storm. In grace, He stilled the tempest, but He also rebuked the disciples' lack of faith.

MATTHEW 9

The King now exercised His authority in a new way. He pronounced pardon on a sinner, and straightway opposition was aroused. To the questioning and rebellious hearts He vindicated His authority to forgive sins by a different exhibition of power, the power of healing. The effect was instantaneous and remarkable. The multitudes feared and glorified God.

The record of a triumphal progress of the Shepherd King follows. A ruler, a woman ostracized because of her plague, two blind men, a dumb man possessed with a devil, crossed His path, and all their varied needs He met, and with strong, tender words spoke to all some message of peace and courage. Here also the opposition of His foes manifests itself openly, and the long conflict with the forces of false religion begins. The Pharisees, madly jealous of His power, attribute it to Satan.

This section reveals the attitude of the King to the crowds, and the position of His people as intermediary. There is, first, a general statement of His public ministerial work. Then follows a declaration of the effect produced on Him. "He was moved with compassion." This movement of His compassion is consequent on His vision of the true condition of the crowds, "distressed" and "scattered"; and, as the attitude of the Pharisees proves, they are "sheep without a shepherd."

MATTHEW 10

As a result of this, the King calls, equips, and sends forth His disciples. No work can be done to extend His Kingdom that is not the direct outcome of His compassion. To men in communion with that compassion He first says, "Pray," and then, "Go." This is the perpetual order of the messengers and missionaries of His Kingdom—Compassion, Prayer, Service.

These men are to proclaim the Kingdom, and to accompany the proclamation with signs. The measure of their service is to be the measure of their receiving—"freely." The King forewarns them of persecution, and promises them that before governors and kings the Spirit shall give them the word to speak. All the persecution and misunderstanding will bring them into the truest communion with Him, "the disciple as his Master," "the servant as his Lord." This sense of comradeship with Christ in suffering is the certain cure for its smart.

Then follow words concerning God which are full of the most overwhelming terror, and these are linked with other words perhaps more exquisitely tender than any ever spoken concerning Him. "Able to destroy both soul and body in hell." "Not one of them [sparrows] shall fall to the ground without your Father; but the very hairs of your head are all numbered." With such conceptions of God, who will not dare anything to serve Him?

MATTHEW 11

This picture of John is very full of pathos—from the high triumph of inspired preaching to the solitude and loneliness of a prison. John made as direct application to Jesus as his circumstances permitted. Surely the wisest course possible. Jesus answered him not by verbal assurance, but by the deeds of the Kingdom. The credentials of Christ are ever to be found in His actual works.

The fickleness and worthlessness of public opinion has striking exemplification here. In the ordinary manner of life, Jesus and John were contrasts. The one was a stern ascetic, living in the simplest fashion; the Other was a Man of the people, living in the ordinary way. The first they said had a devil; the Master they charged with gluttony and drunkenness. There is but one thing for any who are called to public service, that is, to go straight on, undeviating in loyalty to God, and deaf to the voices around, knowing that at last "Wisdom is justified by her works."

Christ upbraiding the cities! It seems so contrary to His spirit of love and gentleness, but it is not so. Why does He thus reproach them? "Because they repented not." They persisted in rebellion, and that in spite of the manifestations of His power. There is, then, a condition more deeply degraded, more hopeless, than that of Sodom. The sin against light is far more terrible in itself, and more awful in its results, than sins committed in darkness. Capernaum's rejection of the Son of God is infinitely worse than Sodom's bestiality.

From reproach of cities, the Master turned to prayer. The use of the word "answered" is suggestive, revealing the perpetual fact of communion existing between Christ and God. The note of praise was the response of Christ's heart to the secret of Jehovah.

From prayer He turned back to the crowd with words full of sweetest pity and divinest power. He claims knowledge of the Father, which can be gained only by those to whom He willeth to reveal the Father. And while we pause and wonder who the favored ones will be, there breaks on our listening ears the sweetest of all music. He calls all who labor and are heavy laden, and promises to give them rest by so revealing the Father that to do His will will be the delight of life, the light burden, the easy yoke.

MATTHEW 12

This chapter chronicles direct attacks on Christ. The first was petty and foolish. It is on the question of the Sabbath. The Master gives to His people the true conception of the sanctity of the Sabbath. It is established, and remains, for "the Son of Man is Lord of the Sabbath." "How much is a *man* better than a *sheep?* Why, then, rescue a sheep and neglect a man?

The second attack was characterized by malicious hatred; it was an absolute denial of the sovereignty of God. Satan is cast out by Satan. The absolute folly of the position is revealed in the Lord's reply. Only two forces are at work in the world, the gathering and the scattering. Whoever does the one contradicts and hinders the other. Beelzebub and the demons of whom he is prince are breaking up, destroying, scattering! Christ's work is the opposite, healing, saving, gathering.

The third attack was a manifestation of contemptuous unbelief. "Master, we would see a sign from Thee." Christ revealed the true reason for their unbelief, "an evil and adulterous generation."

The last attack would be to Him the bitterest of them all. Mark gives us an insight into it that we miss in

Matthew (Mark 3:21-35). Jesus' friends, even His mother, are so far out of sympathy with Him as to believe Him mad, and to desire to put Him under restraint. Of this He makes occasion to declare the blessedness of the relation that the subjects of the Kingdom bear to Him. It has been wrongly imagined by some that the Lord's language here shows disrespect for His mother, as though she had grieved Him. This is surely to miss the deepest truth in His statement. The relationship with Him into which those come who do the will of His Father is as dear as that of brother and sister and mother.

MATTHEW 13

This chapter contains the seven parables of the Kingdom. The reason for the parabolic teaching of Christ is set forth here. This first parable was spoken to the multitudes (verses 2,3). Its explanation was given to the disciples only (verses 10-18). "The word of the Kingdom" is the seed (verse 19). The result is dependent on the one who hears, and on how he hears.

The second parable was spoken to the multitudes (verse 34). Its explanation was given to the disciples only (verse 36). Another sowing is going on in the world's broad fields side by side with that of the Son of Man. The final extermination of evil is not to be found during sowing, but lies in the period of harvesting at the end of the age. The character of this age is thus clearly revealed as mixed.

The figure of a great tree in the Scriptures is ever of great power. It is so used of the king of Assyria, of Pharaoh, and of Nebuchadnezzar. This particular parable says nothing of the nature of the tree, whether it is good or bad. It is simply a revelation of this one aspect of force in the world, the greatest of all, and such Christianity undoubtedly has become. Birds lodging in the branches most probably refers to elements of corruption which take refuge in the very shadow of Christianity. How much the Kingdom has suffered by harboring the unclean birds very few rightly appreciate.

The figure of leaven is uniformly used in Scripture to typify evil. This is no exception to the rule. All the outward manifestations of Church life have become more or less corrupt, contaminated by the evil leaven which was introduced into the Church of Jesus Christ by paganizing influences. That which produces fermentation issues in disintegration, and leaven is the very principle of decay in active condition.

The next three parables were spoken not to the multitudes, but to the disciples, and they reveal the present age from the divine standpoint rather than in its manifestation of the Kingdom to the world. The treasure hid in the field is the Church, and the Finder is the Lord Himself. The special treasure is His heavenly people, but the whole field is His. Nothing will finally be lost save the abominable and whosoever worketh or maketh a lie. The same truth is presented in the next parable. The merchant is the Master. The Church is the "pearl of great price." We have not bought Him. He has bought us. The last general parable teaches the mixing of the present results of work, and points to the end of the age and the sorting that will then take place.

From teaching His disciples, the Lord went to Nazareth, and there "did not many mighty works because of their unbelief."

MATTHEW 14

The presence and activity of the true King filled the false ruler with alarm. Herod sacrificed John to his lust. Once Herod had heard John, and the remembrance of former conviction was still with him, but the grip of sensual intoxication was greater than the voice of conscience. Yet in the sight of heaven it was Herod who perished, not the prophet. "When Jesus heard of it" (verse 13), that is, of Herod's surmise, He went to the desert. The crowds followed Him. "He healed their sick," and with five loaves and two fishes fed 5,000 men, besides women and children.

'Twas springtime when He blessed the bread,
'Twas harvest when He brake.

The Master Himself felt the need of getting away at times from the multitudes into places of loneliness and prayer. Familiarity with the crowd only produces hardening. Familiarity with God issues in a perpetual resensitizing of the heart, which prevents hardening.

The familiar story of the storm on the lake is full of exquisite beauty. The Master in His place of quiet retirement has not forgotten His disciples, and in the moment of their need comes to them strong to deliver, mighty to save. This story is daily repeated in the life of some storm-tossed soul. At the first we often fail to recognize Him as He approaches through the wind and over the sea. Wait patiently, and over the howling of the storm will sound the infinite music of His voice: "Be of good cheer. It is I. Be not afraid."

MATTHEW 15

The question was not of cleanliness, but of ritual. This washing of hands to remove imaginary evil was a part of the tradition of the elders. Against the binding of such burdens on men our Lord passionately protests. "The commandment of God" (verse 3). This is the one and only burden that men ought to bear, and this fact our Lord proceeded to enforce by illustration and teaching.

Then going into Tyre and Sidon, we have one of the sweetest stories of them all—the mother heart carrying the need of her daughter with unswerving faith to Him who had created the love of mother! How strange at first appear His silence and rebuff. The reason for His attitude is revealed in the result which followed. He knew how strong her faith was, and His method manifested that faith in all its beauty. How perpetually the very best of character is hidden, until for its forthshining our King seems to hide His face.

Another manifestation of the unlimited resources, unmeasured power, and ungrudging grace of the King follows. These people were most probably heathen or semi-heathen, gathered from the region of Decapolis (Mark 7:31). Our Lord had confined His journeyings and ministry to the chosen people to whom He had been sent, but true to the divine intention concerning that chosen people, when strangers and aliens came to Him He gave them blessing without stint.

What a marvelous exhibition we have of the slowness of faith in these disciples, who, notwithstanding what they had seen the Master do with five loaves and two fishes among 5,000 men, yet questioned Him how they should feed a smaller crowd, 4,000 men, with more supplies, seven loaves and a few fishes. Yet are we much better than they? How often past deliverances seem to have no power to deliver us from present anxiety.

MATTHEW 16

What a very wonderful fact in the life and ministry of Jesus is His power of suppressing the marvelous powers

He possessed. He never used them save in divine wisdom and love. How easily He could have given a sign which would have startled and overwhelmed. It would have been wasted so far as the purpose of His life and ministry, the establishment of the Kingdom of heaven, were concerned. This accounts for the solemn word to the disciples which they were so slow to comprehend, "Beware of the leaven of the Pharisees and Sadducees." Here again notice the blindness of these disciples. It really looks as though the two miracles of feeding had impressed them with the importance of taking "loaves," rather than with being with Christ. Thus do men put the emphasis in the wrong place.

Now the King is rejected! Here is the first hint of a new departure. All the principles and privileges of the Kingdom are to be embodied in a new society among men, the Church. The creation of the new society is the outcome of the refusal of men to accept the King. That refusal will presently be culminated in the Cross. That Cross, then, is to be the way of the creation of the Church. So the King begins to speak of His coming passion (verse 21). From this His loyal subjects shrink. They are as yet subjects of the King only. The wisdom and love of God are beyond their present comprehension, and they tremble and protest. Therefore came the searching word to them. Members of the Church, those who will follow Him henceforth during the period of His rejection, must in the necessity of the case do so by the way of the Cross. The best and only preparation is that they should deny self, and themselves go to the place of crucifixion. From this time these men were amazed, and estranged, and followed afar, until at Pentecost they were baptized into a vital union with their Lord.

MATTHEW 17

"After six days." Days of silence. No record have we of what transpired in those days. The strange declarations of the Cross had crushed the hearts of these men. Now to three of their number, as special training for special work, was granted this wondrous vision of glory. The true force and meaning of all this they did not comprehend until the Spirit came. That then the value of the experience was appreciated is evident from Peter's reference to the vision (II Peter 1:16-19).

Again a contrast! There the mountain; now the valley. There glorified saints; here the lunatic. There the King in His heavenly glory; here His representatives baffled and beaten. And why? For lack of faith! Not for lack of intellectual assent—though even that today seems in danger of vanishing—but for lack of that living faith which yields the whole being to the King's unquestioned control. Wherever there is such faith, even though small as a grain of mustard seed, the mountains become plains. Yet how glorious it is that when need can find its way beyond the failing disciples to their Lord He is never beaten or unable. With what quiet and Kingly majesty He accomplishes all we fail to do. That is the great comfort. The final issue of this fight with demons does not depend on us, but on Him.

MATTHEW 18

What a sad state of heart prompted this question! How absolutely opposed to the whole genius of the Master's teaching and example! He replied by an act, and a statement growing out of that act. The child in the midst was a revelation of the truly great character. To rob a child of its child character is to make it stumble, and the words of Jesus leave no room for doubt how such an act is abhorred by God. The journey into the wilderness is a journey to restore childhood to a wanderer, for it is not the will of God that a "little one" should perish. The essential fact in the transformation Christ works is that He changes the great ones into little children.

Out of the desire for greatness will spring actual trespass of one against another. With such trespass our Lord dealt from the standpoint of the duty of the injured, and not of the one who inflicts the injury. 1. Tell him his fault. You have no right to ignore it, for so you injure the wrong-doer. 2. Failing this first method, take one or two others. 3. Failing that, tell it to the church. 4. Then if that fail, "let him be unto thee as a heathen man and a publican." What does that signify? That I am to despise and oppress him? Certainly not. The Christian's attitude toward a "heathen man and a publican" must be a passionate desire to help and save. This is emphatically taught in the parable which answered Peter's question. It is in this connection that the Master utters the memorable words which contain the most perfect statement of true ecclesiastical policy. The gathering of souls in the name of Jesus constitutes the Church, which has authority to deal with the wrong-doer. Then let it be noted that the seat of authority is not in human agreement, but in the presence and Lordship of Jesus.

MATTHEW 19

The Pharisees approached Him with a question concerning divorce. The force of His reply is in the words "*from the beginning.*" He had no opinions apart from the will and intention of God. As God willed, so let it be! "Why did Moses then command?" His answer is a contradiction of their main position. "Moses . . . *suffered.*" He did not command, but because of the people's hardness of heart he suffered. Marriage, not celibacy, is the law of life, yet the Master recognizes that celibacy will be the condition of some, and does not condemn it when it arises from one of three causes, the necessity of birth, the action of men, the voluntary act for the sake of the Kingdom of Heaven. This is a dark saying not intended for all, as the words of Jesus indicate.

It is beautifully fitting that having reiterated the irrevocable divine law relating to marriage, thus emphasizing the value of family life, He should now show His direct and wonderful interest in and tenderness toward children. In this place the word "such" does not primarily refer to the child character, but to children; and so the Master that day claimed all child life as belonging to His Kingdom.

The picture of this young man would be perfect to any but the clear vision of Christ. Yet the words of the Master prove that He saw the imperfections, and, moreover, they suggest that the young man was also conscious of them, "If thou wouldst be perfect." "Follow Me" is the Master's supreme word to him. Submit, obey, follow! And then with rare skill the Lord sets His mark on the supremest thing hitherto in the young man's life, and that which is his greatest hindrance—his wealth. "He went away sorrowful." Yet "Jesus . . . loved him."

MATTHEW 20

One great principle of rewards is laid down in this parable. It is that they will be given, not according to length or amount of service, but according to fidelity to opportunities.

The Master was now taking the last journey to Jerusalem, fully conscious of its deep significance in His mission. Beyond the Cross He saw the glory of the new life. He called His disciples to Him, and told them of His coming death and resurrection. Here as in every case during the last sad days His account of His own suffering to come is broken in on by some little question of precedence among them. We are tempted to be angry with them. He was not. Patiently He laid down for them the principles of true greatness, service even unto sacrifice.

In the neighborhood of Jericho He performed a gracious act. While on His way to ratify in actual word and deed what, in effect, has already taken place—His rejection as King—two needy men sought a favor of Him as "the Son of David," a manner of address that signified their acknowledgment of His Messiahship. Straightway His compassion was touched, and He exercised His wondrous power to answer their prayer, and gave them sight.

MATTHEW 21

In this cleansing of the Temple for the second time—He had done the same at the outset of His ministry—the Lord revealed His conception of the secret of all civic righteousness and strength. He revealed for all time the laws of civic purity. He came to His city and His Temple, which He cleansed so that the very sources of the streams of influence being pure the streams must become pure.

The cursing of the fig tree was the only miracle of judgment that Jesus wrought, and the principal force of it is not direct, but parabolic. He had a perfect right to make what use He chose of the creations of His own power to teach His lessons.

We now come to the beginning of the last conflict. The chief priests and elders confronted Him, and openly challenged His authority. He met their question with another. He had been baptized by John, and at that baptism had received the anointing of authority for public ministry. Now He asks them what was the authority for John's baptism. They could not say, "Of men," for they were cowards. They would not say, "Of heaven," for they were hypocrites. So, with a calm dignity, conscious of the fact that He had already answered them, He refuses to enter further into the question of authority.

Our Lord now exercised his authority by speaking in their hearing authoritative parables directly applicable to them, as they themselves discovered.

MATTHEW 22

The first two parables contained the history of the Hebrew nation up to the slaying of the Son. This one is prophetic. It presents the sin of this people in the light of the day of grace. The King sends His messengers first "to call them that were bidden." "They would not come." A second appeal is made—the mission of the Holy Spirit through the apostles. Of this the people made light. Each went to the material interest of the moment, his farm, his merchandise. The only attention they paid to the messengers was to persecute and kill them. Then came the King's armies, and the city was destroyed. Within forty years of the crucifixion of Jesus this was literally fulfilled.

Then we have a new departure by the King's enemies in their methods of attack. They endeavored to entangle Him in His talk. They propounded three questions: 1. A semipolitical question. 2. A question involving a great doctrinal dispute. 3. A question touching morality.

In His replies Jesus manifested in a wonderful manner His perfect familiarity with all the relations of life here and hereafter, and revealed the ignorance and wickedness of His questioners: 1. Duty to Cæsar exists, and is conditioned in responsibility to God. 2. The conditions of the spiritual world cannot be measured by material conditions. 3. Those are the greatest words of the law which include all the rest. Then with one startling question, He revealed their ignorance of mysteries of their own writing and history.

MATTHEW 23

This chapter is one of the most sublime and awful in the whole inspired volume. It records the last words of Jesus to the crowds. He summed up, He reached His verdict, He pronounced sentence.

It is awful in its majesty, terrible in its resistless force. With what relentless persistence and unfailing accuracy He revealed the true condition of the leaders of the people, their occupation with externalities and pettiness, and their neglect of inward facts and weightier matters.

Here, indeed, if ever, we have "thoughts that breathe and words that burn." One can almost feel the withering force of His strong and mighty indignation—indignation directed, not against the people, but against their false guides. And yet behind it all is His heart, and the "woes" merge into a wail of agony, the cry of a mother over her lost child.

MATTHEW 24

Passing from the city, the disciples drew their Master's attention to the stones of the Temple, and He told them that this glorious building would be demolished so that no single stone would be left upon another.

He went on to the Mount of Olives, and His disciples came to Him privately for more specific teaching on the great subjects suggested by His closing address to the crowds, and His prophecy concerning the Temple. In order to understand the teaching of this chapter we must distinctly bear in mind the questions which our Lord answered. They are three, and occur in verse three: 1. "When shall these things be?" 2. What shall be the sign of Thy coming?" 3. "What shall be the sign of the end of the age?" The disciples did not so tabulate their questions. In all probability they presented them as one request, supposing that all these things would happen simultaneously. Jesus' answer was directed mainly to correct this misapprehension.

Answering the first question, the Master carefully distinguished between "these things" and "the end." The former He declared must come to pass, but the latter is not yet (verse 6). Moreover, He distinctly told the nearness of them. "Verily I say unto you, This generation shall not pass away, till all *these things* be accomplished" (verse 34). Here again He most carefully distinguished between "*these things*," and "*the coming of the Son of man.*" The former He practically dated, saying that the then existing generation should not pass until all was fulfilled. "*The coming,*" He says, cannot be dated, for the time is known only to the Father.

The question concerning His coming He answered by declaring that when He does come there will be no doubt or question. He ended with a solemn injunction to "watch" (verse 42).

With reference to the third question as to the end of the age, He said: 1. "It is not yet" (verse 6). 2. It shall be "when this Gospel of the Kingdom shall be preached in the whole world for a testimony unto all nations" (verse 14). What this may really mean is a big question. Some claim that this has already been done, and that therefore the end of the age is necessarily close at hand. This conclusion is open to grave doubt. Everything depends on the meaning of the words, "for a testimony."

MATTHEW 25

"Then." This gives us the time in which the Kingdom of Heaven will be likened unto ten virgins. That Kingdom passes through many phases, but just before the coming of the King this will be its character. Note especially that the *ten* virgins are required to give a correct idea of the Kingdom.

Again, to interpret the next parable rightly, we must remember it concerns the *servants* of the King. He has not committed His goods to rebels, but to His own. To apply this parable to all men is to suppose that the absent Lord has committed the stewardship of His goods to rebels as well as to subjects. No greater mistake could be made. When He comes, the slothful and unprofitable will be cast out, not because they did not believe or because they had rebelled, but because they had neglected the opportunities which He had committed to them. How solemn is the teaching of the parable for all His servants. What am I doing with my Lord's talent? Neglect may bring about awful loss. I may be saved only as by fire.

The Lord then referred to His apocalypse, His coming in glory. The judgment is not of the saints, nor is it of the race considered as individuals. It is, as He so very distinctly declared, the judgment of the nations. There are three classes. Those on the right—sheep; those on the left—goats; and "these My brethren." He separates between sheep and goats according as they have treated His brethren.

MATTHEW 26

The Lord now reverted to the theme of His coming suffering, telling the disciples with great definiteness of the time—"after two days"; and of the event—"The Son of Man is delivered up to be crucified." Meanwhile the priests and elders were assembled in secret conclave, plotting how they might secure Him in order to silence His voice by putting Him to death.

Whether the story of the alabaster cruse was in chronological order is of little moment. It is a revelation of perhaps the most wonderful and touching expression of love the Saviour ever received, and leads to the most dastardly act to which He was ever subjected. Mary's love is the brightest gleam, and Judas' treachery the darkest shade.

Jesus ate the Passover feast with the handful of His loyal subjects, and one other. Never in all the history of that great feast had it been so sublimely kept. It was the culmination of the old, and the attitude of the old to Him was marked by the presence and act of Judas. He was the true representative of the nation at that board. Before the new feast (growing out of the old in the infinite grace of God by that dark act of treachery symbolic of the nation's awful failure) was instituted, Judas had gone out (John 13:30).

The story of Peter follows. He was not the only one sure of himself. Every man among them shared the confidence (verse 35). Yet there was not one among them equal to one hour's vigil with Him.

No words can help us to contemplate the Master in Gethsemane's dark hour. Let us read these words alone, prayerfully, approaching this sacred place of His agony in silence and adoration.

Having faced and conquered the most terrible trial of loneliness, and having rebuked in gentle tones of remonstrance the sleeping three, the King now turned to face His foes. Neither in the annals of the historian nor in the realm of fiction is there anything that can equal the degradation of the unholy trial, the base devices to find a charge to prefer against the Prisoner, the illegal tricks to secure a verdict of guilty which would ensure the death penalty. As one reads this story one wonders more and more at the greatest miracle of all, the patient suffering of the spotless One. There is but one explanation. Let each of us today take time to repeat it in the lurid glare of the light of that iniquitous council chamber, *"He loved me, and gave Himself for me."*

MATTHEW 27

The morning saw the plot hatched in the night carried into effect. This is chronicled in the first two verses of the chapter. The picture of Judas in his remorse is very terrible.

Pilate stands out as a warning against the policy of expediency. He was convinced of the innocence of Jesus, and his conscience—perhaps more acute that day than it had been for a very long time—very plainly revealed to him that his duty lay in releasing the Prisoner. However, he endeavored to secure himself and his position, and so flung Christ and conscience away at the same time.

Let us note the persons gathered around the Cross. The soldiers of Rome, for the most part debased, brutalized men. Simon of Cyrene, compelled to bear the Cross, yet surely discovering its message. Chief priests, scribes, elders, filled with malice and envy, and mocking Him, yet even in their mockery uttering, under constraint of God, great truths. "He saved others; Himself He cannot save." Thieves, the companions of His Cross and death, divided then and forever by their attitude toward Him. A group of women in the distance watching all. That mixed crowd was surely a prophecy. All sorts and conditions of men have been attracted by that Cross, and have been influenced by it according to the manner of their approach. Some have watched. Some have mocked. Some have been healed.

There was not one of His apostles to bury Him! The two men who attended to this sacred service were Joseph of Arimathea and Nicodemus (John 20: 39). Two women watched the burying. If it were not so inexpressibly sad as a revelation of hard-hearted unbelief, it would be ludicrous to notice His enemies' foolish attempt to guard the dead body of Jesus. Was the irony of Pilate conscious, one wonders, when he said, "Make it as sure as ye can"?

MATTHEW 28

"He is not here, He is risen!" That, surely, is the sweetest music. How beautifully it crowns the King. His enemies have rejected Him, and have proved their malice by handing Him over to their common, their last, their most terrible enemy—Death. The King proves His Kingship by overcoming that enemy in His dying, and on this Easter morning, the first, stands on His own earth again, having grappled with and vanquished the great foe of the race.

In verses 8-20 we have a glimpse of the living One. All the suffering is behind, the conflict is won. Now the heavens receive Him for a season. He will come again to reign over the whole earth.

Before His departure He gathered around Him His band of apostles and gave them the great commission, urgent with the urgency of His "GO," wide as the world in its scope, strong as the strength of Deity, and resourceful as He is Himself, for He promised to be always with the messengers, even to the end of the age.

So ends the Gospel of the King.

He came and declared the laws of the Kingdom, and revealed its beauty in His life and its beneficence in His deeds. His own would have none of Him, and in unholy coalition with Gentile powers uttered the verdict, "We will not have this Man to reign over us." They slew Him. Yet the last note is not that of man's rejection, but of God's exaltation, and we gather around the risen One, and cry, Long live the King!

Mark

MARK 1

The introductory words of this Gospel according to Mark are characterized by brevity. Mark at once announces his theme, "The beginning of the Gospel of Jesus Christ, the Son of God," and then in rapid, clear sentences declares the mission and message of the forerunner.

The Man of God's will comes from the obedience of Nazareth to the obedience of the life of public ministry. As to words, how brief the story of the temptation, yet how much force and meaning are compressed into it. Four points are especially to be noticed. 1. "The Spirit driveth Him." 2. "He was in the wilderness forty days, *tempted of Satan.*" 3. "He was with the wild beasts." 4. "The angels ministered unto Him."

The calling of two pairs of brothers is recorded. This was the call to service, "I will make you to become fishers of men."

A remarkable testimony to Jesus Christ was borne by a demon, "Thou art the Holy One of God." What a confession of the victory of Christ! In spite of all the attacks of hell, He was still untouched, unharmed of evil.

From the synagogue our Lord passed to the home. His hand of gentle love and omnipotent force takes hold of the dry, fevered hand of a woman, and imparts the coolness of healing and the power to serve.

News of the two miracles spread, and the crowds gathered. With perfect ease our Lord healed many, and cast out many demons! Such pressure of the crowds made it necessary that He hold communion with the Father. Next morning, very early, while darkness still lingered, He rose before any of the others, and stole away to a desert place to commune with God.

The disciples told Him that all were seeking Him, and He immediately decided to go elsewhere. The story of the leper is full of a subtle charm that never loses its power over the hearts of men. The quick "I will" of Jesus, the touch proving at once His great tenderness toward the man, and His perfect confidence in Himself, are exquisite illustrations of the grace and tenderness of this "Servant of all."

MARK 2

A great principle of the exercise of power by the Master is revealed in the words, "When He saw their faith." There can be no doubt that the word "their" includes the whole party, both the man himself and those who brought him.

From the house to the seashore He passed, and the multitudes followed Him. Rapidly and forcefully the story of Levi is told. Called to follow. All abandoned. A feast made, and Jesus the principal Guest, with many of Levi's friends and associates present. Again the scribes and Pharisees were exercised. "He eateth and drinketh with publicans and sinners." The Master's words explain the whole meaning of His sociability. He went to the feast of the publican as a Physician, *to heal.*

A third question on observance of the Sabbath was raised because the disciples had plucked ears of corn on that day. Our Lord replied: 1. The Sabbath is universal, not Jewish, "the Sabbath was made for *man.*" 2. Jesus claimed it as His own. "The Son of man is Lord even of the Sabbath." 3. There are circumstances in which it is permissible to break the letter of the Sabbath law. "Did ye never read what David did, *when he had need,* . . . ?" 4. Any application of the Sabbath law which operates to the detriment of man is out of harmony with divine purpose. "The Sabbath was made for man, *and not man for the Sabbath.*"

MARK 3

This is one of the few occasions on which it is said that Christ was angry. Particularly note the reason for His anger: "When He had looked round about on them with anger, *being grieved at the hardening of their hearts.*" What a picture these next verses give us of the thronging of the crowds! Perhaps there is no other picture in the Gospels quite equal to it for life, and color, and movement.

The time had now arrived for setting apart His workers. 1. "He . . . calleth unto Him whom He Himself would." 2. "They went unto Him." 3. "He appointed twelve, that they might be with Him, and that He might send them forth." The chosen are "appointed" to two things, first, to be with Him; and, second, to be sent forth.

Here is chronicled the effect which the news of His ceaseless activity had on His kinsfolk at Nazareth. These brothers of the Lord never had had any great confidence in Him, and in all probability He spoke out of the depth of His own experience when He said, "A man's foes shall be they of his own household."

No more solemn and awful words ever fell from the lips of Jesus than those in which He referred to "eternal sin" (see R.V.). That sin is the sin against the Holy Spirit, the deliberate, wilful, and final rejection of His ministry. His kinsfolk, the account of whose setting out to Him is contained in the earlier part of the chapter, here arrive. They were come, from whatever motive, to hinder Him in His work. It must have cost Him suffering to know that neither His mother nor His nearest relations understood that He was carrying out the will of God.

MARK 4

In verses 1 and 2, and 10 to 12, we have the explanation of the reason of the parabolic teaching of Jesus. He clothed divine truth in picture forms that men might more easily look upon it and learn it, just as He Himself was veiled in human form that men might have some vision of God suited to their capacity.

In verses 3 to 9, and 13 to 20, we have the parable of the sower. He is the Sower. The results following His sowing are indifference, shallowness, insincerity, fruit.

The illustration of the lamp reveals the responsibility entailed by privilege. Light is bestowed that it may lighten.

The parable of development (verses 26-29) is peculiar to Mark's

Gospel. It is concerned with the responsibility of the disciples for sowing the seed and gathering the harvest. The parable of the grain of mustard seed we have dealt with in Matthew, to which we may refer.

One of the most beautiful touches in this narrative, though full of sadness, is contained in the words, "They take Him with them, *even as He was*, in the boat." It reveals the weariness of the Master, and how at His word they hurriedly departed with Him that He might have opportunity for rest. How much better had they not disturbed Him. Far better to weather a storm in perfect confidence in Him than to enter a calm He creates, if the price of it is a rebuke from His lips for lack of faith.

MARK 5

Nevertheless the men of Gadara "began to beseech Him to depart from their borders" (verse 17). The price was too heavy; *their pigs were destroyed.*

There is heartbreak here. Jairus fell at His feet, and said, "My little daughter is at the point of death." *"And He went with him."* Of course He did! Exposition is superfluous. The procession to Jairus' house halted. The deep compassion of the Master's heart could not pass on without coming into very close dealing with this poor, broken, lonely, ostracized woman. However, contact that heals must always issue in confession that glorifies.

"Thy daughter is dead." Jesus was as quick as affliction's stroke—"Fear not, only believe." "The child is not dead, but sleepeth." "Talitha cumi." Wooed by such tones, the child spirit will come from the farthest spheres. He is not here now in bodily presence, and our darling went, and we were left desolate. Nay, not desolate. Surely it was that she heard Him say, "Talitha cumi," and our little lamb arose, and went *to Him.*

MARK 6

"He could there do no mighty work." Not that He in Himself was unable, for His hands laid on a few sick folk brought healing, but that the condition of wilful and persistent unbelief limited the power of the people to receive.

This is the first sending forth of the twelve. There are three definite points of equipment, and they cover the whole area of necessity, from minute detail to the utmost limit of their work. 1. They were "to go shod with sandals." 2. They were to go two by two. 3. They were to go provided with His authority. His parting instructions were very simple, yet drastic. They went, and preached, and healed.

The fame of Jesus spread, and reached the court of Herod. He, utterly depraved, and unscrupulous, trembled with fear. Why should Herod have feared? The very fame of Jesus was a continuity of the messages of the forerunner; and Herod, unable to recognize the King, feared the gruesome reappearance of the dead. So does sin make cowards of men when the Light approaches.

The messengers returned to tell Jesus their doings and teachings, and they went away together. The crowds saw them departing, and outran them round the shore. When He saw that waiting multitude, with its deep need, He was moved with compassion and "began to teach them many things." Then He fed them. Then He sent the disciples away. The reason for this is found in John 6: 14, 15, where we are told, "They would have taken Him by force and made Him a King." He would have no kingship based only on a selfish satisfaction.

MARK 7

In strong and clear language the Master denounced tradition as contrary to the commandment of God. 1. Things from without do not defile, and therefore are not sin. Temptation is not sin. 2. Only that is sin which comes from within, which is the deliberate outcome of the determining will of man. 3. Such determinings are the sources of defilement. 4. The list of evil things which the Master gives includes every possible form of evil, and these defile a man when they proceed from him in acts. 5. Such acts are committed only by the will of man.

The story of this woman is full of beauty. Hers was the faith that recognized the importance of Jesus' dictum that the children should first be fed, and consented to abide in His household as only a dog if she might have the crumbs of His table. His was the giving which recognized that her submission to divine arrangement and faith in the love of God raised her at once into the true sphere of blessing. She was spiritually, and therefore most truly, a daughter of the covenant.

The story of the healing of the deaf man is an instance of our Lord's freedom from any stereotyped method. Could we but understand all the facts of the man's condition, and all that the Master wished to do for him, we would see the necessity for every step in the process.

MARK 8

This was the second miracle of feeding. Our Lord knew whence these people came, and was solicitous for them on their long journey home if they departed without food. The miracle was the result.

The warning given to the disciples was consequent on the request of the Pharisees for a sign from heaven. This desire for a sign beyond those given was, and is, a danger. Those who live in unbroken communion with God do not seek for signs, but find them in all the miraculous movements of the most commonplace hours.

Here we have another, and perhaps the most remarkable, of the miracles which were wrought in stages.

The Master was approaching the end of His mission, and He gathered around Him His disciples. He questioned them on the opinions of men concerning Him. He then sought one other testimony, and that from those whom He had chosen. It is this view of the question and answer that reveals the value and preciousness of Peter's confession, "Thou art the Christ." Superior to all the rest, the One to whom all the others were but forerunners. The very Messiah!

Peter's position in what followed was not an altered one. How could the Messiah who was to restore the kingdom do so if the elders of the people rejected and killed Him? The new teaching introduced now for the first time was full of surprise. It is worthy of notice here, as in other instances in the last days of Jesus, that all this mistake arose, on Peter's part, from a partial attention to the Master's words. If he had grasped the promise, "after three days rise again," how different must have been his attitude.

Turning from private dealing with His disciples, and addressing them and the multitudes, our Lord laid down the stern, inexorable law of His Kingdom.

MARK 9

Here we see four men who have passed without death into the atmosphere and society of the heavens. One only of the four is there by His own right. Pure and spotless humanity stands in the glory of the unsullied light, and holds familiar converse with the spirits of just men.

We pass from the mountain to the valley. There we see Jesus, the baffled disciples, the father, the departing demon tearing his victim. The majesty and power of the Lord are manifested. Again He led these men through Galilee in privacy, and taught them, and the subject was still the Cross.

MARK 10

The Pharisees raised a question concerning the marriage relation. The Master went to the root of all things in the words, "From the beginning of the creation." The supreme and final authority is not the permission of a human lawgiver, but the will and intention of God.

It was in this connection that Jesus took the children in His arms and blessed them, laying His hands on them.

The story of the rich young ruler reveals the need of control. The way to find it is to follow the Master. The Master told His disciples that riches were always a snare. It is ever hard for a rich man to enter, but with God the impossible is possible.

"Jesus was going before." The disciples followed with an unnamable and awful dread upon them. Jesus was interrupted by James and John. With what tender patience He talked to them. The ten were indignant with James and John. This indignation of the ten is no more worthy of imitation than is the ambition of the two. Indignation and ambition were alike based on selfishness and desire for greatness.

The story of Bartimaeus reveals anew the readiness and power of Christ to aid.

MARK 11

This is the one occasion in the life of Jesus on which He of set purpose, and in such a way as to be understood of the crowds, took the position and accepted the homage of a King.

Afterward the disciples wondered as they saw the withered fig tree. (For the miracle see notes on Matthew 21: 18-22.) This wonder was caused by Jesus' evident power; *they* did not question His right. Having in a brief and pregnant sentence revealed the secret of His power in such a case to be faith, He uttered some most remarkable words on prayer.

There is an underlying consideration in the cleansing of the Temple. The part of the Temple where this traffic was carried on was the court of the Gentiles. His words, "a house of prayer for *all the nations,*" claimed the right of worship for Gentile as well as Jew, and denied the value of service rendered to some at the expense of any. The reputed masters of the Temple approached this newcomer, and demanded to know "in what authority" He was acting. The true Master of that Temple (for, observe, He had spoken of it as "My House") was dealing with men who were not sincere. He took them back to the last voice from heaven, and because they had not heard or obeyed that voice, declined to give them any further revelation.

MARK 12

In this parable of the vineyard the Lord very graphically sketched for those people their own national history, and condemned them thereby. "They perceived that He spake the parable against them." These words would seem to intimate that the rejection of the Saviour by these rulers of the people was more a sin against light than we sometimes imagine. They had a clear comprehension of what He meant, but they set their hearts and wills against Him.

A coalition of religion and politics, Pharisees and Herodians, approached as if seeking after truth, and proposed a problem. With perfect ease, without resort to any subterfuge, Jesus replied. Cæsar's things to Cæsar, God's to God.

Next, the Sadducees came to Jesus, proposing a possible situation involving the resurrection. Our Lord replied by declaring their ignorance. "Is it not for this cause that ye err, that ye know not the Scriptures, nor the power of God?" (verse 24).

Next a scribe asked a very subtle question. In answer, our Lord restated the essential truth of the unity of God, and then uttered the two great commandments, showing that they were great, not by comparison, but by inclusion.

Having answered the questioners, the Lord now carried the conflict into the camp of the enemy, and asked them a question. He played no trick with them in order to "catch them in their talk." He was revealing a truth, and His question led men into a place where they might see something of the divine method and understand His own position and mission.

Then followed a description of the scribes as He saw them: self-centered men, desiring all the outward show; oppressors, devouring widows' houses; hypocrites! For a pretense making long prayers. Unholy men. Receiving greater condemnation.

And once again we are face to face with the Master's keen observation of all that passed around Him, but this time in another application. As He saw the emptiness of the long prayers, so also did He observe the value of the sacrificial gift; and His estimate declares that those two farthings were worth more in the economy of heaven then all the gifts of the wealthy, which lacked the element of sacrifice.

MARK 13

A casual remark from the lips of one of the disciples drew from Jesus words full of solemnity and full of hope. This stately building was to be destroyed. It was already destroyed in the eyes of Christ by the corruption, the impurity, the blasphemy sheltered within its walls. And yet to those who are with Him, what matter? The Temple is gone, but God abideth, and in Christ by the Spirit is ever near hearts that seek Him. No more long pilgrimages to worship. There where thou art, He is. Then worship!

The account of these final discourses of the Lord are much more fully given and dealt with in Matthew and the notes thereon. The special point of interest for us lies in the closing part of the chapter, from verse 31 to the end. The Lord made three statements closely connected and yet perfectly distinct. 1. He announced the abiding character of His words. 2. He most clearly said that only the Father knows of that day and hour, referring to the question of the disciples as to the time when all things should be fulfilled. 3. He declared the true attitude of His people, "Watch":

> Let the door be on the latch
> In your home;
> In the chill before the dawning,
> Between the night and morning
> I may come.

MARK 14

Mary, conscious of the sorrow of death which was in her Lord's soul, poured out the rarest gift she possessed, and so anointed Him beforehand for His burial. Her name is forever redolent of pure devotion.

Two sets of arrangements are here chronicled, those of Judas and Jesus, yet both converging to the same end under the sovereign will and power of Jehovah. Jesus gathered round Him those who were, according to His own teaching, most nearly related to Him (see 3: 34, 35), and so grafted the new feast on to the old. In this institution of the breaking of the bread as a perpetual feast of remembrance and proclamation, our Lord made His death the central matter in His work. Not His life, or miracles, or teaching, but His death.

Jesus joined His disciples in singing. Most probably they sang the concluding portion of the *Hallel* (Psalms 115-118).

No disciple witnessed the agony of Gethsemane. One was arranging for the Master to be taken by the mob. Eight were left outside the gate. Three were asleep inside. Heaven and hell watched the conflict. In the Garden scene Mark omits incidents full of interest, but gives us a rapid view of the crisis.

The chief actors in all this awful and tragic chapter of human history were the priests. Man's sin had its most awful manifestation in the death of Jesus, and therefore priestism is the most awful form of human depravity in itself, and in the results it produces.

Such a fall as Peter's comes to no man suddenly. The preparation for it lies back in the story, and began arrestingly immediately after his noble confession, "Thou art the Christ." Not until Peter had confessed Him Messiah did Jesus attempt to lead him into the larger truth of the necessity for suffering and death. There Peter failed.

MARK 15

This chapter is one of those that needs little explanation and must ever be read in awe and reverence. Pilate represented the Roman empire, which attempted to secure itself by its ordinary methods of policy and force, and then fell, crushed and broken forever.

Simon was "impressed," that is compelled to His service; but it is most probable that this man became a devout follower of the Master, and that his sons, Rufus and Alexander, also were well known to the early Christians.

We gaze and wonder at the Cross with a great, strange contradiction and combination of emotion—with sadness as we remember that our sin caused Him the pain unutterable, with gladness as we reverently bathe in the river of His grace.

Mark records the great central cry out of the darkness, and we listen and are overawed! Then "the veil of the Temple was rent in twain from the top to the bottom." The barrier 'twixt God and man was destroyed. A new and living way was opened to the presence of God. From that moment the Cross admits to, and excludes from, the Holy Place, according to the relation men bear to Christ.

When Joseph of Arimathea went into the presence of Pilate he contracted defilement, which made it impossible for him to take part in the feast that was approaching. That defilement was made deeper by his contact with the dead. Yet no men had such keeping of the feast as did the two secret disciples, Joseph and Nicodemus, who dared the ceremonial defilement in order with tender hands to care for the Holy One of God, who was never to know corruption.

MARK 16

How completely all His disciples had missed the meaning of His teaching concerning His own resurrection may be gathered from this story. The women were bringing spices to embalm His body. In spite of their failure, He provided for their reception when they came to the tomb. They found a heavenly visitor.

Mark gives us a very condensed account of the Lord's sojourn on earth after His resurrection. There is a very beautiful revelation of His grace and love in appearing first to Mary Magdalene, out of whom He had cast seven demons.

There is a calm dignity about Mark's account of the ascension, which is a very appropriate ending to this Gospel of the Servant. He "sat down at the right hand of God." The Servant of all has taken the place of Chief of all. And yet His triumph is not cessation of activity, for as they go forth to preach the Word everywhere, in obedience to His parting instruction, He works with them, and gives the signs which confirm the truth of their message. Thus the last manifestation of the grace which has been so conspicuous is that He sends us forth to carry on His work; and He is with us.

Luke

LUKE 1

Luke brings us face to face with the Son of Man and the Saviour of the world. The apostle first gives an account of how he did his work. He then tells of Gabriel's visit to Zacharias announcing the birth of the Herald of the Lord, following it immediately with the august account of the coming of this same Gabriel to Mary, and the great annunciation. Her reception of that announcement was in faith and submission to the divine will. Thus we see her co-operating in the purpose of God.

Luke records the first two songs of the new dispensation, the first being a salutation by Elisabeth of Mary as the mother of the Lord, and the second the great *Magnificat* of Mary herself.

The faith of Zacharias, which had trembled in the presence of the divine promise, was restored when he wrote on the slate the name of the babe. This was a return from the point of unbelief, and the exercise of will in the appointed way.

This chapter ends with the third song of the new era, and it takes the form of a prophetic benediction from the lips of a priest of the chosen people. It was a song of salvation, and has within it truth deeper than most likely the singer then understood.

LUKE 2

Jesus was born in Bethlehem, under the yoke of an oppressor. Moreover, by the exigency of the circumstances, He was born amid the homeless crowd. This was according to the divine arrangement and foretelling.

The message of the angel and the chorus of the heavenly host are of especial interest as revealing heaven's outlook on the birth of Jesus. That may be stated by citing two brief sentences. 1. "Glory to God in the highest," 2. "Peace on earth among men in whom He is well pleased."

Simeon and Anna were representatives of the remnant of Israel who were true to the divine ideal and purpose. Simeon in song, and Anna in speech, set forth the praises of God.

The final paragraph of this chapter covers a period of thirty years in the life of our Lord, giving us a picture of the Boy dedicated to the things of His Father, telling, first, of His growth, and then of His advancement until He had arrived at maturity and readiness for His mission.

LUKE 3

Luke marks with great care the time of the ministry of John, employing an emperor, a governor, three tetrarchs, and two high priests to do it. By means of these names a picture of the world at the time is given to us: the empire under Tiberius Cæsar, the commonwealth of Israel divided and governed by four of Rome's vassals, the priesthood degraded by a dual leadership contrary to all the law of God. It was then that the Word of God came to John, the most important event of the time.

With the coming of the Word to him, John became a public figure. Men crowded to listen to him. It was a stern preaching of repentance, and formed the prelude to the music of Messiah's message. Then came the Messiah Himself. At His baptism He received a twofold seal: the direct declaration of the pleasure of God, and the anointing of the Spirit.

At this point Luke speaks of Jesus' age, about thirty, and gives His actual genealogy, tracing it back through Mary and David to Adam.

LUKE 4

As man Jesus was tempted. All the words with which He rebutted the attacks of Satan were quotations from the divine law for the government of human life. The exhaustive nature of the temptation is revealed in Luke's words, "When the devil had completed every temptation." Evil had nothing more to suggest. The thoroughness of the temptation was the completeness of the victory.

The perfect and victorious Man now found His way back to Nazareth, and there, reading from the prophecy of Isaiah, claimed Messiahship definitely.

The account of this induction is followed by a group of pictures revealing different aspects in the work of our Lord. He is seen teaching in the synagogue while the people listened in astonishment. The quietness is disturbed by the cries of a demon-possessed man, and the Lord is seen as Master of the underworld of evil. Next He is revealed as Master of disease, this revelation following that of His authority over evil. He who is able to exorcise demons has no difficulty in dealing with the result of evil in any form.

Then an evening scene, when it was light indeed, and the Lord's unlimited resources were revealed. Finally, His need to be away from the pressing crowds, when He passed to the desert.

LUKE 5

Four of Jesus' disciples, already called into the relation of discipleship, are here called more definitely to service. Taking command of their vessel, to which in all probability they had returned without warrant, they found Him able to direct them in an earthly calling, and by so doing lifting them to the position from where henceforth, they would catch men.

The coming of the leper revealed an advance beyond the common crowd in his attitude toward Jesus. The leper believed in Jesus' power to heal. Luke the physician gives a vivid picture of his condition, "full of leprosy." Nevertheless, the man himself believed in the power of the Lord, but was not sure of His willingness. Quickly and graciously, by touch and word, the Master settled that question.

A picture follows which is a contrast, namely, the doctors of the law critically listening to Jesus while guarding themselves against any new idea. It was then that the strong faith of a few disturbed the assembly when the man who was palsied came on the scene. Jesus spoke the word of the forgiveness of sins to him, whereon Jesus was immediately charged with blasphemy. He demonstrated His authority by healing the man.

Nothing puzzled the religionists of the Lord's time more than His eating and drinking on terms of familiarity with publicans and sinners. Here He revealed the reason for doing so. He was among men as the great Physician.

LUKE 6

In a synagogue our Lord healed the man with a withered hand, and the religious watchers were filled with anger because, according to their view, our Lord had desecrated the Sabbath. Surely, there is no desecration of divine ordinances so powerful as that severe orthodoxy which clogs the stream of compassion. By fulfilling its intention, the Lord of the Sabbath sacredly kept it in restoring this man to health and power.

Luke gives us here the account of our Lord's choosing of the twelve. It is instructive and revealing that Luke tells us that our Lord preceded this election by a night of prayer. In the arrangement of the names we notice that they were placed in double harness, two by two, yet there was but one apostolate.

We have next our Lord's discourse to His disciples, delivered in the hearing of the crowd. The difference between this address and the Sermon on the Mount is, among other things, in the omission here of all contrast between the old system and the new. Here we have the great principles for the blessing of humanity at large. Jesus ended His charge by a claim, quiet in its assumption of authority, and startling also, as He revealed the character which will abide in spite of all storms. Carefully note the threefold condition. 1. "Every one that cometh to Me," surrender. 2. "And heareth My words," discipleship. 3. "And doeth them," obedience.

LUKE 7

Here our Lord passed over the national boundary to bring blessing to the household of a Roman centurion. Of that man the elders said, "He is worthy." The man said, "I am not worthy." Jesus said, "I have not found so great faith, no, not in Israel." It certainly is a wonderful story, showing that the principle of faith is supreme over all privileges of race and birth.

Two crowds are seen meeting outside the city of Nain, one, the Master, His disciples, and a great multitude, approaching the gates; the other, a dead son, his mother, and many people of the city, issuing forth from the gates. As they met, life triumphed over death, sorrow was turned into joy.

Luke now tells of how John sent an inquiry to Jesus which unquestionably was born of his perplexity over the methods of our Lord. Jesus' reply was first that of continuing the work that He was doing, then of speaking of the greatness of John, and finally of seeking from him faith, even though intellectually he might be perplexed.

The scene in the house of Simon the Pharisee is very full of beauty as it reveals our Lord dealing with two entirely different personalities—Simon, cold, dispassionate, satisfied with his own integrity; the woman, conscious of her sinful past, rejoicing in her forgiveness and pouring on Jesus the evidences of her love. Our Lord Himself contrasts the two in the most striking way, revealing the value of moral cleansing as leading to the victory of love.

LUKE 8

Luke here refers to our Lord's journeyings, and reveals the interesting and beautiful fact of how women of wealth provided for him on the material level, ministering to Him of their substance.

At this point Luke records the parable of the sower, which forever divides into four sections those who hear the proclamation of the Word: first, those in whom His truth can produce no results, wayside hearers; second, those whose power of hearing is superficial, rock hearers; third, those in whom other forces impede and check the development of truth, thorny hearers; fourth, those who are responsive.

Following the parable we have the account of a memorable voyage over the sea and back. First came the time of quiet for Himself; He slept. The storm did not wake Him. The disciples woke. He calmed the wind, hushed the sea, and rebuked the disciples.

Reaching the country of the Gadarenes He restored to true life a demon-possessed man, and at the same time destroyed an unholy and forbidden traffic. A deputation of the inhabitants besought Him to depart from their coasts, and He went. He never forces Himself on unwilling hearts.

Our Lord's quick sensitiveness to need which ventures in faith is seen in His consciousness of the touch of a trembling woman as He traveled to the house of Jairus. Again His keen appreciation of the hour of greatest trial is revealed in His words to Jairus, "Fear not, only believe." His supreme authority was revealed as He put the scorners out of the chamber. His sweet, human sympathy is seen in the command to give the little one something to eat.

LUKE 9

As He sent His apostles out, He gave them power and authority. They went forth without any provision for the journey other than the things of spiritual equipment. Rumors of the ministry and power they exercised reached Herod, and he was filled with fear. The apostles returned from their first mission, and our Lord took them to Bethsaida, where He performed the wonder of feeding the crowd. In a remarkable way, that feeding is a parabolic illustration of the method by which those who serve Him are to reach the needs of humanity. Their duty is to yield all they have to Him, and then to obey Him, no matter how mere prudence and worldly wisdom may question the method.

At this point our Lord began the second stage in the disciples' training. In answer to His inquiry, one of their number confessed in full the glory of His Messiahship. He then began to show them the necessity for the Cross. They failed to grasp the significance of the revelation.

The next scene we have is of three of them being taken to the mount, and beholding Him in His transfigured glory, and finding that there, in converse with Moses and Elijah, He was speaking of that self-same Cross.

Descending to the valley, we see first the disciples beaten by demon-possession, and then the Lord exercising His authority and power in freeing the child from that possession.

The chapter closes with illustrations showing that in following Jesus there must be no compromise and no delay.

LUKE 10

The mission of the seventy is recorded only by Luke. They went forth, sent by Jesus. They returned glad in the victories they had wrought in His name. He received them, and declared to them the whole truth concerning the kingdom of evil, in the words, "I beheld Satan fallen as lightning from heaven," and then warned them not to rejoice in their apparent success, but rather in their relationship to that kingdom from which Satan had fallen.

A lawyer asked Him, "Who is my neighbour?" and the story of the good Samaritan is our Lord's reply to that inquiry. We are arrested by the fact that He completely shifted the ground of the question, and by this reply said, in effect, that the question as to who is a neighbor was not so important as the question to whom was he a neighbor.

The account at the close of this chapter of the visit to the house of Martha and Mary is very full of beauty. In His declaration to Martha, "One thing is needful," He was revealing the supreme thing in life. If we would be strong for service in the strength that prevents distraction and unrest, we must know what it is to find time amid all the duties of life to sit at His feet as disciples.

LUKE 11

Watching the Master at prayer, His disciples were inspired with a desire to pray, and requested that they be taught. He responded to them in a fourfold statement. First, He gave them a model. Then He revealed the character of God as He contrasted it with that of the unjust judge. He then gave them the franchise of prayer in the words, "Ask, seek, knock"; and finally revealed the ground of confidence as it existed in the Fatherhood of God.

His casting out of a demon raised criticism by some, to which criticism He replied, "If Satan also is divided against himself, how shall his kingdom stand?" adding the tremendous declaration, "He that is not with Me is against Me, and he that is not with Me, scattereth."

This was followed by our Lord's denunciations of the age. He spoke of it as a generation seeking a sign, and thus proving their blindness, of the rulers as punctiliously particular in paltry matters while neglecting judgment and the love of God, of the lawyers as binding ceremonial burdens upon the people that they would not lift themselves. Thus the blindness of the people is traced back to the blindness and wilfulness of the leaders and teachers. In all the public utterances of our Lord there is much which reveals this same thing, and should cause all those who are called to positions of leadership to realize their great responsibilities.

LUKE 12

Knowing that the enmity of the rulers against Him would proceed also against His disciples, He told them not to be afraid of those who kill the body, remembering ever their Father's care, as revealed in the sparrows, and in the numbering of the hairs of their heads.

His address to His disciples was interrupted by one of the multitude. It was an appeal for action in the matter of the distribution of property. Refusing to arbitrate, He uttered the great parable of the rich fool, declaring unequivocally that "a man's life consisteth not in the abundance of the things which he possesseth."

This was followed by a description of the true attitude of the disciples of Jesus. For the moment let us take out from it certain revealing phrases, "Fear not," "sell . . . and give," "loins girded about," "lamps burning," "men looking for their Lord," "be ye also ready," "the Son of man cometh."

Answering a question of Peter, the Lord then gave another aspect of Christian life. It is watching and waiting for the Lord Himself, which must forever be that which prevents the abuse of trust and wrong relationship between fellow servants.

It was in this connection that our Lord broke out into the great soliloquy which Luke alone records, in which we see Him looking to the ultimate in His mission, the casting of fire, and recognizing that this can be realized only through the passion baptism to which He was moving.

LUKE 13

Someone brought to our Lord an account of a happening which seemed to suggest that those who suffered catastrophe are proved to be "sinners above all." He directly contradicted that view, and in that connection uttered the great parable of the fig tree, revealing the true principles of life.

There follow three full-length portraits: of Jesus, in His attitude toward this woman; of the ruler, and his objection; of the woman herself, a daughter of Abraham under the power of evil.

Luke links two parables of the Kingdom with the rejoicing of the multitude for all the glorious things that were done by Him. The first, the parable of the tree, teaches the growth of the Kingdom into a great power; and the second, the parable of the leaven, its corruption.

Passing on His way our Lord showed that there are limits to the divine mercy, that there will be those who will not be able to enter in. They will be such as are workers of iniquity. It is only against such that the door is shut.

That truth is emphasized by His lamentation over Jerusalem.

LUKE 14

Nothing escaped the notice of Jesus. He saw the guests in the house, and their method of procedure in seeking the chief seats. As He watched, He enunciated two great truths of social application. First, He criticized those seeking precedence; and, second, He criticized a hospitality which was extended in the hope of recompense.

One of the guests, moved by the word of the Master, exclaimed, "Blessed is he that shall eat bread in the Kingdom of God." In the parable that followed, the Lord revealed the divine action in the establishment of His Kingdom, and showed the reluctance of the human heart to fulfil its condition.

When Jesus left the house where He had been entertained, He was followed by great multitudes, to whom He uttered, perhaps in words severer than on any other occasion, His terms of discipleship. These were severance from every earthly tie in order to follow Him, and an actual fellowship in the Cross. This was the occasion, moreover, on which He gave the reason for that severity. It was that the work of God which He had come to accomplish was building and battle. It was necessary that He have those on whom He could depend to complete the building and win the battle.

LUKE 15

Our Lord's attitude toward the sinning multitudes aroused the hostility of the Pharisees, and to them principally He uttered the great discourse of this chapter, consisting of a threefold parable. In its entirety it constitutes a wonderful revelation of the divine heart.

In the first phase, that of the Shepherd, the aspect of grace in the work of the Son is revealed. In the second, the aspect of grace is revealed in the work of the Spirit. The third phase of the parable necessarily unveils the heart of the Father. It shows unending love for the sinner following him to the far country, waiting for his homecoming, and then shining out in the welcome. The divine love is the theme throughout. Love goes to the wilderness. Love continues to seek. Love welcomes home.

The story ends with the account of one of whom we ever speak as the elder brother. It is at least significant that he is not called so in the narrative. The prodigal is spoken of as brother to this man, but he is ever called the "elder son." His attitude forfeited his right to be called a brother. Nevertheless, his story reveals the possibility of living in the father's house and failing to understand the father's heart. This was the failure which characterized those who criticized the work of our Lord.

LUKE 16

The Master had a lesson to teach His disciples on the subject of earthly wealth, and He made use of this unjust steward for purposes of illustration only. The element in the action of the steward which our Lord commended was of foresight and singleness of aim. It was in this connection that He uttered the memorable words, "Ye cannot serve God and Mammon." The whole force, of course, is on the word "serve." When God is served, Mammon is used beneficently. When Mammon is served, the claims of God are ignored.

In this same connection our Lord gave the account of the life and death of two men, throwing clear light on the life beyond. That is seen as connected with, and growing out of, the life here. It is of great importance that it follows closely the teaching concerning Mammon. One of the most radiant of its lessons is that if a man have wealth it is a positive sin for him to use it for his own luxury and ease and remain unmindful of the want and needs that lie at his very gate. Money possessing a man is the direst curse, for it hardens his heart and paralyzes his noblest powers. The money of a God-possessed man is a blessing, for it becomes the means of expressing his sympathy with his fellows.

LUKE 17

The thinking of the Master for His disciples is always that they should live in love. He knew, however, that offenses must come. In that connection He uttered the solemn word of warning, "Woe unto him through whom they come." He then gave instructions on our attitude toward the offender.

There follows the story of the lepers. *Ten* men with a common need lifted a cry of agony in petition to the Son of God. *Ten* men were directed by Him to do what appeared absurd. The law required to show themselves to the priest when they were cleansed. These men were still lepers. Nevertheless, *ten* men trusted Him, and started on the journey. *Ten* men were miraculously healed through obedience, and then *one* man turned back to glorify God. Because of this, the question of Jesus, "Where are the nine?" becomes arresting and revealing, showing, as it does, that He waits for the worship of healed souls, and often is robbed of it.

The Pharisees asked Him when the Kingdom of God would appear, while it was right in their midst because the King Himself was there. This the Lord declared: "The Kingdom of God is in the midst of you." Turning to His disciples, He spoke of the day that lay far ahead in which He would no longer be unrecognized, but revealed in His glory to a faithless and unbelieving age.

LUKE 18

Two parables on prayer are here given. The first insists on its necessity as an alternative to fainting. The second reveals the secrets of prevailing prayer, namely, humility and a deep sense of need. The comparison of the two prayers offered in the Temple precincts will show in the case of the Pharisee a sense of self which almost excluded the consciousness of God, while in the case of the publican the supreme sense was of God. The first was rejected. The other was justified.

It is significant that the three evangelists, Matthew, Mark, and Luke, show that the incidents of the blessing of the children and the rich young ruler were united. Of the children our Lord declared, "Of such is the Kingdom of God." The character that proves citizenship is the character of childhood.

In dealing with the young ruler the truth was emphasized that only through the strait door of absolute renunciation of self is it possible for men to regain the child attitude toward life.

What follows reveals that this renunciation demands the way of the Cross. For a while these disciples shunned the shame and the pain of it. Ultimately, however, every man of them, save Judas, went into the realm of death with Jesus. The incident of the blind beggar reveals that fellowship in that Cross always results in compassion and willingness to help those in trouble.

LUKE 19

Zacchæus was the last convert but one in the ministry of Jesus. Our Lord's method with him is very revealing. He asked for his hospitality, and after receiving it held an unrecorded conversation with him which resulted in the complete revolution of the man's outlook and his activity. It was in this connection that our Lord uttered that supreme word of His ministry, "The Son of Man is come to seek and to save that which was lost."

In close connection He uttered the parable of the pounds. This, by the way, must not be confused with the parable of the talents. In the latter the gifts varied in amount. In this the value was identical. Not all had the same number of talents. All have the pound for trading. The people following Him to Jerusalem "supposed that the Kingdom of God was immediately to appear." In the parable He gave them the program of events. He was going to a far country to receive His Kingdom. During His absence His servants were to trade with His capital for His profit. At His return He would deal with those who had thus been responsible.

Going to Jerusalem, He entered the Temple. As He approached it, all the disciples broke into song. The song is remarkable as an answer to the song of the angels which had announced the birth of Jesus. They then sang, "Glory to God in the highest, peace on earth." These now significantly sang, "Peace in heaven, and glory in the highest." Surely it was an inspired song, with a fuller meaning than perhaps the singers understood. He was going to the death by which He would make a peace in heaven which would issue in peace on earth. Peace with God must precede peace among men.

Jerusalem had failed to learn the things belonging to peace, and this called forth Jesus' tears.

LUKE 20

This chapter records the remarkable happenings gathered around our Lord's entrance into the Temple. By a parable He revealed the awful sin and failure of the Hebrew nation, culminating in His own rejection, showing, moreover, that that sin must result ultimately in the breaking into pieces of the sinning people.

The closing conflicts between the rulers and Jesus constitute the saddest revelation of the depravity of the human heart. Jesus' teaching had driven them into a corner from which there was no escape. They would have laid hands on Him forthwith had they not feared the people. So they sent spies to endeavor to take hold of His speech. Here, as in all cases, man's sin serves only as a dark background to throw into brighter relief the glory of the Saviour. All the rulers' attempts were futile. He answered with infinite wisdom and terrific force all the quibbles they raised, and then uttered in the hearing of all the people the solemn warning and the scathing denunciation of the scribes. These answers of His were not the sharp retorts of smartness, but the final utterances of a wisdom which revealed the ignorance of the questions.

LUKE 21

Here we have another illustration of the fact that nothing could escape the Master's vigilance. Of the gifts being cast into the treasury He was the true Appraiser. He saw the widow as she cast in her gift, and said that she had "cast in more than they all." In the realm of superfluity God does not begin to count. The first entry in the heavenly books is that of sacrifice.

Addressing His disciples, Jesus spoke to them especially about their service and attitude. His words must have come with special force to the men who had heard with what wisdom He had answered the malicious attacks on Him. He declared that they should have "mouth and wisdom." Herein is discovered the secret of the wonderful utterances of these men chronicled in the Acts of the Apostles. Finally, in this connection He uttered the superlative claim, "Heaven and earth shall pass away, but My words shall not pass away." This statement had special application to what He had been saying concerning the future.

Then He laid certain injunctions upon His disciples of the utmost importance. They were first to "take heed to themselves," and things which they were to guard against were named, "surfeiting," "drunkenness," "cares of this life." In view of these responsibilities they were to "watch . . . at every season," and, finally, to make "supplication."

LUKE 22

Here we have the record of final things before the Cross. The priests and the devil are seen in coalition.

As the end approached, the Master is seen with the shadow of the Cross on Him, desiring to eat the Passover with His loved ones. Even in this connection the disciples contend over which of them is to be accounted the greatest.

After the observance of the Passover and the institution of the new Feast, He declared to them, "Satan hath obtained you by asking" (margin). Notice carefully Satan's demand, and that it was granted. This involves the truth that he could not touch the disciples without the divine permission. As at the moment Peter was the man in supreme danger, our Lord singled him out as He said, "I made supplication for thee."

The new order was approaching. The Master was leaving His disciples in His bodily form. It was in this connection He said, "Let him sell his cloke and buy a sword." The word "sword" arrested them, and they produced two, to which action the Master responded, "It is enough." Notice carefully He did not say, "They are enough." He was not referring to the swords, but to the principle He had laid down. Indeed, their eagerness to produce the swords evidenced their slowness to appreciate the spiritual nature of the conflict ahead of them. When presently Peter used one of the swords, the Lord sharply rebuked him.

Passing out, and into Gethsemane, He was followed by His disciples. The supreme revelation of our Lord in Gethsemane is of His complete submission to the will of God as He said, "Nevertheless, not My will, but Thine be done."

Then followed the darkness of which our Lord said to His enemies, "This is your hour, and the power of darkness." Through this hour He passes alone with the firm step of the Conqueror.

LUKE 23

This is the story of the Cross, and, as in dealing with other Gospels, it is best read in reverent quietness and meditation. We see all the forces of evil as represented in the Jewish priests and in Pilate joining hands to secure the murder of Jesus. Dr. Maclaren has remarked that there is something impressive in the unbroken continuity of the clauses in this paragraph which follow one another, linked by a simple 'and,' like the waves of the Dead Sea which roll heavily in dreary succession. It is for us to stand on the margin of that sea of unutterable anguish, and to remember that His submerging was for our deliverance.

What mingled feelings of disappointment and love must have filled the heart of Joseph as he laid the body of Jesus in his garden grave. Nevertheless, the love was the supreme matter, and it found vindication later.

LUKE 24

No human eye saw the resurrection. The women came early, but only to find the stone rolled away. The record of those earliest experiences is full of touching beauty. Luke alone gives us the story of the walk to Emmaus, in which disappointed disciples poured out their story, and in which at last He revealed Himself to them as the Risen One.

Much mystery still surrounds the fact of the resurrection, but the fact abides. There are suggestive points, moreover, in this account of His appearances. He distinctly denied that His resurrection was of His Spirit only, for He invited them to touch His hands and His feet. The evidences of a material body are abundant. Nevertheless, He came to their midst through closed doors, and at last, in bodily form, passed away, superior to the law of gravitation. To speak of the resurrection as supernatural is correct so long as we mean by "natural" the sphere of life in which we are bounded today. There is nothing supernatural to God. We take His facts today, and await His explanation tomorrow.

The last brief picture of Jesus in this Gospel is of His passing into the presence of God, with hands uplifted in priestly benediction.

John

JOHN 1

The Gospel of John brings us into the profoundest facts concerning the Person of Jesus. The first eighteen verses constitute the introduction to the whole Book. The main declaration is found by bringing together verses 1, 14, and 18. In these the Eternal is linked to the temporal, and the temporal is revealed as the interpretation of the Eternal.

The rest of the prologue consists of three parentheses. 1. Verses 2-13, in which the glories of the Word are revealed in the varied processes of God's relation to humanity. 2. Verse 14, an exclamation by John over the glory he beheld. 3. Verses 15-17, which give the double witness of John the Baptist and John the Apostle.

The remainder of the chapter contains an account of John's conflict with the rulers, and of the first things in the ministry of Jesus as Messiah as He gathered His earliest disciples. In it we see a group of men of different temperaments coming into contact with Him, and we observe His varying methods with them, and His winning them to Himself as we hear their differing names and titles for Him, all unified in a recognition of His authority.

JOHN 2

At Cana our Lord wrought what John describes as the "beginning of His signs." It was a sign of power in the realm of creation, and of it being exercised in answer to faith. It was a sign, moreover, of His attitude toward pure joy in the activities of human life.

After a short period of retirement at Capernaum, Jesus went to Jerusalem, and there gave the first outward sign of His official position. The outer courts of the Temple had been turned into a veritable market-place. He cleansed them, and when asked for His authority, in words not then probably understood, He declared that the final sign of such authority would be His death and resurrection. Such an action by our Lord was bound to draw attention to Him. Moreover, while in Jerusalem He wrought other signs, so that many were attracted to Him. It is an arresting fact that whereas, in that sense, they committed themselves to Him, He, knowing them perfectly, did not commit Himself to them.

JOHN 3

Nicodemus would seem to have been one of the finest products of Judaism.

He was thoroughly sincere. Moreover, he was determined to investigate for himself, and so came to Jesus by night, not because he was cowardly, but because he sought a lonely and personal interview. This was the man to whom our Lord revealed the necessity for the new birth. When the statement created difficulty in the mind of Nicodemus, our Lord revealed to him the fact and necessity for the Cross. Whether Nicodemus understood Him it is impossible to say. The ultimate in his story shows that he became a disciple.

The whole history of John the Baptist is characterized by a rugged splendor, but nowhere does his greatness stand out more conspicuously than in the scene recorded here. There was no touch of jealousy, no latent sorrow in his heart as he said, "This my joy therefore is fulfilled; He must increase, but I must decrease." John the evangelist comments on this attitude, showing how reasonable and right was this position. The speech from heaven must, of necessity, be above all other. That witnesses to certainties, not to speculations.

JOHN 4

The words, "He must needs pass through Samaria" are arresting. The final explanation must be found in His dealing with the woman of Samaria. In itself, it is a radiant revelation of His method as He led this woman step by step from an almost flippant carelessness into a confession of discipleship.

It was while dealing with her that the disciples, who had gone away to find food, returned, and they were amazed to see Him talking to a woman. With love for Him, they sought to persuade Him to eat. He took the opportunity to reveal to them the deeper things of His heart, telling them that He had meat to eat that they knew not of, which was to do the will of God. He had been doing that will in dealing with this needy woman.

The sequel of that conversation was His tarrying in the Samaritan city for two days, during which He so dealt with them that they made the great confession, "This is indeed the Saviour of the world."

Leaving Samaria, He returned to Galilee, and He came to Cana. There, at a distance, He wrought a wonder in healing the boy in answer to the father's urgent appeal.

JOHN 5

It was at this time that the conflict between Christ and His enemies, which culminated in His Cross began. A miracle wrought on the Sabbath gave rise to this first outbreak. Throughout this chapter we have incidents colored by this conflict. The first was of the man in Bethesda's porches. In infinite compassion Christ dealt with him and healed him. His enemies objected because the wonder had been performed on the Sabbath; and, in effect, He replied that in the presence of sin and misery God had no Sabbath. He said, "My Father worketh even until now, and I work."

His answer was understood by them as claiming equality with God. It should be carefully observed that He did not deny the accuracy of their deduction, but continued to speak as One who claimed such equality of authority. He declared that the truth of all He was saying was evidenced by His works, and consequently by His Father.

He then rebuked these men for searching the Scriptures and failing to understand them, for had they understood the Scriptures they would have discovered that they led to Him.

JOHN 6

The whole chapter really records things resulting from the conflict recorded in the previous one. Having crossed the sea, Jesus first fed the multitude, and they, enamored of His ability, attempted to take Him by force, and make Him King. This He would not permit. Sending His disciples across the sea He retired to the mountain. Then followed the wonder —recorded also by Matthew and Mark—of His stilling of the storm. Thus it will be seen that He returned to where the conflict had occurred, and immediately, in a discourse, rebuked the people for having been attracted by the wonder in the realm of the material while they neglected the deep spiritual facts of life. Presently they asked Him for a sign. He answered their request by offering Himself to them as bread, the Bread of life.

These men were sense-bound. They did not apprehend His meaning. Continuing, He insisted on the supremacy of the spiritual, as, taking the manna for illustration, He declared, "Your fathers did eat, and died," and, further, "This . . . a man may eat . . . and not die."

The Jews were more than ever mystified, and disputed among themselves. Confronted by this difficulty, our Lord went further still, and spoke in mystic language of the necessity for drinking His blood. The figure was suggestive of a way into life through death and sacrifice.

This fuller unfolding perplexed His own disciples, consequent upon which He inquired, "Would ye also go away?" It was Peter who made the reply, "To whom shall we go? Thou hast the words of eternal life." Nevertheless, at this point some of His disciples broke with Jesus.

JOHN 7

So far, John has recorded incidents in the first year of our Lord's ministry. We now come to a comparatively brief section in which he records happenings in the central and crowded two years. He arrived in Jerusalem at the feast of Tabernacles. His fame had spread, and there was discussion concerning Him there. Having arrived, He taught in the Temple precincts. In doing so He rebuked their attitude, and referred to the miracle wrought on an earlier occasion in the Bethesda porches. On the last day of the feast He stood and made His great utterance concerning the flowing of the rivers, claiming that He was able to satisfy thirst, and, moreover, that those who received such satisfaction from Him should become channels through whom the overflowing rivers should pass.

The religious authorities had sent officers to arrest Him, but owing unquestionably to the wonder of His speech they were unable so to do, for they said when they were asked why they had failed, "Never man so spake." One voice was raised at this point in His defense, the voice of Nicodemus.

At the close of the day "every man went to his own house."

JOHN 8

The end of chapter 7 is closely linked with this, in that after declaring "every man went to his own house," the writer said, "But Jesus went unto the Mount of Olives."

Here we have the story of a return to the Temple, and of Jesus' dealing with the woman in the presence of the rulers. With matchless skill He showed that these men had no right to judge this woman. This He did Himself in matchless grace.

At verse 12 we have a continuation of the line of thought broken off by the introduction of the narrative of the woman. Our Lord made a stupendous claim, "I am the Light of the world," and declared that men following Him would not walk in darkness, but have the light of life. On the basis of that He went on with His teaching, in the course of which He again claimed to work in harmony with His Father, and uttered supreme words revealing His claim for Himself, and showing the blindness and wickedness of those who were opposing Him. His enemies were angry, and asked Him, with evident scorn, "Whom makest Thou Thyself?" It was then that He emphatically said, "Before Abraham was, I am."

JOHN 9

The account of His healing of a blind man follows. Its values are gained very largely in relation to this spirit of opposition which was being exhibited. The case aroused great interest, so much so that the man was arraigned before the rulers, and his attitude before them aroused their anger even yet more, so that they excommunicated him. Then our Lord sought him out, revealed Himself as the Son of God, and received his worship.

Then, again, He declared that He had come into the world in order that the blind might see and those who saw might become blind. His statement that He had come to judge the world meant that He would be the separating One, the One through whom God would judge. The position of men would be decided by their attitude toward Himself. In this teaching there was a hinting and outline of the coming order, but without any clear description of it.

JOHN 10

Continuing, He gave a more detailed picture of that coming order. There was to be a fold, with a door. There was to be a flock, with a shepherd. Entrance to the fold would be by the door. The flock would know and follow the shepherd. Here John declared, "They understood not what things they were that He spake unto them"; and that "therefore" of Jesus shows that what followed in His teaching resulted from their failure to understand. This fuller statement centers on two principal claims of our Lord, "I am the Door," "I am the good Shepherd." Entrance on the new order would be through Him. Of the fold He is the Door. Sustenance and government within the order would be through Him. Of the flock He would be the Shepherd. Such teaching again caused division.

While walking in the porch of Solomon, the Jews asked for some more definite pronouncement. In reply, Jesus referred them to what He had already told them, and then restated the facts of the new order, insisting on the relation between Himself and His Father. All this teaching aroused those opposed to further activity, but their rage was restrained, and they were not able to arrest Him.

JOHN 11

Here we have the account of the last sign wrought by Jesus as recorded by John, namely, the raising of Lazarus. Very beautiful in this connection is the depiction of the sorrow of the sisters, and our Lord's method of dealing with each of them in turn. His approach to the grave revealed some of the deepest things in His own attitude. He was troubled in the presence of the sin and unbelief which had its final expression in death. Nevertheless, He acted with complete authority, and as a sign of His redeeming power raised Lazarus, and restored him to his loved ones.

This last sign raised the opposition of His foes to definite activity. The degraded condition of things is seen in the fact that the chief priests, who were Sadducees, made common with the Pharisees in their action against Jesus. It was at this point that Caiaphas gave his advice characterized by cunning and his contempt for Jesus

As a result, the council determined on the Master's death. It was then that Jesus retired into "a country near to the wilderness," where He tarried for a while with His disciples.

JOHN 12

The shadows of the Passion were now falling across the path of the Christ. In what happened at the supper we have a vivid contrast. Mary and Judas arrest our attention. She, discovering the sorrows of His heart, pressed closely to Him, and sacramentally expressed her love. Judas, blinded in self-interest, criticized her action, and so revealed himself as utterly opposed to the very spirit of the Lord Himself.

From Bethany Jesus passed to Jerusalem, where a stupendous outburst of welcome greeted Him. It was of little worth, as subsequent events proved. Nevertheless, He moved through the worthless present, transmuting it into the triumphant future.

The incident of the coming of the Greeks is full of revelation, for it drew from our Lord that contemplation of His own death and its issue expressed in the symbol of the grain of wheat.

At this point in his narrative, John shows how, notwithstanding all the signs, the people did not believe; and then records what would seem to be the last public testimony of Jesus. It is a summarized statement of His claims, made just as the light of the working day was passing and the hour of darkness was approaching. Nothing can possibly be more sublime than these closing public utterances of our Lord. They are in perfect harmony with the marvelous conception of Him presented to us in this Gospel as the revealed Love and Light and Life of heaven.

JOHN 13

For a time our Lord now devoted Himself to His own, and in this connection we have the account of His washing the disciples' feet. The whole action was Eastern, and was the action of a slave. By what He did and said our Lord intended to emphasize that the supreme action of God is service, and that fellowship with Him demands such action on the part of His followers.

Then, in connection with the Passover feast, Judas was excluded, and our Lord uttered the significant words, "Now is the Son of Man glorified," and this made possible our Lord's final instruction to His disciples. It was in this connection that Peter, strangely perplexed, asked Him the question, "Whither goest Thou?" to which our Lord first replied by showing Peter that he, Peter, could not at that time accompany Him on the pathway. When Peter protested, our Lord showed him that He knew all the weakness lurking within him better than he himself could know it, as He declared that before sunrise he would deny Him thrice.

JOHN 14

There is no real break between the end of chapter 13 and beginning of chapter 14. Therefore continuing, while now including all the disciples, He charged them not to let their heart be troubled. He then answered Peter's original question by saying He was going to prepare a place for them. To Thomas' protest He answered that He Himself was "the way, the truth, and the life"; and to Philip's great exclamation, "Show us the Father, and it sufficeth us," He replied in words that need no comment, "He that hath seen Me hath seen the Father."

Still continuing, He told them that at His departure He would send them Another, who would disannul their orphanage by revealing Himself to them and bringing them into closer association with Him. It was on the basis of this assurance that He said to them, "Peace I leave with you." He carefully described the peace as "My peace." His peace was a heart untroubled and unfearful in spite of all the suffering and conflict ahead of Him. The secrets of that peace were His certainty as expressed in the words, first, "I go to the Father," and, second, "The prince of this world cometh, and he hath nothing in Me."

JOHN 15

Our Lord now uttered the great allegory of the vine. Certain words in it arrest our attention, "the vine," "the branches," "the fruit." The close interrelationship between these is emphasized, and our Lord declared, "I am the Vine, ye are the branches." The vine includes all—root, stem, branches, leaves, and fruit. No figure of speech could more perfectly set forth the intimate relationship between Christ and His own.

In applying the truth, the commandments of the Lord are found in remarkable setting. The first, "Abide ye in My love"; the second, "Love one another." In this connection He dealt with the ministry of the Spirit in this application.

Their relationship to Him, issuing in likeness to Him, must bring on them the hatred and persecution of the world which already had been brought on Him. Jesus declared this hatred to be finally hatred of the Father. The measure in which His disciples produce the fruitage of His life will be the measure of their revelation of the Father, with its protest against worldliness; and so it must be the measure of the world's hatred of them. Nevertheless, in the Comforter there would be a ministry directly for the world. That testimony is to be borne by the Spirit in His co-operation with the Church.

JOHN 16

Throughout these discourses our Lord was preparing His disciples for all that He saw coming to them. He told them that they would have sorrow resulting from their suffering. Because of this, it was necessary that they have the Comforter, and He could come only after the bodily departure of the Lord Himself.

The world was still in the heart of Jesus, and He told His disciples in very clear terms what the office of the Spirit would be in the world. To gather up the teaching, we see that the testimony of the Spirit is to be wholly concerned with Christ, and is to convince the world of sin, righteousness, and judgment. As to His own, the Comforter will guide them into the truth, and into the perfect knowledge of Christ Himself. Here we see they displayed their ignorance, not understanding what He meant by "a little while." This, with great patience, He interpreted to them.

In the closing section of His discourse our Lord told them that He had been speaking in proverbs, but undoubtedly again referring to the coming Comforter, He declared that He was henceforth speaking to them plainly of the Father. All ended with the august words, "I came out from the Father, and am come into the world; again, I leave the world, and go unto the Father." In those sentences we have a declaration of the whole redemptive progress of the Son of God. From the Father into the world; from the world unto the Father.

JOHN 17

This chapter records for us words of our Lord addressed to His Father. In the first movement He was dealing strictly and only with relationships between Himself and the Father, referring to a past glory, and anticipating the coming glory, first, that resulting from the Cross, and then the return to that which had been abandoned.

In the second section He spoke to His Father of His relationship with the men immediately surrounding Him at the time. His prayer for them was not indifferent to the world, although He prayed at the moment not for the world, but for these men as the instrument by which He would yet reach the world. For them He asked that they might be kept from the evil that is in the world, and that to this end they might be sanctified in the truth. These men no longer belonged to the world in its degradation, but they did belong to it for its salvation. This He indicated as He said, "As Thou didst send Me into the world, even so send I them into the world."

Finally, He said, "Neither for these only do I pray, but for them also that believe on Me through their word." Thus He looked on and prayed for the world. Therefore He prayed that they might be one. The closing words of this intercessory prayer reveal our Lord's final purpose for the Church. It is that all His own might be with Him. The first application undoubtedly is to His Cross, with Him in its fellowship; and the last inevitably to the glory, with Him in the glory that will follow.

JOHN 18

From the sacred hours of teaching and prayer our Lord passed to the final acts in His mighty work. This brought Him to Gethsemane, where we have a revelation of His majesty and His meekness. He suffered Himself to be seized and bound, and led away, and so He passed to the court of the high priests.

In all the annals of human crime there is nothing more utterly degraded and despicable than the procedure of what is spoken of as His trial before them. Unable to deal with the situation, they sent Him to Pilate, and once again we have the amazing story of the majesty and dignity of His dealing with this representative of the Roman power. It is quite evident that Pilate would have preferred to release Jesus.

It was during this period that Peter came to the full realization of his appalling weakness as it had been declared to him by his Master. Under the pressure of the hour he uttered the threefold denial. Carefully observe how at this moment of finality and his failure he was not abandoned.

JOHN 19

Here once more we have the story of the Cross, and once again it is a story to be read almost without note or comment. The picture of our Lord led forth and presented to the crowds by Pilate is one of appalling solemnity. Whatever Pilate's intention, the vision of Jesus failed to arouse in the hearts of the multitude any pity for Him, and they clamored for His death. In spite of all Pilate's protests, the clamor continued, and he yielded to it, and handed Jesus over to the mob.

Referring to the Cross itself, John is careful to say that it was when Jesus knew that all things were accomplished that He cried, "I thirst," and after that declared the fulfilment in the words, "It is finished."

Presently we have the beautiful picture of two disciples secretly paying the last tender offices of respect to the body of their Lord. Joseph found Him a grave in a garden, and Nicodemus brought great wealth of spices for His entombment.

JOHN 20

This is the story of a dark morning and a lost Master. The strange excitement of it all is evidenced by the fact that the three disciples named are all seen running. Mary ran to tell the disciples, and John and Peter ran to the grave.

Mary tarrying in the neighborhood of an empty tomb after the disciples had returned to their home is symbolical of what the Church would have been had there been no resurrection. Her cry, "They have taken away the Lord out of the tomb, and we know not where they have laid Him," tells the whole story. It was when she thus spoke that He made Himself known to her as the living One, and she cried out, "Rabboni."

On that memorable resurrection day John records the morning and evening appearances of our Lord. Between the morning interview with Mary and the evening meeting with His disciples He had seen Peter alone, and journeyed with two men who walked to Emmaus. John tells of Jesus appearing in the midst of the assembled disciples. He greeted them with the words, "Peace unto you," showing them His hands and His side. He then repeated the salutation, and declared what their commission would be, and prophetically indicated the power that would be theirs as He breathed on them and said, "Receive ye the Holy Spirit."

Very beautiful is our Lord's dealing wtih Thomas eight days later.

JOHN 21

This chapter undoubtedly added later by the writer is a revelation or manifestation of the risen Christ. Here He is seen interested in His disciples, and caring for their immediate needs, and that in spite of the fact that they had gone back to fishing, although He had charged them to tarry until they were endued with power from on high.

In all the story of our Lord's dealings with His own disciples nothing is more exquisite than this account of the patience and strength of His dealing with Peter. He talked to Peter in that morning hour, and gave him his commission and that of the Church in fellowship with Him. They were to go forth into the world, feeding the lambs, shepherding the sheep, and feeding the sheep. Moreover, there is a touch of human interest in His rebuke of Peter for attempting to discover the divine will concerning another man.

The book ends with the declaration, "There are also many other things which Jesus did, the which if they should be written every one, I suppose that even the world itself should not contain the books that should be written." At the beginning of the story we stand in the presence of the bewildering eternities, and at the close we are thus brought in amazement to a recognition of the infinitudes which have been condensed in the life and activities of a Person on whom we may look, to whom we may listen, and yet who forever defies any to say that is to be said concerning Him.

Acts

ACTS 1

In the opening verse Luke reveals the nature of his first treatise. It had to do with "all that Jesus began to do and to teach." This is followed by the last glimpse we have of the disciples before Pentecost, together with the account of the Ascension. We then see them during the period between the Ascension and the coming of the Holy Spirit. It is interesting to study the list of those who are named as being gathered together with them. Their need for that Spirit for guidance is revealed in an election to fill the place of Judas. Casting lots was wholly out of place, and was never resorted to after the coming of the Spirit. That the action was a mistake is revealed in that in His own time and way God found and fitted an apostle. It is to be noted how in consequence of this initial blunder, Paul had constantly to defend his right to the place of apostleship.

ACTS 2

The first paragraph of this chapter records the first page of the history of the Church. It is seen as it began to form. The separated units of the disciples were fused into the new unity of the Church. Through this new unity God, by the Spirit, addressed Himself to the gathered multitudes. They gave expression to the wonderful works of God in sacred, ecstatic song.

This produced an effect on the city which called forth the first recorded address in the power of Pentecost. It is arresting to see in that address how the apostle first referred to the Old Testament Scriptures, and, second, showed how all their predictions were fulfilled in Jesus of Nazareth.

The result of this message was immediate and glorious. Under conviction produced by the Holy Spirit, the people asked, "What shall we do?" Peter replied, by giving clear instructions, and by testimony and exhortation, until about 3,000 souls were added.

The early Church life is described in verse 42, in which it is said that "they continued steadfastly" in four matters: "in the apostles' teaching," in "fellowship," "in the breaking of bread," in "prayers."

The story ends with a picture of the practical realization of that early fellowship, in which these were the predominant notes: a wholesome fear, a powerful service, a mutual ministry, constant worship, a great gladness, a gracious influence, and perpetual growth.

ACTS 3

The men at the Beautiful Gate of the Temple is the illustration of a constant fact: approximation to God is a habit of humanity in its need. Mendicants are not often found at the doors where an infidel lecture has been delivered. In speaking to the man, Peter revealed the essential meaning of Christianity. He was not able to minister to the man in material things so far as silver and gold were concerned. He was, however, able to communicate to him something which would make him master of his disability.

This miracle attracted the crowd, and Peter at once directed the people's attention to their own God, the God of Abraham, of Isaac, and Jacob, claiming that He had visited them in the Person of Jesus. Faith in His name was the avenue through which God had wrought the wonder. No glory accrued to man from what had happened; none to the man who was healed, for his faith was not brought into play at all; none to the apostles, as they clearly declared.

ACTS 4

Opposition to apostolic preaching and work seems to have originated mostly from the influence of the Sadducees. The preaching of the apostles contradicted all the cardinal elements in the Sadducean philosophy, which is comprehensively revealed later (Acts 23:8). The first note of their preaching was affirmation of the resurrection of the Lord; moreover, they declared later that they had been delivered from prison by an angel, and that they were working with the Holy Spirit.

However, all attempts at suppression produced the contrary result. The three thousand of Pentecost had already grown to five thousand. We now see the apostles for the first time definitely placed on trial. It was a significant bar, consisting of Annas, Caiaphas, and others of the kindred of the high priest. At first no definite charge was preferred. It was a court of inquiry. Peter affirmed that his authority was from Jesus of Nazareth, through whose power the wonder had been wrought. With great daring he charged these very men with the murder of Jesus.

The tribunal was astonished at these men's boldness, and it is arresting to observe that they concluded that "they had been with Jesus."

Confronted with this opposition, the disciples betook themselves to prayer, and they had a new manifestation of power in a new filling of the Holy Spirit.

Here we have the introduction of Barnabas and his action. In a venture of faith he sold his land, and invested its proceeds in the work of God.

ACTS 5

Here we have a terrible story. The account of Ananias and Sapphira stands in vivid contrast to that of Barnabas. The sin was dishonest dealing with the Holy Spirit. The judgment was swift and terrible.

The salutary effect of it was seen in the people's fear of joining this new community. Notwithstanding these things, the work went forward. Multitudes of both men and women were added to the Lord.

The opposing forces are now seen face to face. The enemies of Christ were roused to action. The apostles were arrested and imprisoned, and were supernaturally released. The scene of their appearance before the judges is vivid. On the one side was the most august and representative assembly that could be gathered. On the other, a handful of men who by all human standards were mere nonentities. As the spokesman of the whole Church, Peter addressed the assembly. The Sadducees were filled with anger. Gamaliel was a Pharisee, and really found himself more in agreement with the doctrine of the apostles than with the rationalism of the Sadducees. He advised, therefore, that these men should be left alone. The picture of them going forth rejoicing in suffering is filled with beauty, showing their experience of relationship with Christ.

ACTS 6

The story alternates between the opposition of the outside crowd and the condition of the Church in its own borders. A difficulty arose concerning the distribution of relief which had a national tone. As we consider the story it is very arresting to notice that whereas the complaint had come from the Greeks, all those appointed in the new diaconate bore Grecian names.

In this connection it is declared that "the Word of God increased," "and the number of the disciples multiplied." One of those elected, Stephen, was a remarkable man; as the chronicler says, he was "full of grace and power." His witness brought on him bitter attack, which was popular rather than priestly, the first manifestation of this kind of opposition.

ACTS 7

The charge against Stephen was that he had spoken against the Temple and the Law. His reply consisted of a masterly review of the history of the nation from the calling of Abraham to the rejection of Jesus. He was careful not to speak disrespectfully of the Temple, notwithstanding that he reminded them that the history of the nation was of a God-governed people long before the Temple was erected. Thus reviewing the past, he declared the blindness and hardness of heart of the people, who in the old days, had turned to false gods.

Nothing can be clearer from a study of this defense than the new spiritual concept which had taken possession of these early Christians. The Temple and all its ceremonial were shown to be but incidental, and a passing method in the divine movement.

Such argument and directness could produce but one result. The people's rage was stirred against him. The picture of the martyrdom of Stephen is full of exquisite beauty. A vision of his Lord was granted to him in the hour of his suffering and death. He saw His Lord, not sitting, but standing, thus fulfilling one aspect of His great priesthood. This vision of Christ seems to have shut out the brutality of the mob from the eyes of Stephen, and he saw the mob only in its folly and sin. Committing himself to his Saviour, Stephen prayed that the sin of his murder might not be laid to the charge of his enemies.

ACTS 8

The popular outburst against Christianity evidenced in the martyrdom of Stephen was general. Members of the Church at Jerusalem were scattered throughout Judea and Samaria. How dark the day seemed to be for the infant Church. Nevertheless, the overruling hand of God is seen in the movement. As they were scattered, the members did not cease their work. They went through Judea and Samaria preaching the Word.

Philip, one of the recently chosen deacons, went to the city of Samaria. There a great company of the people believed, but there was something lacking in the work, for they did not receive the Holy Spirit. This gave Simon the sorcerer an opportunity. When Peter and John came the gift of the Spirit was bestowed, and Simon was summarily dealt with.

Then we have an account of the spreading of the movement. The apostles returned to Jerusalem, preaching on the way in many of the villages of the Samaritans. Philip, acting under a direct guidance, took a journey of at least thirty miles, and on the way declared the Word to an Ethiopian eunuch. Thus the truth was presented to the first of the dark-skinned sons of Africa. After his teaching of the eunuch, Philip went to Azotus; and, in turn, journeyed through Judea and Samaria, as far as Cæsarea, preaching in all the cities.

ACTS 9

Opposition, the leader of which seems to have been Saul, continued. Armed with letters from the high priest, he attempted to put an end to the Nazarene heresy. It was on his journey with this intent that he was arrested by Christ. The action of Ananias stands out as a revelation of a man ready for his Lord's command, and carrying it out without any hesitation and with all brotherly love.

How important was the apprehension of Saul is evident at once. He completely devoted himself to the service of his new Lord. This change of attitude in the man necessarily issued in a change of attitude toward him. The persecutor became the persecuted. When, after a lapse of time, Paul came to Jerusalem, the Christian disciples were afraid of him, but Barnabas stood by him.

At this point the book returns to Peter. Two incidents are recorded, one at Lydda, where Æneas was healed; the other at Joppa, where Dorcas was raised from the dead. This paragraph ends with a significant announcement. Peter abode many days in Joppa with one Simon, a tanner. The calling of the tanner was absolutely repugnant to the Jew, and the fact that Peter was willing to tarry in his house is a sign that in spirit he was already learning the lesson of how mere national exclusivism was at an end in the economy of Christ.

ACTS 10

The story of Cornelius is remarkable. In himself, as Luke tells us, he was "a devout man, and one that feared God with all his house, who gave much alms to the people, and prayed to God alway." This man received a direct communication in an open vision.

While God was thus drawing Cornelius toward the Evangel, He was preparing the messenger to declare that Evangel. Peter was astonished, and made his astonishment known, but yielded ready obedience to the prompting of the Spirit, and came to the house of Cornelius.

His discourse there opened with a declaration of a new perception of things which had come to him, a perception breaking down his prejudices and broadening his outlook. In dealing with Cornelius he recognized that the preaching which he and the rest had already heard, the proclamation concerning the Lordship of Jesus according to the herald John, was not enough, and he proceeded to testify to the great facts of the Evangel. The result was that a company of new believers were baptized by the Holy Spirit. After this, and as a sign of the essential baptism, they were baptized with water.

ACTS 11

It is very interesting to note how slowly the prejudices of the Hebrew Christians gave way, and yet how amenable they were to the evidences as they appeared. The apostles and the brethren at Jerusalem felt that Peter had taken a wrong step, yet when he stated all the facts of the case and realized that the work was indeed that of the Spirit, they laid aside their prejudices and followed the light.

The apparent calamity of the scattering abroad of the Christians really issued in the great missionary movement which practically occupies the whole of the remaining part of the book. In Antioch a remarkable work followed the preaching of certain men with the result that the Church at Jerusalem sent Barnabas thither. What he saw gladdened his heart, and, realizing the importance of the movement, he went to Tarsus to seek Saul. Then followed a year's work in Antioch under the direction of these men.

Agabus appears here, and once again in the narrative (21: 10). On both occasions he is seen exercising the prophetic gift in its predictive element. A famine which he announced is matter of history. What is valuable in chronicling it in the sacred record is that it was a crisis which brought out the true Christian spirit of these Gentile Christians. There can be little doubt that they were conscious of the suspicion of the Jewish brethren; yet every man of them, according to his ability, contributed toward the relief which was sent by Barnabas and Saul to the sufferers in Jerusalem.

ACTS 12

Again persecution broke out in Jerusalem, and the first of the apostolic band suffered martyrdom at the hands of Herod. A revealing sentence concerning Herod is that which declares that when "he saw that it [the killing of James] pleased the Jews, he proceeded to seize Peter also." This, however, was not permitted by the divine overruling. The prayer of the assembled Church was heard and answered. It may remain to us a perplexing question why James was slain and Peter delivered. There is no explanation. Nevertheless, the revelation of the facts is reassuring. That God delivered Peter proves His power to have delivered James. That He did not deliver James proves that the death of James was also within the compass of His will, and we know that in the great Unveiling all will be seen to have been right.

There is something very graphic in the contrast between the opposing forces which is incidentally revealed. Baffled, angry, conceited, Herod went to Cæsarea. There a popular demonstration proclaimed him a god. He did not refuse the description and was smitten. Now notice carefully the statement which follows, and which is introduced by the word "But," which suggests a contrast. "The Word of God grew and multiplied." So has it been through all the centuries. Sooner or later, those who have opposed the Christ have been swept aside, while the march of the triumphant Word has never ceased for a moment.

ACTS 13

The first most distinctly missionary movement sprang from Antioch, and was independent of all official initiation. A company of those in Antioch sent Saul and Barnabas, and it is declared immediately afterward they were sent by the Holy Spirit. Saul and Barnabas started on this journey together.

While especially glad to work among the Gentiles, Paul ever began with the Jew and the synagogue. In Antioch in Pisidia we find him reviewing his own history, and proclaiming his evangel. He made it clear to those Jews who listened to him that the whole movement was in harmony with, and, indeed, in fulfilment of, their Scriptures.

Many Gentiles were brought to a

knowledge of the truth and received the blessings of the new covenant. This stirred the enmity of the Jews, and solemnly the apostle officially turned to the Gentiles. The Jews were, as he declared, "unworthy of eternal life" because they had rejected the message; while the Gentiles were "ordained to eternal life," because they believed.

Again persecution followed. The result was that the preachers were cast out. Paul and Barnabas, therefore, shook the dust of Antioch from their feet, and went to Iconium, leaving behind them this new company of disciples filled with joy and with the Holy Spirit.

ACTS 14

In Iconium there was largely a repetition of the experiences at Antioch. Becoming aware of the growing hostility, Paul and Barnabas passed on, and came to Lystra. There is a marked difference between Paul's address here and messages which he delivered to the Jews. In this he recognized and dealt only with Gentile position and thought. He described himself as a bearer of good tidings from the eternal God. Designating their gods, "vain things," he announced the living God.

With relentless anger, the persecuting Jews of Antioch and Iconium followed the apostle to Lystra. Here it is easy to read the statement, "They stoned Paul, and dragged him out of the city, supposing that he was dead"; but it was a fearful experience, and in all probability he would carry the marks of it with him to the end of his journey. How he must have remembered Stephen as the stones rained on him.

Nevertheless, this great missionary pressed forward as far as Derbe, and then turning back on his course, he revisited the very places where he had been submitted to persecution. As he did so, he told the people that "through tribulation we must enter into the Kingdom of God." What emphasis his own bruised body would lend to his word. The statesmanlike qualities of the apostle are manifested in this revisiting of the churches, establishing them, and appointing elders to take the oversight of affairs. Returning to Antioch, the two reported on their work, and so ended the first missionary journey.

ACTS 15

In the work among Gentiles the question of circumcision very naturally arose, and its difficulty is revealed in the calling of a council. That council seems to have opened with much desultory discussion. Then followed the serious contributions. Peter's address is chronicled. In it he faced a supreme fact, that in sending him to the Gentiles God had proved that He made no distinction. The next speakers were Paul and Barnabas, who simply repeated the story of their work. The summing up by James is characterized by wisdom, and his finding was that the Gentiles should not be troubled with anything that was purely Jewish. The difficulty cleared away, the discussion ceased. Remarkable unanimity had been gained, for it is said that the apostles and the elders of the whole Church were in agreement. Paul and Barnabas returned to Antioch, and there was rejoicing when the message was delivered to the church.

A revealing story of sharp division between these two men occurs here. Paul seems to have been afraid of Mark, because he had withdrawn from them on a previous occasion, whereas Barnabas believed in him, and defended him. It is good to remember that subsequently Mark was restored to Paul's favor, as certain references in his letters clearly show.

ACTS 16

Here begins the account of Paul's second journey. At Lystra he found Timothy. His action in the circumcision of Timothy is startling in view of the recent decision of the council. Some charge him with inconsistency, and yet perhaps it was a proof of a larger and deeper consistency.

The beginning of this journey is noted for a remarkable experience. The Spirit compelled Paul to a course against his own inclination. At the end of that journey the man of Macedonia appeared to him, and the movement toward Europe began. They came to Philippi, a Roman colony. There they first went to a Jewish place of prayer, and found there a Gentile woman who worshiped, whom, with her household they baptised.

At last Paul and Silas found themselves in prison, and then occurred that wonderful revelation of Christian courage. In prison they sang with their feet fast in the stocks. They were delivered supernaturally, and the first result was winning the jailor for Christ. It is interesting here to see Paul making use of his earthly citizenship in demanding that his rights should be respected by the magistrates. Undoubtedly, he did this in the interest of others. To suffer wrongfully, without protest, is likely to issue in perpetuation of the wrong and involving others in suffering.

ACTS 17

At Thessalonica and Berea the apostle visited the synagogues, and again in each case persecution arose from the Jews. A sentence which fell from the lips of the leader of the mob shows with what rapidity the Gospel was winning its way. Said they, "These that have turned the world upside down have come hither also."

Passing on to Athens, we have the wonderful account of Paul's action there. The effect on him of what he saw is revealed in the statement, "His spirit was provoked within him as he beheld the city full of idols." When at last he found himself confronting the wise men on Mars Hill he delivered a message characterized by courtesy and clarity from their standpoint, and at last declared to them the great doctrine of the resurrection. Basing his message on what he found among them, with masterly skill he built a structure which led him to this statement of the resurrection. His address consists first of declarations concerning God; second, of declarations concerning man's relationship to God; and, third, a declaration of the position of Christ as vindicated by His resurrection.

ACTS 18

Leaving Athens, the center of the intellectual life of Greece, Paul came to Corinth, its commercial center. There he joined Aquila, and gave himself to the work of tent-making, while reasoning on the Sabbath in the synagogue with both Jews and Greeks. When opposition arose, he turned from the synagogue, and found his base of operations in the house of Titus Justus. Unquestionably the opposition was keen, but he was encouraged as the Lord spoke to him in a vision. The result was that he remained in Corinth for a year and six months.

The opposing Jews at last arraigned Paul before Gallio. Gallio treated these Jews with supreme contempt, and by this fact the overruling God delivered His servant.

At last he left the city and passed to Ephesus, from Ephesus to Cæsarea, from Cæsarea to Jerusalem, where he tarried long enough to salute the Church, and so back to Antioch, completing the second missionary journey.

Then we see him starting on the third journey, going first over old ground. It was in this period that we have the account of a vow. It is perhaps a little difficult to explain, and expositors have taken different views.

The account of Apollos follows. By birth and training he was especially fitted for work in that area. He was evidently a remarkable man, "eloquent, mighty in the Scriptures, instructed in the way of the Lord, fervent in spirit." Nevertheless, it is equally evident that he was limited in his knowledge of Jesus, which knowledge resulted from the ministry of John. It was on account of this he was more carefully instructed by Aquila and Priscilla.

ACTS 19

The result of the work of Apollos was manifest when Paul reached Ephesus. There he found a company of sincere disciples to Jesus as He had been revealed by John. To them Paul declared the truth in its fulness, and they entered into the experience of the new birth by receiving the Holy Spirit.

For two years Paul remained in Ephesus as a center, influencing all the district. A survey of the whole account shows how all kinds of facts and forces were pressed into the service of the Word. Opposition, however, was fierce, and resulted in an uproar on account of the falling off in the sale of the shrines for the Ephesian goddess, Diana. This uproar shows how men, alienated from God, make all life center around the material. So long as the preaching of "the Way" disturbed the thought of men, or even changed some of their habits, it mattered little; but when these changed habits touched the wealth of the craftsmen, opposition resulted. Vested interests are always saying to Christianity what the demons of old said to Christ, "Let us alone." Christianity is always saying in reply what Christ said to the demon, "Hold thy peace, and come out of him."

ACTS 20

Restful and mastered by Christ, Paul was yet restless and resistless in devotion to the enterprise of his Lord. These facts are evident throughout this chapter. We follow him in rapid movements, always calm and confident. After tarrying in Greece for three months, he found that a plot was laid against his life and quickly passed overland. Detained in Troas, he ministered to the saints and strengthened their hearts.

It was while here that Eutychus, overcome with sleep, fell to death, from which Paul raised him.

In taking farewell of the elders of Ephesus the apostle delivered an address characterized by great clarity and beauty. Reviewing his own work, he made no apology. His care for the flock was tenderly expressed. As for himself he was going to Jerusalem bound in spirit, and was certain that suffering awaited him. Yet there was no shrinking. Life itself was not dear to him, his only passion being the fulfilment of his ministry for Christ.

ACTS 21

Passing on toward Jerusalem, Paul and those with him reached Tyre. There the disciples urged the apostle not to go to Jerusalem; but, having received from the Spirit a revelation of all that lay before him, he pressed on.

Presently Cæsarea was reached, and here we get another glimpse of Philip the evangelist. Living at Cæsarea he had four daughters who were devoted to the work of the Lord. While tarrying there Agabus arrived and uttered words of prediction. This prediction harmonized with the apostle's own conviction that he was on his way to suffering. Once again he was urged not to proceed, and once more his devotion overcame all human urgency.

Arrived at Jerusalem, he was received by the elders, and rehearsed the story of the wonderful triumph of the Word among the Gentiles. Here there were those who were opposed to this very work. It was at this time that Paul took the vow of the Nazarite. It is impossible to escape the conviction that in doing so he was mistaken. The only purpose of his action was to maintain peace, which was not achieved.

ACTS 22

Paul's defense as here recorded is a rare and perfect example of Christian argument. He was defending his devotion to work among the Gentiles. In that defense the last word he was permitted to utter was the word "Gentiles." Immediately the fury of the crowds burst out. In that moment of crisis Paul broke once and forever with the trammels of the Judaic system.

At this point we have a remarkable view of the condition of affairs in the church at Jerusalem. Quite evidently there were many who still observed all the forms and ceremonies of the Jewish ritual. They were attempting the policy of compromise.

In connection with the frenzy of the mob we have another case of Paul claiming his rights of earthly citizenship. Suffering for Christ's sake is a holy privilege, but no man has any right to court martyrdom in order to allow men to sin when a protest may prevent them. Paul gloried in the stigmata of Jesus, but he did not fail to prevent scourging when it was in his power legally to do so. Thus it is seen that meekness is not foolhardiness, and courage may express itself in preventing suffering as much as in enduring it.

ACTS 23

By action of the Roman governor, Paul was arraigned before the Jewish Sanhedrin. Hardly had he commenced before he was interrupted and insulted. It was a most trying ordeal for the apostle. It is easily conceivable that he would be dejected in the loneliness of the following night. It was then that the Lord stood by him and said, "Be of good cheer," and assured him that in spite of all opposition he would bear witness also at Rome.

So fierce, however, was the opposition to the apostle that certain men vowed to destroy him. Again God overruled and made the fact known to Paul, through his nephew, as the result of which Paul took action which led to his protection and deliverance. Under Roman escort he reached Cæsarea, and was presented to the governor, who placed him under guard until his enemies arrived.

ACTS 24

Tertullus, who appeared here, was a Roman barrister, it being necessary for the Jews to employ such in presenting their cases before a Roman tribunal. The charges he made were palpably false. His description of Paul as a "pestilent fellow" had no justification whatever. The chief charge was that he was "a mover of insurrections." The baselessness of this charge also is apparent, but the subtlety of it is clear. The only charge which could be substantiated was that Paul was "a ringleader of the sect of the Nazarenes."

Paul's defense is a splendid illustration of the strength and dignity of one who is conscious that he has nothing to hide. His address to Felix was courteous, courageous, and clear. With quiet scorn he denied the charges preferred against him except the one, for he freely confessed that he was "of the Way, which," and there is an evident touch of irony in his words, "they call a sect."

The sequel is full of interest. The decision of Felix was favorable to Paul, who was committed to an indulgent imprisonment, and so protected from his enemies. Felix's subsequent action was prompted by mixed motives, and resulted in his arraignment of Paul before himself and Drusilla, who was the daughter of Herod, who had slain James and was herself a wanton. Paul's reasoning here was characterized by such faithfulness and force as to produce terror in the mind of Felix. Paul remained for two years at Cæsarea. Then Felix being recalled he left Paul in bonds.

ACTS 25

The Jews besought Festus to bring Paul to Jerusalem for trial. This, however, he refused to do. When arraigned before him, Paul again made use of his rights as a Roman citizen, and definitely appealed to Cæsar.

In order to send him to Rome it was necessary that Festus should have a definite charge to prefer against Paul, and it was in order to secure this that he took advantage of the visit of Agrippa to have Paul brought before him. The occasion was made a special one, and the gathering was an impressive one. The leaders attended in full state, surrounded by the military authorities, and all the light and leading of the city. Agrippa was well known for his learning, and for an æsthetic side to his nature. On the other hand, Bernice, who was with him at the time, was his sister, with whom, even at the moment, he was living in incestuous relationship. Paul was called on to tell his story in order that Festus might base a report on it to Rome.

ACTS 26

Agrippa intimated to Paul that he might speak, and the apostle spent a moment in introductory words, and then uttered his great apologia, in which a twofold purpose is evident, first, his own defense, and, second, the declaration of the way of salvation. In defending himself he ignored the charges against him, but explained the change of front in his own career. Thus he dealt with the underlying reason which had prompted his enemies' opposition. He gave the story of his conversion, his commission, his consecration. Throughout it is evident that he was making plain the way of life.

Festus, a Gentile, saw nothing in Paul's discourse save evidences of madness. While Paul was answering Festus, he addressed himself principally to Agrippa, and evidently attempted to constrain him to honesty on the basis of intellectual conviction. Agrippa's answer, accurately translated in the Revision, "with but little persuasion thou wouldest fain make me a Christian," was a contemptuous sneer. Paul's rejoinder was at once dignified and tender. He calmly assumed the authority of his own position, even though he was a prisoner wearing a chain; and then in exquisite tenderness wishing that Agrippa might be such as he was, he added the words, "except these bonds."

ACTS 27

The study of Paul's last voyage reveals some apparently contradictory facts, and yet common in the experience of the saints. On the one hand, difficulties and dangers multiplied. On the other, the divine purpose was being carried out. It would seem as though all forces were combined in an effort to prevent his coming to Rome. On the other hand, we see how all the way he was conducted, cared for, comforted. From first to last no note of complaint was uttered by this servant of the Master.

We have a graphic description of

the storm, in the course of which strictly nautical expressions are used which are arresting. So fierce it was that Luke writes, "All hope that we should be saved was now taken away." It was at this juncture that Paul addressed the people, and his message is a splendid evidence of his confidence in his Master. His, "Be of good cheer," was a word of faith, but it was also the language of reason, for had he not heard his Lord assuring him that he must come to Rome.

Under the stress of the occasion, the human management came at last completely into the hands of Paul, and he took wise precautions to prevent the sailors from leaving the ship. At last all were saved. In this story we surely have a valuable picture of the divine method: God overruling, while man trusts Him and acts. A firm confidence produces a strong courage, and true faith manifests itself in reasonable action.

ACTS 28

On land new perils threatened. While gathering sticks for a fire, a viper fastened on the apostle's hand. Shaking it off, he was unharmed. This convinced those who watched that he was divine, and they sought to worship him. Necessarily, Paul refused such homage. Three months Paul and his companions sojourned there, during which time they received kindness from the inhabitants, and Paul wrought healing, beginning in the house of the governor.

After this long and tedious journey was accomplished, interest naturally centers in the actual arrival at Rome. It may be interesting here to group some statements which cover the movement. "I must also see Rome" (19: 21); "So must thou bear witness also at Rome" (22: 11); "Unto Cæsar shalt thou go" (25: 12); "So we came to Rome" (28: 14).

Met by some of the brethren outside Rome, Paul thanked God and took courage. Then presently he was actually in Rome, and his great opportunity had come. The apostle seems to have had no consciousness of being a prisoner, or, at any rate, he knew that he was "a prisoner of the Lord Jesus Christ." When Paul reached Rome a great day dawned for the Gentile world.

It is arresting to see Paul's loyalty to his brethren after the flesh. Unable to visit the synagogue because of his chains, he called together the elders, and spoke to them of their Messiah, declaring that his chain was worn for "the hope of Israel."

The ending of the Book of Acts is characterized by a lack of finish. Nevertheless, it is illuminative. The apostle dwelt in his own hired house, thus suggesting the Church's independence of all the patronage of the nations of the earth. The burden of his preaching was the Kingdom of God. The closing words are historic and prophetic, "none forbidding him." They tell the wonder of how the overruling Lord made a prisoner in the imperial city for two years an apostle of the King and city yet to be manifested.

Romans

ROMANS 1

Bringing the first and seventh verses together, we find the called apostle writing to the called saints.

As for himself, Paul declared, first, that he was debtor, because a gift had been bestowed on him for the Greeks and barbarians, the wise and the foolish. In verses 16 and 17 we have a statement in brief of the whole argument of the epistle, and a declaration of the Gospel deposit which made Paul a debtor.

It is a Gospel of power, that is, one which is equal to the accomplishment of something infinitely more than the presentation of an ethic. The one condition is named in the phrase, "to every one that believeth." The provision is that God has provided a righteousness for unrighteous men.

The apostle showed, first, the need for salvation by dealing exhaustively with the subject of the ruin of the race. He commenced with the Gentiles, and in this paragraph we have a statement of general principles, an announcement concerning Gentile sin. The Gentiles' sin consisted in that instead of glorifying God they deified that which revealed Him, and yielded themselves wholly to the creature, thus becoming sensualized and degraded.

The apostle then declared the fact of Gentile judgment. Its principle is evident in the threefold expression, "God gave them up" (verses 24, 26, 28). He gave them up in order that their bodies should be dishonored. This issued in the degradation of their spirit, which, acting under the influence of deified physical powers, became the force of vile passions, which, in turn, reacted on the body in all manner of unseemliness. Thus again the issue was a reprobate mind, a mind that had lost its true balance and perspective, and was characterized by all the evil things which the apostle names. The wrath of God is thus evidenced in the corruption following the sin of refusing to act on the measure of light received.

ROMANS 2

It is evident that the apostle here turned to the Jew, though he did not immediately name him. He charged the Jew with the sin of practicing the very evils he condemned in the Gentiles. He is at least as great a failure as the Gentile in the matter of actual righteousness. Godliness, as privileged relationship, is of no value except as it produces actual righteousness.

In verses 21 to 23 the apostle declared the ethical failure of the Jew. This he did by asking a series of questions, every one inferentially charging these people with actual failure in conduct in the very matters which are regulated by the law for which they stand and which they profess to teach.

On the basis of the previous argument the apostle now charged the Jew with what is his principal and most terrible sin. He had become a blasphemer of the name of God among the Gentiles. If the Gentiles had imperfect light, they ought to have received the more perfect light from the people, who, on their own showing, took the place of guide, and light, and corrector, and teacher. But because in the actualities of their outward conduct they had been committing the same sins that their law condemned, the Gentiles had seen no reason to believe, through their testimony, in the one living God, to whom the Jews professed to be related. His name, therefore, had been blasphemed among them by Jewish failure.

Then follow the apostle's conclusive declarations concerning Israel. The bestowed privileges are all valueless. Thus again is the doctrine of justification by faith which does not issue in works declared to be false. The principles underlying this passage are of permanent value and of searching power.

ROMANS 3

Paul here turned to a brief discussion of certain objections. First, "What advantage, then, hath the Jew?" He replied, "Much, every way." He then mentioned only one, which he spoke of as being "first of all," meaning of supreme importance, "that they were entrusted with the oracles of God." Therein lay the supreme advantage of the Jew.

Then arises a new question. If man's faith fails, will God be unfaithful? To this the apostle replied that is it impossible for God to be unfaithful. The faithfulness of God is demonstrated by His unchanging attitude toward man. If man sins, God judges him; if man repents, God forgives him.

And yet still another question logically follows. If sin is the means of glorifying God by demonstrating His faithfulness, is it righteous to punish the sinner? The reply is that unless God punishes sin He has no basis on which to judge the world at all.

So far, the whole argument presents a picture of humanity from the divine viewpoint. It is so terrible in itself as to create a sense of hopelessness in us.

With the words, "but now," the apostle began the declaration of the Gospel. The whole is summarized in the statement that "a righteousness of God hath been manifested." This righteousness of God is at the disposal of those who believe.

The apostle then told of the great provision of grace by first naming the foundation blessing, or justification, "by His grace"; and then announcing the medium through which grace has operated to that end, "the redemption," a word fraught with infinite meaning, to be more fully unfolded as the argument proceeds; and finally naming the Person, "Christ Jesus," who has accomplished the work of redemption, which issues in the justification of the sinner.

The work of the Cross is set at the heart of this Evangel of salvation, and is seen to be a fulfilment of God's purpose, by God's Son, for the vindication of God's righteousness, in the action of God's forbearance.

The result is now set forth in a statement that is as startling as it is gracious: "That He might Himself be just," or righteous; "and the Justifier," or the One who accounts as righteous "him that hath faith in Jesus." This is the glorious Evangel.

ROMANS 4

The apostle now dealt with another difficulty that might arise in the mind of the Jew, showing that the method of grace, namely, imputing righteousness in response to faith, is in harmony with the whole history of Israel. As an illustration of this the apostle took the case of Abraham, father and founder of the nation, and showed how he was accepted and rewarded through faith, and not through works, both by his personal acceptance by God, and by his position as recipient of the promise of a coming deliverance. In this connection was made the declaration which must have been astonishing indeed in the ears of a Jew—that Abraham was the father, not merely of circumcised men according to the flesh, but of all who believe, even though they be in uncircumcision.

The Messianic hope came to Abraham, not through law, for it burned in his heart, and was the center of the nation of which he was the founder at least 400 years before the law was given. The apostle shows the value of this history. It bears testimony which strengthens the faith and confidence of those who look to, and believe in, Jesus. Resurrection life which follows the settlement of the question of sin by our justification is the bestowment of God on those who believe in Jesus.

ROMANS 5

The apostle now dealt with the values of justification. The value to the individual is a threefold blessing. This may be stated in three words—peace, grace, hope.

The soul at peace stands in grace, in the sense of favor. The believer has no fear of God, and so is at peace, and has free access to the divine presence because he stands in favor at the court of heaven. The soul thus justified and standing in favor enters into a new realm of aspiration and hope.

Because of all this, life is changed in its meaning, and tribulation especially is found to be of such a nature as to cause the heart to rejoice.

The apostle now showed the difference between the first and second man, the first and last Adam, in their race headship and the results produced by each. The whole argument is based on the literal accuracy of the account of the fall of man chronicled in Genesis, the apostle making no fewer than nine references thereto in so short a passage. In the case of the first Adam, disobedience issued in sin, judgment, condemnation, death for the race. In the case of the last Adam, obedience issued in grace, justification, righteousness, life for the race. These are coextensive. So far as the evil results of the first Adam's sin have spread, so far do the benefits of the last Adam's work extend.

By faith in Jesus, the last Adam, man can be set free from all the results of the disobedience of the first Adam. By continuity in the disobedience of the first Adam, man is excluded from the values of the work of the last Adam.

ROMANS 6

The apostle declared, "We died to sin," that is, we were set free from our relationship to sin. On that basis he asked his question, How can we live in that to which we have died? Taking baptism as an illustration, he showed that it is the sign of death and resurrection. Therefore the injunction, "Even so reckon ye also yourselves to be dead unto sin, but alive unto God in Christ Jesus." The whole new man is to be yielded to God, and his members are to become instruments of righteousness unto Him. The servant of sin is the slave of sin. The servant of righteousness is the bond servant of righteousness. The past experience of these people witnessed the yielding of themselves to sin, with the result that they were mastered by sin. The present experience is to see the yielding of the members to righteousness with the issue of experimental sanctification.

It is at the close of this statement that we have that verse so full of glorious meaning and so often quoted, "The wages of sin is death; but the free gift of God is eternal life in Christ Jesus our Lord." Sin as the master of the life pays the wage of death in every department of life. The contrast is not merely with reference to the finality, but with reference to the whole process, for God begins with life bestowed as a free gift, which is at once the root and the force, as it will be the final fruitage.

ROMANS 7

Continuing his argument, the apostle showed under the marital figure that a change of covenant changes the center of responsibility.

Then we have one of the great personal and experimental passages of the Pauline writings. The pronouns change from the plural to the singular. The whole of the seventh chapter gives us a picture of the religious experience of Paul up to the time of his meeting with Christ. It deals with his condition before the law, his experience at the coming of the law, and his subsequent experience under the law. He made two statements: "I was alive apart from the law once"; "The commandment came . . . and I died." When was the apostle alive apart from the law, and when did the commandment come, so that he died? When he spoke of having been alive apart from law, he referred to those days of his infancy and childhood in which without consciousness of law there was no consciousness of sin and he was living the life that was without any sense of distance between himself and God. "The commandment came, sin revived, I died." The apostle carefully declared what particular commandment it was that brought home to him this sense of sin. "Thou shalt not covet." In that he discovered that he was violating the divine commandment, and so he died.

The experience next described is of a man seeking the highest. Here is a double experience in the life of one man, doing hated things, and by his very hatred of them consenting to the goodness of the law which forbids them. Terrible indeed is the condition, so terrible that he broke out in that cry that tells the whole story of his inner consciousness. "Wretched man that I am! who shall deliver me out of the body of this death?" While thus the apostle wrote the words which reveal the agony of his past condition, he wrote them from his present sense of victory and deliverance, and so parenthetically answered his question, in the words, "I thank God through Christ Jesus our Lord."

ROMANS 8

The opening sentences of this chapter show a remarkable contrast with the previous chapter. From the fearful sense of condemnation we pass into the consciousness of no condemnation.

Having shown the negative value of the spiritual life as mastery over sin, the apostle now indicated briefly the positive value under the figure of sonship. Children are heirs of the Father's wealth and the Father's home. The apostle kept plainly in view the ground of our claim. "We are joint-heirs with Christ."

The final fact in God's salvation of man is glorification. The apostle first suggested and declined a comparison between the sufferings and the glory. So stupendous and overwhelming is the radiant vision of the ultimate issue of the work of grace, that, set in the light of it, the sufferings of the present time are incomparable. The contemplation of the glory issued in a great certainty. "We know," wrote the apostle. "What is the certainty?" Note its present tense. "All things work." Everything is contributing to the consummation. "Things work together." The "good" toward which "all things work together" is that the sons are to be conformed to the image of His Son.

The magnificent consummation consists of three questions, Who are the foes? Who are the accusers? Who are the separators? In answer to the first, the apostle declared, "God is for us." In answer to the second, he declared that God justifies us. In answer to the third, he declared that none of the terrible things which may form part of the process through which we pass to glory can separate us.

ROMANS 9

The connection between this very remarkable passage and the preceding climax is close. The great certainty of "no separation" is the experience of one in close communion with the Lord experimentally. What the apostle now declared is the outcome of the fact that the sphere of his life is Christ. When this is remembered, we have the key to what else were inexplicable. No man could have written such words unless he were indwelt and dominated by Christ through the Holy Spirit. The first expression is toward his brethren after the flesh. The description of God's purpose for Israel is very fine.

The word "but" with which the sixth verse opens suggests the contrast between the glorious facts concerning Israel just enunciated and Israel's present condition. The great fact is declared that "they are not all Israel, that are of Israel; neither, because they are Abraham's seed, are they all children." God had made a selection from the seed, Isaac and not Ishmael, Jacob and not Esau. The selection in each case was based upon an underlying purpose of God which the apostle calls "the purpose of God according to election." The underlying principle of the action of God is His mercy and His compassion.

The apostle took an illustration from the opposite condition. Pharaoh is an example of the result of unbelief and wilful setting of the heart against the right. The figure from Jeremiah of the potter and the clay must be interpreted by the character of God. The quotation from Hosea is used here in a wider sense than by the prophet himself. The writer is referring to such as were, according to the flesh, outside the covenant. The quotation from Isaiah re-emphasizes the fact that not all Israel after the flesh shall be saved, but a remnant only. This again is by divine choice.

In conclusion, he declared the reason of the determining choice in each case. The choice of God is of those who believe.

ROMANS 10

The apostle ever had in mind the Master Himself when he spoke of the righteousness of God. The idea of that righteousness, held by Israel was due to their misunderstanding of the written law, their ignorance of its true meaning, because they had not known Christ. Paul knew perfectly well that nothing so soon compels a man to cease seeking to establish his own righteousness as a vision of the righteousness of God. On the way to Damascus he was going about establishing his own righteousness; but a vision of the righteousness of God at once brought him to the position of submission to it.

The apostle then discussed the way of righteousness according to the plan of God in contrast with the attempt that Israel was making to establish its own righteousness. The great statement is made in the words, "Christ is the end of the law unto righteousness to every one that believeth."

A series of questions reveals the importance of the work of preaching the Gospel. There can be no calling on One not believed in; there can be no belief in One not heard of; there can be no hearing without a preacher.

From among the number of those who heard the glad tidings published by the missionary messengers, only some were elect. They were such as not only heard, but hearkened and believed. The last quotation from Isaiah defines exactly the divine attitude—hands spread out continuously toward a rebellious people. The will of God is the salvation of all such, and He has elected to salvation those who believe.

ROMANS 11

This discussion now gives rise to a new question, "Did God cast off His people?" They were created a nation in order that through them all the nations should be blessed. Failing to realize the divine intention concerning their own national life, they consequently and necessarily failed to fulfil that intention concerning the nations outside. God, however, does not allow the outside nations to suffer, but in infinite grace works through the fall of His earthly people toward enriching the whole world.

Most carefully and solemnly should the apostle's words be noted, "Behold then the goodness and severity of God." His severity is manifested in cutting off the natural branches because of unbelief. His goodness is evidenced in His reception of the Gentiles on the basis of their belief.

A doxology closes the whole doctrinal statement of the epistle. The outburst of rapturous praise was the result of the apostle's consciousness of the wonderful victory of God through Christ over all the opposing forces of evil, and His solution in infinite wisdom of the problems that baffle the intellect of man. The notes of the doxology are first a recognition of the depth of the riches of God's wisdom and knowledge, and then of man's utter inability to understand.

At the close of this section it is important to remember that the only interpretation of the inscrutable wisdom and operation of God is to be found in the revelation of His grace in Jesus, which is the foundation doctrine of the whole epistle.

ROMANS 12

The word "therefore" links all that is now to be said with everything that has gone before. Because of the grace of God, the believer is called to certain attitudes and actions. The very first of these is personal abandonment to God.

In what sense is it possible to present the body to God? The true ideal is to use it in all its powers according to the good and acceptable and perfect will of God. The spirit is evidently God's. The body, therefore, is presented to God. The mind is thus renewed according to the will of God.

Having declared the true attitude of the Christian life to be sacrifice to the will of God, the apostle now proceeds to show how that sacrifice will be expressed. All of chapters 12 and 13 is really occupied with this subject. Chapter 12 shows the evidence manifested in personal life, and chapter 13 as regards the world.

The first positive proof of abandonment to the will of God is humility. Here, of course, it is spiritual humility. There is always danger that one who has solemnly dedicated everything to God will on that very account become puffed up, and there is no pride more objectionable than spiritual pride.

Humility is manifest in using a gift to fulfil the function of the body rather than to glorify self. Wherever such humility exists genuine love necessarily follows. It is valuable to notice carefully the relation between these personal and relative injunctions concerning love; the first reveals the mind of love; the second, shows the method of love.

Such self-emptied, love-centered devotion to the will of God will alone make possible obedience to what follows.

ROMANS 13

The apostle now showed what attitude the believer will take toward the world. The first thing dealt with is submission to authority. These powers are of God. The believer's submission to the will of God is manifested in the world by his obedience to properly constituted authority. The very statement of the case, however, inferentially reveals another side of the question. The believer subjects himself to the power when he fulfils the true intent of his calling and office. Paul's own case will give examples of rebuking rulers.

Again, abandonment to the will of God is evidenced before the world by the discharge of all just debts. This is summed up in the first injunction, "Owe no man anything save to love one another." Always to owe love is to render it impossible to defraud in matters of purity, of life, of property. Thus, as the apostle declares, "Love, therefore, is the fulfilment of the law."

Thus ends the section dealing specifically with the requirement of the Christian's submission to God, personal humility in love, relative submission to love. These are the true credentials of the life abandoned to God in spirit, soul, and body.

The apostle then declared what is the perpetual incentive to realization of the abandonment of life, in both its inner and its outward manifestations. Darkness is everywhere. The children of the Lord are to walk as in the day, even though as yet the night is round about them. They already feel the breath of the morning moving through the darkness, and, casting off the garments of the night, they are to clothe themselves with the armor of light and watch for the first gleam of the breaking dawn.

ROMANS 14

The apostle now turned to discussion of some of the difficulties which may arise in the Christian Church. Dealing with the question of the animals sacrificed to idols he laid down a supreme principle that it would be well for us ever to remember. Every man stands or falls to his own Master. The same principle applies to the observance of days. The court of appeal is the mind loyal to Christ.

The deduction from the discussion has to do with our attitude toward each other. When I pass judgment on my brother, I am usurping the very throne of God. He alone knows all the facts, and alone is able to pass a judgment, and this right He reserves to Himself. The sphere of judgment open to us is not our brother's life and action, but our own. The test by which we are to judge is the welfare of our brother.

This judging of one's self by the standard of the well-being of another now leads the apostle to show what is the highest and noblest exercise of freedom, namely, the abandonment of a right, if need be, for the good of a weak brother.

The apostle summed up the whole question by appealing for such conduct as will make for peace and mutual edification. This, however, by no means issues in anything approaching looseness of moral conduct, for the apostle lays down in this connection what is perhaps the most searching and severe test of conduct in the New Testament, "Whatsoever is not of faith is sin." That is to say two things: first, that a person devoted to the Lordship of Jesus sins when acting from any motive other than confidence in, and obedience to, Him. How many individual questions of conduct, on which we are anxious to obtain outside opinion, would be settled if this principle were always remembered and obeyed.

ROMANS 15

The most powerful argument for Christian conduct is the example of Christ. He pleased not Himself. The injunction to receive one another is an injunction addressed to Jews and Gentiles. Throughout the letter the apostle had defended the Gentile against the self-satisfied national pride of the Jew, and the Jew against the probable contempt of the Gentile. This is the final injunction on the subject.

Paul closed his argument with a benediction, "The God of hope." What a wonderful title, suggesting that God is the reason for all the hope that brightens the way, and that because He is Himself full of hope. The Christian should be the greatest optimist because of the optimism of God.

Thus having ended the epistle as it was concerned with its great statement of doctrine, and the application thereof to life, the apostle turned to personal matters. Concerning the triumph of the Gospel, he declared, "Christ wrought through me." How glorious a commentary on the true position of the Christian worker! In speaking of his appointment, the apostle used language which indicates a phase of priestly office too often lost sight of. He had ministered the Gospel so that there had been an "offering up" of the Gentiles. Too often the priests of the Lord stand empty-handed in the holy place in this respect.

Very touching and beautiful was his request for their prayers. Notice the subjects he suggested for prayer. First, that he "may be delivered from them that are disobedient in Judea." Then also that his ministration, that contribution he is taking from the churches of Asia, may be acceptable. These prayers were most assuredly answered. Yet how often the answer to prayer differs from our expectations. What matters it if it be "through the will of God"? That was the qualifying petition which was finally answered. It is this confidence which lends power to this closing benediction, "May the God of peace be with you all. Amen."

ROMANS 16

In the salutation twenty-six persons are named. Two-thirds of these names are Greek, which, in all probability, are names of persons the apostle had actually known in his work in Asia. Phoebe was specially recommended. His old friends, Priscilla and Aquila, were evidently back in Rome again (Acts 18:2). The chief interest of this passage centers, however, in the apostle's incidentally revealed consciousness of the interrelationships of the saints as being dependent on the common relationship to Christ. Notice carefully the phrases which indicate this. "In the Lord," "In Christ Jesus," "Unto Christ," "In Christ," "In the Lord," "In the Lord," "In the Lord,"

"In the Lord" (verses 2,3,5,7,8,9,10, 11,12,13). Thus the impulse of love, the bond of service, the principle of fellowship are always union with Christ.

The consciousness of unity in Christ so evident in the salutations now caused a solemn word of warning. In a scathing sentence the apostle refers to teachers that "serve . . . their own belly."

Fitting is the benediction at this point, reminding all who are confronting conflict of the channel through which the promise of ultimate victory has been made possible of fulfilment: "The grace of our Lord Jesus Christ be with you." How beautiful is this revelation of fellowship in service in the closing salutations. For instance, Tertius, who had written the words as Paul dictated them, was also a fellow laborer; and he adds his greeting to the rest. Gaius, too, his host, sends his message of love. A man of note, Erastus, the treasurer of the city, and one of whom we know only that he was "the brother."

All closes with a doxology in which the apostle thinks of that perpetual purpose of love which, having been kept in silence through ages, has now been manifested in this Evangel, that through all the coming ages there may be the song of glory to God; and he reverently ascribes the glory to whom it is thus evidently due.

I Corinthians

I CORINTHIANS 1

The epistle is to the Church. Its messages are only for those who have been brought into fellowship with Jesus Christ. The character of the Church is indicated in the words, "sanctified in Christ Jesus, called saints." The equipment of the Church is indicated in the phrase, "enriched in Him."

The foundation proposition of the epistle is that the Church is called into the fellowship of Jesus Christ. The first part of the letter is corrective. It deals with evidences of the dominance of the carnal nature, and the first is of the divisions which had arisen among them. Paul first beseeches them to "speak the same thing," to "be perfected together in the same mind and in the same judgment."

These factions, created by disputes in the realm of the "wisdom of words," were the result of the folly of failing to appreciate the marvelous wisdom of that great "Word of the Cross" which was the foundation on which their faith was built, and which brought them into sacred union with Jesus Christ, and therefore with each other. The apostle shows the unutterable folly of those who were attempting to deal with Christian truth after the manner of that "wisdom of words" which characterized the age, and who were thus causing schism in the body of Christ. "The Word of the Cross" contradicted the whole method and result as it revealed the wisdom of God and the ultimate discomfiture and overthrow of all that the age most valued.

I CORINTHIANS 2

The apostle reminds the Corinthian Christians that when he first came to them he did not come with excellency of speech, or of wisdom, but with "the Word of the Cross." Yet there must be no foolish imagining that there is no wisdom, or that the Christian teacher has no deep and sublime subjects with which to deal. The apostle says, "We speak wisdom, however." And yet the wisdom was such as could be taught only among those who were full grown. Babes and feeble ones in Christ could not be led into the deep things of God. For them there must be the simple proclamation of the word of wisdom, without its explanation and unfolding.

What, then, is this wisdom? It is a mystery, hidden from the world's wisdom, but known of God and revealed by His Spirit. It could come to man only through the direct and distinct revelation of the Spirit of God. It is pre-eminently important that this should ever be borne in mind. "The Word of the Cross" is not the ultimate of human reasoning. All mere philosophies of the mind have failed to explain it, as the wisdom of the world had failed to discover it. It is the Word of God hidden from ages, and spoken at last only by that Spirit of God "who searcheth all things, yea, the deep things of God." This revelation, moreover, could not be received by the natural man.

Here it is well to understand Paul's meaning by his use of the term "natural." He invariably speaks of man unregenerate as the natural man, putting him in contrast with man regenerate, who is the spiritual man. Thus the reason why "the wisdom of words" is folly becomes apparent.

I CORINTHIANS 3

The reason for the schisms was that these people were carnal. "Jealousy and strife" are evidences of carnality.

Proceeding, Paul declared the true value of the Christian ministry. "For we are God's fellow-workers." The sublimity of their work is evidenced by the fact that they are co-operating with God. The foundation of the building is Jesus Christ. On that great foundation other men are building. Some of the work is precious and permanent, of the nature of gold, silver, costly stones. It may be some of it is unworthy—wood, hay, stubble. The nature of the work is to be revealed in the great fire baptism, which is to be the final process before the completion of God's great building. Thus it is evident that the matter of supreme importance is the building.

The purpose of the building is revealed in the statement, "Ye are a sanctuary of God." The word "sanctuary" here is of especial value as indicating not merely a temple, but a temple appropriated to its true use, a building set apart to God for His own dwelling.

In the light of this statement concerning the Church the apostle wrote the solemn warning, "If any man spoil the temple of God, him shall God spoil." The apostle sums up and endorses his argument that the "wisdom of the age" is foolishness with God.

If a man turn from this foolishness to the wisdom of God he possesses all things. The teachers themselves—Paul, Apollos, Cephas; all the facts that touch personality and affect it—"the world," "life," "death," "things present," "things to come"—all these are possessed by the man who has learned his own folly and glories alone in the Lord. Such a man not only possesses, he is possessed. He is Christ's! And, yet again, the final safety is God Himself, for "Christ is God's."

I CORINTHIANS 4

Christian teachers are "ministers of Christ." That defines their responsibility. They are "stewards of the mysteries of God." That defines their work. What dignity does this double statement suggest?

In view of this, to Paul it was "a very small thing" what judgment men might form of him. The Lord at His Coming will pronounce the judgment. It would seem as though this faithful steward of the mysteries of God feared lest the very impetuous sweep of his anger against the folly of the schism-makers would be misunderstood, and he hastens to write tender words as he closes this section. His purpose is not to shame them, but to admonish them. They are his "beloved children."

Looking back over the argument, it is clearly seen that the final test of wisdom is always power. Herein is the difference between the "wisdom of words" and "the wisdom of God."

The "wisdom of words" has no moral lift in it. On the other hand, the "wisdom of God" is manifested in the "Word of the Cross." By that Word men are not merely mentally illumined, they are morally saved. Put the teachers of psychology or philosophical systems down in the midst of corrupt Corinth, or in later cities, with their own writings as the textbooks, and how much can they do to lift the burden, break the chain, quench the passion, and out of a ruined humanity reconstruct a divine manhood? Put down in the same city a Salvation Army lassie who utterly lacks all words of wisdom, but who lives and prophesies the "Word of the Cross," and watch the issue. The result of power is the true test of wisdom.

I CORINTHIANS 5

The apostle now passed to derelictions. The first was lack of discipline. A case of immorality had brought no sense of shame to the church, and no action had been taken. The woman was called to immediate and drastic dealing therewith, and was to act in harmony with the apostle's instruction finally by "the power of the Lord Jesus." The man must be severed from all the advantages of church fellowship.

The reasons for these strong measures were the ultimate salvation of the excommunicated man and the purification of the church. The whole teaching emphasized that there must be no toleration of evil in the church.

I CORINTHIANS 6

The apostle now passed to another dereliction. Disputes in the church were being submitted to heathen tribunals. What these matters were we are not told. The teaching of the apostle is clear, and has application for all time. Disputes among saints should be settled between saints, and wholly within the confines of the church. The argument as to the fitness of the saints for the work is that as they will finally have to judge angels, surely they ought to be able to judge things pertaining to this life. The apostle declared that it is better to bear wrong than to appeal for right to a tribunal of unrighteous men. His argument as to the unfitness of unbelievers is that "the unrighteous shall not inherit the Kingdom of God."

Under certain circumstances lawful things may not be right for the Christian. First, lawful things may not be expedient, and, second, lawful things must not gain mastery. In the compass of the first limitation, namely, expediency, the whole outlook of the Christian is undoubtedly included, not merely personal right, but the culture of the life; and, moreover, relative responsibility concerning others. Things which are lawful in themselves if they do not directly tend to profit both the individual and those who may be influenced by the individual are inexpedient.

The second limitation is that things which are perfectly lawful must not be permitted to obtain mastery over life. With a passing reference to the question of meats, the apostle deals with the sin of fornication. How high and stately is the ground of his argument, that the body is now a member of Christ and is for the Lord. The person joined to the Lord "is one spirit," and therefore, all the functions and powers of the life must be dominated by that spirit.

I CORINTHIANS 7

Certain difficulties had arisen in the Corinthian Church concerning which they had sent inquiries to Paul. He now answers their questions. These answers contain principles of permanent application.

The principles concerning marriage may thus be simply stated: First, marriage is in itself honorable and right. Second, where married union of converted and unconverted men and women is concerned, the believer, at least, is not to take the initiative in bringing about a dissolution. The supreme thought in the apostle's mind throughout this whole section is the relation of the Christian to the Lord. That must be zealously guarded. Everything else must be subservient to it because of the urgency of the Lord's business. The apostle then leaves it to each to make personal settlement of all these difficulties in the light of this supreme relationship.

Let the daughters of the King settle the question of marriage always and only within this sphere, consenting or refusing, according as such action will help or hinder their highest realization of the fulfilment of His glorious purposes.

I CORINTHIANS 8

The apostle next dealt with the subject of "things sacrificed to idols." The question evidently was whether the members of the Church in Corinth ought under any circumstances to eat parts of the heathen sacrifices which were sold in the market places for general consumption as food. In dealing with the question the apostle, by contrasting knowledge and love, laid down a principle that is of far wider application than the subject itself demands. He shows that "knowledge puffeth up," while "love edifieth," or "buildeth up"; and thus at once reveals love rather than knowledge as the true principle of action.

If knowledge is the simple principle and as an idol is nothing, sacrifices offered to idols have no meaning or value. The evident deduction is that in the light of knowledge a man may eat most certainly. Howbeit the apostle says not all men have that knowledge. Some have been used until now to the idol. They have considered it real, and their judgment, while evidencing the weakness of their knowledge, is nevertheless real to them.

The Christian principle of love demands consideration of the weakness of them; consequently the question whether such meat is to be eaten by the Christian must ever be decided on the basis of that principle. The apostle summarizes the whole position in the superlative words with which this section closes, "If meat causeth my brother to stumble, I will eat no flesh for evermore, that I cause not my brother to stumble."

I CORINTHIANS 9

The words, "my defence to them that examine me is this," reveal the opposition to him in Corinth. The two words, "defence" and "examine," are purely legal, and are in the language of the courts of justice. The apostle is speaking of himself as on his defense and under examination. The apostle declares that his right in the case of the Corinthians at least is based on his work. Whatever relation he may bear to others, he is an apostle to them at least, for they are the very seal of his apostleship in that they are, as he has said previously, his children in the Gospel.

While defending his rights, he declared his abandonment of them in the power of that compulsion of the Gospel through which he became all things to all men. The same principles are here enforced by a general illustration. The apostle used the race as an illustration, and laid down this one simple principle, "So run that ye may attain." The goal is always to be kept in view, and all present action is to be governed by the passion for reaching that goal and receiving the crown. There is therefore to be self-control in all things, in order that there may be ultimate victory.

The solemn closing words reach the very heart of the argument. The apostle, speaking now of himself, again for the sake of illustration, declares that he runs not uncertainly; that he fights not as beating the air; that he brings his body into bondage, even by buffeting, and all this because he sees the terrible possibility of himself being rejected, even though he has been a herald to others; the meaning of which most evidently is that failure to regulate life so as to help others imperils our own salvation.

I CORINTHIANS 10

A great warning based on an illustration in Israel's history is contained in these words, "Wherefore let him that thinketh he standeth take heed lest he fall." To this warning the apostle adds that there is no necessity for such falling, because the very temptations that come to man are under the divine control, and are limited to the capacity of the tempted, while out of them God always makes a way of escape.

Carefully connect the opening injunction here with the closing declaration of the previous verse. "God . . . will . . . make also a way of escape. . . . Wherefore, my beloved, flee from idolatry."

Then the apostle gives the greatest argument of all for the Christian position. In sudden and startling fashion he puts the Christian feasts into contrast with the idol feasts.

Then followed a definite answer to their questions. The tests of Christian action is expediency. The test of expediency is edification. The test of edification is the good of the other. Everything closes with instructions. Things sold in the shambles may be eaten, no question being asked. Things set on the table at a Christian feast may also be eaten, without asking questions. If, however, at any gathering someone should challenge a believer by saying that the meat on the table had been offered in sacrifice, then for the sake of the man who raises the question, and for the sake of his conscience, the believer is to refuse to partake.

Finally, he condenses all into the form of two governing principles. First, "Do all to the glory of God"; second, "Give no occasion of stumbling."

I CORINTHIANS 11

Another Corinthian question concerned the position of woman and her true attitude in the exercise of divinely bestowed gifts. He declared that woman's true position is subservience to man. The nature of that subservience, however, the apostle was also very careful to indicate. God is equal with Christ. God co-operates with Christ. God is the Head of Christ.

Then follows a touch of purely local color. The women in Corinth itself, whose heads were shaven and went uncovered, were women of shame. The apostle therefore enjoined woman exercising gifts of ministry to do so with those outward manifestations of her true relationship to man which are proper and becoming.

However, the great value to us of this teaching is its recognition of the right of women to pray and prophesy. The question of wearing a veil is of no permanent importance. Not wearing a covering for the head in this country has not the significance that it had in Corinth.

The last matter to be discussed was the Lord's Supper. Grave abuses had arisen, and in order to correct these abuses the apostle told the story of the institution of the Supper. In brief words, the apostle declared the value of the feast to the world. The arresting word is "proclaim." The Supper of the Lord, observed by the saints from year to year, from century to century, is the one outward and visible sign and symbol of His death. It is to continue until He Himself shall return. Instituted in the concluding days of His First Advent, it must be maintained until He come.

And thus that dark betrayal night
With the last advent we unite,
By one long chain of loving rite,
Until He come.

I CORINTHIANS 12

Now the apostle turned from the corrective section of his letter to the constructive as he proceeded to deal with the spiritualities which negative the carnalities. These are those of the unifying Spirit (12), the unfailing law of love (13,14), and the ultimate triumph of resurrection (15).

In the establishment of the Lordship of Jesus is the creation of a new unity. This unity, however, has its perfect variety. The unifying force is God, in the three Persons of His Trinity—the Spirit, the Lord, God. The variety in the unity is created by gifts, ministrations, workings. For this great service of co-operation the Church is gifted by the Spirit, directed by the Lord, energized by God.

The apostle emphasized under the figure of the body the union of those who minister with the Lord. There is diversity of function in the unity of the body. The key statement is, "for the body is not one member, but many." This fact is again simply stated in conclusion. The body is one in its totality of separate members. Christ the Head directs all the activity of the whole of the members, and so of the body itself. The members, responding to that central authority in the power of their own functions created by the Spirit, at once fulfil their ministry, contribute to the fulfilment of the ministry of the body, and exhibit the glorious wisdom of the directing Lord.

The section closes with the injunction, "Desire earnestly the greater gifts," and, said the apostle, in effect, I will show you the most excellent way to obtain them. What, then, is the most excellent way? The answer comes in the two chapters following. It is the way of love.

I CORINTHIANS 13

The apostle dealt with love, its values (verses 1-3), its virtues (verses 4-7), and its victory (verses 8-13).

The values of love are discovered in the fact that, apart from it, all the best things are worthless.

Its virtues are shown with force and beauty. Every sentence is simple and sublime, and the whole contains a perfect analysis of love.

Passing from this description of the virtues of love, the apostle now showed how it is supreme because of its victory. The first element is its duration —"Love never faileth." The thought in the word translated "faileth" is falling off, like the leaves of a flower Love never loses its life principle. To emphasize the truth of his affirmation, the apostle now put love into comparison with excellent things, things indeed to be desired as gifts; and showed how, while they are transient, love is permanent. He added the final word in demonstration of the proof when he compared love no longer with the things that pass, but with the things that abide, and yet declared it to be the greatest—"Now abideth faith, hope, love, these three; and the greatest of these is love."

It is the greatest because it is the reason and strength of the others. If it were possible to lose it, faith would fail, and hope would die. It is the greatest, moreover, because it is the real heart of the spirit's union with God and the light of its understanding of Him.

I CORINTHIANS 14

The apostle now submitted certain gifts to the test of love. Prophesying is desirable because it edifies others. Then as to Tongues. It was a gift that enabled men to speak to God, perhaps in prayer, perhaps in praise, most probably in both ways; its effect on the man who had the gift was to strengthen his spiritual life. Its effect on others was valueless unless it was accompanied by interpretation. The apostle declared that if he came to them speaking with tongues it would not profit them. If a man had the gift of tongues, he should also pray for the gift of interpretation.

He then declared the effect produced by the wrong principle of desiring gifts. Where, instead of the most excellent way of love, the desire was glorification of self, malice most certainly crept into the heart. Against this the apostle especially warned them, urging them to the simplicity and ignorance of childhood as to malice, and to the maturity of men in mind.

Definite instructions for the orderly exercise of the gifts follow. These consist of general principles, which may be tabulated thus:

(1) The test of the possession of a gift is subordination to authority.

(2) The man who is ignorant is hopeless; let him be ignorant. (Some of the texts read, "Let him be ignored.")

(3) The "most excellent way" is to love.

(4) The gift of tongues is not, however, to be despised nor denied.

(5) Then, finally, a word covering the whole. "Let all things be done decently and in order." The word "decently" means with comeliness, with beauty. Thus the organization of the Church is to carry on all its exercises with that beauty which issues from the impulse of love, and that orderliness which is the result of law.

I CORINTHIANS 15

The last fact of the "spiritualities" is the resurrection, and the apostle first gives the proof of the resurrection of Christ. His final proof was his own experience.

It is evident that there were some in the Corinthian Church who were holding rationalistic views and denying resurrection. To deny resurrection is, of course, to deny Christ's resurrection, and to do this is to do away with Christianity. If Christ rose not, then the apostolic testimony concerning God is false, for that has been that He raised up Jesus. If that testimony is false, then also are the doctrines of the forgiveness of sins and the ultimate salvation of men.

The further result is that those who have fallen asleep in Christ, that is, who have passed away in quiet confidence, resting their souls on Him, have perished.

The suppositions are swept aside by the apostle's, "But now." "But now," seeing that men are loosed from sins, and that all the other facts are thereby demonstrated, the foundation truth of Christ's resurrection is absolutely demonstrated.

Having dealt with all the glorious issues of the resurrection, the apostle's argument turns to the manner of resurrection. Two things are certain. These two matters he argues at length: first, that there will be continuity of personality in resurrection; and, second, that there will be a difference in the risen one.

The ultimate injunction of the epistle should be read in connection with the fundamental proposition (1:9). To understand the meaning of this injunction aright we should carefully inquire what the work of the Lord is. His work, as He Himself clearly declared, is to seek and save the lost. That, then, is the work of the Church. In this work we are called to steadfastness, that is, continuity and perseverance and unmovableness, that is, steadfastness even in spite of opposition; and to be always abounding, that is, to overflowing service more than the mere observance of duty.

I CORINTHIANS 16

The last chapter of the epistle is local and personal. In the first sentences important principles are revealed as to the true method of Christian giving. It is to be regular and systematic rather than occasional and spasmodic. It is to be personal and alone, for laying by in store does not mean placing in a collection basket in a meeting, but privately apportioning and guarding.

There follow references full of suggestive beauty to Timothy, and Apollos, and injunctions which are epigrammatic and forceful, "Watch ye," "Stand fast in the faith," "Quit you like men," "Be strong." These four injunctions are really but two, the first two being complementary and correlative, and also the last two.

The letter ends with matters of a personal nature, all of which breathe the same spirit of love and fellowship. Finally, the apostle took the pen into his own hand. Let it be noted at once that the character of what he wrote is defined by the opening, in which he declares that he is writing a salutation; and by the closing, which speaks of the grace of the Lord Jesus, and Paul's love to all. Between these lie the words which some have thought of as malediction. As a matter of fact, they have nothing of the spirit of anger. They contain the solemn statement of an established fact, something from which there is no more escape than from the certainty of death to any who are deprived of sustenance; or from the necessity for penalty to those who violate the laws of nature. Paul's view of the Lordship of Jesus is such as to drive him to declare that if any man love not the Lord, there is no alternative other than His anathema.

II Corinthians

II CORINTHIANS 1

The second letter to the Corinthians was evidently the outcome of the first. The apostle opened with the usual introduction, laying emphasis on his apostleship by the will of God, coupled with the salutation of grace. He wrote of a great trouble through which he had passed, and rejoiced in the comfort that had come to him, and, still more, in the ability to comfort others that had come to him from his experience.

Speaking of God as the "God of comfort," he said that experience of divine comfort in affliction enables us to comfort others. He tenderly recognized the aid afforded him by the prayers of the Corinthians, speaking of his deliverance as their gift to him.

It is evident that some in Corinth had charged him with fickleness of purpose in that he had not come to them as he had intimated he would do. Against this charge he now vindicated himself. He told them why he had not come to them. It was out of love for them; he wanted to spare them, and called God as witness. Yet immediately the apostle is careful to say that he had no lordship over their faith, that his only purpose was to minister to their joy, and that their standing was in faith, not in anything that he might say or do.

II CORINTHIANS 2

What a remarkable light is thrown on his first letter by his declaration that he wrote it "out of much affliction and anguish of heart," and "with many tears." Referring thus to his first letter, Paul singled out from it the flagrant case of the incestuous person, speaking of him wih extreme delicacy. It is evident that, for the most part, the Church at Corinth was in accord with the apostle, for they had carried out his injunction, and had disciplined the wrongdoer. Also, the result had been salutary in his case, for the apostle writes of the guilty man being in danger of being "swallowed up with his overmuch sorrow." He now urged the congregation to manifest their love by restoring the man to fellowship. As the apostle had urged them to exercise discipline to defeat the foe, he now counseled them to manifestation of love for the man, also to defeat the foe.

Perhaps nowhere in the New Testament is the subject of the ministry so clearly set in relation to its sublimities. The apostle described the triumphant nature of the true work of the ministry. The figure is of a Roman triumph. In such a triumph the conspicuous personages were the victor and the vanquished. The apostle spoke of himself and those engaged in the ministry as victors. Their work is likened to a long triumphant march. That is Paul's estimate of the true nature of the ministry. So great a conception is it that he exclaims, "Who is sufficient for these things?" The words that follow are really connected with what precedes the question; they declare that the reason for the victory lies in the fact that there has been no corrupting, or making merchandise, of the Word of God.

II CORINTHIANS 3

The apostle declared that the Church is the supreme credential of the power of the ministry. The Corinthian Christians are "known and read of all men." This, however, was not the deepest truth. They were the epistle of Christ. The author and the Writer of the living epistle is Christ; the pen or instrument is the apostle. The ink, or means of accomplishing the revelation, is the Spirit. The true credentials of Christian ministry are always such epistles.

Then follows a comparison between the ministry of the old economy, which was of the letter, and that of the new, which is of the Spirit. What, then, is the difference between the letter and the Spirit? The letter reveals, the Spirit realizes. The revelation of the letter can do no other than destroy, for man, standing in its light, finds his own imperfection and becomes conscious of his own inability. The Spirit, realizing in man that which the letter presents to man, corrects his inability and imparts life.

The glory of the letter flashing on the life of man could but reveal his sin and announce his death. Moses, the minister of the letter, must veil his face, because the issue of his message is death to those to whom it is delivered. "But we all, with unveiled face beholding as in a mirror the glory of the Lord, are transformed into the same image from glory to glory, even as from the Lord the Spirit." The supreme power of the ministry, therefore, lies in the fact that it is the declaration of a message of transforming life by the Spirit, which is demonstrated by the transformation wrought in those who declare that message.

II CORINTHIANS 4

Continuing about the ministry, the apostle said, "We faint not," "we have renounced the hidden things of shame," "we preach . . . Christ Jesus as Lord." Hearing, some perish because "the god of this world hath blinded their minds," and that because of "unbelief." The god of this world is able only to blind the minds of the unbelieving.

This ministry, so full of triumph for such remarkable reasons, is yet exercised through great tribulation. The treasure is in earthen vessels, and these are subject to affliction. Yet there is in this a reason and a value. It is that the "exceeding greatness of the power may be God." From that initial statement the apostle proceeds to contrast in a very remarkable way these two things—the vessel, which is earthen, and the power, which is divine. The earthen vessel is pressed on every side, but because of the power it is not straitened. It is often perplexed, but never to the point of despair; "pursued, yet not forsaken; smitten down, yet not destroyed."

This is the revelation of a great principle of all successful work. It is through travail that others live, through out-going virtue that others are healed, through breaking the earthen vessels that the light flashes out on the pathway of others. These tribulations are endured because of the certainties which give strength even in the midst of tribulations.

This very "affliction worketh" the glory. Affliction is not something to be endured in order to reach glory. It is the very process which creates the glory. Through travail comes birth. Through suffering comes the triumph. Through dying comes the living.

II CORINTHIANS 5

The vision of the house of God, and the coming at last to the Lord, throws its light on, and explains the value of, the groaning and the burden of the tabernacle, of the period of absence from the Master. "Absent from the body," "at home with the Lord." This reveals the consciousness. No strangeness, no sense of having to keep up an appearance, "at home with the Lord." The passing of all that is strained, and the coming of the perfect ease of naturalness. Surely Paul was right. The affliction is light when placed in the balance against the weight of the glory.

The twofold impulse of the ministry is revealed, "the fear of the Lord" (verse 11), "the love of Christ" (verse 14). This fear of the Lord is the constant and passionate anxiety rightly to respond to the love of Christ which constraineth.

All this means that the ministry is the work of reconciliation, and its burden is summarized in the majestic and magnificent declaration, "God was in Christ, reconciling the word unto Himself." On the basis of this great declaration the apostle makes his first appeal, beseeching the Corinthians to be reconciled to God.

II CORINTHIANS 6

The injunction, "We intreat also that ye receive not the grace of God in vain," harmonizes in method with many others used by Paul. Let your conduct harmonize with your position in grace. With what powerful argument does he make his appeal! As "ambassadors on behalf of Christ," as though God were "intreating by us," "working together with Him we intreat." These arguments are made powerful by the method of all the apostle's ministry, which he goes on to describe.

These descriptions may be divided into groups: first, actual bodily toil endured in "patience . . . afflictions . . . distresses . . . stripes . . . imprisonments . . . tumults . . . labours . . . watchings . . . fastings"; and all these in much patience.

He then passes to facts which are mental: "pureness . . . knowledge . . . longsuffering . . . kindness." And, finally, to those which are spiritual: "The Holy Spirit . . . love unfeigned . . . the word of truth . . . the power of God . . . the armour of righteousness on the right hand and on the left."

The apostle broke out in his second appeal for consecration. The best possible analysis of this is dividing it into appeals and arguments. The appeals are: "Be not unequally yoked with unbelievers," "Come ye out from among them, and be ye separate . . . and touch no unclean thing," "Let us cleanse ourselves from all defilement of flesh and spirit, perfecting holiness in the fear of God." The arguments are, first, a series of questions, and then the recitation of great promises: "I will dwell in them, and walk in them; and I will be their God, and they shall be My people." "I will receive you, and will be to you a Father, and ye shall be to Me sons and daughters."

II CORINTHIANS 7

The section culminates in an appeal full of local coloring and suggestion. In a great cry he gave expression to the hunger of his heart when he wrote, "Make room for us" (see margin). He then declared that he had wronged no man, that he had corrupted no man, that he had taken advantage of no man.

Almost afraid lest such a statement should embitter them by creating a sense of shame, as though he would rebuke, he immediately declared that this was not his purpose, and proceeded to emphasize his love for them, going through his personal experiences to demonstrate it. He told them of his sorrow in Macedonia. He told them of the new joy and gladness that flooded his heart when Titus came and told him that they had received and been obedient to his letter, that it had caused them such sorrow as to produce in them repentance. He told them yet again of the great added joy that had come to him because they had refreshed the soul of Titus, for the apostle had boasted to Titus of them, and they had proved worthy of his boasting.

His final word was one of magnificent hopefulness, thrilling with great joy. "I rejoice that in everything I am of good courage concerning you." Perhaps there is hardly a chapter in Paul's writings in which the heart of the man is more perfectly revealed, and the charm of it is found in the natural humanness which is manifested, and yet which all the while is under the constraint of that love of Christ which makes the fear of the Lord the supreme motive in all life and service.

II CORINTHIANS 8

The apostle now turned to the subject of the collection for the saints at Jerusalem, concerning which he had written in his previous letter (I Corinthians 16). He cites the example of the churches in Macedonia. They gave themselves (1) to the Lord, (2) to the apostles and fellow saints. This action of the Macedonian Christians is in harmony with the Spirit of the Christ. While careful to tell them that he is not speaking by way of commandment, he yet gives them his judgment, and it is that as it was they who were to begin in this matter, so it was they who should certainly complete the act.

He then lays down the true principle on which gifts are acceptable to God. It is readiness, so that the value of a gift is never reckoned intrinsically, but by a man's possessions. The apostle is careful to avoid any chance of misinterpretation in financial matters. "We take thought for things honourable, not only in the sight of men." It is urgent that nothing should be done which is open to misunderstanding by men of the world. Against this the apostle carefully guarded by seeing to it that such things were attended to by duly accredited persons, himself sedulously avoiding the handling of money.

II CORINTHIANS 9

In concluding this subject of the collection for the saints the apostle declares that he desires that their giving should be glad and spontaneous. He excludes two methods of giving, "grudgingly," that is, very literally, sorrowfully. It is the giving of those who have not first given themselves, and consequently are conscious of the loss of that which is given. "Or of necessity," that is, giving as simply an act of duty, and not from an impulse of delight. On the contrary, he says, "God loveth a cheerful giver."

He then recites the advantages of giving. The first of these is that giving will fill the wants of the saints. That in itself is good, but the outcome is even better. Through such ministry gifts will cause glory to God.

And yet again, they will bring the intercession of those they have helped, a harvest of precious value. The final word concerning this whole subject is an expression of thanks to God for His unspeakable gift, for the apostle knows that the remembrance of it will do more than all his argument to stimulate the generosity of those who have received the inestimable blessing.

II CORINTHIANS 10

Here begins the third division of the epistle, in which the writer vindicates his authority. Here he seems to have more especially in mind the minority who have been opposed to him.

While walking in the flesh, that is, of course, living on human levels and being conscious of all the limitations of his body, he assures them that he does not war according to the flesh, but that his warfare is in "casting down imaginations, and every high thing that is exalted against the knowledge of God, and bringing every thought into captivity to the obedience of Christ."

They have been looking at the outward things. This he explains later by quoting their own words. "His letters . . . are weighty and strong; but his bodily presence is weak, and his speech of no account." In all probability those who were his chief opponents, and with whom he deals in this section, are those who constituted the Christ party referred to in his first epistle.

The apostle declares that if a man make such a claim, "even as he is Christ's, so also are we." Thus he does not exclude this man from relation to Christ, but claims that the man has no right to exclude him. The apostle declines, however, to adopt the principle of self-glorying on which his opponents were acting. The whole motive and method of their work is self-centered, and their glorying is therefore of the same nature. His sphere lies even beyond the Corinthians, and, moreover, he is looking to entering into that through their co-operation.

Here again is revealed a true principle of work, that its enlargement grows out of itself. Every toil undertaken under divine direction creates new forces for still larger opportunities. Thus the true object of glorying is the Lord. Workers who are obedient to His arrangement have something to glory of, while those arrogating to themselves places and programs are, for lack of authority, driven to the expedient of self-commendation. The apostle finally declares that self-commendation does not mean approval. That comes only from the commendation of the Lord.

II CORINTHIANS 11

Having thus stated the true grounds of glorying, and being about to make his boast (such action having been made necessary by the opposition), the apostle has so little love for it that he commences with an apology, and a very explicit declaration of his deepest reason for doing it. He is jealous with a godly jealousy, that is, with a jealousy after the pattern of the jealousy of God, which is always the jealousy of wounded love.

The extreme difficulty of the case was that while preaching the same things, those in opposition were creating divisions by personalities, and therefore Paul was bound to save them by personal boasting.

He commenced this boasting with the remarkable statement that he was "not a whit behind the very chiefest apostles." It has been said that this is a sarcastic reference to the false teachers, but it is far more probable that in harmony with his constant defense of his own apostleship he first declares his equality with all the apostles on the basis of his divine appointment to this office.

Then followed the threefold glorying in the exercise of his apostolic office among the Corinthians, in its manner, in its method, and in its motive.

So that if he himself must needs glory, it shall be in the things that concern his weakness, while he calls God to witness to the truth of the things he writes. And of these things of weakness the first is the escape from Damascus, in which was nothing to create the spirit of fleshly boasting, and yet it was his open door to apostleship and service.

II CORINTHIANS 12

The boasting continues. However, it takes on a new and startling characteristic. In his apostleship there had been something supernatural, something not to be finally explained. Of this, he will glory. As to the method, Paul himself declares his ignorance. However, there was no uncertainty about the great fact that he received revelations not to be accounted for by any merely natural hypotheses, neither were these revelations given to him for communication, for again he affirms that he "heard unspeakable words, which it is not lawful for a man to utter."

The purpose of the revelations was evidently to give him courage and confidence in his work. The peril lay in the danger of his becoming "exalted overmuch." In order to prevent this, came the "thorn in the flesh." "Now," says the apostle, "will I rather glory in my weaknesses, that the power of Christ may rest upon me."

The letter was now coming to a close, and the apostle was careful to make perfectly clear what had been his attitude in writing. His dealing with them had been conditioned in a threefold fact: first, in the sight of God; second, in Christ; third, for their edifying. This paragraph shows an unveiling of the heart of the true spiritual teacher, yearning in love over his children, desiring earnestly their highest welfare, caring little for their approval of his conduct but much for their approval by God. Out of such desire he delivered his message, conscious of its authority because he speaks in Christ.

II CORINTHIANS 13

In view of his intention to visit them again the apostle urged them to personal examination. They were to test themselves, and to prove themselves whether they were in the faith. The reason for his appeal, he urged, was not that he might be approved, but that they might do right.

All this long-continued argument of the apostle can hardly be read without a consciousness of his deep anxiety that the Corinthians should understand him, and know that the only motive prompting him in all his dealings with them was love of them. And yet, while thus anxious that they should understand him, he desired far more that they should be right themselves with the Lord.

The last words are words of cheer. A series of brief exhortations is first given, indicating what the Corinthians' true attitude should be. "Farewell," which here is not equivalent to "Good-bye," but rather to "Rejoice." "Be perfected," or "Be fully equipped." "Be comforted," an injunction carrying the thought back to the beginning of the letter, in which the apostle dealt so fully with the comfort of God, which comes to all the afflicted. "Be of the same mind," carrying the thought back still further, to the beginning of his first letter, in which he introduced his first corrective section by a similar injunction. "Live in peace," the all-inclusive word, for peace pre-supposes purity, and is the very condition of power.

After the injunctions comes the declaration, "The God of love and peace shall be with you."

The whole passage closes with the benediction. First, "the grace of the Lord Jesus Christ," because it is through Him grace has had its epiphany, and through Him we have access to the Father. Then "the love of God," for that lies ever at the heart of all blessing, being the infinite fountain from which the streams flow forth. And, finally, "the communion of the Holy Spirit," for it is through such fellowship that the blessings of grace are realized and the love of God is shed abroad in the heart.

Galatians

GALATIANS 1

In the beginning of most of his epistles Paul definitely declares his apostleship. In this instance, in a parenthesis, he defends that declaration more emphatically than in any other introduction. The absence of personal salutations is marked. He does not, however, omit the salutation of the Gospel. Grace and peace are for them also.

As there are no words of personal salutation, so also there are no expressions of thankfulness for the Galatians' condition. Instead of the usual, "I thank my God," we find him writing, "I marvel." These people were "so quickly," that is, so easily "removing" from the Gospel. There were those who troubled them. These troublers were perverting "the Gospel of Christ." They were insisting on fleshly ceremonies (3:1, 3), on the observance of days (4:10), on circumcision (5:2), and on a new legalism (5:4). This was utterly subversive of the evangel of the Cross. The apostle showed the completeness of the Gospel by telling his own story.

The divine element throughout is clearly marked. There was, first, the revelation to him of Jesus Christ, then the revelation in him of the Son of God, and, finally, such revelation through him that the churches of Judæa, though they did not know his face, glorified God in him.

GALATIANS 2

Having dealt with the divine origin of his teaching, the apostle now proceeded to show that his teaching was confirmed by the conference he had with the elders at Jerusalem fourteen years after his conversion. Of the false brethren he declared that their purpose was to bring the followers into bondage, and it is evident they desired that Titus, who accompanied him, should, because he was a Greek, submit to the rite of circumcision. Against this Paul resolutely set his face, absolutely refusing to submit, because he understood the reason of the claim.

Of the visit of Peter to Antioch we have no record in the Acts, but the story is perfectly plain as Paul tells it. Peter's action was of so grave a nature that the apostle, of set purpose, rebuked him before the whole company of believers.

Then follows the great fundamental statement of doctrine. The ultimate purpose of law was to drive men to Christ, through whom they would live to God, and so be independent of all the law's restrictions. Therefore, to put oneself under law again was to break the purpose of law, which was to end itself.

In this connection the apostle wrote that wonderfully comprehensive statement, "I have been crucfied with Christ; and it is no longer I that live, but Christ liveth in me; and that life which I now live in the flesh I live in faith, the faith which is in the Son of God, who loved me, and gave Himself up for me." Here we have the true Christian life, in both its negative and positive aspects.

GALATIANS 3

Here begins the second division of the epistle, in which Paul deals with the doctrine of liberty. He begins with the exclamation, "O foolish Galatians, who did bewitch you?" He then inquired, Did they receive the Spirit by the works of the law, or, having begun in the Spirit, are they now perfected in the flesh? Was their suffering in vain? Was that Spirit supplied, and those miracles wrought by the works of the law?

The answers to these questions are perfectly clear, and reveal a positive doctrine. The true sons of Abraham are they who are of the faith. "As many as are of the works of the law are under a curse." This the apostle shows to be so. The Scripture says, "The righteous shall live by faith"; while the law says, "He that doeth them shall live in them."

What, then, was the value of the law? It was a temporary arrangement only, until the coming of the Seed. It was a divine arrangement, for it was "ordained through angels by the hand of a mediator," Moses. Therefore the law leads on to the coming of the Seed, the Christ, through faith in whom the promise made to faith may be realized. The work of the law was to keep men in ward, and to shut them up unto the faith "afterwards to be revealed." Thus "the law has become our tutor to bring us unto Christ." The "tutor" is really one who exercises discipline and watches over conduct. Then the law was simply a disciplinary custodian, until Christ, who would open the prison door, and would set the prisoner free. Thus the new-born are Abraham's seed, not according to, or by the way of, law, but according to promise. This is the great doctrine of liberty from the law.

GALATIANS 4

He now declared the process of freedom. "God sent forth His Son . . . under the law." Thus the law He kept was justified, and He lived thereby. But more than this, He bore its penalty, and so procured justification and life for those who, while under its tutelage, had broken it.

The result of this is that they are sons, and now cry "Abba, Father." Under the old bondage God was not known. But now they have come to know God. The return of these Galatian Christians to this ignorance is indicated by their observance of days and months, and seasons and years, that is, to Judaism. The fear expressed at the close of the last paragraph leads to a tender and beautiful personal appeal by the apostle. He beseeches them to become as he is—free from all these things, for he says, "I also am become as ye are."

He contrasts with himself those who have been troubling them, introducing the passage referring to them with the word "they." He does not deny their zeal, but declares their motive to be evil, and ends with an outcry over them like that of a mother. This is the final application of the doctrine of liberty. All that system which lived in the realm of boasted relation to Abraham he characterizes as being in the position of Hagar; and carrying his argument concerning the relationship of faith to its logical conclusion, he claims that the true Jerusalem from above is the mother of the saints. "We," he says, speaking of those who are in Christ, are the "children of promise," and, consequently, the bondwoman is to be cast out.

GALATIANS 5

The whole law of liberty is stated in the sentences, "For freedom did Christ set us free," "stand fast therefore," and "be not entangled again in a yoke of bondage."

He then refers first to circumcision. If a man receive circumcision, Christ will profit him nothing; he has become a debtor to the whole law. If a man desire to be justified by the law, he is severed from Christ, he is fallen from grace.

The positive side of this is then stated. Faith working through love is the great principle of all conduct. The apostle then proceeded to a correction of popular mistakes concerning freedom. The idea that liberty means the absence of all restraint is false. The true use of freedom is stated in the injunction, "through love be servants one to another." The emergence from bondage through Christ is the passing into a sphere of life in which all the powers should act under the dominion of the true motive—love. In answer to an inferred question how such love is possible, the injunction is, "Walk by the Spirit, and ye shall not fulfil the lust of the flesh."

The contrast between flesh and spirit is then made. First, "the works of the flesh." These are operations in the realm of death. Then "the fruit of the Spirit." This refers to an operation in the realm of life. As the apostle has said that the whole law is summed up in the word "love," so now it is evident that the one fruit of the Spirit is love. All the words following form an exposition of the meaning of love, an analysis of the experience resulting therefrom.

GALATIANS 6

Having dealt with the conduct of liberty thus broadly, the apostle now made some detailed application of the principles enunciated, giving an important illustration pertinent to the whole question of the relation between himself and the Galatian Christians. They were to communicate to the necessity of the teachers in all things, remembering that God is not mocked. He is a God of law and order, and as the sowing is, so must be the reaping.

The conclusion of the epistle opened with a personal touch as the apostle referred to the large characters in which he had written. Finally, he summarized the whole subject of the false teachers. The principle on which they had attempted to compel the Galatians to be circumcised was the desire to make a fair show in the flesh in order that they might escape persecution. As against this, the apostle declared that he desired only to glory in the Cross. This glorying is experimental. Through that Cross the world had been crucified to him, and he to the world; and in that very personal crucifixion which had endured persecution and suffering he gloried, and in naught beside.

He then pronounced peace and mercy on those who walk by that rule, glorying only in the Cross, and "upon the Israel of God." What a touch of splendid independence there is in the words, "Henceforth let no man trouble me; for I bear branded on my body the marks of Jesus." The very shame and suffering and persecution which the false teachers would escape the apostle declares have stamped him with the true insignia of his office. The scars on his body left by the stripes and the stones speak of his loyalty to, and fellowship with, his Master, and render him splendidly independent of all human opinion and declining to be troubled by any man. The whole letter closes with a benediction.

Ephesians

EPHESIANS 1

The theme of this letter is pre-eminently of the Church as the medium for the accomplishment of the divine purpose. Those addressed are described as "saints," and as "the faithful in Christ Jesus." These the apostle greets in the words, "Grace to you, and peace from God our Father and the Lord Jesus Christ." Grace is the river flowing from the heart of God. Peace is the consciousness of the trusting soul.

The letter itself begins with a great benediction in which the apostle speaks as a member of the Church, declaring the blessedness of God and the blessedness of the Church through God. In dealing with the subject of the Church, he first writes of its origin. It is predestined to be "holy and without blemish," and that to the praise of the glory of the divine grace. The method of His predestination is threefold: redemption (verse 7), revelation (verses 8 to 12), realization (verses 13 and 14).

This doctrine of grace creates in the heart of the apostle desires for the saints which are constantly expressed in prayer. He prays that they may have "a spirit of wisdom and revelation," and this by having "the eyes of their heart enlightened."

All this in order that they may know, first, the vocation, and, second, the power. The vocation of the Church is here described as the "riches of the glory of His inheritance in the saints." God has an inheritance in His people, and it is that of the Church as a medium through which His grace is to be manifested. The apostle prays, moreover, that they may know "the exceeding greatness of His power." This he described as "the working of the strength of His might," and gave as supreme illustration the resurrection and ascension of our Lord.

EPHESIANS 2

The next subject is the edification or building of the Church. The materials of the building are found amid things which are absolutely opposed to the will and purpose of God. From this material God, who is rich in mercy, finds the material for His building. The process is that in Christ Jesus those found are made alive, are raised up, and made to sit with Him.

The purpose for which the building is created is then distinctly told in the words, "That in the ages to come He might show the exceeding riches of His grace in kindness toward us in Christ Jesus." If the heart is overwhelmed by the splendor of the vision suggested, it is comforted by the declaration immediately following, "We are His workmanship."

Following on, the apostle shows how these materials are to be unified into one building. Jew and Gentile are to be united in Christ. Though they were "far off," they are to be "made nigh." Thus Jew and Gentile are admitted into the one household of God.

Finally, we have the revelation of the foundation, "Built upon the foundation of the apostles and prophets, Christ Jesus Himself being the chief Cornerstone." It is evident that the geometrical figure in the mind of the apostle was of a pyramid, for in the pyramid the cornerstone is the key to the whole structure. This can hardly be said of any other form of building. The building is then described as "a holy temple in the Lord," and its purpose that it should be "a habitation of God in the Spirit." The creation of the temple is the result of the work of Jesus. The incoming of the Spirit is making use of the appropriated temple according to the intended purpose.

EPHESIANS 3

God's dwelling in the Church is not finality. It is equipment for the fulfilment of the divine purpose. The apostle claims a stewardship in the mystery of the Church, and declares the astounding fact that "unto the principalities and the powers in the heavenly places might be made known through the Church the manifold wisdom of God." In his Corinthian letter the apostle showed that the Word of the Cross is the wisdom of God. Therefore, through the Church is to come the proclamation to the unfallen ones of the infinite Grace of God. Heaven will have much music, but none so full of infinite meaning as the song of the ransomed.

Called forth by the stupendous magnitude of his theme, the apostle again speaks of the fact that he is praying for them. Through a series of consecutive petitions he reaches the statement of his final desire. It is "that ye may be filled unto all the fulness of God."

The doctrinal section of the letter ends with the doxology, "Unto Him, the glory in the Church and in Christ Jesus." Thus the inherent blessedness referred to in the opening benediction (1:3) finds its expression in the Church and in Christ Jesus. So stupendous are the ideas developed in this letter that in the presence of them faith must stagger, save as it is recognized that God bestows power equal to the accomplishment of the great purpose. He is One "that is able to do," and that, moreover, "exceeding abundantly above all that we ask or think." Finally, he declares that this ability is "according to the power that worketh in us."

This doxology is full of a sublimity which is characterized by simplicity. "Unto Him be the glory," that is, the great purpose; "in the Church and in Christ Jesus," such the wondrous medium; "unto all the generations of the age of the ages," that the immeasurable duration.

EPHESIANS 4

The apostle at once proceeded to apply this great doctrine to the present life of the Church. From the heavenly calling he passed to the earthly conduct. The matter of first importance is maintenance of the unity of the Spirit. The fact of that unity is then declared. "There is one body, and one Spirit"; the function of the instrument so described is revealed in the words, "one hope of your calling." He then showed how the unity is created: "one Lord," the Object of faith; "one faith," centered on the one Lord; "one baptism," that of the Spirit. The great result is "one

God and Father of all, who is over all, and through all, and in all."

The ascended Christ received gifts, and bestowed them "for the perfecting of the saints unto the work of ministering, unto the building up of the body of Christ."

Having referred to the ascension of Christ, the apostle linked that ascension to His descent. These Christians are called to the maintenance of unity, and how each one is equipped for such obedience is then declared. Grace sufficient is supplied to each until all shall attain to the fulness of the stature of Christ.

In order to realize these things there must be an absolute turning away from the old manner of life in accepting the new. In a series of eight remarkable contrasts the apostle showed the difference between the old and the new. In order to fulfil these injunctions, it is solemnly charged, "Grieve not the Holy Spirit of God." Putting away all these things of the old is the work of the Holy Spirit, as is also the realization in life and character of the things of the new. If we will let the Spirit have His way, we shall find these evil things wither and die, and it will be possible, in the power of the new life, to obey the positive injunctions. If, on the other hand, we cling to, and indulge in, the things condemned, we shall cause sorrow to the great Indweller.

EPHESIANS 5

All that the apostle had been saying was emphasized by the statement of their relationship to God as he called them to be "imitators of God." Again he urged them to put off the old and put on the new. In the old are things of darkness. Believers are to walk as children of the light. That light is found in Christ, "Christ shall shine upon thee."

In the final movement the apostle makes a contrast between false excitement and true enthusiasm, between being "drunken with wine" and being "filled with the Spirit." The whole teaching here is emphasized by the words, "Walk worthily of the calling." In order to do this, we find two principal injunctions: "Grieve not the Holy Spirit of God" (4:30), and "Be filled with the Spirit" (5:18).

Dealing with the Christian household the apostle first revealed the divine conception of the sacredness of the marriage relation. The ideal is presented as conformity to the pattern of the relationship existing between Christ and His Church. The wife yields her complete allegiance to an absolutely self-sacrificing love. Therefore, in his relationship the husband is mastered by a self-emptying devotion. Thus the heads of the household are called on to bear such relation to each other as is worthy of the high calling of the Church, made possible by the glorious union existing between her and her Lord.

EPHESIANS 6

The teaching now turned to the next relationship of importance in the Christian household—the relationship of parents and children. Children are to yield obedience, and thus be set free from all care and anxiety. When the period of childhood passes, obligation does not cease. They are still to honor father and mother.

The responsibility of parents is referred to only with regard to the father. Thus the apostle emphasized that the chief responsibility for training a child should rest with the father. In the exercise of parental authority there must always be the principle of reasonableness, that the obedience of the child may be constrained by love.

The next relationship in the Christian household is that between servants and masters. Service is to be rendered, ever remembering that the final standard must come from the

Lord Himself, and is to be rendered as to Him. Masters also are to rule always from the standpoint of loyalty to Christ. The master's relation to his servant will depend on his relation to his own Master in heaven.

The apostle now turned to the subject of conflict. Life on earth after the pattern of the heavens is bound to bring the soul into conflict with all the forces that are opposed to God. He recognized that behind all the opposition of man is the more terrific opposition of spiritual powers. If, however, there is the revelation of a terrible conflict, there is no room for cowardly fear. Perfect provision is made for the saint. Concerning this armor the apostle has two injunctions. First, "Put on the whole armour of God"; second, "Take up the whole armour of God," indicating equipment and actual conflict. Then the saint is "to stand," and "to withstand," and, "having done all, to stand." The letter ends with personal matters, every one of which is interesting and suggestive, and, finally, the benediction.

Philippians

PHILIPPIANS 1

This letter is in itself a revelation of Christian experience. The word "sin" is not mentioned. The flesh is referred to only that it may be ignored. It is characterized by a revelation of the mind of love. Associating Timothy with himself, the apostle described Timothy and himself as the "servants of Jesus Christ."

Declaring that he thanks God upon all his remembrance of Philippians, he tells them that he is praying that their "love may abound yet more and more in knowledge and all discernment." Such an experience will enable them to "approve the things that are excellent," and so "be sincere and void of offence unto the day of Christ."

Thrice over he referred to his bonds. He declared that these "have fallen out unto the progress of the Gospel," and that in three ways. First, "throughout the whole prætorian guard and to all the rest," the fact that he is a prisoner of Christ has been manifest. Second, therefore, an effect had been produced on his brethren. They had become confident through his bonds. And yet again reference is made to a Judaizing element in the Church. On every hand the Lord is magnified.

In view of all these things the apostle was able to write, "To me to live is Christ, and to die is gain." Then he stated his mental debate. From the purely personal aspect it would be very far better that he should depart. The triumph, however, is on the side of sacrificial service, for his remaining will minister to progress and joy in the faith of others. From the standpoint of personal experience he wrote to them concerning their fellowship, and declared that "to you it hath been granted on the behalf of Christ . . . to suffer."

PHILIPPIANS 2

The apostle now urged those to whom he wrote to fill his joy to the full. In order to do this he indicated two causative facts which suggested two resulting experiences, and then referred to conduct issuing therefrom. The facts are "exhortation in Christ" and "fellowship in the Spirit." When these are realized and submitted to they create that frame of mind which issues in such manner of life as is for the progress of the Gospel.

In a stupendous and stately passage the mind of Christ is revealed. The master principle is love, first as the motive of self-emptying, and, second, as the reason of divine exaltation. In His Self-emptying, Christ passed from sovereign authority to obedient service, which led ultimately to the death of the Cross, in which He was able to deal with sin and provide redemption.

The issue of such Self-sacrificing love and action resulted in the enthronement of that mind of love. God highly exalted Him, and gave Him the name that is above every name, with the avowed purpose that all should submit to Him.

In order to obtain obedience to the initial injunction to have the mind of Christ, the apostle now shows the secrets of ability to obey. First, there must be recognition of the fact that it is God who wills and works in the believer; and then the consequent deduction as this fact of salvation is worked out in fear and trembling. The result will be that in the midst of a crooked and perverse generation the believers will be seen as lights in the world. Throughout this teaching, incidentally, we have a revelation of how remarkably Paul himself was actuated by the mind of Christ. Though in prison, the missionary impulse was strong in him, and his passion for the progress of the Gospel and the blessing of others affected all his thinking and his doing.

PHILIPPIANS 3

This is the great chapter of the autobiography of Paul. First, he emphasized the story of his past in a most remarkable way. Then referring to these things as gains (the word in the original is plural) he declared he counted them loss. The vision of Christ immediately showed him the worthlessness of everything in comparison.

He then brought up the story of his life to the time of his writing. It would then be about thirty years after meeting the risen Lord that he counted his gains but loss. He now wrote, "I count all things to be loss." After thirty years of tribulation and trial such as few men have known, there was no regret in his heart.

The supreme passion of his life was that he might "know Him, and the power of His resurrection, and the fellowship of His sufferings." Having thus looked at his past and declared his present attitude, he spoke of his sense of limitation, and declared that there remained for him but one thing, which was to press toward the ultimate realization of conformity to his Lord spiritually, mentally, and physically.

He then urged those to whom he wrote to walk by the same rule. Referring to the false walk of certain people, he described the true walk as inspired by the consciousness of heavenly citizenship, and having as its direction the complete realization of salvation at the Advent of the Lord. Those referred to as walking in a false way are seen as diametrically opposed to this idea. In their case the Cross is made of none effect, and the whole mind is materialized and sensualized. The end of such conduct is perdition, and the apostle, even with tears, warns the saints at Philippi against the peril of such conduct.

PHILIPPIANS 4

Passing from particular to general instruction, the apostle first enjoined the grace of rejoicing. Twice he repeated his injunction. Moreover, he charged the Philippians that forbearance toward all men should be manifested. Continuing, he showed that the cure for anxiety is supplication with thanksgiving. In this connection he used that remarkable phrase, "the peace of God." Observe it carefully, the peace *of* God, His quietness as serenity, based on His infinite knowledge and unlimited power. Well does the apostle declare that it passes all understanding. This is the peace which is to guard the heart of such as make their requests known to God. To know that He knows, to be sure that He cares, to obey in the confidence that He is able to accomplish all His perfect will, is to have the heart at rest, and the thoughts guarded against anxiety, and free for highest service.

The mind thus guarded by the peace of God is set free to think on the highest things which Paul here named. Drawing to the conclusion of his letter, the apostle expressed thankfulness for the love manifested to him by the saints at Philippi, and declared that in all things he had learned the secret of rest in the midst of varying circumstances. That secret is ultimately revealed in the words, "I can do all things in Him that strengtheneth me."

The deepest reason for his thankfulness for their care is not selfish, but that their giving meant that fruit increased to their account. What a fulness of thought there is in the declaration so familiar, and yet forevermore surprising. "My God shall supply every need of yours, according to His riches in glory in Christ Jesus."

The doxology constitutes a fitting expression of the experience of the Christian. This prisoner of the Lord Jesus recognizing his relationship to God, ascribes to Him the glory and is thus seen superior to all the limitations which characterized his position. The last words are those of personal and tender salutation by the pronouncement of the single and inclusive benediction of the grace of the Lord Jesus Christ.

Colossians

COLOSSIANS 1

This letter is correlative to the Ephesians, and shows the glory of the Head of the Church as at her disposal. After expressing his thankfulness for the faith, love, and hope of the saints, Paul tells them that he was praying that they might "be filled with the knowledge of His will," and declares that the reason of such prayer is that they may "walk worthily of the Lord."

Provision is made for this in the twofold fact that they have been "delivered" and "translated." Set free from the dominion of sin, they are "translated . . . into the Kingdom of the Son of His love." It is here that Paul set forth the glories of the Person of the Redeemer in a passage that is unique for its revealing beauty. Of the invisible God, He is the Image. As to the creation, He is the First-born, that is, the One who has pre-eminence both as Originator and Sustainer. As to the Church, He is the Head, and now is described as "First-born from the dead." The apostle summarized the whole truth concerning the glories of the Person of Christ in his declaration, "It was the good pleasure of the Father that in Him should all the fulness dwell."

It is the purpose of God, through Christ, "to reconcile all things to Himself." The means of reconciliation is the Cross. The issue of the reconciliation is that those who were "alienated . . . enemies in your mind in your evil works" are to become "holy . . . without blemish . . . unreprovable." In this connection the apostle claims that to him had been committed the stewardship of the truth concerning the Church as the medium through which the glorious purpose of God would be accomplished. Therefore, the aim of this epistle, and, indeed, of all apostolic work is admonishing and teaching every man toward the realization of perfection in Christ, because that issues in the perfecting of the whole Church.

COLOSSIANS 2

If for a moment we glance back at the passage beginning with 1:24 and ending with 2:3, we find reference to a threefold mystery: the first, the Church, which is the Body of Christ; then the secret of life in the individual believer, "Christ in you, the hope of glory"; finally, the deepest mystery of all, "the mystery of God even Christ." The apostle declared his reason for having so carefully stated this doctrine of Christ and the Church. It is that the Colossian Christians might not be deluded.

The central declaration of the epistle is found in this chapter, "For in Him dwelleth all the fulness of the Godhead bodily, and in Him ye are made full, which is the Head of all principality and power."

As the apostle approaches the personal and practical application, he shows what this relationship of the believer to Christ means in two fundamental respects. Union with the death of Christ means union with His work of reconciliation. Union with the resurrection of Christ means union with all the glories of His Person.

Certain perils were threatening the Church at Colossæ with which the apostle dealt. Some were attempting to bring believers into bondage to external observances, and the apostle warned them against such. The other peril was putting Christ at a distance by allowing intermediation between the soul and Him, even that of angels.

The perils against which the apostle warned these Colossians have often recurred in the history of the Church. By pledges and promises according to human ordinances a man is constantly in danger of worshiping his own will. By submission of the conscience to human intervention an unwarranted subservience is created. How true it is that there may be a development and strengthening of the lower side of human life in self-denial, in submission to false authority, and in the mere bruising of the body. There can be no such result where the soul is living in conscious experience of death with Christ and life in Him.

COLOSSIANS 3

The believer is to "seek the things . . . above." The word "seek" marks aspiration, desire, and passion. The things above are those of the empire of Christ. In order to seek these things the mind must be set on them. The believer's responsibility is revealed, first, in response to the union with Christ in death, in putting to death the things of the earth, of which a list is given. Also the things of the spirit which are evil must be put off. These too are named.

Then follows the application in the matter of our union with Christ in life, and the apostle again shows the things that manifest such union. The final and inclusive word in this application is, "Whatsoever ye do in word or in deed, do all in the name of the Lord Jesus, giving thanks to God the Father through Him."

A section of practical illustrations of application follows in the case of husbands and wives, children and parents, servants and masters.

COLOSSIANS 4

The true purpose of life for the saints and faithful in Christ is to the maintenance of a twofold relationship—toward God, and toward those who are without. The first is covered by prayer as it includes adoration, confession, and petition. This life must be sedulously cultivated. A necessary element in such a life is watchfulness. Yet such watchfulness is not to be characterized by anxiety, for it is to be "with thanksgiving." Cheerfulness is to mingle with cautiousness.

Toward "them that are without" the saint is to walk in wisdom. This again is closely linked with the prayer life. Moreover, the speech of the saint is to be characterized by grace and salt, that is by courteousness, and yet by the qualities which prevent corruption.

The letter closes with references that were local and personal. The references to Tychicus, Onesimus, Aristarchus, Mark, and Jesus, are characterized by Paul's recognition of their excellences. The one picture that stands out is that of Epaphras. Evidently when the letter was written he was with Paul, and there was striving in prayer for that Church of which really he was a member. In this description of Epaphras we have an insight into his character. He was praying for them that they might "stand perfect and fully assured in all the will of God." What greater prayer is it possible for any to offer for loved ones than this, and what greater service can anyone render than thus to strive in prayer on behalf of the loved ones? The final words have in them a touch of pathos. Taking the *stylus* from the one to whom he had been dictating, he wrote words which indicate at once his sense of limitation and his desire for sympathy, "Remember my bonds."

I Thessalonians

I THESSALONIANS 1

This letter was intended as a message of comfort and instruction to those who were in the midst of persecution. In writing, the apostle associated himself with Silas and Timothy. He commenced by referring to the great truth of the Church's safe position as being "in God the Father, and the Lord Jesus Christ"; and then declared the foundation facts of Christian character. They are, first, the "work of faith," by which the apostle referred to the belief through which believers entered into relationship with Jesus Christ; second, the "labour of love," referring to the whole activity of life after belief; and, third, "the patience of hope," referring to the strength issuing from the expectation of the return of the Lord.

The Gospel had come to them "in power and in the Holy Spirit, and in much assurance." The result was that they "became imitators," and "an example." As a result, the Word of the Lord had sounded forth far and near. This result followed from the fact that the Gospel was, indeed, in power. There is a vital connection between the description of their discipleship and their activity. The "work of faith" consisted in turning "unto God from idols," the "patience of hope" in waiting "for His Son from heaven." Throughout the letter these great facts are recognized, and illustrated, and applied.

I THESSALONIANS 2

It is evident that some of the Jews in Thessalonica had been discounting the apostle in his absence. He very definitely defends himself against such detraction, asserting that his preaching had been with boldness, characterized by thankfulness, full of tenderness, and prosecuted with earnestness. The faith they had exercised demonstrated that the Gospel was "not . . . vain." Their "work of faith" was the credential of the apostle's spiritual authority. His authority is further emphasized by their "labour of love." Having received the Word, and so working the "work of faith," they had treated it as the very Word of God, and served even in suffering. To "serve the living and true God" ever means a "labour of love," that is to say, it is obedience to the law of love in the impulse of love, and this inevitably results in suffering in the midst of those who are antagonistic to God's revelation of His will through the Lord Jesus.

Finally, in answering the charges against himself, the apostle referred to the Lord's return. He speaks of himself as "bereft" of the Thessalonians for a short season, but qualifies the statement by saying that this is "in presence, not in heart." It is the Coming of the Lord that he looked forward to as the one reward of all present toil and pain and suffering. They are at once his hope, his joy, his crown.

Very beautiful is this turning of the apostle's thought to the ultimate vindication of his work. The detractors were busy attempting to undervalue this work, and to cast aspersions on his character, his honesty, and his tenderness. All this will finally be answered in the splendor and the glory of that moment when the Lord shall receive to Himself in glory those who "turned . . . from idols to serve a living and true God, and to wait for His Son from heaven."

I THESSALONIANS 3

The special purpose of the next movement in his letter was the strengthening of the Thessalonians in their sufferings. Their "work of faith" had brought them into a place of service which entailed suffering. In this connection, the apostle makes personal reference to having sent Timothy to them, while he was left alone in Athens. Whereas Athens was a burden on his heart, his love for the Thessalonians prompted him to this action. Timothy had brought him a message telling of their "faith and love that filled him with gladness." In view of this loyalty he again referred to the great light of hope, the coming of the Lord, praying that his way might be directed to them, and that they might abound in love.

Thus in the midst of their suffering the apostle's words flashed on them the light of that glorious moment when character would be perfected, and the stress and strain of the process pass into the perfect realization of a glorious result. At the advent of the Master all the aspirations of the believing soul toward perfection of character would be realized and fulfilled. Toward that glorious finality all present life should move, and waiting for the Son which creates the "patience of hope" is thus seen to be the most profound and potent inspiration to holiness of life and character.

I THESSALONIANS 4

At this point in his letter the apostle turned to exhortation. Timothy's report concerning the Thessalonians' condition had indicated that they needed some words of kindly warning.

The first subject is personal purity. Their life was lived in a city characterized by great moral looseness. The condition of the unregenerate Gentiles is revealed in the arresting phrase which describes them as living "in the passion of lust," and declares that the reason was that "they know not God." Hence the necessity for a life of purity among the members of Christ. Their attitude toward each other was to be that of love, while that toward those who "are without" was that they should be quiet, and attend to their daily work, thus bearing testimony to the power of the Gospel in life. No testimony is more powerful for God than that a life fulfilling the "daily round, and the common task," which is characterized by the renunciation of idols, and illuminated by the hope of the coming of the King.

It is evident that some of these Thessalonian Christians had fallen on sleep, and that, somehow, those remaining were afraid lest these departed ones had missed the realization of the glorious hope of the advent of Jesus. To correct that impression the apostle now dealt with the great subject, especially to show the relation of the advent to those who had thus fallen on sleep. They had been living in the "patience of hope." The apostle now declares that they who have fallen asleep will take precedence at the advent. Therefore, sorrow for the departed ones must not be the sorrow of despair. These loved ones are at present with the Lord, and at His Coming will accompany Him. What we may reverently describe as the program of the advent is then given. The Lord Himself will descend. Then the dead in Christ will rise, and receive the eternal body. Then the living will be caught up in the clouds, and the final truth is declared in the words, "So shall we ever be with the Lord."

I THESSALONIANS 5

Under the figure of a camp in which fully armed soldiers are waiting for the break of day, while those not expecting this are sleeping and drunken, the apostle shows that those waiting for the Son are children of light, and therefore called upon to live in watchfulness and sobriety.

In view of the glorious certainty of hope the apostle urged them to continue in the "labour of love" in serving "a living and true God." There follow brief injunctions (verses 17-20) which perfectly set forth the true attitude demanded of the saints. Every one of the injunctions will bear close examination.

The apostle finally declared his desire and assurance concerning these Thessalonian Christians. His desire was that they might be sanctified wholly by "the God of peace Himself." That entire sanctification is described as the preservation of "spirit and soul and body at the Coming of our Lord Jesus Christ." The letter closes with words that are entirely personal. Conscious of the difficulties of his own position at Corinth, from where he had written, the apostle craves their co-operation in prayer. The last words are of most sacred benediction. Their faith and love and hope are all centered on the Person of the Lord Jesus Christ. Through Him grace had been manifested for their salvation; in Him they stood in the grace which conditioned their service and their growth; and at His Coming the grace of the first epiphany would merge into the glory of the second. Thus the apostle committed the Thessalonians to the grace of the Lord Jesus Christ in order to establish them in faith, in love, and in hope.

II Thessalonians

II THESSALONIANS 1

Evidently, this letter was intended primarily to correct certain mistakes which the Thessalonians were making concerning the Second Advent. They were failing to distinguish between the two phases, the Day of the Lord and the coming of the Lord. In his introduction the apostle again referred to their faith and their love, but not to their hope. The peculiar peril now threatening them was to be found in this matter.

The apostle proceeded to deal with "the revelation of the Lord Jesus." He is to be revealed "from heaven with the angels of His power in flaming fire." The revealing is to be for a definite purpose. It will exclude from His face and His glory all who are disobedient. The connection of the saints with that apocalypse is declared to be rest first, and, finally, they are to constitute the medium through which the Lord Jesus' glory will be manifested and marveled at. The terrors of His revealing are not for the saints, and in the age following His revelation the saints are to be associated with Him, and to be the channels through which the truth of His glory will be made known.

"To that end," that is, with such a consummation in view, the apostle proved that God might count them worthy of such calling, fulfilling every desire and good work, the deepest desire of his heart being that at last, in the fulness of interrelation, Christ might be glorified in them, and they in Christ.

II THESSALONIANS 2

The apostle now stated clearly the order of events connected with the Second Advent of Jesus. He first announced the distinction between the two things that they were evidently confusing: "the Coming of our Lord Jesus Christ" and "the Day of the Lord." For the first they are to wait, for it is to be the occasion of the gathering together of the saints to Himself. The second cannot come until certain other matters have been accomplished. He earnestly warns them against confusing the hope of the coming of Jesus with the fact of His manifestation to the world, in which "the Day of the Lord" will be ushered in. The signs of that Day will be a falling away, and, finally, the manifestation of evil in a person whom he now describes.

Having thus referred to that manifestation of the man of sin the apostle described the then present condition of affairs, which condition, by the way, remains until this time. Two forces are in conflict. The one he described as "the mystery of lawlessness," and the other as "One that restraineth." The first is the essential spirit of evil. It is described as a mystery on account of the secret and subtle method of its working. The other force is referred to as a Person. That Person is holding the mystery of lawlessness in check. Clearly, the reference is to the work of the Holy Spirit. This will continue until the Spirit is "taken out of the way." That will be the occasion for the heading up of evil in a person, and so also the occasion of the revelation of Jesus, and the destruction of the man of sin. The apostle charged the Thessalonians to "stand fast, and hold the traditions."

II THESSALONIANS 3

In conclusion the apostle urged them to pray for him that the preaching of the Word in other places might be with power and victory. He affirmed his confidence in them, and expressed his desire for their continual patience.

In a very practical way he rebuked those who were neglecting their earthly calling, making themselves chargeable to the care of others. As he had not withdrawn himself from the ordinary avocation of his life while ministering the Word to them, it was of the utmost importance that they should walk by the same rule. The true attitude of "waiting for the Son" is ever unceasing fidelity to all the responsibilities of the present.

In view of this, the apostle laid down the principle that "if any will not work, neither let him eat." Any view of life which makes work distasteful and causes its neglect is wrong.

The letter closes with the apostle's words of tender desire for these Thessalonian Christians. He does not forget their troublous circumstances, and he supremely desires peace for them. However, for him, peace is associated only with the Lordship of Jesus, whom he here speaks of as the "Lord of peace," and whose presence he evidently considers will assure the Thessalonians that very blessing.

The personal salutation and the apostle's declaration that such signature is guarantee of the genuineness of his writing were for their safeguarding against spurious communications, such as had caused them trouble in the matter of the Advent. There is the addition of one little word in this final benediction as compared with its form in the first Epistle. It is the word *"all."* Thus the apostle takes in those whom he had been rebuking and correcting, and so reveals the greatness of his heart and his love.

I Timothy

I TIMOTHY 1

This letter is an apostle's letter to a young minister having oversight of the church in Ephesus. The first part of the letter deals with the Church, its doctrine, its devotions, and its ministry. Difficulties existed in that "certain men" were teaching erroneous doctrine. In all probability, the reference was to the Gnostic heresies. The apostle shows the relation of "sound doctrine" to the law which the Gnostics were misinterpreting. Enumerating the evils resulting from such false teaching, he shows how they are contradictory to that "sound doctrine" which is according to the "Gospel of the glory of the blessed God." Let Timothy charge these men not to teach the "different doctrine" which has such evil results, for the Gospel is a helpful doctrine.

Mention of the Gospel calls forth an exceedingly beautiful passage which is at once a song and a testimony. The apostle illustrates the beauty of the Gospel from his own experience. He had passed through stages, having been first a blasphemer, then a persecutor, and, finally, injurious. His salvation had come through faith. On that personal experience he now dogmatically affirmed the trustworthiness of the Gospel. He summarizes the Gospel in the simple statement, "Christ Jesus came into the world to save sinners." Addressing Timothy as a captain of the host of God, he charges him to wage a good war. This he will accomplish by "holding faith, and a good conscience." The apostle emphasized the urgency of the charge by a warning in which he cited instances of those who had failed.

I TIMOTHY 2

The apostle then turned to the public devotions of the Church. As the Church is the medium for proclamation of the doctrine of truth, so also is it the instrument of intercession as between men and God. The apostle used words that cover the whole ground, "supplications," "prayers," "intercessions," "thanksgivings." Christians in those days were being charged with rebellion against earthly government. The prayers of the Church disproved the charge. Such prayer is according to the will of God, and harmonizes with the perfect provision He has made for salvation.

Turning to the matter of the demeanor and position of women, we must remember that Paul was dealing with affairs in Ephesus. Behind the picture of the Christian woman as

SPORTS	ESPN2	68	36	68	28	28	-	38	24	28	28	(N) **cc**	**Racing** (N)	
	ESPNC	69	-	69	27	27	-	-	-	27	27	**2-Minute Drill**	**2-Minute Drill**	**Sportscentury:** Hawkins **cc**
	FOXSS	40	37	22	29	29	15	34	-	29	29	**You Gotta See This!**	**You Gotta See This!** (N)	**Boxing:** Fight Ti From Indio, Cali
	GOLF	66	-	66	-	-	-	-	-	-	-	**Golf Academy**	**Golf Central** (N)	**European PGA G**
	SPEED	67	60	67	-	-	67	-	44	-	-	**SBK 2001** (N)	**MotorWeek** (N) 'G'	**American Muscle Car** (N)
MOVIES	HBO	7	71	14	62	62	5	21	14	62	62	**Movie (5:30):** Never **cc**	**Movie:** Brokedown Palace (1999) are jailed in Thailand for drug sm	
	HBOP	74	72	74	-	-	-	-	-	-	-	**Movie (5:30):** Anna and the King (1999) Jodie Foster. **cc**		**Movie:** Titan A.E Drew Barrymore
	HBOS	75	73	75	-	-	-	-	-	-	-	**Movie (5:45):** Nixon (1995) Anthony Hopkins, Joan Stone's portrait of America's 37th president. 'R' c		
	MAX	14	74	-	65	65	22	15	21	65	65	**Movie (6:30):** Invasion! (1999) Campbell Scott. 'PG-13' **cc**		**Movie:** I Love Tr porters team u
	MC	73	-	-	68	68	-	19	-	68	68	**Movie (6:45):** In the Line of Fire (1993) Clint Eastw Secret Service agent battles a vicious assassin. '		
	SHOW	72	77	2	67	67	20	17	3	67	67	**Movie (6:00):** The Boyfriend School (1990) 'PG-13'		**Movie:** Scream cat killer stalks
	CHAN	**T**	**A**	**M**	**RP**	**Y**	**C**	**R**	**C**	**G**	**L**	**7PM**	**7:30**	**8PM**
	A&E	36	41	18	38	38	36	22	15	38	38	**Law & Order** "Causa Mortis" 'PG' **cc**		**Biography** "San phisticated Bab
	AMC	27	42	-	34	34	-	33	-	34	34	**Three Stooges cc**		**Movie:** Racing V school pals hav
	ANPL	38	-	38	42	42	-	-	-	42	42	**Amazing Animal Videos** 'G'	**Planet's Funniest Animals**	**Planet's Funniest Animals**
	BET	59	56	39	52	52	1	-	30	52	52	**106 & Park: Top Ten Live**	**BET.com Countdown** (N)	**Hits From the S**
	BRAVO	37	-	-	-	-	-	-	-	-	-	**St. Elsewhere** "Whistle Wylie Work"		**Movie:** River's keep mum afte
	CART	53	29	53	-	-	-	-	40	-	-	**Scooby**	**Courage the Cowardly Dog**	**Ed, Edd n Eddy** 'G'
	COM	52	53	38	56	56	-	-	-	56	56	**Daily Show** 'PG' **cc**	**Stein's Money cc**	**Movie:** Roman turer helps a n
	CMTV	51	45	51	49	49	38	-	34	49	49	**Nonstop Country**		
	DIS	71	75	59	44	44	21	-	16	44	44	**Princess Diaries cc**	**Movie:** Zeus and Roxanne (1997 Quinlan. A dog and a dolphin f	
	DSC	35	38	34	40	40	35	28	32	40	40	**Wild Discovery** "Clever Critters" (N) (Part 2 of 2) 'G'		**Face Makers** '
	E!	49	57	-	-	-	-	-	-	-	-	**Celebrity Homes** 'PG'	**Coming Attractions** 'PG'	**Mysteries & Scandals**
	EWTN	57	-	57	-	-	-	-	-	-	-	**Our Lady of the Angels Monastery Daily Mass**		**Life on the Ro** In)

Billy Graham | COMMENTARY

Sometimes, we have nowhere to go but up

Q. *I've never had anything to do with God, but a friend of mine who is a Christian said the other day that God will get my attention some day, whether I like it or not, even if I have to hit bottom first. Is that true?*

Why wait to find out if it is true or not? And why wait to discover the peace and joy only God can bring into your life? I have never met a person who came to Christ late in life who didn't wish they had come much, much sooner.

Yes, sometimes we do have to hit bottom before we will listen to God, although when that occurs, we are usually responsible for what has happened, not God. The problem, however, is that even when some people hit bottom, they still may not hear God's voice and turn to him. They have resisted him for so long that their hearts have become hardened and insensitive toward God. The Bible warns, "A man who remains stiff-necked after many rebukes will suddenly be destroyed – without remedy" (Proverbs 29:1).

I pray that you will stop and realize you are on a dead-end road. Only Christ can give you meaning in life right now, and only he can give you hope for eternal life. Jesus warned, "wide is the gate and broad is the road that leads to destruction, and many enter through it" (Matthew 7:13).

I wonder if you have turned your back on God because you have a false idea of what it means to follow him. Perhaps you think God will restrict you and make your life miserable. But Jesus said, "I have come that they may have life, and have it to the full" (John 10:10).

Billy Graham: Billy Graham Evangelistic Association, P.O. Box 779, Minneapolis, MN 55440.

here portrayed is that of many of the women of the Greek communities, and it was to save the women of the Church from any conformity to debased ideals that these passages were written. The adornment of women in the Church must not be external decoration, but the general demeanor. The word "apparel" in this connection has reference to much more than mere raiment. It is the garbing of the whole life in its external manifestation. This garbing should result from internal sobriety, which means the perfect equipoise and control of life. The true place of woman is indicated by a reference to the original order in the case of Adam and Eve. Out of that history comes the occasion of woman's travail, and the apostle declared that in that supreme sorrow she will be saved, if her character is what has been already described.

I TIMOTHY 3

Turning to the government of the Church, the apostle deals with two orders, bishops and deacons. The bishop is an overseer, whose duty it is to watch over the flock. The apostle describes the qualifications necessary to fulfil the office: (1) character (verses 2,3), (2) temperament (verses 4,5), (3) experience (verse 6), and (4) reputation (verse 7). The description of the deacon has unquestioned reference to the order instituted in the early days, as recorded by Luke (Acts 6:1-6). According to this, they were to be "men of good report, full of the spirit of wisdom." There is not the slightest warrant for looking on the office in any sense as inferior. Its function was different, but not less important. The business of the Church ever needs to be carried on by men of highest character and deepest spirituality. All this will be seen as the instructions of the apostle are pondered.

The purpose of all the apostle had written was that men might know how to behave themselves in the Church. A remarkable and singularly beautiful description of the Church follows. It is the house of God, and therefore it is the pillar and ground of truth. The essential glory of the Church is "the truth." Having shown this, the apostle describes the truth in words which constitute a verse of perfect poetry. There have been varied renderings of this passage. That of Humphreys in the *Cambridge Bible* is very illuminative.

> Who is flesh was manifested,
> Pure in Spirit was attested;
> By angels' vision witnessed,
> Among the nations heralded;
>   By faith accepted here,
>   Received in glory there!

I TIMOTHY 4

Having thus dealt with the Church, the apostle showed Timothy how he was to fulfil his responsibility. He had a duty toward the truth, and therefore toward the Church. In order to correct errors which would arise, Timothy was to give definite instruction. Abstinence from lawful things is a matter for personal decision and action, and must never be made a necessity of religious life or godliness. The apostle then described the secrets of strength for those who were called upon to defend the truth against error. A faithful saying, and worthy of acceptation, is that God is "the Saviour of all men, specially of them that believe."

The teacher must be such a man as to carry conviction. The injunction, "Let no man despise thy youth," has the force of, "Do not be despicable." How Timothy may fulfil this injunction is then stated. He is to be an example of the believers in godliness of life.

The apostle's final instructions concerning Timothy's duty to the truth are strikingly comprehensive in their description of the true method and habit of the Christian minister. They may be divided thus: (1) his public work (verse 13), (2) his private work (verses 14,15), and (3) his general attitude, and its consequent issue (verse 16). The greatest power of the preacher is personality; continuity in his work is the way of his salvation, and so also the way of salvation for others.

I TIMOTHY 5

Timothy's demeanor toward men and women was now described, and demands careful study and attention. As for men, seniors are to be treated with respect, while the younger men are to be treated as brethren.

Of women, he is to treat the elder as mothers, and the younger as sisters. The large section devoted to widows indicated peculiar local conditions and dangers. Hence the careful instructions.

At verse 17 we find the term "elders" used in a more specific sense, referring undoubtedly to those who held office in the Church. These were to be held in honor and provided for. Order must be maintained, and discipline enforced, yet in such a way as befits the elders' honorable position. The true Church order must ever be "first pure, then peaceable." The responsibility resting on Timothy was so great that the apostle charged him to act in the sight of God, of Jesus Christ, and the elect angels. Apparently turning aside for a moment, and thinking of Timothy's "often infirmities," he gave him personal and practical advice.

I TIMOTHY 6

The final injunction of the apostle concerning Timothy's duty toward his flock had to do with his dealing with Christian slaves. The master must not treat them with contempt. They are to recognize that the slaves are serving Christ, and so make their service the opportunity of testimony to the power of the Gospel. Service will be rendered more readily and faithfully because impulsed by love.

The apostle then reverted to the prime occasion of Timothy's appointment to Ephesus, which was the presence and action of false teachers. To these he referred in scathing words. In this connection occurs a sentence which flashes a fierce light into the inner working of the minds of these teachers as the apostle refers to them as "supposing that godliness is a way of gain." To this evil the apostle opposes the great truth that "Godliness with contentment is great gain." The contrasting ideas are arresting. According to these false teachers, godliness is a means of gaining much. According to Paul, godliness is the gain of being content with little.

An appeal is then made to Timothy, who is addressed, "O man of God." The note of the appeal is threefold, "flee," "follow," "fight." He is to flee the things of evil, to follow those of truth, and thus to fight the good fight of faith. The strength for the conflict is found in the life eternal. Moreover, there is to be a great epiphany, when the supreme and absolute Lordship of Jesus is to be revealed. That is to be the supreme inspiration of service and of conflict.

The final charge to Timothy brought to the mind of the apostle the peril which threatened those who were rich. He describes the true attitude of the Christian man possessed of wealth, showing (1) his true state of mind, (2) his proper use of wealth, and (3) the secret strength of realization. The epistle closed in an outburst of personal appeal full of force and beauty.

II Timothy

II TIMOTHY 1

The second letter to Timothy was written from prison. Paul, conscious of the evil existing in the Church, forecast the terrible days that were coming. He was conscious also of the grave responsibility resting on Timothy. He introduced his letter by a revelation of his affection for Timothy, and his thankfulness for him.

His first appeal had to do with Timothy himself. He charged him to "stir up the gift" he had already received, and not to be "ashamed . . . of the testimony." The qualities of the gift were described as consisting in capacity for oversight, and government in the Church. This must not be exercised in a spirit of cowardice. The kindling to a flame of such a gift would not make the pathway easy. A twofold incentive was revealed in the greatness of the Gospel committed to him as a deposit, and his own experience and convictions.

In this paragraph we have five main assertions, "I was appointed," "I suffered," "I am not ashamed," "I know Him," "I am persuaded." There is yet another, which is subsidiary in the sense of being resultant, "I have believed." Looking back, he wrote, "I was appointed." Thinking of the present, he declared, "I suffered," "I am not ashamed," "I know Him." Looking to the future, he said, "I am persuaded."

II TIMOTHY 2

In order to fulfil the ideal revealed in the instructions, Timothy was charged to "be strengthened in the grace that is in Christ Jesus." The apostle employed three figures of speech, the soldier, the athlete, and the husbandman, as revealing the methods by which Timothy might be strengthened in grace. The ultimate command is, "Remember Jesus Christ."

The apostle next referred to his own experiences again. Briefly, but vividly, he said, "I suffer hardship unto bonds, as a malefactor." Paul was now in prison for the second time, and was ranked as one of the lowest criminals. Nevertheless, he was jubilant over the fact that "the Word of God is not bound." It is in fellowship with Christ that such experience is granted. "If we died with Him, we shall also live with Him; if we endure, we shall also reign with Him." This declaration is followed by the solemn warning, "If we shall deny Him, He also will deny us," for God must be faithful to Himself.

The apostle then turned to the subject of Timothy's responsibility as to the Church. This is revealed as threefold: first, the exercise of power (verses 14-19); second, the exercise of love (verses 20-23); and, third, the exercise of discipline (verses 24-26). In the presence of difficulties created by a wrong teaching, Timothy must show himself a workman skilled in the specific calling of handling the Word of truth. The goal of ambition is "approved unto God." The method is, "Give diligence . . . a workman." The work, "rightly dividing the word of truth."

The duty of Timothy in the exercise of discipline, and the manifestation of love are then set forth. The apostle grants the existence of mixture in the Church. Separation from fellowship with the unworthy is a condition of fitness for the highest forms of service. The apostle urged this consecration in a threefold injunction, the key words of which are "flee," "follow," "refuse."

II TIMOTHY 3

Clearly seeing trouble coming from the teaching of those who were "holding a form of godliness, but having denied the power thereof," the apostle referred to his own manner of life and service as affording an example of what Timothy's experience must necessarily be. He referred to his "teaching," his "conduct," his "purpose," and his "faith," his "longsuffering," his "love," and his "patience." The results of such life and service had been persecution and suffering. Out of all these things he had been delivered, for while the difficulties of the pathway had been great, the strength and faithfulness of the Lord had been greater.

Finally, in this connection the apostle turned to Timothy's responsibility concerning the truth. The first word marking that responsibility is the word, "abide." The apostolic teaching at this point reveals Paul's estimate of the qualities which constitute the values of the Scriptures. "Teaching" refers to the authoritative quality which constitutes the foundation on which the building is to go forward. "Reproof" is testing. "Correction" refers to bringing back into the true line. "Instruction" refers to training by discipline, toward consummation. The Scriptures, therefore, provide the foundation on which to build, a method for testing the building in course of erection, a force equal to correcting mistakes, and the supply for carrying out the enterprise to perfection.

The purpose throughout is to make complete the man of God, but this perfection of the instrument is not the ultimate goal. That is reached in the work which the complete man of God is to perform. The sequence is suggestive, and if we study it from the effect to the cause we see what was evidently in the mind of the apostle. The matter of supreme importance was the work committed to Timothy. In order to do this he must himself be complete. In order to reach this completeness his character must result from the power of the Holy Scriptures. In order to obtain this he must abide therein.

II TIMOTHY 4

As the result of these charges, the apostle shows what Timothy's attitude must be toward those over whom he has oversight. There are four things which he must do. "Preach the Word," "reprove," "rebuke," "exhort." The qualities of the Word which are of value in building personal character are to be used in carrying out relative responsibility.

Then follow what are, in all probability, the last written words of Paul preserved to us. His position was that he was already "being offered." This was a reference to his consciousness that his life was drawing to a close. He referred to that coming experience as a "departure."

Looking back over the years of service, he had no lament, but triumphant thankfulness. Three phrases indicate his consciousness of that service, "I have fought," "I have finished," "I have kept." Looking to the future, he declared that a crown was laid up for him. He then referred to his associates. Demas had left him, having loved the present age. Crescens was away in Galatia, Titus in Dalmatia, both probably carrying out some mission. Luke was still by his side. Mark was absent, but Timothy was charged to bring him with him when he came. Tychicus was also absent in Ephesus. It is in some senses a sad picture, yet it glows with light. The final section is purely personal. Paul commissioned Timothy to bring a cloak, some books, and certain parchments.

It is impossible to read the close of this letter without seeing how remarkably the apostle had been brought into active fellowship with his Lord. His last words were of the nature of a prayer of desire, expressive of all he felt that Timothy would need in the midst of the difficulties and dangers of his position in Ephesus, "The Lord be with thy spirit." If this desire were fulfilled, the faithfulness of Timothy would be assured.

The closing sentence, "Grace be with you," is such as would be expected from Paul. The one theme of all his preaching and teaching had been grace. The way of grace is the way of the Lord's fellowship; it is by grace that the Master abides with the spirit of His servant.

Titus

TITUS 1

Titus is not mentioned in the Acts of the Apostles. From the letter we learn that he was a convert of the apostle. Moreover, we know that he was a Greek.

This letter reached him while he was in Crete, amid peculiar circumstances; his mission was to set the church in order. Therefore the apostle enjoined him to appoint elders. He defined the function of the elder as that of the steward of God, and showed that the function would be fulfilled by loyalty to "the faithful word which is according to the teaching." Only men of character were to be appointed to such office. The elder must be blameless as a family man, in personal character, and in his relation to truth.

There were Judaizing teachers in Crete, and the apostle laid down an important principle for dealing with them: "To the pure all things are pure, but to them that are defiled and unbelieving nothing is pure." This cut clean across the teaching of those referred to, which consisted in insistence on certain ritualistic commandments. Titus was charged to "reprove them sharply." There are forms of evil which demand the surgeon's knife. The reason for the severity is that the highest purposes of love may be real ized.

TITUS 2

The apostle then proceeded to show what the behavior of aged men, aged women, and young men in the Church should be. In connection with the behavior of bond-servants Paul employed what is perhaps the most beautiful description of godly behavior when he said, that "they may adorn the doctrine of God our Saviour in all things." While it is still only a theory doctrine lacks the manifestation of beauty. When, however, it is realized and manifested in human life its beauty at once appears. The value of a theory is always supremely apparent in the results it produces.

If these were the duties of the Church, the apostle now proceeded to show what were the resources at the disposal of every Christian. In a passage of singular beauty and power he declared the fourfold value of the grace of God. That grace appeared in the First Advent, and brought salvation to all men. Salvation, then, is the fundamental fact. It brings cleansing from sin, and enlightenment. Grace then proceeds to teaching. This teaching conditions the life of man in relation to all the forces with which it comes in contact. The word "soberly" refers to the world within; "righteously," to the world around; and "godly," to the world above. The life of the Christian is set in the light of the Second Advent, when there will be an epiphany of glory. All this is then set in the light of the work of Christ. The salvation which grace brings is experimentally the redemption from iniquity which Christ accomplishes. The instruction which grace imparts is the perfection which issues from identification with Christ. The denial of ungodliness results from the possession by God which Christ ensures. The hope which grace presents is the impulse to the service which Christ creates.

TITUS 3

The final section of the epistle has to do with the Church and the State, dealing with the duty of the Church, arguments impelling to the fulfilment of duty, and the method of realization. The duty of the Church is to submit to authority, to be ready for every good work, to be free from evil speech, and to be gentle and meek.

In order to fulfil these ideals, Christian people should remember their own past, and treat with pity those who are yet "foolish, disobedient, deceived." The threefold memory of what we were, of how the change has been wrought, and of what we are, will serve to create the spirit of subjection to authority, equip us for honest toil, silence all evil speech, and generate an unceasing compassion.

Titus was charged to "affirm confidently" these important things. The whole charge to Titus reveals the truth concerning every minister to whom is committed the oversight of the flock of God. For himself the apostle charged him to shun the things unprofitable and vain, and to maintain discipline.

The epistle closes with reference to Tychicus, Apollos, Artemas, and Zenas. The very mention of these names indicates the growth of the Christian movement.

The final word concerning occupations shows clearly the duty of members of the Christian Church to contribute to the support of those devoted to the work of the ministry.

The closing benediction harmonizes with the opening salutation. It is a benediction of grace, the only difference being that whereas at the beginning it was addressed to Titus, at the close all those to whom he ministered were included. For fulfilment of the work as steward of the house of God, and for the Church's submission, grace is needed and supplied.

Philemon

PHILEMON

The letter to Philemon is of a personal nature. In all probability Philemon was a native of Colossæ, and a member of the Church there. While the letter is addressed to him, his whole household and the whole Church were included.

The apostle began by expressing his thankfulness for Philemon. His purpose was to seek an action by Philemon in harmony with his Christian position. The real reason of the letter emerges when Paul appealed to Philemon, rather than commanded him, to certain action in the case of Onesimus, his runaway slave. Paul based his appeal on his personal love, the fact that he was such a one as "Paul the aged"; and also on the change that had been wrought in the man Onesimus. He drew two portraits of the man by the use of two words. He had been "unprofitable." He was now "profitable," or, to be more correct, he was "well profitable," that is, completely so. Therefore the appeal to Philemon was to take Onesimus back because of the change that had taken place in him, and to receive him no longer as a slave but as a brother.

The letter closed with the expression of the apostle's hope that he would be able to visit Philemon, and the request that a lodging be prepared for him. Salutations from the little group who were with him in Rome and the benediction brought the letter to its close. The benediction had to do with grace, which is here described as "the grace of our Lord Jesus Christ." Of course, it was the grace of God, but it is here described as that of our Lord Jesus Christ, because in Him was manifested the effect of the grace of God in human life.

Hebrews

HEBREWS 1

The first words of this epistle plunge to the heart of the subject. Two truths are revealed: the first, God; the second, that God has revealed Himself. Two periods of revelation are referred to, that "of old time," and that "at the end of these days." These periods are contrasted. The first was characterized by diversity. The new is characterized by unity. The whole argument is to show the superiority of the speech that has come through the Son.

His glories are set forth in a sevenfold description. He is "Heir of all things," Creator of the ages, Effulgence of the glory of God, "the very Image of His Substance," the Upholder of all things, the Purifier of sins, joint Ruler with "the Majesty on high."

His superiority to all that had preceded Him is first shown with reference to angels. The argument occupies this and most of the next chapter. The subject is introduced by seven quotations from the Old Testament in which His relationship to God as Son, His superiority in the matter of the divine service, and His sharing of the divine throne, are set forth. The majority of the quotations are from the Psalms.

HEBREWS 2

Here we have the first of a series of warnings uttered in connection with the arguments. If the ministrations of angels had been of so steadfast a character, how much more the speech of the Son. The danger against which this section utters its warning is drifting away from this final speech. The inevitable answer to the question, "How shall we escape?" is that seeing that the Son has made the way of deliverance for those who have broken the law administered by angels, there is no hope of escape for those who refuse to hear and obey Him.

Continuing the argument concerning the superiority of the Son to the angels, the writer declares that for a period the Son had been made lower than the angels. Through this humiliation, and the victory wrought therein, He passed back to the place of sovereignty, into which He brings man, to whose level He had passed in becoming lower than the angels. Thus He is seen occupying the position of authority as the result of that descent wherein He took human form. Three quotations are given which prove His identification with men, even to the point of calling them brethren. Thus

He has taken His seat at the right hand of the Majesty on high, resuming His original position of supremacy, with the added right accruing from His humiliation and victory. He had passed angels in His great descent. He had passed them again in His glorious ascent. Thus the superiority of the Son to the angels is supremely established.

HEBREWS 3

The argument now passed to the second claim of superiority, that over all human leaders. He is first seen as superior to Moses and Joshua. He is "the Apostle" completely fulfilling the function represented by the work of these two; He is also "High Priest," thus realizing everything suggested in the position of Aaron.

The position of Moses was that of a servant in the house of God. His faithfulness was shown in that he made all things according to the pattern. The spiritual house of God consists of the "holy brethren" and the "partakers" of the divine calling, and over them Christ is the Head.

Then follows a second solemn exhortation and warning. The readers are reminded by another quotation from their Scriptures of what had happened in the wilderness. The heart was hardened by unbelief, and therefore they were shut out from rest. In view of this example these readers are warned against the peril of being "hardened by the deceitfulness of sin."

The argument of warning returned to the first illustration, and shows how many who came out of Egypt never entered the promised land. This was because they had sinned. The sin is described as disobedience, the disobedience of unbelief. If, then, because of unbelief in the servant Moses, men were excluded from rest, how much more will that be so in the case of those who are disobedient to the Son.

HEBREWS 4

The picture of the whole generation who perished in the wilderness is brought to mind, and the question is, What did they lack, and why did they perish? They did not lack the message of "good tidings." It was preached to them. They did not fail to hear the message. The reason was that "the word of hearing did not profit them, because it was not united by faith with them that heard." Where faith is lacking, the provisions of God are unavailing.

Nevertheless, the purpose of God abides, and seeing that some have failed, the offer is repeated, this time by the superior speech of the Son. Therefore the urgent appeal in the first verse.

Closely in connection, the writer deals with the superiority of the Son over Joshua. He completed that in human leadership in which Moses failed. He led the people in. Nevertheless they did not enter into rest.

The declaration unquestionably concerns the Son. "He that is entered into His rest hath Himself also rested from His works, as God did from His."

The writer then turned to the question of the superiority of Christ as Priest. Christ is revealed as One who has passed through the heavens, and now is seated at the right hand of the Majesty on high. On the basis of that believers are urged to hold fast their confession. The Son, as Priest, is "touched with the feeling of our infirmities." The second appeal, therefore, is, "Let us draw near with boldness." The boldness referred to is confidence in the understanding and tenderness and ability of the enthroned Priest.

HEBREWS 5

The writer proceeded with the same argument as he instituted a contrast.

The two essential qualifications of a priest are capacity for sympathy, and the vocation of God. These are perfectly fulfilled in Christ, who is appointed by God to Priesthood after the order of Melchisedek. His sympathy is demonstrated by the declarations concerning Him that through "prayers," "supplications," "strong crying," "tears," He entered into all human experiences, and learned obedience through the things which He suffered. It should be noted that this does not mean that He learned to be obedient, but that He entered into the experience of obedience. Through this process He became "the Author of eternal salvation."

Having thus introduced the great subject, the writer declared his sense of the difficulty he experienced in dealing with it, because his readers were dull of hearing, having to be taught when they should be teaching, having to be fed with milk when they should be receiving solid food.

HEBREWS 6

This chapter consists of the third appeal and warning. The appeal is that they should leave the first principles and press on to perfection. The things referred to were Jewish, and all have spiritual fulfilment in Christ. Then there occurs the solemn and indeed an awe-inspiring warning.

Much controversy has waged around these verses. There can be no doubt that those described are such as have been brought into living relationship with Christ. Of no unregenerate persons can it be said that they were "enlightened," "tasted of the heavenly gift," "tasted the good word of God, and the powers of the age to come." No person can be a partaker of the Holy Spirit save through faith in Jesus Christ, and all such are born again, and are members of Christ.

The peril described is not stumbling, but falling away, that is, final and positive apostasy. The danger is deliberate, ultimate rejection of Christ.

The supreme illustration of the persistence of faith in the Old Testament is Abraham's. His encouragement was God's oath. Ours is that selfsame oath, ratified in the Person of the High Priest who has entered into the Holy Place as our Representative.

HEBREWS 7

The writer now takes up again the subject of the Priesthood of Jesus after the order of Melchisedek. Melchisedek is called "Priest of the Most High." His name means king of righteousness. He is called "King of Peace." The one instance of the exercise of his priesthood in the Old Testament reveals him administering sustenance, imparting blessing, and instituting communion. The similarity between him and his priesthood and Christ and His priesthood is so remarkable that it does appear as though the appearance of Melchisedek to Abraham was one of the Christophanies of the Old Testament.

The writer then turned to the subject of the superiority of Christ to the priesthood of Levi. That priesthood had failed to perfect anything. The right of the Priesthood of the Son was vested with His own Personality. He had an endless life, and this implies the absolute perfection of His nature, and, consequently, the continuity of His Person. The superiority of the Priesthood of the Son consists in that through Him a better hope was given to men through which they might draw nigh unto God, and so ultimately realize perfection.

The contrast is made vivid in two particulars. First as to the oath of appointment; and, second, as to the perpetuity of the office. Beyond the Son there is no necessity for any priest, for that God has appointed Him by oath forever. He is therefore "able to save to the uttermost," because "He ever liveth to make intercession."

HEBREWS 8

Having established the fact of the superiority of Christ, the argument now proceeds to deal with the superiority of the relationships consequent thereupon. The central verity is set forth in the words, "We have such a High Priest." Because this is so, His ministry must be superior in all its details. It is so in the place of its exercise. In position and localization He is not on earth. He rules over the whole spiritual House, "which House are we," in which God dwells, and in which He is the perfect and prevailing Priest.

The result of this more excellent ministry and place of ministry is a better covenant. In a quotation from Jeremiah the writer claims that in and through Christ the new order which prophets saw and foretold is realized.

The superiority of the covenant is threefold. First, it is written on the heart, and so is internal rather than external. Second, it is inclusive, for its far-reaching scope men will not need to teach each other concerning God. Finally, it is based on that incalculable blessings of the forgiveness of sins, the putting away of those things which so long had stood between man and God. The writer ends by saying that the old "is nigh unto vanishing away" because of the coming of the new.

HEBREWS 9

Because of the better priesthood and the better covenant a better worship is established. First, the sanctuary is described. Christ is set forth as the One who has entered into a greater Tabernacle through a greater service. His entry into the Holy Place is "once for all," because He has for ever dealt with sin.

The superiority of the sacrifice is emphasized, for it is able to "cleanse the conscience from dead works to serve the living God." The words used here to describe the central mystery of redemption are arresting. Christ is seen suggestively as Priest and Sacrifice. He offered Himself "through the eternal Spirit."

On the basis of this great sacrifice the new Priest had entered into the Holy Place. A testament or a covenant always becomes operative through death. Moses had initiated the service of the tabernacle of old by the shedding of blood. So Christ, "once at the end of the ages," having "put away sin by the sacrifice of Himself," initiated a new covenant of life through the gateway of death.

The pre-eminent thought in this section is that now in the priesthood of Christ a place of worship, unlocalized and unlimited, is provided. Wherever is found the soul who will come to God through Him, there He is as Priest, with the value of His own sacrifice, providing redemption and acceptance; and, moreover, having exhausted judgment in the process of His death, He hides from coming judgment all who trust in Him, changing the dread of that awful assize into the glorious hope of His own second appearing.

HEBREWS 10

The writer now deals with the subject of the better worship. In this connection he again quotes from the prophecy of Jeremiah in order to emphasize the prediction of the new covenant concerning the forgiveness of sins. Through this offering and sacrifice of Christ, the worshipers are brought into a relationship with God in which there is no more consciousness of sin, but, instead, a delight to do God's will, and so is fulfilled the second part of Jeremiah's prediction.

The provision made in Christ lays

a new responsibility on those who understand it. The veil has been rent, and a way has been made into the Holiest of all. Those who enter through this rent veil may do so boldly. That responsibility is described as threefold, "Let us draw near," "Let us hold fast," "Let us consider one another."

A solemn warning dealing with the sin of possible apostasy follows. Those guilty of such sin have "trodden under foot the Son of God . . . counted the blood . . . an unholy thing . . . done despite unto the spirit of grace." If this great way of salvation, this mightiest sacrifice of all is refused, no other sacrifice remains. The work of Jesus is God's uttermost possible for the salvation of man. If this be rejected, by such rejection man deliberately chooses for himself the only possible alternative, which is the vengeance of God. Concerning that the writer says, "It is a fearful thing to fall into the hands of the living God."

The warning ends with words full of hope. They had endured, taking joyfully the spoiling of their possessions, and are urged not to cast away their boldness. Faith was the abiding condition of the old economy, and so it is also of the new.

HEBREWS 11

Then follows a series of illustrations of the power of faith taken from the history of the Hebrew people. The first is that by faith men know that the ages have been fashioned by the Word of God.

After this comes the rapid survey of the triumphs of faith. Abel worshiped on the basis of sacrifice. Enoch walked in days of general defection. Noah worked as against all outward appearance. Abraham obeyed the divine call, obtained a son contrary to the course of Nature, and offered him at the apparent risk of bitterest disappointment. Isaac predicted the line of divine activity. Jacob blessed the sons of Joseph. Joseph provided for moving his bones to the land of his fathers. Moses was preserved as a child by his parents, made choice as a man, and established the nation. The nation itself made its exit from Egypt, and, finally, found its way into Canaan. Then comes the story of a woman outside the covenant who, acting on the principle of faith, was included in the record of its triumphs.

Then comes a list of names, every one of which has its own story of triumph through faith; and, immediately succeeding, a list of deeds and victories accomplished in the same power. The pathway of faith had been a pathway of suffering, and those who have thus endured are described as being such "of whom the world was not worthy."

The fruitfulness of faith in all these instances is yet more clearly revealed in that none of them received the promise. Faith was strong enough to enable them to endure even to the end, postponing the final realization until the purposes of God should be wrought out in the history of men.

HEBREWS 12

After this rapid survey of the past, the writer makes his great appeal. It is that we "consider Him" who is "the Author and Perfecter of faith."

The final appeals of the Epistle fall into four sections. In the first two the causes of weakening faith are recognized (verses 4-13 and 14-17). In the third we have an epitomized statement of the arguments of encouragement (verses 18-24), and, finally, we have the last appeal and warning (verses 25-29).

Dealing with their suffering, the writer rather reminded them that they had not yet "resisted unto blood." Glancing at the passage we notice these words, "chastening," "chasteneth," "chastening," "chasteneth," "chastening," "chasten," "chastened," "chastening." The repetition of the word is the insistence on the recognition of a principle. It suggests discipline which is a method of fatherhood, and, though a process of pain, a means to a glorious end. Another cause of failure may be disputes or differences, hence the injunction to "follow after peace . . . and . . . sanctification." Maintenance of peace always depends on the realization of sanctification in experience.

The writer graphically states the contrast between the old and the new economy in order to strengthen faith that may be wavering. The old was filled with majesty, as the descriptive phrases prove; but those who believe in Christ are not come to these things, but rather to Mount Zion, and the realm of spiritual realization.

The ultimate exhortation of the epistle then occurs. The Epistle opened with a declaration that God had spoken, and now the writer says, "See that ye refuse not Him that speaketh."

HEBREWS 13

The last chapter contains a series of general exhortations. It is evident that the letter was sent to those whose faith was being challenged and weakened, and whose love, therefore, was cooling. These are enjoined to love in its simple fact, then in its manifestation toward the stranger, and, finally, in tenderness to those who are in bonds. Paul enjoined them to purity and contentment.

Having dealt with matters of their inner life, he showed their true relationship toward teachers, truth, worship, service, and the overseers of the flock. Jesus Christ, concerning whom the whole epistle has been written, is declared to be unchanging. Therefore they, too, are not to be carried away by strange teaching.

The final words of the letter constitute a great prayer combined with personal messages. Paul's prayer for them is that they may be made perfect to do the will of God. The ground of confidence in this prayer is made clear by the statements surrounding the petition itself. It is prayer to the God of peace, who, through Jesus Christ, is "working in us that which is well-pleasing in His sight." Everything closes with the inclusive benediction, "Grace be with you all."

James

JAMES 1

James wrote to Christians in the midst of temptation and trial. He showed first that the issue of testing is that they "may be perfect and entire, lacking in nothing." It is therefore to be looked upon as a means of blessing and received with joy. He clearly pointed out that God is never the Author of temptation as enticement toward evil, and in a passage full of remarkable force revealed the process of such temptation. It is an appeal through desire to some perfectly legitimate need of life, but suggests its attainment in illegitimate ways. If such enticement be rejected the victory is won.

James showed that the Word of God is the stronghold for faith in meeting temptation. Therefore the Word should be received "with meekness." Thus, and thus only, will it be possible under temptation to save the soul. James employed the figure of a man looking at himself in a mirror, and going away, and forgetting his likeness, which is graphic. The man who endures temptation is he who, looking into the law of liberty, continues therein.

This action dealing with the effect of faith on temptation closes with a remarkable contrast between the false and the true in religion. The word "religious" here occurs only in the New Testament, and is a somewhat remarkable word. It indicates all manner of external observances, and in this connection stands in direct contrast to the phrase, "pure religion." In all pure religion the deepest fact is the recognition of relationship to God, and this expresses itself in compassion, which drives men into touch with those in affliction and consecration, which keeps them unspotted from the world.

The whole section teaches us that temptation is not from God, but that in the divine economy it is overruled for the good of the saint.

JAMES 2

Proceeding, James dealt with the effect of faith on conduct. It makes it impossible to show any respect of persons on the ground of the possession of worldly wealth. To show such respect shows that the faith of Jesus Christ is not held. In His eyes wealth or poverty is nothing. The corrective, therefore, for such failure is to be found in the exercise of a faith like that of Christ, which, seeing God, respects men, and gives them the place of honor according to their relationship to Him.

In this connection is found one of the strongest passages in the whole of the letter, revealing the value of faith, and its utter uselessness where it fails to express itself in works. A faith that does not issue in conduct harmonizing with its profession cannot save, is dead in itself, and is barren. The interrelationship between faith and works is illustrated in the cases of Abraham and Rahab, the one the father of the faithful, and the other a woman outside the covenant. In each case faith was the vital principle, but it was demonstrated to be such by the works which it wrought. A faith which does not express itself in conduct is as dead as a body from which the spirit has departed.

The closing declaration summarizes all the section, and is, indeed, the central truth of the whole epistle. Faith will produce action true to the word which it professes to believe. If there be contradictory action, there is therefore no true faith. What man believes he actually does. Therefore true conduct is ever the outcome of true faith.

JAMES 3

The writer now proceeded to show the effect of faith on speech. Beginning with the warning against every man setting up to teach, he proceeded to deal with the power of speech. He likened the tongue to the bit in the mouth of a horse, and to the helm of a ship. Surely a contrast between the tongue set on fire by hell and the tongue of fire is suggested. Speech ever waits for inspiration, and such inspiration comes from the depths of evil or from the Spirit of the living God. Follows a contrast between the wisdom which is described as being "earthly, animal, devilish," and the true wisdom in which the deepest fact is purity. The resulting purity is the character described as "peaceable," that is, desiring peace; "gentle," that is, forbearing; "easy to be entreated," that is, amenable to reason; "full of mercy," that is, capable of forgiving; and "full of good fruits," that is, actually engaged in kindness; "without variance," that is, consistent in the sense of being even and regular in tone and temper; "without hypocrisy," that is, without deceit or acting a part. Evil wisdom produces tempest and conflict, strife and malice. The wisdom from above has the manifestations of calm and certainty, of quietness and love.

The closing words, "the fruit of righteousness is sown in peace for them that make peace," suggest the propagative power of peace. All this teaching shows the effect of faith on that natural character from which speech springs, and therefore it reveals the effect of faith on speech itself.

JAMES 4

The writer now dealt with the effect of faith on character. Everything depends on desire. To attempt to satisfy a natural desire without reference to God is futile, and issues in internal conflict and outward warfare and strife. The writer inquired, "Doth the Spirit which He made to dwell in us long unto envying?" It is self-evident that the Spirit of God does not create desire which issues in envying.

The divine corrective of such a condition is, first, that God "giveth more grace . . . to the humble." In the infinite grace of God there is ample supply to counteract all the forces of evil. The responsibility is revealed in a series of injunctions. With regard to Satan, first must be submission to God, and then resistance. It is not enough, however, to draw nigh to God and then to be careless in conduct. "Draw nigh to God, and He will draw nigh unto you." In the sense of the resulting nearness it is possible to cleanse the hands, that is, to correct the conduct; and to purify the heart, that is, to make right the character.

Such attitudes of life will result, first, in right relationship with man. Living faith in God ever creates in the heart of man the consciousness that his judgment of another may be partial and mistaken, but only God knows the deepest facts. Therefore faith in God means a dependence on Him that is actual and active. It is in connection with this argument that the principle is laid down that "to him therefore that knoweth to do good and doeth it not, to him it is sin." The reference is to the saying, "If the Lord will." Thus it is shown that the neglect of any right habit, even in speech, is of the nature of sin.

JAMES 5

Approaching the conclusion of his letter, the writer addressed a terrible indictment and solemn warning to the rich. He showed the failure of possessions, and how they may become the curse of life.

Selfish life which results in oppression of the poor and consequent robbery of God is known by God. The teaching reveals remarkably the divine passion for justice.

To those who suffer, the writer addressed words full of tender comfort. He called them to patience. All that was said at the beginning of the letter concerning the value of trial in the life is taken for granted. Remembering that God is working through all these processes toward bringing the fruit to maturity and ripeness, it is necessary that His people have patience.

The final paragraph of the epistle contains advice and instructions for differing experiences and needs. "Is any . . . suffering?" "Is any . . . cheerful?" "Is any . . . sick?" Those who are in suffering are charged to pray. Those who are in circumstances of good cheer are to express themselves in praise to God. In dealing with sickness it is most important to remember that here sickness is connected with sin; the raising of the sick is united with forgiveness of sin. The particular cases of sickness were those which were evidently the result of wrongdoing. In such cases the elders were to be called to act. The use of oil is in itself the indication for such necessity. Any other interpretation would make it a matter of superstition. The Christian man, however, will never depend on natural means alone. While recognizing the place and importance of means, the divine action is also recognized as the ultimate in all healing. The value of this exercise of confession and forgiveness is emphasized by the words with which the epistle closes.

I Peter

I PETER 1

Like the letter of James, the purpose of this was to establish those who were passing through a period of suffering and testing. In his introduction the apostle used the name Jesus had given him, "Peter." He described those to whom he wrote as "elect . . . according to the foreknowledge of God," and "in sanctification of the Spirit." He approached the subject of the testing of their faith by reminding them of the heavenly nature of their vocation. The final issue thereof is an inheritance, all the characteristics of which are in direct contrast to the inheritances of earth.

Approaching the actual fact of their trials, the apostle turned the light of the great hope on them. Joy should be theirs in the consciousness that the issue of the testing would be the vindication of their faith at the revelation of Jesus Christ.

This wonderful salvation had been the subject of inquiries and research by the prophets of old, and angels desired to look into the matter. Having set the testing of their confidence in relation to its purpose, the apostle proceeded to practical exhortation, and dealt, first, with individual responsibility, and afterward with relative responsibility. The personal attitude is described as girding up the loins of the mind, with hope perfectly set on assured consummation. The strongest argument is then used. It is that they have been redeemed, brought from slavery into the liberty of children. That redemption was provided at infinite cost. The apostle then passes to relative injunctions, and the first calls them to the maintenance of unfeigned love of the brethren.

I PETER 2

In order to obey the injunctions, those to whom Peter writes are urged to put away all such things as are contrary to the spirit of love. In order to do this they will long for the sustenance of the Word.

All this leads to the subject of the testing of their confidence. Describing the Church as a building, Peter declared the cornerstone is the living Christ, from whom the preciousness is derived, which is to manifest the excellencies of God to the world. The description of the Church is systematic and exhaustive. It is a race, and this suggests its life principle. It is a priesthood, and so has right of access to God. It is a nation, and so is under His government. It is a possession, and so is actually indwelt by Him.

The application of these principles

immediately follows. The first result will be abstention from fleshly lusts, and behaving themselves among outsiders in a seemly manner; they will silence slander, and vindicate God. Peter then showed what should be the relation of the separated nation to the world powers. It was to be submission to authority. In short, crisp sentences he charged them, "Honour all men. Love the brotherhood. Fear God. Honour the king."

Then he showed how these things would apply. Servants will yield obedience to their masters as unto Christ. The service rendered will be the opportunity of manifesting the very Spirit of Christ.

I PETER 3

The marriage relation was then dealt with, and special emphasis was laid on the fact that the true adornment of woman is found in her character rather than in her dress. Husbands are charged to dwell with their wives according to knowledge. The final reason for the fulfilment of this ideal is that prayers be not hindered.

Passing to the subject of suffering which invariably follows loyalty to Christ, the apostle quoted from the Psalms. That shows that the eyes of the Lord are on the righteous and His ears open to their supplication. With regard to evil, His face is on them. In the light of these facts the power of any to harm the followers of God is challenged. One supreme responsibility rests on them, and it is beautifully expressed in the words, "Sanctify in your hearts Christ as Lord." The issue of such loyalty will be that the very persons who revile will be put to shame.

In strengthening his brethren for suffering the apostle had cited the example of Christ. In this connection occurs a statement which has given rise to differing interpretations, and even to controversy. The simple meaning of it is that when He was put to death in the flesh, Christ passed into a new life of the spirit. In that life He went and preached to the spirits in prison. What His message was we are not told. Why only those disobedient in the days of Noah are mentioned is not stated. What the purpose or result of Christ's preaching was, is not revealed. On all these points we may form our own conclusions, but we have no authority for anything approaching dogmatic teaching.

I PETER 4

The whole force of the argument which the apostle has used in speaking thus of the Christ was to show these saints how through suffering Christ reached a triumph, and to call them to arm themselves with His mind. Let them act by ceasing from sin and all the gratifications of the flesh which had characterized their past.

Injunctions followed the argument. The light of the future is turned on the past, "The end of all things is at hand." The effect of this certainty is then stated in its personal and relative aspects. The individual is to be of sound mind and sober unto prayer. The ultimate purpose is that God may be glorified in all things.

The apostle's last words of comfort for those in the midst of testing is that "fiery trial" is not "strange." The process is watched by God and made a means of grace.

Such results, however, do not follow suffering, which is the consequence of sin. Where persecution is the result of relationship to Christ let there be no shame, but rather rejoicing. Let them accept the name and glorify God in it by fulfilling its true meaning, and manifesting itself in life. Seeing that judgment begins at the house of God, there is no room to doubt the punishment of those who in evil life persecute its members. Remembering that these fires of persecution are watched by God, and never allowed to harm His own, let them commit their souls to Him. Thus the attitude of quiet patience is enjoined on all who suffer for the sake of the Name they bear.

I PETER 5

Finally, the apostle proceeded to strengthen his brethren for conflict. The first matter dealt with was the general orderliness of the Church. He enjoined the elders that they care for the flock. Their office is twofold, to attend or feed, and to keep watchful oversight. They are not to lord it over the flock, but are to serve the flock, not, indeed, as under the authority of the flock, but under that of the Lord and Master, the Chief Shepherd. The younger are to be in subjection, and that is ever in the Church of God the place of honor. Let there be humility, and beyond that no anxiety, for "God careth."

Having thus dealt with the orderliness of the Church, the apostle turned to the conflict. The adversary is named, and his method is described. He is neither careless nor neutral. His business is the destruction of all good. He is seeking whom he may devour. The attitude of the Christian toward this foe is to be soberness, and watchfulness, actual conflict, steadfastness in faith. The soldier must never be off duty. Seeking the enemy must be answered by watching the saint. Moreover, there must be actual fighting, and that can be only as the soldier stands firm and strong in faith.

A very beautiful incentive to fighting is given in conclusion. We are not alone. Our brethren in the world are all fighting. Our battle is not our own merely. It is theirs also. They fight for us, and we for them. Our defeat harms them as well as ourselves. The epistle closes with some personal words, and the final benediction of peace.

II Peter

II PETER 1

This Epistle was addressed to the same persons as was the first. Its purpose was to strengthen them in view of dangers threatening them within the Church. The apostle addressed them as having "like precious faith" with himself. He first reminded them of great principles of preservation. All things pertaining to life and godliness are granted through the knowledge of Him who called them by His glory and virtue. Because of this perfect provision the saints are called to diligence in the development of their resources. Faith is the root principle, and this must be developed until it reaches the ultimate fruitage, which is love.

As the apostle wrote, he was conscious of his approaching departure. He was remembering the glory that had flamed on him on the mount of transfiguration. On that mount he had heard the Lord speak of His exodus. He now used the same word in referring to his own departure. On the mount he had seen the "power" and "coming" of the Lord Jesus, and here he dealt with those two great facts. What he had then seen had confirmed the prophecies of the past, which had been a lamp shining in a dark place.

II PETER 2

Turning to the subject of the perils threatening the Church, two are referred to—false teachers, and a materialization of mind which follows on such teaching. As in old days there were false prophets, so we are told there will be false teachers. Hence the necessity for watchfulness. The teachers referred to are those who deny the Lord. The apostle illustrated the effect of such false interpretation by the example of Lot, who, being a righteous man, yet lost his influence in Sodom.

In burning and searching words he described the characteristics of those whom he had in mind. After the severest denunciation he pictured them in their luxurious living, giving themselves over to every form of license. Balaam is given as an illustration of the evil of the love of hire. By two phrases he described graphically such teachers. They are "springs" luring thirsty souls with the hope of satisfaction, but "without water." They are "mists driven by a storm," and this tells the deepest truth concerning these men, who, so far from ministering rest and peace, are themselves servants of unrest and disturbance.

We find here no dainty handling

of false teaching. The apostle shows that the effect of false teaching is ever the denial of the power of Christ. Denying His Lordship issues in every form of evil. To deny the Lord in any particular is to loosen the bondage of the soul to Him, and to open the door for the incoming of all evil.

II PETER 3

False teaching which denies the power of Christ issues in false thinking which denies the Coming of Christ. There will be mockers who will walk in lust and make sport of the great hope of the Church, declaring that things will ever continue as they have continued. To strengthen his readers against this peril, the apostle reminded them of the prophecies, and the commandment of the Lord, and said further that what appears to be delay is due to the long-suffering of God, with whom time does not exist.

The day of the Lord will come. It will be destructive. It will be constructive. We may hasten that day by holy living and godliness. The results of this knowledge should be diligence to create the character for which He will seek, to create it by loyalty to His Lordship, and patience during the delay.

The final exhortation is twofold. "Beware." To be forewarned is indeed to be forearmed. The certainty of the truth of the things of Christ will enable the trusting soul to detect error and to produce a carefulness and steadfastness in life. That marks the attitude of caution. "Grow!" Standing in grace and knowledge the soul is in the soil and atmosphere for development. Let there be growth by response to these things. Growth is the condition of increasing strength and abiding steadfastness.

The writer ends with a brief and comprehensive doxology of glory to the Lord and Saviour in the present and the future; that is, in response to His power, and by way of His Coming. The soul is established against all possibilities of perils in Him both now and forever.

I John

I JOHN 1

This is possibly the last apostolic message to the whole Church. It is complementary to the Gospel of John. Its subject is fellowship with God, into which believers are introduced through their union with Christ.

The whole fact of the mission of our Lord is declared to be a manifestation of eternal life. Concerning this John wrote, "We have heard," "we have seen," "we beheld," "our hands handled." The purpose of the manifestation was to bring men into fellowship with God. Through the manifestation of eternal life, and our reception of it by faith, we have fellowship with the Father. This means fellowship in Light, Love, and Life.

The first great message of the "word of life" to men is that "God is light." The place of fellowship therefore is that of walking in the light of God. In God there is no darkness, neither can there be. If, then, "men love darkness rather than the light," they are excluded from the fellowship of God.

Because of perpetual imperfection even in our most holy things there is need of a constant cleansing, which is provided in the "blood of Jesus His Son." Light makes sin known. The sins of the past are forgiven, and the soul is cleansed from all unrighteousness.

I JOHN 2

Affirming that the purpose of his writing is that we sin not, the writer declared that even if we sin, provision is made by which it may be put away. The tests whereby we may know our relation to light are stated with regard to God, and with regard to our fellow men. The proof that we know God is that we keep His commandments. It is possible to know a great deal about God intellectually and still live in rebellion against Him. God is known in His Son. To be joined to Him and to abide in Him is to be transformed to His likeness. The supreme commandment, then, is to love. Love of the brethren proves a walk in light. Hatred of the brethren demonstrates darkness.

In dealing with the perils of darkness John made the groundwork of his appeal their experience in Christ. That appeal was made to "little children," "young men," "fathers." These are warned against worldliness, which is described as "the lust of the flesh, the lust of the eyes, and the vainglory of life." Fellowship with God means the love of the Father, which makes

Him the supreme consciousness of the soul. Having that love, the things of the world pass away.

The second peril to fellowship is the Antichrist. The spirit of Antichrist is to deny that Jesus is the Christ, which involves the denial of the Father and the Son. Any system of teaching which makes Jesus anything less than He is set forth to be in the Gospel writings is the expression of Antichrist. The Church of God needs ever to be on the watch against such tendencies and such teachings. To be influenced by purely human philosophy and wisdom will ever bring the Church into bondage to Antichrist. Therefore, let the "little children abide in Him," that so at His Coming there may be boldness and not shame.

I JOHN 3

The letter now passed to a discussion of the fellowship of the saints with God as love. The hope born of love will have as its inevitable result the purification of those possessing it. The apostle shows that in Christ there is no need for anyone to sin, and that if one does he violates the very life principle which makes him a child of God. The proof of fellowship with God as love, therefore, is to be found in righteousness of conduct and love manifested toward our brethren.

The result of such fellowship with God as love will inevitably be the world's hatred of us. The love of God for man is spiritual and perfect, and according to light, which always rebukes sin. It is this element which stirs up the hatred of men. Notwithstanding this, the hatred of the world is to be answered by loving, and that expressed even in material matters. Our love is to be in deed and in truth, rather than in word and with the tongue. The test by which we may ourselves know we are of the truth is a heart at rest before God. Doubt or uncertainty of mind is ever productive of harm. Boldness toward God is the result of a quiet and peaceable experience. The place of peace and power is abiding in Him. Abiding in Him means obedience: "he that keepeth His commandments abideth in Him." The apostle names the commandments. They are two in number, and include all other matters. The first is that we should believe in Jesus Christ, and the second that we should love one another.

I JOHN 4

Two closely related perils threaten our fellowship with God as love, false prophets and the spirit which actuates them. Teaching is to be tested by the indwelling Spirit. All who refuse to confess that Jesus is Lord do so because they are of the world. At the root of every heresy concerning Jesus there has been worldliness in some form. To degrade the Person of Christ is to shake the foundations of faith. There can be no character which is according to God when the creed concerning Christ is a denial of the Spirit's test.

The apostle then makes an appeal by the employment of two arguments. First, that the nature of God is love, and therefore those who are His children should love. The second, that God has manifested His love.

The argument and appeal now issue in the declaration that no man has seen God, but the essence of the unseen God has been revealed in Christ, and now is to be revealed through His children. There is only one manifestation of God which is prevailing and powerful, and that is love. This is seen in the Son. All the glories and perfections of the Son are ours in Him. That is the apostle's consciousness of the glorious perfection of the provision which lends sternness to the words, "If a man say, I love God, and hateth his brother, he is a liar."

To every person in actual union with God in Christ, love is possible. This, moreover, is not a privilege merely; it is a stern duty. The world still waits for the knowledge of God, which can come only through His revelation in the love of His children.

I JOHN 5

The final subject is our fellowship with God in life. This is fundamental, and is shown to be so. The relationship between the life of God and the love of God is self-evident, and that is equally true concerning the life of God and the light of God.

Thus is brought out most clearly the true nature of Christianity. It is first and last and always life. Fellowship with the light of God is not possible to those who are alienated from His life. The experience and activity of His love never come to those abiding in spiritual death.

Seeing that the fundamental aspect of fellowship with God is fellowship in life, and, moreover, seeing that man enters into life by believing, the apostle now gives the witness on which faith takes hold. The first is the truth that Jesus Christ came by water and blood. The reference is certainly to two essential features in the coming and work of Jesus. The water signifies the purity of His human life as consecrated to God and symbolized in His baptism by John. The blood refers to that passion baptism which was the supreme occasion and clear evidence of Jesus' own fellowship with God in love.

Three bear witness to these things: the Spirit of life, the water of light, the blood of love. These three agree in One, and that One is the Son of God.

The concluding words of the writer declare the reason for his writing. His purpose was confirmation of their confidence in God, which was calm and contained. The chief exercise of that confidence is manifested in intercession, that is, in prayer for others who are not walking in light. All closes with the group of certainties, and an injunction against idols.

II John

II JOHN

This letter to the "elect lady" is principally concerned with the Truth, the word being constantly repeated. The apostle wrote with conviction of the importance of Truth in its effect on life. In declaring his joy that the children of the elect lady were walking in Truth, he wrote the central commandment, "that we love one another." Love is obedience to light, that is, to Truth. It is of the utmost importance that love should be of the true nature. Any consent to darkness out of a so-called charity is not love. Loyalty to the Lord is the true way of love, and anything which compromises that is false, and eventually violates love.

The reason for the letter is discovered in the words, "deceivers are gone forth." The heresy of these teachers was the denial of the Incarnation, "Jesus Christ coming in the flesh." The apostle referred to supposedly progressive teaching. There were those who were "going on." Progress which denies fundamental Truth is retrogression. All development which is destruction is disastrous. So important is this that the apostle urged that no hospitality or greeting is to be given to those who by false teaching imperil the life and light and love of the believer.

The teaching of the letter may thus be summarized. Christianity is love. Love is dependent on the light of Truth. To deny the Truth is to make love impossible. The continued experience of fellowship is dependent on the continued fact of fellowship in love and light and life. The continued fact of fellowship is proved by the continued experience of fellowship.

III John

III JOHN

It is probable that the Gaius to whom this letter was sent is the Gaius of Corinth (I Corinthians 1:14). Its subject is hospitality as revealing love, and the apostle uttered a warning against schism. As in the letter to the "elect lady," the keynote is Truth. In that John warned against false hospitality. Here he commands true hospitality. He charged Gaius to set forth certain evangelists "worthily of God." This is a remarkable phrase, and probably means, first, that Gaius was to see in these men the messengers of God, and, second, that he was to act as a child of God.

In striking contrast to Gaius stands Diotrephes. The whole truth about him is revealed in the words "Diotrephes, who loveth to have the preeminence." That is the essential violation of love. His heterodoxy was of spirit and temper rather than of intellect.

Another character introduced in the letter is Demetrius. In all probability he was the bearer of the letter, and John quoted him in direct contrast to Diotrephes.

The central statement of the epistle is in the words, "He that doeth good is of God: he that doeth evil hath not seen God." Doing good is to be interpreted by the subject of the letter, namely, hospitality. Those who thus act in love do so because they are of God, that is, related to Him in the fellowship of life. Such were Gaius and Demetrius. Those who act selfishly do so because they have no fellowship with God. The writer closes with words anticipatory of a meeting, and a message of peace.

Jude

JUDE

The subject of this epistle is apostasy. Apostasy is shown to be wilful return to ungodliness. Two classes are dealt with: those who "kept not," and are therefore "kept"; and those who "keep themselves," and are "kept from stumbling."

The faith was in peril, and Jude wrote urging that they should contend earnestly for the faith. The faith for which he pleaded was a life of loyalty to the Lord. The danger was created by the presence and influence of certain men who were making the grace of God an occasion for lasciviousness.

Three illustrations were given of the evil results of apostasy, those of Israel, angels, and the cities of the plain.

The fundamental wrong of the men referred to was insubordination: they were "setting at nought dominion, and railing at dignitaries." The influence of such men is like that of Cain, hatred and murder; of Balaam, seduction and lying; of Korah, envy and rebellion. In a passage full of fiery force, Jude denounced the evil of these ungodly men.

The subject of the true attitude of believers in face of all these perils is dealt with. First, there is to be recognition of the danger. It has two distinguishing marks. The first is that their influence is that "they make separations," and the second is that their temper is sensual, not spiritual. In the presence of these perils it is important that believers should "keep yourselves in the love of God." This is to be done by building on faith, praying in the Spirit, and looking for mercy.

There is a relative duty. "On some have mercy," that is, those in doubt. "Some save," that is, probably, such as had been snared. These are to be snatched from the fire. "On some have mercy with fear," refers possibly to the Libertines themselves.

The epistle closes with a glorious doxology which ascribes to God the Saviour all honor for that He is able to accomplish the salvation of His trusting ones in two ways, which are all-inclusive: as to continuity, "able to guard you from stumbling"; and as to consummation, "to set you before the presence of His glory."

Revelation

REVELATION 1

The theme of this Book is found in its opening sentence, "The Revelation of Jesus Christ." This should be borne in mind from first to last, and our object should be to see Him as He is here revealed.

John opens with a greeting to the seven churches in Asia, employing the words "grace" and "peace." He then emphasized that the words were from God through Christ, who claims to be "the Alpha and the Omega."

The first Revelation of Jesus Christ is of Him in His glory as John beheld Him in the isle that is called Patmos. He is seen as "a Son of man," nevertheless, in His Person removed from all others in the amazing splendor of His glory. Human were breasts, and head, and hair, and eyes, and feet, and voice, and hands, and mouth. Superhuman was the golden girdle, and pure wool-whiteness, the flame of fire, the burnished brass, the many waters, the holding of the stars, the activity of the sword, and the splendor of the sun.

The effect produced on John by the vision was to make him appear "as one dead." In that condition he heard the voice saying, "Fear not; I am the First and the Last, and the Living One; and I was dead, and behold, I am alive for evermore, and I have the keys of death and of Hades." The touch of that Hand, and the sound of that Voice equipped John to receive the unveiling which through him was to be given to the churches. Immediately following, the commission to write was given to John, and the relation between the Lord, His ministers, and the churches was set forth.

REVELATION 2

The next movement in the Book consists of the unveiling of the Lord in His relation with the Asian churches, and therefore with His Church. It is impossible in such brief notes as these necessarily are to deal with the details of these letters. They may be treated in two ways. The first is the revelation of differing Church conditions continuing throughout the whole of the Christian era. The second is treating them as covering successive periods in that same era. We may now follow the latter method.

The letter to the Church at Ephesus reveals apostolic conditions. The period was one of toil and patience, characterized by attempts to corrupt the doctrine by impure practice. It was a period in which the Church lost its first love.

The letter to the Church at Smyrna

covers the period of pagan persecution. The result of that persecution was the purification of the Church. The letter said that the Lord knew the difficulties of the situation and also that in spiritual power the Church was rich.

The letter to the Church at Pergamum covers the period during which the Church passed under the blighting patronage of an earthly power. Satan, the prince of the world, had his throne at the heart of the Roman Empire, and there the Church dwelt. There were those faithful souls who held fast the Name, but the church received and tolerated evil things.

The letter to the Church in Thyatira covers the central period in the Church's history. It was again a period of persecution. It covered what we speak of as the Dark Ages, in which a shameless harlot had usurped power in the Church of Jesus Christ.

REVELATION 3

The letter to the Church in Sardis covers the period of the Reformation. The Church was addressed as "dead." Yet there were things remaining which were not dead, but "ready to die." The address is largely to that living remnant. The charge to be watchful was not spoken to death, but to life. Christ's message to the period was a call to establish the things that remained.

The letter to the Church at Philadelphia covers the great period of evangelization which, ushered in by the Puritan movement, broke into its full power in the Evangelical Revival. In this time the Church is seen following her Lord as never before and cooperating with Him in His purposes.

The letter to the Church at Laodicea describes the final period prior to the advent of the Lord. It is, indeed, a dark and terrible picture. The Church is seen in a lukewarm condition. It is, however, the Church of the excluded Christ. Nevertheless, though excluded, He waits, knocking at the door and seeking admission.

In these seven letters there are two statements of our Lord's common to every one: "I know," and "I will." Thus He is seen presiding over the affairs of the Church with perfect understanding of conditions obtaining in the churches, and declaring His authority as He condemns or commends. He walks in the midst of the lampstands, holding in His hands the stars, and reveals both His knowledge and His authority in every message.

REVELATION 4

This chapter introduces us to the Revelation of Christ in His government of all world affairs in which a most remarkable vision of the heavenly order is presented to us. Everything is seen as surrounding the throne. Four and twenty elders are seated round about that throne. In an inner circle are four living creatures, symbolically described as, the first like a lion, the second like an ox, the third as a man, and the fourth like a flying eagle. The whole interest centers in Him who sits on the throne. No suggestion of shape is given. The appearance is likened to that of two precious stones, jasper and sardius.

The seer gazing on the heavenly order saw and heard perfect worship. The first note was uttered by the living ones; in the high and holy exercise they have no rest day or night, they offer glory and honor to Him who occupies the throne. This ascription is followed by prostration before the throne as elders cast their crowns before Him who sits thereon.

So ends the vision of the essential heavenly order. The symbolism is majestic and sublime, and while there may be many differing interpretations, the fundamental truths are self-evident. At the center of everything is an occupied throne. Gathered around it are those who appreciate the character of the One enthroned, and submit themselves to His government. The light of that vision shone for the seer on all the darkness and the gloom which presently was to be revealed to him.

REVELATION 5

In this chapter we have John's vision of the heavenly arrangement for earthly administration. The program lies in the hand of the One who sits on the throne. It is written, but sealed, and none can know it. This fact produced a great sorrow in John, so that he wept much, seeing that none was able to take the book and unloose the seals in order that the heavenly program might be carried out on the earthly level.

But now appeared the Lamb, whose advent was heralded by the most wonderful music it is possible to imagine. In the great movement the living ones and the elders and countless thousands of angels joined with the whole creation of God. As in the vision of the heavenly order in the previous chapter the fact of the Throne was the supreme revelation, here is revealed the equally glorious fact that the administration of the will of God in earthly affairs is committed to Christ.

If indeed the earlier vision of the heavenly order prevents panic, this vision inspires the heart with thrills of joy, and, perforce, causes it to express itself in ceaseless song. To see the scroll on which is written the story of the divine purpose and program in the pierced hand is to prepare to sing the song of assurance amid all the strange and otherwise perplexing events which are to follow. Holiness is thus established on the central throne, and acts through Him who is forever the Exponent of the Infinite Love. This leaves no room for doubt that whatever happens will be in accord with strictest justice and tenderest compassion. Happy is the man who in the midst of all the problems and perplexities of the present age remains forever conscious of the established heavenly order and of the method of earthly administration.

REVELATION 6

We now pass to that section of the Book in which, under the heavenly order by earthly administration, events proceed toward the great consummation. The Lamb, holding the book, breaks the seals.

The apostle heard the voice of one crying, "Come," and he beheld one who symbolized kingliness and goes "forth conquering, and to conquer." This is the Antichrist, Satan's most complete counterfeit of the Christ Himself.

The breaking of the second seal reveals the issue of the reign of Antichrist, war and carnage. The earth is plunged into all the terrors of the despotism of false authority.

The opening of the third seal brings a revelation of the want that follows war and carnage. A commercial despotism springs up which makes scarce the necessities of the millions and leaves untouched the oil and the wine which are the luxuries of the wealthy.

The breaking of the fourth seal shows the fourth phase of misrule. Death in all its most terrible forms, by sword, famine, pestilence, and by wild beasts, sweeps away the fourth part of the earth.

On the opening of the fifth seal John heard the cry of the saints slaughtered for their loyalty to the Word of God. The end is not yet.

The opening of the sixth seal is immediately followed by premonitions of the coming One. Over all the government of the false are signs of the established order of the true. The earth itself is shaken, the sun is blackened, the moon becomes as blood, the very stars of heaven fall. The effect on earth is one of absolute and abject terror.

REVELATION 7

Under the sixth seal we have seen and heard the portents of coming divine intervention. At the sounding of the seventh seal these will be resumed. Chapter seven describes a pause, and first deals with events on earth. Restraining angels are seen holding in check the hurricane of divine judgment.

After the account of the sealing of an elect number, the seer turns to contemplate a vision in heaven. It is that of a multitude so great that no man could number it. The multitude was diverse and yet unified. The diversity was of earth. National peculiarities, tribal characteristics, popular distinctions, and lingual differences are all still apparent. This earthly variety is incorporate in heaven's harmony. All stand before the throne, equally ready for service.

This great multitude is composed of those who had come out of the great tribulation. They are now seen in heaven. Very beautiful and tender is the description of their condition. Service has superseded suffering, and all sorrow has been banished. The salvation they celebrate has lifted them to a place of immeasurable blessedness.

REVELATION 8

The seventh and last seal on the scroll is broken. On earth uproar and strife follow as at Babel, but in heaven silence for half an hour. Then follows the sounding of trumpets initiating activities leading to the ultimate manifestation of the King.

At the sounding of the first trumpet a great storm breaks over the earth. At the sounding of the second, terrific disturbance occurs in the sea. At the sound of the third comes a terrible poisoning of the waters, bringing death. At the sounding of the trumpet of the fourth angel the third part of the light of the sun, moon, and stars is eclipsed. Through all these movements God is seen speaking to men of His throne and His power, which they have ignored. They all describe the operations of punitive judgment. Between the sounding of the fourth and fifth trumpets an eagle is seen proclaiming the coming of a threefold woe, but the fact of the proclamation is evidence of the long-suffering of God. That surely is the explanation of the eagle's proclamation in the midst of the sounding of trumpets.

REVELATION 9

At the sounding of the fifth trumpet the procedure of judgment takes a new form, passing from the material to the spiritual. The loosing of Satan is suggestive of the manifestation of satanic agency under the permission of God. Demons come forth, a terrible army, and scatter among the sons of men. It is noticeable that their power and time are limited by the government of God. The most terrible aspect of this visitation is that stricken men seek for death and are not able to find it.

The sounding of the sixth trumpet introduces a period of judgment in more terrible forms. Immense hosts of hitherto restrained powers of darkness sweep over the earth. The worship of demons is clearly mentioned in this connection as one of the manifestations of evil. The unholy traffic with the spirit world will issue in the devastation of men by these very spiritual agencies.

The closing declaration here is indeed terrible. Notwithstanding the awful dispensation of death, men unsmitten will not repent, but will continue in the same demon worship, with its consequent sins of murder, sorcery, and fornication.

REVELATION 10

Still under the period of the sixth trumpet, an interlude follows, chronicling events preparing for the sounding of the seventh and last trumpet. An angel comes to make a most important announcement, namely, that there shall be no more delay, that at the sounding of the seventh trumpet by the seventh angel the mystery of God will be finished.

The seer was now commanded to take the book and to eat it. This figure of eating the book is familiar, and suggests the feeding of the soul on the Word of God. It is to that that the seer was called anew. Such feeding brings men into fellowship with Christ and God. There is a fellowship in joy, and the book is sweet; in sorrow also, for there is bitterness; and yet again in service, for those so eating must prophesy. This threefold experience comes to all who study the unfoldings of divine purpose and process. The joy of the assurance of the divine government is ever accompanied by the signs of sorrow over the ruined and unrepentant and unbelieving. This twofold consciousness had its central manifestation in history when Jesus wept over Jerusalem and pronounced doom on it. Thus, as the revelation of the final judgments are about to be given, the man admitted to the secret of the Lord is called on to share in the joy and sorrow and service.

REVELATION 11

John is called on to measure the temple. In such measurements the court of the Gentiles is not to be recognized. It shows God dealing with the world through His chosen people.

The account of the two witnesses must be taken in connection with the recognition of the temple. Their work will be to tell the will of God to an age in rebellion against Him. No malice is able to accomplish the destruction of these witnesses until their work is ended. When that is done they are slain, and there is the appalling sound of an apostate race rejoicing in the silencing of the voices of truth. The triumph of evil is terrible, but it is short-lived. Ultimately, the witnesses are raised from the dead and taken into the heavenly places. Through them God sets the supernatural ministry of truth over against the supernatural influences of demon power and worship. When at last evil seems to triumph, it secures its own defeat.

At last, the seventh angel sounds and ushers in the final movements before the complete victory of the King. Voices in heaven declare that the rule of the world has been taken over by God and His Christ. The occasion gives cause for profoundest thankfulness, and the elders in the presence of the Supreme Royalty fall on their faces and worship. In their praise impending events are set forth, to be more fully described later.

REVELATION 12

In this and two subsequent chapters we have an interpolation in the account of the actual procedure. Two signs are described, a woman and a dragon, between whom is antagonism. Symbolically, it covers the story of the ages. The ultimate conflict between the dragon and the woman and the final defeat of the dragon will be shown presently. A description is given of a conflict between principalities and powers, fallen and unfallen. Perfect victory is gained through the blood of the Lamb and His word of testimony.

The heavens rejoice, and all inhabiting them at the exclusion of the foe. He is cast down to the earth, and there is a manifestation of his malice and power on the earth level for the short time remaining to him. This power, however, will be definitely restricted. In this whole description there is a vivid unveiling of the nature and malice of the devil contending in the heavens to the last in terrible mental conflict with all the hosts of light; then, when finally cast out from the heavenly places, turning with renewed fury and force on those who have been associated with Christ. Amid these terrible scenes we are never allowed to lose sight of the might and majesty of God, who checks all the underworld of evil.

REVELATION 13

Still reviewing the process, a beast is seen as the agent of Satan. It is the Antichrist, who is counterfeit of Christ. He appears with the signs and symbols of kingship. He is characterized by attractiveness, for the whole earth wonders after him, and is constrained to worship. It is the ultimate blasphemy of the counterfeiting of God's anointed King by Satan.

Yet another beast is portrayed, and in him the deception is still carried forward further. The methods he employs are a counterfeiting of those which mark the activity of the Spirit. Nevertheless, they are all rendered valueless by the erection at the center of his propaganda of an idol representative of his master. As the counterfeit ever demonstrates the existence of the genuine, so the genuine makes opportunity for the presence and activity of the counterfeit. Imitations have ever formed the gravest perils in the history of the Church and the world, and the devil's final attempt to gain the government of the race will thus be an appalling attempt to imitate the Person of God's crowned and anointed King. The mental enlightenment of the race by that time will admit of no positive denial of the existence of God or of the reality of the spiritual. The world, therefore, must be deceived by misrepresentation.

REVELATION 14

The attention of the seer was now turned again to the heavenly order. The redeemed are seen standing with the Lamb, a company of obedient souls who follow Him "whithersoever He goeth."

In distinction from the seventh angel who had sounded the trumpet John now refers to "another angel." At this point the unfallen angels are described as exercising a remarkable ministry on earth. The first of them proclaims eternal good tidings. Yet another proclaims the fall of Babylon.

The Gospel calling men to submission having been sounded, and the defeat of Babylon announced "another angel, a third," goes forth with a message of warning. In this proclamation the continuity of the divine recognition of human will is evident. All are called on to choose. The beast and the prophet insist that men receive their mark, and those refusing are slain. On the other hand, God's angel messenger warns against receiving that mark.

It is in that connection that it was announced, "Blessed are the dead which die in the Lord from henceforth." To those who through terrible suffering are faithful unto death will be granted the way of entry on the higher service.

A double view of impending judgment is given in the figures of the harvest and the vineyard. As to the harvest, it is briefly stated, "He that sat on the cloud thrust in His sickle on the earth, and the earth was reaped." That sweep of the sickle in the right hand of the Son of man is a perfect symbol of the final and all-inclusive judgment. The figure of the vintage is an angel holding a sickle and gathering "the clusters of the vine of the earth."

REVELATION 15

Seven angels having seven plagues constitute that which "finished the wrath of God." First, the seer beheld the sea of glass and, standing by, the victorious host who had overcome the beast. They are seen, not as defeated and killed, but as triumphant and living. They sing the song of Moses, which is the song of law, and the song of the Lamb, which is the song of love. They have learned perfectly how law and love mingle and merge in the divine economy. The burden of song is praise to the Lord God Almighty. His words, His ways, His character, His acts are all referred to. Through all the terrible times of stress and strain these souls have walked by faith. Now for them at last faith is lost in sight, and they chant the praise of God whom they served even at the cost of suffering and death.

Following this vision of the victorious hosts, John beheld the opening of a temple in heaven. It is "the temple of the tabernacle of the testimony." From it come the seven angels having the seven final plagues. To these angels the bowls of wrath are given by one of the living ones. Behind these angels is seen in the temple the glory of God in such magnificence and majesty that none can know it until the judgment is fulfilled.

REVELATION 16

A condensed and graphic description of the processes of judgment on the rebellious and sinful race follows. Evil has wrought itself out to its most terrible expression, and now it is to be smitten without mercy.

Everything opened with a great voice sounding from the temple. Terrible physical suffering follows the pouring out of each of the first four bowls. The fifth angel pours his bowl, and the kingdom of the beast is wrapped in darkness. Notwithstanding the unimaginable terror of their condition, the evil men still "blasphemed the God of heaven," and "they repented not of their works."

The sixth angel pours his bowl, and there is a change in the method of judgment. The great river Euphrates is dried up. The drying up of this river makes easy the gathering together of the kings of the earth to do battle against the hosts of God. Then comes Har-Magedon.

In the midst of all this John seems to hear a word of Christ, and answers it in a parenthesis. It announces His coming, and pronounces blessing on those who watch. In all these processes of judgment it would seem that a remnant was continually being lifted into the position of submission and loyalty, and every now and again some such word as this declares the watchfulness and tenderness of God and His readiness to receive and rescue from the judgments those who turn to Him.

The seventh angel pours his bowl upon the air, and the voice from the temple is again heard crying, "It is done." The all-permeating power of God which has operated in beneficent gentleness now shakes the earth, and the judgment of Babylon takes place. Yet again it is written that men still blaspheme God.

REVELATION 17

We now come to the true unfolding of the nature of Babylon and the detailed account of the judgment to fall on her. The name on the forehead of Babylon commences with the word "Mystery." Babylon stands for the whole system of organized godlessness in the history of the human race. In its course it has been surrounded by every kind of material splendor, "arrayed in purple and scarlet, and decked with gold and precious stones and pearls." Through the ages, men turning from the vision of God have seen only the material glory of evil.

As the seer gazes on the fearful vision he wonders with a great wonder.

The angel then proceeds to explain the meaning of the vision. The beast represents the temporal authority which has been the strength of all spiritual harlotry. The heads refer to successive world powers which had risen and fallen. The powers having existed and passed at the time of John's writing were Egypt, Assyria, Babylon, Persia, and Greece. The one then existing was Rome, and still there was one to come. Ten kings remained who would finally act with the beast, having one mind with him. These will act against Babylon, and also against the Lamb, but He will overcome them.

Very striking is the seer's declaration of the overruling of God in the words, "God did put it in their hearts to do His mind, and to come to one mind, and to give their kingdom unto the beast." Thus the angel's explanation ends with a manifestation of the perpetual truth that all godlessness carries within itself the elements of its final defeat and overthrow.

REVELATION 18

The vision of the destruction of Babylon as directly resulting from the government of God is now given. It is announced, "Fallen is Babylon." Her condition is described as that of a habitation of demons, the prison of unclean spirits. Nations, kings, and merchants who have lived and ruled and traded on the principles of Babylon are involved in her fallen condition. A remnant is called out from Babylon before the destruction comes. The angel pronounces a retributive sentence, "As she rendered . . . according to her works."

The fall of the city produces entirely opposite effects on earth and in heaven. The earth is plunged into mourning. The heavenly and spiritual world rejoices. From the beginning, Babylon had been in opposition to heaven. It had lived under the impulse of things seen, while denying the unseen things. At last it is overthrown, and there is rejoicing of the righteous.

A symbolic act follows, the casting of a great millstone into the sea by an angel. The result is that Babylon "shall be found no more." The overthrow is to be absolute, irrevocable. The reason for this is stated as threefold, first, "Thy merchants were the princes of the earth"; second, "With thy sorceries were all the nations deceived"; finally, "In her was found the blood of prophets and of saints, and of all that have been slain upon the earth."

REVELATION 19

We now come to the things leading up to the establishment of the Kingdom. There are three great movements of praise: one by a great multitude who have been slain; the second by the elders and the living ones; finally, a mighty chorus which John describes by a threefold similitude as "the voice of a great multitude," "the voice of many waters," "the voice of mighty thunders." This precedes the marriage of the Lamb. The harlot is no more. The true Bride is manifest.

A word of blessing is pronounced on those bidden to this marriage ceremony.

Now comes the actual manifestation of Jesus to the world, and the judgment already foretold is described from the standpoint of His activity. The principle of His procedure is that He is "faithful and true" in character, and judging in righteousness in conduct. On His head are many diadems, suggesting His imperial sway over every realm of life. His name is "The Word of God." On His thigh is written "KING OF KINGS, AND LORD OF LORDS." This glorious King in His manifestation is accompanied by His armies.

As the heavens are opened, and the King and His armies are manifested, an angel is seen standing in the sun, and in figurative language is heard announcing the coming victory. The massed powers of godlessness are gathered with the awful purpose of making war against the true King. The battle is immediately joined. There is no indecision, no varying fortunes. The King and His armies are supernatural. It is the hour when heaven is touching earth, and the victory is with heaven.

REVELATION 20

Victory having been gained over the earthly manifestation of godlessness, it remains to deal with the power lying behind. The archenemy is described as "the dragon," "the old serpent," "the devil," and, finally, as "Satan." In this grouping of names is a remarkable unveiling of the very essence of evil.

A brief and the only account of the thousand years follows. It will be a time of perfect earthly government under the King appointed and anointed by God. That government will be administered by those who have lived by faith in the supernatural.

The description then turns to millennial issues. Evidently even during that period there will be those who have never submitted to essential righteousness. Satan is loosed out of prison to gather them together, and once more they act in definite hostility to the reign of righteousness. The issue is that Satan loses his usurped dominion forever. He is nevermore to be god of the world nor prince of the power of the air.

Then follows the account of the great assize. Books are opened, and a book. In the books things are written. Those whose names are in the book enter into blessedness. Those whose names are not found entered there are judged according to the things written in the books.

There comes a final movement. Death and Hades are cast into the lake of fire. Deepest death would seem to consist in the destruction of the possibility of dying. Beyond these words it is impossible to go in speculation, of hope or despair. Whatever that final sentence may mean, it is the sentence of Him who occupies the Great White Throne.

REVELATION 21

The endless end of evil has passed before the vision of the seer, and he now observes the resultant order. The holy city appears. Toward a city of God men had looked through long generations. Now it is manifested. God comes to abide with men. There is a new order of things, characterized by laughter without tears, life without death, singing without mourning, content without crying, pleasure without pain.

As John beheld the vision he heard a voice saying, "Behold, I make all things new," and he was charged to write. All things come to pass, because He is the Alpha and the Omega.

As one of the angels who had the seven bowls had summoned the seer to behold the great harlot, so now the same, or another of the seven angels, summoned him to behold the Bride in the glory of the great city. Radiant indeed is the revelation. It is a city of exclusion, having a wall great and high; and of inclusion, having gates opening in every direction. The names of the tribes on the gates suggest the varied temperaments of human life made pure as incorporated in the new social order. The names of the apostles of the Lamb on the foundations signify that the service of suffering has been the very foundation on which the city is built. No temple of localized worship is found, but the presence of God is everywhere known and felt. Beyond the city is the new earth, with nations and kings walking in the light of the glory of God. Excluded from it are all unclean things.

REVELATION 22

Still gazing at the city, the seer beheld the great river of water of life. On its banks is the tree of life, yielding fruit, and leaves for the healing of nations. And once more the apostle declares there shall be no more curse.

The great unveiling is accomplished. It ended with the declaration of the established Throne, and of the unending reign of the saints. What follows is of the nature of ratification and enforcement. The divine word concerning the authority and value of the book is that the words are "faithful and true." In order that those who have received the unveiling should ever be on the alert, it is announced, "Behold, I come quickly." The word "quickly" might with accuracy be rendered "suddenly." A blessing is pronounced on those who keep the words of the prophecy.

John now adds his own name to the ratification of the book, declaring that he had heard and seen all of which he had written.

The angel charged him not to seal the words of the prophecy, and the tendency to permanence of character is revealed (verse 11).

Following the charge of the angel, once again the voice of the great unveiled One is heard reaffirming the suddenness of His coming, and declaring that His reward is with Him. In majestic simplicity He introduces Himself as "I, Jesus," and describes Himself in terms of mystical magnificence as the "Root of David," and, moreover, as David's Offspring.

John writes his solemn testimony against tampering with this narrative of unveiling. The final announcement of Jesus is, "Yea, I come quickly." To this John writes in reply, "Amen, come, Lord Jesus." This is the perfect acquiescence of the trusting soul.

The wonderful book ends with the simplest of benedictions: "The grace of the Lord Jesus be with the saints, Amen."